P9-DGK-961

ENVIRONMENTAL LAW HANDBOOK

Twelfth Edition

J. Gordon Arbuckle
F. William Brownell
David R. Case
Wayne T. Halbleib
Lawrence J. Jensen
Stanley W. Landfair
Robert T. Lee

Marshall Lee Miller
Karen J. Nardi
Austin P. Olney
David G. Sarvadi
James W. Spensley
Daniel M. Steinway
Thomas F. P. Sullivan

Government Institutes, Inc.
Rockville, MD
1993

WITHDRAWN

Tennessee Tech Library
Cookeville, TN

Government Institutes, Inc., 4 Research Place, Suite 200,
Rockville, Maryland 20850

Copyright © 1993 by Government Institutes. All rights reserved.
Published April 1993.

3   2   1

No part of this work may be reproduced or transmitted in any
form or by any means, electronic or mechanical, including
photocopying, recording, or any information storage and
retrieval system, without permission in writing from the publisher. All requests for permission to reproduce material from
this work should be directed to Government Institutes, Inc.,
4 Research Place, Suite 200, Rockville, Maryland 20850.

The reader should not rely on this publication to address specific
questions that apply to a particular set of facts. The authors and
publisher make no representation or warranty, express or
implied, as to the completeness, correctness or utility of the
information in this publication. In addition, the authors and
publisher assume no liability of any kind whatsoever resulting
from the use of or reliance upon the contents of this book.

ISSN: 0147-7714
ISBN: 0-86587-350-X

Library of Congress Catalog Card Number: 92-75400

Printed in the United States of America

SUMMARY TABLE OF CONTENTS

TABLE OF CONTENTS

CHAPTER 2: LIABILITIES AND ENFORCEMENT

CHAPTER 3: RESOURCE CONSERVATION AND RECOVERY ACT

CHAPTER 5: CLEAN AIR ACT

CHAPTER 7: OIL POLLUTION ACT OF 1990

CHAPTER 8: SAFE DRINKING WATER ACT

CHAPTER 9: COMPREHENSIVE ENVIRONMENTAL RESPONSE, COMPENSATION, AND LIABILITY ACT

CHAPTER 12: ASBESTOS

CHAPTER 13: FEDERAL REGULATION OF PESTICIDES

CHAPTER 14: EMERGENCY PLANNING AND COMMUNITY RIGHT-TO-KNOW ACT

CHAPTER 15: OCCUPATIONAL SAFETY AND HEALTH ACT

ABOUT THE AUTHORS

J. Gordon Arbuckle

Gordon Arbuckle is a partner in the Washington, D.C. law firm of Patton, Boggs, & Blow and works in the Denver office. He has practiced environmental and natural resources law for over 20 years and has written and spoken extensively on the Clean Water Act, and other areas of environmental law. In addition, Mr. Arbuckle played a major role in developing and securing enactment of the Deepwater Ports Act and the Deep Seabed Hard Mineral Resources Act, as well as certain provisions of other environmental laws. Mr. Arbuckle has represented clients in petitions filed under RCRA and in hearings on Clean Water Act permits. Mr. Arbuckle is also an author of the *Environmental Health and Safety Manager's Handbook*, the *Emergency Planning and Community Right-to-Know Act Handbook*, and has written several articles concerning criminal liability under environmental statutes.

F. William Brownell

William Brownell is a member of the Hunton & Williams law firm's Energy and Environmental Team in Washington, D.C. His practice covers a broad range of environmental law issues in proceedings before federal agencies, state and federal courts, and Congress. He has represented clients in many of the major rulemakings and judicial review proceedings under the Clean Air Act, as well as in citizen suits and enforcement actions. Mr. Brownell's practice also extends to issues arising under many other environmental statutes. He is a member of the American Bar Association's sections on Administrative Law and Natural Resources Law. He speaks and writes frequently on environmental and administrative law issues, and is an author of the *Clean Air Handbook*.

David R. Case

David Case is General Counsel for the Hazardous Waste Treatment Council, a trade association of hazardous waste firms in Washington, D.C. He was formerly with the law firm of Crowell & Moring where he specialized in environmental law. He was a chairman of the Environmental Pollution Committee and deputy chairman of the Council of Natural Resources and Lands of the Federal Bar Association. He has authored articles and lectured on environmental regulation under RCRA, Superfund, the Clean Air Act, the Clean Water Act, and other federal and state environmental programs. Mr. Case received his B.A. from Amherst College, his LL.B Cantab. from Cambridge University, and his law degree from the University of Michigan Law School.

Wayne T. Halbleib

Wayne Halbleib is Counsel to the Energy and Environmental Practice Group of the law firm of Mays & Valentine in Richmond, Virginia. He provides environmental and occupational safety and health compliance and enforcement counseling, as well as litigation services for banks, corporations, trade associations and local governments throughout Virginia. Mr. Halbleib was an assistant attorney general for the Commonwealth of Virginia and also served as the first state director of the SARA Title III Office in Virginia's Department of Waste Management. He regularly lectures and writes on a wide variety of environmental issues.

Lawrence J. Jensen

Lawrence Jensen is a partner with Holland & Hart where he concentrates his practice on environmental regulatory and legislative matters, with a special emphasis on water and waste issues. Prior to joining the firm, he served with the U.S. EPA as general counsel and assistant administrator for water with responsibility for managing EPA's Safe Drinking Water Act programs. He also served with the Department of the Interior as an associate solicitor, dealing with oil and gas leasing issues, public land management programs, and water rights. Mr. Jensen has lectured extensively on environmental regulatory and water quality issues.

Stanley W. Landfair

Stanley Landfair is a partner with the law firm of McKenna & Cuneo in its Los Angeles office and specializes in environmental law, administrative law, and state and federal litigation. He provides TSCA counseling to many companies in the chemical, aerospace and electronics industries and has litigated numerous actions arising under TSCA, FIFRA, NEPA, the Freedom of Information Act and the Federal Food, Drug and Cosmetic Act, as well as many civil and criminal actions in state and federal courts. Previously, Mr. Landfair was a judicial law clerk in the U.S. Court of Appeals for the Fourth Circuit. He also served as a Judge Advocate in the U.S. Navy, and was chief trial counsel at the Naval Legal Service Office in Japan.

Robert T. Lee

Robert Lee is an attorney in the Washington, D.C. office of Troy, Gould & Mott, where he specializes in environmental compliance and litigation, including all facets of hazardous waste management and remediation and major Superfund litigation. Previously, he served in the Environmental Enforcement Section of the Land and Natural Resources Division of the U.S. Department of Justice. He has also been a government contract attorney, trial judge and trial attorney with the Office of the Judge Advocate General of the U.S. Air Force. He frequently lectures and writes on a variety of environmental issues.

Marshall Lee Miller

Marshall Miller is a partner in the Washington, D.C. office of the law firm of Baker & Hostetler, where he specializes in the areas of environmental law, occupational health and safety, and international transactions. Mr. Miller was previously special assistant to the first administrator of the U.S. Environmental Protection Agency, chief EPA judicial officer, associate deputy attorney general in the U.S. Department of Justice, and deputy administrator of the Occupational Safety and Health Administration. He was educated at Harvard, Oxford, Heidelberg and Yale.

Karen J. Nardi

Karen Nardi is a partner in the San Francisco office of McCutchen, Doyle, Brown & Enersen, where she specializes in compliance issues and administrative law proceedings. She has assisted clients involved in underground tank cleanups, the closure of property contaminated with hazardous wastes, and the cleanup of complex groundwater problems in the Silicon Valley. She was also a legislative analyst for the California state legislature on resources, land use, and energy. Ms. Nardi's co-author, **John J. Gregory**, is an associate in the San Francisco office of McCutchen, Doyle, Brown & Enersen. He has experience in solid and hazardous waste regulatory compliance counseling and litigation, including underground storage tanks, contaminated property cleanups, cost recovery litigation and environmental audits. He is also a civil engineer and was an engineering consultant on soils and groundwater.

Austin P. Olney

Austin Olney, a partner in the Washington, D.C. office of LeBoeuf, Lamb, Leiby & MacRae, heads the firm's Maritime Department. For the last 13 years he has specialized in representing domestic and foreign clients on marine safety and pollution matters. Previously, Mr. Olney served as secretary of natural resources and environmental control for the state of Delaware. He also served as counsel to the U.S. House of Representatives Committee on Merchant Marine and Fisheries. Mr. Olney holds an A.B. degree from Harvard University and a J.D. from Georgetown University Law Center.

David G. Sarvadi

David Sarvadi is an associate with the Washington, D.C. law firm of Keller and Heckman where he specializes in occupational and environmental health and safety. Mr. Sarvadi is also a certified industrial hygienist and has been involved in the environmental and occupational health fields for more than 20 years. He holds a master's degree in Hygiene from the University of Pittsburgh and a J.D. from George Mason University in Virginia.

James W. Spensley

James Spensley serves as special counsel to the Denver law firm of Holme Roberts & Owen. He worked for the President's Council on Environmental Quality after NEPA was first enacted and assisted in the development of the first federal guidelines on preparing an environmental impact statement. As counsel to several committees of the U.S. House of Representatives, he managed the first and only amendment to NEPA and was involved in developing other major environmental legislation concerning atmospheric science, ocean dumping, and environmental research and development issues. In addition, Mr. Spensley serves as an adjunct professor of law at the University of Denver, and lectures at the University of Colorado. He holds a science degree in Industrial Engineering and a law degree from George Washington University National Law Center.

Daniel M. Steinway

Daniel Steinway is a partner in the Washington, D.C. office of Anderson, Kill, Olick & Oshinsky. He has served as minority counsel for environmental matters on the Committee on Science and Technology of the U.S. House of Representatives, and as an attorney-advisor with the U.S. Environmental Protection Agency's Office of Enforcement. He is also a vice chairman, Subcommittee on Alternate Energy Sources, in the Section of Natural Resources Law of the American Bar Association and is the chairman of the Steering Committee, Environmental Law Committee of the Federal Bar Association. Mr. Steinway received a B.S.E. from the University of Michigan and a J.D. from the George Washington University National Law Center.

Thomas F. P. Sullivan

Thomas Sullivan was an attorney in Washington, D.C. who has been in the forefront of the environmental field since the 1960s. He gained experience in industry before practicing law and representing clients in the environmental field. He has authored and edited numerous books such as *The Greening of American Business, Environmental Health and Safety Manager's Handbook,* and *Environmental Information Sources.* He is a regular lecturer internationally on environmental topics and currently serves as president of Government Institutes. Mr. Sullivan has undergraduate degrees from Cardinal Glennon College and St. Louis University, and a law degree from Catholic University.

PREFACE

This *Twelfth Edition* of the *Environmental Law Handbook* marks its 20th anniversary. During these years it has gained recognition as the pre-eminent authoritative resource in its field.

For this new twelfth edition we have invited no fewer than fourteen nationally recognized experts—representing major law firms and institutions from coast-to-coast—to completely rewrite the *Environmental Law Handbook*.

The goal of the *Environmental Law Handbook*, however, has remained constant through all of its editions: to give its users reliable, accurate compliance information by some of the most respected people in the field in each subject area—all presented in a clear, concise manner, with a minimum of legal jargon.

This new edition begins with a chapter on the "Basics of Environmental Law" to provide a foundation to understand and apply the information in the chapters that follow.

Discussion then moves to a look at "Liabilities and Enforcement"—that is, the negative consequences of failure to comply with the requirements of environmental laws and regulations, which can range from "traffic ticket"-like administrative fines to criminal prosecution for a growing number of unfortunate individuals.

Each of the major environmental, health, and safety laws and issues are then covered in individual chapters on the Resource Conservation and Recovery Act; Underground Storage Tanks; Clean Air Act—with emphasis on the changes brought about by the 1990 amendments; Water Pollution Control; Oil Pollution Act; Safe Drinking Water Act; Comprehensive Environmental Response, Compensation, and Liability Act; National Environmental Policy Act; Toxic Substances Control Act; Asbestos; Federal Regulation of Pesticides; Emergency Planning and Community Right-to-Know Act; and the Occupational Safety and Health Act.

We hope that readers of this text will find it to be a comprehensive and useful reference. I encourage all those who want in-depth coverage in a given area to see the many additional references listed in the back of this handbook.

As always, I welcome the opportunity to hear personally from our readers as to how well this flagship publication, as well as all of our products, continues to meet our mutual goals of compliance with the spirit as well as the details of the ever-increasing number of laws and regulations.

Thomas F.P. Sullivan
President
Government Institutes, Inc.

April 1993

Chapter 1

BASICS OF ENVIRONMENTAL LAW

Thomas F. P. Sullivan, Esquire[1]
Government Institutes, Inc.
Rockville, Maryland

This chapter gives the basics of the environmental law field, so that the reader has a foundation to comprehend and apply the information provided in the chapters that follow.

1.0 ENVIRONMENTAL LAW AS A SYSTEM

Environmental law is more than simply a collection of statutes on environmental subjects. The field is one which cannot be mastered simply by learning the specific requirements of some individual laws impacting the environment. Over the past few decades, "Environmental Law" has evolved into a *system* of statutes, regulations, guidelines, factual conclusions and case-specific interpretations which relate one to another. The system is complex in itself and is made even more challenging by the difficulty of the interdisciplinary subject matter to be regulated (health, safety and environment) and the problems which the law often has in dealing with the scientific issues and uncertainties nearly always faced in environmental cases.

Understanding this environmental law system, its unifying principles and the ways in which the individual elements work together to achieve the system's objectives is a challenge for those who try to comply with environmental laws. This book provides assistance in meeting that challenge.

2.0 DEFINING OUR SUBJECT MATTER—WHAT IS ENVIRONMENTAL LAW?

The key to understanding a system as complex as environmental law is the definition of the subject. The best definition, I believe, is:

> The environmental law system is an organized way of using all of the laws in our legal system to minimize, prevent, punish or remedy the consequences of actions which damage or threaten the environment, public health and safety.

---

[1] Author's Note: The author wishes to acknowledge J. Gordon Arbuckle, Esquire, who provided major contributions to this chapter. For this, the author is indebted to him. The author also thanks James Aloysius Hogan, Esquire, for his assistance in the preparation of these materials.

This definition reflects the great expansion over the years of the term "environment" to encompass the protection of public health and workers' safety in addition to the environment.

By this definition, what makes a law or regulation a part of the environmental law system is not its label or original function but the purpose for which it is used. It would be a mistake, for example, to assume that a compilation of the federal environmental statutes would include the entire body of environmental law. It would also be a mistake to think that the criminal code or the Administrative Procedure Act does not contain important environmental laws.

When we talk about the "environmental law system," then, we are referring to all aspects of our legal system—the Constitution, statutes, regulations, rules of evidence, rules of procedure, judicial interpretations, the common law and, indeed, the criminal law—to the extent that these elements are being applied towards environmental ends. "Environmental law" is best defined—not as a book or compilation of certain laws, but, instead, as a *system* for using *all* of the laws for environmental, public health and safety purposes.[2]

In summary, environmental law encompasses all the protections for our environment that emanate from the following sources:

1. laws: federal and state statutes and local ordinances,
2. regulations promulgated by federal, state and local agencies,
3. court decisions interpreting these laws and regulations,
4. the common law,
5. United States Constitution and state constitutions, and
6. treaties.

2.1 How a Federal or State Environmental Law is Made[3]

Federal and state legislative processes are similar; the federal procedure is used here for illustration. First a bill is introduced in either the House of Representatives or the Senate. Bills are referred to committee for consideration. The committee(s), in considering a bill, may hold hearings, study, investigate, and issue a report and a recommendation on whether or not the bill should pass. When a bill is reported out of committee, it is placed on a calendar in the respective house, considered, debated, and, if passed, becomes an act.

In the environmental field, the House and Senate generally pass different bills, and a conference of House and Senate representatives is

---

[2] An article by Robert G. Schwartz entitled "Criminalizing Occupational Safety Violations: The Use of Knowing Endangerment Statutes to Punish Employers Who Maintain Toxic Working Conditions" excellently illustrates both the expansion of the term "environmental law"and the utilization of seemingly non-environmental statutes toward environmental ends. 14 *Harvard Environmental Law Review* 487 (1990).

[3] For a more comprehensive treatment of how laws and regulations are made the reader is referred to Al Coco's, *Finding the Law* (Government Institutes, 1982).

needed to resolve the differences. After passage in both the House of Representatives and the Senate, the act is sent to the President of the United States. The act will become law if it is signed by the President of the United States or if the act is not vetoed within ten days.

This often is a long and arduous process resulting in confusing language to embody the compromises necessary to obtain agreement among all the differing factions and thus a majority vote and the approval of the President.

2.2 How Environmental Regulations Are Made[4]

Environmental statutes generally empower an administrative agency, like the U.S. Environmental Protection Agency (EPA), to develop and promulgate regulations. The President may also empower an executive agency to promulgate regulations through an executive order.

Rule-making is a process of publishing proposed regulations in the *Federal Register;* providing opportunity for the public to comment either through submission of written comments or through public hearings that concern the regulations; and publishing final regulations in the *Federal Register*, which have the force and effect of law when they become effective. Annually the regulations are combined into the *Code of Federal Regulations* (*C.F.R.*).

3.0 LAWS THAT ESTABLISH COMPLIANCE OBLIGATIONS

The natural resource laws such as the Endangered Species Act and those related to fish, wildlife, oil and gas exploration, forests and mining are covered in the *Natural Resources Law Handbook* published by Government Institutes. Although they are important for protection of our ecology, we have elected to approach them from the natural resource perspective. In this *Environmental Law Handbook*, we focus herein on environmental laws, specifically those intended to protect the human environment, health and safety.

3.1 Major Environmental Laws

Subsequent chapters of this book describe the regulatory programs in place under the major federal environmental statutes. These environmental laws define most of the substantive compliance obligations of the environmental law system. The major federal environmental statutes do not, however, operate alone. There are other components of "environmental laws" that supplement or complement the programs which the federal environmental statutes establish.

3.2 State Statutes and Regulations Implementing the Federal Statutes

Many of the federal statutes, like the Clean Air Act or Clean Water Act, establish federal-state regulatory programs in which the states are

---

[4] *See* Coco, *op. cit.*

given the opportunity to enact and enforce laws, meeting federal minimum criteria, to achieve the regulatory objectives which the Congress has established. In most instances where the states have had the opportunity to take over regulatory programs in their jurisdictions, they have done so. States are generally the primary permitting and enforcement authorities subject to federal intervention only if they do not enforce effectively or rigorously enough.

Generally, the states are not precluded from enforcing criteria more stringent than those required by the federal laws, and are given considerable leeway to follow enforcement interpretations which may not be fully consistent with those applied at the federal level. Thus the laws and interpretations used to apply and enforce the federal laws may vary considerably from state to state and these variations may not be readily apparent. Government Institutes has published a comprehensive environmental law handbook on each state. Reference should be made to these to fully understand all the environmental obligations in a specific state.

3.3 State Laws Independent of the Federal Requirements

The trend is for states—particularly certain states like California and New Jersey—to take initiatives to provide their citizens and their environment with protection beyond that generally available under the federal statutes. Examples of laws generated by this trend include:

- **Toxic Waste Minimization Laws** like one in Massachusetts[5] which imposes mandatory waste reduction objectives on companies which use or generate toxic or hazardous wastes.

- **Environmental Full Disclosure Laws** like California Proposition 65,[6] which requires extraordinary efforts to make the public aware of health risks associated with products or environments to which they are exposed.

- **Property Transfer Environmental Laws** - like the New Jersey law,[7] which requires extensive investigation and cleanup of contaminated sites before they are sold or transferred.

- **State Groundwater Protection Laws** - Although the federal government has not yet adopted comprehensive groundwater protection legislation, many, if not most of the states, have detailed permit programs.[8]

---

[5] Massachusetts Toxics Use Reduction Act added by St. 1989, c. 265, §3, approved July 24, 1989.

[6] California Safe Drinking Water and Toxic Enforcement Act, adopted as Prop. 65 in 1986, Cal. Health and Safety Code §§25249.5-25249.13 (West Supp. 1987).

[7] NJ Stat. Anno. 13:1K-6 et seq., Environmental Cleanup Responsibility Act L. 1983, c. 330, §1.

[8] Ground Water Permit Act (Cities, Villages, and Municipal Corporations), Neb. Rev. Stat. 1943, 46-638 *et seq.*, Ground Water Exploration and Protection Act, Kan. Stat. Anno. 82a-1201 *et seq.*; Ground Water Basin Protection Act (Porter-Dolwig), Cal. Water Code §12920 *et seq.*

The list could go on, including state citizens' action laws, laws compelling response at hazardous substance sites not on the federal superfund list, facility siting laws, laws governing the operation of publicly owned treatment works and landfills, asbestos abatement and so on. State laws in many states may be a more important factor in dictating the focus of compliance programs than the laws which exist at the federal level. Commensurate attention is clearly warranted.

3.4 Tax Laws

There is a trend at both the state and federal levels towards using the tax laws to create incentives towards environmentally benign products and activities and disincentives against products and activities considered to be environmentally detrimental. Gas guzzler taxes, recycling tax credits, taxes on use of virgin materials, taxes on hazardous waste generation and excise taxes on various products are among the approaches which have been adopted or seriously discussed. These approaches and other economic incentive-oriented strategies will clearly be more vigorously promoted in the future.

3.5 Business Regulatory Laws

The Federal Trade Commission and a number of state attorneys general have initiatives to use their ordinary business regulatory authorities to police environmental claims made for products. The Securities Exchange Commission has for some time required full disclosure of environmental liabilities in statements and reports falling under its jurisdiction.

The innovative abilities of both state and federal officials will continue to be applied to effective utilization of all the laws in their arsenal in an effort to enforce increasingly stringent standards of protection for health, safety and the environment. The limits on this kind of creativity are yet to be seen and are unlikely to be reached in the immediate future because environmental protection is a political asset.

3.6 Local and Municipal Laws

Localities do have great powers to control the location and operation of facilities within their jurisdictions and are often able to effectively utilize this authority. Active community involvement and participation in consideration of local ordinances is, for a number of businesses, essential to continued ability to operate profitably. While it is difficult to generalize, issues which warrant particularly careful attention include the operation of the local waterworks and waste treatment plants, local recycling initiatives and associated product initiatives, zoning and noise control ordinances, nuisance laws, air emission requirements, landfill restrictions or closures, local emergency planning and initiatives relating to waste site cleanup. In every instance, the impact of this kind of local action can be as immediate and severe as that of any taken at the state or federal level. From the perspective of an environmental law compliance program, local does not mean trivial. It means immediate, important, largely un-reviewable, and deserving of considerable attention. Effective environmental compliance requires acceptance of these facts of life.

3.7 Environmental Law and Judicial Decisions

As the courts interpret the environmental laws and regulations and apply them to specific factual situations, they are continually determining what the law actually means in factual situations. In order to gain the proper understanding of court decisions, a basic knowledge of the United States court system is needed. The courts and their role are described later in this chapter.

3.8 Common Law

Underlying the development of legal theory in the United States is a body of rules and principles relating to the government and security of persons and property which had its origin, development and formulation in England. Brought to the American colonies by peoples of Anglo-Saxon stock, these basic rules were formally adopted in the states in which they were in force after the American Revolution. Known as the "common law," these principles are derived from the application of natural reason, an innate sense of justice and the dictates of conscience. The common law is not the result of legislative enactment. Rather, its authority is derived solely from usages and customs which have been recognized, affirmed and enforced by the courts through judicial decisions.

It is important to realize that "common law" is not a fixed or absolute set of written rules in the same sense as statutory or legislatively enacted law. The unwritten principles of common law are flexible and adaptable to the changes which occur in a growing society. New institutions and public policies; modifications of usage and practice; changes in mores, trade, and commerce; inventions; and increasing knowledge—all generate new factual situations which require application and reinterpretation of the fundamental principles of common law by the courts.

As the courts examine each new set of facts in the light of past precedent, an orderly development of common laws occurs through a slow and natural process. Thus, the basic principles underlying American jurisprudence remain fundamentally constant, evolving slowly and progressively.

The common law, so far as it has not been expressly abrogated, is recognized as an organic part of the jurisprudence of most of the states. The major exception is Louisiana jurisprudence, which is based on Roman law—a relic of French rule prior to the Louisiana Purchase. However, since the state court systems have functioned independently of each other, subject only to federal review in cases of national importance, the common law varies slightly from state to state.

The common law actions that we will discuss in subsequent sections are civil suits in which the plaintiff (the party bringing the lawsuit) seeks to remedy a violation of a right. Civil actions are distinguished from criminal proceedings. Criminal actions are those in which the state seeks to redress a breach of public or collective rights which are established in codified penal law. Subsequent sections of this chapter review the three most frequently used types of common law actions that can be the basis of a lawsuit in the pollution control field.

4.0 COMMON LAW ENVIRONMENTAL REQUIREMENTS: TORTS

"Tort" is the word used to denote a common law civil wrong for which a court will provide a remedy.

A tort arises from the existence of a generalized legal duty to avoid causing harm to others, through acts of omission, as well as of commission. Every adult person is obliged to fulfill a duty of care for the personal and property rights of others while engaged in daily life. Carelessness in exercising this responsibility may give rise to a cause of action (a lawsuit) by means of which the injured party may seek restitution. This duty is noncontractual; that is, it does not arise from an explicit promissory agreement between the parties to the action. So a tort is also distinguished from a contract right which is dependent upon the contract itself.

Tens of thousands of tort lawsuits have been filed involving asbestos cases and other toxic chemical litigation. These cases have prompted some writers to allege that the 1990s is the era of "toxic torts." It is clear that tort law will be of increasing interest in the environmental field in the future as more and more tort lawsuits are filed.

The three types of torts most commonly encountered in the environmental field are: (1) nuisance, (2) trespass and (3) negligence, which are each described in the following sections.

4.1 Nuisance

Nuisance is defined as "that activity which arises from the unreasonable, unwarrantable or unlawful use by a person of his own property, working an obstruction or injury to the right of another or to the public, and producing such material annoyance, inconvenience, and discomfort that the law will presume resulting damage."[9]

The general rule is that a person may use his land or personal property in any manner he sees fit. However, this rule is subject to limitation: The owner must use his property in a reasonable manner. A nuisance arises whenever a person uses his property to cause material injury or annoyance to a reasonable neighbor.

In determining whether a given act constitutes a nuisance, the court considers the nature of the act itself. The discomfort must amount to a

---

[9] *Black's Law Dictionary* 1065 (6th ed. 1990).

material injury or annoyance. It must tangibly affect the physical or mental health of ordinary people under normal circumstances or conditions.

4.1.1 Noise Nuisance

The most common form of environmental nuisance is noise pollution. Noise produced by human activities is a common environmental problem. In order to constitute a nuisance in the legal sense, generally, noise must be of such magnitude and intensity as to cause actual or psychological discomfort to persons of ordinary sensibilities. Noise from the operation of an industrial plant constitutes an actionable nuisance if it affects injuriously the health or comfort of *ordinary* people in the plant's vicinity to an *unreasonable* extent. The courts and legislatures have had difficulty in setting an absolute standard, so this determination rests on the facts.

O'Neill v. Carolina Freight Carriers Corp.[10] is an example of a "noise nuisance" case in which a homeowner was awarded both an injunction and damages against the operators of a nearby business. In this case, the plaintiffs showed that they were ordinary people and that the noise from trucks and loading operations at a terminal located immediately adjacent to their home was unreasonable. It caused them loss of sleep and prevented general enjoyment of their home. The court ruled that the truck terminal noises between 11:00 p.m. and 6:00 a.m. were unreasonable and that every property owner must make reasonable use of his land so as not to cause unnecessary annoyance to his neighbors.

In the *O'Neill* case, the facts lead readily to a conclusion of injury to health because the noise during the night could logically cause loss of sleep and resulting injury to health.

The case of *Rose v. Chaikin*[11] presents another interesting situation in which noise constituted a nuisance. On the New Jersey Shore just north of Atlantic City, the energy conservation-minded and environmentally conscious Joseph Chaikin erected a windmill on his residence. When it began to produce offensive noise exceeding levels permissible under the controlling city ordinance, Joel Rose and other neighbors initiated suit to enjoin the operation of the windmill.

The court announced the following standard: "The essence of a private nuisance is an unreasonable interference with the use and enjoyment of land. The elements are myriad. . . . The utility of the defendant's conduct must be weighed against the quantum of harm to the plaintiff. The question is not simply whether a person is annoyed or disturbed, but whether the annoyance or disturbance arises from an unreasonable use of the neighbor's land. . . . Unreasonableness is judged not according to exceptionally refined, uncommon or luxurious habits of living, but according to the simple tastes and unaffected notions generally prevailing among plain people."[12] Due to

---

[10] 156 Conn. 613, 244 A.2d 372 (1968).

[11] 187 N.J. Super. 210 (1982).

[12] *Ibid.* at 216.

the unreasonable character, volume, frequency, duration, time, and locality of the noise, the court issued an injunction against any further operation of the windmill.

There is no fixed standard as to what degree or kind of noise constitutes a nuisance. The circumstances of each case must be considered independently. Generally, the key determination is whether or not the noise is unreasonable and causes some physical or psychological harm. This determination varies from one community to another and from one period of time to another depending on local attitudes and customs.

4.1.2 Other Nuisances

Smoke, dust, odors, other airborne pollutants, water pollutants and hazardous substances have also been held to be nuisances.

The *Ozark Poultry Products* case provides an example of an odor being classed as a nuisance.[13] In this Arkansas case, nine homeowners in the vicinity of a poultry plant brought suit to abate the odor nuisance created by operation of the plant. They claimed that odors from the poultry plant caused them to feel nausea and to lose sleep at night. On the witness stand, the plant manager admitted that operation of the plant violated existing law. The court found the plant to be a public nuisance, and the homeowners obtained a court order to close the plant unless conditions causing the nuisance were corrected within a time limit established by the court.

In 1984 Vernon Lever sued Wilder Mobile Homes, Inc.[14] because Wilder's improperly maintained sewage treatment lagoon emitted offensive odors that interfered with gardening, family picnics, and church groups at Lever's residence. The court found that, "In South Carolina 'anything' causing inconvenience or damage, or interfering with the enjoyment of life or property is a nuisance [Citation omitted]. More to the point, it is a nuisance to use property in such a way that annoying or injurious odors are emitted."[15] Accordingly, the appellate court affirmed that Wilder Mobile Homes, Inc. was liable for maintaining a nuisance.

It should be noted that air pollutants only constitute a nuisance under certain circumstances. Normal air is usually considered as that common to a locality and so varies from one area to another. To be a nuisance, the air pollution must cause harm and discomfort to ordinary people to an unreasonable extent.

In the case of *Chicago v. Commonwealth Edison*[16] the court refused to issue an injunction against alleged air pollution. The court found that although the public had a right to clean air, the notion of pure air has come to mean clean air consistent with the character of the locality and the attending circumstances. The court ruled that the city had failed to answer

---

[13] *Ozark Poultry Products, Inc. v. Garmon*, 251 Ark. 389, 472 S.W. 2d 714 (1971).

[14] *Lever v. Wilder Mobile Homes, Inc.* 322S.E.2d692 (S.C.App. 1984).

[15] *Ibid.* at 693-4.

[16] 24 Ill. App. 624, 321 N.E. 2d 412, 7 Env't. Rep.Case. (BNA) 1974.

the threshold question of whether Commonwealth Edison's Indiana facility caused substantial harm so as to constitute an actionable invasion of a public right. In order to be entitled to injunctive relief a substantial harm or injury must be clearly demonstrated. This case is a strict interpretation of the law of nuisance because it was a request for an injunction to cease operation which would have a broad impact on employment and local economics. If the action had been for damages, the court may have decided it differently by not using a strict interpretation of the law.

In *Harrison v. Indiana Auto Shredders*,[17] the Seventh Circuit Court of Appeals also refused to permanently enjoin operation of an automobile shredding and recycling plant based on a nuisance action. The court held that under the evidence presented and in the absence of an imminent hazard to health or welfare—none of which was established—the defendant could not be prevented from continuing to engage in its operation. In addition, the court believed that the operation should be allowed a reasonable time to correct any defects not posing threats of imminent or substantial harm.

In essence, the courts were not convinced by the evidence presented in these last two cases that harm caused by the alleged nuisance was so great as to justify forcing the defendant to cease operation. If these facilities were shut down, many families would be injured by the forced unemployment. So the weighing of equities by the court resulted in a determination based on all the evidence presented in favor of allowing continued operations. This is generally called "balancing the equities."

Individuals may sue for private injuries resulting from a public nuisance. In *Anderson v. W.R. Grace & Co.* the plaintiffs claimed that contamination of the groundwater from which they drew their water constituted a nuisance that caused their illnesses. The court found that, "The right to be free of contamination to the municipal water supply is clearly a 'right common to the general public,' thus interference with that right would be a public nuisance."[18] The court pointed out that while the general rule is that common rights are to be vindicated through suit by a public official, when a plaintiff has sustained "special or peculiar damage," an individual action may be maintained. Since injuries to a person's health are by their nature "special and peculiar," the court allowed plaintiffs to seek damages for their special injuries.

The Earthline Corporation, a subsidiary of SCA Services, Inc., attempted to operate an industrial waste recovery, treatment, storage and disposal site on a 130-acre site in Illinois. Ninety acres are located within the Village of Wilsonville and the remaining acres adjacent to the village. The operation accepted hazardous wastes and toxic substances. The Village sued Earthline to stop the operation and also to require the removal of those hazardous wastes and toxic substances that had been deposited on the

---

[17] 528 F.2d 1107, 8 Env't Rep. Cas. (BNA) 1569 (7th Cir. 1975).

[18] 628 F.Supp. 1219 (D.Mass. 1986).

site.[19] The court ruled that the site was a public/private nuisance, issued an injunction against Earthline's further operation of the site and required them to remove all wastes and contaminated soil.

It is most important to note that this case was decided against SCA even though there was no showing that SCA had violated any government regulation. Compliance with government regulations is not a defense against a common law nuisance action. Also, the lower court decision emphasized that a nuisance does not require a showing of any negligence on the part of the defendant. Nuisance and negligence are distinct torts, and except in the cases of nuisances created by negligence, liability for nuisance does not depend upon the existence of negligence. Negligence is not an essential or material element of a cause of action for nuisance and need not be pleaded or proved especially where the thing complained of is a nuisance per se or a public nuisance or results from ultra-hazardous conduct on the part of the defendant. A nuisance is a condition and not an act or a failure to act on the part of the person responsible for the condition.

4.1.3 Some Defenses to Nuisance Actions

Nuisance actions have often been decided by balancing the equities (weighing the impact of the injuries to respective parties involved in litigation). In any balancing of the equities, the good faith efforts of the polluter, while not absolving him, would be a factor.[20]

The availability of pollution control devices is, of course, a significant factor that can be considered by the court. For example, in *Renkin v. Harvey Aluminum*,[21] the court noted Harvey Aluminum's failure to keep pace with technological advances in pollution controls. In that case the court ordered adoption of such controls.

In general, courts are moving to strict liability for environmental nuisances so that practically speaking, there are no good defenses. The solution is: do not create nuisances. If you have an existing nuisance, you are best advised to abate it.

4.1.4 Coming to a Nuisance

"Coming to a nuisance" is the phrase used to describe a defense that the complainant or plaintiff affected by the nuisance moved into the area where the "complained about activity" had already been in existence.

An example of "coming to a nuisance" occurs when someone moves onto property near to an airport or industrial complex and then complains of the nuisance that existed prior to his moving there. Generally, the fact that an individual purchases property with the knowledge of the existence of a nuisance or that he came to the nuisance will not defeat his right to the

---

[19] *Village of Wilsonville v. SCA Services, Inc.,* 77 Ill. App. 3d 618, 396 N.E. 2d 522 (1979), aff'd 86 Ill. 2d 1, 426 N.E. 2d 824 (1981).

[20] *McElwain v. Georgia Pacific,* 245 Or. 247, 421 P.2d 957 (1986).

[21] 226 F. Supp. 169 (D. Or. 1963).

abatement of the nuisance or recovery of damages[22] nor will his right to recovery be affected if the property is sold to another while the lawsuit is pending.[23]

However, some cases have held that if the complainant came to a nuisance, this constitutes a defense to a nuisance lawsuit. This minority view is probably a result of an old axiom of law that one who voluntarily places himself in a situation whereby he suffers an injury will not prevail. The test of liability in these cases is often the knowledge of the plaintiff regarding the consequences of his conduct.

The majority rule, however, is that the fact alone that a person moved into the vicinity of a nuisance by purchasing or leasing property in the area does not bar him from complaining in an action against the continued operation or maintenance of the nuisance.[24] The majority rule is based on the theory that the right to pure air and the comfortable enjoyment of property belong to property as much as the right of possession and occupancy. If population where there was none before approaches a nuisance, it is the duty of those liable to put an end to it.

4.2 Trespass

Trespass is commonly divided into two types:

1. **Trespass to chattels** is an injury to or interference with the possession of personal property, with or without the exercise of personal force. This trespass involves destruction of personal property, taking from the possession of another, or a refusal to surrender possession.

2. **Trespass to land** is an unlawful, forcible entry on another's realty. An injury to the realty of another or an interference with possession, above or below ground, is a trespass, regardless of the condition of the land and regardless of negligence.

Both types of trespass are categorized as intentional interferences with property. However, the concept of intent in trespass is subtle and tricky. In order to support a lawsuit under the theory of trespass to land, the Second Restatement of Torts, §163, Comment b, indicates that the intent necessary is simply an intent to be at the place on the land where the trespass allegedly occurred. For a trespass to chattels lawsuit, as long as the defendant voluntarily interfered with the personal property, trespass to chattels will be appropriate. For both types of trespass, the "intent" requires no wrongful motive. For example, it is no defense that the defendant thought the land or chattels were his own. The property right is protected at the expense of an innocent mistake.[25]

---

[22] *Fertilizing Co. v. Hyde Park,* 97 U.S. 659 (1987); *Rentz v. Roach,* 154 Ga. 491, 115 S.E. 94 (1922); *Vann v. Bowie Sewerage Co.,* 127 Tex. 97, 90 S.W. 2d 561 (1936) are a few cases.

[23] *Abbott v. City of Princeton, Texas,* 721 S.W. 2d 872 (Tex.App. -Dallas 1986).

[24] A comprehensive article on this subject is found in 42 A.L.R. 3rd 344 (1972). This article includes a listing of cases by jurisdictions that recognize the majority rule.

[25] Prosser and Keeton on Torts 87 (5th ed. 1984).

Trespass to land is the type of trespass action that is generally used in pollution control cases. In an action for trespass to land, entry upon another's land need not be in person. It may be made by causing or permitting a thing to cross the boundary of the premises. The trespass may be committed by casting material upon another's land, by discharging water, soot or carbon, by allowing gas or oil to flow underground into someone else's land, but not by mere vibrations or light which are generally classed as nuisances.

In the case of *Martin v. Reynolds Metal Co.*,[26] the deposit on Martin's property of microscopic fluoride compounds, which were emitted in vapor form from the Reynolds' plant, was held to be an invasion of this property—and so a trespass.

The line between trespass and nuisance is sometimes difficult to determine. "The distinction which is now accepted is that trespass is an invasion of the plaintiff's interest in the exclusive possession of his land, while nuisance is an interference with his use and enjoyment of it."[27]

Negligence and trespass have also been used interchangeably as seen in the case of *Stacy v. VEPCO*.[28] In this case, the court ruled that there was "negligence and/or trespass on the part of VEPCO" because of damage caused to Stacy's trees by emissions from VEPCO's Mount Storm plant. It is interesting to note that the court in this case was convinced by the expert meteorologist's testimony that the emissions could travel the 22-mile distance from the plant to damage the trees. The important point to remember is that courts can and do minimize the importance of the form of the action—namely, whether it is a nuisance, trespass or negligence—but endeavor to make a relatively just decision based on all the evidence presented.

4.3 Negligence

"Negligence" is "the omission to do something which a reasonable man, guided by those ordinary considerations which ordinarily regulate human affairs, would do, or the doing of something which a reasonable and prudent man would not do."[29] Negligence is that part of the law of torts which deals with acts not intended to inflict injury.

The standard of care required by law is that degree which would be exercised by a person of ordinary prudence under the same circumstances. This is often defined as the "reasonable man" rule, what a reasonable person would do under all the circumstances.

In order to render the defendant liable, his act must be the proximate cause of injury. Proximate cause is that which in the natural and continuous sequence, if unbroken by an efficient intervening act, produces injury and without which the result would not have happened.

---

[26] 221 Or. 86, 342 O. 2d 790 (1959), *cert. denied,* 362 U.S. 912 (1960).

[27] Prosser and Keeton on Torts 622 (5th ed. 1984).

[28] 7 Env't. Rep. Cas. (BNA) 1443 (E.d.Va. 1975).

[29] *Black's Law Dictionary* 1032 (6th ed. 1990).

Nissan Motor Corp. v.Maryland Shipbuilding and Drydock Company[30] exemplifies a negligence action in an environmental case. The shipbuilding company's employees failed to follow company regulations when painting ships, allowing spray paint to be carried by the wind onto Nissan's cars. The shipbuilders had knowledge of the likely danger of spraypainting, yet failed to exercise due care in conducting the painting operations in question. This failure to exercise due care amounted to negligence.

Persons harmed as a result of careless and improper disposal or handling of hazardous waste can recover for their losses under a negligence cause of action. Indeed, state and federal courts have long recognized this common law theory of recovery against defendants who engage in the negligent disposal of pollutants such as hazardous waste.[31] Where negligence can be established, it is no defense that the negligent action was in full compliance with all government regulations[32] and permit conditions.[33] On the other hand, noncompliance with regulations or a permit may be *prima facie* evidence (proof without any more evidence) of liability in some states.[34]

Generations of creative lawyers have eased the burden of proving negligence or fault in some circumstances by developing the negligence theories described in the following two sections.

4.3.1 Violation of a Statute or Ordinance Can Be Negligence

Generally, the violation of a statute or ordinance which was passed to promote safety is negligence, but the violation of such law does not of itself give rise to civil liability. The plaintiff must show that the violation of the law was the proximate cause of the injury. The violation of a statute or ordinance which is not designed to prevent the sort of harm about which the plaintiff is complaining is not negligence.

An example of the application of this doctrine in an environmental lawsuit is the case of *Springer v. Schlitz Brewing Company.*[35] Mr.and Mrs. Springer owned a large farm downriver from a newly constructed Winston Salem, N.C., brewery of Schlitz. They sued Schlitz for overloading the city's sewage treatment, causing it to pollute the Yadkin River, resulting in fish kills and so interfering with their fishing rights. In North Carolina, as in many other states, a landowner has a right to the fishing, agricultural, recreational and scenic use and enjoyment of the stream bordering his land. A city sewage ordinance prohibited the discharge of pollutants that interfere with the city's waste treatment process.

---

[30] 544 F.Supp. 1104 (1982).

[31] See, e.g., *Knabe v. National Supply Div. of Armco Steel Corp.*, 592 F.2d 841 (5th Cir. 1979).

[32] *Greater Westchester Homeowners Assoc. v. City of Los Angeles*, 26 Cal. 3d 86, 603 P.2d 1329 (1979), 160 Cal. Rptr. 733, *cert. denied*, 499 U.S. 820 (1980).

[33] *Brown v. Petroland, Inc.*, 102 Cal. App. 3d 720, 162 Cal. Rptr. 551 (1980).

[34] See *Martin v. Hersog*, 288 N.Y. 164, 126 N.E. 814, 439 N.Y.S. 2d 922 (1920).

[35] 510 F.2d 468, 7 Env't. Rep. Cas. (BNA) 1516 (4th Cir. 1975).

In this case the plaintiff did not, according to the court's opinion, prove that Schlitz was negligent in the conventional sense. Instead, the court looked to the theory that violation of a city sewage ordinance is negligence "per se." The appeals court directed that the jury should decide if Schlitz violated the city's ordinance. If the jury decides that the ordinance was violated, then the violation is negligence per se; and if the negligence proximately causes injury, then the industry is liable irrespective of any good faith efforts on the part of the defendant.

So, violations of environmental or pollution control statutes or ordinances which are generally designed to protect the public health or safety could result in a successful negligence lawsuit by the injured party even though there is no factual showing of negligence.

4.3.2 Strict Liability and Dangerous Substances

The assessment of liability for damages without requiring a showing of negligence is called "strict liability." A landowner keeping a potentially dangerous substance on his land which, if permitted to escape, is certain to injure others, must make good the damage caused by the escape of the substance, regardless of negligence on his part.

This strict liability theory is very old. It was used in a 1907 case in which oil escaped into the Potomac River in Washington, D.C. and resulted in injury to boats in a downstream boathouse.[36] In this case, it was determined that a potentially dangerous substance is anything which, if permitted to escape, is certain to injure others. This description of a potentially dangerous substance is so broad as to include oil in the case under discussion as well as thousands of other substances in subsequent litigation.

The reasoning for this strict liability standard is that, when persons suffer loss, no good reason can be found to charge the loss against anyone who did not contribute to it. But if someone is engaged in an ultra-hazardous or dangerous activity for profit, he should bear the burden of compensating others who are harmed by his activities.

In making the determination of whether an activity is ultra-hazardous, courts have traditionally scrutinized six factors: (1) the existence of a high degree of risk, (2) the likelihood that resultant harm will be great, (3) the ability to eliminate risk by exercising reasonable care, (4) the extent to which the activity is not common in the community, (5) the appropriateness of the activity to the place where it is carried on, and (6) the activity's value to the community.

Not surprisingly, courts have applied strict liability theories in cases involving the disposal of hazardous waste and hazardous materials management.

In *Crawford v. National Lead Company*,[37] Ohio residents who lived near a federally owned uranium metals production plant alleged that the

---

[36] *Brennan Constr. Co. v. Cumberland*, 29 App. D.C. 554 (1907).

[37] 784 F.Supp. 439 (S.D. Ohio 1989).

defendants failed to prevent the emission of uranium and other harmful materials from the plant and that this failure caused emotional distress and diminished property values. The court examined the six factors listed above and determined that the provision of uranium in various forms to nuclear facilities throughout the country is an abnormally dangerous activity.

The court then looked to the elements of strict liability for harm caused by an abnormally dangerous activity:

1. One who carries on an abnormally dangerous activity is subject to liability for harm to the person, land or chattels of another resulting from the activity, although he has exercised the utmost care to prevent the harm.

2. This strict liability is limited to the kind of harm the possibility of which makes the activity abnormally dangerous.[38]

Ruling that emotional distress and property damage will support a claim of strict liability in Ohio, the court ruled in favor of the residents.

Strict liability takes on a huge role in the burgeoning environmental law field. In fact, the Environmental Protection Agency itself states, "[M]ost of the statutes which the EPA administers are strict liability,"illustrating its widespread use.[39]

Take, for instance, the courts' application, developed over the past decade and a half, of strict liability to the Federal Water Pollution Control Act. As recently as September 19, 1991,[40] the federal courts have recognized the application of strict liability to the Federal Water Pollution Control Act, referring back to the grandfather of this line of cases, *United States v. Earth Sciences, Inc.*[41]

In *United States v. Earth Sciences, Inc.*, a gold leaching operation owned by defendant Earth Science discharged cyanide into the Rito Seco Creek in Costilla County, Colorado during the process of separating gold from ore. Earth Sciences argued that the pertinent statute made only intentional discharges unlawful. The court stated, "The regulatory provisions of the FWPCA were written without regard to intentionality, however, making the person responsible for the discharge of any pollutant strictly liable."[42]

---

[38] Restatement (Second) of Torts §519 (1977).

[39] *Environmental Protection Agency Civil Penalty Policy* (February 16, 1984) at 24.

[40] *United States v. Winchester Municipal Utilities*, 944 F.2d 301 (6th Cir. 1991).

[41] 599 F.2d 368 (10th Cir. 1979)

[42] *Ibid.* at 374.

5.0 LAWS THAT ENFORCE PERMITS, PROHIBITIONS AND PENALTIES

Although the environmental law's mechanisms for enforcing its mandates are essentially the same as those available in other legal disciplines, there are distinctive aspects to the overall enforcement package—the ways in which the available mechanisms are used together to effectively compel fulfillment of the environmental compliance obligations.

5.1 Permits

Perhaps the most distinctive aspect of environmental enforcement is its extensive and effective use of permitting mechanisms. Particularly with laws as complex and technical as most of the environmental statutes, it is critical that there be an effective mechanism for bridging from generalities like "Effluents shall be treated in compliance with best available technology" to specifics like:

> Permittee is authorized to discharge from outfall number 001 "x" pounds per day of pollutant "y," subject to the condition that the discharge be monitored in accordance with specified protocols and that periodic reports be provided.

The permit fulfills this need by, in effect, establishing the "law" for a particular discharge or activity. The requirement to obtain a permit and operate in compliance with it is an individualized and highly effective way of insuring that regulators are notified of releases or activities of which they need to be aware. It is also an effective way of assuring and demonstrating that the person required to comply is on notice of his obligations. The role of permits in bridging the substantive requirements of the environmental laws—notification, discharge controls and so forth—and the other enforcement mechanisms is discussed below.

Permitting requirements, however, are by no means the only weapon in environmental law's enforcement arsenal.

5.2 Enforcement Provisions of the Federal and State Environmental Statutes

Each of the major federal environmental statutes provides an array of enforcement tools to compel compliance with its mandates. Generally, these include:

- **Civil Penalties** ranging from $10,000 to $50,000 per violation or day of violation
- **Administrative Orders** to respond or abate, enforceable by civil and criminal sanctions
- **Civil Action for Relief** including prohibition or mandatory injunction enforced by judicial decree

- **Citizens' Civil Actions**—to compel compliance with or collect damages for violation of the statute
- **Criminal Sanctions** against organizations and responsible individuals for misrepresentation or knowing or negligent violation of the statutes

There is no doubt that the federal environmental statutes and the regulations under them present a formidable set of reasons for a business or other organization to institute programs for aggressive compliance with the environmental laws. They are supported and complemented by similar enforcement provisions in the state environmental statutes as well as in local laws and ordinances.

5.3 General Purpose Criminal Laws

The last major category of "environmental laws that enforce" are laws from the criminal code, originally enacted to punish more traditional crimes, which have been adopted and adapted to the prosecution of crimes which are essentially environmental. The criminal code provisions which have proven particularly useful in this connection include:

- Prohibition Against False Statements to the Federal Government— 18 U.S.C. 1001
- Mail Fraud Statutes—18 U.S.C. 1341, 1343
- Conspiracy Laws—18 U.S.C. 371

Even more traditional criminal laws, such as the murder statutes, have been used, at least at the state level, to successfully prosecute environmental offenses. These non-environmental laws have become almost as important as the environmental statutes in defining the liability of violators.

The environmental law enforcement package, then, is a carefully structured combination of methods—environmental and general purpose, traditional and newly conceived—which work together to bring bad consequences to those who fail to fulfill their environmental compliance obligations. This interaction has been extremely effective and will become even more formidable as the environmental law system matures.

6.0 LAWS THAT DEFINE THE ENVIRONMENTAL LAW PROCESS

Having discussed the substantive mandates of the environmental laws and the enforcement methods which make compliance mandatory, we now need to examine the organic and procedural environmental laws—the laws that establish the framework within which the system operates. Although "organic and procedural laws" is not a term which, at first impression, offers great promise of maintaining the rapt attention of those who would toil in the environmental law vineyard, closer consideration may yield a different conclusion. The fact is that many of the questions which are most critical to successful compliance efforts and most difficult for environmental practitioners to answer fall within this category:

- What level of government has authority to regulate?
- What protections are available to the regulated?
- How do questions of scientific fact get answered?
- Who can go to court and who pays for it?

Answers to these and similar questions—critical to the resolution of environmental cases—are found not in the "environmental" statutes or regulations, but in organic laws such as constitutions—federal and state—and city charters, and procedural laws such as Administrative Procedure Acts, judicial codes and rules of evidence. These determine how our overall legal system works in environmental contexts as well as in others. It is, of course, impossible in one chapter of one volume to do more than highlight some of these important requirements which are particularly germane to the subject at hand.

6.1 The Organic Laws—Constitutions and Charters

In our system, the powers of government and the rights of individuals are defined primarily in the "organic acts" by which governments are created—constitutions in the case of federal and state governments and, generally, charters in the case of local governmental units like cities and counties. These laws provide the foundation for the environmental law system just as they do for the legal system in general. We look to this foundation to give us answers to the most basic and often most important questions encountered in environmental practice.

6.1.1 Federal, State and Local Roles

A question which arises in the development of environmental regulatory programs revolves around which level of government—state, federal or local—is to play the primary role in regulating particular activities affecting the environment. The federal government is a government of limited authority which may act only through the exercise of the enumerated powers granted to it under the Constitution. In practice, however, the enumerated powers—particularly the power to regulate interstate and foreign commerce—have been broadly construed and there are few, if any, recent instances where federal laws enacted to protect the public health and welfare have been held to be in excess of constitutional authority.

Once federal authority has been exercised, and a federal system of regulation has been established, important questions arise about the continuing ability of state and local governments to operate in that same area. While state and local governments have broad "police powers" to do what is necessary to protect the health and safety of their citizens, that authority may be displaced where a scheme of federal regulation, pursuant to enumerated authority, preempts the field of regulation and precludes the further exercise of state and local authority. The judicial trend in these "preemption cases" is towards upholding continued state authority except where the U.S. Congress has explicitly expressed a clear intention to fully occupy the field and displace state authority to regulate. The trend in the

Congress is to explicitly preserve the states' continuing authority to regulate.

6.1.2 Commerce Clause

One line of constitutional cases dealing with this question of "who can regulate?" involves the issue of whether, even in the absence of preemptive federal action, a state or local law may be unconstitutional because it improperly restrains interstate or foreign commerce.

Article I, Section 8, of the U.S. Constitution is called the "Commerce Clause." It grants to Congress the authority ". . . to regulate Commerce with foreign Nations, and among the several States, and with the Indian Tribes." If the courts find that state statutes or regulations impermissibly burden interstate commerce, then they are unconstitutional and unenforceable.

It is well settled that a state regulation validly based on police power does not impermissibly burden interstate commerce if the regulations neither discriminate against interstate commerce nor operate to disrupt its required uniformity. Where there is a reasonable basis to protect the social, as distinguished from the economic, welfare of a community, the courts will not deny this exercise of sovereign power and hold it to violate the Commerce Clause.

Very recently the U.S. Supreme Court examined a Commerce Clause case involving Alabama's Emelle facility, the nation's largest commercial hazardous waste landfill and one of our oldest. For disposal of hazardous waste at the Emelle facility, Alabama charged $72.00 more per ton for waste generated *outside* Alabama than it did for waste generated *inside* Alabama. The Supreme Court ruled that the additional fee discriminated against hazardous waste generated in states other than Alabama and that such burdensome taxes on interstate commerce were forbidden.[43]

Another Commerce Clause case involved the Chicago ordinance banning the sale of detergents containing phosphates.[44] The Seventh Circuit Court of Appeals held that the ordinance did not violate the Commerce Clause because, although it had some minor effect on interstate commerce, the benefits far outweighed these effects, and the ordinance was a reasonable method of achieving a legitimate goal of improving Lake Michigan.

Another result favorable to legislators was reached in Missouri when the constitutionality of the City of Columbia's five-cent refund on beverage containers was challenged.[45] "The declared purpose of the ordinance is to reduce littering and to promote recycling and reuse of empty beverage

---

[43] *Chemical Waste Management, Inc. v. Hunt*, ---U.S.---, 112 S.Ct. 2009, 119 L.Ed.2d.2d121, 60 U.S.L.W. 4433, 34 ERC 1721, 22 Envtl. L. Rep. 20909 (1992); See also *Fort Gratiot Sanitary Landfill, Inc. v. Michigan Dept. of Natural Resources*, ---U.S.---, 112 S.Ct. 2019, (1992).

[44] *Proctor and Gamble Co. vs. Chicago*, 509 F.2d69, 7 ERC 1328 (7th Cir 1975), *cert. denied*, 421 U.S. 978 (1975).

[45] *Mid-State Distributing Company v. City of Columbia*, 617 S.W.2d 419 (Mo.App. 1981).

containers."[46] The Court held, "The Columbia ordinance does not discriminate between intrastate and interstate commerce."[47]

The trend is definitely to try to uphold environmental legislation, the rationale based on a balancing of environmental benefits against detrimental effects.

We can expect the debate along these lines to intensify and revitalize as international laws and treaties establish product standards and regulate activities, like marine transportation, potentially affecting the environment. While questions of "unreasonable burden" may be philosophically the same in the global context as within the national borders, the political dynamics and level of complexity will increase radically and new solutions may indeed be required.

6.1.3 Equal Protection

Another category of cases of interest to the environmental field are those limiting the ability of federal and state governments to regulate conduct under the Constitutional mandate of "equal protection."

Section One of the Fourteenth Amendment to the Constitution prohibits governments from denying to any person the equal protection of the laws. This provision has been applied, essentially, to prevent inappropriate discrimination between regulated entities or categories.

In Hawaii several environmental groups sought to stop an interstate highway project known as the "H-3" project.[48] Congress thwarted their efforts in 1986 when they passed Public Law No. 99-591. Section 114 of this law provided for specific exemption of the H-3 project from federal "4(f) statutes" requiring that no public parks, wildlife refuges, or historical sites be used for any project unless "no feasible and prudent alternative" exists and unless harm to the area is minimized.

The environmental groups asked the court to hold that section 114 violated the equal protection component of the U.S. Constitution. They argued that the right to a healthy environment is an "important" individual right and that Congress violated constitutional principles of federalism in enacting a provision which discriminates against the citizens of Hawaii. They claimed that section 114 "creates an arbitrary classification [based on state citizenship] by denying residents of Hawaii the environmental protections provided by the 4(f) statutes."

The U.S. Court of Appeals for the 9th Circuit ruled against the Hawaiian environmental groups, remarking that no court had ever found a right to a healthy environment to exist. The court held that Congress had the power to exempt specific projects from certain federal laws, and that

---

[46] *Ibid*, at 421.

[47] *Ibid*, at 430.

[48] *Stop H-3 Association v. Transportation Department*, 870 F.2d 1419, 29 ERC 1390 (CA 9th Cir. 1989).

exempting this particular project did not amount to arbitrarily or categorically discriminating against Hawaii.

Courts generally hold that for a classification to violate the constitutional guarantee of equal protection, there must be a showing that there is no reasonable basis for the distinction. A law is presumptively valid. Unless clear and convincing proof demonstrates that a law is arbitrary and unreasonable, the law must be upheld. The result is that few laws are ever held to violate the equal protection clause.

So, effective arguments have been made that there is a need to limit the number of regulators by either giving all power to the states and keeping the federal government out or vice versa. The end result of all these arguments has been continued reaffirmation that, in environmental contexts, federal, state and local governments will continue to exercise concurrent, but not always coordinated, jurisdiction. This fact of life is one of the things that makes this field a challenge.

6.2 The Courts' Role

While the organic laws define the authorities of the legislative and executive branches of the government as well as the judiciary, to understand the law as applied, one must understand the courts' role.

6.2.1 State and United States Court Systems

There are two primary judicial systems in the United States: (1) the state and local courts, established in each state under the authority of the state government, and (2) federal courts, set up under the authority of the Constitution by the Congress of the United States.

The state courts have general, unlimited power to decide almost every type of case, subject only to the limitation of state law. State and local courts are located in every town and county and are the tribunals with which citizens most often have contact. The great bulk of legal business, such as divorce, probate of estates, traffic accidents and all other matters except those assigned to the U.S. courts is handled by these state and local courts.

The U.S. courts, on the other hand, have the authority to hear and decide only selected types of cases, which are specifically enumerated in the Constitution. The U.S. courts are located principally in the larger cities while state and local courts are found throughout the country.

6.2.2 United States Court System

The structure of the U.S. court system has evolved throughout the historical development of our country. The Constitution merely provides: "The Judicial Power of the United States, shall be vested in one Supreme Court, and in such inferior Courts as the Congress may from time to time ordain and establish." Thus, the only court which is constitutionally indispensable is the Supreme Court. The authority to establish and abolish other U.S. courts is vested in and has been exercised by the Congress.

The United States court system is pyramidal in structure with three levels. At the apex of the pyramid stands the Supreme Court of the United States, the highest court in the land. On the second level are the 14 United States courts of appeals. On the third level are the 94 United States District Courts.

A person involved in a suit in a U.S. court may proceed through the three levels of decision. Generally, the case will first be heard and decided by one of the courts on the district court level. If either party is dissatisfied with the decision, it will usually have a right of review in one of the courts of appeals. Then, if still dissatisfied, it may petition for review in the Supreme Court of the United States. However, review is granted by the Supreme Court only in cases involving matters of national importance.

This pyramidal organization of the courts serves two purposes. First, the Supreme Court and the courts of appeals can correct errors which have been made in the decisions of the trial courts. Secondly, the higher courts can assure uniformity of decision by reviewing cases in which two or more lower courts have reached different decisions.

State courts have a similar pyramid structure, with a basic court of original jurisdiction, an appellate court and then a supreme court. Often states do not use the same terminology in naming their courts. So, at the state level the nomenclature can be confusing, but the system of a lower court deciding a case in the beginning with opportunity for review of the decision by appellate courts is the same as in the federal system.

6.2.3 Courts in Practical Perspective

From a practical viewpoint, when you learn about a judicial decision of interest to you, ask which court decided the case. If the Supreme Court of the U.S. decided the case, it is a very important decision for the entire country. If a local court decided the case, it is generally of little interest nationally but of major interest to that local jurisdiction. However, any decision on a point of law is better than none at all.

Also, be aware that courts do differ in their opinions. There are many examples of two lower courts reaching conflicting opinions on a point of law. This is an extremely difficult concept for many to accept. If you are originally trained in engineering or the sciences, you are probably accustomed to dealing in data and facts. To move into the realm of "ifs" and "yes, but" seems like going from the world of black and white into a world of gray. For those who find this troubling, remember that in almost everything, we are talking about degrees of certitude. The field of environmental law may involve a higher degree of incertitude than most other areas because of its newness and changeability. As a result, you do your best to understand what is the meaning of the laws, regulations and court opinions, and you then take into consideration the degree of certitude involved in a particular legal issue before proceeding to a decision.

Also, keep in mind that your court system, although hailed as one of the fairest systems ever developed by mankind, is subject to human frailties. Human interactions like those of dealing with judges, lawyers, plaintiffs, defendants and jurors are another source of uncertainties.

6.2.4 Court Jurisdiction and Forum Shopping

The question of which court has jurisdiction can be a complex issue. Also, the question of the specific court in which a case is initiated is generally a key move in the overall strategy for winning a lawsuit. This is called "forum shopping." When initiating a lawsuit a good lawyer will evaluate which court is more inclined toward his client's position. For example, the judges of the U.S. Courts in the District of Columbia are known for their pro-environmental record. So organizations such as the Environmental Defense Fund (EDF) and the Sierra Club are inclined to initiate their lawsuits in the U.S. District Courts for the District of Columbia. Industrial firms are generally more inclined to file a lawsuit in a district court in Louisiana or other such geographic area with a more conservative judicial record.

6.2.5 When Can Courts Act?

According to Article III, Section 2, clause 1, of the United States Constitution, federal courts can only act on actual "cases" or "controversies," meaning:

1. "moot" questions cannot be decided,

2. "advisory opinions" cannot be issued,

3. cases must be "ripe" for decision—concrete and focused, having reached "finality" on the part of the executive and legislative branches, and not premature and abstract,

4. "collusive" and "feigned" cases will be dismissed, and

5. parties must have standing to sue.

The following examples illustrate these principles.

In *Woodland Private Study Group v. New Jersey Department of Environmental Protection*[49] the U.S. Court of Appeals for the Third Circuit ordered a complaint dismissed as moot when 3M (the Minnesota Mining and Manufacturing Company) and R&H (the Rohm and Haas Company) challenged the New Jersey Spill Compensation and Control Act as unconstitutional. Before their case was decided, however, the New Jersey Supreme Court in two different cases performed what the court called "judicial surgery" on the act, bringing it into conformity with the federal constitution. Both 3M and R&H agreed in letters to the court that this action rendered their case moot, and it was dismissed.

In *TJ Baker, Inc. v. Aetna Casualty and Surety Co.*,[50] plaintiff Baker was named as a potentially responsible party (PRP) for environmental pollution at several sites. Aetna Casualty and Surety Co. had issued

---

[49] 846 F.2d 921, 27 ERC 1911 (3rd Cir. 1988).
[50] 28 ERC 1237 (DC NJ 1988).

comprehensive general liability [CGL] insurance policies to Baker, and Baker sought "partial summary judgment on the legal interpretation, under New Jersey law, of a provision contained in the CGL policies which defined an 'occurrence'—the event which triggers coverage under each policy."

"What the plaintiff seeks, in essence, is an advisory opinion on the state of New Jersey law regarding the widely-used 'occurrence' definition in CGL policies. This requested ruling would not require an examination of any of the facts, disputed or otherwise, involved in this matter, nor would this determination dispose of any claim or any part of any claim asserted by plaintiff."[51] Accordingly, the federal district court dismissed the case, illustrating the rule against issuing advisory opinions.

Ripeness was the issue in *In re Combustion Equipment Associates, Inc.*[52] There the EPA sent the appellant a letter naming it a *potentially* responsible party (PRP) for groundwater contamination at two landfill sites. The appellant sought judgment that any CERCLA liability it may have had was discharged by its subsequent Chapter 11 bankruptcy reorganization. The court ruled that there was no finality to the EPA's action of naming the appellant a PRP, and since there was not yet any determination that appellant was actually responsible, there might never be a need to assess the effect of the bankruptcy reorganization on such responsibility. The court dismissed the action as not ready or "ripe" for determination.

6.2.6 Who May Sue?

To sue, a party must have "standing" or an appropriate individuated interest in the outcome of the case. In the 1989 case of *McCormick v. Anshutz Mining Corp.*,[53] the plaintiff, Walter McCormick, alleged that Anshutz Mining had violated CERCLA. However, McCormick testified in deposition that he had not been injured in any way by alleged discharges of pollution from a mine owned by Anshutz Mining. While McCormick was worried that he might be exposed to *future* liability because he had been in charge of the refinery at the mine until it was closed, "The mere possibility of future injury is not enough." Hence, the court dismissed McCormick's case for lack of standing.

In the context of actions to compel or obtain review of agency actions, the required interest is described in the Administrative Procedure Act (APA). Under APA, standing exists only when a plaintiff can satisfactorily demonstrate that (a) the agency action complained of will result in an injury in fact and that (b) the injury is to an interest "arguably within the zone of interests to be protected" by the statute in question.

The leading cases addressing the "injury in fact" question are cases involving the National Environmental Policy Act and environmental impact statements. The key case is the Supreme Court decision in *Sierra*

---

[51] *Ibid.*, at 1239.

[52] 838 F.2d 35, 27 ERC 1227 (2nd Cir. 1988).

[53] 29 ERC 1707 (DC Emo 1989).

Club v. Morton.[54] This case involved the recreational development of the Mineral King Valley. The question in *Sierra v. Morton* was: What must be alleged by persons who claim injury of a non-economic nature to widely shared interests to give them standing? The court recognized that environmental well-being, like economic well-being, is an important ingredient of our society. The fact that environmental interests are shared by the many rather than few does not make them less deserving of legal protection. But the "injury in fact" test, according to the Court, requires that the party seeking review be himself among the injured. The Sierra Club did not allege and show that it or its members would be affected in any of their activities or pastimes by the development. So the Court ruled against them. However, this has since proven to be an easy matter to remedy by the plaintiffs alleging that an aesthetic or other non-economic interest was injured. So the Sierra Club established in this decision that environmental interests could be the basis for standing.

In a subsequent Supreme Court case, *SCRAP v. U.S.*[55] the Supreme Court gave some law students standing to sue the Interstate Commerce Commission (ICC) in a rate increase case involving recyclables. The Supreme Court ruled that standing to sue was demonstrated by the students, showing that they used forest and streams in the Washington, D.C. area for camping and hiking and that this was disturbed by the adverse environmental impact caused by the nonuse of recyclable goods brought on by the ICC rate increase on recyclable commodities.

In one of its most recent visits to the case or controversy and standing issue the Supreme Court has indicated that environmental organizations do not get a free ride to judgment but must allege and prove individuated injury in fact. In *Lujan v. National Wildlife Federation,*[56] the Supreme Court reversed a decision which held that two affidavits filed on behalf of the National Wildlife Federation had satisfactorily alleged injury in fact, even though they were not specific as to the actual injury. The affidavits were filed in support of a challenge to a program of the Bureau of Land Management. The Court stated that "whether one of respondent's members has been, or is threatened to be, 'adversely affected or aggrieved' by Government action—Rule 56(e) is assuredly not satisfied by pleadings which state only that one of respondent's members uses unspecified portions of an immense tract of territory, on some portions of which mining activity has occurred or probably will occur by virtue of the governmental action."[57]

The U.S. Supreme Court's current trend is definitely to make it harder for a plaintiff to establish standing to sue. The 1992 case of *Lujan v. Defenders of Wildlife*[58] continues this trend. This lawsuit challenged the

[54] 405 U.S. 727 3 Env't. Rep. Cas. (BNA) 2039 (1972).

[55] 412 U.S. 669 (1973)

[56] 110 S.Ct. 3177 (1990).

[57] *Id.* at 3189.

[58] 110 S.Ct. 3177 (1990).

view that U.S. agencies' funding of development projects overseas does not have to comply with the Endangered Species Act. The court did not rule on the question of whether the law's provisions extend to overseas projects, but rather dismissed the case on the legal ground that the plaintiffs lacked standing to sue. One of the plaintiffs in this lawsuit, Joyce Kelly, had asserted that she would suffer harm because the Bureau of Reclamation's project to rebuild the Aswan Dam in Egypt threatened the endangered Nile crocodile. Amy Silbred said she would be harmed by the Mahaweli water resource project in Sri Lanka, funded by the U.S. AID, which threatened the endangered Asian elephant and leopard.

Justice Scalia, writing for the court majority, said that although both women had visited the area of the projects and alleged their intention to return, that was not enough to demonstrate that they were in immediate danger of suffering harm. He said plaintiffs must prove they suffer individual, concrete harm as a result of the government's procedural violation to have standing to sue.

6.3 Defining The Rights of the Regulated and Limits of Governmental Authority

While we normally think about "Constitutional Rights" in contexts other than environmental law, there is little doubt that the scope and availability of rights which some regard as "fundamental freedoms" will continue to be matters of vigorous contention in this field. Some of these areas of debate are summarized below.

6.3.1 Search Warrants and the Fourth Amendment

The Fourth Amendment of the Constitution provides that:

> The right of the people to be secure in their persons, houses, papers, and effects, against unreasonable searches and seizures shall not be violated, and no Warrants shall issue, but upon probable cause, supported by oath or affirmation and particularly describing the place to be searched and the persons or things to be seized.

The warrant issue arises most frequently in connection with the collection or obtaining of evidence. Evidence is necessary for any civil or criminal enforcement program. However, federal and state evidence collection is limited by Fourth Amendment prohibitions. Generally warrants are only sought after entry is refused, because there is no need for a search warrant when the owner or operator has given his consent.

The courts have held that the Fourth Amendment applies to the corporate entity as well as to the private citizen. The Supreme Court has held that the requirement for a search warrant even applies to routine inspections.[59] In the *Camara* case, the Court held that the warrant requirement applied to a municipal health inspector's search of a private

---

[59] *Camara v. Municipal Court of San Francisco*, 387 U.S. 523 (1967).

residence. A similar conclusion was reached with respect to a fire inspector's attempted search of a commercial warehouse.[60] In these cases, the Court indicated that a lesser degree of "probable cause" would be required for an administrative search warrant than for the typical criminal search warrant. So there can be routine periodic searches of all structures in a given area based on an appraisal of conditions in the area as a whole rather than on a knowledge of conditions in a particular building. The reasonableness of such inspections is to be weighed against the invasion of rights that the search entails.

In November of 1989, the Supreme Court of Pennsylvania upheld warrantless, unannounced inspection provisions of Pennsylvania's Solid Waste Management Act.[61] The act allowed a Department of Environmental Resources (DER) employee to go into a "transfer station" where trash was compacted, since the employee entered the transfer station "to ascertain the compliance or noncompliance by any person or municipality with the provisions of this act." The DER employee had seen one of the appellant's loaded trash trucks enter the transfer station, which the appellant had not been issued a permit to operate. The court reasoned that the "Colonade-Biswell exception"[62] to the warrant requirement of the Fourth Amendment allows greater latitude to conduct warrantless inspections of commercial property because "the expectation of privacy that the owner of commercial property enjoys in such property differs significantly from the sanctity accorded an individual's home..."[63]

To avoid this need for search warrants, Congress has authorized warrantless searches in some statutes. In the famous *Barlow* case[64] the constitutionality of these legislative waivers was reviewed by the Supreme Court. The Court held that Section 8 of the Occupational Safety and Health Act (OSHA), which authorized warrantless inspections, violated the Fourth Amendment prohibition against warrantless searches and was unconstitutional. Despite this Constitutional protection, the wisdom of demanding a warrant for a normal inspection is dubious at best, and few businesses challenge inspections without warrants because to do so indicates that a problem probably exists. The warrant requirement does put some minimal restraint on the federal government's ability to conduct repetitive or needless inspections.

The Environmental Protection Agency (EPA) has avoided any test of the constitutionality of the warrantless search authorizations given to them by Congress in the Noise Control Act and the Resource Conservation and Recovery Act by not challenging the issue. If an EPA inspector is refused

---

[60] *See v. City of Seattle*, 387 U.S. 541 (1967).

[61] *Com., DER v. Blosenski Disposal Serv*, 523 Pa 274, 566 A2d 845, 30 ERC 1835 (1989).

[62] *Colonade Catering Corp. v. United States*, 397 U.S. 72, 90 S.Ct. 774, 25 L.Ed.2d 60 (1970), *United States v. Biswell*, 406 U.S. 311, 92 S.Ct. 1593, 32 L.Ed.2d 87 (1972).

[63] *Com., DER v. Blosenski Disposal Serv.*, 566 A2d 845, 848 (1989).

[64] *Marshall v. Barlow's Inc.*, 436 U.S. 307 (1978).

admission, EPA, as standard procedure, will then obtain a search warrant and not even try to use the statutory authority. This avoids the constitutional confrontation.

It is common, in the field of environmental law, to find exceptions to the general rules. An example of an exception to the search warrant requirement is the so-called "open fields" exception described in the Supreme Court case, *Air Pollution Variance Board v. Western Alfalfa.*[65] In this case, an inspector of a Division of the Colorado Department of Health entered the premises of Western Alfalfa Corporation without its knowledge or consent to make a Ringelmann reading of plumes of smoke being emitted from the company's chimneys. Western Alfalfa Corporation claimed that the inspection violated the Fourth Amendment by entering its property to collect evidence without a search warrant. The U.S. Supreme Court ruled that the inspector was within an exception to the Fourth Amendment and had not violated the rights of Western Alfalfa Corporation. The Court held the general rule to be that the act of conducting tests on a defendant's premises without either a warrant or the consent of defendant constitutes an unreasonable search within the Fourth Amendment. However, in this case the inspector did not enter the plant or offices. Basically he sighted what anyone in the area near the plant could see in the sky. He was on the defendant's property, but there was no showing that he was on premises from which the public was excluded. The Court held that there is an "open fields" exception to the constitutional requirement for a search warrant which was applicable in this case.

A more recent case describing the "open fields" exception is in the interesting 1992 case of *Forsythe v. Commonwealth of Pennsylvania.*[66]

After various discussions with appellant Barb Forsythe about the condition of her property, Larry Smith, Franklin Township's code enforcement officer, periodically inspected her premises. Smith observed "numerous junked cars, piles of trash, washers, mailboxes, wheel rims, water heaters, concrete blocks, and miscellaneous car parts on her property."[67] Barb Forsythe claimed she was operating a "recycling center" and admitted she had a business sign with the designation "Jay's Auto Parts" erected at the entrance to her yard. Forsythe was convicted of operating a junkyard without a license.

On appeal Forsythe argued that because enforcement officer Smith had entered her property without a warrant, her conviction should be overturned. The appellate court disagreed, however, noting that "[t]he condition of [appellant's] land was easily ascertainable from a public road. She could have no expectation of privacy in an open field."[68] Since the only

---

[65] 416 U.S. 861, 6 Env't. Rep. Cas. (BNA) 157 1 (1974).

[66] 601 A2d 864 (Pa Cmwealth 1992).

[67] *Ibid*, at 865.

[68] *Ibid*, at 866.

evidence used in her conviction was easily ascertainable from a public road, the open fields exception applied and Forsythe's conviction was upheld.

In the vast majority of practical situations, consent is given for collection of evidence. The consent may be oral or written, and is commonly given by employees simply admitting the inspectors to the company premises or giving answers to oral or written questions by government employees.

One method of avoiding the necessity of obtaining a search warrant is to require the owner or operator of the pollution source to get a permit or license to operate which includes a condition allowing inspections without warrants. The U.S. Supreme Court has not yet ruled on the constitutionality of this method. Since permit systems are now being used more and more by federal, state and local agencies to control pollution, this method of obtaining desired evidence will be the trend of the future and provides the government with the consent needed.

6.3.2 Prohibition Against Self-Incrimination: The Fifth Amendment

The Fifth Amendment to the Constitution prohibits compulsory self-incrimination. The protection applies in criminal cases. If the government agency collecting the evidence will use it only for civil actions, such as fines or injunctions, the Fifth Amendment is not applicable. In addition, the Fifth Amendment applies only to persons and not to corporations or partnerships.

In *Braswell v. United States*[69] the Supreme Court reiterated many of the protections against self-incrimination. The petitioner Randy Braswell purchased and sold timber, land, equipment, and oil and gas interests through his two corporations. When a federal grand jury subpoenaed Braswell as president of both corporations to produce the corporations' books and records, Braswell claimed that according to the Fifth Amendment he should not be compelled in any criminal case to be a witness against himself.[70]

In the decision Chief Justice Rehnquist explained that the Fifth Amendment neither applies to "collective entities" such as corporations, unions or partnerships, nor to people acting as agents of collective entities. Rather, the Fifth Amendment applies to people in personal capacities and protects individuals' private papers. Notably, a sole proprietorship is considered personal and is protected by the Fifth Amendment.

The Supreme Court ruled against Braswell. Because the subpoena identified Braswell as an agent of "collective entities,"—specifically, president of the corporations—the Fifth Amendment's protections did not apply. If, on the other hand, Braswell had been operating sole proprietorships as he had in the past, he would have been protected by the Fifth Amendment.

---

[69] 487 U.S. 11 (1988).
[70] Fifth Amendment.

Most environmental statutes provide penalties for both individuals and corporations. Therefore, in a case where the evidence or samples taken might be used in a criminal action, the person in authority at the place where evidence is to be taken should be advised of his rights to remain silent, to an attorney, and that any evidence taken may be used against him in a subsequent criminal action. If these rights are not formally observed, the evidence so collected may not be admissible in a criminal action. See section 6.5.6 of this chapter also.

6.3.3 Due Process, the Fifth and Fourteenth Amendments

The requirement that government entities provide due process of law is found in the Fifth and Fourteenth Amendments.

The Fifth Amendment to the U.S. Constitution says: "No person shall . . . be deprived of life, liberty, or property, without due process of law; nor shall private property be taken for public use, without just compensation."

The Fourteenth Amendment to the U.S. Constitution states: "Section 1 . . . No State shall make or enforce any law which shall abridge the privileges or immunities of citizens of the United States; nor shall any State deprive any person of life, liberty, or property without due process of law; nor deny to any person within its jurisdiction the equal protection of the law."

The Fifth Amendment prohibition applies to federal government and the Fourteenth applies to states.

An example of the application of the legal concept of due process is found in the case, *Construction Industry Ass'n. v. Petaluma.*[71] In this case the Court held that a city ordinance that limits issuance of new building permits to achieve a goal of preserving "small town" character, open spaces and low density population does not violate the due process clause of the Fourteenth Amendment.

The Court's opinion explained that, to satisfy the due process mandate, zoning regulations must find their justification in some aspect of the police power asserted for the public welfare. The Court found that the concept of the public welfare is sufficiently broad to uphold Petaluma's desire to preserve its small town character, open spaces and low density population.

The due process argument was used against the beverage container ordinance of the City of Bowie, Maryland.[72] The Court ruled that there was not a violation of due process since there was not a showing that the police power was exercised arbitrarily, oppressively or unreasonably. The opinion also held that a law should not be held void if there are any considerations of public welfare which can support it.

---

[71] 522 F.2d 897, 8 Env't. Rep. Cas. (BNA) 1001 (9th cir. 1975), *cert. denied,* 424 U.S. 924 (1976).

[72] *Bowie Inn v. City of Bowie,* 274 Md. 230, 335 A.2d 679, 7 Env't. Rep. Cas. (BNA) 2083 (1975).

6.3.4 Police Power and Due Process

Police power is the inherent right of a government to pass laws for the protection of the health, welfare, morals, and property of the people within its jurisdiction. Police power may not be bartered away by contract. It extends to all public needs. It may be put forth in aid of what is sanctioned by usage or what is held by prevailing opinion to be greatly or immediately necessary for public welfare. By exercise of reasonable police power, government may regulate the conduct of individuals and of the use of their property and, in some instances, take property without compensation.

Although the police power of a state is very broad, it is not without limitation. It is always within the power of the court to declare a law void which, although enacted as a police regulation, is not justified as such. In other words, a law enacted as a police regulation must be reasonable. If the law is unreasonable or exercised in an arbitrary manner, it is taking life, liberty or property without due process of law. Two examples of allowable exercise of police powers are given above in Section 6.3.3.

Another example of the valid exercise of police power which did not violate the due process principle was in the Supreme Court case, *Village of Belle Terre v. Borass.*[73] In this case a New York village ordinance restricted land use to one-family houses and precluded occupancy by more than two unrelated persons. The Court held this ordinance to be a valid exercise of the city's police power, stating:

> A quiet place where yards are wide, people few, and motor vehicles restricted are legitimate guidelines in a land use project addressed to family needs. The police power is not confined to elimination of filth, stench, and unhealthy places. It is ample to lay out zones where family values, youth values, and the blessings of quiet seclusion and clean air make the area a sanctuary for people.

The case of *Browning-Ferris Industries (BFI) of Alabama, Inc. v. Alabama Department of Environmental Management* [ADEM][74] illustrates the interplay of police power and due process rights. BFI was trying to open a hazardous waste facility when the Alabama legislature passed the Minus Act prohibiting hazardous waste facilities to open without prior legislative approval. BFI challenged the statute as violative of the Fourteenth Amendment's Due Process Clause.

The court announced that the storage of hazardous waste is an appropriate area for control by the Alabama legislature under its police power. "The Court emphasizes that the Constitution does not foreclose legislative restrictions on hazardous waste facilities. Such restrictions

---

[73] 416 U.S. 1 (1974).
[74] 710 F.Supp. 313, 30 ERC 1166 (M.D. Ala. 1987).

appear to this Court to be essential for the protection of the health and safety of Alabama residents."[75]

However, the federal court found that the statute provided absolutely no standards by which to decide for approval of hazardous waste facilities. The court stated that, "the guarantee of due process...demands only that the law shall not be unreasonable, arbitrary and capricious and that the means selected shall have some real and substantial relationship to the object sought to be obtained.... [Citation omitted.]"[76] Thus, while in an area appropriate for police power protection, the pertinent provision of the Minus Act was held an unconstitutional violation of due process.

6.3.5 Prohibition Against Taking Property Without Compensation

The Fifth Amendment to the Constitution states that "... private property [shall not] be taken for public use, without just compensation."

Despite numerous court opinions on this issue, the line between "takings" which require compensation and valid exercises of "police power" which do not require compensation has never been clearly drawn. It is difficult to predict the outcome when the principles in this area are applied to factual situations.

It may be said that the state takes property by eminent domain because it is useful to the public. This taking requires compensation. When the state takes property because it is harmful, it is done under the police power and does not require compensation. What is useful to one person may be harmful to another. So, the perspective of all the conditions and circumstances is often the determining factor in choosing between useful and harmful.

The problem often comes down to one of degree. In both circumstances damages result. If the damage is suffered by many similarly situated and is in the nature of a restriction and ought to be borne by the individual as a member of society for the good of the public, it is a reasonable exercise of police power not requiring compensation. However, if the damage is so great to the individual that he ought not to bear it under generally accepted standards, then courts are inclined to treat it as a "taking," or unreasonable exercise of police power requiring compensation.

This "taking" issue has been in the forefront of noteworthy litigation. One important case involved the denial of operational drilling permits in the Santa Barbara Channel, *Union Oil v. Morton*.[77] In this case the court reviewed the question of the degree to which government may interfere with enjoyment of private property by exercise of police power without compensation, and concluded that there was not a simple answer to this question. The courts under a variety of tests have recognized that regulation of private property can become so onerous that it amounts to a taking of that property. The court in this case held that a permanent unconditional

---

[75] *Ibid*, at 30 ERC 1169.

[76] *Ibid*, at 30 ERC 1168.

[77] 12 F.2d 743, 7 Env't. Rep. Cas. (BNA) 1 587 (9th Cir. 1975).

suspension of permits to install drilling platforms is a taking that requires compensation or violation of the Fifth Amendment.

Two cases decided by the U.S. Court of Claims confirm that failure to issue permits can constitute a taking. The cases, *Florida Rock Industries, Inc. v. United States*, No. 266-82L (Cl. Ct. July 23, 1990), and *Loveladies Harbor, Inc. v. United States*, No. 243-83L (Cl. Ct. July 23, 1990), both were the result of lengthy administrative proceedings which led to the denial of permits under Section 404 of the Clean Water Act. The major import of the court's decisions is twofold: (1) under certain circumstances, the Government's denial of a permit to fill wetlands under Section 404 of the Clean Water Act is an interference with a property owner's legitimate entitlement to the proposed use of its property, and is thus compensable under the Takings Clause; and (2) in determining the market value of such property following the taking, recreational and/or conservation uses carry minimal value.[78]

A series of cases have held that airport noise can constitute a taking of property rights. In the landmark case of *United States v. Causby*,[79] the Supreme Court held that frequent low flights over the Causby's land by military aircraft landing at a nearby airport operated by the United States constituted a taking of the Causby's property without compensation in violation of the Fifth Amendment of the Constitution. The noise from the aircraft rendered it impossible to continue the property use as a commercial chicken farm. Although the flights did not completely destroy the enjoyment and use of the land, they were held to be so low and frequent as to constitute a direct and immediate interference with the full enjoyment of the land, limiting the utility of the land and causing a diminution in its value, and therefore constituted a taking under the Fifth Amendment.

In another major Supreme Court decision on this issue, *Griggs v. Allegheny County*,[80] the Court held that Allegheny County, which owned and operated the Greater Pittsburgh Airport, was liable for a taking of property under the Fifth Amendment where the noise from taking off and landing at the airport on flight paths over the Griggs' property rendered the property undesirable and unbearable for residential use. The Court saw no difference between the county's responsibility to pay for land on which runways were built and its responsibility for air easements necessary for airport operation. The glide path for the northwest runway is as necessary for the operation of the airport as is a surface right-of-way, wrote the Court. Several states have interpreted their own constitutions to require compensation under less strict circumstances when noise from aircraft has

---

[78] In *Loveladies*, the court placed such value at $1,000 per acre, while in *Florida Rock* it was set at a "nominal" $500 per acre for "future recreational/water management purposes. . . to a government agency".

[79] 328 U.S. 256 (1946).

[80] 369 U.S. 84 (1962).

diminished the market value of the homeowner's property. Interference must be substantial and sufficiently direct in the majority of jurisdictions.

Trade secrets also may be the subject of takings. In *Ruckelshaus v. Monsanto Company*,[81] Monsanto objected to data-disclosure and data-consideration provisions of the Federal Insecticide, Fungicide, and Rodenticide Act (FIFRA), alleging that these provisions amounted to a taking without just compensation in violation of the Fifth Amendment. The Supreme Court held that to the extent that Monsanto, as an applicant for the registration of pesticides, had an interest in its health, safety and environmental data cognizable as a trade-secret property right under Missouri law, that property right was protected by the taking clause of the Fifth Amendment.

While the constitutional rights of individuals and organizations may be more difficult to uphold in contexts where these private rights arguably contend with public rights to a safe and healthy environment, it has often been suggested that constitutional rights are most important in the most unpopular cases and it is here we need to work the hardest to uphold them. The Constitution is, and will continue to be, a major aspect of environmental law.

6.4 Administrative Law and Procedure

As with most areas of law, the business of environmental law is to find the facts and decide what to do about them. While the substantive and organic laws outlined above will greatly affect the way this business is conducted, the required procedures will be influential in determining the outcomes of cases. In cases where there is significant scientific opinion on both sides of an issue, the critical issue is not what the facts are, but who has the burden of proof and what must be done to carry it. In a case where an administrative agency has made a decision, the issue is not whether the rule or decision is good or bad, but whether it was within the agency's authority, consistent with required procedures, and otherwise in accordance with law. The critical questions of environmental practice—the cutting edge issues of science, risk assessment, application of technology and analytical methods—are often resolved not through the scientific and engineering disciplines, but through argument and procedural determinations. Any detailed discussion of the rules for those determinations is well beyond the scope of this text. However, a few brief comments may be helpful.

Administrative law may not be a favorite course in law school, and it is probably not an area in which the average lawyer has much experience. It is probable, however, that administrative law issues are at or close to the heart of somewhere between eighty and ninety percent of all disputes concerning the federal environmental laws and regulations. And there is no

---

[81]467 U.S. 986, 104 S.Ct. 2862, 81 L.Ed2d 815 (1984).

doubt that a basic familiarity with the administrative process will substantially improve the effectiveness and understanding of those who deal with environmental law.

Following is a thumbnail sketch of the most important things we need to know about administrative law.

- Administrative agencies have no inherent or residual authority but can act only pursuant to authority "delegated" to them in the statutes enacted by Congress. If an agency acts beyond the scope of its delegated authority, its action is illegal and void.

- Agencies' opinions in interpreting their own regulations and the statutes they administer will, particularly if consistently held over a substantial period of time, be granted deference by the courts.

- Agencies must act in accordance with the procedures specified in their enabling legislation, or, if no other procedures are specified, in accordance with the Administrative Procedure Act. The required procedures normally entail publication in the *Federal Register*, opportunity for public comment, sometimes a public hearing, response to public comment and final publication.

- Agencies must act in accordance with their own rules and regulations. Failure to follow those rules results in invalid actions.

- Agencies must maintain a docket or record in support of their action and there must be evidence in that record to support the agency action. The record must be open for public examination throughout the period when public comments are being received.

- Agency actions may not be "arbitrary and capricious" . . . which means that there must be at least some evidence in the record to support the agency decision. When a statute specifically requires so, agencies must support their decisions with "substantial evidence." Although the difference between "some evidence" and "substantial evidence" is somewhat obscure, agencies hate substantial evidence requirements.

- Agency decisions may be appealed to the courts under either specific judicial review provisions in the enabling statutes or the general provision in the Administrative Procedure Act. You can't go to court, however, unless you have standing, the issue is "ripe," you have exhausted administrative remedies and a final agency decision has been issued.

- On appeal, administrative agency actions are generally upheld in the absence of some glaring procedural defect or a clearly inadequate record. However, these circumstances occur frequently and successful appeals, while not the rule, are far from a rarity.

6.5 Rules of Evidence

Most environmental issues don't get to court, but of those that do, the majority of them probably involve the questions of who did it and what does it take to prove it. Some of these questions turn on evidentiary determinations, others on questions of responsibility, liability sharing and contribution. Here is a summary of some of the major concepts.

6.5.1 Burden of Proof and Presumptions

Where, as is very often the case, the scientific facts of a controversy are being hotly debated in the scientific community or the facts are otherwise unclear, the outcome of the case may turn on the question of who has the "burden of proof" and the obligation of going forward with the evidence.

Fortunately, in our legal system, plaintiffs in civil cases normally have the burden of proving their cases. They must do so by a "preponderance of the evidence." However, attorneys and courts have developed special liability concepts, like strict liability, to shift the burden to defendants in some circumstances. Since the party with the burden will often lose the case, the question of who bears the burden of proof is one of the most contentious issues in civil litigation in the environmental context.

In criminal cases, the prosecutor has the burden of proving guilt "beyond a reasonable doubt" and defendants are presumed innocent until proven guilty, though that presumption is not always reflected in public opinion.

Finally, where the issue involves an effort to set aside an agency regulation or other action, there is a presumption of validity and the contesting party has the obligation of proving conclusively that the action is arbitrary and capricious, unsupported by the evidence or otherwise not in accordance with law.

6.5.2 Hearsay

Hearsay is evidence which depends for its truth or falsity solely upon statements of a person other than the witness. Hearsay, in itself, has no evidentiary value. The witness cannot be cross-examined regarding hearsay, because the statements are those of another. Generally, hearsay is inadmissible, but there are numerous exceptions.

In the case of documents, a statute usually provides for an official custodian or witness who will certify to their authenticity or validity to overcome the hearsay objection.

6.5.3 Opinion Evidence

Generally, the testimony of a witness is confined to a statement of concrete facts based upon his own observation or knowledge. However, expert opinion evidence, though often based largely on hearsay, opinions, or conclusions not normally admissible into evidence, is admissible when it concerns scientific or technical matters and is presented by an appropriately qualified expert. Non-expert witnesses may be asked to express an opinion to help understand what was observed, but conjecture is not admissible.

An expert can generally be found for either side of a case. For example, the prosecutor will have his psychiatrist testify that the defendant is sane while the defendant's psychiatrist is testifying he is insane. This type of divergent opinion evidence is common in environmental litigation.

The major issues in these cases are whether scientific evidence is credible, reflective of the weight of scientific opinion and sufficient to support a verdict or submission to a jury. Judicial thinking on these issues varies widely from case to case and is clearly in a transitional, uncertain state.

6.5.4 Witnesses

Generally, all persons are competent to testify, but their credibility can be attacked. Leading questions (ones which suggest an answer), may generally only be asked of unwilling witnesses or adverse parties. A witness must answer all questions asked which will provide information on the issue under investigation—unless this testimony may subject the witness to criminal prosecution. The opposing party has a right to cross-examine the witness. If the witness refuses to answer on cross-examination, his entire testimony may be expunged from the record. Generally, cross-examinations are limited to facts on which a witness testified during direct examination.

6.5.5 Privileged Communication and Environmental Audits

Privilege is an exception to the rule that the public has the right to know every man's evidence. The reason for the exception is public policy.

In environmental lawsuits, the concern is with the attorney-client relationship. It is the duty of a lawyer to preserve his client's confidences. This duty outlasts the lawyer's employment.

The concept of privileged communications can be used not only in lawsuits but also when providing legal advice in connection with environmental audits and assessments. Thus, though there is no absolute assurance that the privilege can be maintained, it may be useful to have a lawyer supervise the information-gathering process during an audit and establish procedures for controlling access to all documents generated during the audit.

6.5.6 Your Own Reports as Evidence Against You

Many of the environmental laws and regulations require reports or data to be filed with the government. Even the reports to the Securities and Exchange Commission require disclosure of information on pollution. Most of these reports are available to the public and to competitors.

The extent to which the results of an investigation or inspection are available in private liability litigation remains uncertain. A corporation is not protected by the self-incrimination provisions of the Fifth Amendment to the U.S. Constitution. So, it may not object to the use of its records as evidence against it.[82]

6.5.7 Samples or Physical Evidence

One of the common evidentiary problems raised in court cases involves physical evidence. In environmental cases, the evidence is often a sample or

---

[82] *Essgee Co. v. U.S.*, 262 U.S. 151 (1923). Also see Section 6.3.2 of this chapter.

some data. Some of the key issues normally involved with physical evidence are: (1) has the evidence or data been altered or contaminated, (2) was the equipment used in evidence collection properly calibrated, (3) were scientifically acceptable and standard methods of analysis used in evaluation and (4) who has handled the evidence (chain of custody)?

In order to lay a proper foundation for the admission of evidence, an attorney should be able to present the principals in the "chain of custody" to testify as to their involvement and their appropriate expertise in the proper handling of the evidence. The courts will frequently require the parties to stipulate authenticity of evidence to avoid this tedious form of proof. In legal terminology, "to stipulate" is to agree initially on conduct or evidence for the purpose of shortening the legal proceedings.

6.5.8 Evidence Collection and Constitutional Rights

A problem that may arise in the collection of evidence concerns the Fourth Amendment or Constitutional rights of corporate entities and private persons.

The Fourth Amendment to the U.S. Constitution prohibits all unreasonable searches and requires a search warrant for most investigations. However, no search warrant is needed in three situations: (1) when there is an emergency, (2) when the owner or operator gives his consent, or (3) when the samples could be taken from outside of the property (open fields exception). See the previous section on search warrants.

In most states, search warrants are used for searches for the implements or fruits of a crime and not for mere investigation of conditions which may lead to either civil or criminal penalties. A few states authorize a special kind of search warrant, sometimes called an inspection warrant, which may be used to investigate conditions.

The Fifth Amendment prohibition against criminal self-incrimination was described earlier. In evidence collection involving criminal charges against private parties, this Fifth Amendment right must be properly observed or the courts will not allow evidence to be introduced in the case. The Fifth Amendment protections apply only to private persons and not to corporations or partnerships.

7.0 JOINT AND SEVERAL LIABILITY AND CONTRIBUTION

The concept of joint and several liability in toxic tort and clean-up cases springs from the extreme difficulty of apportioning liability among, say, numerous contributors (for example, to a hazardous landfill). Under this concept one party can be held liable for all of the costs of an action. In such a case it is the responsibility of the one party to identify others to share the liability. The theory is that the public or the injured party should not bear the risk and cost of sorting out these complex situations but, instead, should rest the burden on those who caused the problems. These issues of contribution and liability sharing were among the most hotly contested issues of the eighties, and the dispute will continue into the nineties and perhaps beyond. The "public" may eventually "win" this dispute but then, as usual, will pay for its victory with "transaction costs added" for good measure. There clearly is a need for improved procedures to determine and assess responsibility for environmental harms.

8.0 ORGANIZING FOR ENVIRONMENTAL COMPLIANCE

Once a basic understanding of the environmental law system and its requirements is achieved, the next step is to apply that knowledge to attain or maintain an acceptable compliance posture in the organizations you advise or act for. The last approach to the development of an effective compliance program rests on the basic premise that aggressive compliance is the most effective protection.

Books have been written—notably Government Institutes' *Environmental, Health & Safety Manager's Handbook*—discussing and detailing the elements of an appropriate compliance organization. The following principles derived from this text may be instructive:

- Everyone is responsible for environmental law compliance and, to protect against individual liability, everyone should continually demonstrate due concern and diligent efforts to comply.
- Providing appropriate education and training as well as sufficient informational resources is a good demonstration of concern for compliance and key to a successful environmental management program.
- The best answer to the question of what can be done to prevent violations and minimize liability is an appropriate corporate "culture" or management structure formulated with a view to environmental objectives and aggressively implemented.
- Outside consultants and counsel can help, but can't comply for you any better than they could run your company. The objective of an effective program is to provide the organization's officers and employees with the knowledge, resources and motivation required to meet and exceed requirements.
- After your compliance system is in place, periodic "audits" to verify compliance and identify areas where compliance can be improved will be helpful. "We had a good program but got sloppy" is not a mitigating factor, but an aggravating admission of failure. Don't start what you don't intend to finish and don't do anything halfway.

9.0 ENVIRONMENTAL LAW KNOWLEDGE IS CRUCIAL

The need for a working understanding of the environmental law system is probably more crucial now than it ever has been. Our actions and inactions, what we know and—perhaps most importantly—what we ought to know, can have dramatic effects on the financial well-being of organizations as well as the financial and personal futures of the individuals who work for them. Failure to know is no excuse. Under the legal theory of constructive knowledge, for those involved in the environmental field, knowledge may be presumed.

Knowledge of and strict adherence to the mandates of the environmental laws is not a luxury for companies and organizations. Financial viability and profitability—the bottom line for businesses—and personal freedom—the bottom line for individuals—may rest on this knowledge and how we use it. I hope this handbook will be helpful in that connection and that you aggressively seek more information and learning in the future.

For additional information, the reader is referred to the related books and courses listed at the end of this handbook.

Chapter 2

LIABILITIES AND ENFORCEMENT

J. Gordon Arbuckle
Patton, Boggs & Blow
Denver, Colorado
Washington, D.C.

1.0 OVERVIEW

Environmental liabilities are the negative consequences of failure to comply with the requirements of environmental laws and regulations. The environmental law system provides an array of types of liabilities ranging from "traffic ticket"-like administrative fines to criminal prosecutions. Selection among these types of consequences is based on factors such as the nature of the violation, the culpability of the offense, the consequences of the violation, the specific environmental law or regulation which has been violated, and the identity of the person who decides to pursue action against the violator.

These various types of liabilities, and factors determining the consequences of a given violation, are discussed in this chapter. Let's look first, however, at the underlying philosophy—the purposes to be achieved by the liability consequences of the environmental law system.

2.0 PURPOSES OF ENVIRONMENTAL LIABILITIES

There are four generally recognized purposes for the imposition of liability as a consequence of violation of environmental laws:

1. To encourage compliance or to deter non-compliance with legal standards of care concerning human health and the environment (that is, to influence behavior);
2. To punish wrongdoers or those who fail or refuse to comply with environmental laws;
3. To require the responsible parties to correct the damage, clean up the problem, or pay the costs of doing so; and
4. To require responsible parties to make the injured whole by paying damages.

The first two purposes, deterrence and punishment, are accomplished primarily by penalties, which can be either civil/administrative or criminal in nature. Such penalties are provided for in most environmental statutes as well as in general-purpose criminal laws. Furthermore, damage actions under generally recognized common law theories such as trespass, public nuisance, and other so-called "toxic torts" may also have a deterrence or punitive aspect in that damage awards may include exemplary or punitive damages.

The third primary purpose of imposing liability—correction, clean-up, or remediation—is accomplished largely by requirements to respond, or to pay the cost of another's response to environmental harms which responsible persons, organizations or their predecessors have created or participated in creating. Response requirements are generally imposed by environmental statutes. The Clean Water Act (CWA), the Resource Conservation and Recovery Act (RCRA), and the Comprehensive Environmental Response, Compensation, and Liability Act (CERCLA or Superfund), are particularly significant sources of this kind of response requirements.

The final primary purpose of the environmental law liability scheme is to compensate or "pay damages" to victims and make them whole. This goal is achieved by imposing upon liable parties a requirement to compensate victims for the harms or injuries which result from environmental offenses or lack of due care. Such compensation may be required not only for adverse health effects, but for economic and natural resource injuries. Although compensation requirements are included in various environmental statutes (see for example, CERCLA, and the Oil Pollution Act of 1990), the common law and civil damage suits prosecuted under it remain the major sources of compensation requirements in environmental contexts.

3.0 FORMS OF LIABILITY

The various liabilities, or consequences, which accomplish the above purposes fall into three general categories: *penalties* (civil and criminal), *remedy requirements* and *compensation requirements*. Volumes have been, and will continue to be, written concerning each of these liability categories. The following summary discussion is intended only as a short, functional map of the liability framework.

3.1 Penalties—Administrative/Civil and Criminal

Penalties are sanctions designed to punish the commission of a prohibited act or the omission of a required act. Thus, penalties may be (and are!) imposed regardless of whether the offensive conduct resulted in actual injury to a person or property. In other words, the familiar "no harm, no foul" rule does not apply to environmental penalties. Harm is an aggravating factor which tends to increase the amount of a fine or length of imprisonment, but proof of harm is not an essential precondition to the imposition of a penalty.

Penalties are classified as administrative/civil or criminal based on the process by which they are imposed and the degree of blame or culpability which attaches to the act or omission being prosecuted. Culpability generally results from either the intent of the violator or his ability or inability to demonstrate "due care."

3.1.1 Civil/Administrative Penalties

Virtually all environmental statutes provide for enforcement of their requirements and prohibitions by civil/administrative penalty proceedings. Even with the increased use of criminal penalties (discussed infra.), civil and administrative actions continue to be the mainstay of governmental enforcement efforts concerning environmental matters.

Civil/administrative penalties under environmental statutes normally take the form of monetary fines ranging from $5-25,000 per violation.[1] Lest these amounts appear affordable, it should be noted that each day in violation of a statute is often deemed a separate violation.

These penalties are assessable upon the mere occurrence of the prohibited act or omission. No element of intent, recalcitrance or blameworthiness is required, although such "state of mind" of the offending party may be considered an aggravating factor by the enforcing party when determining how severe (and expensive) a penalty will be imposed.

Civil penalties are imposed by judicial actions filed in civil courts. Administrative penalties, on the other hand, may be directly imposed by agency administrative order without the need for court involvement, except in the case of an appeal of the administrative action or in an enforcement proceeding arising from the penalized party's refusal to pay.[2] Whether the enforcing agency can impose a civil fine by administrative order or needs to go to court in order to do so depends on the statute under which the agency is acting to impose the sanction, since some environmental statutes authorize administrative penalties and others do not. Not surprisingly, where administrative penalties are authorized by statute, an enforcing agency will prefer, at least in the case of minor fines, to follow that route rather than go to court. Administrative procedures may be less burdensome to the agency, and provide less protection to the liable parties than civil actions. Furthermore, although administrative decisions can be appealed in court, the trend is clearly for reviewing courts to show great deference toward administrative decisions.

Where administrative penalties are authorized, some statutes, like the Clean Water Act, the Comprehensive Environmental Response, Compensation and Liability Act and the Emergency Planning and Community-Right-to-Know Act[3], provide for two classes of penalties.[4] The lower level of penalty (generally referred to as a "Class I" administrative penalty) is limited in the amount per violation or the total amount (generally $10-25,000) and may be imposed with minimal procedural formalities and no hearing on the record. Higher level administrative penalties ("Class II")

---

[1] *See, e.g.* CAA § 113(d)(g); CWA § 309(d); CERCLA § 109(a),(b); EPCRA § 325; ESA § 11; FIFRA § 14(a); MPRSA (Ocean Dumping) § 105; RCRA § 3009(g); SDWA (Safe Drinking Water) § 1423(b); SMCRA § 518; TSCA § 16(a).

[2] *See, e.g.,* §113(d) of the Clean Air Act.

[3] 33 U.S.C. §1319(g)(2), 42 U.S.C. § 9609(a),(b), 42 U.S. §11045(b)].

[4] CWA § 319(g)(2); CERCLA § 109(a) and (b); EPCRA § 325(b).

may run $25,000 per day of violation and may not be imposed without an on-the-record administrative hearing. Where substantial penalties are involved, most agencies tend to avoid the expense and effort of conducting administrative hearings by electing the judicial route where that option is available. This approach usually results in an informally negotiated settlement.

Civil penalties are generally assessable against "any person" who violates, or against the "owner/operator" or "person in charge" of a facility or entity which violates. There is little doubt that civil fines may be imposed against both violating organizations and responsible individuals. However, civil/administrative penalties are normally focussed on companies or organizations, rather than individuals, unless the enforcer perceives a compelling point to be made or problem to be avoided.

Aside from the obvious central issues of "Who is alleged to be responsible?" and "Did that party violate?," there are two primary questions to be addressed in a civil penalty proceeding: "How many violations have occurred?" and "What is the amount of the fine for each violation?"

Where the question is "how many," the enforcers talk about "aggregation" of penalties: Is each day of violation a separate violation? Each parameter exceeded? Each parameter each day? When you think about the mathematical implications of these questions, it is easy to see how typical fines, under statutes which provide maximum penalties of $25,000 per violation, can achieve totals ranging in the millions of dollars. It is beyond our scope to discuss the complex precedents, statutes, regulations, and guidance documents dealing with the counting of violations. The point to be made is that violation counting is important and it is arcane. Painstaking consideration should be paid to this issue in defense or negotiation of penalties.

The second key question—how much to charge per violation—is also complex. The statutes will generally provide that penalties, up to a maximum, will be established based on consideration of factors such as:

> the nature, circumstances, extent and gravity of the violation . . . and, with respect to the violator, ability to pay, any prior history of such violations, the degree of culpability, economic benefit or savings (if any) resulting from the violation, and such other matters as justice may require. [CWA, §309(g)(3)].

Under most of the major environmental statutes, EPA has defined this laundry list with penalty policy "guidance," often complete with computer formulas, which is supposed to tell the enforcers how to develop firm dollar figures. Some enforcers have been heard to refer to this guidance as a "black, voodoo art" and the legal status of the guidance is, at best, unclear. Nevertheless, the guidance documents are available and often provide the only detailed discussion of the manner in which penalties are calculated. Penalty negotiators and defenders need to obtain, read, and understand them. The last thing to be said about civil/administrative penalties is that the vast majority of them are negotiated with the agency prior to being judicially imposed, embodied in compliance agreements which normally also include detailed compliance obligations, and incorporated in judicial decrees settling the case. These are all matters for detailed consideration and discussion. There is a good deal of unwritten lore and "policy" in this context and, for that reason, penalty defense and negotiation is probably best handled by someone who has done it before.

Before quitting this discussion of civil penalties, be aware that the trend is toward increasingly aggressive use of all kinds of penalties, including civil, and that the kinds of numbers we are seeing in the civil penalty context will continue to escalate in amount. Penalty negotiation and defense skills are an increasingly urgent need.

3.1.2 Criminal Penalties

As we have noted, civil penalties attach to the commission of some prohibited act or the omission of what is legally required. Bad intentions, culpability and blameworthiness are not necessary elements of a civil offense and need not be proven in order to assess a civil penalty. Criminal offenses, on the other hand, traditionally have been believed to necessarily involve not only the commission of the prohibited act, but also a showing of bad intent or some other element of culpability—such as reckless or willful misconduct or an act so bad, in and of itself, as to be "per se" criminal.

The public "opprobrium" attaching to persons prosecuted criminally is greater, by orders of magnitude, than that resulting from civil offenses. Of course, it is also significant that criminal convictions can result in imprisonment, while civil offenses cannot. From an enforcement perspective, however, the most important difference between civil and criminal prosecutions is that criminal prosecutions can focus on individuals as well as organizations, and, in a criminal case, the organization can't insulate individuals from the consequences of their conduct.

The enforcers understand this, and also have come to understand that the most effective, perhaps only, way of changing compliance cultures in corporations and other organizations is to change the attitudes and behavior of the individuals in control of those organizations. As a result of this and also, perhaps, other factors such as continuing increases in public environmental concern, the use of criminal sanctions as tools to enforce environmental compliance has increased markedly over the last decade.

According to figures released by the U.S. Department of Justice, criminal indictments for environmental violations have increased from only 40 in FY 1985 to 191 in FY 1992. Similarly, annual pleas/convictions have gone from 37 to 104 in the same time period.[5]

---

[5]Department of Justice Memorandum, re: Environmental Criminal Statistics FY 83 through FY 92, October 27, 1992.

But this may be only the tip of the iceberg. With the exception of the National Environmental Policy Act (NEPA), virtually every environmental statute now provides some form of criminal liability.[6] Currently a significant amount of scrutiny and criticism is being leveled at the Department of Justice by Congress, based on a perceived lack of commitment by the Bush administration to vigorously pursue criminal actions against environmental wrongdoers.[7] Given the combination of such Congressional pressures, a growing public opinion against pollution and polluters, as well as a change in administrations, it is probably safe to say that criminal enforcement in the environmental arena will grow more vigorous and frequent in the coming years.

Furthermore, in both the legislative and judicial processes, traditional distinctions between civil and criminal liabilities in the environmental context are being blurred or obliterated. We are coming to the point where a separate showing of "bad intent" or blameworthiness may not be necessary to prove an environmental crime.

Substantive violations of environmental laws may be reaching the point of becoming criminal per se and the question of whether an act or omission is a civil or criminal offense may have become largely a matter of prosecutorial discretion. However, the cases do provide some direction or factors to look for as elements of a criminal offense.

3.1.2.1 Knowing Violations

Under nearly all of the federal environmental statutes a "knowing" violation or failure to comply with requirements is a crime. The courts have now made very clear that it isn't necessary that one actually know in order to "know." One can be charged with "knowing" when one *should have known*. Several courts have held that companies working in the "highly regulated field" of hazardous waste should know, and are legally responsible for knowing, all requirements for managing hazardous waste correctly or legally. Knowledge of the law may be implied. For example, in the decision in *United States v. Hayes International Corp.*,[8] a prosecution under RCRA based on the theory of implied knowledge, the court rejected several arguments based on the "knowing" element of the statute, and articulated rules under which "knowing" convictions may be obtained under environmental statutes:

1. Mistake of law, grounded in the argument that defendants had no knowledge that a waste was hazardous within the meaning of the

---

[6]CAA § 113(c); CWA § 309(c); CERCLA § 103(b) and (c); EPCRTKA § (b) and (d); FIFRA § 14(b); MPRSA (Ocean Dumping) § 105(b); RCRA § 3008(d); SWDA (Safe Drinking Water) 1423(b); and TSCA § 16(b).

[7]*See, e.g., Preliminary Report on Environmental Prosecution by the United States Department of Justice*, prepared by The Environmental Crimes Project, National Law Center, George Washington University, October 19, 1992.

[8]786 F.2d 1499 (11th Cir. 1986).

regulations or that a permit was required under the statute, was rejected by the court which stated that "it is completely fair and reasonable to charge those who choose to operate in such [highly regulated] areas with knowledge of the regulatory provisions."[9]

2. The Government need not prove a defendant's actual state of mind in order to establish knowledge that a facility receiving hazardous wastes was not permitted. This may be proved circumstantially by showing that the defendant "willfully fails to determine the permit status of the facility."[10]

3. Although not supported by the facts here, the court found that a good faith belief in a material fact that proved to be in error would be a defense to a charge that a defendant acted knowingly.

Thus, this case stands for the proposition that public welfare statutes involving toxic chemicals and hazardous waste have significant public health implications, and that the companies subject to these statutes are highly regulated and may be presumed to have knowledge of the applicable regulatory requirements. Second, this presumed knowledge may be used to prove circumstantially that a defendant is acting in knowing violation of a statute if he or she fails to act in accordance with the strictures of that statute. Under most environmental statutory schemes, "bad intent" is no longer required in order to establish criminal liability, even under a "knowing" standard.

Furthermore, knowledge of violations can be imputed not only to the corporation, but to individuals within the corporation who, by virtue of their responsibilities and authority, should have known of such violations. Individual responsibilities of this sort cannot simply be delegated away. For example, in *United States v. Park*, the Supreme Court held that a corporate officer could be held criminally responsible if such officer had "by reason of his position in the corporation, responsibility and authority either to prevent in the first instance, or promptly to correct, the violation complained of, and that he failed to do so."[11] This rule should encourage corporate managers to read their job descriptions closely, especially since the Justice Department's policy is to indict not only corporations committing environmental offenses, but also the highest ranking individual in a company against whom a case can be proven.

---

[9] 786 F.2d 1503.

[10] 786 F.2d 1504.

[11] 421 U.S. 658, 673 (1975). Park, the president of a large food distribution company was convicted of adulteration of food under the Food, Drug, and Cosmetic Act, even though responsibility for compliance with applicable rules had been delegated to others in the company. Park had received notice that the food in the company's warehouse was being adulterated by rat poison. He had delegated the responsibility for remedying the situation to some employees.

3.1.2.2 *Negligent Violations*

A number of the statutes criminalize the "negligent" violation of their requirements.[12] Compliance duties under these statutes are often broadly stated and failure to comply, coupled with simple negligence, can support criminal charges even if "knowledge" or intent cannot be shown or implied. "Negligence" is simply the failure to exercise due care, and when you are dealing with dangerous chemicals or high risk activities, "due care" is a substantial burden.

In *United States v. Pennwalt*,[13] the company was criminally indicted for a negligent discharge of chemicals in violation of the Clean Water Act as a result of the collapse of a 75,000 gallon storage tank. Pennwalt failed to report the spill correctly in violation of CERCLA, and also was charged with a negligent failure to adequately maintain the storage tank. The company was fined $1.1 million. In a related action, the manager of the Pennwalt plant was fined $5,000 and placed on probation for a period of two years. (Under the new sentencing guidelines, a sentence of imprisonment would now result for such conduct.) This case underlines the importance of both proper and accurate reporting as well as the exercise of "due diligence"—in this case, instituting adequate checks to ensure that equipment and plant are maintained in a safe condition.

3.1.2.3 *Notice Requirements and False Statements*

In addition to the criminal penalties for knowing or negligent violations of their substantive provisions, several of the environmental statutes make it a criminal offense to fail to immediately notify of the discharge or release of certain pollutants or hazardous substances.[14] Others, like the Clean Air and Clean Water Acts, impose mandatory requirements in permits and require notice of non-compliance. Keep in mind that, like the Internal Revenue Code, most of the environmental statutes rely on self reporting as their primary foundation. Because of their fundamental importance to the functioning and integrity of the system, the notice requirements are jealously guarded. Violation of a notice requirement is treated as a serious offense with severe consequences. These "notice" requirements are complex, but are consistently and rigorously enforced. They are a particularly fertile source of prosecutions.[15]

Related to the notice requirements are prohibitions against false statements, like the one found in the Clean Water Act, which provide a basis for prosecution of knowing misstatements in required reports or "render[ing] inaccurate any monitoring device or method required to be

---

[12]*See, e.g.*, CWA, §309(C); CAA, § 113(C)(4).

[13]No. CR88-55T (W.D. Wash. 1988).

[14]*See, e.g.*, CERCLA § 103(b).

[15]*See, e.g.*, CAA, §113(C)(2)(B).

maintained..."[16] This last type of provision deserves special emphasis due to the complexity of monitoring methodology and the great temptation to "put a thumb on the scale" by, for example, monitoring only the times you think you are in compliance or running "preliminary samples" to determine when to sample. This "thumb on the scale" is a criminal thumb and the rest of the body may well be incarcerated along with it.

3.1.2.4 Endangerment

Finally, under the environmental statutes, it is increasingly common to see particularly severe liability attached to crimes of "endangerment"— knowingly, recklessly, or perhaps even negligently creating imminent risks of death or serious bodily injury to persons.[17] It is not necessary for injury to actually occur in order to sustain a conviction for this type of offense. Rather, the placing of another person in "imminent danger" will suffice.

3.1.2.5 Seriousness of Criminal Violations

In digesting this summary discussion of the criminal liability provisions of the environmental law, keep in mind two things. First, criminal violation counts are never lonely—they always travel in packs. Second, the criminal provisions of the environmental statutes are ably assisted by provisions of the ordinary, "garden variety" non-environmental criminal laws which, against the backdrop of the environmental laws' massive information requirements, present extremely formidable tools for the prosecutor's arsenal.[18]

Consider the following:

False Statements

Under 18 U.S.C. Section 1001, a person who knowingly and willfully makes a false statement to the federal government is subject to a fine of up to $10,000 and/or imprisonment up to five years. An example of enforcement of this provision can be found in the indictment of W.R. Grace & Co. in connection with an incident in Woburn, Massachusetts.

Mail Fraud

Sections 1341 and 1343 of 18 U.S.C. penalize the use of the mails, airwaves, or interstate wires in connection with a "scheme or artifice" to defraud, or for obtaining money or property by means of false or fraudulent representations. A case in point is *United States v. Gold*,[19] in which a chemical corporation and its officers were indicted for making false statements to EPA.

---

[16]CWA § 1319 (C)(4).

[17]*See, e.g.*, CAA § 113 (C)(4) and (5) and RCRA 3008(e).

[18]The "Pennwalt" indictment (discussed, *supra*) illustrates how a simple tank failure can yield a multi-count criminal prosecution.

[19] 470 F. Supp. 1336 (N.D. Ill. 1979).

Conspiracy

Section 371 of 18 U.S.C. can be used if two or more corporate employees conspire to violate environmental laws. For instance, in *United States v. Olin Corp.*,[20] the defendants were charged with violation of conspiracy law and 18 U.S.C. Section 1001 in connection with their plan to defraud EPA regarding mercury discharges into the Niagara River. The penalties for conspiracy include fines of up to $10,000 and/or imprisonment for up to five years.

This listing is by no means exhaustive. There have been murder and manslaughter prosecutions for chemical exposures causing death. The limits of the prosecutorial imagination are yet to be fully tested.

The "penalties" aspect of the environmental liabilities framework has become an extremely important factor for consideration in the design and implementation of any organization's environmental compliance program. In most cases, criminal penalties cannot be covered by insurance and are not deductible for tax purposes. Review of this potential liability should reinforce in the minds of all responsible officers and employees the correctness of the conclusion that criminal liability is serious and its potential should be a serious consideration in every organization's consideration of the costs and benefits of aggressive compliance.

3.2 Requirements to Respond

The second component of the liability system is the set of statutory mandates to "clean up" or otherwise remedy the consequences of "releases" or discharges of pollutants to the environment or other impacts of an organization's past or present activities. Unlike the penalty provisions, the focus of these "response requirements" is not on the need to deter or punish violations, but on the need to correct or prevent environmental harm. Where response actions are concerned, there is usually a "no harm, no foul" rule.

There are three statutes of primary concern in the response context. The Clean Water Act and related provisions of the Oil Pollution Act require the owner or operator of a vessel or facility from which any discharge of oil or a hazardous pollutant to surface waters originates to report the spill immediately and either clean it up and remedy its consequences or pay the cost of a government-led cleanup effort.[21] Under CERCLA, persons who generate or participate in the disposal of hazardous pollutants which damage or threaten the environment may be held jointly and severally liable for costs incurred by either the government or private parties which respond to or abate the damage or threat.[22] (Jointly and severally liable means each person who generated or participated in the disposal of hazardous pollutants is subject to liability for the entire cost of cleanup.) CERCLA also

---

[20] 465 F. Supp. 1120 (W.D.N.Y. 1979).
[21] CWA § 311.
[22] CERCLA § 107

imposes notification requirements in the event of any release of a "reportable quantity" of a hazardous pollutant to the environment.[23] Furthermore, the act authorizes EPA or a state to unilaterally order responsible parties to respond to and remedy release or disposal site problems. Failure to comply with such an order, without good cause, subjects the recalcitrant party to liability for up to three times the cost of the ordered cleanup.[24]

Finally, RCRA imposes requirements for "closure" of disposal facilities which, in essence, require clean up and closure of any location at which hazardous wastes have been "disposed of" since November, 1980.[25]

3.3 Requirements to Compensate

The last prong of this system of environmental liability is the requirement to compensate for harm caused by your actions. Compensation of this type usually arises in the context of so-called "toxic tort" suits, and actions to compensate for loss of (or damage to) natural resources. These actions, and any resultant requirements to pay, are *in addition* to any fines and penalties that the federal and state governments may be empowered to seek or impose on the basis of previously discussed violations of environmental statutes.

As is probably obvious, violations of environmental statutes or failure to exercise due diligence in protecting health and the environment can result in damage or injury far greater in scope or persistency than almost any cause, save war. The magnitude of the harm caused by the Exxon Valdez or Chernobyl will be discussed for generations to come. After the response to the damage, following the penalization of the entity which caused the harm, there remains the element of compensation—of either individuals or the public in general—for actual physical damage or injury or loss of resources.

For example, the oil spill at Valdez resulted in the loss of tens of thousands of living creatures of various species and, some will argue, irreparable damage to Alaskan shorelines. Two environmental statutes provide causes of action to compensate "the public" for the loss of such "natural resources." The Clean Water Act prohibits releases into the water of oil or hazardous substances which may affect natural resources, and authorizes the United States to sue to recover for any injury to such resources.[26] Likewise, CERCLA makes responsible parties financially liable for damages or injury to natural resources. [27]

For example, CERCLA provides that "Trustees" of a natural resource can act to obtain compensation for its loss. Trustees are usually state,

---

[23]CERCLA § 103

[24]CERCLA § 107(C)(3)

[25]*See, e.g.,* 40 CFR §§ 264.110, 265.110.

[26]CWA, § 311.

[27]CERCLA, § 107(f).

federal, or American Indian officials with general responsibility for natural resources within their particular jurisdiction. Compensation is available for loss or injury to the resources, whether permanent or transitory. While actions of this type are still somewhat rare, many existing Superfund sites will likely have future natural resource damage claims far in excess of the costs of site remediation. Estimates for natural resource damages at existing Superfund sites have ranged as high as $2 billion.

"Toxic tort" actions are brought by individuals, often in the form of class action litigation, claiming that the environmental damage caused by a company or individual has injured their person or property. Cancer is often claimed to be the physical injury, usually because of a higher number of occurrences in the affected area when compared to other similarly situated locales. Other physical symptoms which have led to these actions range from reproductive effects and higher-than-normal rates of miscarriages down to increased instances of eye or throat irritation.

These actions often arise directly prior to or immediately after a governmental agency initiates an enforcement action under Superfund or a state analog. The role played by those statutes is crucial in that they establish liability for the environmental damage as strict, joint and several. Where there is strict liability, toxic tort claimants are charged only with establishing "causation." That is, the claimant need only establish the link between the violation of environmental duty and the "damage"—personal or physical injury.

Due to the nature of our industrialized society and the numerous causes of disease or injury, toxic tort defendants are often willing to expend great amounts of money in challenging the "causation aspect" of these cases. Such an approach may be an imprudent response, given the current tendencies of juries to be very sympathetic to victims of environmental damage and harsh towards the perpetrators of such damage.

The other primary area of toxic torts recovery is property damage. While this aspect of the problem sometimes is mentioned only as a footnote, it can be economically devastating to a liable party because of the seriousness of the health problems associated with the environmental damage. Entire communities and towns have been literally abandoned as a result of environmental damage. Witness Love Canal in New York and Times Beach, Missouri as examples of the potentially vast scope of undesirable environmental consequences where property damage, as opposed to personal injury, is involved. Causation is usually much more easy to establish in a property damage claim. The right to compensation is also more easily established.

Under an adverse personal injury or property damage judgment, the bottom line—financial damages—may reach well beyond actual pecuniary loss to plaintiff, from emotional distress (including such manifestations as "fear of cancer") to loss in assessed valuation of property to actual relocation costs for an entire town.

Far-reaching actions of this sort are becoming more and more common for a number of reasons. First, the public is more aware of environmental problems and suspicious of symptoms deemed out of the ordinary. Next, compensation is more frequently awarded. Last, the level of expertise in the field is growing and becoming more diversified. Alleged victims in Small Town, U.S.A. can now find an attorney to champion their cause where, five or ten years ago, few with the requisite skills would be available. In short, when faced with an environmental problem, the prudent manager must look beyond resolution of the matter with federal, state and local enforcers and must identify and prepare for potential demands from the affected citizenry. The climate in which we live makes it unwise to stonewall, ignore, or harass the "victim" of environmental pollution.

To summarize: Environmental law consequences take these forms:

1. <u>Civil/Administrative Penalties</u>
   fines
   loss of rights

2. <u>Criminal Penalties</u>
   prison
   fines
   restitution
   loss of rights

3. <u>Remedy Requirements</u>
   clean up costs
   closure requirements
   response requirements

4. <u>Compensation Requirements</u>
   civil damages
   punitive
   compensatory

These liabilities and schemes work efficiently together to achieve the objectives of promoting compliance, punishing violators, cleaning up pollution and making the injured whole.

4.0 WHICH KIND OF CONSEQUENCE APPLIES?

The next important question is "How do we decide the nature and magnitude of the consequences that should be applied in a particular situation?" The answer to this question isn't easy. It must be based on a careful, three-factor analysis which is described here in broad outline.

The nature and seriousness of the consequences to be imposed in a particular situation depend on three major factors:

Gravity of the offense
Culpability (fault) of the offender
Extent of injury or damage

The figure on the next page illustrates the interplay between these three factors.

The object of the game is to not get caught with a black ball that you can't cover with a very light colored ball from the Culpability/Fault column. If you do get caught, you're in serious trouble. If the black ball is in the "gravity" column, it's criminal trouble. If it's in the "damage" column, you're in "pay a lot of money" trouble. If it's in both, you're in both. If you find dark gray balls in several columns, they may be added together to put you in the black—where, in this context, you definitely don't want to be.

Take the following example—your employee is killed in a large tank he is cleaning (black ball in the damage column.) You can show that the accident occurred despite your operation's full compliance with all applicable laws (white ball in the gravity column) and despite your diligent effort to seek out and prevent the circumstances that caused the accident (white ball in the culpability column). In these circumstances, your jeopardy is probably limited to payment of workman's compensation claims.

If, however, we use other gravity factors—such as a failure to comply with relevant OSHA worker "right-to-know" or training requirements, we begin to sense real problems. If we're not in a position to demonstrate diligence—which gets harder under the circumstances—we start thinking seriously about criminal exposure and punitive damages in the law suit. Somewhere between negligence and gross negligence on the culpability scale, criminal consequences—"big trouble"—become probabilities. That point on the scale at which we start thinking of acts as criminal continues to get lower on the bar as the level of diligence we expect from environmental compliance programs increases.

FACTORS THAT DETERMINE CULPABILITY

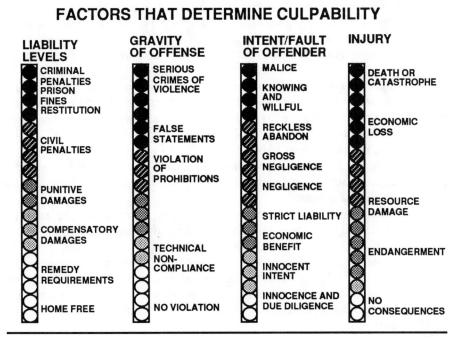

LIABILITY LEVELS	GRAVITY OF OFFENSE	INTENT/FAULT OF OFFENDER	INJURY
CRIMINAL PENALTIES PRISON FINES RESTITUTION	SERIOUS CRIMES OF VIOLENCE	MALICE KNOWING AND WILLFUL	DEATH OR CATASTROPHE
CIVIL PENALTIES	FALSE STATEMENTS VIOLATION OF PROHIBITIONS	RECKLESS ABANDON GROSS NEGLIGENCE	ECONOMIC LOSS
PUNITIVE DAMAGES		NEGLIGENCE STRICT LIABILITY	RESOURCE DAMAGE
COMPENSATORY DAMAGES	TECHNICAL NON-COMPLIANCE	ECONOMIC BENEFIT INNOCENT INTENT	ENDANGERMENT
REMEDY REQUIREMENTS		INNOCENCE AND	NO
HOME FREE	NO VIOLATION	DUE DILIGENCE	CONSEQUENCES

G

So remember—consequences accumulate. Deal with the one you're facing but watch for the ones slipping up behind. Comply with even the technical details of the environmental laws and regulations. *Demonstrated diligence avoids the black ball. Even simple negligence may let it fall.*

Remember also that in the environmental regulatory arena, the rules of the game tend to change.

Major trends in the assessment of consequences include:

(1) Increasing the perceived gravity of environmental offenses,

(2) Reducing the level of intent or culpability required to justify penalty assessment, and

(3) Minimizing of the level of proof required to show causation and collect damages.

All of these trends will tend to impose a higher standard of care and greater liability exposure for organizations as well as for those individuals responsible for environmental risk management and compliance functions.

5.0 INDIVIDUAL LIABILITY—WHO BEARS THE CONSEQUENCES?

The really major trend in the area of consequences, however, involves not so much what the consequences are—but who must bear them.

Under most of the environmental laws, it is clear that the term "responsible person" includes individuals as well as companies. The basic premise of corporate/organizational liability is that a corporation is liable, by imputation, for everything any of its officers or employees think or do in the conduct of the corporate business. There may be a "beyond the scope" defense, but it is severely limited.

The basic premises of individual liability are that officers and employees who directly participate in conduct violating the laws are individually responsible for the violations. They are presumed to know the legal requirements.

Officers, managers and supervisors who do not participate directly in an illegal act, but who occupy positions of authority such that they are in a position to seek out and prevent the act, but fail to do so, are individually responsible for the offense.

The major trend in enforcement philosophy is towards emphasis on individual liability as the most effective way of assuring diligent compliance efforts by companies and organizations.

In the early 1980s the environmental law enforcement community started to ask: "How do we make corporations and other organizations comply? They have no arms, no legs, no conscience—if you cut them they don't bleed, you can't put them in jail, and you can't fine them enough to get their attention."

The answer that emerged in the mid to late 1980s was that "Individuals make a difference in corporations. They are not nameless and faceless. They can go to jail. We can get their attention."

Since criminal prosecutions are the only consequences from which a company cannot insulate its managers and employees, an emphasis on individual liability is therefore also an emphasis on criminal liability.

The trend towards criminal enforcement in the eighties produced serious results.

In 1982, the United States Department of Justice established an "Environmental Crimes Unit" solely for the purpose of prosecuting environmental offenses. Since October 1983, as a result of prosecutions by that unit, more than:

- 704 individuals have been indicted

- 315 corporations have been indicted

- 476 individuals have been convicted

- 240 corporations have been convicted

- $237,647,692 in fines have been paid

- More than 404 years in jail time have been sentenced, with over 206 years of actual confinement.[28]

The Federal Bureau of Investigation, and of course the Environmental Protection Agency, are heavily committed to assisting in this investigation and prosecution effort. Training programs to aid similar efforts at the state level have been underway for some time, and the states have become increasingly active in criminal prosecution of environmental offenses. There is no doubt that criminal prosecutions will continue to play an increasingly important role in providing incentives for compliance with environmental obligations.

The next congress may further accelerate this commitment if it enacts legislation such as the proposed "Pollution Prosecution" and "Environmental Crimes" acts. Criminal prosecutions are also facilitated by continuing legislative and judicial actions reducing the requirement for criminal liability to simple negligence ("knew or should have known"). New federal sentencing guidelines for individuals and organizations will increase the severity of sentences where convictions are obtained. The bottom line is that individual responsibility will be a central theme of environmental enforcement in the nineties. In this context, it would be difficult to overemphasize the principle that every individual is responsible for environmental law compliance and needs to be making a daily demonstration of due concern and diligent efforts to seek out and halt or prevent violation in order to escape liability.

The role of the responsible individual today is more crucial than ever. His/her actions or inactions, what he/she knows, and perhaps most importantly—what he/she *ought* to know—can have a dramatic effect on the financial well-being of the corporation as well as his/her own

---

[28]Source: U.S. Department of Justice Memorandum, re: Environmental Criminal Statistics FY 83 through FY 92. October 27, 1992.

financial and personal future. Knowledge of, and strict adherence to, the mandates of the environmental statutes is no longer applicable only to large companies. Financial viability and profitability—the bottom lines for corporations—and personal freedom—the bottom line for individuals—rest on how effectively and thoroughly the individuals within a corporation do their jobs. That, in turn, depends partly on the individuals but also, in large part, on the organizational climate within which they operate.

6.0 THE FINAL QUESTION—WHO ENFORCES?

The last issue to be examined in this summary discussion of environmental liability is a critical one. Who brings the legal consequences we have talked about to the individuals and organizations which fail in their legal duty to comply with the environmental laws and demonstrate due concern for human health and the environment? In other words, who can sue, or otherwise enforce environmental duties. And the answer, of course, because we're lawyers, is "It depends."

6.1 Government Enforcement

A few of the environmental statutes, like TSCA, can, with limited exceptions, only be enforced by federal action.

Administrative penalties and compliance orders can be issued directly by the agency in charge of the law in question—EPA in most instances. But, where court action is required—as it is in the case of the larger fines, all criminal actions and court injunctions or enforcement orders—EPA must "refer the matter for prosecution by the Department of Justice." The Department of Justice is the government's lawyer. As such it maintains an extensive network of federal prosecutors operating not only from Washington, but also throughout the "several states."

However, most of the environmental statutes, like the Clean Air Act, the Clean Water Act, CERCLA and RCRA, contemplate cooperative federal-state enforcement programs and procedures. Thus, individual states may assume responsibility for legislative implementation in accordance with federal guidelines and subject to federal oversight. In federal-state programs, either the state or the federal government (or sometimes both) can enforce federal environmental statutory requirements. The pervasiveness of the federal government's continuing involvement will vary depending on the particular statute. In nearly all programs, however, careful consideration of both state and federal positions is advisable. It is often a mistake to take comfort in a lax enforcement attitude at either the state or federal level. Not only do attitudes change, but it is uncommon to find such attitudes shared by both state and federal officials.

State statutes, independent of the federal programs, are exclusively enforced by the states, and local laws are enforced by local governments. As such, they merit independent and thorough research.

6.2 Citizen's Suits

One reason that it is often unadvisable to rely on "understanding" governmental enforcement policy is that citizens are playing an increasingly significant role in enforcement of the environmental laws. Criminal prosecutions, of course, remain primarily the province of governmental prosecutors, though even there, bounty provisions like the "Dumpbuster" provision of CERCLA[29], may play a role.

In civil enforcement actions, individuals are often empowered to seek compliance orders or assessment of penalties actions under the "Citizens' Suit" provisions of environmental statutes.[30] Such actions have become increasingly frequent. Even in the absence of government prosecution, citizens are often authorized to act, under the increasingly popular theory of "citizen attorneys general." Because citizen actions are often initiated after lengthy periods of non-compliance, extraordinary fines and penalties are often possible.

Finally, where individuals have suffered monetary damages or incurred clean-up costs as a result of environmental violations or lack of due care for health and the environment, it is becoming easier to recover in traditional common-law "toxic tort" or "cost recovery" actions. Furthermore, statutory rights to collect damages or clean up costs are being created by statutes like the Oil Pollution Action of 1990 and CERCLA.

7.0 CONCLUSION

The public commitment to protection of public health and the environment will only increase in the coming decades. Thus, we can expect to see continued increasingly effective and vigorous efforts by institutions and individuals to assess liability to organizations and individuals which violate our environmental laws or otherwise fail to exercise "due care" for human health and the environment.

These liability concepts have attached themselves to technical legal principles dating back to the Magna Carta which have withstood the test of time. They deserve careful scrutiny and attention, for they most certainly reflect the ethic of our generation and will therefore be enforced.

In the recent words of former EPA Administrator, Reilly:

> Environmental crime is today no less a crime than theft, blackmail or assault. And more and more assuredly, if you do the crime, you'll do the time.

For additional information on this topic the reader is referred to the related books and courses listed at the end of this book.

---

[29]CERCLA, § 109(d).

[30]*See, e.g.,* CAA, § 304; CWA, § 505; CERCLA, § 310; RCRA, § 7002.

Chapter 3

RESOURCE CONSERVATION AND RECOVERY ACT

David R. Case
Hazardous Waste Treatment Council
Washington, D.C.

1.0 OVERVIEW

The United States has the most innovative and protective regulatory program for the management of hazardous waste of any country in the world. Over the last decade, the adage "out of sight, out of mind" has given way to a comprehensive national program that seeks to encourage source reduction, high-technology treatment, and secure disposal of hazardous wastes. Congress has enacted as national policy the mandate that hazardous waste will be treated, stored, and disposed of so as to minimize the present and future threat to human health and the environment.[1] The U.S. Environmental Protection Agency (EPA) and the states have sought to implement this mandate in complex regulations issued under the Resource Conservation and Recovery Act of 1976 (RCRA), as significantly amended by the Hazardous and Solid Waste Amendments of 1984 (HSWA).[2] Over 500,000 companies and individuals in the United States who generate over 172 million metric tons of hazardous waste each year must comply with the RCRA regulatory program.

RCRA is a regulatory statute designed to provide "cradle-to-grave" control of hazardous waste by imposing management requirements on generators and transporters of hazardous wastes and upon owners and operators of treatment, storage and disposal (TSD) facilities. RCRA applies mainly to active facilities, and does not address the equally serious problem of abandoned and inactive sites. Congress established liabilities and mandated remedies to correct problems at those sites in the Comprehensive Environmental Response, Compensation, and Liability Act of 1980, commonly known as Superfund,[3] which is discussed in detail in another chapter.

RCRA is currently divided into ten subtitles, A through J. The most significant of these is Subtitle C, which establishes the national haz-

---

[1] Resource Conservation and Recovery Act, 42 U.S.C. §§ 6901 et seq. (1988). Citations throughout this chapter are to sections of the act, rather than to the U.S. Code. See national policy in § 1003(b).

[2] Pub. L. No. 94-550, 90 Stat. 2796 (1976), as amended, Pub. L. No. 96-482, 94 Stat. 2334 (1980); Hazardous and Solid Waste Amendments of 1984, Pub. L. No. 98-616, 98 Stat. 3221.

[3] 42 U.S.C. §§ 9601 et seq.

ardous waste management program. Subtitle C, which encompasses Sections 3001-3020, establishes the following basic structure for the RCRA program. (See Table 1, below.)

Section 3001 requires EPA to promulgate regulations which identify specific hazardous wastes, either by listing them or identifying character-istics which render them hazardous. Persons managing such waste are required to notify the EPA of their hazardous waste activities.[4]

Persons who generate or produce these wastes (generators) must comply with a set of standards authorized by RCRA Section 3002. These include handling wastes properly and preparing manifests to track the shipment of the waste to treatment, recycling or disposal facilities.

Persons who transport hazardous waste (transporters) are required by Section 3003 to comply with another set of regulations dealing with manifests, labeling and the delivery of hazardous waste shipments to designated TSD facilities. Transporters must also comply with the U.S. Department of Transportation (DOT) requirements relating to containers, labeling, placarding of vehicles, and spill response.

Section 3004 requires TSD facilities to comply with performance standards, including statutory minimum technology requirements and groundwater monitoring, and a prohibition on the land disposal of untreated hazardous wastes. Section 3005 requires owners and operators of TSD facilities to obtain permits which set forth the conditions under which they may operate.

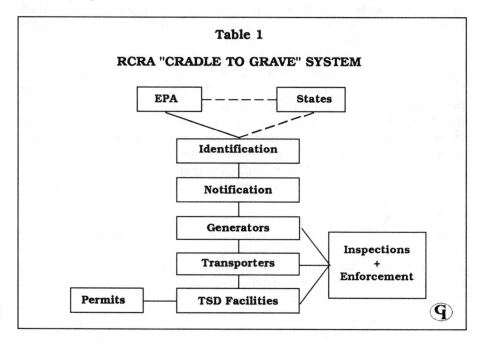

Table 1

RCRA "CRADLE TO GRAVE" SYSTEM

---

[4]Section 3010(a).

Section 3005(e) establishes the "interim status" provision for existing TSD facilities which allows them to remain in operation until a site-specific permit is issued. Owners and operators of interim status TSD facilities must file a timely application for a RCRA permit under Section 3005(a) in order to qualify, and comply with interim status standards in the regulations. The 1984 HSWA sets a timetable for EPA and the states to process and issue final RCRA permits.

Section 3006 of RCRA authorizes states to assume responsibility for carrying out the RCRA program, in lieu of the federal program. The state must administer and enforce a program which is consistent with and equivalent to the federal program. States can adopt more stringent requirements, but the state program may be no less stringent than the federal program. Sections 3007 and 3008 authorize site inspections and federal enforcement of RCRA and its implementing regulations.

Other provisions of Subtitle C include provisions for compiling a state-by-state hazardous waste site inventory; monitoring and enforcement authority against previous owners of TSD facilities; EPA regulation of recycled oil; and controls on the export of hazardous waste.[5]

RCRA has been amended several times since its enactment, most importantly by the Hazardous and Solid Waste Amendments of 1984 (HSWA). The 1984 HSWA mandated far-reaching changes to the RCRA program, such as waste minimization and a national land disposal ban program, discussed below. The amendments made by the 1984 HSWA are extensive. They significantly expand both the scope of coverage and the detailed requirements of RCRA. For example, they require EPA to more fully regulate an estimated 200,000 companies that produce only small quantities of hazardous waste (less than 1,000 kilograms per month). The 1984 amendments also created an entirely new regulatory program, Subtitle I ("eye"), for underground storage tanks containing hazardous substances or petroleum, which affects hundreds of thousands of facilities for the first time.[6] The numerous constraints imposed on those who treat, store or dispose of hazardous wastes in land-based facilities, including restrictions on the disposal of liquid wastes and other common hazardous wastes in landfills, are technically complex. For example, companies using unlined surface impoundments were required to retrofit with double liners and leachate collection systems.

The 1984 HSWA contain many so-called "hammer provisions" that required EPA to implement new requirements by a deadline or a statutory standard went into effect automatically. For example, if EPA had not promulgated the land disposal restriction regulations for all RCRA hazardous wastes by the statutory deadline of May 1990, the "hammer" would have fallen and the unrestricted wastes would have been prohibited from

---

[5]Sections 3012, 3013, 3014, 3017.

[6]Sections 9001-9010. The underground storage tank program is discussed in a separate chapter.

land disposal by operation of statute. There are 72 major provisions in the 1984 HSWA, by EPA's count, and these new requirements are having a substantial impact on every U.S. business that produces hazardous waste.

These major provisions of the Subtitle C program and the impact of the 1984 amendments are discussed in detail below, as are the requirements of other important subtitles of RCRA.

2.0 POLICY GOALS AND OBJECTIVES OF RCRA

Subtitle A of RCRA declares that, as a matter of national policy, the generation of hazardous waste is to be reduced or eliminated as expeditiously as possible, and land disposal should be the least favored method for managing hazardous wastes. In addition, all waste that is generated must be handled so as to minimize the present and future threat to human health and the environment.[7]

Subtitle A also includes a series of objectives designed to achieve these goals, including proper management of hazardous waste in the first instance, minimizing the generation and land disposal of hazardous waste, a prohibition on open dumping, state assumption of RCRA programs, promoting research and development activities for waste management, and encouraging recovery, recycling, and treatment as alternatives to land disposal.[8] These national goals and objectives set by RCRA give direction to EPA's regulatory efforts.

3.0 DEFINITION OF SOLID AND HAZARDOUS WASTE

The starting point for determining the full scope of RCRA's coverage is the broad definition of "solid waste" in the statute. Section 1004(27) states that:

> The term "solid waste" means *any garbage, refuse, sludge* from a waste treatment plant, water supply treatment plant or air pollution control facility *and other discarded material, including solid, liquid, semisolid, or contained gaseous materials* resulting from industrial, commercial, mining and agriculture activities and from community activities but does not include solid or dissolved material in domestic sewage, or solid or dissolved materials in irrigation return flows or industrial discharges which are point sources subject to permits under section 402 of the Federal Water Pollution Control Act, as amended, or source, special nuclear, or byproduct material as defined by the Atomic Energy Act of 1954, as amended (68 Stat. 923). (Emphasis supplied.)

The statute therefore potentially applies to any waste regardless of its physical form. EPA has further defined "solid waste" by regulation, as discussed below.

---

[7]RCRA, Sections 1003(b), 1002(b).
[8]RCRA, Section 1003(a).

The Subtitle C regulatory program of RCRA then covers those solid wastes that are deemed hazardous. As defined in Section 1004(5), the term "hazardous waste" means a solid waste, or combination of solid wastes, which because of its quantity, concentration, or physical, chemical, or infectious characteristics may—

(A) cause, or significantly contribute to an increase in mortality or an increase in serious irreversible, or incapacitating reversible illness; or

(B) pose a substantial present or potential hazard to human health or the environment when improperly treated, stored, transported, or disposed of, or otherwise managed.

These general statutory definitions have been greatly amplified and explained by EPA regulations implementing RCRA, beginning with the framework rule issued on May 19, 1980.[9] These regulations are discussed in the following section which describes the RCRA Subtitle C program in detail.

4.0 SUBTITLE C: HAZARDOUS WASTE MANAGEMENT PROGRAM

4.1 Identification of Hazardous Wastes[10]

EPA has defined solid waste to include any discarded material, provided a regulatory exclusion or specific variance granted by EPA or an authorized state does not apply.[11] "Discarded material" is in turn defined as any material that is abandoned, recycled, or "inherently waste-like."[12] A material is abandoned if it is disposed of, burned or incinerated, or accumulated, stored or treated prior to or in lieu of abandonment. A material is inherently waste-like if EPA so defines it by regulation.[13]

A material can be a solid waste if it is recycled in a manner constituting disposal, by burning for energy recovery, by reclamation, or by speculative accumulation. Materials that are not solid wastes when recycled are materials that are directly used or reused as ingredients or feedstocks in production processes, or as effective substitutes for commercial products, or that are recycled in a closed-loop production process.[14]

---

[9]*45 Fed. Reg.* 33066.

[10]For a more detailed description of the regulatory provisions of RCRA, the reader is referred to Hall, et al., *RCRA/Hazardous Wastes Handbook* (Government Institutes, 9th ed. 1992).

[11]40 C.F.R. § 261.2(a). See 50 *Fed. Reg.* 664 (January 4, 1985). The list of regulatory exemptions appears at § 261.4(a) and is very limited.

[12]40 C.F.R. § 261.2(a)(2).

[13]40 C.F.R. § 261.2(d). EPA has designated dioxin wastes as inherently waste-like.

[14]EPA has proposed amendments to the definition of solid waste to exclude certain in-process-recycled secondary materials that are part of a continuous production or manufacturing process. 53 *Fed. Reg.* 519 (January 8, 1988). This action was taken in response to the court decision in *American Mining Congress v. EPA*, 824 F.2d 1177 (D.C. Cir. 1987).

These interlocking definitions result in EPA regulating a universe of materials that may not commonly be understood to be "wastes" for a particular industry or company. In particular, materials that will be reclaimed or recycled, rather than disposed of, may still be considered solid wastes and therefore hazardous wastes subject to RCRA regulation.

Once a material is found to be a solid waste, the next question is whether it is a "hazardous waste." EPA's regulations automatically exempt certain solid wastes from being considered hazardous wastes. Generally these regulatory exemptions include:

(1) household waste;

(2) agricultural wastes which are returned to the ground as fertilizer;

(3) mining overburden returned to the mine site;

(4) utility wastes from coal combustion;

(5) oil and natural gas exploration drilling waste;

(6) wastes from the extraction, beneficiation, and processing of ores and minerals, including coal;

(7) cement kiln dust wastes;

(8) arsenical-treated wood wastes generated by end users of such wood;

(9) certain chromium-bearing wastes.[15]

EPA has also provided some limited regulatory exemptions under narrowly defined circumstances, such as for hazardous waste that is generated in a product or raw material storage tank, transport vehicle, pipeline or manufacturing process unit prior to removal for disposal. EPA has also adopted a conditional exemption for waste samples collected for testing to determine their characteristics or composition, or to conduct treatability tests.[16]

If a solid waste does not qualify for an exemption, it will be deemed a hazardous waste if it is listed by EPA in 40 C.F.R. Part 261, Subpart D, or if it exhibits any of the four hazardous waste characteristics identified in 40 C.F.R. Part 261, Subpart C. The lists and characteristics are described in the following sections.

4.1.1 Hazardous Waste Lists

EPA has established three hazardous wastes lists. A hazardous waste number is assigned to each listed waste which can be used to identify the waste on biennial reports and other documents, and for purposes of the land disposal ban program. The first list contains hazardous wastes from nonspecific sources (for example, spent nonhalogenated solvents, such as toluene or methyl ethyl ketone).[17] The hazardous wastes on this

---

[15] 40 C.F.R. § 261.4(b).
[16] 40 C.F.R. § 261.4(d).
[17] 40 C.F.R. § 261.31.

nonspecific source list are assigned an "F" number (for example F001 is assigned to various spent solvents). The second list identifies hazardous wastes from specific sources (for example, bottom sediment sludge from the treatment of wastewaters by the wood preserving industry).[18] The hazardous wastes on the specific source list have a "K" number (for example, K048 and K052 are certain petroleum refining wastes). The first two hazardous waste lists are largely self-explanatory. A company need only compare its solid waste stream to those lists to determine if it manages a hazardous waste.

The third list sets forth commercial chemical products, including off-specification species, containers, and spill residues, which, when discarded, must be treated as hazardous wastes.[19] This hazardous waste list actually consists of two distinct sublists. One sublist sets forth chemicals deemed acute hazardous wastes when discarded (40 C.F.R. 261.33(e)). These have a "P" number and are subject to more rigorous management requirements (for example P076 is nitric oxide). A second list contains "U" listed chemicals which are deemed toxic and, therefore, hazardous when discarded (40 C.F.R. 261.33(f)), and which are regulated like other listed hazardous wastes (for example, U002 is acetone).

Hazardous waste regulation under the commercial chemical list can be triggered when a company decides to reduce inventory or otherwise discards a listed commercial chemical product in its pure form. Another situation that may trigger regulation is an accidental spill of the chemical.[20] If a listed commercial chemical is spilled, the spilled chemical and any contaminated material, that is, dirt and other residue, are likely to be discarded and thus become a hazardous waste. Therefore, even companies that generally do not discard or intend to discard any of the commercial chemical products on the list must be prepared to comply with the RCRA hazardous waste regulations in the event of an accidental spill.[21] This may involve, as discussed below, obtaining an EPA identification number and complying, at a minimum, with applicable generator standards. For disposal of small amounts of chemicals or spill materials, the company may qualify as a conditionally exempt "small quantity generator."[22]

Since the RCRA program became effective in 1980, many companies have filed "delisting petitions" with EPA to remove wastes generated at their facilities from the RCRA hazardous waste lists. The granting of a delisting petition exempts the waste generated at a particular facility from the RCRA hazardous waste program. A company seeking a delisting must demonstrate that its particular waste does not contain the hazardous

---

[18] 40 C.F.R. § 261.32.

[19] 40 C.F.R. § 261.33.

[20] 40 C.F.R. § 261.33(d).

[21] See 45 *Fed. Reg.* 76629 (November 19, 1980).

[22] 40 C.F.R. § 261.5. Alternatively, a small spill may qualify as a de minimis loss exempt from the definition of hazardous waste in § 261.3(a)(2)(iv)(D).

constituents for which EPA listed the waste, or any other constituents that could cause the waste to be hazardous.[23]

For example, a company seeking to delist a waste which would otherwise be included under F006 (wastewater treatment sludge from electroplating operations) must show that the concentrations of chromium, nickel, and cyanide for which the waste was listed are below levels of regulatory concern, and also that no other heavy metals or other constituents are present that may cause the waste to be hazardous. EPA must act on a delisting petition within two years of receiving a complete petition.

4.1.2 Hazardous Waste Characteristics

If a waste is not listed as hazardous, the waste is still covered by RCRA if it exhibits one of four hazardous waste characteristics: (1) ignitability, (2) corrosivity, (3) reactivity, or (4) toxicity.[24]

The hazardous waste characteristic of ignitability was established to identify solid wastes capable during routine handling of causing a fire or exacerbating a fire once started.[25] A solid waste is deemed to exhibit the characteristic of ignitability if it satisfies one of the following four descriptions (1) if it is a liquid, other than an aqueous solution containing less than 24 percent alcohol by volume, that has a flash point of less than 140 degrees Fahrenheit (60°C); (2) second, if it is a nonliquid that under normal conditions can cause a fire through friction, absorption of moisture, or spontaneous chemical changes, and burns so vigorously when ignited that it creates a hazard; (3) third, if it is an ignitable compressed gas as defined by the DOT regulations at 49 C.F.R. 173.300; or (4) a waste exhibits ignitability if it is an oxidizer as defined by the DOT regulations at 49 C.F.R. 173.151. An ignitable hazardous waste has the EPA number of D001.

The hazardous waste characteristic of corrosivity was established because EPA believed that wastes capable of corroding metal could escape their containers and liberate other wastes.[26] In addition, wastes with a pH at either the high or low end of the scale can harm human tissue and aquatic life and may react dangerously with other wastes. Therefore, EPA determined that any solid waste is deemed to exhibit the characteristic of corrosivity if it is (1) aqueous and has a pH of less than or equal to 2.0 or greater than or equal to 12.5, or (2) a liquid and corrodes steel at a rate greater than 6.35 millimeters (.250 inches) per year under specified testing procedures. A waste that exhibits the hazardous characteristic of corrosivity has the EPA number of D002.

EPA established the characteristic of reactivity to regulate wastes that are extremely unstable and have a tendency to react violently or

---

[23]40 C.F.R. § 260.22.
[24]40 C.F.R. § 261.3, § 261.20.
[25]40 C.F.R. § 261.21.
[26]41 C.F.R. § 261.22.

explode during management.[27] The regulation lists a number of situations where this may happen which warrant specific consideration (for example, when the waste is mixed with water, when heated, etc.). Since suitable test protocols for measuring reactivity are unavailable, EPA has promulgated a narrative definition of the reactivity characteristic that must be used. A waste that exhibits reactivity has EPA number D003.

The toxicity characteristic is designed to identify wastes that are likely to leach hazardous concentrations of specific toxic constituents into groundwater under mismanagement conditions.[28] This characteristic is determined based on a mandatory testing procedure which extracts the toxic constituents from a solid waste in a manner that EPA believes simulates the leaching action which occurs in landfills.[29] A solid waste exhibits the characteristic of toxicity if, using the test methods prescribed by EPA, the extract from a representative sample of the waste contains contaminants at levels of regulatory concern. The test method is called the Toxicity Characteristic Leaching Procedure, or TCLP. It replaces the Extraction Procedure (EP) Toxicity Characteristic that was initially promulgated by EPA in 1980. The TCLP tests for 25 organic chemicals, 8 inorganics, and 6 insecticides/herbicides. The levels that trigger the toxicity characteristic reflect health-based concentration thresholds and a factor for dilution and attenuation that was developed using modeling of the subsurface fate and transport of contaminants. These hazardous wastes are given EPA numbers D004-D043, depending on the toxic contaminant that causes the waste to be hazardous.

4.1.3 Mixtures of Hazardous Wastes and Solid Wastes

Anyone concerned with hazardous waste management must be aware of the "mixture rule."[30] Under this EPA rule, a mixture of a listed hazardous waste and a solid waste must also be considered a hazardous waste, unless the mixture qualifies for an exemption.[31] The exemptions apply if, for example, (1) the listed hazardous waste in the mixture was listed solely because it exhibits a hazardous characteristic and the mixture does not exhibit that characteristic; (2) the mixture consists of wastewater and certain specified hazardous wastes in dilute concentrations, the discharge of which is subject to regulation under the Clean Water Act, or (3) the mixture consists of a discarded commercial chemical product resulting from

---

[27]41 C.F.R. § 261.23.

[28]40 C.F.R. § 261.24, as amended, 55 *Fed. Reg.* 11862 (March 29, 1990).

[29]40 C.F.R. Part 261, Appendix II.

[30]EPA's 1980 mixture rule and derived-from rule (discussed below) were vacated by the U.S. Court of Appeals in *Shell Oil Co. v. EPA*, 950 F.2d 741 (D.C. Cir. 1991). The court held that EPA did not provide adequate notice and opportunity for comment when promulgating these rules in 1980. At the court's suggestion, however, EPA then re-promulgated the mixture and derived-from rules on an interim basis. 57 *Fed. Reg.* 7628 (March 3, 1992). Congress has now directed EPA to promulgate revisions to these rules, if necessary, by October 1, 1994. Pub. L. No. 102-389.

[31]40 C.F.R. § 261.3(a)(2).

de minimis losses during manufacturing operations. On the other hand, a mixture of a characteristic hazardous waste and a solid waste will be deemed hazardous only if the entire mixture continues to exhibit a hazardous characteristic.

Note that these exemptions apply only when the hazardous waste becomes mixed with other wastes as part of the normal production or waste management process, not when wastes are intentionally mixed to achieve dilution. Such mixing may constitute treatment and could require a RCRA permit.

4.1.4 Derived-from Hazardous Wastes

Of equal importance is EPA's so-called "derived-from rule." Under this rule, a waste that is generated from the treatment, storage, or disposal of a hazardous waste (for example ash, leachate, or emission control dust) is also a hazardous waste, unless exempted.[32] If the waste is derived from a listed hazardous waste, it is considered a hazardous waste until delisting procedures are followed. If the waste is derived from a characteristic hazardous waste, it is not hazardous if it does not exhibit that characteristic. Materials that are reclaimed from solid wastes for beneficial use are no longer wastes, unless the reclaimed material is burned as a fuel or used in a manner constituting disposal (that is, applied to the ground).

4.1.5 Hazardous Wastes Contained in Environmental Media and Debris

Another relevant principle is embodied in the "contained-in rule." EPA has long taken the view that soil, groundwater, surface water, and debris that is contaminated with listed hazardous waste must be regulated under RCRA Subtitle C.[33] The contaminated media and debris are said to contain the listed hazardous waste, and thus to require proper management. EPA has now codified this rule, along with the corollary that debris which is treated so that it no longer contains a listed hazardous waste will no longer be subject to Subtitle C regulation.[34]

4.1.6 Used, Reused, Recycled or Reclaimed Hazardous Wastes

EPA has defined the term "solid waste" to extend coverage to many recycling and reclamation activities.[35] This aspect of the solid waste definition is complex. Conceptually, it requires consideration of two things—the manner of recycling, and the secondary material being recycled.

---

[32]40 C.F.R. § 261.3(b).

[33]EPA's position that the contained-in policy was an interpretive gloss on the mixture and derived-from rules was upheld by the court. *Chemical Manufacturers Ass'n v. EPA*, 869 F.2d 1526 (D.C. Cir. 1989).

[34]40 C.F.R. § 261.3(f), 57 *Fed. Reg.* 37194 (August 18, 1992).

[35]40 C.F.R. § 261.2(c).

The recycling activities that are regulated are (1) use in a manner constituting disposal (for example, land application), (2) burning for energy recovery, (3) reclamation, and (4) speculative accumulation. Secondary materials that are solid wastes when recycled include spent materials, listed and characteristic sludges, listed and characteristic byproducts, commercial chemical products, and scrap metal. These materials are all solid wastes when recycled with two exceptions. Sludges and by-products that are hazardous only by characteristic are not solid wastes when they are reclaimed. Commercial chemical products are not solid wastes when they are either reclaimed or speculatively accumulated.[36]

Materials are not solid wastes when they are directly used or reused as ingredients in an industrial process to make a product, provided the material is not being reclaimed. A material is also not a solid waste when used as an effective substitute for a commercial product, unless the material is burned as a fuel or applied to the land. Finally, a material is not a waste if it is returned to the original process from which it is generated as a substitute for a raw material feedstock, again provided it is not first reclaimed. These provisions reflect EPA's concern to avoid extending RCRA regulation to production activities, as distinct from waste management.

Generally speaking, hazardous wastes destined for recycling are subject to the Part 262 and 263 regulations for generators and transporters, and to the storage facility requirements in Parts 264 and 265.[37]

4.2 Notification of Hazardous Waste Management Activities

RCRA Section 3010(a) requires that any person who manages a hazardous waste (that is, generators, transporters, and owners and operators of TSD facilities) must file a notification with EPA within 90 days after regulations are promulgated identifying the waste as hazardous. EPA has published Form 8700-12 as the Section 3010(a) notification form. The reporting company must identify itself, its location, and the EPA identification numbers for the listed and characteristic hazardous wastes it manages. Notifications must be filed for each site (for example, plant) at which hazardous waste is managed.

Persons managing hazardous wastes under EPA's initial RCRA regulatory program should have filed the Section 3010(a) notification form not later than August 18, 1980.[38] Failure to file makes the transport, treatment, storage or disposal of the hazardous wastes unlawful. Companies that failed to file due to excusable oversight may request that EPA exercise its

---

[36]*Id.* The definition of "sludge" is in § 260.10 and the definitions of "by-product," "scrap metal," "recycled," "reclaimed," and "accumulated speculatively" are found in § 261.1(c). These definitions are critically important to understanding the scope of RCRA's coverage of recycling activities.

[37]40 C.F.R. § 261.6 Certain exemptions are also set forth in the regulation.

[38]45 *Fed. Reg.* 33066 (May 19, 1980).

enforcement discretion and permit continued operation if in the public interest.[39]

Persons who produce, market or burn hazardous waste-derived fuels were required to file a notification by February 8, 1985. These notifications also identified the location and description of the facility, the hazardous wastes involved, and a description of the fuel production or burning activity carried out at the facility.

4.3 Generators of Hazardous Waste

Generators play a crucial role in the overall RCRA hazardous waste regulatory scheme. The failure of a generator to properly identify and initiate the management of a hazardous waste may mean that the waste never enters the "cradle to grave" hazardous waste program. Thus the requirements imposed on generators under RCRA Section 3002 and EPA's implementing regulations at 40 C.F.R. Part 262 are of key concern.

EPA's regulations define the term "generator" as "any person, by site, whose act or process produces hazardous waste identified or listed in Part 261 of this chapter or whose act first causes hazardous waste to become subject to regulation."[40] This definition refers explicitly to the particular site of generation. A corporation with several plants must evaluate and comply with the generator requirements at each facility site.

A generator is initially required to determine whether any of its solid waste is a "hazardous waste" under the criteria described above.[41] The records of any test results, waste analyses, or determinations that a waste is hazardous must be kept for at least three years from the date the waste was last sent to a TSD facility. Most generators retain such records indefinitely. The generator must then obtain an EPA Identification Number before any hazardous waste can be transported, treated, stored or disposed of, and only transporters and TSD facilities that also have obtained their EPA identification numbers can be used.[42]

The generator has the responsibility for preparing the Uniform Hazardous Waste Manifest, a control and transport document that accompanies the hazardous waste at all times.[43] The generator must specify the name and EPA identification numbers of each authorized transporter and the TSD facility or other designated facility that will receive the waste, describe the waste as required by DOT regulations, certify that it is properly packaged and labeled, and sign the manifest certifications by hand.

---

[39] 45 *Fed. Reg.* 76632 (November 19, 1980).

[40] 40 C.F.R. § 260.10(a)(26).

[41] 40 C.F.R. § 262.11.

[42] 40 C.F.R. § 262.12(c).

[43] 40 C.F.R. §§ 262.20 262.23. *See* the Uniform Manifest and instructions, 40 C.F.R. Part 262, Appendix.

In the new era of RCRA, companies must develop new management strategies and technologies to reduce the volume and toxicity of their hazardous wastes. As an action-forcing mechanism, Congress now requires that all generators certify on manifests that:

> I have a program in place to reduce the volume and toxicity of waste generated to the degree I have determined to be economically practicable and I have selected the method of treatment, storage or disposal currently available to me which minimizes the present and future threat to human health and the environment.

A sufficient number of copies of the manifest must be prepared so that all parties listed on the manifest as handling the hazardous waste will be provided with a copy, and a final copy can also be returned to the generator by the TSD facility. A copy of the final signed manifest must be kept for at least three years, although most generators retain copies for a much longer period.[44]

If the manifest is not received back by the generator in a timely or properly executed manner, he must file an "exception report" with EPA or the state. The regulations specifically provide that a generator must contact the transporter and/or the TSD facility to determine what happened to the manifest and the hazardous waste. If, after 45 days from shipping the waste, the generator has not received a manifest with the proper signatures back from the TSD facility, the generator must submit an exception report which consists of (1) a copy of the manifest for which the generator does not have confirmation of delivery; and (2) a cover letter which describes the efforts taken to locate the waste or manifest and the result of those efforts.[45]

A generator, in addition, must properly prepare the waste for transportation off-site. EPA has adopted the DOT regulations issued under the Hazardous Materials Transportation Act, 49 USC §§ 1802 et seq., with respect to the packaging, labeling, marking, and placarding of hazardous waste shipments.[46] In addition to the DOT regulations, EPA requires that any container of 110 gallons or less must be specifically marked with the generator's name, address, manifest document number, and the words:

> Hazardous Waste—Federal law prohibits improper disposal.
> If found contact the nearest police or public safety authority or
> the United States Environmental Protection Agency.

A generator is allowed to accumulate his own hazardous wastes on site without a RCRA storage permit in two related circumstances. First, the generator can accumulate up to 55 gallons of hazardous wastes at or near the

---

[44]40 C.F.R. § 262.40.
[45]40 C.F.R. § 262.42.
[46]40 C.F.R. § 262.31.

point of generation in "satellite accumulation areas."[47] The containers must be properly marked and maintained in good condition, and the waste must be moved into storage once the 55-gallon limit is reached. Second, a generator is also allowed to store hazardous waste on-site prior to shipment for a period of up to 90 days in tanks or containers, provided certain standards are met.[48] The generator must comply with the Part 265 interim status standards for containers and tanks (for example, secondary containment structures) and the requirements for personnel training, contingency planning, and emergency preparedness and response.

A generator must file biennial reports with EPA or an authorized state (some states require annual reports). The biennial report is filed on March 1 of even numbered years for the preceding calendar year, and must include (1) the name, address and EPA identification number of the generator, (2) the EPA identification number for each transporter used, (3) name, address and identification number of each TSD facility to which wastes were sent, and (4) waste identification information including the DOT hazard class, EPA hazardous waste identification number, and the quantity of the wastes.[49] EPA has devised Form 8700-13A for this purpose. The 1984 HSWA requires that the reports now also include information on the "waste minimization" efforts undertaken to reduce the volume and toxicity of the hazardous wastes, and the results actually achieved in comparison with previous years. As a recordkeeping requirement, the generator must maintain copies of the biennial reports (and any exception reports filed) for at least three years.

As a practical matter, in view of the liability imposed by Superfund, discussed in the Superfund Chapter, generators should seriously consider maintaining RCRA waste determinations, test results, manifests, and reports for a lengthy period of time.

Special rules have been issued for persons who export or import hazardous wastes.[50] A generator who intends to export his hazardous waste to a foreign country must first notify EPA in writing at least four weeks before the initial shipment in each calendar year. He must then require the foreign consignee to confirm delivery of the waste, such as by returning a signed manifest. If the generator does not receive a manifest signed by the transporter stating the date and place of departure from the U.S. within 45 days, or written confirmation of receipt from the foreign consignee within 90 days, an exception report must be filed. Annual reports of all exports must be submitted to EPA. A person who imports hazardous waste into the U.S. must initiate the manifest procedures as the generator.

---

[47]40 C.F.R. § 262.34.

[48]40 C.F.R. § 262.34(a). A small quantity generator can store wastes for a longer time period, as discussed below. *See* 40 C.F.R. § 262.34(d)-(f).

[49]40 C.F.R. § 262.41.

[50]40 C.F.R. § 262.50.

4.3.1 Small Generators

As directed by the 1984 HSWA, EPA has promulgated special regulations for small quantity generators that produce hazardous wastes in a total monthly quantity of less than 1,000 kilograms (2,200 pounds).[51] The regulations vary somewhat from the standards that currently apply to hazardous wastes of larger quantity generators. For example, small quantity generators of between 100 kilograms and 1,000 kilograms may accumulate up to 6,000 kilograms (13,200 pounds) of hazardous waste on site for up to 180 days without a permit. If the waste must be shipped over 200 miles, the waste may be stored for up to 270 days.

Besides using the Uniform Manifest, small quantity generators must have their waste treated, stored (except short-term accumulation on site) and disposed of at an interim status or permitted TSD facility, and no longer at a state or municipally licensed landfill. The manifest contains a modified certification of waste minimization for such generators. In almost all other respects, however, small quantity generators of between 100 kilograms and 1,000 kilograms per month are regulated the same as large generators.

Very small generators of less than 100 kilograms per month are still conditionally exempt from RCRA, but they are subject to certain minimum standards.[52]

4.4 Transporters of Hazardous Wastes

A transporter is any person engaged in the off-site transportation of hazardous waste by air, rail, highway or water.[53] Off-site transportation includes both interstate and intrastate commerce.[54] Thus, the reach of RCRA includes not only shippers and common carriers of hazardous wastes, but also the company that occasionally transports hazardous wastes on its own trucks solely within its home state.

Anyone who moves a hazardous waste that is required to be manifested off the site where it is generated, or the site where it is being treated, stored and disposed of, will be subject to the transporter standards. The only persons not covered are generators or operators of TSD facilities who engage in on-site transportation of their hazardous waste. Once a generator or a TSD facility operator moves its hazardous waste off-site—which can be any distance along a public road—he is then considered a transporter and must comply with the regulations.[55]

---

[51]40 C.F.R. § 261.5, § 262.34(d)-(f).

[52]40 C.F.R. § 261.5.

[53]40 C.F.R. § 260.10(a).

[54]Section 3003.

[55]See the definition of "on-site" in § 260.10(a), which by implication defines transportation off-site as any distance along, as opposed to simply going across, a public or private right-of-way.

EPA has promulgated standards for all transporters of hazardous wastes at 40 C.F.R. Part 263. These standards are closely coordinated with the standards issued by the U.S. Department of Transportation under the Hazardous Materials Transportation Act for the shipment of hazardous materials.[56] For the most part, EPA's regulations incorporate and require compliance with the DOT provisions on labeling, marking, placarding, using proper containers, and responding to spills. Of course, all transporters must obtain an EPA identification number prior to transporting any hazardous waste, and they may only accept hazardous waste which is accompanied by a manifest signed by the generator.[57] The transporter himself must sign and date the manifest acknowledging acceptance of the waste and return one copy to the generator before leaving the generator's property.

The transporter must keep the manifest with the hazardous waste at all times. When the transporter delivers the waste to another transporter or to the designated TSD facility, he must (1) date the manifest and obtain the signature of the next transporter or the TSD facility operator, (2) retain one copy of the manifest for his own records, and (3) give the remaining copies to the person receiving the waste.[58] If the transporter is unable to deliver the waste in accordance with the manifest, he must contact the generator for further instructions and revise the manifest accordingly.[59] The transporter must keep the executed copy of the manifest for a period of three years.[60]

The transporter may hold a hazardous waste for up to ten days at a transfer facility without being required to obtain a RCRA storage permit.[61] A transfer facility generally includes a loading dock, storage area, and similar areas where shipments of hazardous wastes are held during the normal course of transportation.

Transporters of hazardous wastes may become subject to the Part 262 requirements for generators if, for example, the transporter mixes hazardous wastes of different DOT descriptions by placing them into a single container, or if he imports hazardous waste from a foreign country.[62] Also, a hazardous waste that accumulates in a transport vehicle or vessel will trigger the generator standards when the waste is removed.

---

[56] 49 U.S.C. §§ 1801, *et seq.*, 49 C.F.R. Parts 171-179.

[57] 40 C.F.R. § 263.11, § 263.20.

[58] 40 C.F.R. § 263.20. Special requirements apply to rail or water transport of hazardous waste, and to persons who transport hazardous waste outside of the United States. 40 C.F.R. § 263.20(e), (f) and (g), § 263.22(b), (c) and (d).

[59] 40 C.F.R. § 263.21(b).

[60] 40 C.F.R. § 263.22.

[61] 40 C.F.R. § 263.12.

[62] 40 C.F.R. § 263.10(c).

If an accidental spill or other discharge of a hazardous waste occurs during transportation, the transporter is responsible for its clean up.[63] The transporter must take immediate response action to protect human health and the environment. Such action includes treatment or containment of the spill and notification of local police and fire departments. DOT's discharge reporting requirements are incorporated into the RCRA regulations.[64] They identify the situations in which telephone reporting of the discharge to the National Response Center and the filing of a written report are required. Transporters are subject to both DOT and EPA enforcement.[65]

The 1984 HSWA affected transporters in minor respects. For example, EPA has established requirements for the transportation of hazardous waste-derived fuels.[66] In addition, railroads are shielded from the RCRA "citizen suit" and "imminent hazard" enforcement provisions (discussed below) if the railroad merely transports the hazardous waste under a sole contractual agreement and exercises due care.

4.5 Treatment, Storage, and Disposal (TSD) Facilities

The term "TSD" is commonly used to refer to the three management activities that are regulated under RCRA Section 3004, and which thus require a permit under RCRA Section 3005. These activities are treatment, storage and disposal of hazardous wastes. Section 3004 directed EPA to establish a comprehensive set of regulations governing all aspects of TSD facilities, including location, design, operation, and closure. The regulations adopted include standards of general applicability and specific requirements for particular types of TSD facilities.[67]

In 1984, Congress added a number of important provisions to Section 3004. These establish, among other things, a ban on the disposal of liquids in landfills, minimum technological requirements (that is, double liners) for surface impoundments and landfills, corrective action for continuing releases at permitted TSD facilities, and controls on the marketing and burning of hazardous wastes used as fuels. Congress also directed EPA to make a number of regulatory decisions under Section 3004 in short order. The most significant provisions set a strict timetable under which EPA must implement a land disposal ban of all untreated hazardous wastes, and establish treatment standards for the wastes. The requirements of the current standards and the impact of the new amendments are discussed below.

First of all, certain basic definitions must be understood. A facility will be regulated as a "treatment facility" if the operator utilizes any method, technique, or process designed to change the physical, chemical, or biologi-

---

[63]40 C.F.R. § 263.30.
[64]See 49 C.F.R. § 171.15 and § 171.16.
[65]45 Fed. Reg. 51645 (August 4, 1980).
[66]40 C.F.R. § 266.33, discussed below.
[67]See 40 C.F.R. Parts 264 and 265, discussed infra.

cal character or composition of any hazardous waste so as to neutralize such waste, to recover energy or material resources from the waste, to render the waste nonhazardous or less hazardous, safer to transport, store or dispose of, or amenable for recovery, amenable for storage, or reduced in volume.[68] There is very little that can be done to a hazardous waste that would not qualify as treatment.

A "storage facility" is defined as one which engages in the holding of hazardous waste for a temporary period, at the end of which the hazardous waste is treated, disposed of, or stored elsewhere.[69] A "disposal facility" is one at which hazardous waste is intentionally placed into or on any land or water, and at which waste will remain after closure.[70] The term "facility" is separately defined to include "all contiguous land, and structures, other appurtenances, and improvements on the land."[71] Clarification of the foregoing definitions can be sought during the permitting process.

A number of different types of TSD facilities and hazardous waste activities are currently exempted from EPA regulation altogether. The list includes the following exclusions:[72]

(1) Facilities that dispose of hazardous waste by means of ocean disposal pursuant to a permit issued under the Marine Protection, Research, and Sanctuaries Act (except as provided in a RCRA permit-by-rule).

(2) The disposal of hazardous waste by underground injection pursuant to a permit issued under the Safe Drinking Water Act (except as provided in a RCRA permit-by-rule).

(3) A Publicly Owned Treatment Works (POTW) that treats or stores hazardous wastes which are delivered to the POTW by a transport vehicle or vessel or through a pipe.

(4) TSD facilities that operate under a state hazardous waste program authorized pursuant to RCRA Section 3006, and which are therefore subject to regulation under the state program.

(5) Facilities authorized by a state to manage industrial or municipal solid waste, if the only hazardous waste handled by such a facility is otherwise excluded from regulation pursuant to the special requirements for conditionally exempt small quantity generators of less than 100 kilograms.

(6) A facility that is subject to the special exemptions for certain recyclable materials, except as provided in Part 266.

---

[68] 0 C.F.R. § 260.10(a). This definition was upheld by the court in *Shell Oil Co. v. EPA*, 950 F.2d 741 (D.C. Cir. 1991).

[69] *Id.*

[70] *Id.*

[71] *Id.*

[72] *See* 40 C.F.R. § 264.1 and § 265.1(c).

(7)   Temporary on-site accumulation of hazardous waste by generators in compliance with 40 C.F.R. § 262.34.

(8)   Farmers who dispose of waste pesticides from their own use in compliance with 40 C.F.R. § 262.51.

(9)   Owners or operators of a "totally enclosed treatment facility."

(10) Owners and operators of "elementary neutralization units" and "wastewater treatment units," as defined in the regulations.

(11) Persons taking immediate action to treat and contain spills.

(12) Transporters storing manifested wastes in approved containers at a transfer facility for 10 days or less.

(13) The act of adding absorbent material to hazardous waste in a container to reduce the amount of free liquids in the container, if the materials are added when wastes are first placed in the container.

The regulations should be consulted for the precise scope of these exemptions.

4.5.1 Standards of General Applicability

As discussed more fully in the permits section below, two categories of TSD facilities currently exist—interim status facilities and permitted facilities. Interim status facilities are those that are currently operating without final RCRA permits based upon a legislative decision to allow continued operation of existing facilities until RCRA permits can be issued. These facilities had to meet a three-part statutory test:

(1)   to be in existence on November 19, 1980, or the effective date of statutory or regulatory changes that render the facility subject to the need for a RCRA permit,

(2)   notify EPA pursuant to RCRA Section 3010(a) of its hazardous waste management activities, and

(3)   file a preliminary permit application.[73]

A facility's interim status ends when the facility receives a final RCRA permit. This in turn is based upon technical standards, issued by EPA or a state with an approved program, which are incorporated into the permit. As discussed in the next section on permits, the 1984 HSWA specified timetables for issuance of final permits to all interim status TSD facilities. All other TSD facilities must obtain an individual RCRA permit before commencing construction.

Separate standards have been issued for interim status facilities[74] and permitted facilities.[75] Both the Part 264 and Part 265 regulations for TSD facilities include standards of general applicability (for example,

---

[73]Section 3005(e).

[74]40 C.F.R. Part 265.

[75]40 C.F.R. Part 264.

personnel training, security, financial responsibility), as well as specific design and operating standards for each different type of TSD facility (for example, storage tanks, landfills, incinerators). The standards of general applicability are discussed first.

An operator of a TSD facility is required to obtain an EPA identification number.[76] The operator must also obtain or conduct a detailed chemical and physical analysis of a representative sample of a hazardous waste before the waste is treated, stored, or disposed of at the facility.[77] This is to ensure that the operator has sufficient knowledge of the particular waste being handled to be able to properly manage it. The facility's waste analysis plan (WAP) deals with such matters as representative samples, frequency of testing and compliance with land disposal verifications.

Operators must install a security system to prevent unknowing entry, and to minimize the potential for unauthorized entry of people or livestock to the active portion of the TSD facility.[78] This may be either a 24-hour surveillance system or a barrier around the facility and a means to control entry, and posted "Danger" signs. Operators are required to prepare and implement an inspection plan specifically tailored to the circumstances at their facility.[79] Permitted facilities located in floodplains or areas prone to seismic activity are subject to location standards designed to reduce the additional risks.[80]

TSD facility personnel are required to be properly trained in the areas to which they are assigned, thus reducing the chances that a mistake due to lack of knowledge of the regulatory requirements might lead to an environmental accident. The training may be by formal classroom instruction or on-the-job training. Facility personnel must be given the training within six months of their employment, and must take part in an annual review thereafter. The program must be directed by a person trained in hazardous waste management procedures.[81] Personnel training should focus on emergency preparations and response procedures.

Special precautions must be taken to prevent accidental ignition or reaction of ignitable, reactive or incompatible wastes. While many of the handling requirements are largely common sense practices, specific steps to protect against mixing of such wastes are included in the regulations. Compliance with the regulations concerning safe management of ignitable, reactive or incompatible wastes must be documented.[82]

Regulations for preparedness and prevention are intended to minimize the possibility or consequences of an explosion, spill, or fire at a TSD

---

[76]40 C.F.R. § 265.11, § 264.11.

[77]40 C.F.R. § 265.13, § 264.13.

[78]40 C.F.R. § 265.14, § 264.14.

[79]40 C.F.R. § 265.15, § 264.15.

[80]40 C.F.R. § 265.18(b), § 264.17(c), § 264.18(a).

[81]40 C.F.R. § 265.16, § 264.16.

[82]40 C.F.R. § 265.17, § 264.17.

facility.[83] Facilities must have, unless unnecessary due to the nature of the wastes handled, the following equipment:

(1)   an internal alarm or communications system,

(2)   a device capable of summoning emergency assistance from local agencies,

(3)   fire and spill control equipment, and

(4)   decontamination equipment.

Operators are required to have a contingency plan for the facility designed to minimize hazards to human health and the environment in the event of an actual explosion, fire, or unplanned release of hazardous wastes.[84] All required equipment must be regularly tested and maintained. Adequate aisle space to allow unobstructed movement of emergency personnel and equipment must also be maintained. Arrangements must be made with local police, fire departments, and hospitals to familiarize them with the facility's layout and hazardous wastes. The TSD facility must also be covered by liability insurance or other financial instruments for claims arising out of injuries to persons or property that result from hazardous waste management operations.[85]

Important recordkeeping requirements apply to TSD facilities.[86] Upon receipt of a manifested shipment of hazardous waste, the operator of a TSD facility must immediately sign, date, and give to the transporter a copy of the manifest prepared by the generator. Within 30 days, the operator must return a completed copy of the manifest to the generator, and retain a copy of all manifests at the facility for at least three years from the date of delivery. All TSD facilities must maintain a complete operating record until closure.[87] The operating record must include, among other things, a description and the quantity of each hazardous waste received and the method and date of its treatment, storage and disposal, the location of each waste within the facility, results of waste analyses, trial tests and inspections.

There are also basic reports which the TSD facility operator is obligated to file with the EPA regional administrator or an authorized state. These include a biennial report of waste management activities for the previous calendar year,[88] an "unmanifested waste" report which the operator must file within 15 days of accepting any hazardous waste that is not accompanied by a manifest,[89] and certain specialized reports, for ex-

---

[83] See generally 40 C.F.R. § 265.30-.49, § 264.30-.49.

[84] See generally 40 C.F.R. § 265.50-.56, § 264.50-.56.

[85] 40 C.F.R. § 265.143(e), § 264.143(f).

[86] See generally 40 C.F.R. § 265.71-.72, § 264.71-.72.

[87] 40 C.F.R. § 265.73, §264.73.

[88] 40 C.F.R. § 265.75, § 264.75.

[89] 40 C.F.R. § 265.76, § 264.76.

ample, an incident report in the event of a hazardous waste release, fire, or explosion.

There are general closure requirements applicable to all TSD facilities, and additional requirements for each specific type of facility.[90] "Closure" is the period after which hazardous wastes are no longer accepted by a TSD facility and during which time the operator must complete treatment, storage or disposal operations. "Post-closure" is the 30-year period after closure when operators of land disposal facilities, such as landfills, must perform certain monitoring and maintenance activities. Generally, the TSD facility must have a detailed written closure plan and schedule, and a cost estimate for closure. The plan must be approved by EPA or the state. It must be amended when any changes in waste management operations affect its terms, and the cost estimate must be adjusted annually for inflation. The closure plan must be followed when the TSD facility ceases operations at the covered unit(s). Post-closure care must continue for 30 years after the date of completing closure, and includes groundwater monitoring and the maintenance of monitoring and waste containment systems.

Financial responsibility requirements have been established to ensure that funds for closure and post-closure care are adequate and available.[91] TSD facilities must use one of the specified financial instruments, such as a corporate guarantee, to provide the closure and post-closure funds.

4.5.2 Standards for Specific Types of TSD Facilities

The standards discussed above are generally applicable to all TSD facilities, from the small drum storage area to the most complex commercial landfill or incinerator. EPA has also promulgated specific design, construction, and operating standards for each different type of TSD facility regulated under RCRA. These include: (1) containers, (2) tanks, (3) surface impoundments, (4) waste piles, (5) land treatment units, (6) landfills, (7) incinerators, (8) thermal treatment units, (9) chemical, physical, and biological treatment units, (10) underground injection wells, (11) containment buildings, and (12) "miscellaneous units."[92] In the years ahead, additional classes of facilities may also be addressed by distinct sets of standards such as these.

Discussion of the detailed regulatory requirements for all of these types of facilities is beyond the scope of this chapter.[93] The following is an overview of the more significant standards that apply to containers and tanks; surface impoundments, waste piles and landfills; and incinerators and industrial furnaces used for hazardous waste burning.

---

[90]*See generally* 40 C.F.R. § 265.110-.120, § 264.110-.120.

[91]*See generally* 40 C.F.R. § 265.140-.151, § 264.140-.151.

[92]40 C.F.R. Part 265, Subparts J-R, and Part 264, Subparts J-X, as amended, 57 *Fed. Reg.* 37265 (August 18, 1992).

[93]These requirements are discussed in detail in Hall, *RCRA Hazardous Wastes Handbook* (Government Institutes, 9th ed. 1991), and in Bauer & Kellar, *Managing Your Hazardous Wastes* (Government Institutes 1992).

A container is any portable device for storing or handling hazardous waste, including drums, pails and boxes. Tank systems are stationary devices constructed primarily of non-earthen materials which provide structural support, and any ancillary piping.[94] The RCRA standards for containers and tanks are basically good housekeeping practices.[95] For example, drums must be maintained in good condition and be handled to avoid ruptures or leaks. Containers must always be kept closed, except when adding waste. Tank systems must be constructed of suitable materials and operated so as to contain the hazardous waste during the tank's intended useful life. Tanks must be operated using controls and practices to prevent overflows and spills. Container storage areas must be inspected at least weekly, and tank systems at least daily, for leaks, corrosion, and other problems. More importantly, almost all container and tank storage areas must be constructed or retrofitted with a secondary containment system to collect spills and accumulated rainfall. Generally, a containment system consists of a diked or bermed concrete (impervious) base with sufficient capacity to collect spillage, and a sump or other method for removing collected liquids. For tanks, the operator can use a lined or diked concrete containment facility, a vault system, or double-walled tanks. Tanks without secondary containment must undergo a structural integrity assessment by a professional engineer.

A surface impoundment is any natural or man-made excavation or diked area designed to hold hazardous wastes containing free liquids, such as pits, ponds, or lagoons. A waste pile is any non-containerized accumulation of solid, non-flowing hazardous waste. A landfill is a disposal facility where hazardous waste is placed in or on the land.[96] The most important performance standards for these land-based facilities are the "minimum technology requirements" (MTRs) enacted in the 1984 HSWA. All new, replacement, and expansion units at surface impoundments and landfills must have double liners, leachate collection systems, leak detection, and groundwater monitoring systems.[97] Waste piles must be constructed with a liner on a supporting base, a leachate collection and removal system above the liner, and surface water run-on controls. The MTR regulations are highly technical and complex, and should be carefully consulted. The groundwater monitoring requirements, for example, call for an extensive scheme for detecting leachate plumes and instituting corrective action when necessary.[98]

Incinerators use controlled flame combustion to destroy hazardous wastes. Recently, industrial furnaces and boilers are increasingly being used

---

[94]40 C.F.R. § 260.10.

[95]*See generally* 40 C.F.R. § 265.170-265.199, § 264.170-264.200.

[96]40 C.F.R. § 260.10.

[97]*See generally* 40 C.F.R. § 265.220-265.230, § 265.300-265.316, § 264.220-264.231, § 264.300-264.317.

[98]*See generally* 40 C.F.R. § 265.90-265.94, § 264.90-264.101.

to burn hazardous wastes as fuels and for destruction. The RCRA standards for these TSD facilities have become more stringent, in large part as a result of the 1984 HSWA.[99] Basically, an incinerator must conduct a detailed waste analysis and trial burn for waste feeds it intends to handle to establish steady state conditions and demonstrate sufficient destruction of hazardous constituents in the waste. The incinerator must achieve a destruction and removal efficiency (DRE) rate of at least 99.99% for the principal organic hazardous constituents designated by EPA for each waste feed. Emission standards are also applied. The incinerator must have continuous monitoring and automatic controls to shut off the waste feed when operating requirements are exceeded.

EPA has also promulgated standards for industrial furnaces and boilers that burn hazardous wastes.[100] Based on Congress' direction in the 1984 HSWA, EPA now requires all persons who produce, distribute, market or burn hazardous wastes as fuel to notify EPA. The invoice or bill of sale for the fuel must bear the legend: Warning This Fuel Contains Hazardous Waste (followed by a list of the hazardous wastes). Such fuels cannot be burned except in qualified utility boilers and industrial furnaces, such as cement kilns. Generators, transporters, marketers and burners of hazardous waste fuels are subject to storage standards for containers and tanks, and to other specific RCRA standards. The owners and operators of boilers and industrial furnaces must comply with detailed technical standards similar to incineration standards, including emission controls, and obtain RCRA permits.

4.5.3 The Land Disposal Ban Program

Perhaps the most significant provision of the 1984 HSWA are the prohibitions on the land disposal of hazardous wastes. These prohibitions are intended to minimize the country's reliance on land disposal of untreated hazardous wastes, and to require advanced treatment and recycling of wastes. Congress began by banning the disposal of bulk or non-containerized liquid hazardous wastes, and hazardous wastes containing free liquids, in landfills.[101]

Next, Congress required EPA to determine whether to prohibit, in whole or in part, the disposal of all RCRA hazardous wastes in land disposal facilities. These include landfills, surface impoundments, waste piles, injection wells, salt domes, and the like. At the same time, EPA was told to promulgate regulations that establish levels or methods of treat-

---

[99] *See generally* 40 C.F.R. § 265.340-265.352, § 264.340-264.351; 40 C.F.R. § 266.30-266.35.

[100] Section 3004(q)-(s); 40 C.F.R. 266, Subpart D.

[101] Congress also directed EPA to minimize the disposal of containerized liquid hazardous wastes in landfills. In order to discourage the use of absorbent materials (e.g., "kitty litter") to reduce free liquids in containerized wastes, EPA's regulations prohibit the landfilling of liquids that have been absorbed in materials that biodegrade or that release liquids when depressed during routine landfill operations. 40 C.F.R. § 264.314-.316, as amended, 57 *Fed. Reg.* 54452 (November 18, 1992).

ment that minimize threats posed by the hazardous waste. If the waste is first treated in accordance with these treatment standards, the treated waste or residue can then be land disposed. In effect, the so-called "land ban" program is really a waste pretreatment program.

Congress set forth a phased program for EPA to implement these land disposal prohibitions. First, EPA has banned the land disposal of dioxin and solvent containing hazardous wastes effective November 1986, unless the wastes are pretreated.[102] EPA set treatment levels based on incineration of non-wastewater solvents, and based on chemical/physical treatment for dilute solvent wastewaters.

Second, EPA has banned the land disposal of certain hazardous wastes (which California had already banned) effective July 1987, unless the wastes are pretreated. The "California list" includes liquid hazardous wastes, including free liquids associated with any sludge, that (1) contain free cyanides greater than 100 mg/1; (2) contain specified concentrations of heavy metals (arsenic, cadmium, chromium, lead, mercury, nickel, selenium and thallium); (3) are acids below a pH of 2; (4) contain more than 50 ppm PCBs; and (5) are solid or liquid hazardous wastes containing halogenated organic compounds at concentrations greater than 1000 ppm.[103]

Third, EPA published a ranking of all other hazardous wastes based on their intrinsic hazard and volume, with a schedule for determining whether to ban the land disposal of such wastes one third at a time.[104] EPA restricted the land disposal of the first-third of the highest priority hazardous wastes on the ranking list in August 1988. EPA set treatment levels for many of the F and K listed wastes in the first-third. EPA extended the ban to the second-third of the ranked hazardous wastes in June 1989. Finally, EPA imposed the land ban restrictions on the third-third wastes, including all characteristic hazardous wastes, in May 1990. Newly listed or identified wastes will be brought under the land ban program in the future.

Congress wanted to promote treatment and recycling of hazardous wastes in lieu of or prior to land disposal. Therefore at the same time EPA promulgated these land disposal restrictions, it also promulgated regulations specifying the methods or levels of treatment that substantially diminish the toxicity or reduce the likelihood of migration of the waste from land disposal facilities. Generally, the treatment standards are based on the levels that can be achieved by the Best Demonstrated Available Technologies (BDAT).[105] In most instances, the treatment

---

[102]40 C.F.R. Part 268. The dioxin containing wastes are those chlorinated dioxins, -dibenzofurans, and -phenols listed as F020, F021, F022, F023, F026, F027 and F028. The solvent wastes are those listed as F001-F005 at 40 C.F.R. 261.31. *See generally* Section 3004(d)-(m).

[103]Disposal by deep well injection is subject to special provisions and a different schedule for implementing the ban.

[104]The ranking and schedule are published at 40 C.F.R. 268.

[105]EPA's decision to use technology-based standards, rather than risk-based standards, was upheld by the court. *Hazardous Waste Treatment Council v. EPA*, 886 F.2d 355 (1989).

standards are expressed as concentrations of constituents in the treated waste. Any treatment technology that meets the concentration-based standard can then be used. If EPA prescribes a specific technology, however, then that method must be used. A company that treats its hazardous waste in accordance with these pretreatment standards will not have the treated waste or residue subject to the land disposal ban.

In the third-third rule, EPA determined that it had legal authority to establish treatment standards below the characteristic level for the ignitable, corrosive, reactive and toxic wastes. However, EPA used this authority sparingly, and generally required only that characteristic wastes be treated by any method, including dilution, that removed the characteristic. Upon judicial review, the court held that EPA must now revise the treatment standards to address the threats posed by any hazardous constituents in these characteristic wastes.[106] The court also ruled that EPA must ensure that hazardous wastes managed in Clean Water Act lagoon systems receive equivalent treatment to that mandated under RCRA.

EPA has limited authority to grant up to a two year extension of the land ban deadlines for specific hazardous wastes if adequate alternative treatment, recovery, or disposal capacity is not currently available. EPA has granted national capacity variances for certain wastes, such as contaminated soil and debris. EPA can also grant a one-year extension, renewable only once, to a company that demonstrates on a case-by-case basis that a binding contractual commitment has been made to construct or otherwise provide alternative treatment, recovery, or disposal capacity, but due to circumstances beyond its control the alternative capacity cannot reasonably be made available by the ban deadline.

Finally, land disposal facilities may submit petitions to EPA which demonstrate, to a reasonable degree of certainty, that there will be no migration of hazardous constituents from a particular disposal unit or injection well for as long as the waste remains hazardous. EPA has granted a number of these so-called "no migration" petitions for deep injection wells.

4.5.4 1984 Amendments Relevant to Used Oil

In the 1984 HSWA, Congress also directed EPA to decide whether to identify used automobile and truck crankcase oil or other used oil as hazardous waste.[107] After substantial delay, EPA finally decided not to list used oil that is destined for recycling as a hazardous waste, but instead to promulgate management standards for used oil collection and recy-

---

[106]*Chemical Waste Management, Inc. v. EPA*, No. 90-1230 (D.C. Cir. decided September 25, 1992).

[107]*See* Section 3014(b). EPA proposed the listing of used oil from motor vehicles and industrial manufacturing processes based on a determination that this used oil typically and frequently contains hazardous contaminants at levels of regulatory concern. 50 *Fed. Reg.* 49258 (November 29, 1985). The final decision was published at 51 *Fed. Reg.* 41900, (November 19, 1986).

cling.[108] These include general facility standards for used oil processors and re-refiners. In addition, EPA decided not to list used oil that is destined for disposal as a hazardous waste, but the hazardous waste characteristics do apply to such used oil.[109]

4.6 Permits

RCRA requires every owner and operator of a TSD facility to obtain a permit.[110] A TSD facility that was in existence on November 19, 1980, or on the date of any statutory or regulatory change that makes the facility subject to RCRA, need only notify EPA of its hazardous waste management activity and file a Part A application to obtain interim status and continue operations.[111] An interim status TSD facility will be issued a site-specific permit in due course. A new TSD facility, or an existing facility that fails to qualify for interim status, must obtain a full RCRA permit before commencing construction, however.

4.6.1 Permitting Procedures and Timetables

A Part A application is a short form containing certain basic information about the facility, such as name, location, nature of business, regulated activities, and a topographic map of the facility site.[112] A Part B application requires substantially more comprehensive and detailed information that demonstrates compliance with the applicable technical standards for TSD facilities.[113] The Part B application may consist of multiple volumes of documentation, including all the written plans and procedures required by the TSD facility regulations.

The final RCRA permit will govern the application of these standards to the particular facility. New facilities must submit Part A and B applications simultaneously; existing facilities that already filed their Part A applications to gain interim status must submit their Part B applications in accordance with statutory deadlines established by Congress, or earlier if requested by EPA or a state.[114]

States authorized under RCRA to administer their own programs are mainly responsible for reviewing applications and issuing permits. EPA regions perform this task in unauthorized states. In the 1984 HSWA, Congress has taken steps to accelerate the permitting of TSD facilities. Congress provided that interim status for any existing land disposal facility be automatically terminated on November 8, 1985, unless the operator

---

[108]The management standards were promulgated at 57 *Fed. Reg.* 41566 (September 10, 1992), and will be codified in new 40 C.F.R. Part 279.

[109]57 *Fed. Reg.* 21524 (May 20, 1992).

[110]Section 3005.

[111]Section 3005(e). See the interim status standards for TSD facilities in 40 C.F.R. Part 265, discussed above.

[112]40 C.F.R. § 270.13.

[113]*See generally* 40 C.F.R. § 270.13-270.21.

[114]Section 3005(c).

had submitted a Part B application for a final permit and a certification that the facility was in compliance with groundwater monitoring and financial responsibility requirements. EPA and authorized states were directed to issue final permits for land disposal facilities by November 1988. Similarly, final permits for interim status incinerators were mandated by November 1989, and for all other interim status TSD facilities by November 1992. If EPA or the state has failed to meet these deadlines, the TSD facility can continue operations provided a timely Part B application has been filed.

After a complete RCRA permit application is filed, the rules in 40 C.F.R. Part 124 establish the procedures for processing the application and issuing the permit. These include preparation of draft permits, public comment and hearing, and the issuance of final decisions. Permit issuance must be based on a determination that the TSD facility will comply with all requirements of RCRA.

HSWA provides that permits for land disposal facilities, storage facilities, incinerators and other treatment facilities can be issued only for a fixed term not to exceed ten years.[115] While permits may be reviewed and modified at any time during their terms, permits for land disposal facilities must be reviewed every five years. At such time, the terms of a permit may be modified to ensure that the permit continues to incorporate the standards then applicable to land disposal facilities.

4.6.2 Corrective Action

Congress also imposed new and stringent corrective action requirements on TSD facilities. All RCRA permits must now require the owner or operator of a TSD facility to take corrective action for all releases of hazardous waste and constituents from solid waste management units at the facility regardless of when the waste was placed in the unit, or whether the unit is currently active.[116] Note that a solid waste management unit can be any tank, lagoon, waste pile, or other unit where any solid waste was placed, and from which hazardous constituents are being released. RCRA permits must contain schedules of compliance for any required corrective action and assurances of financial responsibility for completing such action. If necessary, the operator of the TSD facility may have to take corrective action beyond the facility boundary. This type of authority for cleanup is analogous to Superfund, and will have a very substantial impact on many TSD facilities that need RCRA permits to continue operations.

4.7 State Hazardous Waste Programs

States are authorized by RCRA to develop and carry out their own hazardous waste programs in lieu of the federal program administered by

---

[115]Section 3005(c)(3).
[116]Section 3004(u)-(v).

EPA.[117] To obtain EPA approval, the state program must be "equivalent" to the federal program; must be "consistent" with the federal program and other authorized state programs; and must provide adequate enforcement of compliance with the requirements of RCRA Subtitle C.

Ordinarily, states have at least one year to make regulatory changes consistent with the federal program, and two years if statutory changes are necessary. Congress believed the 1984 HSWA provisions were important to implement quickly, however. Therefore, EPA regulations that implement the 1984 HSWA take effect in authorized states on the same day that they take effect under the federal program. EPA is responsible for implementing HSWA provisions until the state takes over authority. The states can then apply for final authorization for the new requirement after promulgating an equivalent regulation.

This dual administration of the RCRA program means that joint permitting is often necessary, with EPA imposing the HSWA provisions and the state taking responsibility for the rest of the permitting.

4.8 Inspection

RCRA provides that any officer, employee or representative of EPA or a state with an authorized hazardous waste program may inspect the premises and records of any person who generates, stores, treats, transports, disposes of, or otherwise handles hazardous waste.[118] EPA's inspection authority extends to persons or sites that have handled hazardous wastes in the past but no longer do so. The owner/operator must provide government officials access to records and property relating to the wastes for inspection purposes. Copying and sampling are authorized.

In the 1984 HSWA, Congress directed EPA and authorized states to improve and regularize RCRA inspections. EPA and the states must now conduct inspections of all privately-operated TSD facilities at least once every two years. Federally-operated TSD facilities must be inspected on an annual basis. Similarly, EPA must conduct annual inspections of TSD facilities which are operated by a state or local government to ensure compliance with the requirements of RCRA.[119]

All organizations should have an established policy and procedure for handling RCRA inspections, including consideration of whether or not a search warrant should be required.

---

[117]Section 3006; see generally 40 C.F.R. Part 271.

[118]Section 3007. EPA's inspection activities under RCRA Section 3007 are subject to the Fourth Amendment's protection against unreasonable searches or seizures, which the Supreme Court has applied in holding that a warrant is generally required for an inspection by an administrative agency. *See Marshall v. Barlow's, Inc.*, 436 U.S. 307 (1978), which involved the inspection provisions of the Occupational Safety and Health Act.

[119]Section 3007(c)-(e).

4.9 Civil and Criminal Enforcement Actions

EPA can bring several types of enforcement actions under RCRA. These include administrative orders and civil and criminal penalties.[120] Whenever EPA determines that any person is violating Subtitle C of RCRA (including any regulation or permit issued thereunder), it may either issue an order requiring compliance immediately or within a specified time period, or seek injunctive relief against the alleged violator through a civil action filed in a U.S. District Court. Any person who violates any requirement of Subtitle C is liable for a civil penalty of up to $25,000 for each day of violation, regardless of whether the person had been served with a compliance order. A person subject to RCRA cannot rely on EPA to tell him when he is in violation, then take the required corrective action, and thus avoid a penalty. Failure to comply with an administrative order may also result in suspension or revocation of a permit.

RCRA also imposes criminal penalties of up to $50,000, two years imprisonment, or both for persons who "knowingly" commit certain violations. The 1984 HSWA significantly expanded the list of these criminal violations. Fines and imprisonment can be imposed on generators for knowingly allowing hazardous waste to be transported to an unpermitted facility, for knowing violations of federal interim status standards or counterpart state requirements, for knowing material omissions or the knowing failure to file reports required under RCRA by generators, transporters, and TSD facility operators, and knowing transport of hazardous waste without a manifest.

The statute also creates a crime of "knowing endangerment." The purpose of this sanction is to provide more substantial felony penalties for any person who commits the acts described above and "who knows at that time that he thereby places another person in imminent danger of death or serious bodily injury." Upon conviction, an individual faces a fine of up to $250,000 and/or up to fifteen years' imprisonment. An organizational defendant is subject to a maximum fine of $1 million. All of this is part of the message from Congress to EPA and the Justice Department that more rigorous enforcement of the nation's hazardous wastes laws is the federal policy.

4.10 Citizen Suits

Citizen suits are envisioned by Congress and many others as a key enforcement tool for environmental protection. The RCRA citizen suit provision allows any person to bring a civil action against any alleged violator of RCRA requirements, or against the EPA administrator for a failure to perform a nondiscretionary duty. Any person may also petition the EPA administrator for promulgation, amendment, or repeal of any

---

[120]Section 3008.

regulation. Courts are authorized to award costs including attorneys' fees to a substantially prevailing party.[121]

The 1984 HSWA substantially enhanced the role accorded to these suits. The citizen suit provision has been expanded to authorize suits in cases where past or present management or disposal of hazardous wastes has contributed to a situation that may present an imminent or substantial endangerment. However, citizen suits are prohibited (1) with respect to the siting and permitting of hazardous waste facilities (except by a state or local government); (2) where EPA is prosecuting an action under RCRA or Superfund; (3) while EPA or the state is engaged in a removal action under Superfund or has incurred costs to engage in a remedial action; or (4) where the responsible party is conducting a removal or remedial action pursuant to an order obtained from EPA. Affected parties may be allowed to intervene in ongoing suits. Plaintiffs must notify EPA, the state, and affected parties ninety days prior to commencement of a citizen suit.

4.11 Imminent Hazard Actions

In addition, EPA is authorized to bring suits to restrain an imminent and substantial endangerment to health or the environment.[122] EPA construes imminent and substantial endangerment to mean posing a "risk of harm" or "potential harm," but not requiring proof of actual harm.[123]

In response to conflicting federal court decisions, Congress reworded the "imminent hazard" provision in 1984 to clarify that actions which took place prior to the enactment of RCRA are covered by this provision. Thus a non-negligent generator whose wastes are no longer being deposited at a particular site may still be ordered to abate the hazard resulting from the leaking of previously deposited wastes.

The 1984 HSWA also required EPA to provide for public notice and comment, and the opportunity for a public meeting in the affected area, prior to entering into a settlement or covenant not to sue in an imminent hazard action.

5.0 STATE SOLID WASTE PROGRAMS UNDER SUBTITLE D

Regulation of non-hazardous waste is the responsibility of the states pursuant to Subtitle D of RCRA. The federal involvement is limited to establishing minimum criteria that prescribe the best practicable controls and monitoring requirements for solid waste disposal facilities.

In the 1984 HSWA, Congress directed EPA to revise the criteria for facilities receiving hazardous waste from households or from small generators to enable detection of groundwater contamination, and to provide for corrective action, as necessary, and facility siting.[124] Compliance with the

---

[121]Section 7002.
[122]Section 7003.
[123]*United States v. Vertac Chemical Corp.*, 489 F. Supp. 870 (E.D. Ark. 1980).
[124]Section 4010.

minimum requirements determines whether a facility is classified as an "open dump" or not. Disposal of solid waste in "open dumps" (that is, those facilities not meeting the criteria) is prohibited. Existing dumps were allowed to make modifications that would permit them to meet the requirements, and it is the state's responsibility to ensure that such upgrading occurs or that the open dumps are closed.

EPA was not given any enforcement authority, however, for the ban on open dumps. EPA's enforcement authority under RCRA only covers hazardous wastes. EPA cannot take action against a person disposing of nonhazardous wastes in an open dump or against the state for failing to close open dumps, other than terminating certain grant funds available to the state under RCRA. Recognizing this problem, Congress has asked EPA to make recommendations on the need for additional enforcement authorities.[125]

RCRA also envisions that the state, with the help of federal grant funds, will develop regional solid waste management plans. The program is patterned on Section 208 of the Clean Water Act and relies upon a comprehensive regional planning approach to solving solid waste problems. The state is responsible for identifying appropriate management areas, developing regional plans through the use of local and regional authorities, compiling inventories and closing or upgrading existing open dumps, and generally assessing the need for additional solid waste disposal capacity in the area.

Of particular significance is a requirement that states not have any bans on the importation of waste for storage, treatment or disposal, or have requirements that are substantially dissimilar from other disposal practices that would discourage the free movement of wastes across state lines. Although enforcement of this requirement may be difficult, in light of the limited enforcement authority available to EPA, it does evidence a congressional policy for a national approach to solid waste disposal.

6.0 OTHER FEDERAL RESPONSIBILITIES

Subtitle E of RCRA gives the Department of Commerce (DOC) responsibility for developing standards for substituting secondary materials for virgin materials, developing markets for recovered materials, and for the promotion of resource recovery technology generally.

The authorities given to DOC are similar to those assigned to EPA in other sections of the act, specifically Subtitle H on Research, Development, Demonstrations and Information. Nevertheless, DOC has not received sufficient funding to support a major role.

Subtitle F of RCRA requires that all federal agencies and instrumentalities comply with all federal, state, interstate, and local requirements stemming from RCRA, unless exempted by the president. It also requires the federal government to institute a procurement policy that encourages the

---

[125]*Id.*

purchase of recoverable materials which, because of their performance, can be substituted for virgin material at a reasonable price.

7.0 RESEARCH, DEVELOPMENT, DEMONSTRATION AND INFORMATION

In cooperation with federal, state, and interstate authorities, private agencies and institutions, and individuals, EPA is directed to conduct, encourage and promote the coordination of research, investigations, experiments, training, demonstrations, surveys, public education programs and studies. These R & D efforts can relate to the protection of health; planning, financing and operation of waste management systems including resource recovery; improvements in methodology of waste disposal and resource recovery; reduction of the amount of waste generated, and methods for remedying damages by earlier or existing landfills; and methods for rendering landfills safe for purposes of construction and other uses.

EPA was also directed to carry out a number of special studies including the following subjects: small-scale and low technology approaches to resource recovery, front-end separation for materials recovery, mining waste, sludge, and airport landfills.

8.0 MEDICAL WASTE

Congress added a new Subtitle J to RCRA with the enactment of the Medical Waste Tracking Act of 1988. In response to the problem of hypodermic needles and other medical wastes washing up on Atlantic Coast beaches, Congress directed EPA to set up a demonstration program for tracking the shipment and disposal of medical wastes in a selected number of states. The states directed to participate were New York, New Jersey, Connecticut, the states contiguous to the Great Lakes, and any state that petitioned EPA to be included in the demonstration program.

EPA promulgated regulations listing the types of medical wastes to be tracked under the program. These wastes include:

(1) Cultures and stocks of infectious agents and associated biologicals;

(2) Pathological wastes, including tissues, organs, and body parts;

(3) Waste human blood and blood products;

(4) Hypodermic needles, syringes, scalpel blades, and broken glassware;

(5) Contaminated animal carcasses and parts;

(6) Wastes from surgery or autopsy that were in contact with infectious agents;

(7) Laboratory wastes that were in contact with infectious agents;

(8) Dialysis wastes;

(9) Discarded medical equipment that was in contact with infectious agents;

(10) Biological wastes; and

(11) Such other medical waste material as EPA finds poses a threat to human health or the environment.

At the same time, EPA promulgated regulations establishing a demonstration program for the tracking of the listed medical waste. The program provides for tracking the transportation of the waste from the generator to the disposal facility. The generator is required to segregate wastes where practicable, and to use appropriate labels and containers. Medical waste that is incinerated need not be tracked after incineration, but the generator who conducts on-site incineration must report the types and volumes of wastes incinerated during the demonstration program.

EPA and states are authorized to conduct inspections and take enforcement actions under the program. Congress has also made clear that all federal facilities in a demonstration state must comply with all federal, state, interstate and local requirements, including permitting and reporting, that pertain to medical wastes.

At the conclusion of the program, EPA must submit a report to Congress summarizing the results and making recommendations for adequate control of medical waste shipments and disposal. Interim reports are also required.

9.0 CONCLUSION

As the foregoing discussion amply demonstrates, the RCRA program is complex. The 1984 HSWA has added many new requirements which represent a challenge to the will and imagination of the regulated community. Industry has been challenged to find new ways to minimize, treat, recycle and dispose of hazardous waste. These will include the use of innovative and emerging treatment technologies, as well as modifications to production processes and raw materials. Never has the incentive been greater to reuse or reclaim wastes, or to search out new products, processes, and raw materials that do not result in the generation of hazardous waste in the first place.

For a more definitive discussion of this topic, the reader is referred to the RCRA Hazardous Wastes Handbook *and related books and courses listed at the end of this book.*

Chapter 4

UNDERGROUND STORAGE TANKS

Karen J. Nardi[1]
McCutchen, Doyle, Brown & Enersen
San Francisco, California

1.0 OVERVIEW

Underground storage tanks (USTs) are widely recognized as a major environmental problem. They have been the cause of soil and groundwater contamination at thousands of sites throughout the United States. Studies have shown that there are many reasons why USTs cause contamination. Some tanks and associated piping simply corroded or structurally failed during years of use. In other cases, poor past practices resulted in spills when tanks were emptied or when they overflowed during filling.[2]

In 1988, the United States Environmental Protection Agency (EPA) estimated that there were over two million UST systems (which include both the underground storage tank and piping connected to it) located at over 700,000 facilities nationwide. EPA judged that roughly 75 percent of such systems posed the greatest potential for leakage and environmental harm because the UST systems were made of steel without any form of corrosion protection.[3] A recent study suggests that the cost to clean up the nation's leaking underground storage tanks could exceed $41 billion and take over 30 years.[4]

In an attempt to address the widespread problems with USTs, Congress enacted the Hazardous and Solid Waste Amendments (HSWA) of 1984, which in part added Subtitle I,[5] Regulation of Underground Storage Tanks, to the Resource Conservation and Recovery Act (RCRA) of 1976.[6] New RCRA Subtitle I established a federal program for the regulation of USTs which required EPA to adopt regulations for new and existing USTs. EPA issued proposed regulations on April 17, 1987,[7] and adopted final

---

[1]The author gratefully acknowledges the contributions of John J. Gregory, co-author, and Brandt Andersson, editorial assistant.

[2]53 Fed. Reg. 37088-90 (September 23, 1988).

[3]*Id.* at 37095.

[4]Environmental Information, Ltd., *The Underground Storage Tank Market: Its Current Status and Future Challenges*, 3 (1992).

[5]42 U.S.C. §§ 6991-6991i.

[6]42 U.S.C. §§ 6901-699zk.

[7]*See* 52 Fed. Reg. 12662 (April 17, 1987).

regulations on September 23, 1988.[8] EPA also promulgated financial responsibility requirements for owners and operators of USTs containing petroleum on October 26, 1988.[9] Since 1988, EPA has issued several amendments to its UST regulations.[10]

1.1 Objectives of the UST Program

In enacting the UST provisions of RCRA in 1984, Congress had several basic public policy objectives. The statute addresses both the problem of existing tanks which may have caused environmental problems and new tanks that should be designed and operated to eliminate the problems of the past.

One objective of the UST program is to identify existing tanks and require that they either be brought up to certain design and operating standards or be closed. Another purpose is to determine whether existing tanks have leaked, causing an environmental problem. If so, the law requires tank owners and/or operators to take corrective action to address the environmental problem.

For new tanks, the law requires that tanks meet strict design and operating standards and that the government be notified when they are installed. Any tanks that continue to be used must be operated in a way that will minimize the possibility of leaks or spills due to filling or emptying.

The RCRA program also requires the reporting, investigation, and cleanup of releases from USTs. Finally, federal law sets standards for closure of USTs and financial responsibility requirements for persons who own and operate petroleum USTs. The regulations, while detailed, were designed to accomplish these basic objectives.

The RCRA UST program, like many federal laws, is a delegated program. States are given an opportunity to adopt laws and regulations that meet the minimum federal standards. EPA has delegated authority to certain states that have adequate UST programs. In such cases, states (not EPA) are the primary permitting and enforcement authorities for USTs. While states may enforce federal law regarding USTs, state and local laws may be stricter than federal law. Thus, it is very important to check to see whether more stringent state and local laws apply.

This chapter describes the various federal requirements that apply to owners and operators of new and existing UST systems. Many state and local

---

[8] *See* 53 Fed. Reg. 37082 *et seq.* (September 23, 1988), adopting 40 C.F.R. Part 280. On September 23, 1988, EPA also finalized regulations permitting states to run UST programs in lieu of the federal program. *See* 53 Fed. Reg. 37212 (September 23, 1988), adopting 40 C.F.R. Part 281.

[9] *See* 53 Fed. Reg. 43322 (October 26, 1988).

[10] *See, e.g.,* 54 Fed. Reg. 5451 (February 3, 1989); 54 Fed. Reg. 47077 (November 9, 1989); 55 Fed. Reg. 17753 (April 27, 1990); 55 Fed. Reg. 17767 (April 27, 1990); 55 Fed. Reg. 18566 (May 2, 1990); 55 Fed. Reg. 23737 (June 12, 1990); 55 Fed. Reg. 24692 (June 18, 1990); 55 Fed. Reg. 27837 (July 6, 1990); 55 Fed. Reg. 32647 (August 10, 1990); 55 Fed. Reg. 33430 (August 15, 1990); 55 Fed. Reg. 36840 (September 7, 1990); 55 Fed. Reg. 46022 (October 31, 1990); 56 Fed. Reg. 24 (January 2, 1991); 56 Fed. Reg. 38342 (August 13, 1991); 56 Fed. Reg. 40292 (August 14, 1991); 56 Fed. Reg. 49376 (September 27, 1991); 56 Fed. Reg. 66369 (December 23, 1991).

authorities have adopted requirements that apply to UST systems. The reader is strongly encouraged to check and verify compliance with such requirements to the extent applicable. The following aspects are discussed in this chapter:

- **Basic Terminology**—This section describes what UST systems and which owners and operators are subject to the RCRA Subtitle I requirements.

- **Implementation and Enforcement**—This section describes which regulatory agencies are responsible for implementation of the RCRA Subtitle I regulations and the mechanisms available for enforcement.

- **Summary of Reporting and Recordkeeping Requirements**—This section provides a brief summary of the many reporting and recordkeeping obligations that owners and operators of UST systems must comply with.

- **New UST Systems**—This section further describes the notification requirements for owners and operators of new UST systems. A summary of performance standards for new UST systems is also provided.

- **Existing UST Systems**—This section further describes the notification requirements for owners and operators of existing UST systems. A summary of upgrading requirements for existing UST systems is also provided.

- **General Operating Requirements**—This section describes the various operating requirements covering spill and overfill control, operation and maintenance of corrosion protection systems, substance compatibility, and UST system repairs.

- **Release Detection**—This section summarizes the various release detection requirements, methods, and compliance schedules for USTs.

- **Release Reporting, Investigation and Response**—This section describes the various procedures for reporting, investigating, confirming, and cleaning up releases from UST systems.

- **Closure of UST Systems**—This section summarizes the requirements for temporary and permanent closure and change-in-service of UST systems.

- **Financial Responsibility Requirements**—This section briefly summarizes the various financial responsibility obligations facing owners and operators of petroleum USTs.

2.0 BASIC TERMINOLOGY

2.1 Underground Storage Tank Systems

By legal definition, an underground storage tank (UST) is more than just a tank that is buried underground. Tanks and piping systems that are partially below the ground surface may be subject to the UST regulations. To be specific, an UST is defined as:

> Any one or combination of tanks (including underground pipes connected thereto) which is used to contain an accumulation of regulated substances, and the volume of which (including the volume of underground pipes connected thereto) is 10 percent or more beneath the surface of the ground.[11]

Several systems are specifically excluded from the definition of UST under RCRA Subtitle I, including:

(a) Farm or residential tanks of 1100 gallons or less capacity that are used noncommercially for storage of motor fuel;

(b) Heating oil storage tanks that are used on the premises where the tank is stored;

(c) Septic tanks;

(d) Pipeline facilities (including gathering lines) that are regulated under:

  (i) The Natural Gas Pipeline Safety Act of 1968,[12] or

  (ii) The Hazardous Liquid Pipeline Safety Act of 1979,[13] or

  (iii) State laws comparable to the provisions of law referred to in subparagraphs (i) or (ii) above;

(e) Surface impoundments, pits, ponds, or lagoons;

(f) Stormwater or wastewater collection systems;

(g) Flow-through process tanks;

(h) Liquid traps or associated gathering lines directly related to oil or gas production and gathering operations;

(i) Storage tanks that are situated in an underground area (for example, basement) if the tank is situated upon or above the surface of the floor in that area; or

(j) Pipes connected to any of the tanks which are described in subparagraphs (a) through (i) above.[14]

In addition to the above, several systems are specifically excluded from regulation under RCRA Subtitle I, including:

(a) UST systems holding hazardous wastes listed or identified under Subtitle C of RCRA, or a mixture of such hazardous wastes and other regulated substances. Such UST systems would be subject to the hazardous waste requirements of RCRA Subtitle C;

---

[11]42 U.S.C. § 6991(1); 40 C.F.R. § 280.12. Regulated substances are described in section 2.2 below.

[12]49 U.S.C. §§ 1671-1684.

[13]49 U.S.C. app. §§ 2001-2015.

[14]42 U.S.C. § 6991(1); 40 C.F.R. § 280.12.

(b)   Wastewater treatment tank systems that are part of a wastewater treatment facility regulated under Section 402 or 307(b) of the Clean Water Act;[15]

(c)   Equipment or machinery that contains regulated substances for operational purposes (for example, hydraulic lift tanks and electrical equipment tanks);

(d)   UST systems with capacities of 110 gallons or less;

(e)   UST systems that contain a *de minimis* concentration of regulated substances;[16]

(f)   Emergency spill or overflow containment UST systems that are expeditiously emptied after use.[17]

In addition to those systems described above that are otherwise exempt or excluded from the UST regulations, EPA has "deferred" several other UST systems from some of its regulations. These deferred UST systems include:

(a)   Wastewater treatment tank systems;

(b)   UST systems containing radioactive material that are regulated under the Atomic Energy Act of 1954;[18]

(c)   UST systems that are part of an emergency generator system at nuclear power generation facilities regulated by the Nuclear Regulatory Commission under 10 C.F.R. Part 50, Appendix A;

(d)   Airport hydrant fuel distribution systems; and

(e)   UST systems with field-constructed tanks.[19]

No person may install a "deferred" UST system that stores regulated substances unless the system is:

(a)   Capable of preventing releases due to corrosion or structural failure throughout the system's operational life;

(b)   Cathodically protected against corrosion, or otherwise designed or constructed in a manner to prevent the release or threatened release of any stored substance; and

(c)   Constructed or lined with a material that is compatible with the stored substance. Deferred UST systems may be installed at a site

---

[15]33 U.S.C. §§ 1342, 1317(b), respectively.

[16]In its preamble to the final UST regulations, EPA does not define what a *de minimis* concentration is, but states that the implementing agency shall determine on a case-by-case basis if tanks that hold very low or *de minimis* concentrations of regulated substances are to be excluded from the UST regulations. 53 Fed. Reg. at 37108 (September 23, 1988).

[17]40 C.F.R. § 280.10(b).

[18]42 U.S.C. §§ 2011-2286i.

[19]Subparts B, C, D, E, and G of the UST regulations do not apply to any of these deferred systems. 40 C.F.R. § 280.10(c). Also note that Subpart D of the UST regulations does not apply to UST systems that store fuel solely for use by emergency power generators. (40 C.F.R. § 280.10(d).)

without corrosion protection provided a corrosion expert determines that the site is not corrosive enough to cause a release due to corrosion during the operating life of the UST system. For the operating life of the tanks, owners and operators of those systems must maintain records that reflect such a determination.[20]

2.2 Regulated Substances

The RCRA UST program applies to tanks that contain "regulated substances." Any "hazardous substance" as defined in Section 101(14) of the Comprehensive Environmental Response, Compensation, and Liability Act (CERCLA) of 1980[21] is regulated under RCRA Subtitle I. Petroleum and petroleum-based substances that are derived from crude oil, such as motor fuels, jet fuels, distillate fuel oils, residual fuel oils, lubricants, petroleum solvents and used oils are also subject to regulation under RCRA Subtitle I.[22] RCRA Subtitle I regulations do not apply to hazardous wastes because they are regulated under RCRA Subtitle C.

2.3 Owners And Operators

Owners and operators of USTs have certain responsibilities under RCRA Subtitle I. An "owner" is any person who owns an UST that is used for the storage, use, or dispensing of regulated substances on or after November 8, 1984. In addition, any person who owned an UST immediately before the discontinuation of its use prior to November 8, 1984 is considered an owner.[23] Thus, a person who acquires property containing USTs that were abandoned before acquisition of the property and before November 8, 1984 would not be an owner for purposes of the UST program. Also excluded from the definition of "owner" is "any person who, without participating in the management of an underground storage tank and otherwise not engaged in petroleum production, refining, and marketing, holds indicia of ownership primarily to protect the owner's security interest in the tank."[24] This provision is intended to protect lenders or other persons holding security interests in petroleum UST systems that otherwise do not actively participate in the operation of such UST systems.

RCRA Subtitle I defines "operator" as "any person in control of, or having responsibility for, the daily operation of the UST."[25] Unlike regulations for owners, which focus on both current and former owners, these regulations, although not entirely clear, appear to focus only on current operators of UST systems.

---

[20]40 C.F.R. § 280.11(b).

[21]42 U.S.C. § 9601(14).

[22]40 C.F.R. § 280.12.

[23]42 U.S.C. § 6991(3); 40 C.F.R § 280.12.

[24]42 U.S.C. § 6991b(h)(9). This definition appears to apply only to owners of USTs that contain petroleum as opposed to any regulated substance.

[25]42 U.S.C. § 6991(4); 40 C.F.R. § 280.12.

3.0 IMPLEMENTATION AND ENFORCEMENT

3.1 Implementation

EPA has primary responsibility for implementation and enforcement of RCRA Subtitle I. However, the UST program allows for delegation of this authority to states. States may implement, subject to EPA approval, their own UST programs in place of the federal requirements if the state's requirements are "no less stringent" than the federal requirements and provide for adequate enforcement.[26] In addition to the federal program, many states and local authorities have adopted their own UST laws and regulations. Such requirements can, in fact, be more stringent than those provided under the federal regime. Thus, it is important for owners and operators of UST systems to verify compliance not only with federal requirements, but also with state and local requirements.

3.2 Enforcement

EPA has authority under RCRA Section 9006 to issue a compliance order to any person in violation of RCRA Subtitle I.[27] Alternatively, EPA may also commence a civil action in the United States district court for appropriate relief, including the issuance of a temporary or permanent injunction.[28] Failure to comply with an order issued by EPA may result in civil penalties of not more than $25,000 for each day of continued noncompliance.[29] Persons named on an order may request a public hearing to challenge the order within 30 days after the order is served.[30]

EPA may also assess civil penalties against owners and operators who do not comply with UST requirements. An owner who knowingly fails to notify or who submits false information pursuant to the RCRA Subtitle I initial notification requirements shall be subject to a civil penalty not to exceed $10,000 for each tank for which notification is not given or false information is submitted.[31] Owners or operators of USTs may also be subject to civil penalties, not to exceed $10,000 per tank per day of violation for failing to comply with UST requirements relating to leak detection, recordkeeping, reporting, corrective action, closure, and financial responsibility.[32] Similar

---

[26] 42 U.S.C. § 6991c(a), (b)(1). As of September 1992, 10 states have UST programs that have been approved by EPA. Those states are Georgia, Louisiana, Maine, Maryland, Mississippi, New Hampshire, New Mexico, North Dakota, Oklahoma and Vermont. This chapter shall refer to the agency responsible for implementing the federal UST requirements (i.e., either EPA or the state agency with an EPA-approved UST program) as the "implementing agency."

[27] 42 U.S.C. § 6991e(a)(1).

[28] For those states with UST programs that have been approved by the EPA, EPA is required to give notice to the state prior to issuing any order or commencing any civil action. 42 U.S.C. § 6991e(a)(2).

[29] 42 U.S.C. § 6991e(a)(3).

[30] 42 U.S.C. § 6991e(b).

[31] 42 U.S.C. § 6991e(d).

[32] 42 U.S.C. §§ 6991b(c), 6991e(d).

penalties may be assessed for violations of such requirements in any EPA-approved state UST program.

EPA has authority to order owners and operators of USTs to take corrective action for any releases of petroleum when the EPA (or the state) determines that such corrective action will be done properly and promptly by the owner or operator.[33] Under RCRA Section 9003(h), EPA or the state (for EPA-approved state UST programs) may undertake corrective action itself, only if such action is necessary to protect human health and the environment and one or more of the following situations exists:

(a)   No owner or operator can be found to carry out such corrective action within 90 days or such shorter period as may be necessary to protect human health and the environment;

(b)   The situation is such that it requires prompt action by EPA or the state to protect human health and the environment;

(c)   Corrective action costs exceed the amount of coverage required by the RCRA Subtitle I financial responsibility requirements; or

(d)   The owner or operator of the UST has failed or refused to comply with a compliance order of the EPA under RCRA Section 9006, or with an order of the state to comply with corrective action regulations.[34]

Recently, EPA issued a final rule, effective October 28, 1991, establishing procedures relating to the issuance of RCRA Section 9003(h) corrective action orders.[35] The final rule amends regulations provided in 40 C.F.R. Part 24 regarding the issuance of and administrative hearings on corrective action orders. Generally speaking, the rule provides that the same administrative procedures employed for issuance of RCRA Section 3008(h) corrective action orders are to be used for the issuance of RCRA Section 9003(h) orders. Such procedures are less formal and resource-intensive than proceedings that would be required for RCRA Section 9006 compliance orders.[36]

4.0 SUMMARY OF REPORTING AND RECORDKEEPING REQUIREMENTS

Owners and operators of USTs are subject to myriad reporting and recordkeeping requirements under RCRA Subtitle I. The following is a brief overview of the numerous reporting and recordkeeping obligations. Later sections of this chapter discuss how these requirements apply to new tanks as opposed to existing tanks.

---

[33]*See* 42 U.S.C. § 6991b(h)(1)(A).

[34]42 U.S.C. § 6991b(h)(2).

[35]*See* 56 Fed. Reg. 49376 (September 27, 1991).

[36]*Id.* at 49378.

4.1 Reporting Requirements

Initial Notification—Owners and operators of existing and new UST systems are required to notify the appropriate designated agency of the use of such systems. Typically, the state or local regulatory agency is designated to receive such initial notification.[37] These owners and operators also must certify compliance with requirements governing UST system installation, cathodic protection, financial responsibility, and release detection.[38]

Suspected Releases—Owners and operators of USTs must report any suspected releases to the implementing agency.[39]

Spills and Overfills—Owners and operators of USTs must report any spills and overfills from UST systems to the implementing agency.[40]

Confirmed Releases—Upon confirmation of any release, owners and operators of USTs must report such release to the implementing agency.[41] Also note that a release of a hazardous substance equal to or in excess of its reportable quantity must also be reported immediately to the National Response Center and appropriate state and local authorities pursuant to CERCLA and the Superfund Amendments and Reauthorization Act (SARA) of 1986.[42]

Corrective Action—Owners and operators of USTs have several reporting obligations when undertaking corrective action involving USTs, including the reporting of initial abatement measures,[43] initial site characterization,[44] removal of free product from USTs,[45] results of investigations for soil and groundwater clean-ups,[46] and, if required by the implementing agency, submittal of corrective action plans.[47]

Permanent Closure/Change-in-Service—Owners and operators of USTs are required to provide advanced notice of the permanent closure or change-in-service of any UST.[48]

Financial Responsibility—Owners and operators of USTs are required to submit various forms demonstrating financial responsibility for taking corrective action and for compensating third parties for bodily injury and

---

[37]Owners and operators should contact the nearest EPA regional office to determine which agency has been designated for submittal of such notification.

[38]40 C.F.R. § 280.22.

[39]40 C.F.R. § 280.50.

[40]40. C.F.R. §§ 280.30(b) and 280.53.

[41]40 C.F.R. § 280.61.

[42]40 C.F.R. § 280.53, note.

[43]40 C.F.R. § 280.62.

[44]40 C.F.R. § 280.63.

[45]40 C.F.R. § 280.64(d).

[46]40 C.F.R. § 280.(b).

[47]40 C.F.R. § 280.66.

[48]40. C.F.R. § 280.71(a).

property damage caused by accidental releases arising from the operation of petroleum USTs.[49]

4.2 Recordkeeping Requirements

RCRA Section 9005(b), 42 U.S.C. § 6991d(b), provides that any records, reports or information that are provided to implementing agencies shall be made available to the public, except information that has been designated as confidential by the agency.[50] Confidential records, reports or information must be designated as confidential and submitted separately from other records that are otherwise submitted to the regulatory agencies.[51]

Site Corrosion Potential Analysis—Owners and operators of metal USTs and piping that are installed at a site without corrosion protection must maintain records that analyze the corrosion potential of the site and UST systems.[52]

Operation of Corrosion Protection Equipment—Owners and operators of USTs must maintain records of inspections and testing of cathodic protection systems where used.[53]

UST Repairs—Owners and operators of USTs must document and maintain records of UST system repairs.[54]

Release Detection—All owners and operators of USTs must maintain records that document performance claims made by manufacturers of release detection equipment, as well as the results of any sampling, testing and monitoring for releases, and records relating to the calibration, maintenance and repair of release detection equipment.[55] To the extent that owners or operators of USTs use other release detection methods than those prescribed by the RCRA Subtitle I regulations, owners or operators must submit documentation that justifies the use of such other methods.[56]

Permanent Closure—Owners and operators of USTs are required to maintain records of permanent closure or change-in-service of UST systems for at least 3 years after completion of the closure or change-in-service.[57]

Financial Responsibility—Owners or operators of USTs must maintain evidence of all financial assurance mechanisms used to demonstrate financial responsibility under the RCRA Subtitle I regulations.[58] Owners and operators of USTs must maintain their records either at the UST site or at a readily available alternative site. If an UST is permanently closed, owners

---

[49] 40 C.F.R. § 280.106.
[50] *See* 18 U.S.C. § 1905.
[51] 42 U.S.C. § 6991(b)(3).
[52] 40 C.F.R. § 280.20(a)(4), (b)(3).
[53] 40 C.F.R. § 280.31(d).
[54] 40 C.F.R. § 280.33(f).
[55] 40 C.F.R. § 280.45.
[56] 40 C.F.R. § 280.42(b)(5).
[57] 40 C.F.R. § 280.74.
[58] 40 C.F.R. § 280.107.

and operators may mail closure records to the implementing agency if they cannot be kept at the site or at an alternative site.[59]

5.0 NEW UST SYSTEMS

5.1 Notification Requirements

Any owner who brings an UST system into use after May 8, 1986 must notify the designated regulatory agency of the existence of such tank system within 30 days of bringing the UST into use. A standard notification form is usually used. Owners and operators of new UST systems must certify in the notification form that they have complied with various UST requirements, including, for example, requirements for installation of tanks and piping, cathodic protection, financial responsibility, and release detection.[60]

The installer of the UST systems must also certify in the notification form that the methods used to install the tank system comply with industry codes of practice developed by a nationally recognized association or independent testing laboratory in accordance with the manufacturer's instructions. The UST regulations refer to several industry codes of practice that may be used by installers to comply with these requirements.[61]

Finally, any person who sells a tank intended to be used as an UST must notify the purchaser of the various notification obligations for owners of USTs under the UST regulations.[62] Companies that sell property with underground storage tanks should be sure that they advise the buyer of the UST notice requirements. Typically this is done in the purchase and sale documentation.

5.2 Performance Standards

Owners and operators of new UST systems are required to meet several performance standards in order to prevent releases of regulated substances from the systems resulting from either structural failure, corrosion, or spills and overfills. The following sections describe these performance standards.

5.2.1 Tanks

USTs must be properly designed, constructed and protected from corrosion in accordance with appropriate industry codes of practice.[63] An owner may install an UST and corrosion protection system not specified by the regulations as long as the implementing agency determines that the system is capable of preventing the release or threatened release of any

---

[59]40 C.F.R. § 280.34(c).

[60]40 C.F.R. § 280.22.

[61]40 C.F.R. § 280.20(d). *See* 40 C.F.R. 280.22(f).

[62]40 C.F.R. § 280.22(g).

[63]40 C.F.R. § 280.20(a)(1)-(3) specifically addresses tanks constructed of fiberglass-reinforced plastic, steel with cathodic protection, and steel-fiberglass-reinforced-plastic composite.

stored regulated substance in a manner that is no less protective of human health and the environment than other prescribed UST systems.[64]

Owners and operators wishing to install tanks constructed of metal *without* corrosion protection must have a corrosion expert determine that the site is not sufficiently corrosive to cause a release due to corrosion from the UST during its operating life. In addition, for the remaining life of the tank, owners and operators of such USTs must maintain records demonstrating such compliance.[65]

5.2.2 Piping

As with tanks, UST regulations provide similar guidelines and industry codes of practice to follow in the design, construction and corrosion protection of new piping systems. The regulations provide standards for new piping constructed of fiberglass-reinforced plastic and steel with cathodic protection.[66] Similar regulations are provided for piping constructed of metal without cathodic protection. They require the owner and operator to have a corrosion expert determine that the site is not corrosive and to maintain records that demonstrate that the site will remain noncorrosive for the remaining life of the UST piping.[67]

Piping other than that specifically described by the regulations may be constructed if the regulatory agency determines that it is as capable of preventing the release or threatened release of regulated substances as EPA-approved systems.[68]

5.2.3 Spill and Overfill Prevention Equipment

Owners and operators of new USTs must employ spill and overflow prevention equipment to prevent releases that may occur during the filling or emptying of such USTs. Overfill prevention equipment must be capable of either:

(a)   automatically shutting off flow into the tank when the tank is no more than 95 percent full;

(b)   alerting the transfer operator when the tank is more than 90 percent full by restricting the flow into the tank or triggering a high-level alarm;

(c)   restricting flow 30 minutes prior to overfilling and alerting the operator with a high-level alarm one minute before overfilling; or

---

[64] 40 C.F.R. § 280.20(a)(5).
[65] 40 C.F.R. § 280.20(a)(4).
[66] 40 C.F.R. § 280.20(b)(1)-(2).
[67] 40 C.F.R. § 280.20(b)(3).
[68] 40 C.F.R. § 280.20(b)(4).

(d)   automatically shutting off the flow into the tank so that none of the fittings located on top of the tank are exposed to the product due to overfilling.[69]

Spill prevention equipment must be capable of preventing the release of regulated substances into the environment when the transfer hose is detached from the tank's fill pipe.[70] Alternative spill and overflow prevention equipment can be used if owners and operators can satisfactorily demonstrate to the implementing agency that the equipment is no less protective of human health and the environment. No spill and overfill prevention equipment is required if transfers of regulated substances to and from the UST system involve no more than 25 gallons at one time.[71]

5.2.4 Installation

All new tanks and pipes must be properly installed in accordance with appropriate industry codes of practice. Owners and operators must certify, test or inspect such installation to demonstrate compliance with such industry codes of practice.[72]

6.0 EXISTING UST SYSTEMS

6.1 Notification Requirements

Owners of UST systems that were in the ground on or after May 8, 1986 were required to notify the designated regulatory agency of the existence of such tank systems, unless the owner knew that the tank system was subsequently removed from the ground.[73] No notification, however, was required if the UST systems were taken out of operation on or before January 1, 1974. The notice should specify, to the extent known by the owner, the date the tank was taken out of operation, the age of the tank on the date taken out of operation, the size, type and location of the tank, and the type and quantity of substances left stored in the tank on the date the tank was taken out of operation.[74]

Although existing tanks should have been registered by May 1986, states continue to find previously unknown tanks at former gas stations and other businesses. One study estimates that there may be as many as 364,000 existing USTs that are subject to regulation but are still unregistered.[75]

Companies that are considering the purchase of real property typically conduct a "due diligence" review to see whether the property has

---

[69]40 C.F.R. § 280.20(c)(1)(ii), as revised by final rule, 56 Fed. Reg. 38342-45 (August 13, 1991), effective September 12, 1991.

[70]40 C.F.R. § 280.20(c)(1)(i).

[71]40 C.F.R. § 280.20(c)(2).

[72]40 C.F.R. § 280.20(d), (e).

[73]42 U.S.C. § 6991a(a); 40 C.F.R. § 280.22(a).

[74]42 U.S.C. § 6991(a)(2)(B).

[75]Environmental Information, Ltd., *The Underground Storage Tank Market: Its Current Status and Future Challenges*, 13 (1992).

environmental liabilities that the owner will acquire. One item in an environmental due diligence checklist is underground tanks. A prospective buyer can check agency records to see if the property has any registered tanks. Sometimes unregistered tanks are discovered by a prospective purchaser or his consultant during a site inspection.

6.2 Upgrading of Existing UST Systems

All existing UST systems are required, by no later than December 22, 1998, to meet one of the following requirements:

(a)   new UST system performance standards;[76]

(b)   tank upgrading requirements;[77] or

(c)   closure and corrective action requirements.[78]

Existing metal piping systems must also be upgraded to meet the performance standards for new piping systems.[79] Existing UST systems must also comply with new UST system requirements for spill and overfill prevention.[80]

7.0 GENERAL OPERATING REQUIREMENTS

7.1 Spill and Overfill Control

Owners and operators of USTs must ensure that the volume of the tank is greater than the volume of regulated substance to be transferred into the tank *before* the transfer is made, and that the transfer operation is monitored constantly to prevent overfilling and spilling.[81] The owner and operator must report, investigate and clean up any spills and overflows that occur during transfer operations.[82]

7.2 Operation and Maintenance of Corrosion Protection Systems

All owners and operators of steel UST systems that employ corrosion protection must ensure that the corrosion protection systems are operated and maintained to continuously protect those metal components of the UST system that are in contact with the ground.[83] In addition, all UST systems

---

[76] 40 C.F.R. § 280.21(a)(1). 40 C.F.R. § 280.20 details the standards.

[77] 40 C.F.R. § 280.21(a)(2). 40 C.F.R. § 280.21(b) provides upgrading requirements for steel tanks, including requirements relating to the upgrading of the interior lining of the tanks and cathodic protection. Specific industry codes of practice are referenced.

[78] 40 C.F.R. § 280.21(a)(3). 40 C.F.R. § 280 subparts F and G describe the requirements.

[79] 40 C.F.R. § 280.21(c) notes that the industry codes of practice and standards listed in 40 C.F.R. § 280.20(b)(2) may be used to comply with the upgrading requirements.

[80] 40 C.F.R. § 280.21(d) specifies that the requirements in 40 C.F.R. § 280.20(c) are to be followed.

[81] 40 C.F.R. § 280.30.

[82] *See* Section 9.8 of this chapter and 40 C.F.R. § 280.53 for requirements regarding the reporting and clean-up of spills and overfills.

[83] 40 C.F.R. § 280.31(a).

equipped with cathodic protection systems must be inspected for proper operation by a qualified cathodic protection tester in accordance with specific regulatory requirements.[84] Owners and operators of UST systems using cathodic protection must keep and maintain records of the operation of the cathodic protection systems.[85]

7.3 Substance Compatibility

Regulations require owners and operators to use UST systems that are made of or lined with materials that are compatible with the regulated substances that are stored in the UST systems.[86]

7.4 UST System Repairs

Any repairs made to UST systems must be performed in a manner that will prevent releases due to structural failure or corrosion as long as the UST system is used to store regulated substances. Regulations specify that repairs to UST systems must be properly conducted in accordance with appropriate industry codes of practice.[87] Metal pipe sections and fittings that have released regulated substances as a result of corrosion or other damage must be replaced.[88] Repaired tanks and piping must be tightness tested within 30 days following the date of completion of the repair, except if alternative methods are used to verify the sufficiency of the repair.[89] Cathodic protection systems must be tested within six months following the repair of any cathodically protected UST system.[90] UST regulations require owners and operators to maintain records of each repair for the remaining operating life of the UST system.[91]

8.0 RELEASE DETECTION

8.1 General Requirements and Schedule

Owners and operators of new and existing UST systems must provide a method or combination of methods of release detection that can detect a release from any portion of the tank and connected underground piping that routinely contains regulated substances. There are several requirements that govern the installation, operation and performance of release detection equipment and methods for tanks.[92] Owners and operators of suction and pressurized piping systems must also comply with applicable release

---

[84]40 C.F.R. § 280.31(b) and (c) provide frequency and inspection criteria.
[85]40 C.F.R. § 280.31(d).
[86]40 C.F.R. § 280.32.
[87]40 C.F.R. § 280.33(a)-(b).
[88]40 C.F.R. § 280.33(c).
[89]40 C.F.R. § 280.33(d).
[90]40 C.F.R. § 280.33(e).
[91]40 C.F.R. § 280.33(f).
[92]*See* 40 C.F.R. § 280.43.

detection requirements for those piping systems.[93] The date by which owners and operators of UST systems must comply with release detection requirements depends on when the tank and piping systems were installed.[94] Those requirements are being phased in. One study estimates that some 350,000 active USTs will have to undergo monthly leak detection procedures for the first time in 1993.[95] Any existing UST system that cannot apply a method of release detection that complies with applicable release detection requirements must be closed by the date such compliance was required.[96]

8.2 Methods of Release Detection for Tanks and Piping

UST regulations set forth several methods of release detection that may be used for tanks and piping. Such methods for tanks include product inventory control, manual tank gauging, automatic tank gauging, vapor monitoring, groundwater monitoring, interstitial monitoring between the tank and a surrounding secondary barrier, or any other approved method of release detection.[97] Release detection methods for piping include automatic line leak detectors, line tightness testing, vapor monitoring, groundwater monitoring, interstitial monitoring, or any other approved method designed to detect a release from any portion of the underground piping that routinely contains regulated substances.[98] Release detection methods must be capable of detecting a leak rate specified in the regulations for each method with a probability of detection of 95 percent and a probability of false alarm of 5 percent, unless the release detection method was permanently installed prior to December 22, 1990.[99]

8.3 Specific Requirements for Petroleum USTs

USTs containing petroleum products must be monitored at least every 30 days for releases.[100] The 30-day monitoring requirement does not apply to those UST systems that (1) meet the performance standards for new and upgraded tank systems,[101] and (2) employ monthly inventory control or monthly manual tank gauging in conjunction with tank tightness testing.[102]

---

[93] *See* 40 C.F.R. §§ 280.41(b) and 280.44.

[94] *See* 40 C.F.R. § 280.40(c).

[95] Environmental Information, Ltd., *The Underground Storage Tank Market: Its Current Status and Future Challenges*, 3 (1992).

[96] 40 C.F.R. § 280.40(d).

[97] *See* 40 C.F.R. § 280.43 for specifications on tank size and appropriate gauging methods.

[98] 40 C.F.R. § 280.44.

[99] 40 C.F.R. § 280.40(a)(3). Note, however, that the permanent installation date for automatic line leak detectors is September 22, 1991.

[100] 40 C.F.R. § 280.41(a).

[101] 40 C.F.R. §§ 280.20-280.21.

[102] Tank tightness testing must be performed at least every five years until either December 22, 1998 or ten years after the tank is installed or upgraded, whichever is later. 40 C.F.R. § 280.41(a)(1).

UST systems that do not meet the performance standards for new or upgraded USTs may use monthly inventory controls or manual tank gauging in conjunction with annual tank tightness testing until December 22, 1998 when the tank must be upgraded or permanently closed.[103] Owners and operators of tanks with capacities of 550 gallons or less may use weekly tank gauging in lieu of other release detection methods.[104]

Underground piping systems must also be monitored for releases. Underground piping that conveys regulated substances under pressure must be equipped with an automatic line leak detector and have annual line tightness testing or monthly monitoring.[105] Underground piping that conveys regulated substances under suction must either have line tightness testing conducted at least every three years or use monthly monitoring. Suction piping may be exempt from release detection requirements if it meets specific design and construction standards.[106]

8.4 Specific Requirements for Hazardous Substance UST Systems

Until December 22, 1998, owners and operators of existing hazardous substance UST systems must employ release detection that at least meets the requirements for petroleum UST systems. After December 22, 1998, all existing hazardous substance UST systems must comply with the release detection requirements for new hazardous substance UST systems.[107] Regulations require new hazardous substance UST systems to have secondary containment systems and be checked for evidence of a release at least every 30 days.[108] Similarly, underground piping that conveys hazardous substances must also be equipped with secondary containment and, if under pressure, must also be equipped with an automatic line leak detector system.[109]

Other methods of release detection for hazardous substance USTs may be used if approved by the implementing agency. Owners and operators, however, must demonstrate to the implementing agency that the alternative method can effectively detect a release of the stored hazardous substance. Owners and operators must provide information to the implementing agency on effective corrective action technologies, health risks, chemical and physical properties of the stored substances, and the characteristics of the UST site, and must obtain agency approval to use the alternative release

---

[103] 40 C.F.R. § 280.41(a)(2).

[104] 40 C.F.R. 280.41(a)(3).

[105] 40 C.F.R. § 280.41(b)(1).

[106] 40 C.F.R. § 280.41(b)(2).

[107] 40 C.F.R. § 280.42(a).

[108] 40 C.F.R. § 280.42(b). The regulation notes that the provisions of 40 C.F.R. § 265.193 regarding containment and detection of releases for hazardous waste storage tanks may be used to comply with the release detection requirements for hazardous substance USTs.

[109] 40 C.F.R. § 280.42(b)(4).

detection method before installation and operation of the new hazardous substance UST system.[110]

9.0 RELEASE REPORTING, INVESTIGATION AND RESPONSE

9.1 Overview

EPA has estimated that the nation might spend $32 billion to investigate and clean up chemical releases and spills from underground storage tanks. A recent study suggests that figure might exceed $41 billion and take over 30 years. [111] Cleanups typically involve excavation of contaminated soil and testing to see whether underlying groundwater has been affected. If groundwater has been contaminated, the cost of a cleanup can escalate rapidly. In many cases, on-site methods of soil treatment such as soil vapor extraction are needed to remove contaminants from areas such as those beneath buildings where excavation is impractical. This section discusses the legal requirements for reporting, investigating, and cleaning up releases from USTs.

9.2 Reporting of Suspected Releases

Owners and operators of UST systems must report any suspected release to the implementing agency within 24 hours or another reasonable time period specified by the implementing agency.[112] UST regulations identify several conditions which would require reporting:

(a) The discovery of regulated substances released at the UST site or in the surrounding area.[113]

(b) Unusual operating conditions observed by owners and operators, including for example, the erratic behavior of product dispensing equipment, the sudden loss of product from the UST system, or any unexplained presence of water in the UST. Regulations note that the reporting of such unusual conditions is not required if the UST system equipment is found to be defective but not leaking and is immediately repaired or replaced.[114]

(c) Monitoring results from any required release detection method which indicate that a release may have occurred. Reporting is not required if the release detection monitoring device is found to be defective and is immediately repaired, recalibrated or replaced, and if additional monitoring does not confirm the initial result or,

---

[110]40 C.F.R. § 280.42(b)(5).

[111]Environmental Information , Ltd., *The Underground Storage Tank Market: Its Current Status and Future Challenges*, 2-3 (1992).

[112]40 C.F.R. § 280.50.

[113]40 C.F.R. § 280.50(a).

[114]40 C.F.R. § 280.50(b).

in the case of inventory control release detection monitoring, a second month of data does not confirm the initial result.[115]

9.3 Release Investigation and Confirmation

UST regulations require all owners and operators to immediately investigate and confirm *suspected* releases of regulated substances within 7 days or another reasonable time period as specified by the implementing agency.[116] Unless another procedure is approved by the implementing agency, owners and operators are required to take additional steps as described in the sections below.

9.3.1 System Test

Owners and operators must conduct tightness testing of the UST and associated piping to determine whether a leak exists. Should such testing indicate the presence of a leak, owners and operators must repair, replace or upgrade the UST system and begin corrective action to remedy any release. No further investigation is required if testing results do not indicate the presence of a leak and environmental contamination was not the basis for suspecting a release. Owners and operators must conduct a site check, as described below, if environmental contamination has been observed at the site, even though testing results do not indicate the presence of a leak.[117]

9.3.2 Site Check

If environmental contamination is observed at the UST site, owners and operators must evaluate whether a release has occurred from the UST system. If test results indicate that a release has occurred, owners and operators must begin corrective action in accordance with UST regulations. If test results do not indicate that a release has occurred, further investigation is not required.[118]

9.4 Initial Release Response

Once a release from an UST system is confirmed, owners and operators must comply with various corrective action requirements. Owners and operators must perform certain initial response actions within 24 hours of a release, or within another reasonable period of time determined by the implementing agency. Those actions include reporting the release to the implementing agency, taking immediate action to prevent any further release of the regulated substance into the environment, and identifying and mitigating any fire, explosion, and vapor hazards that may be associated with the release.[119]

---

[115] 40 C.F.R. § 280.50(c).
[116] 40 C.F.R. § 280.52.
[117] 40 C.F.R. § 280.52(a).
[118] 40 C.F.R. § 280.52(b).
[119] 40 C.F.R. § 280.61.

9.5 Initial Abatement Measures

Following release confirmation, owners and operators of UST systems must also perform certain abatement measures. Those measures include:

(a) removal of as much of the regulated substance from the UST system as is necessary to prevent further release to the environment;

(b) visual inspection of any aboveground or exposed belowground releases and prevention of any further migration of such releases into surrounding soils and groundwater;

(c) continued monitoring and mitigation of any additional fire and safety hazards posed by vapors or free product in subsurface structures;

(d) remediation of any hazards posed by contaminated soils that are excavated or exposed as a result of release confirmation, site investigation, abatement or corrective action activities;

(e) if not already determined, investigation for the presence of a release where contamination is most likely to be present at the UST site; and

(f) investigation to determine the possible presence of free product and removal of free product as soon as practicable.[120]

UST regulations require owners and operators to submit to the implementing agency a report summarizing the initial abatement steps taken and any resulting information or data within 20 days of release confirmation or within another reasonable time period specified by the implementing agency.[121]

9.6 Initial Site Characterization

Owners and operators must also assemble information about the site and the nature of the release, including information gained while confirming the release or completing the initial abatement measures. Such information must include at least:

(a) data on the nature and estimated quantity of release;

(b) data from available sources and/or site investigations concerning surrounding populations, water quality, use and approximate locations of wells potentially affected by the release, subsurface soil conditions, locations of subsurface sewers, climatological conditions, and land use;

(c) results of the site check; and

(d) results of the free product investigations.

---

[120]40 C.F.R. § 280.62(a).
[121]40 C.F.R. § 280.62(b).

Owners and operators must submit this initial site characterization to the implementing agency within 45 days of release confirmation or according to a schedule required by the implementing agency.[122]

9.7 Free Product Removal

Where investigation has indicated the presence of free product, owners and operators must remove free product to the maximum extent practicable as determined by the implementing agency.[123] Owners and operators must prepare and submit to the implementing agency a free product removal report that describes conditions and the measures taken to abate the presence of free product.[124]

9.8 Investigations for Soil and Groundwater Cleanup

Owners and operators must also conduct investigations of soil and groundwater at the area of release, the release site, and the surrounding area possibly affected by the release if any of the following conditions exist:

(a) Groundwater wells have been affected by the release;

(b) Free product is found to need recovery;

(c) Contaminated soils may be in contact with groundwater; and

(d) The implementing agency requests an investigation, based on the potential effects of contaminated soil or groundwater on nearby surface water and groundwater resources.[125]

Owners and operators are required to submit information collected from such investigations as soon as practicable or in accordance with a schedule established by the implementing agency.

9.9 Reporting and Cleanup of Spills and Overfills

Spills and overfills must be contained and immediately cleaned up. Owners and operators must report any spill and overfill incident to the implementing agency within 24 hours, or other reasonable time period specified by the implementing agency, and begin corrective action if there are:

(a) spills or overfills of petroleum exceeding 25 gallons or another reasonable amount specified by the implementing agency, or that causes a sheen on nearby surface water; and

(b) spills or overfills of hazardous substances that equal or exceed its reportable quantity under CERCLA.[126]

---

[122] 40 C.F.R. § 280.63.

[123] 40 C.F.R. § 280.64.

[124] 40 C.F.R. § 280.64(d).

[125] 40 C.F.R. § 280.65.

[126] 40 C.F.R. § 280.53(a). For designation and reportable quantities of hazardous substances under CERCLA, *see* 40 C.F.R. Part 302.

Owners and operators are required to contain and immediately clean up spills and overfills in amounts less than those described above, but are not required to report such incidents. However, the regulations provide that if such cleanup cannot be accomplished within 24 hours or another reasonable time period as specified by the implementing agency, owners and operators must immediately report such incidents.[127]

9.10 Corrective Action Plan

The implementing agency may require owners and operators to submit a corrective action plan for contaminated soils and groundwater.[128] In such instances, owners and operators typically will prepare the plan according to a schedule and format established by the implementing agency. In some instances, owners and operators may choose to voluntarily submit a corrective action plan for contaminated soil and groundwater. The corrective action plan must provide for adequate protection of human health and the environment as determined by the implementing agency. Upon approval of the corrective action plan by the implementing agency, owners and operators must implement the plan and monitor, evaluate and report the results of such implementation in accordance with a schedule and format typically established by the implementing agency.[129]

Owners and operators may begin cleanup of soil and groundwater before a corrective action plan is approved by the implementing agency. However, owners and operators must first notify the implementing agency of their intention to begin clean-up, and they must comply with any conditions imposed by the implementing agency. Owners and operators must then incorporate those self-initiated clean-up measures into the corrective action plan that is submitted to the implementing agency for approval.[130]

10.0 CLOSURE OF UST SYSTEMS

10.1 Temporary Closure

Occasionally, owners and operators will discontinue use of USTs for an extended period. However, owners and operators must continue to comply with requirements governing the operation and maintenance of corrosion protection and release detection systems, as well as requirements for release reporting, investigation, confirmation, and corrective action if a release is suspected or confirmed during the period of temporary closure. Compliance

---

[127] 40 C.F.R. § 280.53(b). UST regulations also note that pursuant to 40 C.F.R. §§ 302.6 and 355.40, a release of a hazardous substance equal to or in excess of its reportable quantity must also be reported immediately (rather than within 24 hours) to the National Response Center under Sections 102 and 103 of CERCLA, and to appropriate state and local authorities under Title III of SARA.

[128] 40 C.F.R. § 280.66(a).

[129] 40 C.F.R. § 280.66(c). *See also* 40 C.F.R. § 280.67.

[130] 40 C.F.R. § 280.66(d).

with release detection requirements is not necessary as long as the UST is empty.[131]

If an UST system is temporarily closed for 3 months or more, owners and operators, in addition to the above requirements, must leave vent lines open and functioning and cap and secure all other lines, pumps, manways, and ancillary equipment.[132] If an UST system is temporarily closed for more than 12 months and does not meet either performance standards for new UST systems or the upgrading requirements for existing systems (excluding spill and overfill requirements), then owners and operators must permanently close the UST system, unless the implementing agency provides an extension of the 12 month temporary closure period.[133] Owners and operators must complete a site assessment in accordance with 40 C.F.R. § 280.72 before applying for such an extension.

10.2 Permanent Closure/Change-in-Service

Before beginning either permanent closure or a change-in-service[134] of an UST system, owners and operators must notify the implementing agency, at least 30 days before beginning such activities, of their intent to undertake such activities unless such action is in response to corrective action associated with any release from the UST system.[135] For permanent closure, tanks must be emptied, cleaned, and either removed from the ground or filled with inert solid material.[136] Before permanent closure or a change-in-service is completed, owners and operators must conduct a site assessment to evaluate whether releases have occurred at the UST site. Corrective action must be undertaken if contamination is encountered during the site assessment.[137]

For UST systems that were permanently closed before December 22, 1988, the implementing agency may direct owners and operators to assess the area involved in the UST closure and may close the UST system in accordance with UST regulations if releases from the UST are determined to pose a current or potential threat to human health and the environment.[138]

Owners and operators must maintain records of closure or change-in-service that are capable of demonstrating compliance with the regulatory requirements. The results of any site assessment must be maintained for at least three years after completion of permanent closure or change-in-service by the owners and operators who took the UST system out of service, the

---

[131] *See* 40 C.F.R. § 280.70(a).

[132] 40 C.F.R. § 280.70(b).

[133] 40 C.F.R. § 280.70(c).

[134] A change-in-service is described as the continued use of an UST system to store a nonregulated substance. 40 C.F.R. § 280.71(c)

[135] 40 C.F.R. § 280.71(a).

[136] 40 C.F.R. § 280.71(b).

[137] 40 C.F.R. § 280.72.

[138] 40 C.F.R. § 280.73.

current owners and operators of the UST system site, or by the implementing agency if the records cannot be maintained at the closed facility.[139]

11.0 FINANCIAL RESPONSIBILITY REQUIREMENTS

11.1 Applicability and Compliance Dates

Owners and operators of all petroleum UST systems that are subject to the UST regulations must demonstrate an ability to pay for cleanups and to compensate third parties for bodily injury and property damage caused by accidental releases arising from the operation of petroleum USTs.[140] Called the "financial responsibility" requirements, Congress intended that these requirements be phased in over time. EPA has set a time schedule by which owners and operators of petroleum USTs are required to comply with the financial responsibility requirements. Compliance dates depend on the number of USTs that are owned, as well as the net worth of the owner.[141]

UST regulations are silent as to whether financial responsibility requirements are to apply to owners and operators of hazardous substance USTs. At one time, EPA stated that it planned to develop regulations for such USTs in the future. No such regulations, however, have been proposed as of September 1992.[142]

An owner or operator is no longer required to maintain financial responsibility after the UST has been properly closed or, if corrective action is required, after corrective action has been completed and the tank has been properly closed.[143]

11.2 Amount and Scope of Financial Responsibility Required

Owners or operators of petroleum USTs must demonstrate financial responsibility in at least the following *per-occurrence* amounts:

(a) $1,000,000 for owners or operators of petroleum USTs that are located at petroleum marketing facilities, or that handle an average of more than 10,000 gallons of petroleum per month based on annual throughput for the previous calendar year;

(b) $500,000 for all other owners or operators who operate petroleum USTs.[144]

---

[139] 40 C.F.R. § 280.74.

[140] Financial responsibility regulations state that if the owner and operator of a petroleum UST are separate persons, only one person is required to demonstrate financial responsibility. However, both parties are liable in the event of noncompliance with the financial responsibility regulations. 40 C.F.R. § 280.90(e).

[141] *See* 56 Fed. Reg. 66369 (December 23, 1991) (amending 40 C.F.R. § 280.91(d)). *See also* 40 C.F.R. § 280.92(i) and (j).

[142] *See* Office of Underground Storage Tanks, Environmental Protection Agency, *Dollars and Sense, A Summary of the Financial Responsibility Regulation for Underground Storage Tank Systems* (December 1988), 1.

[143] 40 C.F.R. § 280.109.

[144] 40 C.F.R. § 280.93(a).

Owners or operators of petroleum USTs must also demonstrate financial responsibility in at least the following *annual aggregate* amounts:

(a) $1,000,000 for owners or operators of 1 to 100 petroleum USTs; and

(b) $2,000,000 for owners or operators of 101 or more petroleum USTs.[145]

11.3 Allowable Financial Responsibility Mechanisms

There are several ways owners and operators of UST systems can demonstrate compliance with the financial responsibility requirements. An owner or operator may use any one or combination of the following mechanisms: self-insurance, guarantee, liability insurance or risk retention group coverage, surety bond, letter of credit, other state-required mechanism, state fund or other state assurance, trust fund, and standby trust fund. An owner or operator may substitute any alternate financial assurance mechanism provided that at all times the owner or operator maintains an effective financial assurance mechanism or combination of mechanisms that satisfies the financial responsibility requirements.[146]

Over forty states have set up "tank cleanup funds" to help private parties pay for UST cleanup work. It is estimated that these state funds are collecting nearly $1 billion a year through gasoline taxes and other sources.[147] Many UST owners and operators look to these state funds to comply with the RCRA financial assurance requirements because of the difficulty in obtaining private insurance. These state funds have been an important factor in speeding the investigation and cleanup of the thousands of UST sites throughout the country.

11.4 Reporting and Recordkeeping Requirements

Owners or operators must maintain evidence of all financial assurance mechanisms used to demonstrate compliance with financial responsibility requirements until released from the requirements. The type of evidence to be maintained by the owner or operator depends on the financial assurance mechanism used.[148] An owner or operator must maintain an updated copy of a certification of financial responsibility that follows the wording provided in the regulations. The owners or operators must also submit evidence of financial responsibility to the implementing agency, under certain conditions.[149]

---

[145] 40 C.F.R. § 280.93(b).

[146] 40 C.F.R. § 280.95-104.

[147] Environmental Information, Ltd., *The Underground Storage Tank Market: Its Current Status and Future Challenges*, 2 (1992).

[148] *See* 40 C.F.R. § 280.107(b).

[149] *See* 40 C.F.R. § 280.106-107.

12.0 CONCLUSION

Finding and cleaning up existing chemical spills from leaking underground storage tanks and enforcing strict standards for new tanks present a serious challenge to the government and to private companies responsible for USTs. The regulations facing owners and operators of UST systems are numerous and can be confusing.

The basic purpose of the federal UST program is five-fold: (1) To identify existing tanks and require that they be removed or upgraded; (2) to clean up past problems caused by USTs; (3) to require new tanks to meet strict new standards; (4) to require that all tanks be operated to minimize the possibility of leaks and be properly closed; and (5) to require the reporting, investigation, and cleanup of UST spills and releases. This chapter has described only the federal requirements for underground storage tanks. More information may be obtained from the nearest regional office of EPA or EPA's RCRA/Superfund UST Hotline.[150] States and local governments may have additional, stricter requirements for USTs. States may also have "tank cleanup funds" to reimburse companies for the cost of cleaning up UST sites.

For a more definitive discussion of this topic, the reader is referred to UST Management: A Practical Guide, *4th Edition. Also, see related books and courses listed at the end of this book for information on state requirements.*

---

[150]EPA's RCRA/Superfund UST Hotline: 1-800-424-9346.

Chapter 5

CLEAN AIR ACT

F. William Brownell
Hunton & Williams
Washington, D.C.

1.0 OVERVIEW

Over the past two decades, the Clean Air Act has evolved from a set of principles to guide states in controlling sources of air pollution (the 1967 Air Quality Act) to a series of detailed control requirements (the 1970, 1977, and 1990 amendments to the act) that the federal government implements and the states administer. The Clean Air Act regulatory programs have traditionally fallen into three categories.

First, all new and existing sources of air pollution are subject to ambient air quality regulation, through source-specific emission limits contained in state implementation plans (SIPs). Second, new sources are subject to more stringent control technology and permitting requirements. Third, the act addresses specific pollution problems, including hazardous air pollution and visibility impairment.

In 1990, Congress amended this three part system of regulation in significant respects (for example, by revamping the system of hazardous air pollution regulation and by addressing new air pollution problems such as acid deposition), and added a fourth program—a comprehensive operating permit program to focus in one place all of the Clean Air Act requirements that apply to a given source of air pollution. This chapter reviews briefly each of these categories of regulatory requirements, with a particular focus on changes made by the 1990 amendments to the act.

2.0 AIR QUALITY REGULATION

The centerpiece of the Clean Air Act is the national ambient air quality standard (NAAQS) program. The NAAQS's address pervasive pollution problems, and have been established for sulphur dioxide (SO_2), nitrogen oxides (NO_x), particulate matter, carbon monoxide (CO), ozone, and lead.[1] For each of these pollutants, NAAQS's are set at a level designed to protect public health with an adequate margin of safety

---

[1] See 40 C.F.R. Part 50 (1990).

(referred to as the "primary" NAAQS), and to promote public welfare (the "secondary" NAAQS).[2]

NAAQS's are to be reviewed and revised as appropriate every five years.[3] As a practical matter, EPA has had difficulty meeting this schedule. Nevertheless, EPA is currently considering whether to revise the NAAQS for SO_2, particulate matter (measured as particles with a median aerodynamic diameter of 10 microns or less, or "PM–10"), and ozone.

The NAAQS's are implemented through source-specific emission limitations established by states in SIPs.[4] The Clean Air Act sets minimum criteria for SIPs, the stringency of which depends upon whether an area attains or does not attain the level of air quality specified in the NAAQS.

3.0 STATE IMPLEMENTATION PLANS

Sections 107 and 110 of the Clean Air Act give each state primary responsibility for assuring that air quality within its borders is maintained at a level consistent with the NAAQS. This is achieved through the establishment of source-specific requirements in SIPs addressing the primary and secondary air quality standards. The Clean Air Act contains substantive and procedural requirements governing the development and approval of these SIP requirements.[5]

3.1 Requirements Regarding SIP Plans

As amended in 1990, §110(a)(2)(A)-(M) requires that all SIPs must be adopted after reasonable notice and public hearing, and must include the following information:

Enforceable emission limitations (subsection A). A SIP must include enforceable emission limitations and other control measures, including economic incentives and timetables, as necessary to comply with the act.

Air quality data (subsection B). A SIP must include provisions for developing data on ambient air quality to be made available to EPA.

Enforcement (subsection C). A SIP must establish a program for enforcement of emission limitations and control measures. The operation of existing stationary sources, however, will also be subject to regulation and enforcement under the operating permit program established under Title V of the 1990 amendments.

Interstate air pollution (subsection D). A SIP must prohibit emissions activities that interfere with attainment and maintenance of the NAAQS, prevention of significant deterioration requirements, or visibility protection in another state. A SIP must also include provisions insuring compliance

---

[2]CAA §109.
[3]*See* CAA §109(d).
[4]CAA §110.
[5]*See* CAA §§110 and 172.

with sections of the act relating to interstate and international air pollution abatement.[6]

Adequate personnel, funding, and authority (subsection E). A SIP must provide assurances that the designated control authority has adequate resources and power to carry out the SIP under state or local laws.[7] The state must also retain ultimate responsibility for implementation and enforcement despite any delegation of authority.

Monitoring and emission data (subsection F). A SIP must require monitoring and periodic reporting of emissions by stationary sources. The state must correlate emission reports with relevant emission limitations and make the reports available for public inspection.

Contingency plans (subsection G). A SIP must provide authority for certain emergency powers similar to the provisions contained in section 303 of the act, and for adequate contingency plans to restrict emissions of pollutants that present an imminent and substantial danger to the public.

Revision of the SIP (subsection H). A SIP must provide for revision as necessary to take into account any revisions to the NAAQS, any improved methods of attainment, or any finding by EPA of substantial inadequacy of the current plan.

Part D requirements (subsection I). A SIP must meet the requirements of Part D of the act, relating to areas that do not attain the NAAQS.

Preconstruction review and notification requirements (subsection J). A SIP must meet the requirements of Part C (relating to the prevention of significant deterioration program for approval of construction of major new sources of air pollution).

Air quality modeling (subsection K). A SIP must provide for air quality modeling and submission of related data as prescribed by the administrator, for the purpose of predicting the effect of the emissions of any regulated pollutant on ambient air quality.

Permit fees (subsection L). A SIP must include provisions requiring the owner or operator of each major stationary source to pay, as a condition of any permit, fees to cover the reasonable costs of reviewing, acting on, and enforcing the permit, until superseded by a fee program under Title V of the 1990 amendments.

Local consultation (subsection M). A SIP must provide for consultation with and participation of local political subdivisions affected by the plan.

3.2 Procedural Requirements Regarding SIP Development

The SIP is a constantly evolving regulatory document that must be updated as federal requirements and local conditions change. The procedures used to implement SIP requirements are summarized below.

States are responsible for developing SIPs and keeping them up-to-date. SIPs must be submitted to EPA, however, for review and approval.

---

[6]*See* CAA §§115 and 126.
[7]*See* CAA §128.

Until a SIP submittal is approved by EPA, it is enforceable only as a matter of state, not federal, law.

States must ensure that SIPs are adequate to attain and maintain the NAAQS, and must revise SIPs within 3 years of issuance of any new or revised NAAQS (or such shorter time as is prescribed by EPA). Moreover, whenever the administrator finds that a SIP is "substantially inadequate"[8] (i) to attain or to maintain a NAAQS; (ii) to mitigate adequately interstate pollution (see CAA §§176A, 184); or (iii) to comply with any other requirement of the act, the administrator must publicly notify the state and establish reasonable deadlines for SIP revisions.[9]

SIP revisions required in response to a finding by EPA of plan inadequacy (that is, a "SIP call") must correct the deficiency and meet all other applicable requirements of CAA §110 and Part D (addressing additional requirements for areas that do not attain the NAAQS). In order to facilitate submittal of adequate and approvable plans, EPA issues written guidelines, interpretations, and information to the states and the public.[10]

Clean Air Act section 110(k)(1) outlines the requirements for EPA action on new and revised SIP submittals. Generally, within sixty days of receiving a plan or plan revision, the administrator will determine whether the submission is "complete." (Completeness criteria were published in 56 Fed. Reg. 42216 (1991).) If, after six months, the administrator has failed to determine whether these criteria have been met, the SIP submittal is automatically deemed complete. If, however, the administrator determines that the plan or any portion of the plan does not meet the completeness criteria, the state is treated as not having made the submission.[11]

Once a plan submission is deemed complete, the administrator is required to approve or to disapprove the plan within 12 months. A plan that meets all of the applicable requirements of the act will be approved in whole. However, the administrator may also approve a plan in part, or approve a plan revision on condition that the state will adopt specific enforceable measures within one year. This is referred to as a "conditional" SIP approval or a "committal" SIP.[12]

If a state fails to make a required submission, or if the administrator disapproves a SIP submission in whole or in part, EPA must promulgate a Federal Implementation Plan (FIP) for the state within two years of the date on which the SIP submission was required. A federal plan is not

---

[8]CAA § 110(a)(2)(H).
[9]CAA §110(k)(5).
[10]*See* CAA §172(d).
[11]CAA §110(k)(l)(A), (B) & (C).
[12]CAA §110(k)(2), (3) & (4).

required, however, if the state corrects the deficiency before the expiration of this two year period.[13]

3.3 Sanctions for Failure to Develop an SIP

If a SIP deficiency has not been corrected within 18 months of notice from EPA, the administrator may choose either to cut off federal highway funds, or to require additional emissions offsets of at least two-to-one for new or modified sources seeking new source permits, until the state has corrected the deficiency.[14] The administrator may also withhold support grants for air pollution planning and control programs. Further, if the administrator finds "lack of good faith," or if the deficiency has not been corrected within six months after imposition of one of the above sanctions, both of the above sanctions are to apply until the state has come into compliance.[15] Additionally, any ban on new source construction in place under the 1977 amendments to the act remains in place until the administrator approves a plan correcting the SIP deficiencies.[16]

3.4 Additional SIP Requirements in Nonattainment Areas

Title I of the 1990 amendments contains additional requirements for SIPs in areas that do not attain the NAAQS, including specific requirements addressing nonattainment areas for CO, fine particles (or PM-10), and the two precursors of ozone—volatile organic compounds (VOCs) and NO_x. The amendments emphasize an incremental approach to meeting attainment of the NAAQS for each of these pollutants. That is, attainment deadlines have been relaxed as compared to the 1977 Clean Air Act, but more stringent control requirements apply as an area's nonattainment problems become more severe. Specific nonattainment provisions are highlighted below.

3.4.1 Substantive Requirements for Nonattainment SIPs

In addition to complying with the general requirements for SIPs discussed above, nonattainment area SIPs must include the following additional provisions:

Reasonably available control technology. Plans must provide for all reasonably available control measures for major sources as expeditiously as practicable with adoption, at a minimum, of reasonably available control technology (RACT) for existing sources.[17]

Reasonable further progress. Plans must provide for such "annual incremental reductions" in emissions of nonattainment pollutants as are required by Title I of the 1990 amendments, or as are reasonably required by

---

[13]CAA §110(c)(1).
[14]*See* CAA §179(b)(1).
[15]CAA §179(a) & (b).
[16]CAA §110(n)(3).
[17]CAA §172(c)(1).

EPA in order to assure reasonable further progress in attaining the NAAQS by the applicable date.[18]

Inventory of current emissions. Plans must include a provision for obtaining a current inventory of actual emissions from all sources of the nonattainment pollutant(s), including periodic revisions as may be required by EPA.[19]

Permits for new and modified major stationary sources. Plans must require permits for the construction and operation of new or modified "major stationary sources" anywhere in the nonattainment areas. Plans must contain the more restrictive requirements of the nonattainment new source review program.

Quantification of new emissions to be allowed. Plans must expressly identify and quantify emissions that will be allowed in accordance with all new source permits and demonstrate that such emissions will be consistent with the achievement of reasonable further progress and eventual attainment.[20]

Contingency measures. Plans must provide specific measures that will automatically be implemented if the area fails to make reasonable further progress or to attain the NAAQS by the applicable date.[21]

Equivalent techniques. The administrator may allow, upon application from the state, the use of equivalent modeling, emission inventory, and planning techniques, provided that they are not, in the aggregate, less effective than the methods specified by EPA.[22]

3.4.2 Specific Nonattainment Pollutants

The 1990 amendments contain detailed substantive requirements applicable to specific nonattainment pollutants. These requirements increase in stringency as the severity of the nonattainment problem increases. The amendments also set new deadlines for attainment, again depending upon the severity of the nonattainment problem.

Ozone.[23] Ozone nonattainment areas are designated as marginal, moderate, serious, severe, or extreme, depending on the severity of the nonattainment problem. Marginal areas must attain the ozone NAAQS within three years of enactment of the 1990 amendments (that is, by November 15, 1993), moderate areas within six years, serious areas within 9 years, severe areas within 15 years, and extreme areas (Southern California) within 20 years.

New provisions address the obligation of existing sources to install reasonably available control technology (RACT). EPA is required to list

---

[18]CAA §§171(1), 172(c)(2).

[19]CAA §172(c)(3).

[20]CAA §172(c)(4),(5).

[21]CAA §172(c)(9).

[22]CAA §172(c)(8).

[23]*See* CAA §§181-185B.

source categories for which control technique guidelines for RACT have not been published, and then to publish the guidelines pursuant to a rolling schedule contained in the legislation. Stationary sources that are not otherwise covered by a control technique guideline and that emit certain levels of VOCs will also be required to install RACT. States with ozone nonattainment areas will have to revise their SIPs to address various new requirements, including annual, incremental reductions in emissions of VOCs. Finally, states are given authority to require NO_x emission reductions in ozone nonattainment areas that are ranked as having "moderate" or more serious nonattainment problems, and EPA is required to develop guidance with respect to control techniques for NO_x reductions.

Finally, SIP revisions for ozone nonattainment areas must include provisions addressing mobile source emissions, including (1) vehicle inspection and maintenance programs (including "enhanced" I&M programs for areas classified as "serious" or worse), (2) gasoline vapor recovery rules (for areas classified as "moderate" or worse), (3) clean fuel vehicle programs and transportation control measures (for areas classified as "serious" or worse), and (4) work-related vehicle trip reduction programs (for areas classified as "severe" or worse).[24]

Carbon Monoxide.[25] CO nonattainment areas are designated as either moderate or serious. Moderate areas must attain the CO NAAQS by December 31, 1995, and serious areas by December 31, 2000.

The 1990 amendments require that states with CO nonattainment areas include in their plans specific emission reduction requirements (for example, RACT for major sources and mobile source fleet requirements) that must be met by specific deadlines in order that the overall deadline for attainment be met. If a state fails to meet these interim "milestones," EPA must impose sanctions and require revisions to the SIP to ensure compliance.

With respect to mobile source emissions, SIP revisions must include (1) enhanced vehicle inspection and maintenance programs (both for "serious" areas and for certain "moderate" areas), (2) transportation control measures (for "serious" areas), and (3) oxygenated gasoline requirements (for "serious" areas).[26]

PM-10.[27] All PM-10 nonattainment areas are initially classified as moderate, and are to be reclassified later as serious if the area cannot practically attain the PM-10 NAAQS by December 31, 1994. Serious PM-10 nonattainment areas are given until December 31, 2001 to attain the NAAQS.

The 1990 amendments contain requirements for PM-10 similar to those for ozone and CO nonattainment areas. For example, states must implement all reasonably available control measures for major sources, and designate

---

[24]CAA § 182.

[25]See CAA §§ 186-87.

[26]CAA § 187.

[27]See CAA §§ 188-90.

periodic emission reduction milestones until attainment is achieved. EPA is directed to promulgate control technique guidelines for reasonably available control measures and best available control measures for PM-10 emissions from both major stationary sources and area sources.

As with ozone and CO, PM-10 SIP revisions are to provide for automatic implementation of contingency measures if the area fails to attain the PM-10 NAAQS by the mandated deadline. States are to adopt these contingency measures as regulations prior to the deadline for attainment, to ensure that these back-up measures can go into effect without delay if the target date is missed.

4.0 NEW SOURCE CONTROL PROGRAMS

In enacting the 1970 and 1977 amendments to the act, Congress expressed concern that the costs of retrofitting existing sources with state-of-the-art control technologies could be prohibitively expensive. Congress concluded that it would be more cost-effective to require high levels of technological performance at new sources, because they have more flexibility as to location and design than do existing sources.[28] As a result, new sources are subject to more stringent levels of control under the act than existing sources.

4.1 New Source Performance Standards (NSPS)

Under §111 of the act, Congress required the EPA administrator to identify categories of new and modified sources that contribute significantly to air pollution which endangers public health or welfare. To date, EPA has identified 61 such source categories, including most major industrial processes.[29]

For these source categories, EPA must set emission standards that reflect the "degree of emission reduction achievable" through the technology that the agency determines has been "adequately demonstrated" to be the best, taking into consideration "non-air quality health and environmental impacts and energy requirements."[30] NSPS may be promulgated as design, equipment, work practice, or operational standards where numerical emission limitations are not feasible.

Each NSPS in 40 C.F.R. Part 60 identifies the types of facilities (for example, in terms of size and type of process) to which the standards apply. Generally, the NSPS's apply to any facility so identified on which construction is begun after the date of *proposal* of the NSPS. In addition, the NSPS's apply to facilities that are "reconstructed" or "modified" after the date of proposal of the NSPS's.

Once set, NSPS's serve as the *minimum* level of control that can be required at new or modified sources through the new source preconstruction permitting program (discussed below). In theory, NSPS's must be reviewed

---

[28]S. Rep. No. 91-1196, 91st Cong., 2d Sess. 15-16 (1970).

[29]*See* 40 C.F.R. Part 60 (1990).

[30]CAA §111.

at least every four years and, if appropriate, revised through notice and comment rulemaking.[31] In practice, further review of NSPS takes place only infrequently.

Partly as a result of the infrequent revision of NSPS's, the 1990 amendments mandate several revisions to specific NSPS's. For example, the 1990 amendments repeal §111(a)(1) of the act, which includes the percentage reduction requirement for large fossil fuel-fired boilers (1990 amendments §403(a)), and require the administrator to promulgate revised NSPS's for this source category by November 15, 1993. The administrator must propose by January 1, 1993 revised NSPS's for NO_x emissions from fossil-fuel fired steam generating units.[32] The amendments also require promulgation of revised NSPS's for municipal waste combustors by November 15, 1991 (promulgation is currently anticipated by August 1993).[33] Finally, the amendments set a new regulatory schedule for source categories that were listed under §111, but not regulated, prior to enactment of the amendments.[34]

4.2. New Source Review

Large new sources of air pollution (and, under certain conditions, major modifications to large existing sources) are subject to preconstruction review and permitting under the Clean Air Act. The nature of the permitting requirements depends upon whether the source is to be located in an area that attains, or has failed to attain, the NAAQS for the pollutant in question.

Sources located in attainment areas are subject to the prevention of significant deterioration (PSD) permit program; sources in nonattainment areas are subject to the nonattainment program.[35] The PSD program applies to sources that have the potential to emit over 250 tons per year (tpy) of a regulated pollutant, or over 100 tpy of a regulated pollutant if the source falls within one of 28 listed source categories.[36] The nonattainment program applies to sources that have the potential to emit at least 10-100 tpy of the nonattainment pollutant, depending upon the pollutant in question and the seriousness of the nonattainment problem in the area where the source is located.[37]

4.2.1 The PSD Program

Under the Clean Air Act, before one can construct a "major" (that is, 100/250 tpy) new source (or undertake a "major modification" of an existing

---

[31]CAA §111(b)(1)(B).

[32]CAA §407(c).

[33]CAA §129(a).

[34]CAA §111(f)(1).

[35]The PSD Program is contained in Title I, Part C, of the Clean Air Act, and the nonattainment program is contained in Title I, Part D of that law.

[36]*See* 40 C.F.R. §52.21(b)(1) (1990).

[37]*See, e.g.,* CAA §182(b)-(e).

major source) in an area that attains the NAAQS, one must obtain a permit under the PSD program.[38] In order to receive a PSD permit, the owner or operator of a proposed new source must show that the source (1) will comply with ambient air quality levels designed to prevent deterioration of air quality (the "PSD increments"), and (2) will employ "best available control technology" (BACT) for each pollutant regulated under the act that it will emit in "significant" amounts.[39] BACT is defined as the "maximum degree of [emission] reduction ... achievable," taking into account economic, energy, and environmental factors.[40] BACT must be at least as stringent as any NSPS applicable to the source category.

Traditionally, the BACT determination has been a matter of state discretion, based on a balancing of the economic, energy, and environmental impacts of alternative control technologies.[41] In December 1987, however, EPA issued guidance (referred to as the "top-down" BACT guidance) that, as applied, substantially restricted state discretion in making BACT determinations. In response to a judicial challenge, EPA agreed in 1991 to issue a *Federal Register* notice clarifying its position on BACT review. While a proposed rule clarifying BACT was scheduled to be issued in late 1992, there remains some question as to whether a proposal will in fact be issued.

BACT review applies to any regulated pollutant that a source has the potential to emit in a significant amount. Traditionally, BACT review has focused on *both* criteria pollutants and air toxics. The 1990 amendments to the act, however, state that substances listed under the new air toxics program are *not* subject to the PSD program.[42] Since the air toxics list is extensive (that is, 189 substances and compounds are currently listed), this provision should obviate the need for BACT review of regulated hazardous air pollutants once states revise their PSD programs in response to the 1990 amendments. However, states may also choose to continue to require such analyses under state law.

While the BACT determination is perhaps the most important and controversial aspect of PSD permitting, a variety of other issues also must be resolved in order to receive a permit to construct a new source, or to modify an existing source. As noted above, the applicant must show that the proposed source will not cause or contribute to exceeding either NAAQS or PSD increments.[43] The applicant must show that the proposed source will not adversely impact other air quality-related values, such as visibility. And state permitting authorities may require the applicant to consider the implications of any proposed BACT decision for control of air toxics.

---

[38]*See generally* 40 C.F.R. §52.21.

[39]"Significance" levels are provided at 40 C.F.R. §52.21(b)(23).

[40]CAA § 169(3).

[41]*See, e.g.*, 1980 PSD Workshop Manual I-B-2.

[42]CAA §112(b)(6).

[43]*See* CAA §§163, 166.

4.2.2 The Nonattainment Program

In areas that have not attained the NAAQS for a given pollutant (that is, "nonattainment" areas), new major stationary sources, or major modifications of existing major sources, must receive a nonattainment permit before construction can begin. A "major" source for purposes of the nonattainment program is generally one that has the potential to emit in excess of 100 tpy of a nonattainment pollutant. The 1990 amendments lower this threshold for areas with more serious nonattainment problems (for example, to 50 tpy for VOC and NO_x in serious ozone nonattainment areas, to 25 tpy for severe areas, and to 10 tpy for extreme areas). Moreover, in areas that attain NAAQS for some regulated pollutants but not for others, both PSD and nonattainment permits may be required.

States are responsible for implementing the nonattainment permit program. State permit programs must include, among other things, a requirement that major new or modified existing sources commit to achieve the "Lowest Achievable Emission Rate" (LAER). The LAER is to be based on "the most stringent emission limitation" contained in any SIP, or that is "achieved in practice" by the same or a similar source category, whichever is more stringent. If the owner or operator of the proposed source can demonstrate that the most stringent technology is not feasible for the proposed facility, the next most stringent level of control can be established as the LAER.

In order to ensure progress towards attainment of the NAAQS, the state permit program must also require that the proposed new or modified source offset its potential to emit nonattainment pollutants by securing emission reductions from nearby facilities at a greater than one-to-one ratio. In section CAA §173(a)(1)(A), the administrator is given authority to set rules for determining the "baseline" against which emission offsets are to be credited, and EPA has issued extensive guidance on this issue.[44] Moreover, under the Clean Air Act Amendments of 1990, the offset ratios that apply in ozone, CO, and PM-10 nonattainment areas increase as the nonattainment problem becomes more severe. For example, the offset ratio in ozone nonattainment areas varies between 1.1 and 1.5 to 1, according to the seriousness of the area's nonattainment problem.

Finally, the source owner or operator must certify that its other sources are in compliance (or on a schedule to comply) with all applicable air quality requirements, and that the benefits of the proposed source outweigh its environmental and social costs.[45]

4.3 The Reconstruction and Modification Rules

As noted above, new source requirements apply not only to new sources, but to existing sources that are "reconstructed" or "modified."

---

[44]*See, e.g.*, 51 Fed. Reg. 43814 (1986) (Emissions Trading Policy Statement); 40 C.F.R. Part 51, Appendix S.

[45]*See* CAA §173(a).

Reconstruction. EPA promulgated the "reconstruction" rule in 1975 to address projects designed to extend the useful life of existing industrial facilities.[46] The rule defines when a project to rebuild an existing facility becomes so extensive that it is substantially equivalent to replacing the facility "at the end of its useful life."[47] Significantly, the reconstruction rule applies only to the NSPS program, and *not* the PSD or nonattainment permit programs.

In general, work to rebuild or to replace parts of an existing facility triggers the reconstruction rule when the project involves expenditures that are 50 percent or more of the capital cost of a comparable new facility.[48] Triggering the reconstruction rule does not, however, automatically result in application of NSPS. Rather, recognizing that control technology standards developed for new facilities may not be appropriate for reconstructed facilities, EPA has provided that NSPS's will not be applied to reconstructed facilities where the NSPS's are shown to be technologically or economically infeasible, or where consideration of costs, remaining useful life, and potential emission reductions make it inappropriate to apply NSPS's.[49]

When EPA promulgated the reconstruction rule, it stated that it did not anticipate that many facilities would trigger reconstruction review, and that it would address more specific concerns with "life extension" of existing sources in rulemakings establishing NSPS's for specific source categories.[50] It is important, therefore, to examine the NSPS's rules applicable to individual source categories for further guidance on when capital expenditures trigger application of NSPS's.

Modification. Unlike the reconstruction rule, the modification rule can trigger application of the PSD and nonattainment permit programs as well as NSPS's. The modification rule has the same basic elements for all of these programs. First, there must be a "physical or operational change" at the source. Second, this change must "result in" an "increase in emissions" of a regulated pollutant. Third, the modification rules list specific activities (for example, routine repair, replacement, and maintenance) that do not constitute a modification, even if there is otherwise a physical or operational change that results in an emissions increase.

Application of the modification rule has been the subject of much controversy as a result of the so-called *WEPCo* decision.[51] Under the administrative determinations that led to this decision, EPA suggested that virtually *any* activity designed to restore lost capacity at an existing industrial facility (for example, as a result of equipment breakdown), and

---

[46] 40 Fed. Reg. 58417 (1975); 40 C.F.R. §60.15 (1989).

[47] 40 Fed. Reg. 58417 (1975).

[48] 40 C.F.R. §60.15(b)(1) (1989).

[49] 40 C.F.R. §60.15(b)(2), (f) (1989).

[50] 39 Fed. Reg. 36948 (1974).

[51] Wisconsin Electric Power Company ["*WEPCo*"] v. Reilly, 893 F.2d 901 (7th Cir. 1990).

that does not constitute "routine repair, replacement, or maintenance," would trigger NSPS's and must be preceded by preconstruction permit review. The U.S. Court of Appeals for the Seventh Circuit largely accepted EPA's position regarding NSPS's, but rejected key elements of its position regarding the PSD permit program.

While Congress made several attempts to address and to clarify the *WEPCo* decision in the 1990 amendments to the act, the final legislation contained no generic "fix." Administrator Reilly, however, committed to undertake administrative action to clarify the modification rule along the lines of the Administration's legislative proposal.[52] These clarifying rules were promulgated in July 1992.[53]

The final *WEPCo* rule has two parts. First, the preamble to the rule contains the Agency's interpretations of the existing modification rules. These interpretations confirm that the agency will in most respects return to its pre-*WEPCo* interpretations of the modification rules. For example, under this interpretive rule, the agency will not calculate an "emissions increase" in the case of a proposed modification based on a comparison of past actual emissions and future potential to emit, but rather will apply a past-to-future-actual comparison. Moreover, the agency will continue to apply an exclusion for pollution control projects under the new source permitting rules. These interpretive rulings are important since they apply to *all* industry, whereas the formal legislative rule discussed below applies only to large utility boilers.

Second, the agency clarified certain aspects of the modification rules as applied to large utility boilers subject to the acid deposition program (Title IV) of the 1990 amendments. This rule has several general characteristics. First, the rule confirms that new source permitting requirements will not be triggered when a facility has experienced equipment failure and has merely undertaken a project to return the facility to its former, representative production capacity. Second, while the rule confirms that pollution control projects do not trigger new source review, it tightens the traditional pollution control exclusion as applied to large utility boilers by calling for a showing of net environmental benefit in conjunction with such projects. Third, the rule confirms that the test for new source review is whether a specific project "results in" (that is, causes) an increase in emissions. As a result, where an emissions increase occurs as a result of an increase in system demand, new source review is not required.

5.0 SPECIFIC POLLUTION PROBLEMS

Besides establishing generally applicable air quality and control technology requirements, Congress in the Clean Air Act has addressed several specific pollution problems. The most important of these programs

---

[52]Letter from William K. Reilly, EPA, to Michael Boskin, Council of Economic Advisors (Oct. 26, 1990).

[53]57 Fed. Reg. 32314 (1992).

involve air toxics emissions, acid rain, visibility degradation, and chlorofluorocarbon (CFC) emissions. The act also addresses the special concerns presented by mobile source emissions.

5.1 Air Toxics

Congress in the 1990 amendments altered the scheme for regulation of air toxics under section 112 of the Clean Air Act from health-based to technology-based regulation. The following discussion summarizes the key elements of this new air toxics regulatory program.

5.1.1 Pollutants and Source Categories Subject to Regulation

Under the 1990 amendments, 189 substances will be regulated,[54] including both hazardous organics and metals. Moreover, substances can be added to or deleted from this list after rulemaking.

The act provides that any stationary source emitting more than 10 tons per year of any of the listed substances, or 25 tons of any combination of the substances, is considered a major source and is subject to regulation under the major source program. EPA must examine other sources for regulation under an "area source" program, which must be developed within five years of enactment (that is, by November 15, 1995).

In July 1992, EPA published a list of all major source categories and subcategories of hazardous air pollutants, such as oil refineries, chemical plants and the like, which are to be regulated under §112.[55] In September 1992, EPA followed this list of source categories with a draft schedule for promulgation of emission standards, which specifies when each of the listed source categories will be regulated over the next two-to-eight years.[56]

5.1.2 Maximum Achievable Emission Limitations

For each listed major source category, EPA must promulgate standards requiring the installation of technology that will result in the "maximum degree of reductions" that it determines is "achievable." (This requirement has been referred to as the "maximum achievable control technology," or "MACT," standard.) EPA is to base the standard on the best technology currently available for the source category in question, and these standards must be at least as stringent as the level achieved in practice by the best controlled source in the source category (for new source MACT standards) or for the best performing group of sources (for existing source MACT standards).[57]

The first proposed MACT standards, referred to as the hazardous organic National Emission Standards for Hazardous Air Pollutants (NE-

---

[54]*See* CAA §112(b). Prior to 1990, EPA had addressed 33 substances under §112. *See* 40 C.F.R. Part 61 (1990).

[55]57 Fed. Reg. 31576 (1992); *see* CAA §112(c).

[56]57 Fed. Reg. 44147 (1992).

[57]*See* CAA §112(d).

SHAPS) or "HON," were signed by the EPA administrator in November 1992. This proposal addresses emissions of 149 air toxics from 370 synthetic organic chemical manufacturers, and from seven types of non-synthetic organic chemical manufacturing processes, including styrene/butadiene rubber production, polybutadiene production, chlorine production, pesticide production, chlorinated hydrocarbon use, pharmaceutical production, and miscellaneous butadiene use. The proposed standards require control of emissions from distillation, reactor and air oxidation process vents, waste water operations, storage vessels, transfer operations, and equipment leaks.

EPA must also establish regulations allowing exemptions from the MACT standards for existing sources under certain conditions. For example, if a source demonstrates that it has achieved a voluntary reduction of 90 percent or more in emissions of a hazardous air pollutant before proposal of the MACT standard (95 percent for hazardous air pollutants that are particulates), it may be eligible for an extension of the MACT compliance deadline.[58] Final rules implementing this early reduction program were signed by the EPA administrator in November 1992. According to the agency, 66 commitments from 32 companies at 47 plants had been made to the early reductions program as of November 1992.

5.1.3 Residual Risks

Because the MACT standards are technology– rather than health–based, the 1990 amendments provide for a second phase of regulatory controls aimed at protecting public health with an "ample margin of safety." This health-based inquiry would generally take place no later than eight years after a MACT standard had been established for a source category. For known or suspected carcinogens, further control under this subsection is required if the MACT standard does not reduce life time risk to the most exposed individual to a level of less than one-in-one million.[59]

5.1.4 Control of Accidental Releases

The 1990 amendments also require EPA to promulgate regulations to control and to prevent accidental releases of regulated hazardous pollutants or any other extremely hazardous substances.[60] Owners and operators of facilities at which such substances are present in more than a threshold quantity will have to prepare risk management plans for each substance used at the facility. EPA may also require annual audits and safety inspections to prevent leaks and other episodic releases.

5.2 Acid Rain

One of the major new regulatory programs of the 1990 amendments concerns the control of SO_2 and nitrogen oxides (NO_x), precursors of acid deposition. The centerpiece of Title IV of the 1990 amendments is the

---

[58] *See* CAA §112(i)(5).

[59] *See* CAA §112(f).

[60] *See* CAA §112(r).

establishment of an emissions allowance and trading program for SO_2. EPA has recently concluded several rulemakings containing the basic provisions governing this new system.

For example, on October 26, 1992, EPA issued final rules addressing acid rain permits, SO_2 emission allowance tracking and trading, emissions monitoring, excess emissions penalties and offset plans, and the administrative appeals process.[61] EPA also issued the standard forms needed for permit applications and compliance plans. Final SO_2 allowance allocation rules are expected in early 1993.

Sources subject to emission limitations under Title IV will be assigned SO_2 allowances under formulae prescribed in the statute.[62] An allowance is defined as an authorization to emit one ton of SO_2. A plant's annual SO_2 emissions will not be allowed to exceed the allowances allocated to or otherwise acquired by a plant for a given calendar year, or the plant's owner/operator will be subject to penalties that are designed to be more costly than compliance. The 1990 amendments specify that allowances are not a property right and can be limited, revoked or modified.

The act makes specific SO_2 allowance allocations to Phase I utility boilers (that is, boilers that must meet reduction targets by January 1, 1995), and specifies formulae for other boilers. EPA is currently applying these formulae to develop unit-specific allowance allocations.[63] A unit's allowance allocation is made part of its Title IV permit. In addition, source owners and operators must submit compliance plans addressing implementation schedules, including whether the source owner or operator intends to obtain additional allowances in order to comply with the act.[64] For Phase I utility boilers, permit applications and proposed compliance plans are due by February 15, 1993.

EPA's Title IV regulations set up an allowance auction to be held annually.[65] Anyone eligible to hold allowances may purchase at the auction. In addition, holders of allowances can also contribute to the auction and receive a pro rata share of the monies collected. The act specifies that the auction is to be conducted so as to ensure the orderly functioning of the national market for allowances and to preserve competition in the electric power industry. EPA is given the option of discontinuing or altering the frequency of the auction by undergoing another rulemaking if it determines that an auction is not necessary.

The act also establishes a reserve of allowances that owners and operators of new utility units can purchase from the agency as a last resort if they cannot obtain them elsewhere. To be eligible to purchase from the reserve, owners and operators will have to show that they have made

---

[61] 40 C.F.R. Parts 72–78

[62] *See* CAA §403; 57 Fed. Reg. 29940 (1992) (proposed allowance allocation rule).

[63] *See* 57 Fed. Reg. 29940 (1992).

[64] CAA §408.

[65] *See* CAA §416.

honest efforts to purchase from other allowance holders. Moreover, owners and operators of new units must make a "vigorous showing" that allowances are not otherwise available. The regulations implementing the reserve system are to set strict criteria for establishing the requisite showing for access to the reserve.[66]

The agency is also working on regulations addressing criteria and procedures for allowing owners and operators of industrial and small utility sources to opt voluntarily into the Title IV program, by electing certain sources normally not eligible to receive allowances.[67] The purpose of this section is to increase the amount of allowances available, while expanding the scope of sources subject to the Title IV control requirements. Sources that opt into the program, of course, would be subject to all of the permitting and monitoring requirements of this program.

Title IV of the act also addresses emissions of nitrogen oxides (NO_x). Under §407 of the act, EPA was to establish allowable emission rates for NO_x emissions from coal-fired electric utility boilers by May 1992. These rules were proposed in November 1992, and are scheduled to be promulgated in mid-to-late 1993.

By January 1, 1994, EPA is to undertake a study of whether sources should be allowed to exchange NO_x for SO_2 emissions.[68] Trading of NO_x for SO_x emissions is not allowed without additional legislation.

5.3 Visibility Protection

5.3.1 Best Available Retrofit Technology

In the 1977 Clean Air Act Amendments, Congress established a national goal of eliminating "any" manmade visibility impairment in "mandatory Class I areas,"[69] and required that states make "reasonable progress" towards attaining that goal. To achieve that progress, states are to develop through the SIP process requirements for best available retrofit technology (BART) and long term strategies that address sources contributing to visibility impairments in Class I areas.

In 1980, EPA adopted regulations addressing SIP requirements for visibility impairment, and directed states to focus regulatory attention on sources that cause "plume blight" (that is, visible plumes in a Class I area). Another more controversial issue—the regulation of sources contributing to "regional haze"—was specifically deferred.

During the 1980s, EPA found that, for all but one state and one Class I area, there were no sources to which plume blight could be "reasonably attributed." Accordingly, in reviewing the adequacy of SIPs, EPA concluded

---

[66]*See* CAA §416.

[67]CAA §410.

[68]CAA §403(c).

[69]Mandatory class I areas include international parks, national wilderness areas and national memorial parks which exceed 5,000 acres in size, and national parks which exceed 6,000 acres in size, if the areas were in existence on August 7, 1977. CAA §162(a).

that the 1980 visibility rules could be satisfied by incorporation of procedural requirements into SIPs to ensure that visibility impairment would be addressed (for example, through establishment of BART limits) if it were to occur. For Arizona and the Grand Canyon, however, EPA concluded that visibility impairment could be "reasonably attributed" to the Navajo Generating Station (an electric utility plant), and therefore initiated a regulatory program to address this issue.

In 1987, EPA undertook a study involving the release of an artificial tracer from the stacks of the Navajo Generating Station. Based on this study and extensive public comments, EPA published a formal BART rule on October 3, 1991 that calls for 90 percent scrubbing on a plant-wide, annual average basis.[70] This proceeding establishes an important precedent for future efforts to regulate existing sources that contribute to visibility impairment.

5.3.2 Visibility Impairment and the New Source Review Program

Under the deterioration PSD permit program, before a permitting authority can issue a permit authorizing construction of a new or modified source, it must consider whether emissions from the proposed source "will have an adverse impact on air quality-related values (*including visibility*)" (emphasis added).[71] Based on this provision, Federal Land Managers (FLMs) have recently raised the issue of visibility impairment in a number of new source permit proceedings. The Forest Service, for example, has developed a workbook to guide local FLMs in deciding whether proposed new sources would have an adverse impact on the air quality-related values of Class I areas. This workbook indicates that current air quality in many Class I areas is already in the "adverse" category, and advises FLMs to question whether the licensing of any new source might further contribute to these "adverse" conditions. The National Park Service has taken a similar approach (for example, with respect to facilities proposed for the vicinity of the Shenandoah National Park), urging that proposed new facilities obtain offsetting emission reductions to ensure that there is no contribution to adverse effects on visibility.

5.3.3 Visibility Impairment and the 1990 Amendments

The 1990 amendments to the act add to the regulatory program for visibility in several respects. First, Congress authorized a $40 million, 5-year research program to evaluate what more, if anything, ought to be done about Class I area visibility impairment. The decision on further regulation is to be based, in part, on an assessment of whether compliance with other programs of the 1990 amendments (for example, the acid rain program) would solve air quality problems in the Class I areas. Interim

---

[70]56 Fed. Reg. 50172 (1991).
[71]*See* CAA §165(d)

findings from this study are to be issued by EPA by November 1993, and the final report is to be issued by late 1995.

Parallel to these efforts, Congress established a procedure for creating Visibility Transport Commissions made up of governors from states with sources that contribute to interstate air pollution in Class I areas. These commissions are to produce recommendations about the need for additional visibility regulation within four years after their creation.

5.4 Stratospheric Ozone Protection

New Title VI of the Clean Air Act Amendments of 1990 addresses stratospheric ozone depletion and global warming. While the 1977 amendments to the Clean Air Act had dealt with this issue in less comprehensive fashion, Title VI repeals and replaces those provisions by establishing a program for the phaseout of ozone depleting substances generally along the lines called for by the *Montreal Protocol*.

Pursuant to Title VI, Congress has established initial lists of so-called Class I substances (that is, chlorofluorocarbons, halons, carbon tetrachloride, and methyl chloroform) and Class II substances (that is, hydrochlorofluorocarbons). EPA is directed to list additional substances as warranted, and to assign ozone-depletion and global warming "potential values" to each listed substance.

Beginning in 1991, it is unlawful for any person to produce any Class I substance in an annual quantity greater than certain percentages specified in a table set forth in the statute. Exceptions are made for "essential uses" of methyl chloroform, for medical devices that employ Class I substances, and where aviation safety (*for example*, nondestructive testing for metal fatigue and engine corrosion) demands the use of such substances. Beginning in 2000 (or 2002 for methyl chloroform), all production of Class I substances is prohibited. Title VI also calls for the complete phaseout of the use and production of Class II substances (again, with an exception for medical devices) by 2030. The Bush Administration initiated efforts to accelerate this schedule for phasing out ozone-depleting substances.

EPA is further directed to establish transferable "allowances" for the production and use of Class I and Class II substances, and to issue regulations concerning (1) the safe use, recycling, disposal, and release of Class I and Class II substances from appliances and industrial process refrigeration, (2) the servicing of motor vehicle air conditioners, (3) the eventual prohibition of nonessential products using Class I and Class II substances, and (4) the labeling of products made with or containing Class I and Class II substances. Title VI also orders EPA to develop a "safe alternatives" policy.

While EPA has issued final rules for the Class I substances phaseout and the allowance program, the agency has missed several other regulatory deadlines under Title VI. Under the statute, on July 1, 1992, it became unlawful for anyone to knowingly vent or release a Class I or Class II substance from an appliance or industrial process refrigeration. A proposed rule for the implementation of this requirement, however, has not yet been issued. Similarly, while proposed rules have been issued regarding nonessential products (in January 1992) and labeling (in May 1992), final rules have not yet been promulgated. A final rule on the servicing of motor vehicle air conditioners was issued in July 1992.

5.5 Mobile Sources, Fuels, and Fuel Additives

Besides addressing stationary source issues, the 1990 amendments substantially tighten mobile source emission standards. The amendments require automobile manufacturers to reduce tailpipe emissions of hydrocarbons (HC) and NO_x, for example, by 35 percent and 60 percent, respectively, beginning with 40 percent of the vehicles sold in 1994 and increasing to 100 percent of vehicles sold in 1996.[72] The amendments also require a further 50 percent reduction in mobile source emissions of these pollutants beginning in 2003, unless EPA finds that these more stringent standards are not necessary, technologically feasible, or cost effective.

In addition to establishing new mobile source emission standards, the amendments establish two new fuel-related programs designed to achieve emission reductions.[73] The first of these fuel programs—the reformulated fuel program—requires the use of reformulated gasoline in certain CO and severe ozone nonattainment areas beginning in 1992 and 1995, respectively. Among other things, reformulated gasoline must be blended to achieve reductions in volatile organic compounds and toxic tailpipe emissions. Regulations implementing this provision were proposed in July 1991, and supplemented in April 1992.

The second fuel program is the clean fuel vehicle program. Under this program, automobiles operating on "clean alternative fuels" (for example, methanol, ethanol, natural gas, and reformulated gasoline) must meet even more stringent emission standards. The clean fuel vehicle program will be implemented in two ways: (1) by establishing a California pilot test program which requires the production and sale of 300,000 clean fuel vehicles annually by 1999; and (2) by requiring operators of centrally fueled fleets of ten or more vehicles in certain CO and ozone nonattainment areas to purchase and use clean fuel vehicles beginning in 1998.

While Congress clearly envisioned the continued use of traditional emission control technology to achieve the emission reductions required by the amendments, the success or failure of the new program for clean fuels will have a dramatic impact on future emission control programs throughout the country.

6.0 THE OPERATING PERMIT PROGRAM

Prior to 1990, the only permit program contained in the Clean Air Act was the preconstruction permitting program for new and modified sources.

---

[72]*See* CAA §202.
[73]*See* CAA §§211(k) and 241-50.

Existing sources were regulated through provisions established in SIPs, rather than through source-specific operating permits.[74]

Title V of the 1990 Clean Air Act Amendments changed the basic approach to source-specific regulation under the act, by requiring each state to develop and implement an operating permit program for *all* sources of air pollution. The purpose of this new permit program is to consolidate in a single document all of the federal and state regulations applicable to a source, in order to facilitate source compliance and enforcement. Permit programs will be administered by the states, but EPA will retain authority to review and to approve not only the overall permit program, but also each individual permit issued by the state.

In July 1992, EPA issued final regulations addressing the minimum requirements for state operating permit programs.[75] Based on these minimum requirements, states must develop and submit Title V operating permit programs to EPA for approval by November 1993. EPA must act on those programs within one year of submittal (that is, by November 1994). Once the state permit programs have received EPA approval, sources have one year to submit permit applications. States may, however, require the submittal of permit applications even before final EPA approval of state programs.

Accordingly, the next two-to-three years will be critical to the implementation of the Title V operating permit program. To prepare for this new program, it is important to understand the minimum program criteria set forth by EPA in the recently promulgated 40 C.F.R. Part 70 rules.

6.1 Applicability

Section 70.3(a) of the regulations requires a state program to provide for the permitting of at least the following sources:

1. Any major source, defined in section 70.2 of the rules as any stationary source belonging to a single major industrial grouping and that is:
    (i) a major source under section 112 of the act;
    (ii) a major source of air pollutants that directly emits or has the potential to emit 100 tons per year or more of any air pollutant (including any major source of fugitive emissions of any such pollutant); and
    (iii) a major source as defined in Part D of Title I of the act.
2. Any source subject to a standard, limitation, or other requirement under section 111 of the act;

---

[74]While EPA issued guidance in the mid-1980s addressing how a state, through its SIP, could create a federally enforceable operating permit program, few states took advantage of this guidance.

[75]57 Fed. Reg. 32295 (1992).

3. Any source subject to a standard or other requirement under section 112 of the act (a source is not required to obtain a permit solely because it is subject to regulation under section 112(r) dealing with accidental release prevention);
4. Any affected source under Title IV of the act; and
5. Any source in a source category designated by EPA.

A state may defer for five years Title V regulation of nonmajor sources. EPA plans to complete a rulemaking to consider further deferral for or permanent exemption of specific categories of nonmajor sources within five years of the date on which the agency first approves a program deferring regulation of such sources.[76] Section 70.5(c) also allows the states to develop exemptions for insignificant activities because of size, emission levels, or production rate. The rules preclude establishment of exemptions, however, if they would interfere with the determination or imposition of any applicable requirement or the calculation of fees.[77]

6.2 Permit Applications

A source subject to the Title V program must submit a complete permit application—including a compliance plan describing how the source plans to comply with all applicable requirements—to the state permitting authority within one year after the permit program becomes effective.[78] An interim, partial, or full permit program becomes effective upon approval by EPA.[79] If EPA establishes a permit program upon failure of the state to submit an approvable program, the program becomes effective upon promulgation. EPA is currently working on a federal operating permit program, which will appear as 40 C.F.R. Part 71 and which will apply when states fail to implement Title V.

The permitting authority must determine whether an application is complete within sixty days of receipt. Unless the permitting authority requests additional information or otherwise notifies the applicant of incompleteness within this time period, the application is deemed complete.[80]

A permit application must contain all information listed in §70.5(c), including (i) all emissions of pollutants for which the source is major and all emissions of regulated air pollutants; (ii) identification of all points of emissions; (iii) emissions rate in tons-per-year and in other terms necessary to establish compliance; (iv) description of air pollution control equipment; and (v) identification of all air pollution control requirements. A state permit program must provide for standard application forms.

---

[76] *See* 40 C.F.R. §70.3(b)(1) and 57 Fed. Reg. 32253.

[77] *See* 57 Fed. Reg. 32273.

[78] *See* §70.5(a)(1), §503(a) of the Act. However, section 70.5(a)(1)(i) stipulates that the permitting authority may establish an earlier date for submission of a permit application.

[79] *See* §70.4(g).

[80] *See* §70.7(a)(4).

In general, if a source submits a timely and complete permit application, failure to have a permit is not considered a violation of the requirement to operate with a permit until the permitting authority takes final action on the application.[81]

6.3 Permit Issuance

The permitting authority must take final action within 18 months after receiving a complete application.[82] However, anticipating the administrative burden of establishing the new permitting program, Congress section 503(c) provided for a three-year schedule for acting on initial Title V permit applications. Under §70.4(b)(11), the permitting authority must act on one third of the permit applications received in the first year of the program in each year over a three year period. EPA makes clear in the preamble to the rules that "act on" means final action rather than initial review.[83]

In general, the permitting authority must issue permits for a fixed term of no more than five years. Each permit must include the elements listed in §70.4(a), including: (i) applicable emission limitations and standards, (ii) monitoring and related recordkeeping and reporting requirements; (iii) a permit condition prohibiting emissions of sulfur dioxide exceeding any allowances held under Title IV of the act; (iv) a severability clause to ensure continued validity of remaining permit requirements if any provisions are challenged; (v) a statement that the permit may be modified, revoked, reopened, and reissued or terminated for cause; and (vi) a provision to ensure that a source pays fees consistent with an approved state permitting fee schedule.

The permit also must contain the compliance requirements listed in §70.6(c), including (i) compliance certification, testing, monitoring, reporting, and recordkeeping requirements to assure compliance with the permit (including any terms needed to "fill gaps" in applicable compliance requirements); (ii) inspection and entry requirements for permitting authority officials; and (iii) a schedule of compliance and regular progress reports consistent with that schedule.

Finally, the permit must "specifically designate as not being federally enforceable . . . any terms and conditions included in the permit that are not required under the act or any of its applicable requirements." Such terms and conditions are not subject to Title V requirements regarding permit issuance, permit modification, and EPA and affected state review. Any terms not otherwise designated, however, *are federally enforceable.*

6.4 EPA and Affected State Review

Section 70.8(a) requires the permitting authority to provide to EPA a copy of each permit application, draft permit, and final permit issued

---

[81]*See* §70.7(b).

[82]*See* §70.7(a)(2).

[83]*See* 57 Fed. Reg. 32266.

under Part 70. If EPA objects to a proposed permit within 45 days of receipt, the permitting authority may not issue the permit. Under section 70.8(c), EPA must object to issuance of any proposed permit deemed not to be in compliance with the requirements of Part 70. If the permitting authority fails to revise and resubmit the proposed permit to EPA within 90 days of receipt of the objection notice, EPA must issue or deny the permit.[84]

If EPA does not object to the proposed permit, any person may petition the agency to object within sixty days after expiration of the 45-day EPA review period. The petition must be based on objections to the permit that were raised with reasonable specificity during the public comment period, unless the petitioner demonstrates that it was impracticable to raise such objections within that period, or unless the grounds for the objection arose after that period. If EPA objects, the permitting authority may not issue the permit until the objection has been resolved. A petition for review does not stay the effectiveness of a permit if it was issued after the EPA's original 45-day review period.[85]

The permitting authority must also give notice of each draft permit to any affected state on or before the time public notice is provided.[86] An affected state is one whose air quality may be affected *and* that is contiguous to the state in which the source is located or within 50 miles of the source.

6.5 The Permit Shield

Section 504(f) of the act provides that compliance with the permit shall be deemed compliance with applicable provisions of the act *if* the permit includes the applicable requirements, *or* the permitting authority makes a determination that such requirements are not applicable and the determination is included in the permit.

In the final Title V rules, EPA has adopted a narrow interpretation of the permit shield. Section 70.6(f) provides that the permitting authority may include expressly in a permit a statement that compliance with the conditions of the permit shall be deemed compliance with any applicable requirements *"as of the date of issuance"* (emphasis added) *if* (i) the applicable requirements are specifically identified in the permit, *or* (ii) the permitting authority determines in writing that other requirements specifically identified do not apply to the source and the permit includes that determination. If the permit does not expressly state that a permit shield applies, then no shield will be presumed.

6.6 Permit Revision and Operational Flexibility

In the Title V rules, EPA has established several categories of permit revisions. These requirements were the subject of intense debate throughout

---

[84]*See* §70.8(c).
[85]*See* §70.8(d).
[86]*See* §70.8(b)(1).

the rulemaking, with industry generally arguing for limited review of permit revisions and environmental groups and state agencies in favor of more extensive review. At the heart of this debate is the issue of how much flexibility a source should have to change its operations without having to undertake a full-blown permit proceeding.

6.6.1 Administrative Permit Amendments

An administrative permit amendment is a revision that corrects typographical errors, identifies a change in name or related information, requires more frequent monitoring, allows for an ownership change, incorporates into a permit requirements from preconstruction review permits under an EPA-approved program, or makes a similar change.[87] The permitting authority must act on an administrative permit amendment application within 60 days after receipt. No public notice is required for administrative amendments.[88]

Administrative amendments may be implemented immediately upon the filing of an application. No permit shield is available for administrative amendments, except where the terms of a preconstruction permit are incorporated into a Title V permit through the administrative amendment procedure (this can be done only where the state's preconstruction permit program incorporates all of the procedural protections of the Title V program).

6.6.2 Permit Modifications

A permit modification is any revision that cannot be accomplished as an administrative amendment. The rules require states to "provide adequate, streamlined, and reasonable procedures for expeditiously processing permit modifications." States may do so by adopting the procedures outlined in the Title V rules or through other procedures that are "substantially equivalent."[89]

Minor Permit Modifications. Minor permit modifications are subject to limited review requirements and more streamlined procedures.[90] The minor permit modification procedures can be used only for modifications that do *not* (i) violate any requirement applicable to the source; (ii) involve significant changes to existing monitoring, reporting, or recordkeeping requirements; (iii) require or change a case-by-case determination of an emission limitation or other standard; (iv) seek to change or establish a permit term or condition for which there is no corresponding underlying applicable requirement; and (v) constitute a significant permit modification under the state program (see below).

---

[87] *See* §70.7(d).

[88] *See* §70.7(d)(3)(i).

[89] *See* §70.7(e)(1).

[90] *See* 70.7(e)(2).

Within five working days of receipt of a minor permit modification application, the permitting authority must notify EPA and affected states of receipt of the application. EPA has 45 days to review the application. Within 90 days after receipt of the application or 15 days after the end of EPA's 45-day review period, whichever occurs later, the permitting authority must issue or deny the modification or make a finding that the modification is not subject to the minor modification procedures.[91]

The state may allow sources to implement the changes identified in a minor permit application immediately, albeit at the risk of the source owner or operator. Under section 70.7(e)(3), a series of minor modifications can be grouped together for processing if they fall below certain emission thresholds. States may not provide a permit shield for minor modifications.

Significant Modifications. Significant modification procedures must be used for modifications that do not qualify as minor modifications or as administrative amendments.[92] The state must determine what constitutes a significant change. The rules specify that, at a minimum, every significant change in existing monitoring permit terms or conditions and every relaxation of reporting or recordkeeping permit terms or conditions shall be considered significant.

Significant permit modifications are subject to the procedural requirements applicable to permit issuance and renewal, including the requirements for public participation and review by affected states and EPA. The permitting authority must design the review process to complete review of "the majority of significant permit modifications within nine months after receipt of a complete application."[93]

6.6.3 Operational Flexibility

Section 502(b)(10) of the act requires state permit programs to include provisions to allow changes within a permitted facility without requiring a permit revision, if (1) the changes are not modifications under Title I of the act, (2) they do not exceed the emissions allowable under the permit, and (3) the source gives EPA and the permitting authority written notice of the change at least seven days in advance (unless the permitting authority sets a different time for emergencies). Implementation of this provision has been controversial, with state agencies and environmental groups arguing for public notice and agency review.

The final Title V regulations include operational flexibility in the mandatory elements for a state permit program.[94] The rules include the following three means of providing operational flexibility:

---

[91] *See* §70.7(e)(2)(iv).
[92] *See* §70.7(e)(4).
[93] *See* §70.7(e)(4)(ii).
[94] *See* §70.4(b)(12).

- The rules stipulate that the program *shall* allow permitted sources to make §502(b)(10) operational changes without requiring a permit revision (operational changes are changes that are not modifications under Title I of the act, that do not relax monitoring or reporting requirements, and that do not exceed the emissions allowable under the permit).

- The rules *allow* programs to provide for permitted sources to trade increases and decreases in emissions in the permitted facility, where the applicable SIP provides for such emissions trades but the permit does not, without requiring a permit revision.

- The program *must* require the permitting authority to issue permits that contain terms and conditions allowing for the trading of emissions increases and decreases in the facility solely for the purpose of complying with a federally enforceable emissions cap that is established in the permit independent of other applicable requirements.

6.6.4 Off-Permit Operations

Section 70.4(b)(14) authorizes states to allow changes that are not addressed or prohibited by the permit to be made without a permit revision. Under this section, each change must meet all applicable requirements and may not violate any existing permit term or condition. Moreover, sources must provide contemporaneous written notice of the change.

6.6.5 Alternative Operating Scenarios

By far the best way to ensure operational flexibility is to write a permit that allows operation under any reasonably anticipated operating scenario. Section 70.6(a)(9) specifically requires states to include in Title V permit programs the authority to issue permits that include alternative operating scenarios. A source owner or operator would merely have to give notice of a change in operating scenarios, and no permit revision would be required. In addition, in the preamble to the final Title V rules, EPA recognizes that an appropriate way to avoid the need for permit revisions is to base permit terms and conditions on reasonably conservative assumptions regarding source emissions and operations.

6.7 Permit Fees

Section 70.9(b) requires states to establish a fee schedule that results in collection of revenue sufficient to cover permit program costs. The costs to be covered are listed in §70.9(b)(1). EPA will assume that the fees are adequate to cover costs if the fees are equal to $25 per year multiplied by the total tons of the *actual* emissions of each regulated pollutant emitted.[95]

---

[95]*See* §70.9(b)(2).

The fees must be increased annually by the percentage increase in the Consumer Price Index.[96]

A state fee schedule may include emissions fees, application fees, service-based fees or other types of fees.[97] The permitting authority must demonstrate that the fee schedule selected will result in the collection of fees sufficient to meet program requirements.

7.0 ENFORCEMENT OF THE CLEAN AIR ACT

The 1990 amendments to the Clean Air Act give EPA and the courts much broader authority to enforce the substantive provisions of the act, and significantly increase the civil and criminal penalties for violations.

7.1 Civil Enforcement

One of the most significant changes in civil enforcement under the 1990 amendments to the act is the ability of the administrator to bring administrative enforcement actions against violators directly without going through the Department of Justice (DOJ) and the courts. The administrative enforcement provisions, modeled after similar provisions in the Clean Water Act, authorize the administrator to impose administrative penalties of $200,000 or more if the administrator and the attorney general agree that a stiffer penalty is appropriate. The administrator must give written notice to the alleged violator. The violator then has 30 days within which to request an adjudicatory hearing. Administrative enforcement is attractive to EPA because it not only allows EPA to avoid having to coordinate first with DOJ, but also enables EPA to reach agreements with violators more quickly than in litigation.

The amendments also authorize the agency to establish a "field citation" program for minor violations. This program would allow agency officials inspecting a facility to issue environmental "traffic tickets" with fines of up to $5,000 per day per violation. Violators may request a hearing or simply pay the fine.

In addition to expanding the Agency's authority to enforce the act, the amendments also authorize private citizens to seek civil penalties for violations of the act. Under the pre-1990 act, when citizens brought suits against EPA for failure to perform a nondiscretionary act or against a particular source for violations of the statute, the court only had authority to order EPA to take action or to order the source to comply. The statute now enables courts to assess civil penalties in citizen suits, the money from which will be deposited into a fund to help finance EPA's enforcement actions. As under the original citizen suit provision, plaintiffs must provide at least 60 days notice of the action to the administrator, the state, and the alleged violator.

---

[96]*See* §70.9(b)(2)(iv).
[97]*See* §70.9(b)(3).

To underscore how serious Congress is about enforcement of the Clean Air Act, it has authorized EPA to pay a "bounty" of up to $10,000 to anyone who provides information that leads to a criminal conviction or civil penalty.

7.2 Criminal Penalties

The Clean Air Act imposes criminal liability on "any person" who knowingly violates the statute, and makes a knowing violation of the act a felony offense. Significantly, the definition of "person" includes individuals as well as corporations and partnerships, and while some enforcement provisions can only be enforced against "senior management personnel" or "corporate officers," the knowing violation provisions of the act can be enforced against *anyone* involved in the violation. The 1990 amendments have increased fines to $250,000 per day per violation and up to 5 years in jail. Corporations are subject to even larger fines, up to $500,000 per violation.

The amendments have also expanded the crimes related to record-keeping. Individuals are subject to fines of up to $250,000 and two years in jail not only for making false statements to the agency, but also for failing to file or maintain records or reports required under the act. Corporations face fines of up to $500,000 for the same violation. This provision is particularly important for Title V permittees, because the Clean Air Act requires each permittee to certify at least once a year that the permitted facility "is in compliance with any applicable permit, and to promptly report any deviations from permit requirements . . . ."[98]

Knowing failure to pay any fee owed to the government under the act, such as permit fees, is also a criminal act and is punishable by fines of up to $250,000 and one year in jail for individuals and fines of up to $500,000 for corporations. Penalties are doubled for repeat offenders.

Two new sections of the Clean Air Act impose criminal penalties for *knowing or negligent* release of air toxics which place another person in "imminent danger of death or serious bodily injury." An individual who *knowingly* releases any hazardous air pollutant or any "extremely hazardous substance" which places another person in "imminent danger of death or serious bodily injury" is subject to fines of up to $250,000 per day and up to 15 years imprisonment. Corporations may be fined up to $1 million per day. This provision requires actual knowledge that the release placed others in imminent danger of death or serious bodily injury. Lack of actual knowledge, however, does not let a violator altogether off the hook. The statute also imposes criminal liability on persons who *negligently* place others in imminent danger of death or serious bodily harm.

An individual who negligently releases any air toxic which places another person in "imminent danger of death or serious bodily injury" is subject to fines of up to $100,000 and up to one year in jail. Corporations may

---

[98]CAA §503(b)(2).

be fined up to $200,000. Because it criminalizes negligent behavior, this provision has serious implications for anyone with responsibility for environmental compliance and creates a particular need for effective compliance procedures and a clear delineation of responsibilities for ensuring compliance.

In addition to stiffer criminal penalties for violations of the Clean Air Act, Congress has required EPA to substantially increase the number of criminal investigators to enforce all environmental laws. The Pollution Prosecution Act of 1990 requires EPA to have at least 200 trained criminal investigators by October 1995.

7.3 Compliance Audits

In light of the expansion of criminal liability under the act, any company whose activities are subject to environmental regulation is well-advised to implement an internal compliance program. Regular comprehensive audits will reduce the chance of criminal actions against the company by enabling the company to detect and correct problems early on and will be considered a mitigating factor by a court imposing penalties.

A common concern in connection with environmental audits is how to deal with violations once they are discovered and whether the company must report them to the agency. Title V specifically requires permittees to report any deviation from a permit requirement to the agency, and failure to do so carries civil and criminal penalties of its own. A comprehensive internal compliance program, however, can reduce a permittee's potential liability for violations.

The Department of Justice recently released guidelines on the factors prosecutors should consider in making criminal enforcement decisions under federal environmental statutes. The guidelines state that it is the policy of the agency to *encourage* self-auditing and voluntary disclosure of environmental violations by the regulated community. To that end, the agency lists several factors that will weigh against criminal enforcement action including regular, comprehensive environmental audits, timely voluntary disclosure of violations, honest efforts to remedy noncompliance, an effective internal disciplinary system, and prompt, honest efforts to reach compliance agreements with federal and state authorities. Thus, although the company will have an affirmative duty to report violations of the act when it discovers them, voluntary disclosure and cooperation with enforcement authorities should mitigate against enforcement action based on those violations.

8.0 CONCLUSION

The Clean Air Act as amended in 1990 contains numerous complex regulatory requirements. Over the next decade, EPA will be faced with implementation responsibilities that far surpass those that have been assigned to virtually any other administrative agency. The magnitude of EPA's regulatory responsibilities is reflected in EPA's July 1992 update to its "Implementation Strategy for the Clean Air Act Amendments of 1990" (a planning document originally released by the agency in January 1991). The July 1992 update lists 65 proposed and final actions the agency had taken in response to the 1990 amendments, and an additional 141 activities scheduled to take place by December 1993. As can be seen, the Agency's regulatory agenda will continue for the foreseeable future to be heavily influenced by Clean Air Act implementation activities.

Putting in place the numerous new programs called for by the 1990 amendments will of necessity foster the development of new approaches to rulemaking and new administrative procedures. The recently enacted legislation on negotiated rulemaking,[99] for example, is receiving much attention in proceedings to implement the act. The Federal Advisory Committee Act[100] will receive close scrutiny as the agency attempts to integrate formal and informal advisory committees into the traditional rulemaking structure. Interpretive rulings, policy guidance, and adjudication will increasingly be used to implement general statutory requirements as statutory deadlines make it increasingly difficult for the agency to conduct rulemaking.

As a practical matter, these developments will call on those affected by the Clean Air Act to become involved earlier than ever before in the implementation process. This will require more careful monitoring of agency priorities and schedules in order to identify issues that may be of interest before formal regulatory proceedings are announced. The flexibility needed for reasonable implementation of the act may come, in the final analysis, from the informed exercise of discretion by states implementing federal standards and guidance.

Finally, enforcement of environmental laws will receive more attention as the rules implementing the 1990 amendments are put in place. Owners and operators of industrial facilities will need to define their compliance obligations promptly and thoroughly, and to develop appropriate compliance/audit strategies.

In sum, as the 1990 amendments are implemented, clean air regulation will have a greater impact on day-to-day business decisions than perhaps any other piece of environmental legislation. Given the breadth of the act and of the new EPA enforcement powers, comprehensive environmental planning will be crucial to sound business decisions.

For a more definitive discussion of this topic, the reader is referred to the Clean Air Handbook *and related books and courses listed at the end of this book.*

---

[99]Public Law No. 101-648 (November 29, 1990).

[100]5 U.S.C.A. App. 2 §§1 *et seq.*

Chapter 6

WATER POLLUTION CONTROL

J. Gordon Arbuckle
Patton Boggs & Blow
Denver, Colorado
Washington, D.C.

1.0 OVERVIEW

Federal Water Pollution Control Law seeks to protect one of the major environmental media—surface water—by requiring that the discharge of pollutants to those waters be controlled or prevented.

The water pollution regulatory framework is the product of many years of historical development (some would say a lengthy period of trial and error). The "modern" statute—the "Clean Water Act" (CWA) 33 U.S.C. § 1251, Pub. L. No. 95-217, 91 Stat. 1567 (1977)—is entering its third decade of effectiveness and today functions as a complex and reasonably efficient amalgam of nearly all of the regulatory and enforcement tools that have proven effective in environmental contexts.

The CWA program continues to function as something of a laboratory for environmental regulation. We will understand it best by first looking at its historical roots and then turning to a functional analysis of its mechanisms and the ways they work together.

2.0 A BRIEF HISTORY

We have had federal laws governing discharges of waste to surface waters since enactment of the Refuse Act in 1899.[1] That early law, however, focused primarily on the protection of navigation. We did not begin to see real concern over the quality of water in streams and lakes until the late 1940s, when public health concerns over bacterial contamination of drinking water led to federal programs to assist states in the construction and operation of waste treatment plants.[2] Under the Water Quality Act of 1965, the federal government began to help states and interstate compact organizations to establish and enforce water quality standards for surface waters in their jurisdictions. Thus, prior to 1970, standards, generally set by the states, established allowable concentrations of pollutant parameters for various water bodies. These standards were supposed to be used to formulate individualized permit limitations for each discharger.

Although this approach was theoretically attractive, it worked badly in most states. Major problems included:

---

[1]33 U.S.C. § 407.
[2]62 Stat. 1155 (June 30, 1948).

- Inability to determine precisely when a discharge violated applicable standards;
- Inapplicability of federal-state water quality standards to intrastate waters;
- Lack of state initiative in making load allocations required to set enforceable discharge standards; and
- Cumbersome enforcement mechanisms and the requirement of state consent for federal enforcement.

Although a few states made the water quality approach work, it was clear by 1970 that an effective nationwide approach required a permit program based on federal minimum "end-of-pipe" effluent criteria enforceable directly against the discharger.

In short, the process of protecting a designated quality of a receiving stream involved insurmountable technical and political challenges and was largely ineffectual. Thus, prior to 1970, the federal/state program to protect surface waters was largely unworkable and there was no effective program to directly enforce environmentally oriented limits on the discharge of pollutants to water.

Events like the Santa Barbara oil spills of 1969 and Earth Day 1970 made Congress anxious to get into the business of protecting the environment. Comprehensive federal water pollution control legislation was one of the first big initiatives. Unfortunately, while the Clean Air Act passed in 1970, the water pollution control bill ran into opposition and only a limited law, the Water Quality Improvement Act of 1970,[3] dealing with oil spills and treatment of sewage from toilets on recreational boats, could be enacted at that time. At about this same time courts and citizens groups were discovering that the Refuse Act penalized discharges of pollutants which had not been approved by the Army Corps of Engineers and provided a "bounty" to citizens who provided information for the government to bring actions to enforce those permit requirements. Based on this discovery and in order to remedy Congress' failure to enact comprehensive legislation, the Nixon administration "found" the Refuse Act, adapted it as a pollution control law and declared that all industrial dischargers would have to obtain Refuse Act permits and meet appropriate treatment standards in order to continue operation.

As we've noted, the Refuse Act is an archaic 1899 statute designed to protect navigation. It does, however, prohibit almost all discharges into navigable waters or tributaries thereof, unless a permit is obtained from the Corps of Engineers prior to commencing the discharge.[4] By using this authority to require all industrial dischargers to apply for and obtain permits, the granting or denial of which would be based on environmental factors, the administration was able, for

---

[3]Pub. L. 91-467, 84 Stat. 91

[4] The only exception recognized by the statute is for "refuse matter . . . flowing from streets and sewers and passing therefrom in a liquid state." Thus, the regulation of stormwater discharges, which has proven controversial under the Clean Water Act, see § 6.2 below, is more difficult to address under the Refuse Act, though the stormwater exception is to be narrowly applied, and does not include industrial waste. *Crawford v. National Lead Co.,* 29 ERC 1048, 1054 (S.D. Ohio 1989).

the first time, to pose a credible threat of prosecution. Hundreds of criminal cases were prosecuted under the Refuse Act, as such prosecutions were the only mechanism for enforcement provided by the Refuse Act.

The Refuse Act was not drafted as a comprehensive water pollution control statute. Consequently, the permit program encountered severe problems:

- The act provided no standards for the grant or denial of permits, nor were any regulations promulgated to provide such standards;
- As a result of a court decision, *Kalur v. Resor*,[5] environmental impact statements had to be prepared for every permit decision, further taxing the inadequate staff in charge of processing the applications;
- Penalties under the act were thought by many to be inadequate; and
- The relationship of the act to other federal and state water pollution control efforts was unclear and created considerable confusion.

Thus the Administration's bold initiative and the administrative and legal problems it created convinced *everyone* of the need for a comprehensive *modern* water pollution statute.

In late 1972, over President Nixon's veto, Congress finally passed such legislation, Public Law 92-500.[6] This statute made the Environmental Protection Agency (EPA) responsible for setting nationwide effluent standards on an industry-by-industry basis and required EPA to set such standards on the basis of the capabilities of both pollution control technologies and costs to the regulated industry as a whole. EPA had to follow a stringent timetable for setting these standards.

The act continued requirements for water quality standards so that more stringent discharge standards could be imposed where technology-based effluent standards were insufficient to assure that the quality of receiving waters did not deteriorate to, or remain at, unacceptable levels. States could take over the administration of the permit program when state control programs met rigorous federal standards.

The basic framework of the 1972 act—national effluent limitations, water quality standards, the permit program, special provisions for oil spills and toxic substances, and a publicly-owned treatment works (POTW) construction grant program—proved reasonably sound and remains in place, with some modification, today.

Although the Federal Water Pollution Control Act (FWPCA) contained virtually all of the tools and enforcement mechanisms that the Clean Water Act contains today, EPA stumbled in the implementation process by making the wrong decision on what pollutants to regulate. It decided to concentrate on oxygen demanding materials (for example, biochemical oxygen demand, suspended solids), which primarily affected wildlife and aesthetics, and failed to

---

[5] 335 F. Supp. 1 (D.D.C. 1971). The relationship between the National Environmental Policy Act (NEPA) and current Clean Water Act permit requirements is explored in the Chapter on NEPA and in following sections of this Chapter.

[6] 33 U.S.C. § 1251-1376, 86 Stat. 816 (1972).

adequately emphasize the *toxics* perceived to threaten the health of humans and indeed, "life on earth as we know it."[7]

As usually happens when EPA drops the ball, the agency was sued by the environmentalists.[8] The case was settled by a 1976 consent decree—called the Flannery Decree —which refocused all of the CWA enforcement tools on toxics control and spelled out a detailed toxics strategy which is the heart of the CWA program as it exists today.

The Flannery Decree was essentially adopted into statutory law by the Clean Water Act amendments of 1977.[9] The Flannery Decree is still in effect, and its mandates to EPA about how to administer the CWA remain an important factor in its implementation.

A decade later, in 1987, the act was amended to take care of unfinished business—tightening the focus on toxics dischargers, forcing action on toxics-oriented water quality standards, attempting to resolve longstanding problems with the effort to regulate storm water runoff and to strengthen the enforcement mechanisms. These amendments brought the act full circle: discharge standards are now to be tightened beyond technology-based minimums to assure that water quality standards for toxic pollutants are met.

In 1990, after the *Valdez* oil spill, the Oil Pollution Act of 1990 moved the CWA oil and hazardous substance discharge requirements into the modern era by making prevention, removal, and restoration high priorities of the program, with potent enforcement tools and adequate funds to make these priorities felt by the regulated community.

3.0 RESULTING REGULATORY SYSTEM: CLEAN WATER ACT

Forged in this crucible of litigation and politics, the Clean Water Act is perhaps the most tested, most innovative and most enforceable of our federal environmental statutes. It has been the testing ground for most of the regulatory approaches used in the environmental laws, and, if you can understand this program, you can deal with most of the others. The act provides a clear statement of goals and objectives and effectively marshals a number of functional regulatory elements toward their achievement. The goals and elements are summarized below.

3.1 Goals, Objectives and Policies

Like many of the environmental statutes, CWA begins with a statement of "goals, objectives, and policies," which, though they are not legal mandates, play an important role in interpretation. All of the act's operative provisions must be construed to achieve the act's goals, objectives and policies as the Congress has seen fit to state them.

---

7 Rachel Carson, *Silent Spring*, Houghton Mifflin, Boston 1962.

8*NRDC v. Train*, 8 E.R.C. 2120 (D.D.C.), modified, 12 E.R.C. 1833 (D.D.C., 1979).

9Pub. L. No. 95-217, 91 Stat. 1567 (1977).

CWA's stated objective is to "restore and maintain the chemical, physical and biological integrity of the nation's waters." To achieve that objective, the act establishes as "national goals"

- achievement of a level of water quality which "provides for the protection and propagation of fish, shellfish and wildlife" and "for recreation in and on the water"; and
- elimination of the discharge of pollutants into surface waters.

and a "national policy" that:

- the discharge of toxic pollutants in toxic amounts be prohibited.

While the goals, objectives and policies may not be mandatory—the times set for achieving the goals have long since passed—they *are* serious. They mean something and they need to be kept in mind as we try to understand the specifics about the way CWA works.

For example, the "restore and maintain" language of the *objective* has been held to mean at least that we need to have a serious "non-degradation" policy to prevent waters from becoming more polluted than they were when the act first passed in 1972.

The first *goal*—the "water quality" goal—protects both the survival and propagation of fish, shellfish and wildlife and must also provide for "recreation in and on the water." Note that it is not a standard to generally protect human health—but is limited to recreational uses.

The "elimination" or "no discharge" goal, originally intended to favor land application systems, remains in the law to emphasize the need to reuse and recycle process water and chemicals.

The toxics policy, though the meaning of the term "toxic pollutants in toxic amounts" is obscure, was the principal support for the Flannery Decree, and has been a primary focus of the act's implementation since 1977. It is pursuant to this requirement that we focus on human health effects in drinking water when we establish water quality criteria.

3.2 Functional Elements—Achieving Goals and Objectives

With this beginning statement of goals, objectives and policies as its foundation, CWA arrays a formidable set of regulatory tools and mechanisms into an effective, coordinated approach to their achievement. This approach has the following primary elements:

- A process for cooperative federal/state implementation;
- Prohibition of discharges, except in compliance with CWA;
- A permit program, to authorize certain discharges and to regulate those discharges which are permitted;
- A system for determining the limits to be imposed on discharge;
- A system for preventing, giving appropriate notice of and responding to spills;
- Special provisions for certain discharges and activities;
- Encouragement of public treatment facilities; and, finally
- Strong enforcement mechanisms.

Each of these elements will be discussed in some detail in the rest of this chapter.

3.3 Federal/State Implementation Process

The CWA program is a federal/state program—which means that the federal statute sets mandatory minimum requirements for regulatory programs, but that states are given both considerable flexibility as to the means of meeting the minimums and a nearly free hand when it comes to imposition of requirements more stringent than those required under CWA.

The more important federal/state coordination provisions in the CWA include sections 401 and 402, which spell out the process by which states assume responsibility for the discharge permit program in their jurisdictions; the EPA's continuing role in state programs (it has a permit by permit veto), section 402(d); and the states' role in federal permit issuance (the state must certify compliance with its applicable standards or waive certification before a permit can issue, section 401. Section 303 sets out in great detail the planning and allocation tasks which states are expected to perform in the water quality planning process, and section 304 outlines in similar detail the technical support, guidance and other documentation which EPA is expected to provide in support of the state efforts. Section 309 spells out the federal government's continuing enforcement role, which is substantial whether or not the state has assumed the permitting function.

Although most states have assumed the permitting function and EPA's involvement in those states most often takes the form of support and oversight, the Agency's presence is never for long forgotten. Perhaps because of the technical sophistication of many of the issues arising under the act, state resources are often inadequate to fund the science needed for authoritative answers. Particularly in cases which are not of the garden variety, federal actions and interpretations continue to be predominant factors in determining the outlines of policies for state implementation. The potential of federal enforcement also continues to be a gorilla in the closet, likely to come out if the state requests it or if the agency is generally dissatisfied with either a particular company's zeal for compliance or a state's vigor in enforcing it.

To summarize, the federal/state context of CWA regulation means that, though we will deal perhaps most often with the states, recognition and accommodation of the underlying federal role is important to understanding and coping with CWA programs. Federal precedents, technical guidance and, indeed, personalities and bureaucratic imperatives, will continue to influence the application of requirements at the state and local levels and must be taken into account in management and planning. The scope and applicability of the CWA federal/state program is determined primarily by the prohibition against discharges which is discussed in the next section.

4.0 DISCHARGE PROHIBITION

Borrowing from the Refuse Act experience, the drafters of the Federal Water Pollution Control Act (later to become the CWA) established at the new law's central core, a broad prohibition against "the discharge of any pollutant by any person. . ." except in compliance with the act's permit requirements, effluent limitations and other enumerated provisions.[10] The effect of this general prohibition is to shift the burden. In the absence of a prohibition, the enforcers would have the burden of proving non-compliance with legal mandates. The prohibition imposes on the discharger the burden of showing that the discharge complies with the act and applicable regulations. Though this seems like a minor matter, its practical impact is most substantial. The burden of proving compliance in order to defend against substantial civil and criminal penalties makes it prudent and probably necessary for everyone engaged in activities within the prohibition's scope to exercise considerable diligence to avoid the peril of prosecution.

Since the scope of the prohibition determines the breadth of the act's coverage and consequently the magnitude of compliance burdens, the limits of the prohibition's coverage have been debated in detail since the act's early days. In briefly discussing the primary issues in that debate, let's start by looking at the precise words of the prohibition:

> Except as in compliance with...this title, the discharge of any pollutant by any person shall be unlawful.[11]

The term "discharge of a pollutant" is defined to mean "any addition of any pollutant to navigable waters from any point source" and "any addition of any pollutant to the waters of the contiguous zone or the ocean from any point source other than a vessel or other floating craft."[12]

From this language, it can readily be deduced that the issues in controversy have been:

What is a "pollutant?"
What is "addition?"
What is a "point source?"
What are "navigable waters?"

We will look briefly at each of these terms.

4.1 Pollutant

Although the definition of "pollutant" in section 502(6) of the act includes only the materials specifically listed in that section,[13] the definition is nevertheless quite broad and has been broadly interpreted to include virtually all waste material, whether or not that material has value at the time it is discharged.[14]

---

[10] Section 301(a), 33 U.S.C. § 1311(a).

[11] Section 301(a), 33 U.S.C. § 1311(a).

[12] Section 502(12), 33 U.S.C. § 1362(12).

[13] Dredged spoil, solid waste, incinerator residue, sewage, garbage, sewage sludge, munitions, chemical wastes, biological materials, radioactive materials, heat, wrecked or discarded equipment, rock, sand, cellar dirt and industrial, municipal, and agricultural waste discharged into water.

[14] See *Weinberger v. Romero-Barcelo*, 456 U.S. 305 (1982) (bombs dropped on naval target range held to be pollutants); *United States v. Standard Oil Co.*, 384 U.S. 224 (1966) (accidental discharge of gasoline held to be pollutant discharge under the Refuse Act).

4.2 Addition

The act's requirement that there must be an addition of a pollutant in order for a discharge to be prohibited has been successfully used in some situations to preclude the imposition of limitations on the discharge of materials in a waste stream which are present only by reason of presence in intake waters, if the intake water is drawn from the same body of water into which the discharge is made and if the pollutants present in the intake water are not removed by the discharger as part of his usual operations.[15] Nor does the term "addition" include discharges of water from dams, even if a dam's operations adversely affect the temperature and dissolved oxygen content of the water.[16]

4.3 Point Source

The point source element of the discharge definition has been one of the most difficult aspects of the program. Section 502(14) of the act defines the term "point source" to include "any discernible, confined and discrete conveyance, . . . from which pollutants are or may be discharged." The "may be" language is important because it means that permits are required for facilities such as surface waste impoundments from which discharges are not normally anticipated, except under unusual but foreseeable conditions such as excessive rainfall. The "discrete conveyance" language of the definition is so comprehensive as to cover a number of types of discharges, such as storm sewers, irrigation return flows and the like, which are not efficiently regulated through the issuance of permits. For this reason, a number of statutory and administrative exemptions from the point source definition or the scope of the permit program have been adopted. These include irrigation return flows, the discharge of sewage from vessels regulated under section 312 of the act, effluent from properly functioning marine engines, certain agricultural and silvicultural discharges, and certain discharges of dredged or fill material regulated under section 404 of the act. Regulations also exclude from the point source definition storm water discharges which occur outside urbanized areas, provided that the runoff is not from lands or facilities used for industrial or commercial activities. The 1987 amendments amend section 502(14) in order to codify the exclusion of agricultural storm water discharges from the definition of point source. The application of point source limits to the storm water discharges which are not so excluded has been a matter of extreme difficulty, and is discussed in some detail later in the chapter.

4.4 Navigable Waters

"Navigable waters" is defined by the act 33 U.S.C. § 1362(7), to include all "waters of the United States." The term "waters of the United States" is defined by EPA regulations[17] to include (1) navigable waters; (2) tributaries of navigable waters; (3) interstate waters; and (4) intrastate lakes, rivers and streams (a) used by interstate travelers for recreation and other purposes, or (b) which are a source

---

[15] 40 C.F.R. § 122.45(h).

[16] *National Wildlife Federation v. Gorsuch*, 693 F.2d 156 (D.C. Cir. 1982).

[17] 40 C.F.R. § 122.2.

of fish or shellfish sold in interstate commerce, or (c) which are utilized for industrial purposes by industries engaged in interstate commerce. The intent of this definition is to cover all waters over which the broadest constitutional interpretation would allow the federal government to exercise jurisdiction.[18] The definition clearly covers wetlands, and the Supreme Court has upheld an expansive definition of wetlands under regulations governing dredge-fill activities under section 404 of the act.[19] Few exclusions to the definition have been recognized and those which have been accepted to date seem to be limited to situations where the waterway in question is wholly confined on the property of the discharger, does not result in any flow beyond the property line, and is not available for significant public use. There have been a few cases, like *Hoffman Homes, Inc. v. EPA,*[20] which have pointed towards a narrowing of the definitional scope of the term "navigable waters," but it appears that these are both aberrational and short-lived.

One remaining major issue is the extent to which discharges to publicly or privately owned sewage systems constitute discharges to waters of the United States so as to be subject to the National Pollution Discharge Elimination System (NPDES) permit requirement. A discharge to a sewage system which is not connected to an operable treatment works is a discharge subject to the NPDES program, but a discharge to a publicly owned treatment works which is capable of meeting its effluent limits is excluded from the NPDES permit requirement.[21] All industrial dischargers to POTWs are required to comply with general pretreatment standards[22] and many must also comply with industry-by-industry ("categorical") standards, promulgated together with effluent limitations for each industry. (See section 2.0 above.) There are permit requirements for discharges to treatment works which give the EPA substantial discretion to consolidate or issue separate permits as needed to meet effluent standards.

To summarize, though there are important exclusions, the scope of the prohibition against discharge without a permit is exceedingly broad. The basic intent is to regulate all pollutants discharged from all facilities and most contaminated areas into virtually all waters in the United States. It is difficult to imagine a release to surface water which would not fall within the prohibition's scope.

5.0 PERMIT PROGRAM

Perhaps the most distinctive element of the Clean Water Act regulatory framework, the "NPDES permit program" is coordinated with the prohibition to translate the blanket preclusion of all discharges into a set of sixty thousand or so specific conditional authorizations to discharge. In doing so, it defines for each

---

[18] *NRDC v. Callaway,* 392 F. Supp. 685 (D.D.C. 1975).

[19] *United States v. Riverside Bayview Homes, Inc.,* 474 U.S. 121 (1985).

[20] 961 F.2d 1310 (7th Cir. 1992)

[21] 40 C.F.R. § 122.3(c).

[22] 40 C.F.R. Part 403.

individual discharger his permissible level of release into waters of the United States.

"NPDES" stands for "National Pollutant Discharge Elimination System." It is a system of requirements to obtain permits for the commencement or continuation of any discharge of pollutants to surface waters. As we've noted, the discharge of pollutants without a permit is prohibited. So, to avoid a violation, we have to notify the authorities about the nature and circumstances of any anticipated discharge by filing a permit application. Based on the information in the application—and it is often extensive—the issuing authority can determine and notify the applicant of the limitations and conditions upon which discharge will be permitted. Those conditions normally include requirements to minimize the discharge through treatment and to demonstrate continued compliance with those requirements through monitoring and reporting obligations. While we most commonly think of the permit requirement in connection with process waste discharges, permit applications can be filed for routine and foreseeable spills associated with operations, and this is often a sensible approach. The permit program has proven to be an almost indispensable element of effective environmental regulation. It gives the issuing authority precise information concerning the discharger's activities and permits precise advice to the discharger as to what is permissible. Because of this importance, the requirement to file applications and report compliance or non-compliance based on accurate and current data is jealously maintained and vigorously enforced. Parallel, but not identical, permit type requirements are applicable to persons who discharge, not directly but through publicly owned treatment works.

Against this general background, let's consider the specific elements of the NPDES program in more detail. First we'll examine typical permit conditions, then we'll look at the procedures by which permits are issued.

5.1 Permit Conditions

An NPDES permit performs two basic functions in the Clean Water Act regulatory process. It establishes specific levels of performance the discharger must maintain, and it requires the discharger to report failures to meet those levels to the appropriate regulatory agency.

Many conditions typically included in industrial permits are either negotiable or susceptible to legal attack. Accordingly, proposed permit conditions should be carefully analyzed; if inappropriate, modified; and, if need be, contested. The more significant permit conditions are discussed below.

5.1.1 Monitoring and Reporting

The monitoring requirements in an NPDES permit are critically important, especially with the emergence of biomonitoring as a requirement for some sources. The effectiveness of the permit program in assuring compliance with applicable effluent limitations, water quality standards, pretreatment standards and other requirements established pursuant to the act will depend, in major part, on the effectiveness of monitoring and data maintenance requirements included in permits pursuant to section 308.[23] Under that section, EPA is authorized to require the owner or operator of any point source to establish and maintain specified records, make specified reports, install, use and maintain monitoring equipment and methods, take specified samples, and provide other information which EPA may reasonably require. As with the permit program in general, the states have the opportunity to administer their own monitoring programs and, upon obtaining EPA's approval of an appropriate monitoring program, the state becomes the monitoring authority for all point sources within its jurisdiction.

The enforcing authority will have the right to enter the premises of the discharger at any reasonable time, inspect the records required to be maintained, take test samples and so forth. All data obtained under section 308 is required to be open to the public except to the extent non-disclosure is necessary to protect trade secrets. This public disclosure requirement is an essential underpinning of the act's provision for citizen enforcement actions against non-complying dischargers.

The NPDES regulations specify the manner in which effluent limitations are to be included in permits and thus imposed on permittees.[24] The monitoring requirements in various sections of Part 122 are intended to assure compliance with the limits included in permits. Under these provisions, limits are to be imposed and monitoring is to take place at the point of discharge except in limited situations where monitoring at point of discharge is infeasible. The regulations do provide the permit issuer with authority to require monitoring of internal waste streams in certain situations, such as where the final discharge point is inaccessible, where wastes at the point of discharge are so diluted as to make monitoring impracticable, or where interference among pollutants at the point of discharge would prevent detection or analysis. A permittee is required to monitor waste streams, as specified in his permit, to determine (1) compliance with the limitations on amounts, concentrations or other pollutant measures specified in the permit, (2) the total volume of effluent discharged from each discharge point and (3) otherwise as required by the permit.[25]

The permit must include requirements for maintenance and proper installation of the monitoring equipment, must specify monitoring methods and frequencies adequate to provide reliable data regarding the volume of flow and quantity of pollutants discharged, and must specify the test methodology to be used in analyzing the samples taken. If the applicant believes that the monitoring requirements specified in a draft permit are inadequate to yield accurate data, the regulations put on him the burden of requesting additional monitoring requirements which are sufficient to achieve an acceptable degree of accuracy. Compliance with the effluent limits set in the permit will be assessed through application of the monitoring methods which the permit provides. Thus, unless

---

[23] POTWs subject to the act's permit requirements must also require industrial dischargers to monitor their discharges to the POTWs.

[24] 40 C.F.R. §§ 122.44, 122.45.

[25] 40 C.F.R. § 122.44(i).

inadequate monitoring requirements are contested during the permit issuance procedures, it may be difficult to use such inadequacy as a defense in any later enforcement action.

Monitoring records, including charts from continuous monitoring devices and calibration and maintenance records, must be maintained for a minimum period of three years, and that period may be extended by request of the permit issuing authority at any time.[26] As the statute of limitations applicable to permit violations is the five-year limitation in 28 U.S.C. § 2462 (1988),[27] it would be wise to maintain the records for that longer five-year period.

The results of monitoring must be reported periodically to the permit issuing authority on forms provided by the authority. Frequency of reporting is governed by the terms of each individual permit and must be at least annual. In addition to the periodic reporting requirement, certain toxic discharges must be reported within 24 hours.[28] Failure properly to monitor and to report is a violation of the permit and any person who knowingly makes any false statement in monitoring records, monitoring reports, or compliance or non-compliance notifications is subject upon conviction to substantial fines and criminal penalties, both under the Clean Water Act and under the applicable provisions of the federal criminal code, including 18 U.S.C. § 1001.

It is evident from the foregoing that the monitoring requirements may occupy a considerable amount of employee time and require the installation of sophisticated sampling devices, extensive analysis and testing, and detailed recordkeeping and reporting. Many companies may find it appropriate to develop additional in-house technical capability in order to meet the section 308 requirements as imposed in the permit.

5.1.2 Schedules of Compliance

Although the act itself establishes firm deadlines for the achievement of the required levels of treatment, the issuing authority has considerable latitude to require compliance or interim steps towards compliance at earlier dates. The act also provides mechanisms to extend compliance deadlines in limited situations, as where compliance is dependent on connection to a yet-to-be-constructed public treatment works or where use of innovative technology is involved. Most of the statutory bases for extensions, however, have now expired.

5.1.3 Effluent Limitations

Where a permit is issued prior to the publication of effluent limitations for a particular pollutant or applicable industrial category or subcategory, the determination of the precise effluent limitations to be included in the permit are to be based on "professional judgment," which is obviously more flexible than

---

[26] 40 C.F.R. § 122.41(j).

[27] *See, e.g., Chesapeake Bay Foundation v. Bethlehem Steel Corp.*, 608 F.Supp 440, 446-50 (D.Md. 1985); *Connecticut Fund for the Environment v. Job Plating Co.*, 623 F.Supp 207, 211-13 (D.Conn. 1985); *Atlantic States Legal Foundation v. Al-Tech Specialty*, 635 F.Supp 284, 287 (N.D. N.Y. 1986).

[28] 40 C.F.R. §§ 122.41(k)(6), 122.42(a). The non-compliance reporting requirements are specific and detailed and should be carefully reviewed by all permittees.

published rules. This situation is most likely to arise pending promulgation of new limitations for toxic pollutants, or in connection with facilities for which no specific set of limitations is wholly applicable.

Even after promulgation of limitations, the applicant may in certain cases seek modification of limits in the permit, and there is also considerable opportunity for the permitting authority to impose discharge limitations more stringent than the "base-level" effluent guidelines where necessary in order to meet water quality standards, water quality related effluent limitations, the requirements of state planning processes, or other applicable limitations. Thus, there is considerable room for discussion regarding limits to be imposed in permits and a careful engineering analysis of proposed permit limits is a prerequisite to intelligent evaluation and negotiation of permit requirements. By the same token, once a permit has been issued on the basis of "Best Professional Judgment" and it proves more stringent than the promulgated regulations require, the 1987 amendments included an "anti-backsliding" provision which made it quite difficult to relax stringent permit conditions a discharger is actually meeting.[29]

5.1.4 Additional Effluent Limitations

Until recently, NPDES permits normally specified four or five pollutants as being subject to effluent limitations; a far greater number are now included in permits as a result of EPA's toxics strategy. EPA's NPDES permit application and related regulations (section 122.21) require extensive waste stream analysis in order to file permit applications, extensive cataloging in the application of virtually all chemicals in the waste stream, and imposition of controls on the discharge of those chemicals. Implementation of these requirements complicates the permit process and requires more extensive monitoring than was true in the past.

5.1.5 Duration and Revocation

Permits may be valid for terms of up to five years, and may be subject to revocation or modification based on a very minimal showing of "cause." A discharger's interest in connection with the permit process will generally be best served by obtaining a permit with the maximum duration and with as much specificity as is obtainable in regard to the possible grounds of revocation or modification. On the permit's expiration, the permittee, in order to obtain reissuance, must demonstrate compliance with any more stringent criteria which have been promulgated during the term of the original permit. Under EPA's rules, the completed permit application must be filed at least 180 days in advance of the existing permit's expiration date. Prudent practice suggests earlier filing in case the application is found incomplete in some respect.

5.1.6 Other

Depending on the precise nature of the applicant's operation, consideration might be given to bypass and upset provisions, start-up exclusions and so forth. Those who will be responsible for complying with the permits are well advised to make every reasonable effort to predict potential compliance problems and

---

[29] CWA, § 402 (o).

discuss them fully during the permit issuance process rather than in later enforcement proceedings.

5.2 Permitting Procedures

Under section 402 of the Clean Water Act, the EPA is the issuing authority for all NPDES permits in a state until such time as the state elects to take over the program's administration and obtains EPA approval of its program. As of August 1992, 18 states and territories did not have approved NPDES programs; EPA functions as the issuing authority for permits in their jurisdictions.[30] As of August 1992, thirty-eight states and the Virgin Islands have approved state NPDES permit programs.[31] The 1987 amendments gave EPA the authority to approve partial state permit programs, with the proviso that the program be complete within five years of program submission. This revision should increase the number of states with NPDES programs.[32] Where the state is the issuing authority, permitting procedures are generally comparable to the EPA procedures discussed below, with certain exceptions. For example, the states, unlike EPA, are not required to provide for an evidentiary hearing, though many do. Where the state is the issuing authority, procedures for judicial review of permit issuance are those provided under the state's administrative procedure act rather than under the Clean Water Act and the federal Administrative Procedure Act. State permit issuance is not a federal action subject to the requirements of the National Environmental Policy Act.[33]

Permits issued by states are subject to review by EPA, and a state permit may not be issued if the EPA administrator objects within 90 days after the state's proposed issuance. EPA may issue its own permit to the discharger if EPA objects to the state permit.[34] The administrator must state the reasons supporting the objections and must provide a statement of the limitations and conditions which would be included in the permit if it were to be issued by EPA. States are entitled to a public hearing regarding the administrator's objections, and if the objections are not resolved at the hearing or otherwise, the administrator can issue the permit. EPA has the authority to withdraw its approval of a state program and take over the entire program administration if it finds that the state is not carrying out the program in accordance with the act's requirements. This authority has not been exercised.

---

[30] The states and territories without an approved program are: Alaska, Arizona, District of Columbia, Florida, Guam, Idaho, Louisiana, Maine, Massachusetts, New Hampshire, New Mexico, Oklahoma, Puerto Rico, Samoa, South Dakota, Texas, Commonwealth of the Northern Marianas, and Trust Territory of the Pacific.

[31] 57 Fed.Reg. 37163 (Aug. 18, 1992).

[32] CWA, § 402(n).

[33] See *Chesapeake Bay Foundation, Inc. v. Virginia State Water Control Bd.*, 453 F. Supp. 122 (E.D.Va. 1978).

[34] See *Champion International Corp. v. EPA*, 850 F. 2d 182, 28 ERC 1013 (4th Cir. 1988) which upheld EPA's veto of a North Carolina permit on the ground that it failed to assure compliance with water quality standards downstream in Tennessee. EPA then issued a more stringent permit.

Procedures for permit issuance are generally as follows: A permit application, on the appropriate form, must be submitted to the EPA regional administrator (or the state, if it is the issuing authority) at least 180 days in advance of the date on which a proposed discharge is to commence or the expiration of the present permit, as the case may be. Where EPA is the issuing authority, it will require for new dischargers the submission of a new source questionnaire before it will process the permit application. This questionnaire serves as the basis for an EPA determination as to whether the facility is a "new source." If the facility is determined to be a new source, the applicant will be required to prepare an environmental assessment for EPA's use in determining whether an environmental impact statement is required by the National Environmental Policy Act.[35]

After the application is filed, the district engineer of the Corps of Engineers must be given an opportunity to review the application to evaluate the impact of permit issuance upon anchorage and navigation. Other federal agencies, and specifically the Fish and Wildlife Service of the Department of the Interior and the National Marine Fisheries Service of the Department of Commerce, are provided a similar opportunity to comment on the application.

Where EPA is the issuing authority, the state in which the discharge will occur must be provided with an opportunity to review the application. Based on that review, the state is asked to certify, pursuant to section 401 of the act, that the permitted discharge will comply with applicable provisions of sections 301, 302, 303, 306, and 307 of the act. Since provisions in sections 301 and 303 deal with the question of compliance with state water quality standards, the state, in effect, is asked to certify that the discharge in question will comply with all limitations necessary to meet water quality standards, treatment standards, or schedules of compliance established pursuant to any state law or regulation. In one recent case, the Court of Appeals has reversed the grant of an NPDES permit because EPA failed to consider and assure compliance with downstream state water quality standards.[36]

Although the applicable regulations would appear to require the applicant for an NPDES permit to provide EPA with the required certification, in practice EPA forwards applications received without a certification to the appropriate state and keeps the state advised throughout the permit proceedings. If a state does not either certify or deny certification within a reasonable time after the receipt of the permit application, it will be deemed to have waived the certification requirement. Because this time period starts to run on the state's receipt of an application, it is advisable for the applicant to send a copy of the application to the state rather than waiting for EPA to do so. EPA is barred from issuing any NPDES permit unless the state has either certified the permit or waived its right to certify.

In processing the application, the issuing authority makes tentative determinations as to whether a permit should be issued, and, if so, as to the

---

[35] CWA, § 511(c).

[36] *Oklahoma v. EPA*, 31 ERC 1741 (10th Cir. 1990).

required effluent limitations, schedules of compliance, monitoring requirements and so forth. These tentative determinations are organized into a draft permit, and the discharger is normally given an opportunity to review and comment on this draft. The public is given notice of the permit application proceeding and the issuing authority's preliminary determinations with respect thereto.[37]

The regulations provide for a period of not less than 30 days during which the public may submit written comments and/or request that a public hearing be held. The issuing authority is required to hold a public hearing if there is a significant degree of public interest in a proposed permit or group of permits. The public must be notified of such hearings and interested persons must be given at least 30 days in which to prepare for the hearings. Following the public hearing, the issuing authority issues a final determination regarding permit issuance after taking into account the comments received. Where the final determination is substantially unchanged from the tentative determination outlined in the original public notice, the issuing authority must forward a copy of the determination to any person who submitted written comments regarding the permit. Where the issuing authority's decision substantially changes the tentative determinations and draft permit, public notice must be given.

Within thirty days following the date of the notice of final determination, any interested person may request an evidentiary hearing or a legal review to reconsider the determination.

The granting of an evidentiary hearing or legal review stays the effective date of all contested provisions of the permit.[38] The hearing is an on-the-record, quasi-judicial proceeding presided over by an administrative law judge. The decision reached on the basis of the evidentiary hearing[39] may be appealed to the EPA administrator.[40] Where EPA is the issuing authority, the entire permit issuance proceeding, of course, is subject to judicial review under the federal Administrative Procedure Act. This review, however, takes place in the Court of Appeals, not the District Court. Where the state is the issuing authority, the state administrative procedure act probably governs.

Contested provisions of the permit become effective, and a final permit is issued, upon completion of these review proceedings. The issuance of a permit under the Clean Water Act will be deemed to fulfill the permit requirements of the Refuse Act of 1899, as well as those under the act itself, except for requirements under section 307(a) covering discharge of toxic pollutants presenting human health risks. It should be noted, however, that issuance of a permit does not mean that no further action will be required during the permit term. As the permit makes clear, additional applications must be filed and processed whenever modifications to the facility or method of operation will

---

[37] If a variance request or other effort to secure relaxation of generally applicable effluent limits is indicated, it is appropriate to submit the request at this point in the proceedings. If this is done, a stay of further action on the permit, pending disposition of the request, would be appropriate.

[38] 40 C.F.R. § 124.16(a).

[39] Id., § 124.81.

[40] Id., § 124.91.

result in changes to the discharge. Thus, keeping permits up-to-date will often be a continuous endeavor.

The last, but perhaps the most important, point to be made in this discussion of NPDES permits is that the compiler's job is not over, but just beginning, when the permit is issued. Once it is issued, scrupulous attention must be paid to the business of monitoring and demonstrating compliance with the permit as well as with making certain that the facility continues to operate in the manner portrayed in the permit application. The requirement to notify the permitting authority of significant changes in operations is often overlooked with unfortunate consequences. Managing the process of permit compliance is a challenging and painstaking, but clearly essential, effort.

5.3 Determining Discharge Limits

Given the importance of permits in the Clean Water Act regulatory process, it is obvious that the question of what limits go in the permit is one of considerable significance.

Three basic criteria are commonly used to determine the level of control required at the point of discharge. We can require that the effluent be treated to the limits of available or practicable technology; we may require that the discharge be limited so as to maintain a specified level of quality in the receiving medium—for example, a level of water quality in a stream which is suitable for maintenance of a balanced population of fish, shellfish and wildlife and for water contact recreation; or we may limit the discharge as may be necessary to minimize health or other risks—such as toxicity.

The Clean Water Act's approach to establishment of discharge limits uses all three methods. Technology-based effluent limitations—"best available" or "best conventional" technology—establish the *baseline* level of treatment to be met for all discharges. More stringent treatment—beyond the technological baseline—may be required if necessary to achieve water quality standards or avoid effluent toxicity problems. Similar technology, toxicity or water quality-based "pretreatment" requirements are applicable to facilities that send their waste to publicly owned treatment plants rather than discharging directly to surface waters. The technology-based effluent limitations are established by EPA in notice and comment rulemaking proceedings based on evidence as to the level of treatment achieved by exemplary operations. Until applicable limits are formally established, the limits put in permits are determined on the basis of "best professional judgment."

Where adopted limits are applicable, there is limited ability to vary the application to individual facilities even where those facilities may differ fundamentally from those considered in establishing the effluent limits.

Water-quality-based effluent limits are harder to establish because of the need to model or assess the fate of pollutants in specific receiving waters in order to determine the limits to put in the permits. This is particularly true for permits which must address numerous pollutant parameters in the permitted discharge.

Limits based on effluent toxicity are also difficult due to the absence of agreement as to what is meant by "toxic pollutants in toxic amounts." Biological monitoring methods to determine "whole effluent toxicity" are touted by some as an approach to resolution of this difficulty.

Having thus outlined the general philosophy of establishing discharge limits, let's look at some details.

The CWA mandates a two-part approach to establishing effluent limitations for industrial discharges: (1) nationwide base-level treatment to be established through an assessment of what is technologically and economically achievable for a particular industry; and (2) more stringent treatment requirements for specific plants where necessary to achieve water quality objectives for the particular body of water into which that plant discharges. According to some commentators, Congress intended EPA to implement this combination of standards in a way that would force control technology innovation.[41]

5.4 Toxic Pollutants

Although the CWA broadly defined pollutants subject to regulation and permitting, it furnished little guidance before 1977 with regard to toxic pollutants. For that reason, and because the 1972 act imposed unrealistic deadlines on EPA's limited staff, EPA focused almost entirely on high-volume "conventional" pollutants such as biochemical oxygen demand (BOD), suspended solids (SS) and acidity and alkalinity (pH) when it developed the effluent limitations required by the act. As long as this approach was followed, EPA's basic system of effluent limits and permit requirements failed to address the dangers posed by more toxic pollutants such as chlorinated organic chemicals, heavy metals, pesticides and so forth, and at the same time may have overemphasized removal of solids and oxygen-demanding materials contained in conventional wastes.[42] Regulation of "toxic" pollutants was thought to be the exclusive province of section 307(a) of the act, which authorized EPA to identify and regulate, on a chemical-by-chemical rather than industry-to-industry basis, substances which it could prove have toxic effects on identified organisms in affected waters.

Because of the stringent burden of proof and extensive procedures which the pre-1977 section 307 required, EPA failed to establish a workable program to control the discharge of toxic pollutants. Only a limited number of substances were identified as toxic substances; long delays were encountered before final effluent limits were adopted for any of them.

EPA's failure to develop an effective toxics control strategy under the 1972 act led the Natural Resources Defense Council (NRDC), an environmental organization, to sue the Environmental Protection Agency. That litigation was settled, and in the process of settlement, EPA and NRDC developed a policy which focused all of the regulatory mechanisms provided by the 1972 act upon the effective regulation of toxic or priority pollutant discharges. In developing

---

[41] *See, e.g., Chemical Manufacturers Association v. Natural Resources Defense Council,* 470 U.S. 116, 156 (1985) (Marshall, J. dissenting) (and sources cited therein).

[42] It should be noted, however, that conventional treatment frequently, if unintentionally, removes substantial amounts of the more toxic wastes.

this policy, the parties identified (1) the pollutants which would be the primary subject of regulation; (2) the industries which would be the primary concern in applying the regulations; and (3) the methods of regulating toxic discharges with the act's existing legal mechanisms. The agreements reached in these negotiations were embodied in a settlement decree,[43] and were adopted by Congress as a blueprint for a toxics control strategy in the 1977 amendments, and to a certain degree in the 1987 amendments.

The decree mandated full use of all the available regulatory tools under the act with a specific focus on the identified "priority pollutants." Pursuant to the decree, EPA was to develop a program to regulate the discharge of 65 categories of "priority pollutants" (now including at least 126 specific chemical substances—see the appendix at the end of this chapter) by 34 industry categories which include over 700 subcategories. More than 70 percent of the nation's industries were affected by the decree.

The consent decree required adoption of best available technology effluent limitations for each priority pollutant in each industrial category by June 30, 1983. These limitations had to be applicable to at least 95 percent of the point sources in each identified industry category or subcategory. Similar technology-based requirements had to be adopted for new sources and sources discharging into publicly owned treatment works. The basis for excluding a category of point sources from the toxic-focused system of technology-based effluent limitations is quite limited.

In addition to these stringent industry-by-industry toxic effluent limits, the consent decree made specific provision for full implementation of the waterway segment-by-segment approach, discussed below.

The NRDC consent decree provided a judicial mandate for full use of the Clean Water Act's enforcement mechanisms in a carefully tailored effort to reduce discharges of toxic pollutants.

The 1977 amendments largely adopted the technology-based aspects of this mandate and enacted them into federal statutory law. The amendments:

- adopted the consent decree list of priority pollutants as the list of toxic substances to be given primary emphasis in the implementation of the Clean Water Act;
- required adoption of best available technology (BAT) effluent limitations for each listed substance;
- permitted EPA to add to or remove items from the list of "toxic" substances;
- required compliance with BAT effluent limitations for toxic pollutants subsequently added to the list within three years of the establishment of the limitations;
- provided a new system for upgrading and enforcing pretreatment regulations based on both the effluent limitations on the discharge from publicly

---

[43] *NRDC v. Train,* 8 E.R.C. 2120 (D.D.C. 1976), modified, 12 E.R.C. 1833 (D.D.C. 1979).

owned treatment works and the intended use of the sludge from the facilities; and

- authorized EPA to adopt regulations establishing best management practices to control the discharge of toxic pollutants in the form of runoff or other uncontrolled discharges from industrial plant sites, parking lots and so forth.

The 1977 amendments did not, however, fully replace the consent decree. Instead, that decree has been the primary mechanism by which the toxics control program has been modified. The consent decree was amended in 1979 to reflect the changes made by the 1977 amendments and to respond to the operational problems perceived by EPA since the decree was originally issued in 1976.[44] The modification also expanded the permissible bases upon which EPA may exclude substances from regulation pursuant to the consent decree. Pursuant to the deadlines extended in the decree, EPA has now promulgated effluent limitations for all 34 industry categories, or decided for some that insufficient levels of toxic discharge were occurring to warrant such regulation. Challenges to the consent decree have twice been rejected by the courts.[45]

Under the revised consent decree, the EPA can exclude industry categories from regulation of certain substances where only "trace amounts" of the substance are found. The administrator is also authorized to exclude pollutants from coverage under the direct discharge effluent limitations if the amount and toxicity of such pollutants within a category or subcategory does not, in his judgment, justify the development of regulations having nationwide applicability. Seven industry categories of the 34 listed ones have been so excluded.

The basis for excluding pollutants from the applicability of standards was similarly expanded. EPA is authorized to make such exclusions when it finds that the amount and toxicity of all incompatible pollutants discharged by a category or subcategory taken together is so small that regulations of nationwide applicability governing pretreatment of those pollutants is not justified. Three pollutants of the list of 129 have been so excluded.

In the water quality standards area, the modified consent decree has had little effect because of EPA's long delays in identifying the affected wastes and developing a control program. The 1987 amendments put teeth in this portion of the consent decree by imposing a two-year deadline for the states to identify water bodies which fail to meet water quality standards because of toxic discharges by particular point sources, and by requiring the imposition of additional effluent limitations on such responsible point sources, and compliance with them, three years after that.

The consent decree as confirmed by the 1977 and 1987 amendments and modified by the court has transformed the entire Clean Water Act program and focused EPA and industry attention on the most dangerous pollutants. The industry-by-industry technology-based effluent limitations have been transformed

---

[44] 12 E.R.C. 1833 (D.D.C. 1979).

[45] *Environmental Defense Fund v. Costle,* 636 F.2d 1229 (D.C. Cir. 1980); *Citizens for a Better Environment v. Gorsuch,* 718 F.2d 1117 (D.C. Cir. 1983), *cert. denied,* 467 U.S. 1219 (1984).

from limited requirements focused on three or four conventional pollutants to a very specific system of limitations potentially applicable to 126 or more different pollutants as well as whole effluent toxicity for each industry category. Water quality standards will become far more important to industry, especially now that the technology-based standards have been promulgated, and deadlines set to impose more stringent discharge limitations on the basis of water quality standards.

5.5 Industrial Effluent Limitations

5.5.1 Required Level of Treatment—Technology-Based Limits for "Existing" Direct Discharges

Section 301(b) of the 1972 act provided for the establishment of nationally applicable technology-based effluent limitations on an industry-by-industry basis. These effluent limitations were to establish a nationwide base-level of treatment for existing direct discharge sources in every significant industrial category. This level of treatment was to be achieved in two phases. For "existing"[46] industrial discharges, section 301 directs the achievement:

> by July 1, 1977, of effluent limitations which will require application of the best practicable control technology currently available, and by July 1, 1983, of effluent limitations which will require application of the best available technology economically achievable.

As the time for achievement of best practicable technology (BPT) is long past, its primary relevance now is as a basis for setting subsequent standards or, as discussed below, in regulating discharges of conventional pollutants.[47] EPA defined BPT as the "average of the best existing performance by well-operated plants within each industrial category or subcategory." The word "control" in section 301 emphasized Congress' expectation that, in establishing the 1977 effluent guidelines, EPA would emphasize end-of-pipe treatment rather than in-plant control measures. EPA did so. However, section 304(b)(1) of the act makes it clear that the alternative of in-plant process changes may be considered, at least for the purpose of determining whether a proposed effluent limitation is "practicable." Under the statute, the word "practicable," was to be read together with the provisions of section 304(b)(1)(B), and so required that effluent limitations be justifiable in terms of the "total cost of (industry-wide) application of (the required) technology in relation to the effluent reduction benefits to be achieved." This determination was to take into account a number of specific factors such as the age of the equipment and facilities involved, the process employed, and non-water quality environmental impacts. Thus, in developing the BPT limitations, the Environmental Protection Agency was required to make what amounted to a cost-benefit balancing test that took into account a broad

---

[46] The act's "existing discharge" provisions will in fact apply to some newly constructed facilities since they cover any source for which a new source performance standard (see Part 3.3) has not been proposed.

[47] EPA recently and successfully invoked the BPT provisions in setting revised standards for the organic chemicals industry. *See Chemical Mfrs. Assn. v. EPA*, 870 F.2d 177 (5th Cir. 1989).

range of specific engineering factors relating to the ability of plants within a category or subcategory to achieve the limits. The BPT definition was essentially unchanged by the 1977 amendments.

EPA defined best available technology (BAT) as the "very best control and treatment measures that have been or are capable of being achieved." The agency can consider in-plant process changes in addition to end-of-pipe treatment measures in establishing these limitations, which had a 1983 compliance deadline under the 1972 act. Although EPA is required to consider the cost of achieving the required effluent reduction in determining whether a BAT limitation is economically achievable, it is not required to balance cost against effluent reduction benefit as it is in the case of the BPT standards. The engineering factors required to be considered—age of equipment and facility, process employed, process changes, non-water quality environmental impacts and so forth—are the same for BAT as for BPT.

The BAT definition was essentially unchanged by the 1977 and 1987 amendments, but its scope of applicability was radically altered and its date for attainment was extended until 1989. The BAT effluent limitations now focus primarily on the priority pollutants listed in the NRDC consent decree and on additional toxic pollutants identified pursuant to section 307(a) of the act. These effluent limitations have now been promulgated—several years late in some cases—for all industry categories listed in the consent decree, except that, for some industries, EPA has determined that the industry discharges too few toxic pollutants to warrant regulation under this provision. For pollutants not listed in the consent decree but identified as toxic pollutants under section 307(a)(1) of the act, compliance with BAT effluent limits is required no later than three years after the date on which the limitations are established.

The "conventional" pollutant measures, which were the primary focus of EPA's pre-1977 BAT effluent limitations, are specifically excluded from the scope of coverage of the BAT limits provided by the 1977 amendments. Those pollutants are subject to an entirely new treatment standard established for the first time in the 1977 amendments—best conventional pollutant control technology.

The best conventional technology (BCT) effluent limitations were, like the BPT and BAT limitations, to be adopted on an industry-by-industry basis but were to apply for each affected industry only to pollutants which were identified as "conventional." The compliance deadline for the BCT limitations was March 31, 1989. The 1977 amendments specifically included within the definition of "conventional pollutants" biological oxygen demand (BOD), suspended solids (SS), fecal coliform bacteria, and pH. EPA is authorized to include additional pollutants within the definition of conventional pollutants, but to date has added only oil and grease to the statutory list of conventional pollutants.[48] The act specifically excludes heat from the conventional pollutant definition as there are special statutory provisions for thermal discharges.[49] The BCT limitations were

---

[48] 40 C.F.R. § 401.16.

[49] CWA, § 316.

to be adopted by EPA based on a consideration of the reasonableness of the relationship between the cost of attaining a reduction in effluents and the effluent reduction benefits which will result. The cost of providing treatment to comply with these limits was expected by Congress to be generally comparable to the cost of achieving the secondary treatment limitation for publicly owned treatment works. As with BPT and BAT limits, EPA was required, in adopting best conventional technology effluent limits, to take into consideration factors such as the age of the equipment and facilities involved, the process employed, engineering aspects, process changes and non-water quality environmental impacts (including energy requirements).

Congress anticipated that EPA, in developing the best conventional technology limits, would review the old BAT limits for conventional pollutants and reduce the stringency of such limits to the extent indicated by the economic justification and cost comparability with secondary treatment requirements.

EPA's first effort at developing BCT regulations was reversed because the agency failed to consider cost-effectiveness adequately in the development of these rules.[50] EPA then promulgated revised regulations and methodology, which are far less costly than the original rules. In most industry categories, EPA's new methodology resulted in BCT limitations no more stringent than those established for BPT.

The last of the three categories of technology-based effluent limits for existing industry direct discharges provided in the 1977 amendments is the system of effluent limitations to be adopted for "nonconventional nontoxic" pollutants. This is essentially an "everything else" category which applies to all pollutants other than those identified as priority pollutants, toxic pollutants or conventional pollutants under the preceding sections of section 301. To date, only about ten substances have been so regulated; most could probably be regulated just as well as either toxic or conventional pollutants. Compliance is required three years after the date the limitations are established by EPA regulations, or March 31, 1989, whichever is sooner.

5.5.2 Required Level of Treatment—Technology-Based Limits for "New Source" Direct Discharges

The establishment of effluent limitations for "new sources" (defined as any facility or major modification, the construction of which is commenced "after the publication of proposed regulations" prescribing an applicable standard of performance) is separately dealt with in section 306 of the act. Although the general approach for establishment of new source performance standards under section 306 is similar to the approach for the establishment of section 301 effluent limitations (discussed in the previous section) there are significant differences both as to the level of treatment required and the manner of applying the limitations established. These differences remain important because of EPA's delay in promulgating many BPT and BAT limitations, and because the new source standards

---

[50] *American Paper Institute v. EPA*, 660 F.2d 954 (4th Cir. 1981)

will govern the addition or replacement of certain equipment at an existing discharger.[51]

Section 306(a)(1) of the act defines the term "standard of performance" as

a standard for the control of the discharge of pollutants which reflects the greatest degree of effluent reduction . . . achievable through application of the best available demonstrated control technology, processes, operating methods, and other alternatives, including, where practicable, standards permitting no discharge of pollutants.

The primary difference between these criteria and the section 301 criteria is the requirement in section 306 that EPA consider not only pollution control techniques, but also various alternative production processes, operating methods, in-plant control procedures and so forth. Accordingly, in the establishment of section 306 new source performance standards (NSPS), alternatives or supplements to end-of-pipe treatment will be emphasized. Production process alternatives, which, though less economic, may have a significantly reduced pollution potential may, as a practical matter, be required.

A second major difference regarding criteria for development of new source performance standards is the absence of the kind of requirements for detailed consideration of economic and technological factors which are established by section 301 for existing source effluent limitations procedures. This absence reflects a presumption that if a source is yet to be constructed, there is greater flexibility to alter total facility design so as to achieve stringent effluent limitations. Thus EPA has greater discretion in the promulgation of new source performance standards than it does with respect to existing sources.

A third, and major, factor to be taken into account when considering the applicability of new source performance standards is that the act provides almost no flexibility for moderating the impact of those standards when applied to specific facilities. The "fundamental factors variance" and other modification authorities provided by the act are not applicable in the new source situation and, accordingly, strict conformity with the new source performance standards, where applicable, is essential.

Finally, where EPA is the issuing authority, the issuance of a permit for a new source discharge is a federal action subject to the review requirements of the National Environmental Policy Act.[52] Thus, where the issuance of a new source discharge permit is found to be a major action with a significant effect on the environment, an environmental impact statement will be required. The result will be both substantial delay in the issuance of the new source permit and the potential inclusion of stringent requirements in permits which are issued, requirements which may address a host of other environmental issues besides water pollution discharges and the quality of receiving waters.[53]

---

[51] 40 C.F.R. § 122.29(b).

[52] CWA § 511(c), 40 C.F.R. Part 6.

[53] There are serious questions about the legality of EPA including additional environmental requirements based on NEPA in an NPDES permit. *See Natural Resources Defense Council v. EPA*, 822 F.2d 104 (D.C. Cir. 1987).

Because a determination that a facility is a new source significantly affects both the stringency of applicable treatment standards and the length of time required in order to obtain a permit, the question of when a facility "commences construction" for purposes of applying new source performance standards has proven controversial. This issue is addressed in considerable detail by section 122.29 of EPA's NPDES regulations, court decisions, and opinions of EPA's General Counsel. The question remains difficult because it depends so heavily on the facts of each case. Companies planning new facilities or major modifications of older ones should carefully review these factual and legal issues with counsel early in the planning process.

Section 306 does offer both to new and modified sources one protection which is not available to existing sources under section 301. Section 306 specifically provides that any new facility constructed to meet all applicable new source standards of performance in effect as of the time it is constructed may not be subjected to any more stringent standards for ten years from the date construction is completed or for the period of depreciation under the Internal Revenue Code, whichever is shorter. This protection from more stringent standards of performance, as EPA construes the act, is inapplicable to any more stringent permit conditions which are not technology-based—that is, limitations based on water quality standards or toxic pollutant prohibitions—or to any new permit conditions which govern pollutants not controlled by the applicable new source performance standards with which the facility complied at the time of construction. It should be noted that, on the expiration of the ten-year protection period, immediate compliance with the standards in effect at the time of such expiration will be required. No implementation period for compliance with those standards will be allowed.

5.5.3 Effluent Guidelines for Additional Source Categories

The act requires EPA to make periodic revisions of effluent guidelines for industry categories as technology improves and economics change.[54] The initial set of industry categories was specified in part by section 306(b)(1)(A) and has been expanded with time by EPA.

Section 304(m) was added by the 1987 amendments. This new provision requires EPA to establish and to publish a schedule for the annual review and revisions of existing effluent guidelines.[55] This provision also requires the Agency to identify source categories discharging toxic or nonconventional sources for which effluent guidelines have not been published, and to establish a schedule by which enforceable guidelines for these categories are promulgated. The deadline to promulgate such standards was February 1991.[56]

EPA published such a plan in September, 1992.[57] The plan calls for developing new and revised effluent guidelines, which regulate industrial discharges

---

[54] CWA, § 304(b).

[55] *Id.* 304(m)(1)(A).

[56] *Id.* 304(m)(1)(B), (C).

[57] 57 Fed. Reg. 41000 (Sept. 8, 1992).

to surface waters and POTWs. Effluent guidelines are currently under development for nine source categories, and EPA intends to develop 12 new effluent guidelines over an 11 year period. Four of those new rules are specified; the remaining eight will be specified in future plans.

5.5.4 Required Level of Treatment—Technology-Based Limits for Indirect Dischargers (Pretreatment)

Industrial facilities that discharge into publicly owned treatment works (POTWs) are regulated not by the requirements governing direct discharges, but rather by comparable treatment requirements—pretreatment standards—adopted pursuant to section 307(b) of the act. Pretreatment standards are calculated to achieve two basic objectives: (1) to protect the operation of POTWs; and (2) to prevent the discharge of pollutants which pass through publicly owned treatment works without receiving adequate treatment. The dual objectives of the pretreatment program result in a two-part system of controls under the applicable EPA regulations. General requirements are imposed under 40 C.F.R. Part 403 and requirements specific to particular industries, so-called categorical standards, are developed and imposed together with other effluent limitations governing each such industry.

The first part of the general pretreatment regulation focuses primarily on preventing the discharge into POTWs of pollutants which will interfere with the proper operation of the receiving treatment works. This "protection" standard[58] prohibits the introduction into any publicly owned treatment works of:

(i)   pollutants which create a fire or explosion hazard in the POTW, including but not limited to, waste streams which meet the Resource Conservation Recovery Act (RCRA) test for characteristic inflammable waste;

(ii)   discharges with a pH lower than 5.0 unless the works is specifically designed to accommodate such discharges;

(iii) solid or viscous pollutants in amounts which obstruct the flow in a sewer system;

(iv)   discharges, including discharges of conventional pollutants, of such volume and concentration that they upset the treatment process and cause a permit violation (for example, unusually high concentrations of oxygen demanding pollutants such as BOD);

(v)   heat in amounts which will inhibit biological activity in the POTW resulting in interference, but in no case heat in such quantities that the temperature influent at the treatment works exceeds 40° C (104° F) unless the works are designed to accommodate such heat;

(vi)   petroleum oil, nonbiodegradable cutting oil, or products of mineral oil origin in amounts that will cause interference or pass through;

---

[58] 40 C.F.R. § 403.5, as amended, 55 Fed. Reg. 30082 (July 24, 1990).

(vii)   pollutants which result in the presence of toxic gases, vapors or fumes within the POTW in a quantity that may cause acute worker health and safety problems; and

(viii) any trucked or hauled pollutants, except at discharge points designated by the POTW.

These general pretreatment provisions were recently revised and tightened dramatically as a result of the work by Pretreatment Implementation Review Task Force.[59] These changes were intended to assure that the domestic sewage exclusion under section 1004(C) or RCRA did not allow hazardous wastes to escape needed regulation.[60] Consequently, in addition to the substantive requirements noted above, industrial users of POTWs must now provide written notification to the POTW, the EPA regional Waste Management Division Director, and the state hazardous waste authorities "of any discharge which if otherwise disposed of, would be a hazardous waste under 40 CFR part 261."[61] Moreover, if the discharge is of more than 100 kilograms a month of such waste—whether listed or characteristic—the industrial user is to include information about the hazardous waste constituents, mass, and concentration, and estimate these amounts for the following 12 months. The industrial user must certify as part of its notification that it has a RCRA waste minimization program in place. These requirements become effective in February 1991.

As pollutants which are already addressed in existing discharge monitoring reports are exempt from this notification requirement, it is likely that these notifications, when filed, will result in revisions of a number of pretreatment permits and the filing of enforcement actions for discharge of materials not addressed in such permits. As this new rule has received little attention it seems likely that many industrial users will inadvertently violate it.

The second major objective of the pretreatment regulations—preventing the discharge into publicly owned treatment works of pollutants which pass through those treatment works without receiving adequate treatment—is to be achieved by "categorical" pretreatment regulations. These categorical regulations are applicable only to "incompatible" pollutants—that is, pollutants other than biochemical oxygen demand, suspended solids, pH and fecal coliform bacteria, and which are not adequately treated in the POTW treatment process.[62] These categorical pretreatment regulations, like the BAT regulations and new source performance standards, focus primarily on the 34 industries and 65 toxic pollutant categories specified in the NRDC consent decree. For each discharger into a POTW, these categorical standards are intended to result in the same level of treatment prior to discharge from the POTW as that which would have been required had the industrial facility discharged those pollutants directly to the re-

---

[59] 55 Fed. Reg. 30082, promulgating amendments to 40 C.F.R. Part 403 (July 24, 1990).

[60] *See Comite pro Rescate de la Salud v. Puerto Rico Aqueduct and Sewer Authority*, 30 ERC 1473 (1st Cir. 1989) (restricting scope of domestic sewage exclusion under RCRA).

[61] 55 Fed. Reg. 30131, promulgating 40 C.F.R. § 403.12(p)(i) (July 24, 1990).

[62] Additional pollutants may be identified as "compatible" for a particular treatment works if it can be shown that the facility in question adequately treats those pollutants.

ceiving waters. The stringency of these categorical standards can theoretically be reduced through the mechanism of removal credits, which takes into account the removal of these pollutants consistently achieved by the POTW in question. Removal credits, however, will not be available under the statute until EPA completes promulgation of its sewage sludge regulations under section 405 of the act.[63]

Accordingly, the industrial facility discharging into a POTW will be required to achieve, in meeting the applicable pretreatment limits, a level of treatment performance equivalent to the applicable BAT effluent limitations or new source performance standards unless the receiving POTW has an approved pretreatment program and requests removal credits against the applicable pretreatment limit. This removal credit is to be based on the POTW's demonstrated capability to consistently remove that pollutant in its treatment process. In order to qualify for a revision, the POTW must provide consistent removal of each pollutant for which a discharge limit revision is sought, and its sludge use or disposal practices must, at the time of the application and thereafter, remain in compliance with all applicable criteria, guidelines and regulations for sludge use and disposal. EPA modified its regulations in an effort to account for process variations by POTWs,[64] but that effort was reversed by the Court of Appeals.[65]

Pretreatment requirements are directly enforceable by EPA and states with NPDES permit issuance authority, but the EPA regulations contemplate eventual delegation of primary enforcement responsibility to individual POTWs, with EPA and the states receding into the background.

Under the regulations, any POTW (or combination of POTWs operated by the same authority) having a total design flow greater than five million gallons per day must have developed and implemented a pretreatment program by July 1, 1983, if it receives incompatible industrial waste. A POTW must have an approved pretreatment program in order to grant removal credits, although it may grant conditional removal credits while EPA is considering approval of the POTW's pretreatment program. POTW programs must meet funding, personnel, legal, and procedural criteria sufficient to ensure that the POTW's enforcement responsibilities can be carried out. Once the program is developed and approved, the POTW will be responsible for enforcement of the national pretreatment standards. A POTW may exercise enforcement authority through a number of methods including contracts, joint powers agreements, ordinances, or otherwise.

Finally, pretreatment regulations establish extensive reporting requirements for both industrial users and POTWs in order to monitor and demonstrate compliance with categorical pretreatment standards.

---

[63] *Chicago Association of Commerce and Industry v. EPA*, 873 F.2d 1025 (7th Cir. 1989); *Chemical Manufacturers Association v. EPA*, 870 F.2d 177, 257-61 (5th Cir. 1989); *Armco, Inc. v. EPA*, 869 F.2d 975 (6th Cir. 1989).

[64] 40 C.F.R. § 403.7, 49 Fed. Reg. 31221, August 3, 1984.

[65] *Natural Resources Defense Council v. EPA*, 790 F. 2d 289 (3d Cir. 1986), *cert. denied*, 107 S. Ct. 1285 (1987).

The pretreatment regulations significantly affect industries subject to categorical pretreatment standards, as well as other industrial users of POTWs which will have to comply with general pretreatment requirements.

5.5.5 Best Professional Judgment

As is the case with many regulatory efforts, the comprehensive, detailed and formal process outlined above is, as a practical matter, inapplicable in a very large number of the situations where discharge limits are established since, very often if not always, a significant part of the process leading to the discharge under consideration will be in a category for which applicable effluent limits or performance standards are yet to be promulgated. In such cases, the regulations authorize the permit issuer to establish discharge limits based on the exercise of professional or engineering judgment.

Although this approach seems to vest unbridled discretion in the permit issuer, actual practice seems to result in a reasonably careful process of technology assessments, treatability studies and accepted analytical methods to determine the technology to be used and the level of treatment which it will achieve. Though there is no judicial precedent yet, it seems likely that the courts will hold permit issuers to reasonable standards of professional care. This context seems to result in reasonable negotiation of permit limits in most instances. Professional judgment may well continue to yield reasonable case-specific applications of the "best available" or "best conventional" standards.

5.5.6 Variances

The statutory mechanisms to authorize variances from technology-based standards are exceedingly limited. The most broadly applicable of these variances is the fundamentally different factors (FDF) variance. There are also variance mechanisms to recognize use of innovative control technology and in certain limited circumstances from BAT limitations. Other than the FDF variance, there are no variances allowed from toxic pollutant standards and none at all from discharge limitations set to meet water quality standards.

The FDF variance evolved through EPA and court interpretation, and was codified and tightened by the 1987 amendments.[66] The FDF variance was initially applied to the 1977 BPT effluent limitations through the inclusion of a variance clause in each set of effluent limitations regulations. This clause allowed a discharger to demonstrate that the limitations should not apply to its facility because of the existence of factors which were fundamentally different from those considered by EPA in the process of developing the effluent limitations.

The scope of the required variance clause was expanded in the case of *Appalachian Power Company v. Train*,[67] and EPA's recognition of the necessity of some sort of variance mechanism for "fundamentally different factors" was applauded by the Supreme Court in the *Dupont v. Train* case.[68] The need for a

---

[66] CWA, § 301(n).
[67] 545 F.2d 1351 (4th Cir. 1976).
[68] 430 U.S. 112 (1977).

fundamental factors variance arises from the process EPA uses to develop industry-wide effluent limitations under the Clean Water Act. It is impossible to consider all of the factors required to be considered by section 304 in a full and timely fashion for every type of plant in every industrial category. Consequently, there must be some way to weigh factors not fully considered in the regulatory development process when the time comes to apply effluent limitations to a particular facility in the form of an NPDES permit.

Thus, in both the pretreatment regulations and NPDES permit program regulations discussed below, EPA allows dischargers to obtain the fundamental factors variance. The variance is available with respect to the categorical pretreatment regulations, as well as for all of the technology-based effluent limits for existing sources. It is unavailable for new source performance standards (because a facility yet to be constructed has greater design flexibility) or for water quality-related effluent limitations. The Supreme Court has ruled that the fundamental factors variance is available with respect to toxic pollutants under the Clean Water Act.[69] The 1987 amendments have codified the fundamental factors variance in section 301 (n) and made it more difficult to obtain.[70]

In order to obtain a fundamental factors variance, the discharger must show that factors applicable to this facility are fundamentally different from those considered in the development of the effluent limitations guidelines. Factors which section 125.31 of the regulations and section 301(n) of the act allow to be considered as fundamentally different are:

(1)   the nature or quality of the pollutants contained in the waste load of the applicant's process waste water;

(2)   the volume of the discharger's process waste water and effluent discharged;

(3)   non-water quality environmental impacts of control and treatment of the discharger's raw waste load (are these impacts fundamentally more adverse than those considered during the development of national limits?);

(4)   energy requirements of the application of control and treatment technology (are they fundamentally greater than those assessed in developing national limits?); and

(5)   age, size, land availability and configuration as they relate to the discharger's equipment or facilities, processes employed; engineering aspects of the application of control technology.

If it finds that a fundamentally different factor exists, the EPA may adopt alternative effluent limitations for the facility in question. It should be noted that those limits may be either more or less stringent than the effluent limitations with respect to which the variance is granted.

---

[69] *Chemical Manufacturers Association v. Natural Resources Defense Council,* 470 U.S. 116 (1985).
[70] CWA, § 301(n).

The fundamental factors variance is not available simply because the cost of compliance with BPT limitations would force plant closure.[71] Instead, the costs of BPT compliance are relevant in deciding if fundamentally different factors exist at a plant and, if so, whether the alternate effluent limitations are as cost-effective as those imposed on the industry in general.[72] (The language of the 1987 amendments makes it unclear whether cost can be considered at all.)

Under the 1987 amendments, an applicant must show that it raised the fundamentally different factors during the development of the regulation or show why it did not have a reasonable opportunity to raise the factors in such process.[73] The only meaningful relief available for improper application of factors actually considered during the development process is an appeal to the courts. Unless this appeal is taken within 90 days after the applicable effluent limits are published in final form, the right to raise these issues may be waived. These procedural rules make it imperative for affected industries to monitor and to participate in the development and revision of effluent standards applicable to the industry lest this variance mechanism become unavailable.

There are two additional variance mechanisms applicable to discharges of non-conventional, non-toxic pollutants. The first is under section 301(c). Section 301(c) grants the administrator authority to modify the BAT requirements or the related pretreatment requirements affecting nonconventional, non-toxic pollutants if it can be shown that the economic capability of the discharger necessitates less stringent limitations. A further prerequisite to such a modification is showing that it will result in further progress toward elimination of the discharge of pollutants. Though this basis for granting a variance is reasonably broad, the circumstances in which it can be granted are strictly limited. The section 301(c) variance does not apply to the BCT effluent limitations, and section 301(l) of the act precludes the modification of any effluent limitation regulating a toxic or priority pollutant.

Section 301(g) is the second variance mechanism applicable to BAT limitations for several nonconventional non-toxic pollutants—ammonia, chlorine, color, iron, and total phenols—but excludes heat. In the case of sections 301(c) and (g), the utility of the variance is limited by its application only to nonconventional, non-toxic pollutants.

The final statutory basis for modification of BAT and BCT effluent limits and pretreatment standards is set forth in section 301(k). That subsection authorizes the administrator or state issuing authority to issue a permit providing for a compliance date extension of two years if a source seeks to achieve the applicable limits through the use of innovative technology which has the potential for in-dustry-wide application and has a substantial likelihood of achieving greater ef-

---

[71] *EPA v. National Crushed Stone Association,* 449 U.S. 64 (1980), CWA § 301(n)(1)(A).

[72] *Weyerhauser Co. v. Costle,* 590 F.2d 1011, 1036 (D.C. Cir. 1978).

[73] CWA, § 301(n). EPA's regulatory guidance suggests that all such variance applications should have been filed by July 3, 1989, unless the request is related to a later revision of effluent standards for a source category, or in the establishment of new effluent standards for a source category which did not previously have industry-specific effluent guidelines. 54 Fed. Reg. 246 (Jan. 2, 1989).

fluent reduction than the effluent limitations require or will result in significantly lower costs. It is unclear whether this innovative technology variance may be granted for toxic pollutant limits in view of the prohibition against modification of toxic pollutant effluent limitations set forth in section 301(l).

With respect to the 1977 BPT effluent limits, the act provided only one now-obsolete basis for extending the time for compliance.

5.6 Technology-Based Treatment Standards—Publicly Owned Treatment Works

For discharges from publicly owned treatment works (POTWs), section 301 directed that by July 1 1977, they achieve effluent limitations based on secondary treatment, as defined by EPA, and any more stringent limitations necessary to comply with water quality standards or treatment standards imposed by state law. The 1977 and 1981 amendments provided for extension of the 1977 secondary treatment and other deadlines where, because of lack of federal funding or otherwise, planned facilities had not been completed. The extension was to the earliest date on which funding can be provided and construction completed, but in no case later than July 1988. Industrial dischargers whose permits require discharge to a treatment works and who had enforceable contracts for such discharge or who were included in a treatment works facility plan filed with a grant application could be granted an extension on much the same basis as the treatment works itself.

EPA defined "secondary treatment" for purposes of section 301 in 1973 and modified that definition late in 1984.[74] The effluent levels prescribed by these regulations are as follows:

	% Removal 30 day average	Concentration (mg/1) Monthly Average	Weekly Average
BOD(5 day)	85	30	45
Suspended Solids(SS)	85	30	45
Coliform	200/100 ml.	400/100 ml.	
pH	6.0 to 9.0		

The regulations make special provision for upward revision of the "secondary treatment" effluent limits (1) where necessary to take into account storm water infiltration into combined sewers during wet weather periods; and (2) where necessary to take into account the fact that the section 301 and section 306 effluent limitations applicable to major industrial dischargers into the treatment works (those exceeding 10 percent of the design flow) would permit an industrial user to directly discharge greater concentrations than those set forth in the table. In the latter case, the permitted discharge from the POTW which is attributable to the industrial waste received for treatment may be increased to equal, but not exceed, that which would be permitted under the applicable effluent limitations if the industrial facility were discharging directly into a waterway.

In the 1981 amendments, Congress revised the definition of secondary treatment so that such biological treatment facilities as oxidation ponds, lagoons,

---

[74] See 40 C.F.R. Part 133.

and ditches and trickling filters are deemed to be the equivalent of secondary treatment.[75] These modes of treatment are considerably cheaper than other treatment modes, especially for small communities. The changes made pursuant to this standard allow trickling filters and stabilization ponds to meet secondary treatment requirements if the discharge meets the following parameters:[76]

	% Removal 30 day average	Concentration (mg/1) Monthly Average	Weekly Average
BOD(5 day)	65	45	65
Suspended Solids(SS)	65	45	65
pH	6.0 to 9.0		

The relative stringency of the POTW effluent limitations and the fact that, under the 1972 act, POTWs were, for the first time, subjected to effective and directly enforceable federal effluent limitations and permit requirements, gave municipal authorities a strong mandate to rigorously enforce flow and concentration limitations on industrial users of their systems. In some cases, the "pretreatment requirements" imposed by municipal authorities pursuant to this mandate have been more stringent than the federal pretreatment standards discussed above. In addition, as noted below, the increasing need for high levels of performance by POTWs result in new or upgraded facilities which can drastically increase the cost to industry of waste treatment services. EPA and the Department of Justice have made compliance with pretreatment program requirements by municipalities an enforcement priority.

5.7 Water Quality-Related Effluent Limitations

The 1972 act made technology-based effluent limitations the nationwide minimum or base-level of treatment. The act provides several mechanisms by which these discharge limitations are to be tightened in order to protect or maintain adequate water quality in specific bodies of water. These more stringent water quality-based limitations are most often an issue along bodies of water where there is a heavy concentration of industrial dischargers (for example, the Houston Ship Channel), where receiving waters need to be maintained at a very high quality for recreational or other purposes (for example, a trout stream), or where hydrologic modifications for navigation (for example, lock and dam systems) have reduced the capacity of receiving waters to assimilate pollutants.

Under the CWA as amended in 1987, the new section 304(l) will be the most important of several statutory mechanisms for tightening discharge standards over the next five years. This new provision requires tightening of priority and toxic pollutant discharge limitations to meet water quality standards. Sections 301(b)(l)(C) and 302 apply to all categories of pollutants and provide the basic mechanisms by which water quality standards are established and modified. Other sections provide for periodic reviews of water quality by the states and

---

[75] CWA, § 304(d)(4).
[76] 40 C.F.R. § 133.105.

reports to EPA, efforts to preserve lakes and estuaries, and efforts to develop controls on nonpoint sources of pollution affecting water quality.

5.7.1 Toxic Water Quality Standards

The NRDC consent decree contained several provisions addressing water quality standards as they related to priority pollutants. These provisions required EPA to issue water quality guidance for states to use in setting additional discharge standards for toxic or priority pollutants. In addition, the decree required identification of so-called toxic "hot spots," where the application of technology-based standards would not achieve water quality standards. For a variety of reasons, including EPA's slow pace in issuing the technology-based standards and the inherent scientific complexity of establishing water quality standards, these provisions of the consent decree had little effect at the level of the individual discharger.

The 1987 amendments added section 304(l) to the CWA, an addition which adopts several concepts from the consent decree and places enforceable deadlines on their implementation at the individual discharger level.

Section 304(l) requires that each state identify waters within the state where the application of technology-based effluent limitations does not result in the achievement of water quality standards for toxic pollutants. Where non-compliance results substantially from point source discharges of toxic pollutants, the state is to determine which point sources are responsible and to develop individual control strategies for each of these point sources to bring the water body into compliance with water quality standards. By February 4, 1989, states had to submit the list of identified water bodies, together with the affected point sources and the individual control strategies. EPA had 120 days—or until June 1989—to approve or disapprove. If EPA approved the strategy, then the affected dischargers had up to three years—or until June 1992—in which to comply. If EPA disapproved the control strategies, or if a state failed to submit them, EPA then had one year in which to promulgate substitute control strategies. Sources then have three years to comply, or June 1993, if EPA acts on schedule.

EPA has issued detailed guidance about implementation of section 304(l).[77] The assessments of impaired water bodies are to be made primarily on the basis of existing water quality data, as time does not permit substantial additional monitoring to be conducted to identify these water bodies. In addition, EPA's guidance indicates that when individual control strategies are prepared, they should address all pollutant parameters creating water quality problems (for example, ammonia, chlorine and "whole effluent toxicity"), not simply the toxic pollutants identified in the NRDC consent decree.

EPA treated implementation of section 304(l) as a high priority, and as a result completed its review of state plans and individual control strategies on time in June 1989. As a result of these reviews, EPA listed 595 water bodies as

---

[77] 54 Fed. Reg. 1300 (Jan. 12, 1989).

substantially impaired as a result of toxic discharges from 879 point sources, including 240 POTWs. Individual control strategies—NPDES permit proposals—were established for all these point sources. Many of these plans are now in various administrative appeal stages.

Some environmental groups contend that section 304(1) requires EPA to revise NPDES permits for all discharges of toxic pollutants to impaired waters, an interpretation which would dramatically increase the number of NPDES permits which would have to be revised and tightened for toxic pollutants. The Court of Appeals has agreed with parts of this challenge, holding that section 304(1) requires the listing of many more bodies of water as impaired by toxic pollutants.[78] After the listing of additional impaired water bodies, the Court will allow EPA to reconsider its decision not to impose individual control strategies on many sources. Thus the section 304(1) program may apply to many more sources than those listed in the first round of individual control strategies.

Implementation of section 304(1) requires that states have water quality standards in place for toxic pollutants. States normally rely on EPA's guidance documents for the pollutant in question, which is offered under section 304(a). EPA has completed most of the guidance documents for pollutants identified in the NRDC consent decree.

The 1987 amendments amended section 303(c)(3)(B) to require the states to adopt numerical water quality standards for toxic pollutants where possible.

EPA has now announced that where states fail to adopt either numerical toxic water quality standards or mathematical methods to calculate toxic effluent limitations appropriate for water quality, EPA water quality guidelines will become the new state water quality standard.[79] This policy effectively nationalizes water quality standards unless states act to recognize local variations. Though most states are working to adopt new numerical water quality standards for toxic discharges, most have not yet completed the task.[80]

Where numerical standards are impractical, the amended act now requires EPA to issue guidance on biological monitoring methods and for states to use such methods in setting standards and assessing compliance under the act. EPA issued guidance in December 1989 for biomonitoring using five species, three for fresh water, and two for salt water.[81] EPA is also requiring biomonitoring and whole effluent toxicity testing for POTWs discharging more than one million gallons per day, and smaller, if major industrial discharges are present. Some states (for example, North Carolina) began implementing such requirements even before EPA's formal guidance was issued. Biological monitoring is a relatively new concept under the CWA, and its implementation is likely to prove highly controversial.

---

[78] *NRDC v. EPA*, 31 E.R.C. 2089 (9th Cir. 1990).

[79] 55 Fed. Reg. 14350 (April 17, 1990).

[80] *See Id.* for status list of state water quality standards.

[81] 54 Fed. Reg. 50216 (December 4, 1989).

5.7.2 Water Quality Standards Affecting All Pollutants

Section 304(l) is a more tightly focused version of water quality approaches which have been part of the CWA since 1972. The most important of these more general water quality provisions are sections 301(b)(l)(C) and 302.

Section 301(b)(l)(C) requires industrial dischargers and POTWs to achieve no later than July 1977, any effluent limitations more stringent than the minimum technology-based standards which may be necessary to meet applicable federal-state water quality standards. This requirement is incorporated into permits issued by EPA through the state certification requirement under section 401 of the act. Section 302 of the act authorizes EPA directly to establish effluent criteria more stringent than the applicable BAT limits where necessary for the attainment or maintenance in a specific water body of water quality which "shall assure protection of public water supplies, agriculture and industrial uses, and the protection and propagation of a balanced population of shellfish, fish and wildlife, and allow recreational activities in and on the water. . ." EPA has interpreted this section 302 authority as providing a selective tool for the agency to impose more stringent requirements where necessary to protect important water resources. Although this section has received little use to date, it does have great potential impact in that it authorizes EPA to adopt its own effluent limitations for any body of water for which a state fails or refuses to adopt water quality standards sufficient to maintain fishing and swimming uses.

The water quality standards and water-quality related effluent limitations imposed by these two mechanisms can require levels of treatment considerably higher than those required by the technology-related effluent limits, particularly for water bodies with heavy concentrations of dischargers, or exceptionally poor water quality and correspondingly stringent water quality standards, or water bodies with limited assimilative capacity because of hydrologic factors such as dams for navigation and water supply. (These hydrologic modifications are more likely to be a factor with conventional pollutants such as BOD, which break down relatively fast, than for more persistent toxic pollutants.) The potential stringency of these limitations is increased by the absence of any variance provision applicable to section 301 water quality standards. Section 302 does contain a limited variance mechanism for standards imposed under its mandate, including a potential five-year variance from certain toxic pollutant standards. The requirement for compliance with water quality standards is inflexible and mandatory, thus increasing the importance of carefully following the development of such standards as they apply to particular water bodies and dischargers to them.

The procedures for setting water quality standards are quite complex. States, acting pursuant to the procedures set out in 40 CFR § 131.20, are to hold public hearings every three years for the purpose of reviewing and revising state water quality standards. Although EPA issues guidance documents about the effects of various pollutants, it does not set specific minimums for state standards; instead, the rules require that such standards specify and protect appropriate water uses (for example,, water supply, fish, wildlife),[82] and set specific numerical criteria where possible to attain these ends.[83] The state standards must attain Clean Water Act's goal of fishable, swimmable waters wherever attainable, and, at a minimum must maintain the uses designated in the standards and current uses,[84] unless the state can demonstrate that the designated use is unattainable or infeasible for one of a short list of reasons, primarily concerning other physical or biological aspects of the water body.[85] In addition, there shall be no degradation of "outstanding national resource" waters, such as those in national and state parks.[86]

The Clean Water Act's system of discharge limitations is far from completion and faces severe challenges in dealing with multitudes of specific pollutants in many different circumstances. However the system has already overcome major obstacles and the pieces which are in place establish a system which is increasingly effective in minimizing the discharge of pollutants. The discharge limits under CWA are as sophisticated and stringent as any we are likely to see under any environmental law.

5.8 Preventing, Giving Notice of, Responding to Spills

Although the permit mechanism is highly effective for discharges that can be anticipated and controlled, it is of limited use in dealing with events like accidental spills, which may be unpredictable. Since permits, by their nature, can operate effectively only if issued in advance of the event which causes pollution, there is obviously a need to have other methods for dealing with events, like spills, which can't be anticipated or avoided. To meet this need, the CWA imposes pollution prevention planning requirements to minimize the potential for a spill, mandatory spill notification requirements, and provisions assessing responsibility for responding to spills or paying the cost of response.

5.8.1 Spill Prevention

Pollution prevention mandates under the Clean Water Act include requirements to maintain and implement up-to-date Spill Prevention, Control and Countermeasure (SPCC) plans for facilities with total oil storage capacity in excess of 1,320 gallons above ground or 40,000 gallons below ground. These plans, which include physical requirements such as secondary containment capacity, are intended to minimize the consequences of a spill if one does occur. As a result of enactment of the Oil Pollution Act of 1990, we will shortly see SPCC planning requirements made much more rigorous, and extended to cover vessels and to require plans for facilities storing hazardous pollutants other than oil. Many of these plans will, for the first time, be required to be submitted to the federal authority (EPA or the Coast Guard) for review and approval rather than

---

[82] 40 C.F.R. §§ 131.6, 131.10.

[83] 40 C.F.R. § 131.11.

[84] 40 C.F.R. § 131.10(h).

[85] 40 C.F.R. § 131.10(g).

[86] 40 C.F.R. § 131.12(a)(3).

simply maintained at the facility. We can expect SPCC planning to become an increasingly important aspect of CWA compliance.

Congress was highly critical of the unrealistic and unworkable contingency plans in place in Prince William Sound when the *Valdez* spill occurred. The plans overlapped; they were uncoordinated; they assumed far too small a spill, and far too quick a response time in practice. Many of these problems had been identified in drills but not corrected. As a result, a spill cleanup around the Valdez became a multi-year shore cleanup, at a cost of over two billion dollars.

Section 4202 of the Oil Pollution Act rewrites requirements governing national, area, and facility contingency plans. The National Contingency Plan (NCP) is to be revised by August 1991 to reflect the many changes in the statute; area contingency plans are to be prepared or revised; and individual facility SPCC plan requirements must be prepared and considerably updated.

Under section 311(j) prior to the Oil Pollution Act, facilities were to prepare SPCC plans if they stored more than 1,320 gallons of oil aboveground, or 42,000 gallons below ground.[87] Facilities subject to this requirement include those storing vegetable or mineral oils, not simply petroleum products. Thus many food processing companies are subject to these rules.

Section 311(j)(5) now requires tank vessels and offshore and onshore facilities to prepare SPCC plans, and specifies requirements for these plans. An onshore facility is required to prepare SPCC plans if it handles, transports, or stores oil, and if, "because of its location, [the facility] could reasonably be expected to cause substantial harm to the environment by discharging into or on the navigable waters, adjoining shorelines, or the exclusive economic zone."[88] Given the broad definition of navigable waters used under the Clean Water Act, a potential oil discharge to a storm sewer could be sufficient to require preparation of SPCC plans.

The SPCC plan must be a plan to respond, to the maximum extent practicable, to a worst case discharge, and to a substantial threat of such discharge, of oil or hazardous substances.[89] The plan must:

(1)   be consistent with the NCP and area contingency plans;

(2)   identify the person in charge of the facility, who must have authority to implement the plan;

(3)   require immediate communication between the person in charge and appropriate federal officials and response action contractors;

(4)   ensure by contract (or other means allowed under regulation) that adequate private personnel and equipment will be available to remove the worst case discharge to the maximum extent practicable;

(5)   require training, periodic unannounced drills, and equipment testing necessary to assure effective response actions;

---

[87] 40 C.F.R. Part 112.

[88] CWA, § 311(j)(5)(B)(iii).

[89] CWA, § 311(j)(5)(A).

(6)   be updated periodically; and

(7)   be resubmitted for approval with each significant change.[90]

The SPCC plans are to be submitted for federal approval and the language of the statute suggests all such plans must be submitted and approved in order for facilities to continue operations. The legislative history suggests that only a fraction of these will have to be submitted and reviewed; otherwise the Coast Guard or EPA, as the case may be, would be overwhelmed with SPCC plans for small facilities.

The statute requires SPCC plans to be submitted for approval by February 1993. Without submission of such a plan, vessels and facilities are not permitted to continue to operate. Vessels and facilities submitting such plans may continue to operate for up to two years pending such approval. If the statutory time period expires without action by the regulatory agency, or if approval is denied, then the vessel or facility may not continue to store, transport, or handle oil.

These new requirements will place a premium on the early preparation or update of SPCC plans, in part because these plans must assure that a response action contractor is ready to bring adequate cleanup equipment in the event of a spill, and in part because the approval process may be slow. Although it seems unlikely that enforcement officials would in fact require facilities to shut down if regulatory delays slow plan approvals, the facility is in a better position to argue against such a shutdown if it has prepared and filed the needed plans in a timely manner, and has a reputable cleanup contractor ready.

5.8.2 Spill Notification

Section 311 of the CWA requires the owner or person in charge of any vehicle, vessel or facility from which there is a discharge or threatened discharge of oil or a reportable quantity of a hazardous pollutant to notify the National Response Center.[91]

Since 1970, section 311(b)(5) has required that the person in charge of a facility or vessel must make an immediate report to the appropriate federal agency of discharges of harmful quantities of oil to navigable waters. In practice this means that any discharge of oil to the waters must be reported to the National Response Center, which is run by the Coast Guard. Such reports may not be used as the basis for any criminal prosecution against the person reporting, except for false statement or perjury. It is a criminal offense to fail to report, punishable by up to five years in jail.

The Oil Pollution Act completely revised the penalties applicable to discharges of oil, and to violations of the SPCC and other regulations. A new provision, section 311(b)(6), is added, allowing the government to seek administrative penalties of up to $125,000 for violations of regulations or for discharges. This provision is very similar to the administrative penalty provision in section 309(g), and will probably be implemented using the same procedural rules.

---

[90] Clean Water Act, § 311(j)(5)(C).

[91] National Response Center phone number: 800-424-8802.

Under section 311(b)(7), as added by the Oil Pollution Act, much larger civil penalties may now be assessed in civil penalty actions brought in federal court. Any owner, operator, or person in charge may be fined up to $25,000 per day for a discharge, or $1,000 per barrel of oil discharged. Although the daily penalty level is consistent with that provided for violations of other provisions of the Clean Water Act, the quantity-based penalty is new and may reach extremely high levels quickly in the event of a large spill. Civil penalties may be tripled where a discharge results from gross negligence or misconduct. The minimum penalty in such cases is $100,000.

New criminal penalties are provided to punish dischargers. This change was accomplished simply by making the Clean Water Act's criminal penalty provision applicable to discharges in violation of section 311(b)(3). Where such a discharge is negligent, the penalty could be a year in prison and a $25,000 fine; where the discharge was done "knowingly," the penalty could be three years in prison, and a $50,000 fine; where the discharge resulted in placing others in imminent danger of serious bodily injury or death (knowing endangerment), the prison term is fifteen years, and the fine, $250,000 for an individual, and $1,000,000 for an organization. These criminal penalties may be difficult to obtain in practice, however, because of the mandatory self-reporting in section 311(b)(5), and immunity from prosecution for compelled reports written into the statute and from the Fifth Amendment.

5.8.3 Hazardous Substance Spills

Section 311 also governs the discharge of hazardous substances. EPA was slow to implement the hazardous substances provision, and shortly after regulations were promulgated in March 1978, a court enjoined significant parts of the regulations before they became effective. Congress responded to the court's action by amending section 311 to simplify and clarify its provisions along the lines agreed to in a compromise between EPA and the industry plaintiffs in that case.[92] The 1977 amendments were directed toward the two most significant problems identified by the court: the elements necessary to establish what was to be considered a harmful quantity and the relationship of section 311 to the NPDES program.

Pursuant to these amendments, EPA has designated approximately 300 substances as hazardous and thus subject to the section 311 program.[93] In addition, the agency has designated quantities of these substances that may be harmful (called a "reportable quantity").[94] Hazardous substances are placed in one of five categories: X, A, B, C, D. A harmful quantity of a category X substance is one pound, of a category A substance is 10 pounds, of a category B substance is 100 pounds, of a category C substance is 1000 pounds, and of a category D substance is 5,000 pounds.[95]

---

[92] Pub. L. No. 95-576, 92 Stat. 2467 (1978).

[93] 40 C.F.R. Part 116.

[94] 40 C.F.R. Part 117.

[95] 40 C.F.R. § 117.3.

The second principal feature of EPA's hazardous substance regulations is the exclusion of discharges made in compliance with an NPDES permit. Since a primary purpose of the amendments was to limit section 311 to "classic" hazardous substance spills, the regulations specify that they are not applicable to chronic discharges of designated substances if the discharge complies with an NPDES permit.[96] Such discharges, of course, remain subject to regulation under the NPDES program.

Further, if an NPDES facility has intermittent, anticipated spills of hazardous substances (for example, spills into plant drainage ditches), it should determine whether these discharges ought to be brought within the terms of its NPDES permit. The regulations give the facility the option of having such discharges regulated through the NPDES program or pursuant to section 311.

Discharges of hazardous substances may also reach navigable waters through municipal sewers and publicly owned treatment works. Discharges from industrial facilities to a POTW are not covered by the regulations at present. The regulations do apply to all discharges of reportable quantities of hazardous substances to POTWs by a mobile source such as trucks unless the discharger has met certain requirements.[97]

A facility owner or operator who spills a harmful quantity of a hazardous substance must report the spill; failure to do so will subject him to criminal penalties.

5.9 Controlling Non-Industrial Process Waste Discharges

Although the system of effluent limits imposed through the NPDES permit program is an effective means of regulating waste discharges which result from normal industrial or municipal processes and which are amenable to treatment prior to discharge, this system is an inappropriate means of regulating and controlling accidental and unanticipated discharges or discharges which, by their nature, are not subject to confinement and treatment (for example, area-wide or plant site runoff). For this latter class of discharges, the focus of regulation must be on preventing the discharge (in the case of the accidental spill) or on minimizing the volume of pollutants carried (in the case of area-wide and plant site runoff). Since accidental spills and "non-point source" discharges are responsible for a large percentage of the total pollutants introduced into the nation's waterways, the act provides a number of mechanisms, supplemental to the NPDES permit program, to control discharges which are unrelated to industrial process wastes. This system of supplemental regulatory controls is the subject of this section and the next one.

5.9.1 Non-Point Source Pollution

The primary mechanism contemplated by the 1972 act for controlling area-wide, non-point source pollution was the planning and regulatory program created by section 208. Although the section 208 process produced some high

---

[96] 40 C.F.R. § 117.12.
[97] 40 C.F.R. § 117.13.

quality area-wide waste treatment plans, in about 1980, Congress stopped funding this development and implementation of 208 plans. Consequently, little progress has been made in controlling non-point source pollution.

The 1987 amendments made non-point sources of toxic pollutants an important aspect of water quality planning under sections 303 and 304(l). As part of identifying water bodies which fail to attain and maintain water quality standards after compliance with technology-based standards, states must also identify those water bodies which fail to meet standards for toxic pollutants as a result of non-point sources of such pollutants. In section 319 of the 1987 amendments, Congress authorized $400 million over four years to fund state efforts to plan control measures for non-point source controls. Additionally, the 1987 amendments added section 320, the National Estuary Program. Under this provision, states are (among other things) to plan and to implement additional controls on point and non-point sources of pollutants to estuaries included in this program. Although state participation in this estuary program is voluntary, a number of important estuaries (for example, Chesapeake Bay, Puget Sound) are involved, and are apparently being treated as priorities by the states involved.

5.9.2 Storm Water Discharges and Best Management Practices

The regulation of municipal and industrial storm water discharges has been controversial since enactment of the 1972 amendments. That controversy persisted in large part because Congress failed to devise a regulatory program tailored to storm water discharges, leaving EPA the unpleasant choice of regulating all storm water discharges from point sources in the same fashion as process waste water from major industries, or leaving all such discharges unregulated. The first choice is unworkable because of the potentially vast number of such discharges and the high cost of treating all of them; the second choice would have left a number of major discharges of toxic and other pollutants completely unregulated, resulting in significant harm to the environment.

EPA arrived at a middle course, regulating discharges from industrial areas and municipalities above a certain size. The 1987 amendments adopted but substantially modified this approach. The amended act now requires that five categories of municipal or industrial storm water discharges be regulated as NPDES discharges:

1. discharges which have NPDES permits issued as of February 1987.
2. discharges "associated with industrial activity."
3. discharges "from a municipal separate storm sewer system serving a population of 250,000 or more."
4. discharges "from a municipal separate storm sewer system serving a population of 100,000 or more but less than 250,000."
5. other discharges designated by the EPA administrator or the state if such discharge "contributes to a violation of a water quality standard or is a significant contributor of pollutants to waters of the United States."[98]

---

[98] CWA, § 402(p)(2).

For discharges associated with industrial activities, NPDES permits must meet the applicable effluent limitations imposed upon the industry in question. Many industrial dischargers, of course, already have NPDES permits governing the discharge of storm water from plant yards and other ancillary areas. These continue to be regulated under existing permits.

Storm water discharges "associated with industrial activity" which do not currently have permits are subject to different procedures. By February 1989 (two years after enactment), the EPA was supposed to establish permit application requirements for such discharges. By February 1990 (three years after enactment), permit applications were to be filed, and by February 1991, EPA (or the state) was to issue or deny such permit. The permittee must comply with the permit "as expeditiously as practicable, but in no event later than three years after the date of issuance of such permit," or February 1994 if the earlier steps had been completed in a timely fashion.

Large municipal discharges—that is, discharges from storm water sewer systems serving more than 250,000 people—must meet the same schedule for permit application regulations, application filing, and deadlines for permit issuance and compliance. Thus, EPA's application regulations were to be issued by February 1989, permit applications were to be filed by February 1990, EPA (or states) were to decide and issue permits by February 1991, and permittees must comply with them by February 1994.

The 1987 amendments allow the EPA administrator flexibility to issue permits for discharges from municipal storm sewers on either a system or jurisdiction-wide basis. The permit must "include a requirement to effectively prohibit non-storm water discharges into storm sewers." The amendments impose substantive requirements on the permitted discharges. Such permits:

> shall require controls to the maximum extent practicable, including management practices, control techniques and systems, design and engineering methods, and such other provisions as the Administrator or the State determines appropriate for the control of such pollutants.[99]

Although smaller municipal storm sewer systems (that is, those serving 100,000 to 250,000 people) are subject to these same substantive permit requirements, the timetable for applications, permit decisions, and compliance is longer than for large municipal systems. Thus, EPA is supposed to issue permit regulations for these smaller dischargers by February 1991, permit applications must be filed by February 1992, permits must be granted or denied by February 1993, and compliance is required within three years of such issuance, or February 1996, if the timetable is met.

EPA at last published its final regulations concerning NPDES permits for storm water discharges in November 1990.[100] These rules address application requirements for storm water discharges associated with industrial activity and

---

[99] CWA, § 402(p)(3)(B)(iii).
[100] 55 Fed. Reg. 47990 (Nov. 16, 1990).

for discharges from municipal separate storm sewer systems serving a population of 100,000 or more.[101] Unlike the EPA's proposed storm water rules, the final rules require direct permit coverage for all storm water discharges associated with industrial activity, including those that discharge through municipal separate storm sewers.

The storm water regulations do not apply to all discharges of storm water by industries but only to storm water discharges associated with industrial activity. The regulations define "storm water discharge associated with industrial activity" to mean:

> the discharge from any conveyance which is used for collecting and conveying storm water and which is directly related to the manufacturing, processing or raw materials storage areas at an industrial plant.[102]

For a majority of the categories of industries (which are identified at 40 C.F.R. § 122.26(b)(14)(i)-(x)), storm water discharges associated with industrial activity include, but are not limited to, storm water discharges from:

1. industrial plant yards;
2. immediate access roads and rail lines used or traveled by carriers of raw materials, manufactured products, waste materials, or by-products used or created by the facility;
3. material handling sites;
4. refuse sites;
5. sites used for the application or disposal of process waste waters (as defined at 40 CFR Part 401);
6. sites used for the storage and maintenance of material handling equipment;
7. sites used for residual treatment, storage, or disposal;
8. shipping and receiving areas;
9. manufacturing buildings;
10. storage areas (including tank farms) for raw materials, and intermediate and finished products; and
11. areas where industrial activity has taken place in the past and significant materials remain and are exposed to storm water.

However, for a limited number of categories of industries, storm water discharges associated with industrial activity include only storm water discharges from all the areas listed in the previous sentence:

---

[101] "Storm water" means storm water runoff, snow melt runoff, and surface runoff and drainage. 40 C.F.R. § 122.26(b)(13).

[102] 40 C.F.R. § 122.26(b)(14).

where material handling equipment or activities, raw materials, intermediate products, final products, waste materials, by-products, or industrial machinery are exposed to storm water.[103]

The regulations therefore make a critical distinction between facilities identified at 40 C.F.R. § 122.26(b)(14)(xi) and facilities identified at 40 C.F.R. § 122.26(b)(14)(i)-(x). The former types of facilities (which include, *inter alia*, food processors, cigarette manufacturers, clothing producers, furniture makers, printers, pharmaceutical producers, and paint manufacturers) are not regarded as having storm water discharges associated with industrial activity unless the materials or activities specified above are exposed to storm water. Contrarily, storm water discharges from the latter types of facilities (which include, *inter alia*, sawmills, paper mills, chemical producers, petroleum industry facilities, and metal smelters and refiners) are considered to be associated with industrial activity regardless of the actual exposure of these same materials or activities to storm water.

If a facility does discharge storm water associated with its industrial activity, the facility must seek coverage under a promulgated storm water general permit, apply for a permit through a group application, or apply for an individual permit.

A discharger of storm water associated with industrial activity may apply for an NPDES permit through a notice of intent to be covered by a general permit. EPA has promulgated some general storm water permits that indicate what facilities are eligible for coverage by the permits. Obtaining coverage under a general permit should impose a lesser burden on an industrial facility than submitting an individual or group permit application.

Facilities not eligible for coverage under a general permit are required to file either a group or individual permit application. The ability of a facility to obtain a permit under the group application procedure will depend upon whether that facility is a member of the same effluent guideline subcategory or is sufficiently similar to other members of the group to be appropriate for general permit coverage. In determining whether a group is appropriate for general permit coverage, the group applicant should use the factors set forth in 40 C.F.R. § 122.28(a)(2)(ii), the current regulations governing general permits, as a guide.

A group application consists of two parts. Part 1 of a group application requires information concerning the participants in the application and their industrial activities. After approval of Part 1 of a group application by EPA, the applicants must submit Part 2, which requires a percentage of the participants (usually 10%) to provide the detailed quantitative data that all applicants for individual permits must provide.[104]

---

[103] "Material handling activities" include the storage, loading and unloading, transportation, or conveyance of any raw material, intermediate product, finished product, by-product or waste product. 40 C.F.R. § 122.26(b)(14).

[104] 40 C.F.R. § 122.26(c)(2).

Part 1 of a group application must be submitted to EPA by March 18, 1991. Based on information contained in Part 1, EPA will approve or deny the members in the group application within 60 days after receipt. Part 2 of the application must be submitted no later than 12 months after the date of approval of Part 1. Facilities that are rejected as members of a group will have 12 months to file individual permit applications from the date they receive notification of their rejection.[105]

If a facility cannot seek coverage under a general permit and cannot obtain a group permit, then it must bear the considerable burden of applying for an individual permit. To obtain an individual permit, the discharger must provide detailed information about the facility, including, *inter alia*, a topographic map of the facility and a narrative description of certain activities at the facility, such as materials and waste management practices.[106]

In addition, dischargers seeking individual permits must present quantitative data, based on samples of storm water discharges collected during storm events, from all outfalls containing a storm water discharge associated with industrial activity. The sampling must be conducted in accordance with the elaborate regulations set forth in 40 C.F.R. § 122.21(g)(3) and (7).[107] The parameters required to be tested are set forth at 40 C.F.R. § 122.26(c)(i)(E).

Because gathering the data for an individual permit application is very costly, a discharger of storm water associated with industrial activity should, if possible, seek coverage under a general permit (when promulgated) or submit a group application. If, however, an industrial facility must apply for an individual permit, the facility should begin the data collection and the field testing at an appropriately early date, given the extensive data required to be submitted. Individual permit applications must be submitted by the facility to EPA or permitting state by October 1, 1992, or at least 30 days prior to the anticipated date of discharge, whichever is later.[108]

This permit system is the primary mechanism for regulating plant site runoff where toxic and hazardous pollutants are not involved. In addition, section 304(e), which was added by the 1977 amendments, authorizes EPA to require permittees to adopt "Best Management Practices" to control toxic pollutants resulting from ancillary industrial activities. EPA also is authorized to prescribe regulations to control plant site runoff, spillage or leaks, and sludge or waste disposal. The legislative history of this provision indicates that Congress anticipated that EPA's regulations would specify treatment requirements, operating procedures, and other management practices by classes and categories of point source discharges.

---

[105] 40 C.F.R. § 122.26(e)(2).

[106] 40 C.F.R. § 122.26(c)(i)(A)-(D).

[107] These regulations require a grab sample taken during the first 30 minutes (or as soon thereafter as practicable) of the storm water discharge. A flow-weighted composite must also be taken. 40 C.F.R. § 122.21(g)(7).

[108] 40 C.F.R. § 122.26(e)(1).

EPA proposed sweeping regulations to implement the best management practices provisions of section 304(e),[109] but issued final regulations of more modest scope.[110] Both the proposed and final regulations, however, attempt to apply the BMP requirements on an across-the-board basis, instead of by categories, an administrative short-cut which may cause difficulties when EPA applies BMP requirements to particular operations.

The final regulations emphasize BMPs of a procedural nature (especially preventive maintenance and housekeeping) and BMPs requiring only minor construction. EPA stated that these regulations are the first of two or more steps; Spill Prevention, Control and Countermeasure (SPCC) plans for hazardous substances (which have been proposed but never promulgated) and possibly additional BMP provisions are scheduled as regulatory requirements in the future. EPA also writes BMPs into effluent guidelines for some industry categories. As a practical matter, RCRA and CERCLA regulations for handling hazardous wastes or releases of hazardous substances have largely taken the place of additional BMP requirements.

The existing BMP requirements are applicable to all dischargers who use, manufacture, store, handle or discharge any pollutant listed as toxic under section 307 or as hazardous under section 311 and for all ancillary manufacturing operations which may result in significant amounts of toxic or hazardous pollutants reaching waters of the United States. Any BMPs required by a section 304(e) effluent limitations guideline must be expressly incorporated into an NPDES permit, and BMPs may be so incorporated if EPA or the State agency determines this to be "necessary to carry out the provisions of the Act . . . ." These requirements appear to have been specifically contemplated by Congress when it added the BMP provisions in 1977.

In addition, the regulations require the permittee to develop a "Best Management Practices" program, which must be submitted as part of the permit application and which will be subject to all permit issuance procedures. This program must be written, must establish toxic and hazardous substances control objectives, and must establish specific BMPs to meet these objectives. The program must also address a number of points concerning ancillary activities such as materials inventory and compatibility, employee training, visual inspections, preventive maintenance, housekeeping, and security. These requirements will tend to overlap to some extent with requirements under the Occupational Safety and Health Act (OSHA) hazard communication standard, with some RCRA requirements, and some requirements under Title III of SARA.

5.10 Special Provisions

5.10.1 Discharges to Ground Waters

One byproduct of the Clean Air Act and the Clean Water Act has been increased pressure to dispose of waste materials on or below land and the

---

[109] 43 Fed. Reg. 39282 (September 1, 1978).

[110] 40 C.F.R. Part 125, Subpart K.

consequential increased threat of groundwater contamination. However, aquifers are a class of water bodies which the act's definition of "waters of the United States" does not clearly include. Thus, although the act, in section 402(b)(1)(D), requires states, as a precondition to approval of their NPDES programs, to "control the discharge of pollutants into wells," it gives EPA no direct authority to regulate disposal of pollutants by subsurface injection.

Although EPA initially sought to regulate underground discharges pursuant to the Clean Water Act, it met with mixed results. The courts disagreed as to whether EPA had authority to regulate disposal into wells under that statute.[111] EPA now relies on the authority of RCRA and the Safe Drinking Water Act (SDWA) to regulate such discharges and is encouraging the states to develop underground injection control programs pursuant to 40 C.F.R. Part 146.

Part C of the SDWA applies to injection wells. However, well injection is broadly defined as the:

> subsurface emplacement of fluids through a bored, drilled or driven well; or through a dug well, where the depth is greater than the largest surface dimension.

Thus, the state underground injection programs will have broad applicability.

EPA is also regulating the injection of hazardous wastes under the Resource Conservation and Recovery Act. Waste lagoons and ponds will continue to be regulated by EPA and the states pursuant to the hazardous waste program.

Thus, many companies which may be exempt from wastewater discharge regulation under the Clean Water Act because they did not discharge to navigable waters are subject to requirements governing wastewater discharges pursuant to the Safe Drinking Water Act and the Resource Conservation and Recovery Act.

5.10.2 Dredged or Fill Material

Section 404 of the Clean Water Act substantially affects development in areas adjacent to navigable waters. The section stringently controls dredging activity and the disposal of dredged or fill material into navigable water by granting the Corps of Engineers the authority to designate disposal areas and issue permits to discharge dredged and fill material therein, rather than making such discharges subject to the general permit program provided by sections 301, 304, and 402 of the act. The stringency of these requirements has been reinforced by three factors:

- Section 404 has been construed to extend to all waters of the United States,[112] including wetlands which are themselves very broadly defined in a definition upheld by the Supreme Court.[113] Accordingly, the Corps

---

[111] See *United States Steel v. Train*, 556 F.2d 822 (7th Cir. 1977), and *Exxon Corp. v. Train*, 554 F.2d 1310 (5th Cir. 1977). The Seventh Circuit has since decided that regulation of a well under the Clean Water Act is not a bar to regulation of the well under RCRA. *Inland Steel Company v. EPA*, 31 ERC 1527 (7th Cir. 1990).

[112] *NRDC v. Callaway*, 392 F. Supp. 685 (D.D.C. 1975).

[113] *United States v. Riverside Bayview Homes, Inc.*, 474 U.S. 121 (1985).

permit program under section 404 is applicable to many dredge and fill projects which would not have required permits under prior law;

- The Corps has construed section 404 broadly, so as to cover not only disposal of dredged or fill material, as the section would seem to imply, but also the emplacement of dredge or fill material for development purposes and the construction of structures;[114] and

- Section 511(c) of the act covers only permits issued by the EPA administrator, so that section 404 permits, unlike most other permits under the act, are subject to NEPA and possibly to the environmental impact statement requirements.

Congress extensively revised section 404 in the 1977 amendments. The principal change was to authorize the states to establish permit programs for dredge and fill activities in non-navigable waters.[115] In order to establish such a program, a state must comply with extensive requirements prescribed by the act and must obtain EPA's approval of the program. There are also requirements for the state's operation of its program, including a requirement that a copy of each permit application and each proposed permit be sent to EPA. EPA, the Corps of Engineers, and the United States Fish and Wildlife Service have the right to comment on applications and proposed permits, and provision is made for the situation in which EPA objects to issuance of a permit.

A second change authorized the Corps of Engineers (or a state having an approved program) to issue "general" permits for specified categories of activities involving the discharge of dredge and fill materials. To issue such a permit, there must be a finding that the activities in the category are similar in nature and will have minimal adverse effects. Any activity covered by a general permit can be conducted without obtaining an individual section 404 permit so long as the requirements and standards set forth in the general permit are complied with. The Corps expanded the scope of its general permit program to reduce the regulatory burden on a number of activities which involve incidental dredge or fill work.[116] As part of a settlement agreement with environmental groups which had challenged these regulations, the Corps changed these rules to assure that they are only applied in practice to activities which have a minimal environmental impact.[117]

Finally, section 404(f) exempts certain dredge and fill discharges from regulation under section 404 if specified effects on navigable waters are avoided. The activities thus excluded from the scope of section 404 include maintenance operations, the construction of temporary sedimentation basins, temporary farm, forest and mining roads, and several types of agricultural activities.

---

[114] 33 C.F.R. § 323.2 (1).

[115] It is generally thought that, if a state does establish its own program, it will not be subject to NEPA constraints in its permit issuing activities.

[116] 33 C.F.R. Parts 320-330.

[117] 49 Fed. Reg. 37482 (October 5, 1984).

The Corps of Engineers, through the United States attorney for the district in which a violation occurs, has the power to bring enforcement actions in the name of the United States not only to collect penalties of up to $25,000 per day of violation but to compel restoration of areas which have been dredged or filled without a necessary permit, or dredged in violation of permit conditions. Under the 1987 amendments, the Corps may also bring administrative penalty proceedings under section 309(g) of the act. In civil penalty proceedings in district court, the Supreme Court has held in a case involving restoration work and penalties that a defendant in a civil penalty action has the right to a jury trial.[118] The Court's holding may cause the Corps to rely heavily on administrative proceedings because of their flexibility.

In November 1989, EPA and the Corps of Engineers executed a memorandum of understanding, under which the Corps, in exercising its authority to review permits under section 404, will strive to minimize the loss of wetlands. Under this policy initiative, known as the "no-net loss" policy, the Corps is to avoid adverse impacts in its permit decisions as much as possible. The Corps must choose the least environmentally damaging practical alternative. The adverse effects on wetlands are to be minimized as much as possible. Only as a last resort is off-site mitigation to be used.

The policy has proven quite controversial, and may be the subject of legislative amendment. Those critical of the policy contend that it protects many non-tidal wetlands of little ecological value, but at great expense to the regulated community. The oil industry did obtain a clarification of the policy in early 1990 so that it does not apply to tundra areas in Alaska, many of which will meet the technical definitions of wetlands in the summer months.

5.10.3 Ocean Discharge Criteria

Section 403(c) of the act directed EPA to promulgate guidelines for determining the effects of pollution discharges on ocean water quality and other aesthetic, recreational, and economic values of the oceans. No permit for an ocean discharge may be issued unless the permit-issuing authority determines that the discharge will not cause unreasonable degradation of the environment, and permit conditions may be imposed to insure that such degradation will not occur.[119] An ocean discharge applicant may be required to submit substantial additional information about receiving waters. The intent of this provision was to assure that limitations were relaxed only in situations involving deep, fast-moving marine waters which resulted in the rapid mixing of very large quantities of water with the discharge of the pollutants.

The 1981 amendments to the Clean Water Act extended the time for municipalities to apply for waivers of secondary treatment requirements for ocean discharges.[120] The 1987 amendments have tightened the requirements to

---

[118] *United States v. Tull*, 481 U.S. 412 (1987).

[119] 40 C.F.R. Part 125, Subpart M.

[120] Pub. L. No. 97-117, 95 Stat. 1632.

assure that waivers are granted only in unusual circumstances.[121] The intention of the 1987 amendments was to assure that these waivers could not be obtained where the POTWs had no (or an insufficient) pretreatment program, where the effluent volume was very large and receiving waters were shallow and not rapidly mixed, or where in combination with other sources the POTW discharge would interfere with marine waters. Recent EPA enforcement action under CERCLA against dischargers to marine POTWs suggest that relaxations of effluent limits under section 301 will be of little benefit to municipalities in the future.

5.10.4 Ocean Dumping and the Marine Protection Research and Sanctuaries Act

The Marine Protection Research and Sanctuaries Act (MPRSA)[122] was first enacted almost simultaneously with the 1972 Federal Water Pollution Control Act. Except for oil spills and ocean outfalls governed under sections 311, 301(h) and 403 of the Clean Water Act, and several minor exceptions, the MPRSA governs all discharges of wastes to ocean waters within United States' jurisdiction or by United States' vessels or persons to the oceans anywhere.[123]

As a result of numerous amendments, no ocean dumping of industrial wastes is permitted, except in exigent circumstances, and except for sewage sludge from the New York City area, no dumping of sewage sludge is permitted either.[124] The exemptions for New York City and its environs—created by court decision and EPA's failure to issue revised regulations—has recently been terminated by statute, effective in 1991. Recent efforts to extend the deadline have been rejected by the courts.[125] By its terms the statute bars ocean disposal of radiological, chemical, and biological warfare agents and high-level radioactive wastes.[126] Disposal of fish wastes is permitted and is regulated under the Clean Water Act.

Under the amended statute, the only ocean dumping activities of any significance permitted are the disposal of dredged spoil. Under the MPRSA, the Corps of Engineers is authorized to issue permits for transporting dredged materials for ocean disposal.[127] The Corps has promulgated regulations applicable to such activity,[128] which is also subject to EPA's substantive review criteria,[129] unless EPA waives the criteria.[130]

---

[121] CWA, § 301(h).

[122] 33 U.S.C. § 1401-14.

[123] 33 U.S.C. § 1401. Other exceptions include marine sanitation devices under section 312 of the CWA, and emissions from marine engines, fishing wastes, oyster shells, and marine structures. MPRSA, § 1402(f).

[124] § 1412a.

[125] *United States v. Nassau County*, 733 F. Supp. 563 (E.D.N.Y.), aff'd, 31 ERC 1648 (2d Cir. 1990).

[126] § 1412.

[127] MPRSA § 103, 33 U.S.C. § 1413.

[128] 33 C.F.R. Part 324.

[129] MPRSA § 103(b) and (c), 33 U.S.C. § 1413(b) and (c).

[130] MPRSA § 103(d), 33 U.S.C. § 1413(d), 40 C.F.R. Part 225.

EPA is also to establish criteria for designating dump sites and then designate sites for dumping and sites where dumping will not be allowed.[131] When EPA first promulgated its comprehensive ocean dumping regulations, it had not yet done baseline and other studies necessary to determine whether its criteria could be met. Accordingly, EPA designated sites already in use on an interim basis. Environmental groups strongly objected to continued use of sites which had not undergone the requisite studies and review. Following litigation, a consent decree was entered which imposed schedules for EPA to conduct the studies and decide whether to designate 22 interim dredge spoil sites.[132] The Corps may use disposal sites for dredged spoils at locations other than those designated by EPA for disposal of other materials.[133] EPA assumed additional obligations by voluntarily adopting a policy of preparing Environmental Impact Statements (EIS) for all site designations.[134] This policy has proved to be a substantial hurdle in final site designations.

More than 140 interim dredge material sites have been designated, although not all are currently in use.[135] EPA is currently planning to delegate to its regional offices the authority for designated dump sites.

Ocean incineration is considered a type of ocean dumping and therefore requires a permit under MPRSA. Only research permits have been granted to date, and extremely strong opposition has led to the denial of the most recent application for a research permit.[136] This denial has been upheld by the district court, pending the time, if ever, when EPA issues special regulations governing ocean incineration of hazardous wastes.[137] EPA has now indefinitely deferred the issue of ocean incineration regulations, and that deferral decision has been upheld.[138]

General permits may be issued upon application, or by regulation without application, for material having minimal environmental impact which is disposed of in small quantities.[139] EPA has promulgated regulations generally authorizing ocean dumping for the purposes of burial at sea, the sinking of Navy target vessels, and disposal of vessels (subject to specified limitations).[140] Permits for ocean disposal of materials meeting EPA's discharge criteria are called "special permits" and may be issued for three-year terms.[141] Research permits can be issued for some materials with a term of 18 months.[142]

---

[131] MPRSA § 102(a)(g), 33 U.S.C. § 1412(a)(g), 40 C.F.R. Part 228.4.

[132] *National Wildlife Federation v. Costle*, Civ. No. 80-0405 (D.D.C. October 1980).

[133] 40 C.F.R. § 228.4(e)(2).

[134] 39 C.F.R. 16186 (May 7, 1974), 39 Fed. Reg. 37419 (October 21, 1974), 40 C.F.R. § 228.6(b).

[135] 40 C.F.R. § 228.12.

[136] 51 Fed. Reg. 20344 (June 4, 1986).

[137] *Waste Management, Inc. v. EPA*, 669 F. Supp 536 (D.D.C. 1987).

[138] *Seaburn v. United States*, 29 ERC 1597 (D.D.C. 1989).

[139] 40 C.F.R. § 220.3(a).

[140] 40 C.F.R. § 220.3(a).

[141] 40 C.F.R. § 220.3(b).

[142] 40 C.F.R. § 220.3(e).

Surveillance to determine or detect violations of the act is to be conducted by the Coast Guard and other appropriate federal agencies.[143] Violations of the act or of permits issued under it are subject to:

1. an administratively assessed penalty of up to $50,000 per day of violation;
2. injunctive relief in court;
3. criminal penalties of up to $50,000 and/or imprisonment of up to one year;
4. seizure of the offending vessel; and
5. citizen enforcement for injunctive relief in court.[144]

In *Middlesex Sewage Authority v. National Sea Clammers*,[145] the Supreme Court has held that the act does not create a private right of action for damages for fisherman or others economically harmed by violations of the act. Presumably, monetary damages could be sought under common law and admiralty law theories.[146]

5.10.5 Thermal Discharges

Although heat is defined as a pollutant by the Clean Water Act and thereby is subject to technology-based effluent limitations imposed on industrial dischargers and POTWs, Congress included special provisions for the regulation of thermal discharges, in order to avoid unnecessary control costs. If the discharger can show that the technology-based effluent limitations under section 301 or under a new source performance standard are more stringent than necessary to assure protection and propagation of a balanced, indigenous population of shellfish, fish and wildlife in and on the body of water where the discharge is to occur, the administrator or state may adjust the effluent limitation to a less stringent level, which will still assure such protection and propagation.

This provision—section 316—is particularly important to power plants because heat is such a significant part of their discharge and because EPA established a "no-discharge" BAT requirement for heat. Even though this effluent limitation was overturned by the courts,[147] permit issuers often initially propose no-discharge of heat as an effluent limitation under section 402(a).

Section 316 proceedings are quite complex; EPA requires substantial amounts of scientific data. There are difficult questions regarding what the "indigenous" population is, when a population is "balanced," and how heat will in fact affect the aquatic organisms. Nonetheless, this provision does excuse thermal dischargers from control requirements to the extent such requirements are unnecessary to protect the environment.

---

[143] MPRSA, § 107, 33 U.S.C. § 1417.

[144] MPRSA, § 105, 33 U.S.C. § 1415.

[145] 453 U.S. 1 (1981).

[146] *Union Oil v. Oppen*, 501 F.2d 558 (9th Cir. 1974).

[147] *Appalachian Power Co. v. Train*, 545 F.2d 1351 (4th Cir. 1976).

5.11 EPA Construction Grants Program

The stringent treatment requirements imposed on POTWs by the 1972 act made a major federal assistance program a necessity if most municipalities were to be able to construct the facilities necessary to comply with the new effluent limitations. The construction grant program which the 1972 act established in response to this need is one of the largest public works programs now being funded by the federal government. The 1987 amendments converted the grant program into a revolving loan program administered by states beginning in 1990, with moneys disbursed after that time taking the form of loans, the repayment of which will fund additional construction.

Under the grant program enacted by the 1972 act, the federal share of the cost of approved treatment works was originally 75 percent, but that percentage was decreased to 55 percent in 1981, where it remained until replaced by the revolving loan program in 1990. The act and EPA's implementing regulations[148] impose substantial conditions governing factors such as the share of operating costs which industrial users must pay, the eligibility of different parts of the plant and related sewer systems and so forth. The objective is to assure that loans will fund the construction of plants which will meet applicable treatment limits in a cost-effective manner. These conditions can substantially affect the costs of POTW treatment to industrial users.

5.11.1 Revolving Loan Program

The 1987 amendments added a new title, Title VI, to the Clean Water Act, governing federal grants to states for sewage treatment plant construction. Beginning in 1990, EPA is to make capitalization grants to the states for the states to establish revolving loan programs for POTW construction. The states are to administer these loan programs pursuant to agreements with EPA. Under these agreements, states are to pay an additional 20 percent above the federal grant into the state fund.[149] There are requirements for the prompt obligation of loan moneys, and for regular auditing and accounting.

The state agency is to make loans for POTW construction through 1995 according to most of the same substantive criteria used previously to make grants—for example, requirements to minimize infiltration and inflow—and combined sewer overflows, to encourage use of innovative technology, and to achieve at least secondary treatment levels.[150] Funds may also be lent to help with nonpoint source controls and estuarine management plans under sections 319 and 320. Loans are to be made at or below market rates for a term not longer than 20 years, and repayment is to begin within one year of project completion. The loan recipient is to establish a dedicated source of revenue to repay the loans.

If states are found not to be administering their loan programs in compliance with these requirements, then EPA can withhold future federal grant money and reallocate that state's money. States are to prepare annual plans for the use of

---

[148] 40 C.F.R. Part 35, Subpart E.

[149] CWA § 602(b)(2).

[150] CWA § 602(b)(6).

loan moneys after public comment, as well as annual reports documenting how such funds were in fact used.

In 1990, EPA adopted implementing regulations for Title VI.[151] Under these regulations states must enter formal delegation agreements with EPA, identifying the state agency administering the loan program, the program costs, the personnel needed, the accounting system to be used, among other factors. These agreements have a five year term. Under these agreements states are to perform virtually all of the functions in loan review EPA previously performed for grants. Grantees will have the right to dispute state decision before the EPA Region.

Perhaps most noteworthy of these rules is the requirement that construction projects receiving grant assistance undergo state environmental review similar to NEPA scrutiny.[152] These regulations track many federal NEPA requirements including public participation, consideration of alternatives, and careful documentation of the decision process. This environmental review process is, according to EPA, based on sections 602(b)(6) and 511(c). Section 511 sets forth EPA's NEPA obligations for POTW construction grants and other issues under the Clean Water Act; section 603(b)(6) incorporates this provision by reference.

5.11.2 User Charges

When the 1972 act became law, Congress feared that the substantial grant assistance available to municipalities could function as an indirect subsidy to industrial users of the funded treatment works and that this subsidy would give users of POTWs an unfair competitive advantage over direct dischargers. Consequently, the act required that municipalities provide for repayment of that portion of the construction grant allocable to industrial users.

From the industrial user's viewpoint, the Industrial Cost Recovery (ICR) requirement converted the construction "grant" to the equivalent of a long-term, no-interest loan. However, ICR proved quite difficult to administer and was repealed in 1980 after a legislative moratorium on such projects had expired. Some local communities continue to assess ICR payments even though they are no longer required by federal law. Such local ICR requirements are often of questionable legality under state law.

As the cost recovery regulations defined industrial users' proportionate share of the capital cost of new grant-funded treatment facilities, the user charge regulations establish requirements to be met by a municipal system for industrial sharing of the annual operating and maintenance charges of such facilities. Section 204 of the act requires, as a condition of federal construction grant assistance, a finding that the applicant has adopted or will adopt:

> a system of charges to assure that each recipient of waste treatment services within the applicant's jurisdiction . . . will pay its proportional share. . .of the costs of operation and maintenance

---

[151] 55 Fed. Reg. 10178 (March 10, 1990); 55 Fed. Reg. 27095 (June 29, 1990) promulgating 40 CFR § 35.3000-.3170.

[152] 40 CFR § 35.3140.

(including replacement)[153] of any waste treatment services provided by the applicant.

The EPA regulations[154] elaborate on the statutory requirement for proportionate distribution of O&M costs as follows:

> A grantee's user charge system based on actual use (or estimated use) of waste water treatment services may be approved if each user (or user class) pays its proportionate share of operation and maintenance (including replacement) costs of treatment works within the grantee's service area, based on the user's proportionate contribution to the total waste water loading from all users (or user classes).

> To insure proportional distribution of operation and maintenance costs to each user (or user class), the user's contribution shall be based on factors such as strength, volume, and delivery flow rate characteristics.

Quantity discounts to large volume users are not acceptable. EPA's philosophy is that savings resulting from economies of scale should be apportioned to all users or user classes. This policy would not, however, appear to preclude recognition of the other efficiencies that some large volume users are able to provide to the treatment facility to which they discharge. These efficiencies may include flow equalization or other measures to control delivery flow rate. User charges may be established based on a percentage of the charge for water usage only in cases where the water charges are based on a constant cost per unit of consumption and thus may be reasonably reflective of the amount of wastewater discharged. The regulations also specifically provide that an industrial user which discharges, to a treatment works, wastewater containing toxic pollutants that cause an increase in the cost of managing the effluent or sludge from the treatment works must pay for those increased costs. Finally, it should be noted that user charges, unlike cost recovery payments, are to be based on actual use of the facility and not on reserved shares, as is sometimes erroneously asserted by some municipalities.

Appendix B to EPA's regulations sets forth in more detail the guidelines for user charge computations and provides sample formulae for use in that connection. The guidelines are necessarily complex and technical. There is considerable potential for misapplication, particularly by small municipalities. A discharger which is a substantial contributor to a treatment works should thus pay close attention to the municipality's adoption of a user charge system.

As indicated above, the treatment works operator is obligated to develop a user charge mechanism, which will require each user to pay its proportionate share of the cost of waste treatment. This obligation is not fulfilled if, due to the

---

[153] The term "replacement" has been defined by EPA to mean "expenditures for . . . equipment . . . which are necessary to maintain . . . capacity and performance during the service life of the treatment works. . . ."

[154] 40 C.F.R. § 35-929-1.

selection of an inappropriate or defective formula or improper application of the formula selected, industrial users are required to subsidize waste treatment services performed for other users of the system. EPA or state approval of any planned construction grant or loan application could, if necessary, be contested on that basis.

The basic approach in discussions with the POTW operating entity should be to make certain that the formula adopted (1) gives recognition to economies, other than economies of scale, which may be inherent in the nature of the company's discharge (for example, the discharge may occur at non-peak periods, it may be low in suspended solids as compared to domestic sewage) and (2) does not give excessive weight to characteristics of the company's discharge, such as BOD content, which do not result in additional treatment costs. For example, if the cost of the treatment works is primarily flow dependent, a high surcharge based on strength of effluent may well be inappropriate. Numerous other technical questions such as the following may arise and should be addressed:

- If the industrial user pretreats its effluent so that its strength is less than that of domestic waste, shouldn't it be entitled to a cheaper rate?
- Shouldn't an industrial user's charge be reduced if it holds its effluent for discharge at non-peak flow periods, thereby contributing to the efficiency of the treatment works?
- If the particular type of industrial effluent makes the treatment works operate more efficiently, shouldn't that factor be recognized? (For example, iron in industrial discharges is used by some municipalities to help remove phosphorous from waste water.)
- If an industrial user's wastes are phosphorous and nitrogen-deficient, isn't it inappropriate to require that user to pay the portion of plant operation and maintenance expense allocable to removal of those pollutants?
- If a substantial portion of the plant capacity is for treatment of water flowing into the system during periods of rainfall due to infiltration and inflow, shouldn't costs allocable to the treatment of this wastewater be primarily allocated to residential connections which are the primary cause of this circumstance?

These and many other similar questions are commonly answered by local authorities when they develop the user charge system which will be proposed for EPA (or state) acceptance. As user charges are an increasingly important cost component of waste treatment services provided by POTWs, affected users must be alert to the proposal of ordinances establishing new user charge systems and must ask questions such as these when such proposals are made.

5.11.3 Cost Effectiveness and Eligibility

Both POTW officials and industrial dischargers which use POTWs have an immediate and substantial interest in minimizing the costs of constructing and operating such works. The POTW owner-grantee or borrower, however, may be unsophisticated in the waste treatment area (or underfunded) and need technical and other assistance to assure that his waste treatment program is cost-effective.

There unfortunately have been numerous cases where plants have been designed to achieve levels of treatment beyond that required by the applicable permit limits, or with capacities in excess of that necessary to serve foreseeable needs. The procedures mandated for the development of section 201 facilities plans, the preparation of related environmental assessments, and the conduct of value engineering studies provide both industry and concerned citizens with considerable opportunities to help municipalities avoid these wasteful practices.

The final issue which should be considered in any effort to minimize the cost of industrial participation in a loan or grant-funded POTW program is the question of whether all or only some of the elements of the POTW are eligible for federal (or state) loan or grant funding. Treatment works costs which are found to be ineligible must be fully funded by the grantee without benefit of generous state loan programs. The resulting bond costs will be correspondingly higher as localities have to raise money on the open market. Industrial users are generally called upon to pay their proportionate share of the cost of amortizing the required bonds. Thus, where a portion of the facilities is found to be ineligible, industrial users will be called upon to pay not only the costs of the treatment works over its useful life but also their share of the bond interest—at market rates—on that facility.

As federal and state budget deficit problems mount, it seems likely that EPA and states will subject grant and loan applications to increasingly rigorous scrutiny in order to conserve limited grant and loan funds. EPA has narrowly interpreted the act's eligibility provisions as they apply to treatment facilities designed to handle industrial wastes. Thus though the act's definition of treatment works would appear to apply to facilities which handle industrial wastes, EPA's regulations specify that allowable projects do not include "(1) costs of interceptor or collector lines constructed exclusively or almost exclusively to serve industrial users or (2) costs allocable to the treatment for control or removal of pollutants in wastewater introduced into the treatment works by industrial users, unless the applicant is required to remove such pollutants introduced from non-industrial sources." The scope of this exclusion in individual circumstances is subject to considerable interpretation and there are also considerable legal questions regarding the statutory authorization for this provision. Its application does merit careful attention in a number of situations.

5.11.4 POTW Costs to Industrial Dischargers—Summary

The factors referenced above make it clear that users of POTWs are no longer insulated from the substantial costs of complying with Clean Water Act requirements. In many circumstances, POTWs can be an expensive way for an industrial discharger to meet the act's requirements. The economics of alternative on-site treatment and direct discharge should be carefully examined before making or continuing commitments to rely on a POTW as a method of compliance.

5.12 Enforcement

The CWA, especially after the 1987 amendments, provides a number of enforcement options to EPA and the states, as well as a heavily-used citizen suit provision. As companies' potential exposure under these enforcement and penalty provisions can be staggering, even for infractions causing little actual harm, it is important for regulated entities to understand what their potential exposure is under the CWA's criminal, civil, and administrative penalty provisions, as well as for citizen suits.

5.12.1 Criminal Penalties

Section 309(c), the criminal penalty provisions of the CWA, was substantially revised and stiffened by the 1987 amendments. The 1990 Oil Pollution Act extended these criminal penalties to spills and other violations of section 311. Under the amended section 309(c):

- "Negligent violations" in § 309(c)(1) are subject to criminal penalties of not less than $2,500 or more than $25,000 per day of violation, as well as up to one year's imprisonment per day of violation. Penalties and length of imprisonment are doubled for a second offense.

- "Knowing violations" in § 309(c)(2) are subject to fines of not less than $5,000 nor more than $50,000 per day of violation and up to three years imprisonment per day of violation. As with "negligent violations," penalty levels double for second offenses.

- Section 309(c)(3) creates a new class of offense for "knowing endangerment," where a person knowingly violates a permit or other requirement "and who knows at that time that he thereby places another person in imminent danger of death or serious bodily injury." Conviction of "knowing endangerment" requires proof of "actual awareness or actual belief" which may be shown by "circumstantial evidence, including evidence that the defendant took affirmative steps to shield himself from relevant information." The penalty for knowing endangerment is imprisonment for 15 years and a fine of up to $250,000, or in the case of an organization, a fine of not more than $1,000,000. Fines and penalties are doubled for second offenses.

- Section 309(c)(4) strengthened criminal penalties for anyone who files false reports or who knowingly falsifies, tampers, or renders inaccurate any monitoring device or method. Violations are now punishable by a $10,000 fine and imprisonment of up to two years; penalties double for second offenses.

Because negligence violations are potentially criminal, the scope of potential criminal violations under the amended CWA is extremely broad, and reason for diligent attention to compliance.

Additionally, the degree of knowledge required to satisfy the "knowing" requirement may include many situations where a discharger is aware of a violation but continues to operate while seeking to abate the violation. A situation where a discharger has received an administrative order requiring cessation of a violation would likely meet the definition of "knowing" violation if the violation continued unabated. Also of concern are situations where a discharger is asked to accept a limitation it cannot meet in a timely manner, but to rely on the enforcement discretion of EPA, state, or local officials to protect the discharger from enforcement action while the discharger works to meet the new limitation.

The "knowing endangerment" provision is nearly identical to the similar penalty provision in RCRA. In the Clean Water Act context, knowing endangerment becomes an issue where water supplies are contaminated, where pretreatment requirements for toxics are deliberately violated, or where hazardous substances are deliberately dumped in sewers or waterways instead of being sent to a proper treatment, storage, and disposal facility (TSDF) under RCRA. Several knowing endangerment prosecutions have now been initiated for violations of pretreatment requirements, violations which allegedly endangered employees.[155]

In recent years, criminal charges have been brought repeatedly against large and small violators of the Clean Water Act. In addition to the knowing endangerment cases noted above, the United States has obtained indictments against Exxon Shipping for the Valdez spill, against Pennwalt Chemical for negligent violations resulting in a tank failure and spills, against Ocean Spray for knowing violations of pretreatment requirements, and against a number of individuals for violations of dredge-fill requirements. Other cases have resulted in sentences of imprisonment,[156] which are becoming much more common as a result of sentencing guidelines. The statute allows the United States to proceed criminally not only against the companies involved, but also against "responsible corporate officers."[157] Moreover, circumstantial evidence may be used to prove violations of the knowing endangerment provision, including evidence that an officer deliberately shielded himself from knowledge of such violations.[158] Thus a "white heart, empty head" defense will not be legally sufficient.

States also provide criminal penalties for violations of their statutes implementing the Clean Water Act. Moreover, in circumstances involving violations of both the water pollution control statutes and hazardous waste statutes, defendants have been sentenced to prison under state water pollution control laws.

5.12.2 Civil Enforcement Options

Under the Clean Water Act as amended in 1987, EPA acting through the Department of Justice, has a number of civil enforcement options to address violations of the act, the implementing regulations, and NPDES and other permits. These civil enforcement options are usually found in state procedure as well.

EPA can decide to do nothing in response to a violation. There is divided authority for the proposition that EPA need not take enforcement action in

---

[155] *United States v. Borjohn Optical Technology, Inc.*, Cr. No. 89-256 (D. Mass. Nov. 7, 1990).

[156] *See, e.g.*, *United States v. Frezzo Bros., Inc.*, 546 F. Supp. 713 (E.D.Pa. 1982), aff'd, 703 F.2d 62 (3d Cir. 1983).

[157] CWA, § 309(c)(6).

[158] CWA, § 309(c)(3)(B).

response to every reported violation.[159] As a practical matter, EPA must let many infractions pass unpunished because the agency's resources are limited and because it would be inequitable to bring enforcement actions in some circumstances.

If EPA does decide to take civil enforcement action, as opposed to referring the matter for criminal prosecution or initiating an administrative proceeding, the agency may and often does seek both injunctive relief and civil penalties. EPA may seek injunctive relief under either section 504 or section 309(b). Section 504 applies to discharges which present an imminent and substantial endangerment to the health, welfare, or livelihood of persons. (The statute specifically refers to an inability to market shellfish as a factor warranting action under section 504.) In such circumstances EPA may seek an injunction "to immediately restrain any person causing or contributing the alleged pollution to stop the discharge . . . ." A former version of this provision was invoked by EPA to restrain the discharge of taconite tailings in the famous Reserve Mining case[160] in Minnesota, but the emergency provision has received little use since that time.

EPA normally relies upon section 309(b) when it seeks injunctive relief. This section empowers the district courts to enter preliminary and permanent injunctions to restrain and abate violations of the statute, regulations, and permits, including state NPDES permits. If an injunction is issued and subsequently violated, not only are the criminal and civil penalty provisions of the Clean Water Act applicable, but so are the criminal and civil contempt powers of the court. Normally where a Clean Water Act case is settled through entry of a consent decree, EPA will insist on a schedule of stipulated penalties addressing any future violations of the decree. In settlement of several recent cases, EPA has obtained consent decrees requiring the discharger to undertake substantial remedial action to address the environmental problems caused by the discharge.[161]

Where EPA believes that a violation is serious enough for referral to the Department of Justice for civil enforcement action, the agency normally seeks substantial civil penalties. The 1987 amendments increased available civil penalties under section 309(d) from $10,000 per day of violation up to $25,000 per day of violation. Moreover, the amendments changed section 309(d) to set forth a number of factors for the court to weigh in assessing the appropriate amount of civil penalties to assess against a violator, including:

- the seriousness of the violation;
- the economic benefit (if any) resulting from the violation;
- any history of such violations;

---

[159] Compare *Dubois v. Thomas*, 820 F.2d 943 (8th Cir. 1987) and *Sierra Club v. Train*, 557 F.2d 485 (5th Cir. 1977) (no enforcement required) with *Green v. Costle*, 577 F. Supp. 1225 (W.D. Tenn. 1983).

[160] *Reserve Mining Co. v. EPA*, 514 F.2d 492 (8th Cir. 1975). The Court of Appeals modified the district court's injunction to allow the discharger additional time to comply rather than to require immediate cessation of operations. *Id.* at 538.

[161] *United States v. USX Corp.*, C.A. No. H88-558 (N.D. Ind. July 27, 1990); 55 Fed. Reg. 32319, 32320 (Aug. 8, 1990) (proposing approval of decree). Under this decree, USX is to pay a $1.6 million fine and spend up to $7.5 million to study and remedy contaminated sediments.

- any good faith efforts to comply with applicable requirements;
- the economic impact of the penalty on the violator; and
- such other factors as justice may require.

The statute's Polonius-like advice to the district courts about how to calculate penalties is unlikely to result in any sort of uniform penalties being assessed, but may tend to even out some of the extremes on either end of the spectrum.

The amendments did resolve one other civil penalty issue: how should process upsets be treated, particularly where the upset caused a number of pollutant parameters listed in the permit to be simultaneously exceeded? Under the amended section 309(d) "a single operational upset which leads to simultaneous violations of more than one parameter shall be treated as a single violation." Where violations of multiple parameters do not result from an identifiable operational upset, however, the government may try to argue that Congress' silence about that situation means that multiple violations have occurred.

Shortly after the 1987 amendments were enacted, the Supreme Court held in *United States v. Tull*[162] that defendants in civil penalty cases under the Clean Water Act have a constitutional right to a jury trial. The Tull case involved civil penalties imposed for violation of the dredge-fill provisions of section 404. The decision clearly applies to all civil penalty proceedings brought in federal court under the Clean Water Act and other environmental statutes as well. The jury may only decide liability, however; the district judge decides the amount of penalty which is appropriate in the event a violation is found by the jury.[163]

The amounts of civil penalties paid in Clean Water Act cases increased dramatically during the 1980s. There are a significant number of federal enforcement cases where the government has collected over half a million dollars in penalties and several where the government has collected more than a million dollars. Indeed, in one case, involving noncompliance by a number of sewage treatment plants in Puerto Rico, the court assessed a penalty of more than $32,000,000.[164] Civil and criminal penalties are not deductible business expenses for federal income tax purposes, so the financial impact of these penalties on industrial dischargers can be quite severe. As EPA's emphasis on enforcement is increasing, and as the compliance dates for most standards have now passed, it is likely that civil penalties assessed in these cases will continue to increase, as will the attention dischargers must pay to compliance.

5.12.3 Administrative Orders and Penalties

Section 309(a) authorizes EPA to issue administrative compliance orders to persons in violation of their permits or other Clean Water Act obligations. The order may require compliance with an interim compliance schedule or an operation and maintenance requirement in not more than 30 days; permanent

---

[162] 481 U.S. 412 (1987).

[163] Id., at 426-27.

[164] *United States v. Puerto Rico Aqueduct and Sewer Authority*, 25 ERC 1921 (D.P.R. 1987).

compliance is to be required in a time that EPA determines is reasonable under the circumstances. The state is to be sent copies of any such order.

The issuance of an EPA compliance order is a serious matter for a discharger, since failure to comply or at least to make good faith efforts to do so may be the basis to initiate a criminal prosecution for "knowing" violations, or to initiate a civil penalty proceeding where the claim is made that the discharger is recalcitrant or acting in bad faith.

The 1987 amendments added a new Subsection 309(g) which authorizes EPA to initiate administrative penalty proceedings against violators. The Corps of Engineers may also initiate administrative penalty proceedings for violations of dredge fill permits or permit conditions under section 404 of the act. Likewise, under the Oil Pollution Act, the Coast Guard may initiate administrative penalty proceedings for violations of section 311.

The statute provides Class I and Class II penalties, which differ primarily with respect to (1) the limits on what penalties EPA or the Corps can impose and (2) the procedures EPA or the Corps must follow to impose them. The upper limit on the penalty which may be imposed in a Class I proceeding is $25,000 total for the proceeding and $10,000 per violation. The defendant has the right to an informal hearing.

The upper limit on penalties in Class II proceedings is $125,000, with a $10,000 maximum penalty per day of violation. The defendant is entitled to a more elaborate hearing than in Class I penalty proceedings, a hearing before an independent administrative law judge (ALJ). In determining the amount of penalties to be imposed in the event violations are found, the ALJ (or EPA or the Corps, in the case of Class I violations) is to consider the same factors the district court is required to consider in assessing civil penalties under section 309(d).

Administrative penalty proceedings initiated by EPA, the Corps, or by states under comparable state administrative penalty schemes are a bar to citizen suits under section 505 of the act for the same violations if the administrative penalty proceeding is initiated prior to notice that a citizen suit will be filed. This statutory rule is a significant departure from the prior case law rule that state administrative proceedings do not bar citizen suits. Although the new provision does limit citizen suits significantly, citizens may participate in the administrative proceeding.

In the event an unsuccessful defendant disagrees with EPA's (or the Corps' or Coast Guard's) penalty decision, judicial review may be obtained in district court for Class I penalties, and in the court of appeals for Class II penalties. Citizens who commented in the administrative proceeding may also seek judicial review. In order to prevail in such a judicial review, the person challenging the EPA decision must show either that EPA's decision is unsupported by substantial evidence or is an abuse of discretion. Although the statutory language is unclear, it may be read to permit the court to increase penalties where EPA (or the Corps) has abused its discretion to impose too low a penalty.

EPA has proposed a number of administrative penalties since passage of the 1987 amendments. The agency frequently proposes the maximum penalty, thereby shifting the burden to the defendant to show factors mitigating the violation and thus reducing the level of penalties assessed. EPA has used administrative penalties extensively in pursuing pretreatment violations. Often, EPA will bring multiple administrative proceedings to address multiple parties discharging inadequately treated wastes to a single POTW.

5.12.4 Compliance Strategy

The broad enforcement discretion enjoyed by EPA and the states, coupled with the requirement of publicly filing monitoring reports, including those showing violations, requires potential violators to take the initiative in dealing with compliance problems. In the event of a possible violation, a discharger must be prepared to spend substantial time and effort with all relevant agencies. When several parts of EPA and several different state agencies are involved, there is no assurance that they are pursuing a coherent strategy or, indeed, are even talking to each other. Thus the discharger must be prepared to keep all federal and state agencies fully informed, preferably in a way that will ensure the most favorable processing of any potential violations. In doing this, the discharger should attempt to accomplish the following three goals:

- Convince the relevant enforcement agencies of its good faith. The EPA civil penalty policy makes it clear that "recalcitrance" is an aggravating factor and cooperation a mitigating one. Since the enforcement agencies will not, for the foreseeable future, be able to move against every violation, a discharger's good faith or bad faith will be an important factor in deciding who to move against, and, if so, how severely.

- The discharger must attempt to deal with any major health or environmental problems caused by a potential violation in a manner that is as serious as the manner EPA or the state enforcement agency would adopt. Discharges which may create public health problems, or create unique environmental impacts, or which are likely to be the subject of adverse publicity are recognized as aggravating factors in the EPA's civil penalty policy. To the degree possible, special efforts should be made to avoid discharges of such substances and to quickly control and clean up any spill.

- The discharger must realistically appraise not only its chances of ultimately prevailing in any enforcement litigation, but the bureaucratic constraints such as the civil penalty policy on EPA and the Department of Justice in settlement negotiations. In any settlement calculus, a discharger must understand that even a successfully defended enforcement action will likely result in substantial adverse publicity. This negative exposure is not fully overcome by a favorable verdict.

Although these guidelines are not a panacea to the problems involved in dealing with potential enforcement actions, they can reduce the uncertainty surrounding the present enforcement system.

5.12.5 Citizen Suits

Section 505 of the act provides an additional impetus to vigorous enforcement of the act's provisions. It authorizes any person "having an interest which is or may be adversely affected" to commence civil actions either against a discharger, for violation of any effluent standard or limitation under the act, or against EPA for failure to proceed expeditiously to enforce the act's provisions. Experience under the Clean Water Act indicates that citizen suit provisions are highly effective in increasing the number of enforcement actions brought. While the Clean Water Act, unlike the Refuse Act, does not make provision for the payment of a "bounty" to a citizen providing information leading to successful enforcement, it does make specific provision for the payment of attorney and expert witness fees. More importantly, the Clean Water Act plainly authorizes citizen actions, while the Refuse Act, which provides only criminal penalties, was construed by the courts not to permit citizen suits.

Since about 1985 an average of approximately 200 notices of intent to bring citizen suits against dischargers were filed with EPA each year. Giving such notice is the first step in bringing a citizens' enforcement action, and is frequently the start of settlement negotiations between the discharger and the citizens' group. Normally in citizens' enforcement actions which are litigated, the plaintiffs use a discharger's required Discharge Monitoring Reports (DMRs) to establish the discharger's liability. As some courts have held that dischargers are strictly liable for permit violations, intent is not a good defense. Most of the recent citizen suits have been settled on the basis of some combination of:

1. payment of civil penalties;
2. adoption of a compliance schedule;
3. stipulated penalties for failure to meet the schedule; and
4. attorney's fees and costs to plaintiffs.

Although EPA's minimal enforcement efforts in the early years of the Reagan administration were a primary cause of the recent flurry of citizens' enforcement actions, EPA's view of the enforcement action can be an important factor in settlement negotiations. In several cases, EPA has refused to agree to settlement conditions worked out by environmentalist plaintiffs and dischargers, on the ground that the conditions were too generous to the discharger. EPA's leverage in these negotiations is derived from its statutory right to intervene in any citizen's enforcement action. The 1987 amendments have formalized EPA's role in reviewing consent decrees in citizen suit cases, and allow EPA 45 days to object in court.[165]

The bulk of reported citizen enforcement cases have been litigated in Connecticut, New York, New Jersey, the Chesapeake Bay area, Louisiana and California. A number of new cases are contemplated by environmental groups in most parts of the country. Frequently, national environmental groups such as the Sierra Club or Natural Resources Defense Council will work with local environmental groups such as the Connecticut Fund for the Environment or the Chesapeake Bay Foundation.

---

[165] CWA, § 505 (c)(3). The United States has objected to settlements which fail to provide for the payment of civil penalties to the United States. These challenges have had limited success. E.g., *Compare Friends of the Earth v. Archer Daniels Midland Co.*, 31 ERC 1779 (N.D.N.Y. 1990) (rejecting such challenge); *Sierra Club v. Electronic Controls Design, Inc.*, 31 ERC 1789 (9th Cir. 1990).

Courts ruling on motions to dismiss these citizens' suits have generally held that the members of these groups have standing—the right to file the action—and have sometimes extended standing to the groups themselves. In addition, the courts have resolved a number of other potential procedural obstacles to the citizen suits favorable to the environmentalists, holding that:

1. the five-year federal statute of limitations for civil penalties, 28 U.S.C. § 2462, governs these proceedings, and not shorter state limitations periods; and

2. the citizens' suits can be used to recover civil penalties assessed by the court and payable to the federal government, as well as to obtain injunctive relief against the violator.

The primary limitations placed on citizen suits by the courts result from the Supreme Court's construction of section 505 in *Gwaltney v. Chesapeake Bay Foundation* in 1987,[166] and the Court's strict reading of notice requirements in the RCRA citizen suit provision in *Hallstrom v. Tillamook County* in 1989.[167] In *Gwaltney*, the Court held that citizen suits must allege either continuing or intermittent violations; citizen suits may not be maintained for wholly past violations.[168] This limitation has not significantly impaired citizen suits because all the Court has required is a good-faith allegation of continuous or intermittent violation at the time the statutory 60-day notice is given. Indeed, even in the *Gwaltney* case, the lower courts found on remand that there was sufficient evidence to support the claim of a continuing or intermittent violation, and affirmed a penalty of nearly $300,000.[169] Fines of almost a million dollars were recently affirmed in another Chesapeake Bay case, which involved several years of reporting violations by a pretreater.[170] It is evident from this record that citizens' suits can be a potent enforcement tool.

6.0 POLLUTION CONTROL PLANNING IN THE CURRENT REGULATORY CLIMATE

Compliance with the Clean Water Act requirements outlined above would be difficult and costly under the best of circumstances. These difficulties are compounded by inconsistencies in EPA (and state) enforcement policies, EPA's tardiness in developing standards, and the periodic congressional rewriting of statutory requirements for the construction grant program. Consequently, the questions of how the law will be interpreted and enforced are often not amendable to predictable answers. Participation in the development and revision of standards and continuing contact with officials responsible for permitting and

---

[166] 484 U.S. 49 (1987).

[167] 110 S.Ct. 304 (1989). The Hallstrom case requires strict compliance with the 60-day notice requirement in the RCRA citizens' suit provision, similar to section 505 of the Clean Water Act. Unless the provision is strictly adhered to, the citizens' suit may be dismissed.

[168] 484 U.S. 49, 64-67.

[169] *Chesapeake Bay Foundation v. Gwaltney of Smithfield Ltd.*, 890 F.2d 691 (4th Cir. 1989).

[170] *Sierra Club v. Simkins Industries, Inc.*, 617 F. Supp. 1120 (D.Md. 1985), affirmed, 27 E.R.C. 1881 (4th Cir. 1988).

enforcement is necessary if industrial dischargers wish to operate in a more consistent and predictable regulatory environment.

6.1 EPA Standards Development and Revision

The suitability and practicability of the standards and regulations which EPA promulgates under the act are dependent on EPA's thorough understanding of the processes and products to be regulated, the availability of detailed and reliable data on the applicability and limits of available treatment technology, and careful consideration of the economic and environmental impacts involved. Except for industry inputs, most standards (whether done by EPA staff or through outside contractors) tend to be based principally on technical data readily obtainable through review of existing literature. In some cases, these data are outdated, unreliable and inadequate. Thus, absent effective and technically documented participation by industry spokesmen, the standards which EPA promulgates are likely to have unanticipated effects when applied to real world conditions. Particular process or design factors may not have been considered and may be inequitable when applied to a specific plant or product.

Thus, early and active participation in the standards development and revision process, either directly or through appropriate industry organizations, is advisable. Although EPA has completed the development of most standards, the toxics strategy and development of toxics water quality standards and discharge limitations based on them will continue to require such participation, as will the periodic updating and revision of existing standards which are mandated by various provisions of the act. Such participation could properly involve the following steps, which were made especially important by the provisions of the 1987 amendments governing the fundamentally different factors (FDF) variance:

1. Assess the probability that standards (or revisions) applicable to your company's operations will be promulgated.

2. Determine the procedure which will be followed in developing the standard, the contemplated time schedule, and the areas under consideration where data available to EPA may be deficient.

3. Assess the standards development procedure to determine whether it provides for taking into account any unusual aspects of your plant process or product design. Make comments to EPA and any private contractor involved as to how the procedure could be improved.

4. Consider providing EPA and/or the appropriate private contractor any relevant technical data possessed by companies in the industry which is unpublished or otherwise not generally accessible.

5. If the time schedule permits, consider the desirability of industry sponsored research or analytical projects to fill gaps in existing data on available technology or environmental and economic impact. In this connection, consideration should be given to consulting with EPA on the structuring of the project and exploring the possibility of EPA involvement in the conduct of the project.

6. After a proposed standard is published in the Federal Register, the company or its spokesmen should participate in the usual comment procedure and consider the possibility of obtaining judicial review if the standard, as finally promulgated, is still unreasonable. In this connection, it should be kept in mind that if objections to standards are not asserted in judicial review proceedings in a timely manner, then they are waived. Further, it is generally wiser for a company to litigate a standard at a time when it does not stand accused of a violation.

6.2 Negotiation of Permit Conditions

Whether a company's authorization to discharge is in the form of an NPDES permit for direct discharge into a waterway or a contract with a municipality for use of its treatment facilities, the terms and conditions of that permit or contract may be every bit as important, in terms of impact on profits, as a major corporate contract. Moreover, the addition of the anti-backsliding provision by the 1987 amendments make it especially important that the initial permit or contract be correct, as costly errors can be very hard to fix.

These requirements can be the subject of negotiations. Accordingly, pollution control managers should determine the areas in which the act and regulations leave room for negotiation and, based on a careful assessment of the company's long-term interests, should negotiate actively in an effort to obtain favorable permit terms and conditions. These negotiations will be more important and much more complicated if toxic pollutants are involved.

6.3 Discussions With Regional Office and State Officials

No matter how good the standards are or how carefully permits are drawn, there will inevitably be situations where companies are forced to make major investment decisions which are affected by significant uncertainties in determining the applicable environmental control requirements. In these circumstances, serious considerations should be given to obtaining advance guidance from the appropriate EPA regional office and/or state enforcement personnel—whether or not the applicable statute makes provision for obtaining such guidance. A written indication that the cognizant authority has reviewed your proposal and found it acceptable, while perhaps not legally binding, can be of great future benefit. If the proposal is not acceptable to EPA or the state, it may be better to find that out before money has been spent. The chances of acceptance are generally far greater when the company goes to the regulator, rather than the other way around.

6.4 State and Local Planning Activities

Industry would also be well advised to pay considerable attention to the substantial planning requirements which are imposed by the act on state and local governments, especially the numerous water quality planning requirements imposed by the 1987 amendments. The state and regional water quality implementation plans, continuing planning processes and area-wide waste treatment management plans may well be as important as federal rules and regulations in determining a company's future abatement costs. If properly carried out, these planning processes can be of immeasurable aid to business planners in predicting and planning for the future.

Appendix
Section 307: Toxic Pollutants

Acenaphthene
Acrolein
Acrylonitrile
Aldrin/Dieldrin
Antimony and compounds*[171]
Arsenic and compounds
Asbestos
Benzene
Benzidine
Beryllium and compounds
Cadmium and compounds
Carbon tetrachloride
Chlordane (technical mixture and metabolites)
Chlorinated benzenes (other than dichlorobenzenes)
Chlorinated ethanes (including 1,2-dichloroethane, 1,1,1-ethane and hexachloro-
     ethane)
Chlorinated naphthalene
Chlorinated phenols (other than those listed elsewhere; includes trichlorophenols
     and chlorinated cresols)
Chloroalkyl ethers (chloromethyl, chloroethyl, and mixed ethers)
Chloroform
2-chlorophenol
Chromium and compounds
Copper and compounds
Cyanides
DDT and metabolites
Dichlorobenzenes (1,2-, 1,3-, and 1,4-dichlorobenzenes)
Dichlorobenzinine
Dichloroethylenes (1,1-and 1,2-dichloroethylene)
2,4-dichlorophenol
Dichloropropane and dichloropropene
2,4-dimethylphenol
Dinitrotoluene
Diphenylhydrazine
Endosulfan and metabolites

---

[171] *The term "compound" shall include organic and inorganic compounds.

Endrin and metabolites
Ethylbenzene
Fluoranthene
Haloethers (other than those listed elsewhere; includes chlorophenylphenyl ethers, bromophenylphenyl ether, bis (dischloroisopropyl) ether, bis-(chloroethoxy) methane and polychlorinated diphenyl ethers)
Halomethanes (other than those listed elsewhere; includes methylene chloride methylchloride, methylbromide, bromoform, dichlorobromomethane, trichlorofluoromethane, dichlorodifluoromethane)
Heptachlor and metabolites
Hexachlorobutadiene
Hexachlorocyclohexane (all isomers)
Hexachlorocyclopentadiene
Isophorone
Lead and compounds
Mercury and compounds
Naphthalene
Nickel and compounds
Nitrobenzene
Nitrophenols (including 2,4-dinitrophenol, dinitrocresol)
Nitrosamines
Pentachlorophenol
Phenol
Phthalate esters
Polychlorinated biphenyls (PCBs)
Polynuclear aromatic hydrocarbons (including benzanthracenes, benzo-pyrenes, benzofluoranthene, chrysenes, dibenzanthracenes, and indenopyrenes) Selenium and compounds
Silver and compounds
2,3,7,8-Tetrachlorodibenzo-p-dioxin (TCDD)
Tetrachloroethylene
Thallium and compounds
Toluene
Toxaphene
Trichloroethylene
Vinyl chloride
Zinc and compounds

For a more definitive discussion of this topic, the reader is referred to the Clean Water Handbook and related books and courses listed at the end of this book.

Chapter 7

OIL POLLUTION ACT OF 1990

Austin P. Olney
LeBoeuf, Lamb, Leiby & MacRae
Washington, D.C.

1.0 OVERVIEW

The Oil Pollution Act of 1990 (OPA)[1], is far more comprehensive and stringent than any previous U.S. or international oil pollution liability and prevention law. OPA is divided into nine titles. Title I of OPA creates a new section on oil pollution liability and compensation in Title 33 of the U.S. Code.[2] In Title I, OPA imposes strict liability for a comprehensive and expansive list of damages from an oil spill into the water from vessels and facilities. The law contains limits on this liability, but the limits are far higher than under previous U.S. law or international law. These limits are subject to important exceptions. OPA creates a $1 billion supplemental compensation fund for oil spills and details procedures for obtaining access to it.

Title IV of OPA amends provisions of the Federal Water Pollution Control Act[3] concerning oil spills. Title IV expands the authority and capability of the federal government to direct and manage oil spill clean up operations. It requires vessel and facilities operators beginning in 1993 to file detailed oil spill response plans evidencing the availability of private-sector clean up and removal resources. Also in OPA Title IV are amendments to the title of the U.S. Code on shipping and navigation safety.[4] OPA mandates numerous operational requirements for vessels to prevent oil spills, including the replacement, beginning in 1995, of single hull oil tankers and barges with double hull vessels. Title IV of OPA also substantially increases the civil and criminal penalties for causing spills and for violating many marine safety and environmental protection laws.

Of the seven other OPA titles, Title III concerns the implementation of international conventions. Title III does not require the United States to adopt any international conventions on oil spills. Titles II, VI and IX contain technical and conforming amendments to other laws. The remainder of the act addresses subjects primarily concerned with Alaska and is beyond

---

[1]Pub. L. 101-380, August 18, 1990.

[2]33 U.S.C. §§ 2701-2761.

[3]33 U.S.C. §§ 1251-1376, renamed the Clean Water Act in 1977. OPA Subtitles B and C of Title IV make extensive amendments to section 311 of the Clean Water Act, 33 U.S.C. § 1321.

[4]Title 46 U.S. Code.

the scope of this chapter. Title V contains provisions on oil spill prevention and removal in Prince William Sound[5], Title VII sets up an oil pollution research and development program[6], and Title VIII amends the Trans-Alaska Pipeline System Act.[7]

2.0 BACKGROUND

While the grounding of the *Exxon Valdez* on March 24, 1989 and several subsequent accidents in 1989 and 1990 are generally viewed as the inspiration for the enactment of OPA, the law is actually the product of nearly 20 years of Congressional debate on oil pollution liability and tanker safety. This debate frequently centered on whether federal law should preempt state law and whether federal law should be circumscribed by international treaties.

In the 1970s Congress responded to concern over water pollution by enacting the Federal Water Pollution Control Act. Section 311 addressed oil spills from vessels and facilities by imposing strict liability to the federal government for clean up and removal costs.

In addition, three specialized statutes addressed oil spills in specific circumstances: the Trans-Alaska Pipeline Authorization Act,[8] the Deepwater Port Act of 1974,[9] and the Outer Continental Shelf Lands Act Amendments of 1978.[10] These statutes set up strict liability schemes and supplemental compensation funds for spills occurring in their respective areas. Congress also enacted laws to promote safer port operations and safer vessels: the Ports and Waterways Safety Act of 1972[11] and the Port and Tanker Safety Act of 1978.[12]

Individual U.S. state governments also adopted their own oil pollution laws. Although a few states, such as California, Pennsylvania and Maine adopted oil pollution laws in the late 1970s, a majority of the 24 coastal states have enacted special oil spill laws or amendments since 1986.

Roughly contemporaneous with U.S. efforts, the International Convention on Civil Liability for Oil Pollution Damage was signed in 1969 and came into force in 1975.[13] The CLC established a strict liability regime subject to limits on liability for tankers carrying persistent oil. The International Convention on the Establishment of an International Fund for

---

[5] 46 U.S.C. § 2731-37.

[6] 46 U.S.C. § 2761.

[7] 43 U.S.C. § 1653.

[8] 43 U.S.C. § 1651.

[9] 33 U.S.C. § 1517.

[10] 43 U.S.C. § 1801.

[11] 86 Stat. 424.

[12] 33 U.S.C. § 1221.

[13] International Convention on Civil Liability for Oil Pollution Damage, 1969, 9 I.L.M. 45 (1970) (CLC).

the Compensation for Oil Pollution Damage[14] created a supplemental compensation fund, financed by the cargo interests. The Fund Convention was signed in 1971 and came into force in 1978.

Although the United States participated in the diplomatic conferences, neither the CLC nor the Fund Convention was ratified by the United States for two reasons. Their limits of liability were perceived to be too low, and the CLC and Fund Convention would have preempted federal and state law. Nevertheless, partly at the behest of the United States, two protocols to the CLC and the Fund Convention were adopted at a diplomatic conference held in 1984.[15] The 1984 Protocols increased limits of liability, expanded the scope of compensable damages, and increased the size of the supplemental compensation fund. Neither of the Protocols is in force internationally.

Many of the structural and operational requirements of the 1978 Port and Tanker Safety Act were enacted internationally by the Protocol of 1978 Relating to the International Convention for the Prevention of Pollution from Ships, 1973.[16]

3.0 TITLE I: OIL POLLUTION LIABILITY AND COMPENSATION

Title I[17] establishes the federal liability scheme for vessels and facilities that spill oil on waters subject to U.S. jurisdiction. It sets out the scope of the act: the waters, vessels and facilities that OPA applies to. It defines the standard of liability and enumerates compensable damages. The provisions of Title I also set up the claims procedures, financial responsibility requirements, and the uses of the $1 billion Oil Spill Liability Trust Fund.

3.1 Definitions

Section 1001 of OPA contains 37 definitions which are used throughout the entire act.[18] OPA restates verbatim many of the definitions of the Clean Water Act.

Vessels: Except where otherwise limited, OPA applies to all vessels, not just tankers. Consequently, a spill involving fuel from a pleasure craft or bunkers from a general cargo vessel is subject to OPA liability. On the other hand, these vessels are not subjected to the operational and construction requirements that tankers are. Vessels are defined to include "every description of watercraft or other artificial contrivance used, or capable of

---

[14]The International Convention on the Establishment of an International Fund for Oil Pollution Damage, 1971, 11 I.L.M. 284 (1972) (Fund Convention).

[15]Protocol of 1984 to the International Convention on Civil Liability for Oil Pollution Damage and the Protocol of 1984 to the International Convention on the Establishment of an International Fund for Compensation for Oil Pollution Damage (1984 Protocols).

[16]20 I.L.M. 561 (1981).

[17]33 U.S.C. §§ 2701 2719.

[18]33 U.S.C. § 2701.

being used, as a means of transportation on water, other than a public vessel." Public vessels are non-commercial government vessels.

Tank Vessels: These are vessels constructed, adapted to carry, or that carry oil or hazardous materials in bulk as cargo or cargo residue and that are U.S. documented vessels, operate in U.S. waters or transfer oil or hazardous material in a place subject to the jurisdiction of the United States. This definition of tank vessels is not limited to oil tankers and barges, but also includes tankers and barges carrying hazardous materials such as explosives, liquified petroleum gas and liquified natural gas.[19]

OPA provisions vary in scope. For example, OPA liability is imposed only on vessels which discharge oil (section 1002). Financial responsibility requirements apply to all tank vessels carrying oil and hazardous materials (section 1016). Double hull requirements apply only to tank vessels which carry oil (section 4115).

Mobile Offshore Drilling Units (MODUs) are drilling units that are capable of being used as an offshore facility; self-elevating lift vessels are not included in this definition.

Facility is any structure, group of structures, equipment, or device (other than a vessel) which is used for any of the following purposes: exploring for, drilling for, producing, storing, handling, transferring, processing, or transporting oil. The term also includes any motor vehicle, rolling stock, or pipeline used for these purposes. Facilities are further subdivided into onshore and offshore facilities.

Oil covers oil of any kind, including petroleum, fuel oil, sludge, oil refuse, and oil mixed with wastes, other than dredge spoils. The definition goes on to exclude any part of oil which is defined as a "hazardous substance" by the Comprehensive Environmental Response, Compensation and Liability Act (CERCLA).[20] Thus, there is no overlap between the liability provisions of OPA and those of CERCLA.

Person is defined broadly to include both natural persons and commercial and government entities, including states, municipalities, commissions, political subdivisions and interstate bodies.

Owner or Operator is the person(s) who bears the burden for the substantive obligations of OPA. In the case of a vessel this means a person who owns, operates or demise (bareboat) charters a vessel. With respect to facilities, it is those persons owning or operating the facility. For an abandoned vessel or facility, it is the person who would have been the owner or operator immediately prior to abandonment.

Responsible Party is liable for removal costs and damages under section 1002. Generally the term means the owners or operators whose vessel or facility is the source of an oil discharge or which poses the substantial threat of a discharge. For deepwater ports, the responsible party is the

---

[19]These materials are listed at 49 C.F.R. § 172.101.
[20]42 U.S.C. § 9601.

licensee and for offshore facilities the responsible party is the lessee or the permittee of the area in which the facility is located. Public entities are not considered responsible parties in connection with onshore facilities.

Discharge is any sort of emission in the navigable waters, the adjoining shoreline, or the exclusive economic zone. A discharge of oil triggers OPA liability. A discharge of CERCLA hazardous substances[21] triggers OPA containment and removal provisions.

Incident: One or more discharges from the same source constitute an "incident."

Navigable waters means *all* waters of the United States beginning with marshes and extending seaward 12 miles to the limits of the territorial sea. A discharge in these waters or on the adjoining shoreline is covered by OPA.

Exclusive Economic Zone includes those waters which extend seaward 200 miles. Discharges in these waters are also covered by OPA.

Remove or Removal: Under Title IV of OPA, public and private entities are to carry out the effective and immediate removal of a discharge and mitigate or prevent the substantial threat of a discharge. Remove or removal is defined as containment and removal of the oil or hazardous substance from the water and shorelines and taking other actions to minimize or mitigate damage.

4.0 ELEMENTS OF LIABILITY

OPA makes responsible parties for vessels and facilities liable for the results of oil spills without regard to fault, subject only to certain narrow defenses. While this is essentially the same liability that vessel and facility owners and operators had under the Clean Water Act, the damages that can be recovered from them after an oil spill under OPA are potentially much greater.

4.1 Standard of Liability

Section 1002 states that liability under OPA exists "[n]otwithstanding any other provision or rule of law...." This removes any prerequisite to liability such as the requirement that a claimant show physical damage to his property. This also means that a vessel owner is unable to limit his liability to the value of this vessel and its freight under the Limitation of Liability Act.[22]

OPA further states that each responsible party for a vessel or facility is liable for removal costs and damages. This envisions that in some circumstances multiple responsible parties could be liable for the entire amount of removal costs and damages. This is called joint and several liability.

---

[21] 40 C.F.R. § 116.
[22] 46 U.S.C. § 183.

4.2 Removal Costs

A responsible party is liable for all removal costs incurred by the federal government, state governments, or Indian tribes. The only restriction on these removal costs is that they be incurred under the authority of either the Clean Water Act as amended by OPA, or the Intervention on the High Seas Act,[23] which governs discharges in international waters which threaten the United States.

OPA provides that removal costs can include expenses of actions taken by virtually any agency or department of federal, state, and local governments to avert the threat of a discharge, and to ensure the immediate and effective containment, dispersal and removal of the oil or hazardous substance. These costs and expenses could also include those resulting from whatever action is necessary to protect fish, shellfish, wildlife, public and private property, shorelines, beaches, and living and nonliving natural resources.

A responsible party is also liable for any removal costs incurred under authority of state law. Finally, a responsible party is also liable for any removal costs incurred by any person, that is private individuals and organizations, for actions taken which are consistent with the National Contingency Plan.

4.3 Compensatory Damages

In addition to removal costs, OPA makes a responsible party liable for six categories of compensatory damages:[24]

Natural Resource: The United States, states, Indian tribes, and foreign governments are entitled to recover from a responsible party for damages, injury to, destruction, loss of, and loss of use of natural resources. Natural resource damages also include the reasonable cost of assessing those damages.

Real or Personal Property: If an oil spill injures real or personal property or diminishes the earnings from that property, the owner, or anyone who leases that property, may claim damages.

Subsistence Use: Any person who relies on natural resources for subsistence (as opposed to commercial reliance which is covered under loss of profits and earnings) may recover damages for injury to natural resources regardless of who owns or manages those resources.

Revenues: Federal, state, and local governments are entitled to recover damages equal to the net loss of taxes, royalties, rents, fees, or net profit shares resulting from the destruction or loss of real or personal property, or natural resources.

Profits and Earning Capacity: A claimant is entitled to loss of profits or impairment of earning capacity from injury, destruction, or loss of real or personal property or natural resources.

---

[23]33 U.S.C. § 1471.
[24]Section 1002.

Public Services: State and local governments are entitled to recover damages for the net costs of providing increased or additional public services resulting from removal activities, including fire, safety, and health protection.

4.4 Interest

A responsible party, or his insurer, may be liable to a claimant for interest on the amount to be paid in satisfaction of a claim.[25] The interest period begins 30 days after the claim is presented to the responsible party, and continues until the claim is paid. An offer of the amount claimed can suspend the interest period, as will reasons beyond the control of the responsible party. Interest payments are not included in liability limit calculations.

5.0 NATURAL RESOURCE DAMAGES

OPA establishes a standard for measuring natural resource damages applicable to all actions for such damages. Government bodies are identified as the trustees of natural resources to whom a responsible party is liable in the event of damage to their respective natural resources. Each of these government entities is to develop a plan for repairing damage to its natural resources, and the cost of carrying out these plans constitutes the major component of natural resource damages. The federal government is charged with issuing timely regulations for the assessment of natural resource damages.

A responsible party is liable to the federal government, state, and foreign governments, as well as Indian tribes for injury to, destruction of, or loss of natural resources. Authorized representatives of these government entities are to be designated as trustees of their respective natural resources, to present claims for, and recover for damages to, natural resources. The different entities have jurisdiction over natural resources belonging to, managed by, controlled by, or appertaining to them. Where there is joint jurisdiction, the trustees are to exercise joint management or control over the shared resources; no group of trustees can preempt another group.

The designated federal, state, foreign, and Indian trustees are also charged with assessing damages to their natural resources, and determining the assessment costs. They are to develop and implement plans for the restoration, rehabilitation, and replacement of the natural resources of which they are trustees. The plans are also to include provisions for the acquisition of equivalent resources—that is, resources comparable to the injured resources—to restore the damaged ecosystem. This alternative is to be utilized only if the trustees determine that restoration, rehabilitation or replacement is not feasible. The trustees are to determine the cost of implementing these plans. The trustees are also to calculate the diminution in value of the damaged resources pending restoration. These trustee plans

---

[25]Section 1005.

are to provide the basis for the calculation of natural resource damages for which a responsible party is liable.

Also prescribed is the standard measure of damages to natural resources that is to apply to all actions brought under the act. This consists of (1) the cost of restoring, rehabilitating, replacing or acquiring the equivalent of the damaged natural resources; (2) the diminution in value of those natural resources pending restoration; and (3) the reasonable cost of assessing the damage. Since double recovery for natural resource damages is prohibited, government entities and tribes are directed to consolidate their efforts to assess and recover natural resource damages.

The Undersecretary of Commerce for Oceans and the Atmosphere in consultation with the Environmental Protection Agency, the Fish and Wildlife Service, and other affected federal agencies are to promulgate regulations for the assessment of natural resource damages. Trustees' natural resource damage assessments made according to these regulations are treated legally as rebuttable presumptions. This means that they are presumed to be correct; although the presumption can be overcome, the opponent has the burden of proof of doing so.

Amounts recovered by the respective trustees for natural resource damages are to be retained by the trustees in their own trust accounts to be used, without further appropriation, exclusively for the costs of carrying out their restoration plans. Excess amounts are to be deposited in the Oil Spill Liability Trust Fund.

Any person can obtain judicial review of trustees' actions in federal court.

6.0 DEFENSES TO LIABILITY

Strict liability is a legal policy which imposes on a person who engages in a particular activity the responsibility for compensating others for the harm he causes, regardless of fault. OPA makes a responsible party strictly liable for oil spill damages. There are only four defenses which exonerate a responsible party from liability, three complete defenses to liability and one defense to particular claimants.[26]

The complete defenses involve the intervention of outside events: an act of God, an act of war, and an act or omission of a third party. If one or more of these events, or a combination of them, is the sole cause of the discharge or threat of a discharge of oil and the resulting damages or removal costs, then the responsible party is exculpated. However, the responsible party is only able to avail himself of these defenses if he fulfills his other obligations under the act. He must report the spill, he must cooperate and assist with removal efforts, and he must comply with official removal orders.

A responsible party also has a defense to the claims of a particular claimant to the extent that the incident giving rise to the claims is caused by the gross negligence or willful misconduct of the claimant himself.

---

[26]Section 1003.

6.1 Third Party Liability

When a responsible party is able to establish that the threat or spill, and resulting removal costs and damages, were caused solely by the act or omission of one or more third parties, then the third parties are treated as the responsible parties instead of the original responsible party.[27]

However, a third party will be treated as a responsible party only in limited circumstances. The third party cannot be an employee or agent of the responsible party. Nor will the third party be treated as the responsible party if the third party's act or omission, causing the threat or spill, occurred in connection with a contract between the responsible party and the third party, unless the contract only involves carriage of oil by a common carrier by rail. The responsible party must prove that he exercised due care in handling the oil and took precautions against foreseeable acts of the third party and any foreseeable consequences of those actions.

Furthermore, the responsible party must first pay removal costs and damages to any claimant. Only at that point is the responsible party entitled to be subrogated to the claimants' rights and recover the amount for any claims paid from the third party or from the Fund.

7.0 LIMITS ON LIABILITY

The act limits the liability of a responsible party for removal costs and damages to specified dollar amounts depending on the type of vessel or facility involved in the spill.[28] However, egregious or aberrant behavior by a responsible party, or his failure to fulfill his reporting and assistance obligations under OPA, create circumstances in which these limits do not apply.

7.1 The Standard for Limiting OPA Liability

The right of a vessel owner or facility to limit liability is a conditional right. The right to limit is lost if the incident was proximately caused by the gross negligence, willful misconduct or violation of an applicable federal safety, construction or operating regulation by the responsible party.

Similarly, the failure of a responsible party to fulfill his reporting, cooperation and compliance obligations under OPA will render the liability limits inapplicable. The actions of an agent, employee, or contracted party (not including rail common carriers) are considered to be the acts of the responsible party.

These exceptions to the limits on liability are far broader and more numerous than the ones under prior law. Previously, under the Clean Water Act, only if the government could show that the discharge was the result of willful negligence or willful misconduct within the privity and knowledge of the owner or operator, would the limits on liability not apply.[29]

---

[27]Section 1002(d).

[28]Section 1004.

[29]33 U.S.C. § 1321(f)(1).

7.2 Specific Liability Limits

The Oil Pollution Act increases the liability limits for vessel and facility owners or operators from the limits under the Clean Water Act. For vessel owners, the limits have been increased by a factor of almost ten. Furthermore, the Oil Pollution Act limits are now the only limits available for vessels owners, since other statutory limits have been abrogated.

For tank vessels, the limit is the greater of $1,200 per gross ton or either $2 million for vessels 3,000 gross tons or smaller, or $10 million for vessels larger than 3,000 gross tons. For other vessels, the limit is the greater of $600 per gross ton or $500,000. For vessels which carry oil as cargo from outer continental shelf facilities, these limits only apply to liability for damages. The owner or operator of such vessels is liable for all removal costs, without limit, resulting from a discharge.

For onshore facilities and deepwater ports, the limit is $350 million, and for offshore facilities (except deepwater ports) the limit is $75 million plus the total of all removal costs. For outer continental shelf facilities, these limits only apply to liability for damages. The owner or operator of such facilities is liable for all removal costs, without limit, resulting from a discharge.

Liability limits for mobile offshore drilling units which operate as offshore facilities and are involved in a discharge or the threat of a discharge are the same as for vessels. However, if the removal costs and damages exceed the vessel liability limits, then the facility liability limits apply.

These liability limits also apply to third parties. If the act or omission of a third party that causes an incident occurs in connection with a vessel or facility owned or operated by the third party, then his liability is subject to the limits under OPA. In other cases, the liability of a third party is restricted in amount to the limit of the responsible party for the vessel or facility from which the discharge occurred, as if the responsible party were liable.

7.3 Adjustment of Liability Limits

The president is directed to report periodically to the Congress on the desirability of adjusting the statutory limits of liability. No authority is conferred in this section to actually adjust the limits on the liability for vessels in general.

The president does have the authority to adjust the limits on liability for onshore facilities and deepwater ports without an amendment to the statute.[30]

With respect to onshore facilities, the president may set by regulation specific limits of liability between $8 million and $350 million for any class or category of onshore facility.

The secretary of transportation is also required to report on the relative risks associated with the use of deepwater ports as compared with the

---

[30]Section 1004(d).

risks associated with other ports and is authorized to lower the limits of liability by regulation for deepwater ports from \$350 million to \$50 million.

The president may also amend triennially the limits of liability by regulation to reflect significant increases in the Consumer Price Index.

8.0 RECOVERY BY A FOREIGN CLAIMANT

Section 1007 permits a foreign claimant (a person residing in a foreign country or a foreign government) to bring an OPA claim in the United States for a discharge in the territorial sea, internal waters, or adjacent shoreline of a foreign country. Section 1007 is the only specific statutory authority for a foreign claimant to bring an OPA action in U.S. courts.

There are a number of conditions that must be fulfilled for a foreign claimant to bring an OPA action in a U.S. court. These conditions essentially ascertain that the origin of the spill had a strong connection with the United States. The foreign claimant must demonstrate that it has not received compensation for removal costs and damages and, except for Trans-Alaska Pipeline Oil spilled in Canada, that recovery under OPA is provided for in a treaty or executive agreement or by reciprocal right. At present, there are no such agreements or rights.

9.0 RECOVERY BY THE RESPONSIBLE PARTY

A responsible party entitled to a defense to liability under section 1003 or entitled to limit its liability under section 1004 can assert a claim under section 1013 for amounts paid.[31] The responsible party with a complete defense to liability can recover all payments of removal costs and damages. The responsible party entitled to limit its liability under section 1004 can recover amounts paid exceeding the limit.

10.0 CONTRIBUTION AND INDEMNIFICATION

Where multiple parties are involved in an oil spill, any person can bring a contribution action against any other person who is liable or potentially liable under OPA or another law.[32]

No responsible party may divest itself of OPA liability by contract. However, any person potentially liable under OPA may agree to have others contractually assume the responsibility to pay for some or all of those liabilities through insurance contracts or indemnity agreements and hold harmless agreements.[33]

11.0 OIL SPILL LIABILITY TRUST FUND

Some of the principal sections applicable to the creation and operation of the Fund are: section 1012, Use of Fund; section 1013, Claims Procedure;

---

[31]Section 1008.
[32]Section 1009.
[33]Section 1010.

section 1014, Designation of Source & Advertisement; section 1015, Subrogation; and section 6002, Annual Appropriations. Also relevant are section 1007, Recovery by Foreign Claimants; section 1008, Recovery by Responsible Party, and section 9509 of the Internal Revenue Code.[34]

11.1 Abolition of Existing Funds

11.1.1 Deepwater Port Liability Fund[35]

This fund was established in 1974 to pay for cleanup costs and damages associated with deepwater ports. It was funded by a two cent tax on the owners of deepwater port oil. It was never utilized, and its balance of $6.6 million was transferred to the Fund.

11.1.2 Offshore Oil Pollution Compensation Fund[36]

This fund was established in 1978 to cover uncompensated economic losses including removal costs from OCS activities. It was financed by a three cent tax on OCS producers. It, too, was never utilized and its balance of $171 million was transferred to the Fund.

11.1.3 Trans-Alaska Pipeline Fund[37]

This fund was established in 1973 to cover damages and removal costs in excess of $14 million and less than $100 million from vessels carrying oil loaded at the pipeline terminal in Valdez, Alaska. It was financed by a five cent tax on the owners of TAPS oil. Claims against the fund were filed from the *Glacier Bay* and *Exxon Valdez* spills, and may be filed from the *American Trader* spill. The fund is retained under OPA until certification that these claims have been resolved.

11.1.4 Federal Water Pollution Control Act Fund[38]

This was called the "311 or 311(k)" Fund. It was set up in 1973 to be a $35 million revolving fund for federal responses to oil and hazardous substance spills. However, its balance never exceeded $25 million. It was financed through initial appropriations and recoveries from responsible parties. Availability of its funds was subject to appropriation. Its $20 million balance was transferred to the Oil Pollution Liability Trust Fund.

11.2 Preservation of State Funds

OPA preserves the right of the states to establish or continue any state oil pollution compensation fund, or the right of the states to tax for the purpose of oil pollution compensation funds.

---

[34] 26 U.S.C. § 9509.
[35] 33 U.S.C. 1517(f).
[36] 43 U.S.C. 1812.
[37] 43 U.S.C. 1653(c).
[38] 33 U.S.C. 1321(k).

11.3 Funding of the Fund

At the end of 1992 the Fund had a balance of $870 million. This sum resulted from the five cents per barrel tax on oil received at U.S. refineries, or petroleum products entering the United States for consumption, use or warehousing and the integration of existing funds into the Fund. Future penalties from Clean Water Act section 311 violations, Deepwater Port Act violations, and Trans-Alaska Pipeline Authorization Act violations will be paid into the Fund as will be excess natural resource damages.

The Attorney General is authorized to recover any compensation paid by the Fund and all costs of the claim. The Fund is also authorized to borrow up to $1 billion from the Treasury.

11.4 Uses of the Fund

The Internal Revenue Code sets a $1 billion per incident limit on government and private uses of the Fund.

11.4.1 Government Uses:

1. Up to $50 million per fiscal year, including $250,000 at the request of a state, is made immediately available without further appropriation, for federal and state removal and monitoring costs to provide a quick response to an incident.
2. Up to $500 million per incident is provided for natural resource damages.
3. Payment of removal costs and damages must be consistent with the National Contingency Plan resulting from a discharge from a foreign offshore unit.
4. OPA also provides for payment of administrative, operational, and personnel costs and expenses for implementation, administration, and enforcement of the act. Certain of these expenditures are specifically authorized.

11.4.2 Private Uses:

The Fund can be used for payment of uncompensated removal costs and damages consistent with the National Contingency Plan for claims submitted according to the claims procedure. These amounts are available for payment without further appropriation by Congress. Uncompensated claims could result from defenses to liability and liability limits or the financial inability to pay claims.

12.0 CLAIMS

OPA sets up a notification and claims procedure to facilitate the prompt filing and payment of claims for damages from oil spills.[39] Procedures are also detailed for the processing of claims by the Fund. The

---

[39]Section 1013.

Fund is available to satisfy claims which are not fully compensated by the responsible party.

12.1 Designation of the Source and Advertisement

OPA requires the person in charge of a vessel or a facility to report a spill to federal authorities. Failure to notify the authorities is grounds for imposing penalties and abolishing defenses to or limits on liability. Under OPA, upon receiving information about a spill, federal authorities will designate the source and notify the responsible party and insurer. If the spill does not involve damages or removal costs, no designation need be made.

Depending on whether the responsible party accepts liability or not, either the responsible party or the federal authorities will advertise the source of the spill and the claims procedure.[40]

Responsible Party Advertises: If the responsible party or insurer does not deny designation within five days, thus accepting liability for the spill, they must advertise the designation and the claims procedure within 15 days of the designation and continue to do so for 30 days.

Government Advertises: If the federal authorities are unable to designate the source, if the source is a government vessel, or if the responsible party accepts the designation but fails to advertise, the government will advertise at the responsible party's expense.

12.2 Procedure

Claims for removal costs and damages must be presented first to the designated responsible party or insurer. If the responsible party denies liability for the claim, or the claim is not settled 90 days after submission or the date of advertisement, whichever is later, the claimant has the option of bringing a lawsuit against the responsible party or presenting the claim to the Fund.

Claims can be presented first to the Fund if the responsible party denies the designation, if the authorities are unable to designate the source, or if the source is a government vessel. Insufficiently compensated claims submitted according to the claims procedure can be presented directly to the Fund.

Claims are also subject to a statute of limitations. The time limit for presentation of claims is six years after completion of removal action for presentation of claims for recovery of removal costs. Claims for damages must be submitted within three years of discovery of loss. Claims for damages to natural resources must be submitted within three years of discovery of loss or completion of natural resource damage assessment.

13.0 FINANCIAL RESPONSIBILITY

OPA continues the Clean Water Act requirement that owners and operators of vessels and facilities demonstrate the financial capacity to pay

---

[40]Section 1014.

claims up to their limits of liability.[41] However, because the amounts of the liability limits have been increased dramatically, the amounts of financial responsibility which must be demonstrated are also much larger.

13.1 Vessels

The financial responsibility requirements apply to any vessel over 300 gross tons, except a barge (non-self-propelled vessel) which is not carrying oil on board, either as a fuel or a cargo. Thus not only tankers, but also other classes of vessels, such as passenger vessels and cargo vessels, must comply with the financial responsibility requirements.

The requirements also apply to any vessel, regardless of tonnage, which is either transshipping or lightering oil within the exclusive economic zone. The financial responsibility requirements do not apply to vessels in innocent passage or vessels transferring oil not destined for the United States.

13.2 Facilities

The financial responsibility requirements apply to offshore facilities and deepwater ports, but not to onshore facilities.

13.3 Calculation of Financial Responsibility Amounts

For vessels, the owner or operator must show financial responsibility sufficient to meet his limit of liability. For tank vessels carrying oil or hazardous materials, the amount is $1,200 per gross ton. For other vessels, it is $600 per gross ton. The owners or operators of multiple vessels must only cover the limit of liability of the largest vessel.

For offshore facilities, the general requirement is for $150 million of financial responsibility. For deepwater ports, the amount is $350 million. The secretary of transportation may lower these limits. Owners or operators of multiple facilities must cover only the limit of liability of the largest facility.

13.4 Methods of Demonstrating Financial Responsibility

Financial responsibility may be evidenced by one or more of the following methods: insurance, surety bond, guarantee, letter of credit, self-insurance, or "other evidence of financial responsibility." The president (in the case of facilities) and the secretary of transportation (in the case of vessels) may issue regulations which set standards for policy or contract defenses, conditions, and terms.[42] An entity other than the responsible party which provides evidence of financial responsibility is a "guarantor."

13.5 The Role of Guarantor

The stated purpose of having a guarantor of the owner's liability is to "provide claimants with a full range of options for pursuing their

---

[41]Section 1016.
[42]Section 1016(e).

claims."[43] Consequently, OPA requires guarantors to be directly liable to claimants for removal costs and damages, subject to very limited defenses. Claimants are intended to have direct access to recovery, regardless of whether the responsible party is insolvent or otherwise unavailable to pay claims.

13.6 Financial Responsibility Regulations

The regulations relating to evidence of financial responsibility issued prior to the enactment of OPA remain in effect until superseding regulations are issued.[44]

Although the Coast Guard issued a notice of proposed rulemaking on September 1991, as of the end of 1992 final regulations have not been issued.

14.0 SUBROGATION

Any person who compensates a claimant for removal costs or damages is subrogated to all the rights that the claimant may have under OPA and any other law.[45] The Fund is subrogated in respect to any claims it pays and can assume the claimant's rights under any law, including state law.

15.0 LITIGATION AND JURISDICTION

Although OPA channels the resolution of claims first to the responsible party and its guarantor and then to the Trust Fund, courts will consider claims for damages and can be petitioned to review OPA rules. Section 1017 sets out the rules for this litigation and defines the role of state courts.

15.1 Jurisdiction

United States federal district courts have exclusive original jurisdiction over all OPA cases. However, petitions to review OPA regulations are filed with the U.S. Circuit Court for the District of Columbia. A state trial court with jurisdiction over removal costs and damages may consider OPA claims and state claims.

15.2 Limitations

Claims for removal costs must be brought within three years after the removal actions have been completed. Claims for damages must be brought within three years of the date of the discovery of the loss, and in the case of natural resources damages, within three years after the completion of the natural resource damage assessment performed by the trustees. Contribution actions must be brought within three years after judgment on costs and damages or approval of settlement. Subrogation actions must be commenced within three years after the payment of a claim for removal costs or damages.

---

[43]H.R. Conf. Rep. No. 653, 101st Cong., 2d Sess. (OPA Conf. Rep.) 119 (1990).
[44]Section 1016(h).
[45] Section 1015.

16.0 RELATIONSHIP TO OTHER LAWS

Congress declined to enact an exclusive federal oil pollution law and instead chose a system which preserved state law.

16.1 Preservation of State Law

OPA does not preempt state law. State and local governments may impose additional liability or requirements related to oil spills by statute or ruling as well as imposing additional civil or criminal penalties.[46] States may establish oil pollution funds to pay for removal costs and damages. States may also enforce federal financial responsibility requirements in state waters.[47]

16.2 Preservation of Federal Laws

OPA does not affect the Solid Waste Disposal Act.[48] Nothing in the OPA creates a cause of action against federal officials or employees.[49]

16.3 Tanker Design and Construction Standards

The Conference Report states that OPA does not affect the ruling of the U.S. Supreme Court in the *Ray v. Atlantic Richfield Co.*,[50] a case striking down state tanker construction regulations which conflicted with federal regulations. This suggests that federal authority to regulate vessel design and construction is preserved and that OPA does not grant states any additional authority in this area.

17.0 TITLE II: CONFORMING AMENDMENTS

Title II contains conforming amendments transferring the balance of funds under the Clean Water Act[51], the Deepwater Port Act[52], and the Outer Continental Shelf Lands Act[53] to the OPA Oil Spill Liability Trust Fund. The secretary of transportation is also authorized to utilize the Fund for removal activities under the Intervention on the High Seas Act.[54]

18.0 TITLE III: INTERNATIONAL OIL POLLUTION PREVENTION AND REMOVAL

A contentious issue in the OPA debate was United States participation in international oil pollution conventions. Generally, the House of Representatives advocated participation in the international conventions

---

[46]Section 1018.

[47]Section 1019.

[48]42 U.S.C. § 6901.

[49]Section 1018(d).

[50]OPA Conf. Rep. at 122. *Ray v. Atlantic Richfield Co.*, 435 U.S. 151 (1978).

[51]Section 2002.

[52]Section 2003.

[53]Section 2004.

[54]Section 2001.

for reasons of comity international uniformity. On the other hand, members of the Senate found that the international compensation levels were too low and that the preemption of federal and state laws by the conventions was unacceptable.

The compromise proposed in Title III of OPA[55] stated the opinion of Congress that the best interests of the United States would be served by participation in an international prevention and compensation regime that was at least as effective as domestic law.

Title III also contains provisions regarding cooperation between the United States and Canada on oil pollution matters.[56]

19.0 TITLE IV: PREVENTION AND REMOVAL

Title IV is divided into three subtitles. Subtitle A changes many of the laws governing the manning and operation of tank vessels to prevent oil spills. Subtitle B establishes a national planning and response system to insure the prompt and effective removal of oil spills that do occur. Subtitle C substantially increases the severity of criminal and civil penalties that can be imposed on vessel and facility owners and operators for discharges of oil under OPA, the Clean Water Act, and marine safety laws.

20.0 SUBTITLE A: PREVENTION

The OPA contains new or more stringent licensing and operating requirements designed to ensure the safe transportation and transfer of oil and hazardous substance.

20.1 Licensing Requirements: Drug and Alcohol Testing

The secretary of transportation is given the authority to require additional information on driving records, criminal records, and results from drug and alcohol tests of applicants for new merchant mariner's papers, for renewal applicants, and for current holders of licenses, certificates, and merchant mariner's documents.[57] Current holders will be tested for drugs and alcohol on a random, periodic, reasonable cause and post-accident basis.[58]

OPA also adds additional grounds for suspensions and revocations of current papers. Holders of licenses, certificates, and merchant mariner's documents who perform safety sensitive functions may have their papers suspended for drug and alcohol violations. Holders may also have their papers suspended or revoked for a violation of safety or pollution laws and regulations and incompetence, misconduct or negligence.

To insure that all holders of current papers will be subjected to background checks, the terms of all licenses, certificates and merchant

---

[55]Section 3001.
[56]Sections 3002-3005.
[57]Section 4101.
[58]Section 4103.

mariner's documents are changed to five years with five year renewal periods.[59] Existing papers without renewal dates will now be renewed on the date after the enactment of the OPA which is the five-year multiple of the date of issuance.

The master or individual in charge of a vessel may be relieved of command if he is under the influence of alcohol or drugs and is incapable of commanding the vessel.[60]

20.2 Foreign Tank Vessel Manning Standards

The Coast Guard is required to evaluate the manning, training, qualification and watchkeeping standards of foreign countries that issue vessel documentation to determine whether that country's standards are equivalent to U.S. or international standards and whether those standards are being adequately enforced. The Coast Guard is also required to conduct periodic review for each country as well as a post-casualty review.[61]

20.3 Tank Vessel Manning

The Coast Guard is to consider additional factors in formulating manning standards for tank vessels. These factors now include the navigation, cargo handling, and maintenance functions of a tank vessel for protection of life, property and the environment.[62] The secretary of transportation is to initiate a rulemaking on the operation of tank vessels in navigable waters under automatic-pilot or an unattended engine room.

On self-propelled tank vessels, officers and crew members are restricted to working no more than 15 hours in any 24-hour period, or no more than 36 hours in any 72-hour period. For these purposes, "work" includes administrative functions associated with the vessel, whether these functions are conducted on board the vessel or ashore.

20.4 Marine Casualty Reporting

OPA expands existing marine casualty reporting requirements to include marine casualties involving "significant harm to the environment." Casualty reporting requirements for foreign tank vessels are expanded to include casualties occurring in the exclusive economic zone.[63]

20.5 Pilotage Requirements

The secretary of transportation will designate on which U.S. waters tankers over 1,600 gross tons will be required to have a licensed master or mate on the bridge in addition to the pilot. Also, the secretary will

---

[59]Section 4102.
[60]Section 4104.
[61]Section 4106.
[62]Section 4114.
[63]Section 4106(b).

designate waters in the Northwest in which single hull tankers will be required to be escorted by two tugs.[64]

OPA requires non-U.S. flag and Canadian flag vessels to retain a Canadian or U.S. pilot on the Great Lakes. This requirement applies to any vessel, not just to tank vessels.[65]

More stringent requirements are also imposed for Prince William Sound, Alaska.

20.6 Studies and Regulations [Sections 4107-4113]

These sections call for a number of studies and regulations on safety-related issues. The secretary of transportation is required to conduct a study of vessel traffic systems and report the results to Congress.[66] The secretary is required to issue regulations on minimum standards for plating thickness and periodic gauging of plating thickness, as well as minimum standards for and use of overfill devices and tank level or pressure monitoring devices.[67] The secretary is also required to issue regulations on radio equipment for vessels subject to the Vessel Bridge-to-Bridge Radiotelephone Act.[68]

The secretary is to undertake a comprehensive study to evaluate the adequacy of existing navigation laws and regulations for safe operation of tankers.[69] The secretary is to evaluate crew size and qualifications, electronic navigation and position-reporting equipment, navigation procedures, inspection standards, and whether to impose tanker-free zones. The secretary will analyze whether there is a correlation between tanker size, cargo capacity, national origin, and oil spills. The secretary will also consider the use of computer simulators and remote alcohol testing.

Other requirements include a report by the secretary of the army on the feasibility of modifying dredges to be used in cleaning up oil spills,[70] a report by the president on whether liners or other containment devices should be required at shoreside facilities,[71] and a study of the feasibility of a maritime oil pollution prevention training program.[72]

20.7 Double Hull Requirements for Tank Vessels

The requirement that a tank vessel have a double hull goes into effect immediately for a new vessel and according to a phase-out schedule for an existing vessel.[73] The phase-out schedule begins in 1995 and runs until 2015.

---

[64]Section 4116.
[65]Section 4108.
[66]Section 4107.
[67]Section 4109 and section 4110.
[68]Section 4118.
[69]Section 4111.
[70]Section 4112.
[71]Section 4113.
[72]Section 4117.
[73]Section 4115.

Older and larger vessels are retired first. An existing vessel is one for which a contract for construction or for a major conversion has been placed prior to June 30, 1990 and the vessel is delivered under that contract prior to January 1, 1994. Consequently, a future major conversion on an existing vessel could result in that vessel being treated as a new vessel for double hull purposes. Major conversion means a substantial change in the type, carrying capacity, or dimensions of the vessel, or a conversion that substantially prolongs the life of the vessel or makes it a new vessel. A major reconstruction of the hull structure that enhances environmental compatibility also constitutes a major conversion.

20.7.1 Exceptions to the Requirements

New tank vessels are required to be built with a double hull. The only exceptions are vessels used only to respond to oil spills and newly-constructed vessels less that 5,000 gross tons. The latter category must be equipped with a double containment system which has been determined to be as effective as a double hull.

The double hull requirement does not go into effect until the year 2015 in three cases: (1) for vessels unloading at deepwater ports; (2) for vessels delivering to lightering vessels in established lightering zones at least 60 miles offshore; and (3) for existing vessels less than 5,000 gross tons.

20.7.2 Additional or Alternative Requirements

Additionally, the secretary of transportation is directed to complete a rulemaking proceeding to determine whether any structural or operational requirements should be imposed on existing vessels subject to the double hull requirements during the period before the requirement goes into effect. The measures contemplated include hydrostatic loading, and the installation of spill rails or other containment equipment. The secretary is also required to conduct a study and issue a report based on recommendations from the National Academy of Sciences, on whether other structural and operational requirements would provide equal or better protection than double hulls. If the secretary so concludes, he is to propose legislative action. The secretary, also in conjunction with the National Academy of Sciences, is to review periodically the impact of double hulls on environmental safety and is to consider other methods of increasing tank vessel safety.

20.7.3 Title XI Loan Guarantees

The secretary of transportation can provide loan guarantees under the current provisions of Title XI of the Merchant Marine Act, 1936, for the construction of replacement vessels or reconstruction of vessels rendered inoperable by changes in the law. The borrower must be already operating this type of vessel and must agree to use the newly-constructed or reconstructed vessels as replacements. The new vessels must not be larger than the vessels they replace. These provisions essentially restate existing authority.

21.0 SUBTITLE B: REMOVAL

Under OPA federal authorities have the responsibility for averting threats of oil spills and cleaning up ones that happen. These activities are conducted according to the National Response System and the National Contingency Plan. Although the OPA oil spill response system utilizes governmental planning and direction, it relies primarily on private resources to mitigate or remove spills. To ensure the availability of private response personnel and equipment, OPA requires approved individual vessel and facility response plans for vessel and facility owners and operators. Private response efforts are encouraged by conferring immunity from liability for removal costs and damages on those rendering care, assistance or advice in response to a spill.

21.1 Federal Removal Authority

OPA emphasizes federal direction of public and private efforts both of the response to avert the threat of an oil spill and of removal of oil that has been spilled. Under the Clean Water Act, federal authorities were authorized to act at any time to remove oil in the event of a spill or the threat of a spill, but removal could be entrusted to the vessel or facility owner or operator. However, OPA states that federal authorities are to insure the immediate removal of a discharge and mitigate and prevent the substantial threat of a discharge.[74] This authority applies to spills or threats in navigable waters, shorelines, and the waters of the exclusive economic zone. It also applies to situations where federal natural resources are affected.

OPA is more explicit than the Clean Water Act about federal responsibility for responding to the threat of a spill and removing a spill, and it also provides the government with a wider range of alternative actions to accomplish immediate removal. The federal authorities may merely direct or monitor federal, state, and private removal and mitigation actions. More actively, the federal authorities may assume the responsibility and costs of the actions subject to reimbursement from the responsible party. This is referred to as "federalizing" the effort. They may go so far as to remove and destroy a discharging vessel using any means available.

21.1.1 Discharges That Constitute A Substantial Threat to Public Welfare

The federal government has extensive authority over containment and removal of a particular class of spills: those which are deemed to pose a substantial threat to the public health or welfare of the United States. The public health or welfare of the United States includes fish, shellfish, wildlife, other natural resources, or public and private shorelines and beaches. Criteria for identification of these spills, as well as procedures for responding to them, are to be addressed in the National Contingency Plan.

---

[74]Section 4201.

In the case of spills such as the *Exxon Valdez* in Alaska, the *American Trader* in California, and *Mega Borg* in the Gulf of Mexico, the act states unequivocally that the federal government shall direct all federal, state, and private actions to remove the discharge or prevent a substantial threat of a discharge. This delineation of authority is intended to eliminate confusion which allegedly impeded response efforts to such spills.

OPA requires federal direction of federal, state, local, and private response and removal efforts for spills which constitute a substantial threat to public health and welfare. Like lesser spills, they can be federalized by the government who undertakes response and removal and seeks reimbursement from the responsible parties. The federal government also has the authority to remove and, if necessary, destroy a vessel. At least in regard to emergency response measures, the federal government is exempted from contract and employment laws. However, this exemption is not intended to apply to long-term removal actions.

21.2 State and Local Removal Authority

The act specifies federal preeminence in undertaking and directing response actions, but preserves state authority over significant aspects of removal activities. State and local governments may impose additional requirements with respect to removal activities.[75] And, in regard to the conclusion of removal activities, the federal government is required to consult with the governors of affected states before making a determination that removal with respect to any discharge is considered complete.[76]

21.3 Responder Immunity

To induce vessel operators, cleanup contractors, and cleanup cooperatives to undertake prompt and effective measures in response to spills and threats of spills, OPA exempts them from liability.[77] When a person is rendering care, assistance, or advice, he is not liable for removal costs or damages which result from his acts or omissions. However, his acts or omissions must be consistent with the National Contingency Plan or as directed by the federal government. It was also recognized that the National Contingency Plan and federal orders may not cover every detail or eventuality of a spill response. Consequently, responder immunity is extended to actions that are in keeping with the overall objectives of the National Contingency Plan or federal directives.

However, this immunity does not apply to a responsible party, that is, the owner or operator of the vessel or facility from which the discharge originates. It only applies to other individuals or entities whom they retain. Furthermore, although the responder may be relieved of liability

---

[75]Section 1018.
[76]Section 1011.
[77]Section 4201.

for removal costs and damages, that liability is borne by the responsible party.

The immunity does not apply in cases of personal injury or wrongful death, or if the person is grossly negligent or engages in willful misconduct. It does not apply to CERCLA cleanups, either. Nor does OPA immunity prevent states from imposing their own requirements for the liability of persons involved in the removal of oil.[78]

21.4 National Planning and Response System

OPA keeps the National Contingency Plan under the Clean Water Act, which establishes the overall methodology for the containment, dispersal, and removal of oil and hazardous substances.[79] The plan is required to address the assignment of duties and responsibilities among federal departments and agencies, state and local agencies, and port authorities, and sets up Coast Guard strike teams, manned by trained personnel and specially equipped to deal with oil spills. These teams can be called in by the federal on-scene coordinator to provide assistance and training.

The plan also creates a national surveillance and notice system intended to give immediate warning of threatened spills or actual spills to state and federal officials and a national center to coordinate and direct the implementation of the plan.

The plan provides that federal and state officials work jointly to formulate a schedule for the use of dispersants and other chemicals to mitigate or remove a spill, and that the schedule detail both the waters in which it is deemed appropriate to use such chemicals and the amounts of the chemicals that can be used. The plan must now include provisions for the protection of fish and wildlife resources.

OPA also creates a new National Planning and Response System under the Clean Water Act.[80] This system creates a federal, state, and local hierarchy for spill response. The elements of this system are the National Response Unit, Coast Guard Strike Teams, Coast Guard District Response Groups, Area Committees, Area Contingency Plans, and vessel and facility response plans. One of the primary purposes of this system is to prevent duplication of federal and private response efforts. While much of the planning and organization is conducted by public agencies and officials, the objective of this system is to have response equipment and personnel primarily provided by private entities.

Local Area Committees composed of federal, state and local agencies are to be established to prepare, and update periodically, detailed local area contingency plans to respond to a worst case oil discharge, or the threat of such a discharge, from a vessel, offshore facility, or onshore facility in or near the area. These plans must be federally reviewed and

---

[78]Section 1018.

[79]Section 4201.

[80]Section 4202. 33 U.S.C. §1321(j).

approved. The plans must describe the area that they cover and identify any sub-areas of special economic and environmental importance. They are to integrate with the operating procedures of the National Response Unit, other area plans, and individual vessel and facility response plans. The area plans are to list all available federal, state, local, and private response equipment and personnel, as well as firefighting equipment, and are to delegate respective responsibilities between federal, state, and local agencies and owners and operators. The plans are also to contain procedures for obtaining expedited decisions on the use of dispersants.

The president is required to revise and republish the National Contingency Plan (NCP) to ensure coordination among the various response organizations under the act.

21.5 Vessel and Facility Response Plans

Owners and operators of tank vessels, offshore facilities and certain onshore facilities are required to prepare response plans to remove discharges of oil. These plans must be consistent with the National Contingency Plans and Area Contingency Plans. Vessel and facility response plans must identify the qualified individual having full authority to implement removal actions and must require immediate communications between federal officials and private removal contractors. The response plans must identify and ensure by contract or other approved means the availability of private personnel and equipment necessary to remove to the maximum extent practicable a worst-case discharge (including a discharge resulting from fire or explosion) and to mitigate or prevent a substantial threat of such a discharge. A "worst case discharge" for a vessel is a discharge of its entire cargo in adverse weather conditions. For a facility it is the largest foreseeable discharge in adverse weather conditions.

The plans must also describe training, equipment testing, periodic unannounced drills, and response actions of vessel and facility personnel to mitigate or prevent the discharge. The plans must be updated periodically and be resubmitted for approval of each significant change. Removal equipment will be inspected periodically. Vessel and facility owners and operators must have an approved response plan within two years of the date of enactment. However, it is not a defense to liability that an owner or operator was acting in accordance with an approved response plan.

22.0 SUBTITLE C: PENALTIES

OPA significantly increases the severity of criminal and civil penalties resulting from discharges of oil into navigable waters and other offenses contributing to a discharge of oil.

22.1 Criminal Penalties

Under the OPA amendments, a violation of section 311(b)(3) of the Clean Water Act can constitute a criminal offense under section 309, rather than a civil matter.[81] Previously, there was no criminal penalty for a simple negligent discharge of oil. Other existing criminal penalties for deficient operation of a tank vessel have been increased, about five times for individuals and about 10 times for organizations. An organization under federal criminal statutes includes any form of entity other than a natural person.

22.1.1 Clean Water Act Criminal Penalties

Section 309(c)(1) of the Clean Water Act provides that any person who negligently violates section 301 of the FWPCA is subject to criminal penalties.[82]

Section 309(c)(2) provides that any person who knowingly violates section 301 of the act is subject to criminal prosecution.[83]

Section 309(c)(3) penalizes violations involving knowing endangerment.[84] This section is triggered when a person, at the time of committing a knowing violation, has actual knowledge that his actions pose a serious threat to human health and life.

OPA amended section 309(c) to include within its coverage violations of section 311(b)(3). Thus, an oil discharge in violation of section 311(b)(3) now can be treated as a criminal offense.

Under section 309(c)(1) a conviction of negligently discharging oil carries a criminal fine of $2,500—$25,000 per day of violation, one year imprisonment, or both. A prior conviction doubles the fines and term of imprisonment.

Under section 309(c)(2) the crime of a knowing discharge of oil carries a criminal fine of $5,000—$50,000 per day of violation and three years' imprisonment. A prior conviction also doubles the penalties.

If a knowing discharge of oil is committed with the knowledge that another person is placed in imminent danger of death or serious bodily harm, section 309(c)(3) provides a maximum criminal fine of $250,000 and 15 years' imprisonment. For an organization, knowing endangerment carries a maximum fine of $1,000,000.

22.1.2 Criminal Penalties for Failure to Notify

OPA also increases the criminal penalty for failure to notify the appropriate federal official of a discharge of which a person is aware under section 311(b)(5) of the Clean Water Act. The previous penalty was $10,000 and one year imprisonment. The new penalty is a maximum $250,000 fine and five years imprisonment for individuals and a maximum fine of $500,000 for organizations.

---

[81]Section 4301.
[82]33 U.S.C. § 1319(c)(1).
[83]33 U.S.C. § 1319(c)(2).
[84]33 U.S.C. § 1319(c)(3).

22.1.3 Criminal Penalties for Violations of Vessel Inspection, Manning and Operation Requirements

Criminal penalties are also increased for violations of the vessel inspection, manning and operation provisions of Title 46, U.S. Code.[85] Operation of a vessel in a grossly negligent manner, previously a Class A misdemeanor with a penalty of a $5,000 fine and one year imprisonment, now carries a fine of up to $100,000 for an individual or $200,000 for an organization. Should the gross negligence result in death, the maximum penalty for an individual is $250,000 and one year imprisonment and the maximum penalty for an organization is $500,000. The criminal penalty for operating a vessel while intoxicated is identical.

The maximum penalty for a willful and knowing violation of the bulk dangerous cargoes rules in 46 U.S.C. Chapter 37 has been increased from $50,000 and five years' imprisonment to a $250,000 fine and six years' imprisonment for an individual, and a $500,000 fine for an organization. The bulk dangerous cargoes rules govern the design, construction, operation, and manning of tank vessels.

Section 4301(a) eliminates all use immunity for organizations arising from spill notification and eliminates personal derivative use immunity.

Section 4302 strengthens penalties under a number of other marine transportation safety laws.

The maximum penalty for a willful violation of a regulation, order or direction under the Intervention on the High Seas Act,[86] Deepwater Port Act of 1974,[87] and the Ports and Waterways Safety Act[88] has been increased to a fine of $100,000 for individuals and a fine of $200,000 for organizations. If death occurs as a result of a violation, the penalty is a $250,000 fine and one year in prison for an individual and a $500,000 fine for an organization.

22.2 Civil Penalties

In addition to the imposition of criminal penalties, OPA establishes new Class I and Class II penalties for discharges of oil in violation of section 311(b)(3) of the Clean Water Act or for failure to comply with regulations under section 311(j) of the Clean Water Act governing the National Contingency Plan, Area Contingency Plans and vessel and facility response plans. The maximum Class I penalty for a prohibited discharge or for a failure to comply with the contingency or response plan regulations is $10,000 per violation, not to exceed $25,000. This penalty may be assessed only after the guilty party is given notice and a reasonable opportunity to be heard and present evidence concerning the imposition of the penalty.

---

[85]Section 4302.
[86]33 U.S.C. § 1471.
[87]33 U.S.C. § 1501.
[88]33 U.S.C. § 1221.

The maximum Class II penalty for a prohibited discharge or for a violation of a contingency or response plan regulation is $10,000 per day of violation not to exceed $125,000. Procedural prerequisites for the imposition of a Class II penalty are notice and an opportunity for a hearing on the record comporting with the Administrative Procedure Act at which interested persons are afforded the opportunity to testify. Judicial review of the assessment is available otherwise the penalty becomes final 30 days after issuance.

OPA provides an alternative civil penalty scheme for owners, operators, and persons in charge of vessels or facilities. The penalty for discharges violating the Clean Water Act is up to $25,000 per day of violation or up to $1,000 per barrel of oil discharged. If the discharge results from gross negligence or willful misconduct, the minimum penalty is $100,000 and up to $3,000 per barrel of oil discharged. The alternative civil penalties for failure to comply with presidential orders relating to discharges is up to $25,000 per day of violation or an amount up to three times the costs incurred by the Oil Spill Liability Trust Fund resulting from the failure to obey. Failure to comply with contingency plan regulations carries a penalty of $25,000 per day of violation. This penalty can be assessed against any person who fails to comply with the contingency plan requirements and is not limited in applicability to the owner, operator, or person in charge of the vessel or facility. This penalty is imposed by the U.S. District Court.

OPA also sets out a number of criteria to be used in determining the level of civil penalties. The official imposing the penalty, the secretary of transportation, EPA administrator, or judge is to consider the seriousness of the violation, the possible economic benefit to the violator, the degree of culpability, prior violations, efforts of the violator to mitigate or minimize the effects of the discharge, and the economic impact of the penalty on the violator.

Failure to comply with the financial responsibility requirements carries a penalty of up to $25,000 per day of violation.[89] Assessment is by written notice. Criteria to be used to determine the penalty amount are nature, circumstances, extent, and gravity of the violation, degree of culpability, prior violation, and ability to pay. In addition to, or in lieu of assessing a civil penalty, the president may request that the attorney general obtain a judicial order to ensure compliance, including such relief as terminating operations of the company or individual.

23.0 CONCLUSION

The OPA as enacted sets out the general requirements for the progressive oil pollution prevention, liability and compensation regime that Congress adopted. Virtually all of the requirements are subject to further definition and implementation by regulations issued primarily by the U.S. Coast Guard. Many of the OPA requirements for regulations contained dates

---

[89]Section 4303.

by which the regulations were to be issued, usually within one or two years of enactment. The OPA schedule was unrealistic. Two years after enactment, most of the regulations have not been issued, although the regulatory process is underway for nearly all of them. A thorough treatment of the OPA requirements will depend on the contents of those regulations.

For a more definitive discussion of this topic, the reader is referred to the Oil Pollution Act of 1990: Special Report *and related books and courses listed at the end of this book.*

Chapter 8

SAFE DRINKING WATER ACT

Lawrence J. Jensen
Holland & Hart
Washington, D.C.

1.0 OVERVIEW

Until the 1970s, the federal government played only a small role in the regulation of drinking water. For the most part, it limited itself to developing and enforcing drinking water standards that applied only to interstate carriers like railroads and airplanes that provided drinking water to their passengers. It also developed in the 1960s, through the Public Health Service some advisory standards for state drinking water programs that the states largely ignored. In 1974, however, Congress radically altered the federal role by passing the Safe Drinking Water Act (SDWA) and assigning responsibility for its administration to EPA.[1]

SDWA has two principal purposes. The first purpose is to ensure that the water that comes from the tap in the United States is fit to drink. SDWA requires EPA to set national drinking water standards that must be met by the persons who deliver the water to the tap. In this regard, SDWA is somewhat different than the other major environmental statutes in that it regulates the person who supplies a product rather than the person who generates pollution.

The second purpose of SDWA is to prevent the contamination of groundwater, which serves as the principal source of drinking water for 50% of the general population and 95% of the rural population. The most important of the groundwater protection programs is the Underground Injection Control (UIC) Program, which regulates the disposal of liquid wastes underground. SDWA also requires states to develop and implement Wellhead Protection Programs that will prevent the contamination of the surface and subsurface areas that surround wells that supply drinking water to public water systems. Finally, SDWA allows EPA to designate as Sole Source Aquifers those aquifers that constitute the principal source of drinking water for particular communities. Once so designated, federal financial assistance of any type is prohibited to projects that would contaminate the aquifers.

SDWA is, of course, neither the only nor even the most important of the federal environmental statutes that seek to protect groundwater. For

---

[1] The Safe Drinking Water Act was enacted as Title XIV of the Public Health Service Act and is codified at 42 U.S.C. §§ 300f-300j-26.

example, both the Resource Conservation and Recovery Act[2] (RCRA) and the Comprehensive Environmental Response, Compensation and Liability Act[3] (CERCLA), which regulate the management and cleanup of hazardous substances, were enacted, in large part, to prevent and remediate groundwater contamination and both play a more significant role in federal groundwater protection efforts than SDWA. The drinking water standards established under SDWA, however, have become the key federal reference point under RCRA and CERCLA for making prevention and cleanup decisions about groundwater.[4]

2.0 REGULATION OF PUBLIC WATER SYSTEMS

2.1 The Definition of Public Water System

The national drinking water standards established under SDWA apply only to "public water systems." Such systems, however, need not be publicly-owned. The act defines a "public water system" as any system "for the provision of piped water for human consumption," so long as it has "at least fifteen service connections or regularly serves at least twenty-five individuals."[5]

"Water for human consumption" has been held to include not only water that is drunk, but also water that is used for "bathing and showering, cooking and dishwashing, and maintaining oral hygiene."[6] Thus, a system that meets the definition of a PWS will likely still be subject to SDWA standards even if it posts signs warning people not to drink the water it provides.

In its initial regulations implementing the SDWA in 1975, EPA interpreted "regularly serves" as meaning any system that "regularly serves an average of at least twenty-five individuals daily at least 60 days out of the year."[7] EPA gave no explanation of why it added the clarification that a system serve an "average" of 25 individuals daily, although it seems plain that EPA was seeking to interpret the statutory definition of PWS as broadly as possible. In the absence of such a clarification, there would be systems that regularly serve very large numbers of people that could escape regulation simply by showing that there are days when they do not serve 25 people. EPA added the clarification that 60 days of service per year would constitute regular service in order to insure that the act applied to public accommodations that are only open seasonally.

---

[2] 42 U.S.C. §§ 6901-6992k.
[3] 42 U.S.C. §§ 9601-9675.
[4] *Protecting The Nation's Groundwater: EPA's Strategy For The 1990s,* p.31.
[5] SDWA § 1401(4).
[6] *U.S. v. Midway Heights Co. Water Dist.,* 19 Env. L. Rep. 20140, 20142 (E.D. Cal. 1988).
[7] 40 *Fed. Reg.* 59566.

EPA also divided PWS's into two types in 1975: community and non-community. Community PWS's are those that "regularly serve at least 25 year-round residents."[8] There are about 60,000 such systems. Non-community systems are all other systems that otherwise meet the definition of a PWS.[9] The division was made so that drinking water standards that are designed to protect against the adverse effects of long-term or chronic exposure would apply only to those systems whose users would drink the water over long periods of time—that is, systems serving residential populations.

In 1987, EPA recognized that there were many persons served by non-community systems who were also receiving long-term exposure to contaminants in drinking water.[10] These were the persons in schools, factories and offices that provide drinking water to their students and employees from their own water supplies. Such persons were getting a substantial portion of their drinking water each day over a long period of time from systems that were considered non-community and were therefore not generally subject to standards designed to protect against chronic effects. As a result, EPA amended its regulations to include a new type of PWS—the "non-transient non-community water system" (NTNCWS)—and to apply its chronic standards to them. A NTNCWS is a PWS that is not a community system and that "regularly serves at least 25 of the same persons over 6 months per year."[11] EPA has subsequently clarified in a guidance document that to be "regularly served" by a NTNCWS, a person must be served at least 4 days per week for at least 26 weeks per year. There are about 200,000 NTNCWS's.

Drinking water systems like those in hotels that get their water from a PWS and serve only as storage and distribution facilities are not PWS's.[12] However, interstate carriers, like airplanes, are PWS's and must meet the standards, even though they may get their water from another PWS and only distribute it to their passengers. Bottled water providers are not PWS's because they are not providing "piped water." The Food and Drug Administration, however, has made such providers subject to SDWA standards if they distribute their product interstate.[13]

2.2 The Establishment of National Drinking Water Standards

SDWA authorizes EPA to establish two types of national drinking water standards: National Primary Drinking Water Regulations

---

[8] 40 C.F.R. § 141.2.

[9] *Id.*

[10] 52 *Fed. Reg.* 25694, 25712.

[11] 40 C.F.R. § 141.2.

[12] SDWA § 1411.

[13] Federal Food, Drug and Cosmetic Act, 21 U.S.C. §§ 349 and 410. *See also*, 21 C.F.R. Pts. 103 and 129.

(NPDWRs)[14] and National Secondary Drinking Water Regulations (NSDWRs).[15] The primary standards are meant to protect against any "adverse effects to the health of persons" from the consumption of drinking water. They are enforceable against PWS's. The secondary standards, on the other hand, are meant to protect the aesthetic qualities of drinking water, like odor or appearance, and are not enforceable against PWS's under federal law. This distinction between primary and secondary standards is similar to the one drawn between primary and secondary air quality standards under the Clean Air Act.[16]

2.2.1 National Primary Drinking Water Regulations (NPDWRs)

2.2.1.1 The Standard-Setting Schedule

Under SDWA as it was originally enacted, EPA had substantial discretion in deciding which contaminants required a primary standard. However, because EPA was slow to establish many primary standards, Congress sharply reduced EPA's discretion when it amended the SDWA in 1986 and placed EPA under a three-part standard-setting mandate. This statutory mandate has radically altered the pace of standard-setting under SDWA and the consequent regulatory burdens faced by PWS's.

First, Congress required EPA to promulgate standards for 83 contaminants by June 1989.[17] The contaminants to be regulated were specified by Congress, subject to EPA's discretion to make up to 7 substitutions.[18] Although most of the deadlines were not met, EPA had promulgated standards for 76 of the contaminants by July 1992.[19] Indeed, there has been such a torrent of standards with their associated implementation costs imposed on PWS's that the National Governors Conference formally asked EPA in 1992 to place a moratorium on the standard-development process. The governors were particularly concerned about the burdens being placed on the PWS's in small communities. Congress responded to this and other complaints by passing legislation that allows PWS's to skip quarterly monitoring requirements in fiscal year 1993 if an initial test shows no violation.[20]

Second, Congress directed EPA to identify by January 1988 at least 25 additional contaminants that "may have any adverse effect on the health

---

[14] SDWA § 1401(1).

[15] *Id.* § 1401(2).

[16] 42 U.S.C. § 7409.

[17] SDWA § 1412(b)(1).

[18] EPA executed this discretion in January 1988. 53 Fed. Reg. 1892 (Jan. 22, 1988).

[19] Eight VOCs and Fluoride: 50 *Fed. Reg.* 47142, 51 *Fed. Reg.* 11396 and 52 *Fed. Reg.* 25690; coliform and other microbiological contaminants: 54 *Fed. Reg.* 27468 and 27544; 38 organic and inorganic chemicals: 56 *Fed. Reg.* 3526; lead and copper: 56 *Fed. Reg.* 26460 and 30266; 18 synthetic organic chemicals and 5 inorganic chemicals: 57 *Fed. Reg.* 31766. EPA has also proposed standards for radionuclides: 56 *Fed. Reg.* 33050.

[20] Pub. L. 102-389.

of persons and which [are] known or anticipated to occur in public water systems."[21] Under the amendments, EPA must develop standards for at least 25 of the contaminants it identifies within 3 years or by January 1991. This cycle of identifying and regulating at least 25 additional contaminants is then to be repeated indefinitely at three year intervals. EPA published its first Drinking Water Priority list on schedule and updated it three years later.[22] It has not yet, however, established standards for any of the contaminants on the list.

Finally, Congress required EPA to establish standards governing the filtration (December 1987) and disinfection (June 1989) of drinking water supplies.[23] In June 1989, EPA published a combined filtration and disinfection rule that specifies when those two treatment techniques must be employed by PWS's that draw their water from surface waters (or groundwater under the direct influence of surface waters).[24] The filtration rule is unusual in that it requires states to make a case-by-case determination about which of their systems must filter. With estimated compliance costs of more that $3 billion, the filtration and disinfection standards are by far the costliest yet imposed under the SDWA.

2.2.1.2 The Standard-Setting Process

Primary drinking water standards are set through a two-step process. First, EPA determines a Maximum Contaminant Level Goal (MCLG). By statute, the MCLG must be set at the level at which "no known or anticipated adverse effects on the health of persons occur and which allows an adequate margin of safety."[25] MCLGs are not enforceable.

For non-carcinogens, the MCLG is based on the reference dose (RfD). The RfD is an "estimate, with uncertainty spanning perhaps an order of magnitude, of the daily exposure to the human population that is likely to be without an appreciable risk of deleterious health effects during a lifetime."[26] The RfD is derived from the no-observed-adverse-effect-levels (NOAELs) generated from studies of humans or animals. In translating RfDs into MCLGs, EPA seeks to set a standard that will protect a person who drinks two liters of water per day every day for 70 years.

For carcinogens, the MCLG standard setting process is somewhat different. If there is strong evidence that a chemical is carcinogenic, the MCLG is automatically set at zero. This is because EPA has been unable to determine the level at which carcinogens begin to have an adverse health effect. It is therefore conservatively assumed that any exposure to a carcinogen is potentially harmful. If there is only limited evidence that a

---

[21] SDWA § 1412(3).
[22] 53 *Fed. Reg.* 1892 and 56 *Fed. Reg.* 1470.
[23] SDWA § 1412(b)(7)(c) and (b)(8).
[24] 54 *Fed. Reg.* 27486.
[25] SDWA § 1412(b)(4).
[26] 57 *Fed. Reg.* 31781.

chemical is carcinogenic, the MCLG is "calculated using the RfD approach with an added margin of safety to account for possible cancer effects."[27]

Once an MCLG is determined, EPA is required to specify a Maximum Contaminant Level (MCL) that is as close as "feasible" to the MCLG.[28] The MCL is the enforceable standard. Each MCL is usually accompanied by specific monitoring requirements.[29] "Feasible" is defined by the statute as the level that may be achieved "with the use of the best technology, treatment techniques, and other means which the [EPA] finds, after examination for efficacy under field conditions and not solely under laboratory conditions, are available (taking cost into consideration)."[30] EPA must disclose in the standard what technology the standard is based on, but EPA may not require the use of that technology.

When determining what the contaminant level achievable by best technology is, EPA takes several factors into account.[31] First, EPA determines the removal efficiencies of the technology and whether the technology is compatible with other water treatment processes and is widely available. Second, it determines the contaminant level that the technology can achieve when applied to large systems with relatively clean raw water supplies. Third, EPA considers cost by calculating whether the technology would be reasonably affordable to regional and large metropolitan water systems and what the total national compliance cost would be if the MCL were based on the technology. Fourth, EPA considers whether the contaminant level achieved by the technology can be consistently and accurately determined by testing laboratories. Finally, EPA asks whether the contaminant level that can be achieved for carcinogens is protective of public health—i.e., whether it will result in an excess cancer risk to an individual over a lifetime greater than 10^{-4} to 10^{-6}.

If EPA determines that "it is not economically or technologically feasible to ascertain" the contaminant level that is necessary to protect public health, it may require the use of a treatment technique as the standard rather than establishing an MCL.[32] Although not set under this provision, the filtration and disinfection rule discussed above is the best example of the use of a treatment technique as a standard.

Finally, with respect to lead as a contaminant, Congress has directly established certain standards. Because lead can leach out of distribution pipes and fixtures into drinking water as it is carried from a PWS to the

---

[27] *Id.* at 31783.

[28] SWDA § 1412(4).

[29] EPA also requires PWSs to monitor for contaminants for which no MCL has been set. 40 C.F.R. §§ 141.40-141.42.

[30] *Id.* § 1412(5).

[31] 57 *Fed. Reg.* 31797-98.

[32] SDWA § 1412(7)(A).

tap, Congress has required that new pipes, solder flux and coolers used in delivering drinking water be lead-free.[33]

2.2.1.4 Variances and Exemptions

The SDWA allows PWS's to obtain variances and exemptions from the primary standards under some circumstances.[34] These provisions have become increasingly important, especially for small systems, as the number of standards has dramatically increased in the last several years.

If a PWS cannot meet an MCL despite application of the best available treatment technology "because of characteristics of [its] raw water sources," it may receive a variance, but only if the variance will not result in an unreasonable risk to public health.[35] The variance must require eventual compliance with the MCL, but this requirement can be illusory as EPA may specify "an indefinite time for compliance" while the PWS is awaiting the development of new treatment technology.[36] Before the variance becomes effective, notice and opportunity for a public hearing must be given.

A variance may also be granted from a treatment technique if the PWS can demonstrate that the treatment technique is not necessary due to the quality of its raw water supply or if it can demonstrate that an alternative technique is "at least as efficient" in removing a contaminant and agrees to use that technique.[37]

Exemptions from MCLs may be granted "due to compelling factors," including cost.[38] The fact that cost may be taken into account is the primary difference between variances and exemptions. Otherwise, the rules governing exemptions are quite similar to the ones for governing variances. Exemptions must provide for eventual compliance, they may not be granted until notice and opportunity for a hearing has been given and they may not result in unreasonable risks.

Exemptions are effective for one year, with the possibility of an extension for three years. For small systems (those serving not more than 500 connections), repeated extensions may be obtained in certain circumstances.[39] This provision has proved quite important as small systems have struggled to implement the many standards required by the 1986 Amendments.

2.2.1.5 State Programs

Prior to the enactment of SDWA, virtually all states already had a drinking water program. Congress therefore hoped that states would take the lead in enforcing the national standards EPA was required to develop.

---

[33] Id. §§ 1417 and 1461 and 40 C.F.R. § 141.43.

[34] Id. § 1415.

[35] Id. § 1415(a)(1)(A).

[36] 40 C.F.R. § 1412.43(e).

[37] SDWA §§ 1415(a)(1)(B) and 1415(3).

[38] Id. § 1416(a).

[39] Id. § 1416(b)(2)(C).

To this end, SDWA specifies that states shall have "the primary enforcement responsibility for public water systems" as long as their programs meet certain minimum criteria.[40] This means that where the criteria are met, EPA may not directly enforce SDWA requirements against PWS's.[41]

EPA has established a formal process through which states may demonstrate that they are entitled to "primacy" in matters of drinking water.[42] To have primacy, state programs must: (1) have drinking water regulations that are at least as stringent as EPA's; (2) adopt and implement adequate enforcement procedures for their regulations; (3) keep records and report information as required by EPA; (4) provide variances and exemptions, if at all, in a manner that is at least as stringent as specified in SDWA; and (5) adopt and implement an adequate plan for the provision of safe drinking water in emergencies.[43]

To date, all but two of the 57 jurisdictions that qualify as states under the SDWA—i.e., Wyoming and the District of Columbia—have demonstrated "primacy" under SDWA.[44] Although EPA has the authority to withdraw primacy and has threatened to do so, no such action has ever been taken.[45] However, with the proliferation of standards required by the 1986 amendments and the generally sparse federal resources granted to the states to assist in implementation, some states have expressed a desire to give up primacy voluntarily.

2.2.1.6 Enforcement

The SDWA seeks to insure that MCLs are met in two ways. First, it requires PWS's to promptly notify both the regulatory authority and their customers when MCLs or other SDWA requirements are violated.[46] Congress hoped that the requirement to give public notice would act as a positive incentive to compliance by the PWS's as well as alert the public to possible health risks. SDWA was the first of several environmental statutes that now require public notification of violations.[47] Second, the

---

[40] SDWA § 1413.

[41] As discussed below in section 2.2.1.6, even where a state has primacy, EPA may take enforcement actions for violations of NPDWRs or variances or exemptions if a state fails to do so in a timely manner. SDWA § 1414 §1414(a)(1)(B). In addition, EPA may directly enforce violations of the public notification and monitoring requirements and may take appropriate action in an emergency without regard to whether a state has "the primary enforcement responsibility." *Id.* § 1414(c) and § 1431(a).

[42] 40 C.F.R. § 142.10-142.17.

[43] SDWA § 1413.

[44] In certain circumstances, Indian tribes may exercise "primary enforcement responsibility" for SDWA programs on their tribal lands. 40 C.F.R. Part 142, Subpart H.

[45] SDWA § 1413(b)(1).

[46] *Id.* § 1414(c).

[47] *See, for example,* the *Emergency Planning and Community Right-to-Know Act,* 42 U.S.C. §§ 11001-11050.

SDWA provides EPA with a standard complement of traditional sanctions to force compliance where necessary.[48]

Under the public notification rules, PWS's must disclose violations in the local newspaper within 14 days of their occurrence.[49] The newspaper notice is to be supplemented by written notification to each customer through the mail or by hand within 45 days (unless the violation is corrected before the notification is due). Violations that pose acute risks must be reported to local radio and television stations within 72 hours of the violation. In their notices, PWS's are free to explain the violations as they choose, except that EPA specifies language that must generally be used to describe the health basis for the MCL or other requirement that has been violated. PWS's must also notify customers of the results of the monitoring that they are required to do for unregulated contaminants.

On the other hand, whenever EPA finds that a violation of an MCL or of a variance or exemption condition has taken place, it must notify the State and the PWS and then provide "advice and technical assistance" to bring the PWS into compliance.[50] If the state does not then commence an appropriate enforcement action within 30 days, EPA "shall" issue either a compliance order to the PWS or commence a civil action.[51]

An EPA compliance order may not take effect until after notice and an opportunity for a public hearing.[52] Unlike most other major federal environmental statutes, the initial compliance order may not assess administrative penalties. Once an order is violated, however, EPA may assess, through a second order, an administrative penalty of up to $5,000 per violation.[53]

If EPA chooses to proceed in court, it may obtain both injunctive relief and penalties of up to $25,000 per day per violation.[54]

EPA is also authorized to enforce against violations of the public notification and monitoring requirements. Where such violations occur, EPA may proceed without first notifying the state and may seek civil penalties of up to $25,000 or assess an administrative penalty of up to $5,000.[55]

EPA also has broad authority to take appropriate action when the presence of a contaminant in a PWS or an underground source of drinking water presents an imminent and substantial danger to public health.[56]

---

[48] SDWA § 1414.

[49] 40 C.F.R. § 141.32.

[50] SDWA § 1414(d)(1)(A). Of course, EPA has the primary enforcement authority in the two jurisdictions to whom the drinking water program has not been delegated.

[51] *Id.* § 1414(a)(1)(B). It is not clear whether the term "shall" makes EPA's duty mandatory.

[52] *Id.* § 1414(g)(2). 40 C.F.R. Part 1142, Subpart J.

[53] *Id.* § 1414(g)(3)(B).

[54] *Id.* § 1414(g)(3)(A).

[55] *Id.* § 1414(c).

[56] *Id.* § 1431(a).

SDWA may also be enforced by private citizens in federal district court.[57]

2.2.2 National Secondary Drinking Water Standards

Unlike primary standards, secondary drinking water standards are not health-based. Instead, they are meant to guide states in controlling contaminants that "may adversely affect the odor or appearance" of water or other aspects of the public welfare and consequently "may cause a substantial number of persons served by the public water system providing such water to discontinue its use," even though the contaminants pose no risk to public health.[58] Within those guidelines, EPA has discretion to decide what standards are needed. To date, it has issued standards for 15 parameters.[59] The standards may not be federally enforced, but states are free to adopt and enforce them under their own laws.

The most controversial secondary standard and one that is illustrative of the differences between primary and secondary standards was the one set to guard against the mottling of teeth that is caused by exposure to fluoride in drinking water. Although EPA first adjudged the mottling a health effect, it ultimately concluded that only a secondary standard was required because the mottling did not impair the functioning of the teeth.[60]

3.0 REGULATION OF UNDERGROUND INJECTION

It is often said that the federal government lacks a comprehensive groundwater protection program. While this may be true with respect to the myriad surface activities that can affect groundwater, it is not true with respect to most subsurface activities. Under SDWA, the disposal of wastes directly into subsurface areas through wells is regulated by the Underground Injection Control (UIC) Program. EPA estimates that there are almost 400,000 injection wells subject to UIC requirements. By comparison, this is roughly 6 times more UIC wells than there are permitted wastewater discharges under the NPDES program of the Clean Water Act. Under current regulations, the UIC program has its greatest impact on the owners and operators of wells being used for the disposal of hazardous waste, for the reinjection of brine from oil and gas production and for the injection of fluids to aid in the extraction of certain minerals.

3.1 Regulated Injections

The UIC program regulates through a permit system any "subsurface emplacement of fluids by well injection" that "endangers drinking water sources."[61]

---

[57] *Id.* § 1449.

[58] *Id.* § 1401(2).

[59] 40 C.F.R. § 143.

[60] *NRDC v. EPA*, 812 F.2d 721 (D.C. Cir. 1987).

[61] SDWA § 1412(d).

"Well injection" means the subsurface emplacement of fluids[62] through any "bored, drilled or driven shaft, or a dug hole" that is deeper than it is wide.[63]

"Fluids" are "any material or substance which flows or moves whether in a semisolid, liquid, sludge, gas, or any other form or state."[64]

Well injection "endangers drinking water" only if two conditions are met. First, the injection must result in the presence of a contaminant in a potential drinking water source or, as the statute puts it, in an "underground water which supplies or can reasonably be expected to supply any public water system."[65] Such supplies are known as "underground sources of drinking water" (USDW). This means that injection into some groundwater is not regulated. For example, injection into groundwater that has been determined to be "so contaminated that it would be economically or technologically impractical to render that water fit for human consumption" does not require a UIC permit.[66] Second, the presence of the contaminant must: (a) raise the possibility that the PWS will not be able to comply with the national primary drinking water regulations or (b) "otherwise adversely affect the health of persons."

3.2 Substantive UIC Requirements

Injection of any fluid into a well covered by the UIC program is prohibited, except as authorized by permit or rule, and no injection is allowed that would endanger a USDW.[67] Injections into UIC wells that were already in existence at the time EPA developed its regulations were automatically permitted by rule, although most such injections must by now have an individual permit.[68] With the exception of wells in Class V, as discussed below, new wells must obtain an individual permit and must do so before construction of the well commences. Where the conditions applicable to a number of wells in a particular geographic area are similar, an area permit covering all of the wells may be issued.[69]

Unlike the Clean Water Act, the UIC program does not, for the most part, regulate the quality of the fluids being discharged or injected. In other words, owners and operators of UIC wells are not required to treat the fluids prior to injection.[70] Instead, the UIC program regulates the structural

---

[62] The injection of natural gas for purposes of storage is expressly exempted by statute from this definition. *Id.*

[63] 40 C.F.R. § 144.3.

[64] *Id.*

[65] SDWA § 1421(d)(2).

[66] 40 C.F.R. § 146.4 describes which kinds of groundwater may be exempt from UIC regulation. Section 144.7 describes how an exemption determination is made.

[67] *Id.* § 144.11.

[68] *Id.* §§ 144.21 to 144.28.

[69] *Id.* § 144.33.

[70] This is not true for certain wastes subject to the RCRA land bans. *Id.* Part 148. *See also Chemical Waste Management v. EPA*, No. 90-1230, et al. (D.C. Cir., Sept. 25, 1992).

integrity of the wells themselves and the placement of the fluids underground. The general goal of the program is not to regulate how much contamination may be added to a water source without destroying its quality, but to insure that the contaminants never reach the water source. It does this by setting standards designed to prevent the fluids from leaking out of the wells into drinking water sources and, once injected, from migrating out of the injection zone into those sources.

The substantive standards of the UIC program vary depending on the proximity of the well to a USDW and the type of fluids that are being injected. EPA has divided all UIC wells into five classes.[71]

Class I wells are those in which fluids are injected "beneath the lowermost formation containing, within one-quarter mile of the well bore, an underground source of drinking water." They are often thousands of feet deep. There are about 550 such wells in the United States. These wells are further classified by whether they handle hazardous or non-hazardous wastes.

All Class I wells are subject to detailed limitations on where they may be sited and how the wells are to be constructed and operated.[72] The characteristics of the fluids being injected must be monitored, as well as the injection pressure, flow rate and volume. At least every five years, operators must also subject the wells to mechanical integrity tests. At the end of their useful life, the wells must be plugged and abandoned to prevent migration of the fluids from the injection zone. Before obtaining a permit to operate a Class I well, the applicant must demonstrate the financial ability to properly plug and abandon the wells. The applicant must also insure that corrective action has been taken to fix all other wells that penetrate the proposed injection zone and that have been improperly abandoned or plugged.

Class I wells that receive hazardous waste are considered hazardous waste disposal facilities under RCRA and are subject to RCRA permitting requirements. However, such wells are permitted by rule under RCRA as long as they have and comply with a UIC permit,[73] and RCRA corrective action requirements.[74]

As hazardous waste disposal facilities, Class I wells that receive hazardous wastes are subject to the land ban provisions of RCRA. Those provisions ban the land disposal or subsurface injection of certain hazardous wastes unless EPA determines whether and in what manner they may

---

[71] *Id.* § 146.5.

[72] The criteria and standards applicable to wells receiving non-hazardous wastes are in 40 C.F.R. § 146, Subpart B; for wells receiving hazardous wastes the standards are in Subpart G.

[73] 40 C.F.R. § 144.14; this section incorporates many RCRA program elements into the UIC program.

[74] 40 C.F.R. §§ 264.1(d) and 270.60(b).

safely be disposed or injected. 40 C.F.R. Part 148 applies the various land bans to the UIC program.[75]

Operators of hazardous waste injection wells may be exempted from these prohibitions if they make an elaborate demonstration that there will be no migration of hazardous wastes into USDWs as long as the wastes remain hazardous. This demonstration can rely on chemical changes in the waste that render it non-hazardous, or upon a demonstration that the wastes will not migrate into USDWs for 10,000 years.[76] EPA has granted some of these so-called no-migration petitions, but they are difficult and costly to prepare.[77]

Class II wells are those used by the oil and gas industry in connection with conventional oil and gas production, principally for the disposal of produced water. There are some 160,000 such wells in operation, most of which are located in Texas and Louisiana. Like the standards that apply to Class I wells, the Class II well standards also address siting, design, operation and monitoring of the wells and placement of the fluids.[78]

Class III wells are those used by the mining industry to inject fluids to aid in the extraction process for certain minerals, like solution mining of salts or potash or in situ production of uranium or other metals. There are about 21,000 such wells. The standards for Class III wells are found in 40 C.F.R. §§ 146.31-146.35.

Class IV wells are hazardous waste disposal wells in which hazardous or radioactive waste is disposed of *above* or *into* (rather than below, as in Class I) a formation where there is an underground source of drinking water within one-quarter mile of the well bore. Since May 1985, RCRA has specifically prohibited the use of such wells for hazardous waste disposal.[79] Accordingly, there are no standards that apply to the use of these wells. The RCRA prohibition is enforceable under SDWA.

Class V wells are all UIC wells not included in Classes I to IV and comprise the largest class, with over 175,000 wells fitting in this category. They are divided into 32 subcategories and include everything from cesspools and septic systems[80] to salt water intrusion barrier wells, subsidence control wells and wells associated with the recovery of geothermal energy. At present, all injections into Class V wells are authorized by rule and the only requirement on the owners and operators of

---

[75] A recent decision clarified when dilution is adequate treatment for characteristically hazardous wastes that are subject to the "third-third" land ban and are placed in injection wells. *Chemical Waste Management v. EPA*, No. 90-1230, et al. (D.C. Cir., Sept. 25, 1992).

[76] *Id.* at §§ 148.20-148.24.

[77] *See, e.g.,* 55 Fed. Reg. 2691 (Jan. 26, 1990) and 55 Fed. Reg. 19032 (May 7, 1990).

[78] 40 C.F.R. §§ 146.21-146.25.

[79] 42 U.S.C § 6939(b).

[80] Cesspools and septic systems serving single-family homes are not considered Class V wells. 40 C.F.R. § 146.5(e).

such wells is that they report the existence of the wells.[81] EPA is currently working on a set of standards that will govern the use of these wells. Because of the number and variety of Class V wells, the standards are likely to be quite expensive and controversial.

3.3 The State Role in the UIC Program

As with the PWS program described above, a state may exercise "primary enforcement responsibility" or "primacy" over all UIC activities within its borders if its UIC program is formally approved by EPA.[82] A state program must meet certain minimum federal requirements, but may also include different and more stringent state requirements. If a state program is disapproved by EPA or if a state fails to seek primacy, EPA must adopt and implement a federal UIC program for that state. Unlike the PWS program, where all but two jurisdictions have primacy, EPA has had to adopt federal UIC programs in almost two dozen states.[83] In addition, because state UIC programs may be partially approved, there are several states in which the state has primacy over some UIC activities, but not others.

Even after a state assumes primacy over UIC activities, EPA retains important oversight authority. It may enforce state requirements, as discussed below, and may withdraw approval of the state program if the program is deemed deficient.[84] Also, EPA may take action to abate situations that present an "imminent and substantial endangerment" to public health without regard to the state's primacy.[85]

3.4 Enforcement of UIC Requirements

Unlike the PWS program, the UIC program does not require violators to give public notice of their violations. Violators are subject, however, to a full array of administrative, civil and criminal sanctions.

EPA may issue compliance orders for violations and may include in the orders administrative penalty assessments of up to $10,000 per day per violation up to a maximum of $125,000.[86] Violators must be given written notice of any proposed order and must be allowed 30 days in which to request a hearing. Moreover, the public must be given notice of the proposed order and a reasonable opportunity to comment on it.

EPA may also seek civil and criminal sanctions. Courts may assess civil penalties of up to $25,000 per day and may send violators to prison for up to

---

[81] *Id.* §§ 144.24 and 146.52.

[82] The program approval process is set forth in 40 C.F.R. § 145.31. Indian tribes may also apply for and assume primacy over UIC activities on their lands. *Id.* Part 145, Subpart E.

[83] The program status of each state is listed in 40 C.F.R. Part 147. Where the program is administered by EPA, owners and operators should be alert for state-specific adjustments that may have been made to the general federal UIC requirements.

[84] 40 C.F.R. §§ 145.33 and 145.34.

[85] SDWA § 1431.

[86] SDWA § 1423(c).

three years for willful violations.[87] Citizen suits may also be brought by third parties.[88]

In primacy states, EPA may take direct enforcement action against violators, but only after giving them and the state notice and only if the state fails to take "appropriate enforcement action" within 30 days thereafter.[89]

As with the PWS program, the 1986 amendments to SDWA replaced the word "may" with the word "shall" when describing EPA's obligation to enforce and thus raised as yet unresolved questions as to the amount of discretion EPA has to decide whether to take an enforcement action when it becomes aware of a violation of UIC requirements.[90]

4.0 WELLHEAD AND AQUIFER PROTECTION

4.1 Wellhead Protection Programs

The 1986 amendments to SDWA require each state to prepare by June 1989 and to implement by June 1991 an EPA-approved Wellhead Protection Program.[91] The purpose of such a program is to prevent the contamination of the surface and subsurface areas surrounding wells that supply PWS's with drinking water. The requirement reflects a compromise between those who favor the adoption of a comprehensive federal groundwater protection program and those who are opposed to such a program on the grounds that it would necessarily involve the federal government in the land use and zoning decisions that have traditionally been left to state and local authorities.

SDWA requires that each program: (a) specify the duties of the various agencies that will carry out the program; (b) determine the area requiring protection around each wellhead; (c) identify all potential man-made sources of contaminants within the wellhead area; (d) describe a program that will protect the area from the contaminants identified; and (e) include contingency plans for providing alternate drinking water supplies in the event of contamination.[92] SDWA authorizes EPA to award substantial federal grants to states to assist them in the development and implementation of wellhead protection programs, but Congress has appropriated very little money for this purpose.[93]

---

[87] *Id.* § 1423(b).

[88] *Id.* § 1449.

[89] *Id.* § 1423(a)(1).

[90] *Id.* § 1423(a)(1) and (2).

[91] SDWA § 1428. EPA has produced a number of guidance documents to assist states in this effort: *Protecting Local Groundwater Supplies Through Wellhead Protection; Wellhead Protection Programs: Tools for Local Governments; Developing A State Wellhead Protection Program: A User's Guide to Assist State Agencies; Model Assessments for Delineating Wellhead Protection Areas.*

[92] *Id.* § 1428(a).

[93] *Id.* § 1428(k).

Twenty-six states have nonetheless prepared Wellhead Protection Programs that EPA has approved. EPA has no real leverage over those states that have failed to do so: it is not authorized to develop and implement federal plans in the absence of state plans; all it can do is refuse to provide the states with wellhead grants. Moreover, EPA cannot enforce the provisions of the state plans that are in existence, although federal facilities are required to comply with them. Wellhead Protection Programs may be enforceable under state law. Persons operating in wellhead protection areas should therefore become familiar with the state requirements.

4.2 The Protection of Sole Source Aquifers

Where EPA determines that a groundwater aquifer is the "sole or principal drinking water source for an area" and that its contamination would "create a significant hazard to public health," SDWA authorizes EPA to designate the aquifer as a Sole Source Aquifer (SSA).[94]

An SSA designation has two principal legal effects. First, it bars federal financial assistance of any kind to projects whose activities could contaminate the SSA and create a significant hazard to public health.[95] Second, it qualifies local governments having jurisdiction over any SSAs designated before May 1988 for federal demonstration project grants to assist them in the design of "comprehensive management plans" for "critical aquifer protection areas," which are SSAs that meet certain additional criteria.[96] Congress, however, has not yet appropriated any money to fund this grant program.

The practical effect of an SSA designation is primarily political. An SSA designation is seen as a confirmation of the special value of a community's underground drinking water sources and is often used in the struggle to block construction of projects that are seen as potential sources of contamination to those sources. To date, EPA has designated 56 SSAs.

5.0 CONCLUSION

Although the 1986 amendments to SDWA succeeded in greatly accelerating the pace of standard development, they also created severe implementation problems for the many thousands of small PWS's across the country that simply cannot afford to monitor and treat the many contaminants that are now regulated. In the upcoming debate over reauthorization of SDWA, Congress will have to address these implementation problems. Key questions will be: Should state and local governments have more discretion in responding to national mandates?

---

[94] *Id.* § 1424(e). When making an SSA determination, EPA must find that the aquifer supplies drinking water to 50% or more of the population in an area and that no alternative supplies are readily available. Whether an alternative supply is deemed readily available is determined largely by the cost of securing it.

[95] *Id.*

[96] *Id.* § 1427; 40 C.F.R. § 149.3.

Should they be able to decide which environmental risks to address first? Are there better ways to assess the actual risks posed by contaminants? Are the standards based on the best possible science? Are there any ways to insure that there will be more federal money available, especially for the smaller communities, to help with implementation costs? If not, can Congress continue to justify the imposition of national standards? The answers to these questions will be important not just for the quest for safe drinking water, but for national environmental policy generally.

For a more definitive discussion of this topic, the reader is referred to the related books and courses listed at the end of this book.

Chapter 9

COMPREHENSIVE ENVIRONMENTAL RESPONSE, COMPENSATION, AND LIABILITY ACT

Robert T. Lee[1]
Troy, Gould & Mott
Washington, D.C.

1.0 OVERVIEW

1.1 CERCLA's History and Objectives

The Comprehensive Environmental Response, Compensation and Liability Act,[2] commonly referred to as "CERCLA" or "Superfund," was enacted by Congress in 1980. CERCLA's impetus was the emerging realization—as most directly evidenced by the Love Canal tragedy—that inactive hazardous waste sites presented great risk to public health and the environment and that existing law did not address these abandoned disposal sites. CERCLA was designed to respond to situations involving the past disposal of hazardous substances. As such, it complements the Resource Conservation and Recovery Act (RCRA)[3] which regulates on-going hazardous waste handling and disposal.

Over the past twelve years, CERCLA has been roundly criticized by industry as a draconian system which hinders its economic growth and penalizes individual companies by requiring them to perform extensive and costly cleanups without regard to when the original disposal took place or the fact that a company may have exercised due care in handling hazardous materials. At the same time, Congress and the American public have vented frustration over the slow pace of cleanup and the reported waste of taxpayer monies. To many on both sides of these issues, CERCLA has been an expensive failure. CERCLA's future will depend on how Congress deals with the statute when it comes up for reauthorization.

This chapter will discuss CERCLA's major features. It is organized into seven major sections. The first section is an introductory overview of CERCLA. Subsequent sections will discuss CERCLA's primary terms and concepts, remedial provisions, liability provisions, settlement procedures, release reporting requirements, and federal facility requirements.

---

[1]Tonya R. Gaylord and Kenneth A. Veilleux, associates at Troy, Gould & Mott, authored the sections on Natural Resources Damages and CERCLA Section 106 Administrative Orders respectively and assisted in the preparation of this chapter generally.

[2]42 U.S.C. §§ 9601 et seq.

[3]42 U.S.C. §§ 6901 et seq.

1.2 Overview of CERCLA's Provisions

When originally enacted, CERCLA was far less complex than it is today. In 1986, CERCLA was extensively amended by the Superfund Amendments and Reauthorization Act (SARA).[4] SARA added many provisions to CERCLA and clarified much of what was unclear in the original act. However, even after SARA, CERCLA's major emphasis has remained the cleanup of inactive hazardous waste sites and the distribution of cleanup costs among the parties who generated and handled hazardous substances at these sites.

CERCLA's major provisions are designed to address comprehensively the problems associated with hazardous waste sites. CERCLA provides EPA the authority to clean up these sites under what may be generically called its "response" or "remedial" provisions. In doing so, it details the procedures and standards which must be followed in remediating these sites. CERCLA, like most environmental statutes, also contains enforcement provisions. These provisions identify the classes of parties liable under CERCLA, detail the legal claims which arise under the statute, and provide guidance on settlements with EPA. In addition, CERCLA contains provisions specifying when releases of hazardous substances must be reported and the procedures to be followed for the cleanup of federal installations.

1.3 The "Superfund"

One of the most important features of CERCLA is the creation of the Hazardous Substance Superfund to be used by EPA in cleaning up hazardous waste sites. It is to this fund that CERCLA owes its "Superfund" nickname. The Superfund is created by taxes imposed upon the petroleum and chemical industries as well as by an environmental tax on corporations. In addition, general tax revenue is contributed to the Superfund.[5] The SARA Amendments authorized an appropriation of $8.5 million for the five-year period beginning in 1986.[6] In 1990, Congress reauthorized the Superfund program until September 14, 1994 at a funding level of $5.1 billion.[7]

The Superfund may be used not only to pay EPA's cleanup and enforcement costs and certain natural resource damages, but also to pay for certain claims of private parties. Private parties are entitled to payment from the Superfund for EPA-approved cleanups which they have performed.[8] In addition, private parties may file claims for reimbursement when they have performed a cleanup but have been unable to obtain payment from the facility owner or operator,[9] or when EPA has adminis-

---

[4]Pub. L. No. 99-499, Oct. 17, 1986; 126 Cong. Rec. S13112 *et seq.* (daily ed. Sept. 19, 1986).
[5]*See* Title V of the Superfund Amendments and Reauthorization Act of 1986.
[6]42 U.S.C. § 9611.
[7]21 Env't Rep. (BNA) 1243 (November 2, 1990).
[8]42 U.S.C. § 9611(a)(2).
[9]42 U.S.C. § 9612.

tratively required them to conduct a cleanup which is deemed to be arbitrary and capricious or for which they are not liable.[10] However, the Superfund may not be used to finance the remediation of federal facilities.[11]

1.4 Sources of CERCLA "Law"

For those unfamiliar with CERCLA law and lore, finding, let alone understanding, CERCLA's procedures can often be difficult. Many of the procedures that apply in the typical CERCLA matter are set forth in layers of statutory, regulatory, and policymaking documents. While it is true that the foundation for CERCLA is the statute itself, forecasting the government's actions is possible only when one understands the myriad of regulations, policy letters, and papers issued by EPA. These materials detail everything from EPA procedures for remediating contaminated groundwater to collecting stipulated penalties in settlements. Often, EPA staff level employees are *not* aware of many of these policy statements.

2.0 IMPORTANT CERCLA TERMS

An understanding of CERCLA's key terms and phrases is essential in interpreting both the remedial and liability features of CERCLA. Among the most critical terms are those discussed below.

2.1 "Hazardous Substance" and "Pollutant or Contaminant"

CERCLA is designed to address problems and redress complaints associated with "hazardous substances." With the single exception relating to "pollutants or contaminants," discussed below, if a matter does not involve a CERCLA "hazardous substance," it does not fall within the scope of CERCLA. Understanding what constitutes a CERCLA "hazardous substance" is therefore critical.

2.1.1 Definition of "Hazardous Substance"

"Hazardous substances" are defined in CERCLA section 101(14). They are defined by reference to substances that are listed or designated under other environmental statutes. They include "hazardous wastes" under RCRA, "hazardous substances" defined in section 311 of the Clean Water Act, "toxic pollutants" designated under section 307 of the Clean Water Act, hazardous air pollutants listed under section 112 of the Clean Air Act, substances designated under section 102 of CERCLA which "may present substantial danger to public health or welfare or the environment," characteristic hazardous wastes under section 3001 of RCRA, and imminently hazardous chemical substances or mixtures that EPA has addressed under section 7 of the Toxic Substances Control Act (TSCA).

---

[10]42 U.S.C. § 9606(b)(2).
[11]42 U.S.C. § 9611(e)(3).

In order to facilitate the identification of CERCLA hazardous substances, EPA has prepared a list of these substances which is located at 40 C.F.R. part 302.

2.1.2 Quantity of "Hazardous Substance"

It is important to note that CERCLA, unlike most other environmental statutes, contains no requirement that a specified amount of a "hazardous substance" be present before a response action can be taken or a party found liable for a release or threat of release of such substance.[12] This is true in spite of the fact that CERCLA's reporting requirements mandate reporting a release of hazardous substances only when a specified quantity is released.[13] This so-called "reportable quantity" has no effect on a party's liability.[14] The release of any quantity of a "hazardous substance" is sufficient to establish liability. The rationale for the distinction is that CERCLA's response and enforcement provisions are designed to deal with a "release," which is defined as "any spilling, leaking . . . ,"[15] while CERCLA's reporting requirements specifically require that a minimum quantity be discharged before a report need be filed.[16]

2.1.3 Petroleum Exclusion

Excluded from the definition of "hazardous substance" is "petroleum, including crude oil or any fraction thereof."[17] This exception, which has become known as the "petroleum exclusion," plays a significant role in CERCLA since many sites contain petroleum contamination. In many cases, the companies responsible for the petroleum contamination are not liable for CERCLA cleanup costs.[18] This is true even though petroleum contamination *is* addressed under RCRA. The result has been situations in which sites, particularly former gasoline service stations, cannot be the subject of CERCLA actions but can be the subject of actions brought under RCRA.[19]

The meaning of the petroleum exclusion has been the subject of considerable debate as petroleum frequently contains other listed "hazardous substances." The most common of these are the so-called "BTX" compounds—benzene, toluene and xylene. Whether these substances, when present in petroleum, are "hazardous substances" has been the source of controversy. In 1987, EPA's general counsel issued an opinion addressing when

---

[12]*But see United States v. Alcan Aluminum Corp.*, 964 F.2d 252 (3d Cir. 1992)(suggesting concentration might affect apportionment of liability).

[13]42 U.S.C. § 9602. *See infra* section 6.1.

[14]*United States v. Wade*, 577 F. Supp. 1326 (E.D. Pa. 1983).

[15]42 U.S.C. § 9601(22).

[16]42 U.S.C. § 9603.

[17]42 U.S.C. § 9601(14).

[18]*Wilshire Westwood Assoc. v. Atlantic Richfield Corp.*, 881 F.2d 801 (9th Cir. 1989).

[19]*Compare Wilshire Westwood Assoc.*, 881 F.2d 801 (9th Cir. 1989)(CERCLA) *with Zands v. Nelson*, 779 F. Supp 1254 (C.D. Cal. 1991)(RCRA).

such substances, if present in petroleum, are considered hazardous. The opinion states that such substances are not hazardous as long as they are found in refined petroleum fractions and are not present at levels which exceed those normally found in such fractions.[20] In short, indigenous, refinery-added hazardous substances are exempted. The opinion indicates that substances *added* to petroleum as a result of *contamination during use* are not within the petroleum exclusion and that in such cases the substances are considered CERCLA "hazardous substances." This test has met favorable reaction from several courts considering the issue.[21]

2.1.4 "Pollutant or Contaminant"

While the vast majority of actions taken under CERCLA relate to CERCLA "hazardous substances," CERCLA also provides authority for EPA to respond to "a release or substantial threat of release . . . of *any pollutant or contaminant* which may present an imminent and substantial danger to public health or welfare . . . ."[22] Under CERCLA the term "pollutants or contaminants" encompasses just about anything. By definition, such substances include compounds which upon exposure "will or may reasonably be anticipated to cause" certain specified harmful health effects.[23] While EPA can respond to and clean up a site polluted by either a "hazardous substance" or a "pollutant or contaminant," the statute does not authorize EPA to recover its cleanup costs from private parties or to issue an order directing the parties to perform a cleanup when the substance involved is only a "pollutant or contaminant." Only sites contaminated with "hazardous substances" are subject to such actions.[24] Consequently, while the definition of a "pollutant or contaminant" is broad, this breadth of coverage has no practical impact on private parties.

2.2 "Release or Threat of Release"

In order for EPA to undertake a response action under CERCLA, and for liability to attach, there must be a "release" or "substantial threat" of a release of a hazardous substance into the environment. The discharge of a certain quantity of a hazardous substance need not occur for a "release" or "substantial threat of release" to exist. Any quantity, however small, is adequate to trigger CERCLA.[25]

---

[20]United States Environmental Protection Agency, Memorandum from Francis S. Blake to J. Winston Porter, *Scope of the CERCLA Petroleum Exclusion Under Sections 101(14) and 104(a)(2)* (July 31, 1987).

[21]*E.g., Wilshire Westwood Assoc. v. Atlantic Richfield Corp.,* 881 F.2d 801 (9th Cir. 1989); *Washington v. Time Oil Co.,* 687 F. Supp. 529 (W.D. Wash. 1988).

[22]42 U.S.C. § 9604 (emphasis added).

[23]42 U.S.C. § 9601(33).

[24]*See* 42 U.S.C. §§ 9606, 9607.

[25]*United States v. Conservation Chem. Co.,* 619 F. Supp. 162, 233 (W.D. Mo. 1985). *But see Amoco Oil Co. v. Borden, Inc.,* 889 F.2d 664, 670 (5th Cir. 1989)(release of any quantity not sufficient to create liability unless hazard justified response action).

Under CERCLA, the term "release" is defined broadly to include virtually any situation leading to a hazardous substance being freed from its normal container. A "release" thus occurs whenever there is "any spilling, leaking, pumping, pouring, emitting, emptying, discharging, injecting, escaping, leaching, dumping, or disposing into the environment . . . ."[26]

Excluded from the definition of "release" are: releases occurring in the workplace covered by employer claims procedures; emissions from the exhausts of motor vehicles, rolling stock, aircraft, vessels, or pipeline pumping station engines; certain nuclear releases; and the normal application of fertilizer.[27] These exceptions are designed to ensure that workplace-related incidents, nuclear incidents, and exhaust emissions remain regulated by laws other than CERCLA and to avoid interference with agricultural activities. While not specifically excluded from the definition of "release," federally permitted releases (such as releases pursuant to an NPDES permit under the Clean Water Act) are treated differently than other "releases." The only remedy provided under CERCLA for such a release is that under existing law relating to the permit issued.[28]

As with a "release," the term "substantial threat of a release" is interpreted broadly. Courts addressing the issue of whether such a threat exists have generally found a threat whenever objective evidence suggests a hazardous substance might be released absent some affirmative act being taken. Corroding tanks, the presence of a "hazardous substance" in a location where it might freely move in the environment, and abandoned tanks have all been deemed examples of threatened releases.[29]

2.3 "Facility" or "Vessel"

Before a party can be liable under CERCLA's cost recovery and abatement sections, there must first be a release or threatened release from a "facility" or "vessel."[30] Interestingly enough, there is no corresponding requirement for EPA response actions.[31] While this would appear to create situations where EPA might perform a cleanup and be unable to recover its costs, court decisions have so broadly interpreted the definition of "facility" that there is virtually no possibility that such a situation could arise.

CERCLA defines a facility in two parts. First, it lists a variety of things that constitute facilities (for example, building, structure, installa-

---

[26]42 U.S.C. § 9601(22).

[27]*Id.*

[28]42 U.S.C. § 9607(j).

[29]*United States v. Metate Asbestos Corp.*, 584 F. Supp. 1143 (D. Ariz. 1984)(asbestos lying on ground); *New York v. Shore Realty Corp.*, 759 F.2d 1032, 1045 (2d Cir. 1985)(corroding tanks, failure to license facility); *United States v. Northernaire Plating Co.*, 670 F. Supp. 742, 747 (W.D. Mich. 1987)(abandoned drums).

[30]42 U.S.C. § 9607.

[31]42 U.S.C. § 9604.

tion, equipment, pipe or pipeline, or well) and, second, it provides that a facility is also "any site or area where a hazardous substance has ... come to be located."[32] Perhaps it is easier to consider what is not a "facility." Specifically excluded are consumer products in consumer use and vessels. Under CERCLA, the term "vessel" means any craft used as a means of transportation on water.[33]

2.4 "Environment"

The term "environment" under CERCLA is important because a "release" requires the freeing of a hazardous substance into the "environment." Absent this, CERCLA's response and enforcement provisions are not triggered. Like all other CERCLA terms, "environment" is defined broadly to include any surface water, groundwater, drinking water supply, land surface, subsurface strata, and ambient air.

2.5 "National Priorities List"

The "National Priorities List," otherwise known as the "NPL," is an important facet of CERCLA's response procedures. First established in 1981 under section 105(a)(8)(B) of CERCLA, the NPL is part of the National Contingency Plan (NCP) and must be updated annually. CERCLA requires that EPA develop criteria for determining priorities among the various "releases or threatened releases" throughout the nation. These criteria are to be based on risks to public health, welfare, or the environment, taking into account a variety of factors including the extent of population at risk, the hazard potential of the facility's hazardous substances, the potential for contamination of drinking water supplies, and the threat to ambient air.[34] Applying these criteria, EPA scores and ranks the various sites for possible listing on the NPL.

EPA's original scoring system was issued in 1980. In 1990 EPA revised its hazardous ranking scoring system pursuant to the 1986 SARA Amendments.[35]

EPA's decision to list a site on the NPL is considered an action pursuant to the Administrative Procedure Act[36] and subject to notice and public comment. Parties challenging a site listing by EPA must do so within 90 days after EPA's final decision.[37] The failure to challenge a listing during this period operates as a bar to any subsequent challenges.[38]

---

[32] 42 U.S.C. § 9601(9).

[33] 42 U.S.C. § 9601.

[34] 42 U.S.C. § 9605(a)(8)(A).

[35] 55 *Fed. Reg.* 51,532 (1990).

[36] *See* 5 U.S.C. § 553.

[37] *See* 42 U.S.C. § 9613(a).

[38] *See Washington State Dep't of Transp. v. United States Envtl. Protection Agency*, 917 F.2d 1309 (D.C. Cir. 1990).

It is important to recognize that only sites listed on the NPL qualify for long-term remedial actions financed by the Superfund.[39] A site not listed on the NPL may still be the subject of a more short-term removal action.[40]

2.6 "National Contingency Plan"

The primary guidance document for CERCLA response actions is the National Contingency Plan (NCP). The NCP sets forth the procedures which must be followed by EPA and private parties in selecting and conducting CERCLA response actions.

The NCP has been present in various forms since it was first promulgated in 1973. At that time, it was prepared pursuant to the Federal Water Pollution Control Act[41] and designed to address the removal of oil and other hazardous substances. With CERCLA's passage in 1980, EPA was required to expand the NCP to place greater emphasis on the procedures for responding to releases of hazardous substances.[42] The current version of the NCP was promulgated in 1990.[43] Not surprisingly, it is far more comprehensive than all of its predecessors.

The 1990 NCP sets forth the responsibilities of the various organizations (for example, National Response Teams, Regional Response Teams, On Scene Coordinators, Remedial Project Managers) which take part in responses to releases, describes how coordination among these various organizations is to occur, establishes methods and criteria for determining the appropriate extent of response, outlines the procedures to be followed in performing cleanups (remedial actions or removals), and establishes the method by which EPA is to prepare an administrative record to support its actions. What the NCP fails to do is tell EPA the specific type of remedy to employ in each situation. This is largely a matter left to the discretion of EPA in each instance. The vagueness of the NCP on this issue means that the subject of remedy selection is sometimes hotly contested in CERCLA proceedings.

3.0 CERCLA'S REMEDIAL PROVISIONS

Whenever confronting a situation involving the need to conduct a cleanup, EPA has two basic options under CERCLA. It may conduct the cleanup itself and seek to recover its costs from potentially responsible parties (PRPs) in a subsequent cost recovery action, or it can compel the PRPs to perform the cleanup (either voluntarily or involuntarily) through administrative or judicial proceedings.

---

[39] 40 C.F.R. § 300.425(b)(1).
[40] *Id.*
[41] 33 U.S.C. §§ 1251 *et seq.*
[42] 42 U.S.C. § 9605(a).
[43] 40 C.F.R. Part 300.

3.1 EPA's Authority To Act

At CERCLA's core are its provisions setting forth EPA's authority and the procedures EPA must follow in responding to releases. Section 104(a)(1) sets forth the authority to act. Under this section, EPA is authorized, consistent with the NCP, to remove, and to provide for remedial actions relating to, hazardous substances or pollutants or contaminants whenever:

1. any hazardous substance is released or there is a substantial threat of such release into the environment, or
2. there is a release or substantial threat of release into the environment of any pollutant or contaminant which may present an imminent and substantial danger to the public health or welfare.

Thus, this section sets forth the two broad categories of response actions available—"remedial actions" and "removals."

3.2 Categories of Response Actions

3.2.1 "Removal"

Under CERCLA, "removal" actions are undertaken to deal with environmental emergencies.[44] Such actions could include the providing of alternate water supplies to persons whose groundwater has been polluted, the immediate cleanup of hazardous waste spilled from a container, or the erection of a fence around a hazardous waste site. In short, just about any action that tends to diminish the threat of a hazardous waste site and that can be done promptly qualifies as a removal.

Removal actions can occur at a site not listed on the NPL, or they can occur as part of the initial response to a seriously contaminated NPL site which will later be the subject of a more formal and extensive remedial action. For example, investigations of a site which will be the subject of a more extensive remedial action are considered removal actions.[45]

Because the administrative requirements imposed on an EPA removal action are far less than those for a remedial action, removals are frequently done in conjunction with more formal remedial actions.

There are, however, some limitations on removals. Ordinarily a removal action must be capable of being completed within one year and cost no more than $2 million.[46] Exceptions are situations in which:

1. continued action is necessary to respond to an emergency,
2. there is an immediate risk to public health or the environment,
3. the action is part of a larger approved remedial action, or
4. continuation of the removal is consistent with the remedial action to be taken.[47]

---

[44] 42 U.S.C. § 9601(23).
[45] *Id.*
[46] 42 U.S.C. § 9604(c)(1).
[47] *Id.*

The breadth of these exceptions generally means that in situations where EPA wants to continue a removal action beyond one year or above $2 million, it can find a basis for doing so.

3.2.2 "Remedial Actions"

Unlike "removals," remedial actions are long-term, permanent cleanups. Thus, while a "removal" may alleviate an immediate threat to human health or the environment, a "remedial action" is designed to permanently eliminate any threat that a site might pose. While a "removal" can be accomplished in a matter of weeks, "remedial actions" take years or, in some cases, decades to complete. Examples of "remedial actions" include constructing dikes, trenches, or clay covers; excavations; and the permanent destruction or neutralization of "hazardous substances."[48]

3.3 Steps in the Remedial Process

Because "remedial actions" are significantly more complex and costly, more detailed requirements are set forth in CERCLA and the NCP for such actions than for "removals." Not surprisingly, PRPs are also very concerned with the process by which "remedial actions" are selected and conducted by EPA and will often seek to participate in the process used to select such remedies.

3.3.1 Site Identification and Initial Evaluation

Sites are brought to EPA's attention in numerous ways. Site information may be contained in reports of releases submitted either under section 103(a) of CERCLA, or under other federal reporting requirements.[49] Citizens' complaints, investigations by government agencies, and submissions by state agencies are also potential sources of information.[50]

Once brought to EPA's attention, sites with releases or threatened releases are listed in the Comprehensive Environmental Response and Liability Information System (CERCLIS) for subsequent evaluation. CERCLIS contains the official inventory of CERCLA sites and supports EPA's site planning and tracking process.[51]

EPA then assembles information on the site and conducts a preliminary assessment (PA) to determine the scope of the potential environmental problem. The PA, which provides the initial screening of sites, focuses on determining whether the site presents a risk of a release of hazardous substances. A PA may be performed merely by reviewing existing data on the site; if appropriate, a site inspection may also be conducted. The PA may or may not result in a recommendation that further investigation be done.

---

[48]42 U.S.C. § 9601(24).
[49]*See infra* section 6.1
[50]40 C.F.R. § 300.405.
[51]40 C.F.R. § 300.5.

If, after the performance of a PA, it appears that the site presents a threat and that it will score high enough to be listed on the NPL, EPA conducts additional site investigations to gather more data about the hazardous substances at the site, possible human and environmental receptors, and migration pathways. This information is then combined with the information developed in the PA to score the site in accordance with the NPL's hazardous ranking system.

3.3.2 NPL Listing

Formal site scoring is conducted using EPA criteria and scoring procedures set forth in the hazardous ranking system. Among the criteria applied are toxicity of the substances, the location of potential receptors, exposure pathways, threats to the human food chain, and threats to ambient air and groundwaters. Site listing occurs when a score greater than 28.5 is achieved.[52]

Once listed on the NPL, CERCLA's expensive remedial process is committed. Because NPL listing guarantees prolonged and expensive government response actions, challenges to site listing occasionally occur. They have largely been unsuccessful.[53]

3.3.3 Planning Remedial Actions—SCAP

EPA's remedial action timing is tied not only to the nature of each individual site, but also to EPA's concern with meeting congressionally-mandated cleanup numbers.[54] This so-called "bean counting" is an integral part of the overall CERCLA process and explains in part why certain sites appear to languish for years and then suddenly generate a great deal of EPA activity.

EPA's nationwide strategic plan for addressing hazardous waste sites is set forth in its Superfund Comprehensive Accomplishments Plan (SCAP). This document provides details on each site in a computer printout format and specifies those activities which are expected to occur during each fiscal quarter. Analysis of the SCAP can provide any party concerned with a particular site a preview of EPA's long-term planning for the site. In many cases, information will appear in the SCAP before it is widely known to the public.

3.3.4 Remedial Investigation/Feasibility Study

The first major event in the remedial action process after NPL listing is the performance of the Remedial Investigation/Feasibility Study (RI/FS). The RI/FS is the most important facet of any remedial action, because it determines the scope of remedial action to be undertaken. The purpose of

---

[52]40 C.F.R. Part 300 (Appendix A).

[53]*Compare City of Stoughton v. United States Envtl. Protection Agency*, 858 F.2d 747 (D.C. Cir. 1988) *with Tex Tin Corp. v. United States Envtl. Protection Agency*, 935 F.2d 1321 (D.C. Cir. 1991).

[54]*See* 42 U.S.C. § 9616(d),(e).

the RI/FS is to assess site conditions and evaluate alternatives to the extent necessary to select a remedy.[55] EPA then selects one of the alternatives discussed in the RI/FS as the remedy for the site.

As the name implies, the RI/FS consists of two phases, although in practice they are often very interrelated. The first phase is the remedial investigation (RI).[56] The RI, which in many cases can take years to perform, is designed to assess the nature and extent of releases of hazardous substances and determine those areas of a site where releases have created damage or the threat of damage to public health or the environment.

It is during the RI process that extensive soil and groundwater sampling is performed and voluminous reports detailing the results of these investigations are prepared. The purposes of these investigations include determining the nature of the site's geology and hydrogeology, locating the sources of contamination, identifying the type and mobility of contaminants present, and defining the nature of any threat to human health and the environment. In short, the overall purpose of the RI is to collect data necessary to adequately characterize the site for the purpose of developing and evaluating effective remedial alternatives. At the conclusion of the RI, it is expected that EPA will have a reasonably good idea of the sources of contamination, the nature and extent of contamination, and the actual and potential exposure routes.

When enough technical information about the site is available to analyze potential remedies, EPA will then prepare a Feasibility Study (FS).[57] The objective of the FS is to develop a range of remedial alternatives for consideration. As such, the FS evaluates in detail potential remedies for the site, taking into account the findings of the RI. In evaluating options, EPA considers the extent to which each complies with the cleanup criteria specified in CERCLA section 121.[58]

The entire RI/FS process can be extremely costly and time-consuming. Costs, which can range as high as several million dollars, may increase if EPA elects to remediate a site in what are known as "operable units." The use of "operable units"—which represents nothing more than a phased approach to site cleanups—began in the mid-1980s. It is now rare that a major site cleanup does not include the use of operable units. When operable units are used, they ordinarily represent the remediation of a segment of the site. For example, a single site may include three operable units: One operable unit may be designed to address the cleanup and isolation of the sources of contamination at the site; a second operable unit may pertain to remediation of groundwater at the site; and a third operable unit may relate to the remediation of areas adjoining the site. EPA prefers this

---

[55]40 C.F.R. § 300.430(a)(2).

[56]*See generally* 40 C.F.R. § 300.430(d).

[57]*See generally* 40 C.F.R. § 300.430(e).

[58]42 U.S.C. § 9621. *See infra* section 3.5.

approach in order to begin remediation of certain portions of the site, while other portions are undergoing study and evaluation.[59]

3.3.5 Determining the Appropriate Level of Cleanup

3.3.5.1 *General Considerations*

One of the most controversial issues at any CERCLA site is the level or degree of cleanup that must be achieved before the site is considered "clean." At each site, the scope and variety of contamination varies. Moreover, each site's relationship to the public and the environment differs. The bottom line questions are whether the site must be cleaned up to pristine pre-disposal conditions and, if not, what levels of cleanup are adequate.

The issues that arise with regard to cleanup standards include the level of groundwater remediation required, the level of residual soil contamination that will be permitted to remain, and the extent to which site remediation will require excavation of contaminated soils and debris. At the crux of these issues is the question: What levels of risk are acceptable? Since cleanups resulting in the removal of all, or nearly all, risks are more costly and take longer to complete, all parties with a stake in the CERCLA process have concern about how cleanup standards are established.

3.3.5.2 *CERCLA Section 121*

History shows that CERCLA cleanups have become significantly more expensive with each passing year. Costs have been driven upward by the discarding of many formerly acceptable procedures for remediating sites and the substitution of remedies that are designed to achieve far greater permanence and far less residual risk. This trend continued with the 1986 SARA Amendments, which set forth much stricter requirements, making cleanups more conservative and costly. As these costs have risen, many have questioned the need for such expensive cleanups in situations where the risk factors applied are stricter in some cases than risks people encounter every day.

Section 121 of CERCLA sets forth the statutory requirements for cleanup standards. It provides that CERCLA-based remedial actions be in accordance with its precepts and, to the extent practicable, with the National Contingency Plan.[60] Section 121 also requires that remedial actions provide for a cost-effective response. This latter requirement appears to have become a secondary factor applied by EPA in selecting remedies.

In setting forth the factors to be applied, section 121 evidences a clear preference for remedies that are permanent and involve the treatment of

---

[59] 40 C.F.R. § 300.430(a)(1)(ii)(A).

[60] 42 U.S.C. § 9621(a). While Section 121 lists general factors to be applied, the NCP attempts, consistent with the factors listed in section 121, to provide more detailed cleanup requirements. *See* 40 C.F.R. Part 300.

hazardous substances to reduce their volume, toxicity or mobility.[61] This has meant that remedies involving the construction of man-made barriers to "contain" contamination within a designated area are disfavored. At the same time, section 121 clearly indicates that the off-site transport and disposal of hazardous substances without treatment should be EPA's least favored remedial approach. Reading section 121 as a whole, it is clear that Congress' preferred approach is the permanent destruction of hazardous substances through treatment. Various procedures are set forth which drive EPA's remedial decisions in that direction. For example, when hazardous substances are left on-site, section 121 requires that EPA review the adequacy of the remedy every five years. If the review indicates that the remedy is inadequate, EPA must select a new remedy.[62]

CERCLA's greatest impetus towards permanent treatment is the requirement that a remedy achieve all Applicable or Relevant and Appropriate Requirements (ARARs) where hazardous substances are left on-site. Section 121 states that the following are ARARs for the hazardous substance, pollutant, or contaminant concerned:

1. any standard, requirement, criteria, or limitation under any federal environmental law; and

2. any promulgated standard, requirement, criteria, or limitation under a state environmental or facility siting law that is more stringent than any federal standard.[63]

Application of ARARs at CERCLA sites has meant that remedies must achieve the highest cleanup levels established by other federal and state standards. By incorporating requirements from other state and federal environmental statutes and regulations into CERCLA, section 121 ensures that CERCLA remedies will be extremely conservative and costly. CERCLA 121, however, does not specify just what ARARs pertain to a specific site. As a result, the selection of ARARs has become a part of the RI/FS process.

3.3.5.3 Remedy Selection Criteria and ARARs under the NCP

The 1990 NCP attempts to fill in some of the gaps left by section 121 and provide more detail regarding the criteria to be used in both selecting remedies and applying ARARs.

The 1990 NCP provisions regarding remedy selection clearly diminish section 121's mandate that selected remedies be cost-effective. While section 121(a) emphasizes that remedies be cost-effective and does not suggest that cost-effectiveness be less of a factor than other considerations, the NCP relegates cost-effectiveness to merely a measure by which certain other factors are to be evaluated.

---

[61]42 U.S.C. § 9621(b).

[62]42 U.S.C. § 9621(c).

[63]42 U.S.C. § 9621(d)(2)(A).

The NCP sets forth nine criteria which must be applied in evaluating remedies. These nine criteria are in turn divided into three major categories. The first of these three major categories is labeled "Threshold Criteria."[64] There are two Threshold Criteria: (1) overall protection of human health and the environment and (2) compliance with ARARs.

Should a proposed remedy fail to meet both Threshold Criteria, it will not be selected. If the proposed remedy does meet the criteria, it is then evaluated by application of the second major category of criteria, which is known as "Primary Balancing Criteria." Primary Balancing Criteria consist of the following:

1. long term effectiveness and permanence;
2. reduction of toxicity, mobility, or volume through treatment;
3. short-term effectiveness;
4. implementability; and
5. cost

It is during the application of the primary balancing criteria that the NCP provides for the consideration of cost-effectiveness. Cost-effectiveness is determined by evaluating the first three primary balancing criteria to assess overall effectiveness of the remedy. A remedy is deemed cost-effective if its costs are proportional to its overall effectiveness as established by these three criteria.[65] Obviously this appraisal is very subjective, and results can vary widely from site to site.

The final major category of criteria is "Modifying Criteria." Two criteria fall within this category. They are state acceptance and community acceptance. Both modifying criteria are clearly of limited importance since they are merely required to be *considered* by EPA in selecting a remedy.[66] Since that consideration occurs at the very end of the evaluation process—presumably after EPA has a reasonably firm idea of what it desires based upon the other criteria—it can be expected that very strong public and state disapproval would have to exist for a remedy to be discarded.

Since compliance with ARARs is a threshold criterion, determining what ARARs are and whether a remedy will comply with them assumes critical importance. The NCP therefore attempts to expand on the discussion of ARARs contained in section 121. As the phrase implies, ARARs consist of both "applicable" and "relevant and appropriate" standards or requirements. The NCP states that an "applicable" requirement is one which "specifically addresses a hazardous substance, pollutant, contaminant, remedial action, location, or other circumstance found at a

---

[64]*See generally* 40 C.F.R. § 300.430(f).

[65]40 C.F.R. § 300.430(f)(1)(ii)(D).

[66]40 C.F.R. § 300.430(f)(1)(ii)(E).

CERCLA site."[67] Thus, "applicable" requirements at a site with releases into the air or surface water would include those standards addressing air emissions or surface water discharges.

Determining what constitutes a "relevant and appropriate" standard is more difficult. This is largely because of the greater subjectivity involved. The NCP lists several factors to apply in determining whether a standard is "relevant and appropriate":

1. the purpose of the requirement being considered and the purpose of the CERCLA action;

2. the medium (groundwater, surface water, soil, etc.) regulated or affected by the requirement and the medium contaminated or affected at the site;

3. the substances regulated by the requirement and the substances at the site;

4. the activities regulated by the requirement and the remedial action contemplated;

5. any variances, waivers, or exemptions of the requirement and their availability for the circumstances at the site;

6. the type of place regulated and the type of place affected by the release or CERCLA action;

7. the type and size of the structure or facility regulated and the type and size of the structure affected by the release or contemplated by the CERCLA action; and

8. any consideration of use or potential use of the affected resources in the requirement and the use or potential use of the affected resource at the site.[68]

Once determined to apply, an ARAR must be met unless it is waived. CERCLA contains a list of the limited circumstances in which EPA may select a remedy not meeting an ARAR but still permitting hazardous substances to remain on-site.[69] These circumstances are as follow:

1. the selected remedy is only part of a total remedy which will attain the ARAR;

2. compliance with the ARAR will lead to greater risk to human health or the environment than alternative actions;

3. compliance is technically impracticable from an engineering perspective;

4. the remedy will attain an equivalent standard of performance to the ARAR through use of another approach;

---

[67] 40 C.F.R. § 300.400(g)(1).

[68] 40 C.F.R. § 300.400(g)(2).

[69] 42 U.S.C. § 9621(d)(4).

5. with respect to state standards, the state has not consistently applied the standard itself under similar circumstances; and

6. with respect to situations involving Superfund-financed remedies, the need to retain sufficient monies in the Superfund to respond to other sites overrides application of the ARAR to protect public health, welfare, and the environment.

3.3.6 Record of Decision

After completion of the RI/FS, EPA issues a Record of Decision (ROD), which sets forth EPA's selected remedy as well as the factors which led to its selection. The ROD must set forth all facts, analyses of facts, and site-specific policy determinations in sufficient detail for the situation. It must explain how the remedy is protective of human health and the environment, detail applicable ARARs and how they will be attained (or why they are waived), and set forth how the remedy is cost-effective and uses permanent solutions to the maximum extent possible.[70] The ROD must also respond to any public comments on the remedy selected by EPA. Once issued, the ROD must be placed in the administrative record supporting EPA's action at the site.

3.3.7 Administrative Record

The entire remedial process is subject to public notice and comment. In addition, EPA must compile an administrative record. The public,[71] as well as the state,[72] may review and comment on EPA's proposed remedial actions; such comments must be included in the administrative record. The administrative record must also contain EPA's responses to significant public comments received[73] and significant documents considered and relied upon by EPA in selecting its remedy.

The administrative record is critical, not only to the decisionmaking process, but also to any subsequent judicial review of EPA's preferred remedy. Judicial review of EPA's remedy selection decision is limited to the administrative record.[74] Unless review of the administrative record shows EPA's decision to be arbitrary and capricious, the decision will be upheld.

3.3.8 Implementation of the Cleanup Decision

After issuance of the ROD, EPA completes a remedial design (RD). It is through the RD that the ROD's conceptual remedy is reduced to a detailed design permitting its construction and operation. The remedial action (RA) phase involves the construction and operation of the remedy in accordance with the RD. Costs to implement a remedy at a CERCLA site can vary con-

---

[70] 40 C.F.R. § 300.430(f)(5).

[71] 42 U.S.C. §§ 9613(k), 9617.

[72] 42 U.S.C. § 9621(f)(1)(E),(H).

[73] 42 U.S.C. § 9617(b).

[74] 42 U.S.C. § 9613(j)(1).

siderably. Seldom will they be less than $1 million. Not infrequently they can exceed $50 million. More costly remedies are likely in situations of extensive groundwater contamination where long-term "aquifer restoration" is attempted.

3.3.9 Prerequisites to EPA Conducting Remedial Action— State Involvement

As indicated earlier, CERCLA requires that EPA consult with affected states before selecting an appropriate remedial action.[75] CERCLA also provides that EPA cannot proceed with a remedial action using Superfund monies unless EPA first receives certain assurances from the state involved. These required assurances are set forth in CERCLA section 104(c)(3). This section provides that EPA shall not undertake a remedial action unless the state in which the release has occurred first enters into a contract or cooperative agreement with EPA providing that the state will provide future maintenance of the remedial action, ensure the availability of a hazardous waste disposal facility for any necessary off-site disposal, and pay or assure payment of ten percent of the cost of the remedial action, including all future maintenance.[76] A state's inability or unwillingness to meet the ten percent funding requirement can pose a significant barrier to EPA's ability to conduct a Superfund-financed remedial action.

4.0 CERCLA'S LIABILITY PROVISIONS

4.1 Overview

CERCLA contains two basic liability provisions:

1. a provision permitting EPA and private parties to recover their cleanup costs,[77] and

2. a provision permitting EPA to seek a judicial order requiring a liable party to abate an endangerment to public health, welfare, or the environment.[78]

In addition to its two major liability provisions, CERCLA also includes provisions: (1) permitting EPA to take certain administrative actions to compel private parties to undertake actions necessary to protect public health, welfare or the environment; (2) permitting private parties to bring "citizen suits" to enforce CERCLA's provisions; and (3) providing authority for natural resource trustees to bring actions for damages to natural resources.

---

[75] 42 U.S.C. § 9604(c)(2).
[76] 42 U.S.C. § 9604(c)(3).
[77] 42 U.S.C. § 9607.
[78] 42 U.S.C. § 9606.

4.2 CERCLA's Operative Concepts

It is important to understand that there are certain key operative concepts that permeate CERCLA's liability provisions. These concepts, while most directly applicable to CERCLA's cost recovery provisions (section 107), have also been found applicable to CERCLA's abatement provisions (section 106).

4.2.1 Strict, Joint and Several, and Retroactive Liability

Courts have found that CERCLA imposes strict and, in most cases involving multiparty sites, joint and several liability with *no* requirement that a party's hazardous substances have been the cause for the cleanup or response action.

CERCLA's strict liability scheme has been uniformly endorsed by the courts.[79] The basis for CERCLA's strict liability is found in its requirement that "liability" be construed in accordance with the liability standard for section 311 of the Clean Water Act (CWA). As the courts have interpreted CWA section 311 as imposing strict liability, they have had little problem reaching a similar result under CERCLA.[80] Consequently, claims that a party was not negligent or that its activities were consistent with standard industry practices provide no defense to liability.[81]

While CERCLA contains no statutory mandate that liability be joint and several, courts in practice have freely found such liability. In many cases, this has occurred despite the existence of a strong basis for apportionment and despite Congress having *deleted* provisions imposing joint and several liability from CERCLA before its enactment. The deletion, however, has not been viewed as removing the *possibility* of joint and several liability on a case-by-case basis, but as not mandating joint and several liability in all instances.[82] Nevertheless, courts have for the most part readily found joint and several liability whenever there is any evidence of the commingling of hazardous substances by different parties.[83] The practical result of this presumptive joint and several liability has been EPA's ability to sue a few PRPs at major Superfund sites and obtain judicial decisions that each is individually responsible for *all* cleanup costs at the site. While this stance has greatly simplified EPA's task, it has burdened defendants not only with total cleanup costs, but also with the prospect of

---

[79]*E.g., Levin Metals Corp. v. Pan-Richmond Terminal Co.*, 799 F.2d 1312 (9th Cir. 1986); *United States v. Northeastern Pharmaceutical & Chem. Co. ("NEPACCO")*, 810 F.2d 726 (8th Cir. 1986).

[80]*United States v. Chem-Dyne Corp.*, 572 F. Supp. 802 (S.D. Ohio 1983); *New York v. Shore Realty Corp.*, 759 F.2d 1032 (2d Cir. 1985).

[81]*United States v. Conservation Chem. Co.*, 619 F. Supp. 162, 204 (W.D. Mo. 1985).

[82]*United States v. Chem-Dyne Corp.*, 572 F. Supp. 802 (S.D. Ohio 1983).

[83]*E.g., O'Neil v. Picillo*, 682 F. Supp. 706 (D.R.I. 1988). *See infra* section 4.8.4.

pursuing costly contribution actions against parties EPA has elected not to sue.[84]

CERCLA's standard of causation is minimal. In fact, there is arguably no causation requirement with regard to individual defendants at multiparty sites where there has been a release.[85] In CERCLA section 107 cost recovery actions, for example, the issue of causation has been reduced to whether a release or threatened release has caused a plaintiff to incur response costs. It has been stated that a "[c]ausal link between a defendant's release and the plaintiff's response . . ." must be established for liability to attach.[86] However, at multiparty sites it has not mattered whether a party's own waste was released or threatened to have been released as long as some hazardous substance at the site has been discharged.[87]

Finally, caselaw has clearly established that CERCLA liability is retroactive. Thus, parties may be found liable as a result of actions they took long *before* CERCLA's enactment.[88]

4.2.2 Individual and Corporate Liability

One of the unique features of CERCLA's liability scheme is that liability has been found in situations where application of traditional notions of corporate law, such as concepts of limited liability, would exempt individual corporate officers and parent corporations. This breadth of coverage is attributable in part to the flexibility of CERCLA's liability language. In other respects, it is due to the willingness of the courts to use this language to cast the liability net widely in order to achieve what they view as CERCLA's remedial purpose.[89]

CERCLA section 101(20)(A) provided the initial impetus for the courts to discard traditional concepts of individual and corporate liability. This section defines the term "owner or operator" under CERCLA. In so doing, it indicates that the term "[d]oes not include a person, who without participating in the management of a vessel or facility, holds indicia of ownership primarily to protect his security interest in the vessel or facility."[90] Courts have derived from this provision the affirmative implication that a person who *does* participate in management and owns an

---

[84] *See infra* section 4.11.

[85] *But see* discussion regarding causation in Natural Resource Damage Claims, *infra* section 4.10.

[86] *See Dedham Water Co. v. Cumberland Farms, Inc.*, 689 F. Supp. 1223, 1224 (D. Mass. 1988), *rev'd on other grounds*, 889 F.2d 1146, 1151-1154 (1st Cir. 1989).

[87] *United States v. South Carolina Recycling & Disposal, Inc. ("SCRDI")*, 653 F. Supp. 984, 992 (D.S.C. 1984).

[88] *United States v. NEPACCO*, 810 F.2d 726, 732-733 (8th Cir. 1986); *Kelley v. Thomas Solvent Co.*, 714 F. Supp 1439, 1443-1445 (W.D. Mich. 1989).

[89] *See United States v. Mottolo*, 695 F. Supp. 615, 624 (D.N.H. 1988).

[90] 42 U.S.C. § 9601(20)(A).

interest in a business is liable under CERCLA for his company's waste disposal practices.[91]

Based on sections 101(20)(A) and 107(a)(3), which render liable "[a]ny person who . . . arranged for disposal . . . of hazardous substances owned or possessed by such person . . . ," courts have evolved what is termed the "control" test. The control test has been used in determining to what extent individual corporate officers and parent corporations may be found liable. This control test has come to mean that an individual corporate officer or a parent corporation can be found liable if either has exercised control over a corporation's hazardous waste handling and disposal activities.[92] In some cases, courts have held that control over waste handling need not be shown as long as control over the overall business operations of the corporation is shown.[93] Most disturbing from the perspective of the individual corporate officer and parent corporations has been the suggestion in at least one case that simply having the *ability to control* waste disposal activities may be sufficient to create liability—even though such ability to control was *never exercised*.[94]

While some courts have continued to follow traditional notions of corporate law in assessing the liability of parent corporations or individual officers,[95] the clear trend has been to ignore these traditional concepts and determine liability based on CERCLA's developing control test.

4.2.3 Bar Against Pre-Enforcement Review

As indicated above, the process of selecting a remedial action is lengthy and tremendously expensive. Frequently, PRPs, persons living near a site, and environmental groups disagree with EPA's method of performing its studies or with the cleanup plan EPA has selected. For this reason, before EPA incurs the tremendous costs of implementing the remedial action it has selected, one or more of these groups may wish to challenge the action selected by filing a civil suit to enjoin performance of the remedy. CERCLA's provisions facilitating EPA's ability to obtain liability determinations against PRPs are complimented by provisions that, quite literally, make it impossible for these same PRPs, as well as citizens or environmental groups, to challenge EPA's remedial actions until a time of EPA's own choosing.

Section 113(h) limits the jurisdiction of courts to hear challenges to EPA response actions or administrative orders requiring PRPs to perform

---

[91]*United States v. NEPACCO*, 810 F.2d 726, 742 (8th Cir. 1986); *United States v. Bliss*, 20 Envtl. L. Rep. 20,879 (E.D. Mo. 1988).

[92]*United States v. NEPACCO*, 810 F.2d 726 (8th Cir. 1986); *New York v. Shore Realty Corp.*, 759 F.2d 1032 (2d Cir. 1985).

[93]*Vermont v. Staco Inc.*, 684 F. Supp. 822, 831-832 (D. Vt. 1988); *United States v. Kayser-Roth Corp.*, 910 F.2d 24 (1st Cir. 1990).

[94]*See United States v. Fleet Factors Corp.*, 901 F.2d 1550, 1556 (11th Cir. 1990).

[95]*E.g., Joslyn Corp. v. T.L. James & Co.*, 696 F. Supp. 222 (W.D. La. 1988), *aff'd*, 893 F.2d 80 (5th Cir. 1990).

cleanups.[96] Courts have jurisdiction to hear such matters *only* in the following situations:

1. section 107 cost recovery actions or actions for contribution;
2. actions to enforce a CERCLA section 106 administrative order or to seek penalties for violation of such an order;
3. actions for reimbursement under section 106(b)(2) (actions for private party reimbursement from the Superfund);
4. citizen suits under section 310 alleging that a removal action or remedial action violated CERCLA's provisions *after* such actions have been completed, except where a removal action is to be followed by a remedial action in which case the action may not be heard until the remedial action is concluded; or
5. actions brought by EPA under section 106 in which EPA is seeking an order compelling a party to perform a cleanup.

The courts have uniformly held that section 113(h) removes from their jurisdiction any cases seeking to challenge EPA's actions in situations other than those listed above.[97] Indeed, some courts have suggested that any judicial action which might interfere with EPA's ongoing cleanup actions cannot be heard, even if such actions do not directly challenge the remedial action selected.[98]

4.3 EPA's Enforcement Policy

EPA has always used its enforcement authority to pursue the recovery of cleanup costs and to seek judicial orders (consensual or involuntary) requiring PRPs to perform cleanups. However, within the last several years, EPA has adhered to a more aggressive enforcement policy. This policy evolved from a 1989 management review of the CERCLA program conducted by EPA.[99] In essence, EPA's announced policy is one of "enforcement first." Accordingly, when a site requires remediation and PRPs are identified, it is EPA's stated policy to require the PRPs to clean up the site, rather than conduct the cleanup with Superfund monies. EPA's policy is to issue administrative orders under CERCLA section 106 to PRPs prior to the performance of a cleanup by EPA.[100] To support its "enforcement first" policy, EPA has increased its enforcement staff to handle the projected increase in enforcement actions.

---

[96] *See infra* section 4.7.

[97] *E.g., Alabama v. United States Envtl. Protection Agency*, 871 F.2d 1548 (11th Cir. 1989); *Barmet Aluminum Corp. v. Thomas*, 730 F. Supp. 771 (W.D. Ky. 1990).

[98] *North Shore Gas Co. v. United States Envtl. Protection Agency*, 753 F. Supp. 1413 (N.D. Ill. 1990); *United States v. Cordova Chem. Co. of Michigan*, 750 F. Supp. 832 (W.D. Mich. 1990).

[99] United States Environmental Protection Agency, *A Management Review of The Superfund Program* (June 1989).

[100] *See infra* section 4.7.

EPA's "enforcement first" policy will probably lead to increased PRP-financed cleanups. This result is anticipated largely because of the threat of penalties associated with failure to comply with EPA's administrative orders.

4.4 Identifying Responsible Parties

4.4.1 PRP Search

Before it can initiate an enforcement action, EPA must first identify those parties responsible for a site's cleanup. Because many CERCLA sites are the result of disposal activities by hundreds of companies, EPA has developed a highly structured procedure for identifying these companies. EPA initially conducts what is referred to as a "Potentially Responsible Party (PRP) Search." This search is ordinarily performed by an EPA contractor. The process involves obtaining and organizing all available documents associated with the site's operation (for example, invoices, manifests, trip tickets) to determine which entity sent a certain substance to the site.[101] A computer data base, reflecting the quantity and nature of wastes contributed by each responsible party, is often created as a result of this process.

4.4.2 CERCLA Section 104(e)

EPA is aided in its ability to identify PRPs by section 104(e) of CERCLA. This section authorizes EPA to issue information requests requiring a party to provide information to EPA concerning: the nature and quantity of materials it may have disposed of at a site; the nature and extent of any release of a hazardous substance at the site; and information concerning its ability to pay for the cleanup.[102] Section 104(e) also gives EPA the authority to obtain access to vessels and facilities to inspect and copy documents,[103] to enter and conduct sampling at such locations,[104] and to issue orders directing compliance with such requests.[105] Penalties for failure to comply with any request made pursuant to CERCLA section 104(e) can amount to $25,000 per day.[106]

EPA's use of CERCLA section 104(e) information requests is a routine step in the investigative process. Section 104(e) responses form a significant basis for EPA's judgment as to the relative liability of parties. Moreover, since responses to these requests are publicly available, the information they contain may be used by PRPs at multiparty sites to institute contribu-

---

[101]*See* United States Environmental Protection Agency, OSWER Directive 9834.6, *Potentially Responsible Party Search Manual* (1987).
[102]42 U.S.C. § 9604(e)(2).
[103]*Id.*
[104]42 U.S.C. § 9604(e)(4).
[105]42 U.S.C. § 9604(e)(5).
[106]*Id.*

tion actions or allocate damages in cost-recovery actions brought by the government.[107]

EPA has been successful in obtaining sizable penalties from parties who have failed to respond to section 104(e) requests for information.[108] The failure of a party to allow access or properly respond to a CERCLA section 104(e) request for information can result in significant penalties regardless of whether the denial was willful.[109]

4.5 Response Cost Recovery Actions

4.5.1 Overview

The vast majority of litigation under CERCLA is brought pursuant to section 107. This section permits the United States, individual states, or private parties to bring an action to recover costs they have incurred in responding to a release or a threatened release of a hazardous substance. At the same time, section 107 has been recognized as setting forth the basic liability scheme applicable to all causes of action under CERCLA. Traditionally, courts have found that the categories of parties liable under section 107 are also liable under CERCLA's other liability provisions.[110]

4.5.2 Categories of Liable Parties under CERCLA

A liable party under CERCLA section 107 can generally be viewed as any party having some involvement with the creation, handling, or disposal of a hazardous substance at a site. The categories of liable parties include:

1. current owners and operators of the facility or vessel involved;
2. former owners and operators of a facility who were involved with the facility during the time any hazardous substance was disposed at the facility;
3. persons who arranged for disposal or treatment of hazardous substances which they owned or possessed at a facility; and
4. persons who accepted hazardous substances for transport to disposal or treatment facilities or sites which they selected.[111]

In CERCLA jargon, the above categories of liable parties are referred to as: (1) owners and operators, (2) former owners and operators, (3) generators or arrangers, and (4) transporters.

---

[107]42 U.S.C. § 9604(e)(7).

[108]*United States v. Crown Roll Leaf, Inc.*, 29 Env't Rep. Cas. (BNA) 2025 (D.N.J. 1989)($142,000 penalty).

[109]*B.F. Goodrich Co. v. Murtha*, 697 F. Supp. 89 (D. Conn 1988); *United States v. Crown Roll Leaf, Inc.*, 29 Env't Rep. Cas. (BNA) 2025 (D.N.J. 1989).

[110]*United States v. Bliss*, 667 F. Supp. 1298, 1313 (E.D. Mo. 1987).

[111]42 U.S.C. § 9607(a)(1)-(a)(4).

Since CERCLA 107(a) does little more than generally identify the categories of liable parties, it has been left to the courts to address in detail how a party may fit within each category.

4.5.2.1 *Current Owners and Operators*

The first category of liable parties, current facility owners and operators, is the easiest type of liable party to identify. A current owner or operator is the owner or operator at the time a cleanup is performed or at the time litigation is initiated.[112] A current owner or operator is liable regardless of whether it had any involvement in the handling, disposal, or treatment of hazardous wastes at the facility or whether hazardous substances were disposed of at the facility during its period of ownership or operation.[113]

There are few exceptions to current owner/operator liability under CERCLA. One exception exists for state or local governments. Unless they have caused a release or threatened release, state and local governments are not liable as owners or operators where they acquire ownership or control of property involuntarily through bankruptcy, tax delinquency, abandonment, or other circumstances associated with their function as sovereign.[114] An additional exception exists to protect the banking industry. Under the exception, those parties "who, without participating in the management of a vessel or facility, [hold] indicia of ownership primarily to protect [their] security interest . . ." are exempted from owner/operator liability.[115]

Because in some cases it is inequitable to find current owners and operators liable where they have merely acquired a facility after all disposal activities have ceased, Congress created in the 1986 SARA amendments what is known as the "innocent landowner" defense. This defense is available when a current owner or operator can establish that it did not know or have reason to know at the time of purchase that any hazardous substance had been disposed of at the facility. In establishing this lack of knowledge, the current owner or operator must show that before buying the property it undertook "all appropriate inquiry into the previous ownership and uses of the property consistent with good commercial or customary practice . . . ."[116] The defense becomes unavailable if the property is later transferred to another party without the owner/operator disclosing any knowledge of on-site waste disposal gained during his ownership or possession.[117]

---

[112]*City of Philadelphia v. Stepan Chem. Co.*, 18 Envtl. L. Rep. 20133 (E.D. Pa. 1987).

[113]*United States v. Tyson*, 25 Env't Rep. Cas. (BNA) 1897, 1905 (E.D. Pa. 1986).

[114]42 U.S.C. § 9601(20)(D).

[115]42 U.S.C. § 9601(20)(A).

[116]*See* 42 U.S.C. § 9601(35).

[117]42 U.S.C. § 9601(35)(C).

As one may imagine, the "innocent landowner" defense has created a windfall for environmental consulting firms. An entire industry has been built around the defense as corporations have increasingly called upon these firms to conduct the "due diligence" investigations necessary to establish the "appropriate inquiry" required by the defense.

The expansive nature of current owner and operator liability is best reflected in CERCLA's caselaw. Courts have found lessees liable as "owners."[118] Courts also have found corporate officials who actively participated in their companies' management and disposal activities to be "operators" under CERCLA.[119] Parent corporations have been found liable as owners or operators at sites held by subsidiaries where it has been shown that the parents exercised influence over the subsidiaries' management and waste disposal.[120] It has been held that a lender who actively participates in the business of its borrower or whose "involvement with the management of the borrower's facility is sufficiently broad to support the inference that it could affect hazardous waste-disposal decisions . . ." can be an owner or operator of the borrower's facility.[121] State agencies may even be liable as owner/operators when they have actively engaged in activities at sites which have made site conditions worse or led to further releases.[122]

4.5.2.2 *Former Owners and Operators*

CERCLA's liability provisions addressing former owners and operators are ostensibly designed to reach former owners and operators who owned the facility when the disposal of hazardous substances occurred.[123] Unless "disposal" occurred while these parties owned or operated the site, the courts have found them not liable.[124]

Logically one might conclude that a former owner or operator cannot be liable unless there has actually been waste handling and discharge of hazardous substances into the environment during its period of ownership or operation. However, such has not always been the case, in part because the courts have disagreed on what constitutes "disposal."

Some courts have given the term "disposal" a broad meaning. They have suggested that "disposal" can occur in situations where previously

---

[118] *United States v. South Carolina Recycling & Disposal Inc. ("SCRDI")*, 653 F. Supp. 984, 1003 (D.S.C. 1984).

[119] *New York v. Shore Realty Corp.*, 759 F.2d 1032 (2d Cir. 1984).

[120] *United States v. Kayser-Roth Corporation*, 910 F.2d 24 (1st Cir. 1990). *But see Joslyn Corp. v. T.L. James & Co.*, 893 F.2d 80, 83 (5th Cir. 1990).

[121] *United States v. Fleet Factors Corp.*, 901 F.2d 1550, 1557 (11th Cir. 1990).

[122] *CPC Int'l Inc. v. Aerojet-General Corp.*, 731 F. Supp. 783, 788 (W.D. Mich. 1989). *But see United States v. Dart Indus.*, 847 F.2d 144 (4th Cir. 1988)(government entity not liable under CERCLA for activities related to regulatory function).

[123] 42 U.S.C. § 9607(a)(2).

[124] *E.g., New York v. Shore Realty Corp.*, 759 F.2d 1032, 1044 (2d Cir. 1985).

discharged hazardous substances continue to migrate at a site.[125] This interpretation is based upon the fact that, under CERCLA, "disposal" is defined by reference to its definition under RCRA and includes "the discharge, deposit, injection, dumping, spilling, leaking or placing of any solid waste or hazardous waste into or on any land or water . . . ."[126] Under this definition, courts have found that continued migration of hazardous substances constitutes "disposal."[127] Thus, under this concept, former owners/operators can be liable regardless of whether they had any role in disposal activities or even knew that hazardous substances were migrating while they owned the property.

Other courts have taken a more restrictive view of "disposal" for purposes of former owner/operator liability. They have found that continued migration of hazardous substances alone is not adequate. Rather, liability attaches, in their view, only if hazardous substances were introduced into the environment during the former owner's or operator's association with the site.[128]

4.5.2.3 Generators or Arrangers

At most CERCLA sites, the "deepest pockets" fall within the third category of liable parties: "generators" or "arrangers." This is because at most major CERCLA sites many of these parties are Fortune 500 companies.

This category of liable party encompasses more than those who have merely produced or generated hazardous substances. By definition, it includes "any person who by contract, agreement, or otherwise *arranged for disposal or treatment* . . . of hazardous substances *owned or possessed* by such person . . . ."[129] Thus, the major issues associated with this category of liable parties involve what constitutes (1) an arrangement for disposal and (2) ownership or possession of hazardous substances.

Courts have broadly interpreted an "arrangement for disposal or treatment" to reach practically any situation where there has been a relationship between two entities involving the handling and ultimate disposal of a waste containing hazardous substances. Indeed, to be liable as a generator or arranger, a party need not have intended or known that the disposal of hazardous substances would result from the arrangement.[130]

Aside from the traditional situation where the generator of a hazardous substance has arranged for its disposal, "arrangements" deemed sufficient to trigger liability have included: selling a waste material containing hazardous substances to another party for its use in its business,[131]

---

[125]*CPC Int'l Inc. v. Aerojet-General Corp.*, 759 F. Supp. 1269 (W.D. Mich. 1991).

[126]42 U.S.C. § 6903(3).

[127]*United States v. Waste Indus.*, 734 F.2d 159, 164 (4th Cir. 1984).

[128]*Ecodyne Corp. v. Shah*, 718 F. Supp. 1454 (N.D. Cal. 1989).

[129]42 U.S.C. § 9607(a)(3).

[130]*Florida Power & Light v. Allis-Chalmers Corp.*, 893 F.2d 1313 (11th Cir. 1990).

[131]*United States v. A&F Materials Co.*, 582 F. Supp. 842 (S.D. Ill. 1984).

contracting for the disposal of hazardous substances as fill at a construction site,[132] and entering into an agreement for the production of chemicals from furnished raw materials while knowing that the second party's production would lead to the disposal of hazardous substances.[133]

There have been few situations where courts have not found an "arrangement" to exist where the ultimate disposal of a hazardous substance has occurred. One situation where an arrangement has not been found is the sale by one company to another of a useful product (as opposed to a waste) containing hazardous substances.[134] Thus, it appears that characterizing the material sold as a "waste" is important in determining liability under this aspect of the generator or arranger provision.

Generally, courts have tended to ignore CERCLA's apparent requirement that a generator or arranger must have *owned or possessed* the hazardous substance for which there has been an arrangement for disposal. In order to find liability, courts have relied on concepts such as "constructive possession." "Constructive possession" exists when a party has the authority to control the handling and disposal of hazardous substances. Consequently, a waste broker who arranges for disposal can be liable as a generator or arranger despite the lack of actual ownership or possession.[135]

Responding to the nearly impossible burdens of proof which would arise if they had to do so, courts have universally held that plaintiffs need not "fingerprint" a generator's or arranger's hazardous substances at a site. It is sufficient to show that there are hazardous substances "like" those of the generator or arranger at the site and that there is evidence showing that the generator's or arranger's hazardous substances were sent to the site.[136]

4.5.2.4 Transporters

The final category of liable parties under CERCLA encompasses those who have transported a hazardous substance to a site from which there has been a release or threatened release.[137] Parties in this category are typically commercial waste haulers.

Section 107(a)(4), which addresses transporter liability, defines a liable party as one "who accepts or accepted any hazardous substances for transport to disposal or treatment facilities or sites selected by such person from which there is a release or a threatened release." Thus, under this

---

[132]*Jersey City Redevelopment Auth. v. PPG Indus.*, 655 F. Supp. 1257 (D.N.J. 1987).

[133]*United States v. Aceto Chem. Corp.*, 699 F. Supp. 1384 (S.D. Iowa) *aff'd*, 872 F.2d 1373 (8th Cir. 1989).

[134]*Florida Power & Light Co. v. Allis-Chalmers Corp.*, 893 F.2d 1313 (11th Cir. 1990).

[135]*United States v. Bliss*, 667 F. Supp. 1298 (E.D. Mo. 1987).

[136]*E.g., United States v. Wade*, 577 F. Supp. 1326 (E.D. Pa. 1983).

[137]42 U.S.C. § 9607(a)(4).

section a transporter is liable *only if it selected the disposal or treatment site.*[138]

Determining whether transporter site selection has occurred is largely a case-by-case analysis. Any involvement in helping a generator select where to dispose of its waste may be sufficient. The mere fact that a transporter has taken waste to the only state-licensed disposal facility available does not necessarily mean that a transporter did not participate in site selection, particularly when the transporter helped smaller generators identify the facility.[139] Both private haulers and common carriers can be found liable as transporters if they participated in site selection.[140]

4.5.3 Elements of CERCLA Cost Recovery Case

In addition to establishing that a party fits within one of the categories of liable parties, the elements of liability in a CERCLA section 107 cost recovery action include the following:

1. a release or threatened release
2. of a hazardous substance
3. from a vessel or facility
4. which has led to the incurrence of response costs.

Elements 1, 2 and 3 have been discussed in depth earlier in this chapter. The fourth element—incurrence of response costs—warrants greater discussion at this point.

4.5.3.1 *What Constitutes Recoverable Response Costs?*

What constitutes a recoverable response cost is largely determined by reference to CERCLA's definition of "response." CERCLA section 101(25) defines "response" as meaning "remove, removal, remedy, and remedial action, [where] all such terms (including the terms "removal" and "remedial action) include enforcement activities related thereto."[141] "Response costs" thus incorporate any costs associated with a "removal" or "remedial action."

Specific examples of recoverable response costs include costs associated with sampling and monitoring to assess and evaluate the extent of a release or threatened release;[142] costs associated with detecting, identifying, controlling, and disposing of hazardous substances;[143] and costs for the services of environmental consultants and attorneys in preparation of an

---

[138] *E.g., United States v. Hardage*, 761 F. Supp. 1501 (W.D. Okl. 1990). *See also* United States Environmental Protection Agency, *Policy For Enforcement Actions Against Transporters Under CERCLA* (December 23, 1985).

[139] *See generally United States v. Hardage*, 750 F. Supp. 1444 (W.D. Okl. 1990).

[140] *Id.*

[141] 42 U.S.C. § 9601(25).

[142] *E.g., Cadillac Fairview/California, Inc. v. Dow Chem. Co.*, 840 F.2d 691, 695 (9th Cir. 1988).

[143] *Brewer v. Ravan*, 680 F. Supp. 1176 (M.D. Tenn. 1988).

RI/FS and other investigatory and planning activities.[144] While some courts have found otherwise,[145] the majority have also held that EPA's indirect costs (for example, administrative and overhead) are also recoverable response costs.[146] Certain costs have been found not to be recoverable response costs. They include medical monitoring costs[147] as well as lost profits and general damages.[148]

Controversy has revolved around the issue whether attorney fees associated with bringing a CERCLA 107 action are recoverable. Since the definition of "response" includes costs associated with "enforcement," very little dispute has arisen as to whether the EPA can recover its attorney fees. Courts have universally held that Department of Justice (DOJ) and EPA attorney fees and litigation costs associated with bringing a CERCLA action are recoverable response costs.[149] However, the issue has not been resolved with regard to private attorney fees. Many courts have found that private attorney fees are not recoverable response costs.[150] Conversely, other courts have indicated that such costs are recoverable. In doing so, they have suggested that "enforcement" costs are not limited to the government's actions, but extend to private parties seeking to enforce their right in a CERCLA cost recovery action.[151]

As indicated in section 4.2.1, before any response cost is recoverable under section 107, it must be shown that the release or threatened release caused the incurrence of the costs. For example, an adjoining landowner to a site with a threatened release would not be entitled to response costs for the installation of monitoring wells if the wells were installed in response to another unrelated event.[152] This causation requirement is particularly applicable to private cost recovery actions since the CERCLA section authorizing such actions limits recovery to "necessary costs of response."[153] Presumably, "unnecessary" costs are not recoverable; in fact, some courts have suggested that if an action after objective evaluation is not reasonable, the costs should not be recoverable.[154]

---

[144]*Cabot Corp. v. United States Envtl. Protection Agency*, 677 F. Supp. 823, 827 (E.D. Pa. 1988).

[145]*United States v. Ottati & Goss*, 694 F. Supp. 977, 994-997 (D.N.H. 1988).

[146]*United States v. Hardage*, 733 F. Supp. 1424, 1438-1439 (W.D. Okl. 1989); *United States v. R.W. Meyers, Inc.*, 889 F.2d 1497, 1503 (6th Cir. 1989).

[147]*Coburn v. Sun Chem. Corp.*, 28 Env't Rep. Cas. (BNA) 1665 (E.D. Pa. 1988).

[148]*Mola Dev. Corp. v. United States*, 22 Env't Rep. Cas. (BNA) 1443 (C.D. Cal. 1985).

[149]*E.g., United States v. South Carolina Recycling & Disposal, Inc. ("SCRDI")*, 653 F. Supp. 984, 1009 (D.S.C. 1984).

[150]*Fallowfield Dev. Corp. v. Strunk*, No. 89-8644 (E.D. Pa. April 23, 1990).

[151]*General Elec. Co. v. Litton Bus. Automation Sys.*, 920 F.2d 1415 (8th Cir. 1990).

[152]*See Dedham Water Co. v. Cumberland Farms Dairy, Inc.*, 22 Chem. Waste Litig. Rept. 1130 (D. Mass. 1991).

[153]42 U.S.C. § 9607(a)(4)(B).

[154]*Amoco Oil Co. v. Borden, Inc.*, 889 F.2d 664 (5th Cir. 1989).

4.5.3.2 *Compliance with the NCP*

In both private and EPA cost recovery actions, an essential element is that the party seeking such costs must have complied with the provisions of the NCP in incurring such costs. While both EPA and private parties must comply with the NCP, courts have interpreted CERCLA to create a different burden of proof with regard to establishing NCP compliance in each instance. CERCLA provides that EPA is entitled to all costs "not inconsistent" with the NCP,[155] while in private actions such costs must be "consistent" with the NCP.[156] This statutory difference has meant that, in EPA's cost recovery actions, a defendant must prove response costs were inconsistent with the NCP,[157] while the plaintiff seeking response costs in private actions bears the burden of establishing whether its costs were consistent with the NCP.[158]

While courts have uniformly found that failure to comply with the NCP is a barrier to the recovery of response costs,[159] the extent of compliance necessary has been subject to differing interpretations. Since the government is accorded a presumption of consistency, and challenges to its actions are limited to an administrative record—reversible only when arbitrary and capricious—it is not surprising that cases addressing the issue of NCP consistency have largely been in the context of private cost recovery actions. Two approaches for assessing the degree of necessary compliance have evolved. One approach holds that a private party must *strictly* comply with the NCP in order to recover its response costs.[160] Other courts have taken a less restrictive view. They have held that only "substantial compliance" with the NCP is required.[161] This more reasonable approach will likely be the standard of review in the future, particularly because the 1990 NCP sets forth a "substantial compliance" requirement for private response actions.[162]

It should be noted that the NCP creates a presumption that private party costs incurred in complying with a cleanup mandate from EPA are consistent with the NCP.[163] This presumption has been accepted by some courts.[164]

---

[155] 42 U.S.C. § 9607(a)(4)(A).

[156] 42 U.S.C. § 9607(a)(4)(B).

[157] *See United States v. NEPACCO*, 810 F.2d 726 (8th Cir. 1986).

[158] *Amland Prop. Corp. v. ALCOA*, 711 F. Supp. 784, 797 (D.N.J. 1989).

[159] *E.g., Versatile Metals, Inc. v. Union Corp.*, 693 F. Supp. 1563, 1576 (E.D. Pa. 1988).

[160] *Amland Prop. Corp. v. ALCOA*, 711 F. Supp. 784 (D.N.J. 1989).

[161] *Wickland Oil Terminals v. ASARCO, Inc.*, 792 F.2d 887 (9th Cir. 1986).

[162] 40 C.F.R. § 300.700(c)(3)(i).

[163] 40 C.F.R. § 300.700(c)(3)(i).

[164] *United States v. Western Processing Co.*, No. C89-214M (W.D. Wash. July 31, 1991).

4.6 CERCLA Section 106 Abatement Actions

The second major cause of action available under CERCLA arises under CERCLA section 106.[165] This section authorizes EPA to seek judicial relief requiring a PRP to abate an imminent and substantial endangerment to the public health or welfare or the environment because of an actual or threatened release of a hazardous substance from a facility. Such an action may be maintained only by EPA and is not available to private parties.[166] Thus, the purpose of a CERCLA section 106 action for judicial relief is to require liable parties at a site to pay for a cleanup, thus avoiding commitment of Superfund monies for the cleanup.

Most courts have found the general classes of liable parties and elements of proof under CERCLA section 106 the same as those under section 107.[167] The most significant difference is that under section 106 there must also be a situation which "may" present an "imminent and substantial endangerment." To date, this difference between the two causes of action has had little apparent impact. EPA has routinely filed suits containing both causes of action. While paying lip service to the "imminent and substantial endangerment" requirement of section 106, courts have had little difficulty finding that such an endangerment exists since the standard necessary to establish an "imminent and substantial endangerment" is minimal. Caselaw has construed "imminent" to mean, not that the harm must be immediate, but that it could arise in the future if unabated.[168] Similarly, "endangerment" has been construed to mean, not actual harm, but only a threat of a potential harm.[169] It is therefore difficult to imagine a situation with a release or threatened release without there also being an "imminent and substantial endangerment."

Notwithstanding the above, there are differences between CERCLA sections 106 and 107 which can lead to different results. Section 106 provides for equitable relief and states that district courts "shall have jurisdiction to grant such relief as the public interest and the *equities of the case* may require." As a result, some courts have held that certain equitable defenses not available in a section 107 action are available in section 106 cases.[170] A minority of courts have also refused to limit their review of a remedy in a CERCLA section 106 action to EPA's administrative record. In doing so, they have stressed the equitable nature of a section 106 action and the fact that CERCLA section 113's language prohibiting pre-enforcement

---

[165]42 U.S.C. § 9606.

[166]*Velsicol Chem. Corp. v. Reilly Tar & Chem. Corp.*, 21 Env't Rep. Cas. (BNA) 2118, 2121 (E.D. Tenn. 1984).

[167]*E.g., United States v. Price*, 577 F. Supp. 1103, 1113 (D.N.J. 1983). *But see United States v. Wade*, 546 F. Supp. 785, 794 (E.D. Pa. 1982).

[168]*B.F. Goodrich v. Murtha*, 697 F. Supp. 89, 95 (D. Conn. 1988).

[169]*United States v. Conservation Chem. Co.*, 619 F. Supp. 162, 175 (W.D. Mo. 1985).

[170]*United States v. Hardage*, 26 Env't Rep. Cas. (BNA) 1049 (W.D. Okl. 1987).

review limits the scope of judicial review to EPA's administrative record only in situations "concerning the adequacy of any response action *taken or ordered*" by EPA.[171]

Finally, the type of cleanup available under section 106 is arguably different from that available under section 107. Section 106 is designed to "abate" an endangerment, while section 107 is designed to obtain costs associated with responding to a release or threatened release. Full site remediation, which is clearly available under section 107, may not be warranted to "abate" an endangerment in every case. Some courts have noted this limitation.[172] Thus, despite the fact that EPA has indicated it can use section 106 to obtain the same types of cleanups available under section 107, the scope of cleanup under section 106 remains at issue.[173]

4.7 CERCLA Section 106 Administrative Orders

4.7.1 Recent Popularity of Administrative Orders

In addition to authorizing the injunctive relief mechanism,[174] section 106 of CERCLA authorizes EPA to issue a unilateral administrative order to compel a private party to undertake a response action. This enforcement tool was seldom used before SARA's enactment. By 1989, however, in response to criticism that its enforcement program was not sufficiently aggressive and a clearly expressed congressional desire to encourage settlement of lawsuits and private funding of cleanup work, EPA began to use section 106 orders routinely as part of its "enforcement first" policy.

The section 106 order is EPA's most potent enforcement tool and a powerful settlement incentive. CERCLA authorizes EPA to impose stiff penalties for a party's failure to comply with an order, including potential treble damages. Moreover, judicial review is unavailable until EPA decides to initiate an enforcement or cost recovery action. EPA will normally issue section 106 administrative orders only to those parties which are the largest contributors of waste to a site, are financially viable, and against which there is substantial evidence of liability.

4.7.2 Authority to Issue Administrative Orders

Authority for the issuance of a unilateral administrative order is contained in section 106. This section sets forth the following legal prerequisites for issuance of an order:

(a) the existence of:

    (i) an actual or threatened "release"

---

[171]*United States v. Hardage*, 663 F. Supp. 1280 (W.D. Okl. 1987).

[172]*E.g., United States v. NEPACCO*, 579 F. Supp. 823, 840 n.17 (W.D. Mo. 1984).

[173]*See* United States Environmental Protection Agency, *Memorandum On Use and Issuance of Administrative Orders Under Section 106(a) of CERCLA* (September 8, 1983), 41 Env't Rep. 2931, 2935.

[174]*See supra* section 4.6

(ii) of a hazardous substance

(iii) from a facility;

(b) an administrative finding that there is or may be an imminent or substantial endangerment; and

(c) relief that "may be necessary" to abate the imminent hazard.

EPA's finding of imminent and substantial endangerment and its determination of "necessary relief" required to abate the endangerment may well be in dispute. However, PRPs have little opportunity to challenge the existence of these requirements until after the PRP fulfills its obligation under the order or EPA seeks enforcement of the order against a noncomplying party.

4.7.3 Judicial Review of Administrative Orders

A party believing it may have good cause for its refusal to comply with a section 106 order cannot immediately obtain judicial relief to set aside the order. Under CERCLA, the timing of judicial review is essentially determined by EPA. As indicated, section 113 provides that no federal court shall have jurisdiction to review any order issued under section 106 until EPA seeks to enforce its order or sues to recover the costs of undertaking the response action directed in the order.[175]

In addition, CERCLA does not provide a party with a formal opportunity to file public comments that criticize findings made in the order. Instead, it is EPA's policy to offer the respondent a limited opportunity to meet with the agency to discuss the order. The scope of this conference is very narrow. According to an EPA policy statement, the conference is "not intended to be a forum for discussing liability issues or whether the order should have been issued. Instead, the conference is designed to ensure that the order is based on complete and accurate information, and to facilitate understanding of implementation."[176]

Once a party is able to obtain judicial review, the district court will use a deferential standard of review in considering any arguments the recipient might have about the merit of or necessity for EPA's selected response action. The court's review will be limited to material in the administrative record, and the selected response action will be upheld unless the court finds it to be arbitrary, capricious, or not in accordance with law.[177] If not already determined, issues of liability will be tried *de novo*. To the extent they are not connected to the merits or "adequacy" of EPA's chosen response action, issues relating to the existence of "sufficient cause" should also be tried *de novo*.[178] It is unclear under which standard issues relating to the

---

[175]*See supra* section 4.6.

[176]United States Environmental Protection Agency, *Guidance on CERCLA Section 106(a) Unilateral Administrative Orders for Remedial Design and Remedial Action*, OSWER Dir. # 9833.01-a (March 13, 1990).

[177]*See* 42 U.S.C. §§ 9613(j), 9621(a).

[178] *See infra* section 4.7.5.

EPA's legal authority to issue the order—the existence of an imminent and substantial endangerment, for instance—would be determined.

4.7.4 Reimbursement from the Superfund

In an attempt to encourage expeditious compliance with section 106 orders, CERCLA provides that a party who complies with a cleanup order may file a claim against the Superfund to recover costs of complying with the order. However, a party may recover only if that party can show that it was not a liable party under section 107, or that the response action ordered was arbitrary, capricious, or contrary to law.

4.7.5 Penalties for Failure to Comply; Defenses

A party that refuses or fails to comply with a section 106 order may be assessed up to $25,000 per day of the violation.[179] In addition, an unjustified failure or refusal to comply may also result in punitive damages equal to, but not more than, three times the amount of costs incurred as a result of the party's failure to take the action required by the order.[180] Passages in CERCLA's legislative history indicate that the amount of punitive damages will be set by the court, exercising its equitable discretion.[181]

A party may avoid the imposition of penalties by establishing that it had "sufficient cause" for its failure to comply with the order.[182] Only a few cases to date have had occasion to construe the term "sufficient cause"; those that have rely heavily upon statements contained in CERCLA's legislative history.[183] Under these decisions, the party which has failed to comply with the order bears the burden of demonstrating that it has a *reasonable, objectively grounded* belief that:

1. it was not a liable party (as defined in section 107) under CERCLA, or that it had a defense to such liability under section 107(b);

2. it was a *de minimis* contributor to the release or threatened release;

3. the order was legally invalid for some reason (for example, no evidence of an imminent or substantial endangerment);

4. financial, technical, or other inability prevented its compliance with the order[184]; or

---

[179]42 U.S.C. § 9606(b)(1).

[180]42 U.S.C. § 9607(c)(3). *See also United States v. Lecarreaux & Lightman Drum*, 1992 U.S. Lexis 9365 (D.N.J. Feb. 18, 1992); *EPA Policy on Civil Penalties*, 17 Env't L. Rep. 35083 (February 16, 1984).

[181]*See Solid State Circuits v. United States Envtl. Protection Agency*, 812 F.2d 383 (8th Cir. 1987).

[182]42 U.S.C. §§ 9606(b)(1), 9607(c)(3).

[183]*See Solid State Circuits v. United States Envtl. Protection Agency*, 812 F.2d 383 (8th Cir 1987)(providing extensive discussion of defense).

[184]*See e.g., United States v. Parsons*, 723 F. Supp. 757, 763 (N.D. Ga. 1989).

5. the response action ordered was not cost-effective as required by CERCLA section 121(b), or was otherwise inconsistent with the NCP.[185]

Consequently, in order to challenge a section 106 order, "a party must show that the applicable provisions of CERCLA, EPA regulations and policy statements, and any formal or informal hearings or guidance the EPA may provide, give rise to an objectively reasonable belief in the invalidity or inapplicability of the cleanup order."[186]

Given the provisions described above, parties who receive an administrative 106 order have few options under the statute. A party may either comply with the order or face judicial action by EPA. If a party chooses to comply with the order, he may, after fulfilling his obligations under the order, seek reimbursement under section 106(b)(2)(A). The major advantage with this approach is the avoidance of penalties. However, this advantage may be offset by unpredictability about the size of the financial commitment necessary to comply and the lengthy period that funds will be tied up before a reimbursement claim is considered. In the event of noncompliance, the issues would be addressed in a later district court action by EPA to enforce the order or, if EPA funds and implements the response action itself, to recover its response costs plus penalties and punitive damages.

4.8 Defenses to Liability

Generally speaking, there are few affirmative defenses available in a CERCLA action. This is particularly true with regard to CERCLA section 107 cost recovery actions. While the defenses available in a section 106 abatement action appear to be broader, and may include certain equitable defenses, the caselaw in the area is unsettled.

4.8.1 Statutory Defenses

CERCLA section 107 limits affirmative defenses to situations where a release was caused solely by:

1. an act of God;
2. an act of war; or
3. an act or omission of a third party (other than an employee, agent, or party with whom there is a contractual relationship) as long as the defendant exercised due care and took precautions against foreseeable acts of the third party.[187]

Many courts have found that these are the only affirmative defenses available in a CERCLA section 107 action.[188] For this reason, EPA has often

---

[185]*Solid State Circuits v. United States Envtl. Protection Agency*, 812 F.2d 383, 391 n.11 (8th Cir. 1987).

[186]*Solid State Circuits v. United States Envtl. Protection Agency*, 812 F.2d 383, 392 (8th Cir 1978).

[187]42 U.S.C. § 9607(b).

[188]*E.g., United States v. Rohm & Haas Co.*, 669 F. Supp. 672, 675 (D.N.J. 1987).

been successful in having any other defenses raised by a defendant struck early during enforcement proceedings.[189] Nevertheless, in most CERCLA actions a variety of defenses, including many equitable defenses (for example, due care, compliance with existing standards, estoppel), have been raised. In some cases, the courts have appeared willing to go beyond CERCLA's three statutory defenses and consider these additional defenses on the theory that they raise issues relating to apportionment.[190] Thus, despite CERCLA's limited statutory defenses, it is always to a defendant's advantage to raise additional defenses.

The necessity of asserting other equitable defenses is more apparent when one considers the limited instances in which the statutory defenses are available. Each defense is narrowly written and has been narrowly construed by the courts.

There is little caselaw interpreting the *act of God defense*. What caselaw exists suggests that it is to be interpreted narrowly. For example, the defense requires exceptional events rather than mere natural occurrences.[191]

There has also been little discussion of the *act of war defense* by the courts. It remains unclear whether the defense will be limited to releases caused by combat or whether it may extend to releases caused by increased production demands resulting from a war. If consistent with the narrow interpretation given other defenses, it can be expected that the act of war defense will be limited to releases caused by combat.[192]

Most litigation concerning these defenses has focused on the *third party defense*. Since the defense is available only when the third party "solely" caused the release, any involvement, however slight, which the defendant may have had in contributing to the release will make the defense unavailable.[193] In addition, few situations will arise in which the third party will not have had a direct or indirect[194] contractual relationship with the defendant in some way. Leases, employment contracts, waste hauling contracts, and real estate sales contracts can each constitute a connection to the third party which will nullify the defense.[195] The third party defense's most useful application appears to arise in the innocent landowner situation.[196]

---

[189]*E.g., United States v. Dickerson*, 640 F. Supp. 448, 450-451 (D. Md. 1986).

[190]*United States v. Hardage*, 116 F.R.D. 460, 463 (W.D. Okl. 1987).

[191]*United States v. Stringfellow*, 661 F. Supp. 1053, 1061 (C.D. Cal. 1987).

[192]*See FMC Corp. v. United States Dep't of Commerce*, Civ. Action No. 90-1761 (E.D. Pa. February 19, 1991).

[193]42 U.S.C. § 9607(b).

[194]*United States v. Hooker Chem. & Plastics Corp.*, 680 F. Supp. 546 (W.D.N.Y. 1988)(suggesting indirect relationship sufficient to bar third-party defense).

[195]*E.g., United States v. Tyson*, 25 Env't Rep. Cas. (BNA) 1897 (E.D. Pa. 1986).

[196] *See supra* section 4.5.1.1.

4.8.2 Equitable and Other "Defenses"

As indicated, defendants frequently have raised many "defenses" in addition to the three statutory defenses. Some of these defenses have been based upon alleged procedural violations by EPA. Others have been what may be generically categorized as "equitable" defenses. Courts have divided over the availability of these additional defenses. Generally, defenses raising procedural omissions (for example, failure to provide a private party the opportunity to perform a cleanup, failure to notify responsible parties, failure to list a site on the NPL) have been unsuccessful.[197]

Defendants have had more success in raising equitable defenses such as estoppel, unclean hands, and laches. While some courts have ruled that these defenses are unavailable in a CERCLA section 107 action,[198] others have suggested that they may be asserted.[199] Regardless, equitable defenses are more likely to be available in a CERCLA section 106 proceeding since the court is required to render its decision based on the "equities" of the case.[200]

4.8.3 Statute of Limitations

CERCLA contained no specific statute of limitations provision prior to the 1986 SARA amendments. This omission was remedied with the addition of section 113(g), which contains limitation periods for cost recovery actions, natural resource damages, and contribution actions.

With regard to cost recovery actions, section 113(g)(2) sets forth two limitations periods—one for removals and another for remedial actions. It also contains a "tacking" provision which extends the limitation period for removals when they are followed by a remedial action. Response cost claims flowing from a removal action must ordinarily be brought within three years after completion of the removal. However, the government may extend this period by finding that a waiver for continued response is needed. Claims flowing from a remedial action must be brought within six years "after initiation of physical on-site construction of the remedial action." The "tacking" provision arises when a remedial action is initiated within three years after completion of the removal action. In such a case, costs associated with the removal can be recovered with the remedial action costs. Because the limitations periods are tied to whether an event is a "removal" or "remedial action," correctly categorizing an action becomes critical to evaluating the appropriate limitations period.

The limitations period for natural resource damage claims[201] is three years after the latter of either: (1) the "date of the discovery of the loss

---

[197]*E.g., New York v. Shore Realty Corp.,* 759 F.2d 1032, 1046 (2d Cir. 1985). *But see Bulk Distribution Ctrs. v. Monsanto Co.,* 589 F. Supp. 1437, 1448 (S.D. Fla. 1984).

[198]*Kelley v. Thomas Solvent Co.,* 714 F. Supp. 1439, 1451 (W.D. Mich. 1989).

[199]*Mardan Corp. v. C.G.C. Music, Ltd.,* 600 F. Supp. 1049 (D. Ariz 1984).

[200]*United States v. Hardage,* 116 F.R.D. 460 (W.D. Okl. 1987).

[201] *See infra* section 4.10

and its connection with the release," or (2) the date of promulgation of natural resource damage assessment regulations.[202] Since the government's initial effort at promulgating final natural resource damage assessment regulations has been struck by the courts, there is debate over when the limitations period actually begins to run.[203] It has yet to be resolved whether the period runs from the initial, although judicially disapproved, promulgation of these rules or from their subsequent revision to deal with the courts' mandate.

Contribution actions for response costs or damages must be brought no more than three years after: (1) the date of judgment in any action under CERCLA for recovery of such costs or damages, or (2) the date of an administrative order or entry of a judicially approved settlement with respect to such costs or damages.

4.8.4 Divisibility

Traditionally, joint and several liability does not exist where the "harm" is divisible or reasonably capable of apportionment.[204] In such cases, each tortfeasor is liable only for the harm or portion of harm that it individually caused.

At most multiparty sites, responsible parties have had little success in avoiding joint and several liability by arguing that the harm caused is divisible or capable of apportionment.[205] Rather than hear a defendant's arguments on divisibility of harm during the liability phase of the case, many courts have tended to accept EPA's argument that the commingling of wastes renders the harm indivisible. Accordingly, in most cases involving multiparty sites, defendants have been unable to raise divisibility of harm as a partial or total defense to liability. Instead, they have been forced to raise the issue during secondary proceedings to allocate costs among those parties deemed jointly and severally liable. Thus, at sites where several parties have contributed high levels of a hazardous substance and others contributed *de minimis* levels of a far less hazardous substance, each is jointly and severally liable irrespective of its actual contribution.

In a 1992 decision, a federal circuit court demonstrated disapproval of the above approach. It found that commingled waste is not synonymous with "indivisible" harm and suggested that a PRP should be permitted a hearing during the liability phase of a proceeding to establish that the harm was divisible and that its waste could not have contributed to the release because of its relative toxicity, migratory potential, and synergistic capacity.[206] Should other courts follow this decision, defendants will be

---

[202] 42 U.S.C. § 9613(g)(1).

[203] *Ohio v. United States Dep't of Interior*, 880 F.2d 432 (D.C. Cir. 1989).

[204] Restatement (Second) of Torts, Sections 433A, 433B.

[205] *E.g., United States v. Chem-Dyne Corp.*, 572 F. Supp. 802 (S.D. Ohio 1983). *But see United States v. A&F Materials Co.*, 578 F. Supp. 1249 (S.D. Ill. 1984).

[206] *United States v. Alcan Aluminum Corp.*, 964 F.2d 252 (3d Cir. 1992).

provided a real opportunity in future CERCLA litigation involving multiparty sites to avoid the imposition of joint and several liability. In some cases, they may be able to avoid liability altogether. Needless to say, EPA is quite concerned about this decision's impact on its enforcement efforts since more liability hearings to assess divisibility are anticipated.

4.9 "Citizen Suit" Provisions

CERCLA, like other environmental statutes,[207] contains a "citizen suit" provision. This provision permits any "person" to initiate a civil action in two instances: (1) against any other person (including the United States) for violations of any standard, regulation, condition, requirement, or order effective under CERCLA; and (2) against any officer of the United States for failure to perform a nondiscretionary act under CERCLA.[208] With respect to the first type of action, a United States District Court may enforce the standard, regulation, condition, requirement, or order and impose civil penalties for such a violation. In the second type of action, the appropriate district court may order the officer to perform the act or duty.[209]

Prior to initiating a "citizen suit," one must first provide 60 days notice of the intended action to EPA, the alleged violator and, in certain instances, the state involved.[210] This requirement is jurisdictional.[211]

Both responsible parties and environmental groups have attempted to use the "citizen suit" provisions to obtain, either directly or indirectly, review of EPA's remedial action process. These attempts have consistently failed. CERCLA and decisions from the courts make clear that the provisions of CERCLA section 113(h), which limit judicial review of EPA's remedial actions, take precedence over the citizen suit provisions, even when the challenge is only to EPA's procedures in selecting a remedy and not to the remedy itself.[212]

4.10 Natural Resources Damages

The majority of CERCLA actions to date have involved the assessment of liability and damages for costs related to response actions associated with a release. However, the government is increasingly invoking claims under CERCLA's natural resources damages provision to recover costs associated with the loss of a contaminated area's natural resources.

---

[207] *See* 42 U.S.C. §§ 7604 (Clean Air Act), 33 U.S.C. § 1365 (Clean Water Act).

[208] 42 U.S.C. § 9659.

[209] 42 U.S.C. § 9659(c).

[210] 42 U.S.C. § 9659(a),(d)(1),(e).

[211] *Roe v. Wert*, 706 F. Supp. 788, 792 (W.D. Okl. 1989).

[212] *Schalk v. Reilly*, 900 F.2d 1091 (7th Cir.), *cert. den. sub nom.*, *Frey v. Reilly*, 111 S. Ct. 509 (1990).

4.10.1 Statutory Provision

Section 107(a)(4)(C) of CERCLA provides that responsible parties may be held liable for "damages for injury to, destruction of, or loss of natural resources, including the reasonable costs of assessing such injury, destruction, or loss resulting from such a release."[213] While the definition of natural resources is broad in scope and encompasses not only more commonly considered resources such as land, wildlife, fish, and biota, but also air, water, groundwater, drinking water supplies, and any other resources, it is limited to those resources owned, held in trust, or otherwise controlled by a state, the federal government, or Indian tribe. Hence, damages to private property are not recoverable.[214]

Monies recovered for natural resources damages are to be used for restoration or replacement of the resource or for acquisition of an equivalent resource.[215] Regulations interpreting CERCLA's natural resource provisions clearly indicate that natural resource damages are compensatory, rather than punitive, in nature.[216]

Although the government is not required to provide notice to a private party when it initiates a claim against the Superfund for natural resources,[217] CERCLA does contain further limitations on the recovery of natural resources damages. Section 107(f) prohibits recovery for natural resources losses identified in an environmental assessment and thus authorized by permit or license.[218] Moreover, unlike response actions, actions for the recovery of natural resources damages have limited retroactivity; under CERCLA, "[t]here shall be no recovery . . . where such damages and the release of a hazardous substance from which such damages resulted have occurred wholly before December 11, 1980 [the date of CERCLA's enactment]."[219]

4.10.2 Potential Plaintiffs

CERCLA identifies those parties which may assert natural resource damages claims. Specifically, CERCLA provides for designation of federal

---

[213] 42 U.S.C. § 9607(a)(4)(C).

[214] 42 U.S.C. § 9601(16). *See also Lutex v. Chromatex, Inc.*, 718 F. Supp. 413, 419 (M.D. Pa. 1989); *Ohio v. United States Dep't of the Interior*, 880 F.2d 432, 460-461 (D.C. Cir. 1989).

[215] 42 U.S.C. § 9607(f)(1).

[216] *See* 51 *Fed. Reg.* 27,674, at 52,127-52,128 (1986); *see also Ohio v. United States Dep't of Interior*, 880 F.2d 432, 474 (D.C. Cir. 1989).

[217] 42 U.S.C. § 9612(a). *See also Idaho v. Howmet Turbine Component Corp.*, 814 F.2d 1376, 1377 (9th Cir. 1987).

[218] 42 U.S.C. § 9607(f). *See also Idaho v. Hanna Mining Co.*, 882 F.2d 392, 395 (9th Cir. 1989).

[219] *Id. See also United States v. NEPACCO*, 579 F. Supp. 823, 839 (W.D. Mo. 1984), *aff'd in part and rev'd in part*, 810 F.2d 726 (8th Cir. 1986)(pre-CERCLA costs are not recoverable); *United States v. Wade*, 577 F. Supp. 1326 (E.D. Pa. 1983). *But see United States v. Shell Oil Co.*, 605 F. Supp. 1064 (D. Colo. 1985)(retroactivity permitted where damages continued after enactment).

or state "trustees" who are authorized to assess natural resource damages and bring actions for recovery of damages.[220] Although certain courts have extended "trusteeship" to include those municipalities specifically designated by a state, a municipality's ability to pursue natural resource damages remains questionable.[221] Double recovery is not permitted either where there are multiple trustees or where both cleanup and resources restoration costs are claimed.[222]

4.10.3 Historical Inactivity

Throughout the 1980s, the federal and the state governments initiated few actions to recover natural resource damages. This lack of activity resulted in part from section 107's prescription against retroactive application.[223] Moreover, until enactment of SARA, the federal and state governments had relatively easy access to Superfund monies to resolve natural resource damage claims. The monies could be used both to assess the injury to the natural resources as a result of a release and to restore or replace such resources.[224] However, as amended by SARA, CERCLA currently provides that "[n]o natural resource claim may be paid from the Superfund unless the President determines that the claimant has exhausted all administrative and judicial remedies to recover the amount of such claim from the person who may be liable under section 107."[225]

Further contributing to the limited use of CERCLA's natural resource provisions was the difficulty in characterizing the value of natural resources damaged or lost as a result of a release. Although CERCLA included provisions requiring assessment regulations at its enactment, the first of such regulations were not promulgated until 1986.

4.10.4 Assessment Regulations

Section 111 of CERCLA indicates that natural resource damages shall be assessed by those individuals indicated in the National Contingency Plan.[226] In keeping with this mandate, regulations governing such assessments were to be promulgated, including:

> identify[ing] the best available procedures to determine such damages, including both direct and indirect injury, destruction or loss and . . . tak[ing] into consideration factors, including, but not

---

[220] 42 U.S.C. § 9607(f)(2).

[221] *Compare City of New York v. Exxon*, 633 F. Supp. 609, 619 (S.D.N.Y. 1986)(permitting municipal trusteeship); *Mayor & Bd. of Aldermen of Boonton v. Drew Chem. Corp.*, 621 F. Supp. 663, 667 (D.N.J. 1985)(same) *with Town of Bedford v. Raytheon Corp.*, 755 F. Supp. 469 (D. Mass. 1991) (disallowing municipal trusteeship).

[222] 42 U.S.C. § 9607(f)(1).

[223] *See supra* section 4.8.

[224] 42 U.S.C. § 9611(c)(1), (2).

[225] 42 U.S.C. § 9611(b)(2)(A).

[226] 42 U.S.C. § 9611.

limited to, replacement value, use value and the ability of the ecosystem or resource to recover.[227]

In 1986 and 1987, the Department of Interior[228] promulgated two types of assessment regulations dependant upon the associated release: (1) Type A regulations ostensibly for assessing damages resulting from minor releases but actually limited to coastal and marine environment damage[229] and (2) Type B regulations for individual cases whose damages have been caused by more serious discharges.[230] Both sets of regulations became the subject of intense litigation, resulting in their being struck down and remanded to the Department of Interior for revision.[231]

Proposed in April 1991,[232] the new Type B regulations have engendered no less controversy than their predecessor.[233] Among the more vehemently controverted provisions has been the Department of the Interior's position that the three-year statute of limitations extended by SARA would not begin to run until the final promulgation of both the Type B and Type A regulations. Commenters contended that section 113(g)(1), the portion of the statute of limitations section regarding promulgation, had already begun to run from the date the regulations were initially promulgated despite the regulations being later struck and remanded by the court for revision.[234] As a result of comments received during the public comment period on the regulations, the Department of Interior indicated in April 1992 that it would consider yet again revising the proposed regulations.[235]

4.10.5 Prospect of Increased Use

Coupled with the stricter natural resource provisions enacted by SARA, the promulgation of the assessment regulations has substantially increased

---

[227] 42 U.S.C. § 9651(c)(2).

[228] *See* Exec. Order No. 12,316, 46 Fed. Reg. 42,237, 42,240 (1981)(designating Department of Interior as party to promulgate assessment regulations), *superseded by* Exec. Order No. 12,580, 52 Fed. Reg. 2923 (1987). *See also* 42 U.S.C. § 9651(c).

[229] 52 Fed. Reg. 9,042 (1987), *amended at* 53 Fed. Reg. 9,769 (1988); 43 C.F.R. § 11.41(a)(1). *See also Colorado v. United States Dep't of Interior*, 880 F.2d 481, 490 (D.C. Cir. 1989)(limited application of Type A regulations to marine and coastal environments not arbitrary or capricious).

[230] 51 Fed. Reg. 27,674 (1986), *amended at* 53 Fed. Reg 5,166 (1988).

[231] *See Ohio v. United States Dep't of the Interior*, 880 F.2d 432 (D.C. Cir. 1989); *Colorado v. United States Dep't of Interior*, 880 F.2d 481, 490-491 (D.C. Cir. 1989).

[232] 56 *Fed. Reg.* 19,752 (1991).

[233] *Comments of the American Petroleum Institute on Advanced Notice of Proposed Rulemaking (ANPR) on "Natural Resource Damage Assessments,"* 54 *Fed. Reg.* 39,016 (Submitted November 1989); comments of the American Petroleum Institute on Proposed Rule for "Natural Resource Damage Assessments," 56 *Fed. Reg.* 19,752 (1991) (submitted June 1991). *See also Use of Contingent Valuation Methodology to Determine Worth of Resource Questioned*, 23 Env't Rep. (BNA) 919 (1992).

[234] This interpretation of the statute of limitations has been adopted by at least one district court. *See United States v. City of Seattle*, No. C90-395 (W.D. Wash. January 28, 1991).

[235] 57 *Fed. Reg.* 16,850 (1992).

the likelihood of natural resource damage litigation. Individuals identified as trustees in the National Contingency Plan are required to assess natural resources damage, and restoration costs cannot be borne by the Superfund until all administrative and judicial remedies are exhausted.[236] Moreover, assessments conducted in compliance with the assessments regulations are entitled to a rebuttable presumption in proceedings to recover damages from responsible parties.[237] Given these powerful incentives, the federal government or its state counterpart has little reason not to initiate a natural resource action against responsible parties. Moreover, as technical studies increasingly indicate that once-hailed remedial practices such as pump-and-treat technologies cannot return a resource to its original condition or that such restoration is technically impracticable, litigation for "lost use" of natural resources will probably increase.

4.10.6 Proof Issues

The standard for natural resource litigation is significantly different than that for response actions. Under section 107(a) of CERCLA, liability for release of a hazardous substance is based on strict liability and requires no element of causation. The Department of Interior, however, has interpreted natural resources damage actions as requiring a traditional causation analysis typical of tort actions. This interpretation has been affirmed by the courts.[238] Consequently, to prevail on a claim for injury to a natural resource, the trustee must show by a preponderance of the evidence[239] that the defendant's hazardous substance release "was the sole or substantially contributing cause of each alleged injury to natural resources."[240] In so doing, the trustee must show (1) what resource was injured, (2) at what specific locations of the natural resource the injury occurred, (3) when the injury occurred, (4) which release of what substance caused the injury, and (5) by what pathway the natural resource was exposed to the substance.[241] Conversely, defendants carry the burden of proof when asserting as a defense that damages being sought are exempt.[242]

4.11 Contribution Actions

In view of CERCLA's liability scheme, including strict, joint and several liability (in most cases) and few defenses, it is not surprising that contribution actions assume a major role in CERCLA litigation.

---

[236] *See supra* section 4.10.3.

[237] 42 U.S.C. § 9607(f)(2)(C).

[238] *Ohio v. United States Dep't of Interior,* 880 F.2d 432, 470-472 (D.C. Cir. 1989).

[239] *Idaho v. Southern Refrigerated Transport, Inc.,* No. 88-1279 (D. Idaho Jan. 24, 1991)(natural resource damages must be proved by preponderance of the evidence).

[240] *United States v. Montrose Chem. Corp. of California,* 788 F. Supp. 1485 (C.D. Cal. 1991).

[241] *Id.*

[242] *In re Acushnet River & New Bedford Harbor: Proceedings re Alleged PCB Pollution,* 716 F. Supp. 676, 687 (D. Mass. 1989).

Prior to the 1986 SARA amendments, some question existed whether a right of contribution existed under CERCLA. The 1986 SARA amendments resolved the matter by adding section 113(f). This section specifically provides for contribution actions among jointly and severally liable parties and states that in resolving such claims, courts should apply such "equitable factors" as they deem appropriate. This language gives the courts broad discretion in determining cost allocation among jointly and severally liable parties in a contribution action. The factors which appear to be relevant include:

1. the volume of hazardous substances contributed by each party;
2. the relative degree of toxicity of each party's wastes;
3. the extent to which each party was involved in the generation, transportation, treatment, storage, or disposal of the substances involved;
4. the degree of care exercised in handling the hazardous substances; and
5. the degree of cooperation by the parties with government officials in order to prevent any harm to public health or the environment.[243]

While courts are free to apply any other "equitable" factors they deem appropriate, most allocations derive from applying the above factors.

Contribution actions may be brought either during or following a CERCLA section 107 cost recovery action or CERCLA section 106 abatement action.[244] However, in most government enforcement actions, contribution actions are set for hearing after the government's liability case against the primary defendants is resolved.[245]

At many multiparty sites, certain PRPs desire to settle with EPA while others, for whatever reasons, feel that a settlement is not in their best interests. In these cases, EPA may see fit to settle with the first group for less than the full amount of its claim, while reserving the remainder of its claim for an action against the nonsettlors. In such instances, CERCLA provides what is known as "contribution protection" for the settlors. It does so by stating that a party "[which] has resolved its liability to the United States or a state in an administrative or judicially approved settlement shall not be liable for claims for contribution regarding matters addressed in the settlement." [246]

---

[243] *See* H.R. Rep. No. 253, 99th Cong., 1st Sess., pt. 3, at 19, *reprinted in* 1986 U.S. Code Cong. & Admin. News 3038, 3042.

[244] 42 U.S.C. § 9613(f)(1).

[245] *E.g., United States v. Bell Petroleum Serv.*, 19 Chem. Waste Litig. Rept. 152 (W.D. Tex. 1989).

[246] 42 U.S.C. § 9613(f)(2).

5.0 SETTLEMENTS WITH EPA

5.1 Overview

Although certain CERCLA cases have proceeded through trial, these cases are the exception rather than the rule. Settlement is the norm in CERCLA cases, and this preference can be explained for several reasons. From EPA's perspective, settlement is preferable because it conserves Superfund monies as well as EPA's limited resources. Settlements also free EPA's personnel to work on other cleanups. From the perspective of PRPs, settlement is often preferred because it permits them to exercise greater control over the selection and implementation of remedial actions, presumably minimizing costs. PRPs also often prefer settlement to avoid the tremendous costs of litigating a CERCLA case.

This is not to say that the settlement process is smooth or produces results uniformly acceptable to PRPs. Indeed, negotiations can be protracted, contentious, and extremely costly. This scenario is particularly likely at multiparty sites where PRPs must not only negotiate with EPA but also with each other and in some cases with the State where a site is located. While it is EPA's policy to settle, increasingly it has demonstrated inflexibility both with regard to the remedial action selected and with the terms of the settlement agreement. Consequently, many PRPs have begun to question whether settlement is necessarily the best course. Given EPA's policy of routinely issuing section 106 administrative orders, some PRPs have decided to perform cleanups under these orders rather than under a settlement agreement.

5.2 Controlling Authority

Parties attempting to negotiate a CERCLA settlement with EPA often find that the flexibility of the EPA negotiators is constrained both by CERCLA's settlement provisions and by a variety of guidance documents issued by EPA. Moreover, EPA has prepared "model" settlement documents for use by its staff level negotiators. Because of these constraints, truly "negotiated" settlements are not likely to occur.

The SARA amendments added section 122 entitled "settlements." This section sets forth procedures which EPA may follow if it attempts to settle a CERCLA case. EPA's decision whether to invoke the procedures under CERCLA section 122 is discretionary and not subject to judicial review.[247] However, section 122 codifies many of the settlement policies that EPA had followed prior to the SARA amendments. The section should therefore be consulted in detail by any party attempting to settle a CERCLA case, because in many instances it provides specific instructions for when and how various settlement provisions may be used. For example, section 122(f) provides detailed requirements addressing the circumstances in which EPA can provide a covenant not to sue in a settlement agreement. Other sections

---

[247] 42 U.S.C. § 9622(a).

address such issues as partial funding by the Superfund ("mixed funding"), *de minimis* settlements, and public participation in settlements.

Section 122 also contains extensive discussion of "special notice procedures" that EPA may follow when it determines that a period of negotiation would "facilitate an agreement."[248] These procedures provide that if EPA elects to pursue settlement under section 122, it must provide PRPs notice including the names and addresses of all other PRPs, the volume and nature of substances each party contributed to the site (if known), and a ranking of the responsible parties by volume contributed. These special notice procedures also contain provisions authorizing EPA to prepare a "nonbinding preliminary allocation of responsibility" (NBAR) for the PRPs to use in their attempts to allocate costs among themselves. To date, however, EPA has not seen fit to use this provision extensively. This agency reluctance is probably due to the fact that EPA would prefer neither to be bound by the notice provision's requirements nor to lose its flexibility in dealing with potential settlors.

Throughout CERCLA's history, EPA has from time to time issued guidance documents on various issues associated with settlements. In 1985 EPA issued what continues to be its primary settlement policy.[249] This document, which pre-dates the SARA amendments, is generally consistent with CERCLA section 122. It remains the only comprehensive treatment of overall CERCLA settlement policy by EPA. Since 1986 EPA has issued a variety of guidance documents addressing individual settlement topics. Among the topics these guidance documents address are: covenants not to sue,[250] *de minimis* party settlements,[251] stipulated penalties in consent decrees,[252] and "mixed funding."[253] In any negotiation it can be expected that EPA's negotiators will attempt to comply with any applicable guidance document.

5.3 Consent Decrees and Consent Orders

Settlements with EPA are ordinarily memorialized in a consent decree or an administrative order on consent ("consent order"). The difference between the two forms of agreement is that a consent decree is filed with and signed by a federal court, while a consent order does not involve any judicial action. Moreover, any settlement and consent order involving total response costs greater than $500,000 requires approval by the United States

---

[248]42 U.S.C. § 9622(e).

[249]50 *Fed. Reg.* 5,034 (1985).

[250]52 *Fed. Reg.* 28,038 (1987).

[251]52 *Fed. Reg.* 24,333 (1987); 52 *Fed. Reg.* 43,393 (1987).

[252]United States Environmental Protection Agency, *Office of Enforcement and Compliance Monitoring, Guidance on the Use of Stipulated Penalties in Hazardous Waste Consent Decrees*, OSWER Directive No. 9835.2b (1987).

[253]53 *Fed. Reg.* 8,279 (1988).

Department of Justice.[254] Not surprisingly, most parties prefer to have a settlement memorialized through a consent decree as there will be a neutral third party—the judge—available to resolve disputes.

Until recently the terms and conditions of consent orders and consent decrees were often the source of extensive negotiations between EPA and potential settlors. The recent issuance of model consent orders and consent decrees by EPA has severely hindered the opportunity for meaningful negotiations.[255] Experience to date with these model documents suggests that staff level negotiators will be unwilling to vary from most of their provisions.

5.4 Major Settlement Issues

While no two CERCLA settlement negotiations involve precisely the same issues, there are several issues that commonly arise. The frequency with which these issues occur is reflected in the fact that they are the subject of discussion in both section 122 and EPA guidance documents.

5.4.1 "Mixed Funding" and Carve Outs

As discussed earlier, at every multiparty CERCLA site there are parties that wish to settle with EPA and those that cannot or do not. At the same time, there may be a vast quantity of wastes at the site which came from defunct or bankrupt companies. Wastes from these defunct or bankrupt companies have traditionally been referred to as a site's "orphan share." Thus, at most sites those parties which settle will ordinarily account for less than 100 percent of the volume of hazardous substances at the site. In fact, it is not uncommon for many settlements to involve settlors whose cumulative volume of waste represents less than 50 percent of that present at the site.

Settlors in the situations described above are quite naturally interested in avoiding 100 percent of the liability for site remediation and EPA's past response costs. Consequently, they have often sought EPA's payment for a portion (usually the orphan share) of these costs through use of Superfund monies—a process referred to as "mixed funding." At the same time, these settlors will seek to have EPA "carve out" part of its remedial action or costs from their liability and proceed against the nonsettlors for the portion "carved out."

Section 122(b)(1) gives EPA the authority to enter into "mixed funding" agreements whereby EPA agrees to use the Superfund to reimburse settlors a portion of the costs they incur in performing an agreed-upon remedial action. EPA's guidance on mixed funding acknowledges that Congress

---

[254] 42 U.S.C. § 9622(h)(1).

[255] *See* United States Environmental Protection Agency, *Model Administrative Order on Consent for CERCLA Remedial Investigation/Feasibility Study*, OSWER Directive No. 9835.3-1A (January 30, 1990); United States Environmental Protection Agency, *Superfund Program, Model CERCLA RD/RA Consent Decree*, 56 *Fed. Reg.* 30,996-31,012 (July 8, 1991).

recognized the need to consider settlements for less than 100 percent and to use Superfund monies for shares of parties "unknown, insolvent, similarly unavailable, or [which have] refuse[d] to settle." The guidance, which encourages the use of mixed funding in appropriate situations, lists the following factors as considerations in evaluating mixed funding settlements: (1) the strength of the liability case against both nonsettlors and settlors, (2) those options the government may have if a settlement is not reached, (3) the size of the share to be covered by the Superfund, and (4) the good faith of the settlors.[256] The guidance identifies the best situations for mixed funding as those where the settlors offer a substantial portion of remediation costs and where the government has a strong case against financially viable nonsettlors.

EPA's use of mixed funding has been uneven. Despite explicit authority in both CERCLA and EPA's guidance documents, "mixed funding" has been unavailable to deal with the problems of "orphan shares" and nonsettlors at many sites. However, EPA has been more receptive to "carving out" a portion of a remedial action's costs for nonsettling parties to absorb.

5.4.2 *De Minimis* Settlements

At most multiparty sites there are a large number of companies which have disposed of relatively small quantities of hazardous substances. Section 122(g) addresses these so-called *"de minimis"* parties. It encourages EPA to "as promptly as possible" reach a final settlement with such parties and identifies the following types of situations in which a *de minimis* settlement is appropriate:

1. situations where both the amount and toxicity of hazardous substances contributed by a party is minimal compared with other hazardous substances at the facility; or

2. situations where a party is the owner of the property where the facility is located but did not conduct or permit the generation, handling or disposal of hazardous substances at the facility; contribute to the release or threatened release from the facility; or acquire the facility with knowledge that it had been used to store, handle or dispose of hazardous substances.[257]

Aside from the opportunity of an early settlement, *de minimis* parties are ordinarily offered a settlement with *real finality*. In return for what is known as a "premium payment," EPA will ordinarily provide *de minimis* parties a complete covenant not to sue which is revocable only if subsequent information reveals that the party's waste contribution was not truly *de minimis*. This guarantee means that should future problems develop at a site, these *de minimis* parties will not be required to participate in or fund future remediation efforts.

---

[256]*See* 53 *Fed. Reg.* 8,279 (1988).
[257]42 U.S.C. § 9622(g)(1).

5.4.3 Covenants Not to Sue and Reopeners

For most settlors, a settlement with EPA that entails subsequent remediation actions does not represent finality. Because there is great uncertainty at most sites about the effectiveness of the remedial action selected, neither CERCLA nor EPA guidance provides a complete release from future liability.

CERCLA section 122(f) provides that settlements may contain a covenant not to sue. There is no provision for the use of a release. In considering whether to issue a covenant not to sue, EPA is to consider: whether such a covenant is in the public interest, whether it would expedite a response action, whether the settlor is in compliance with the consent decree, and whether the response action has been approved by EPA.

In most cases, however, EPA's covenant not to sue is illusory. CERCLA provides that, except in certain designated instances, a covenant not to sue must be accompanied by an additional provision—known as a "reopener"— which allows EPA to sue for future liability resulting from *unknown conditions*.[258] EPA guidance on covenants not to sue also requires that the reopener provision permit a subsequent suit in situations where *additional information* reveals that the remedy is "no longer protective of public health or the environment." This reopener is required in all settlements except those involving:

1. *de minimis* parties;
2. "extraordinary circumstances" where reasonable assurances exist that public health and the environment will be protected from future releases and where certain enumerated factors (for example, nature of risks, toxicity, strength of evidence, ability to pay, litigation risks, etc.) are considered; and
3. portions of a remedial action that entail:
   (a) the offsite transport of hazardous substances to RCRA-approved disposal facilities where EPA has required offsite disposal after rejecting an alternative permitting on-site or other disposal; or
   (b) the treatment of hazardous substances "so as to destroy, eliminate, or permanently immobilize the hazardous constituents of such substances" such that they no longer present a significant threat.[259]

5.4.4 Stipulated Penalties

CERCLA settlements, whether consent orders or consent decrees, routinely contain provisions for stipulated penalties in the event that a settlor fails to meet certain designated milestone events. The use and amount of these penalties are the subjects of negotiation, but generally EPA seeks to

---

[258] 42 U.S.C. § 9622(f)(6).
[259] *Id.*

extract a penalty amount deemed sufficient to motivate the settlor to meet the deadline set by the agreement.

CERCLA section 121(e)(2) provides for the use of stipulated penalties in consent decrees. EPA's guidance on the use of stipulated penalties in consent decrees has interpreted this provision to require that all consent decrees involving a remedial action contain provisions for stipulated penalties.[260] It is EPA's policy to tie stipulated penalties to compliance schedules, performance standards, and reporting requirements. However, stipulated penalties do not arise if delay is occasioned by a *force majeure* event or, in some situations, where an interim deadline is missed but a final deadline is met.

One of the policy's more disturbing features to settlors is EPA's insistence that stipulated penalties continue to accrue during any delay caused by a dispute under the consent decree. Where the dispute is resolved in EPA's favor, a settlor forfeits the accrued amount. Thus, the policy effectively hinders settling parties from effectively using a consent decree's dispute provisions.

6.0 RELEASE REPORTING REQUIREMENTS

CERCLA sections 102 and 103 provide the basis for requiring certain parties to give notice of a release of hazardous substances. Section 103(a) requires that any person in charge of a vessel or facility notify the National Response Center,[261] as soon as that person has knowledge of any "release" from the vessel or facility of a hazardous substance *equal to or greater than the reportable quantity for that substance*. As indicated in section 2.2, a "release" is defined broadly to include the escape of a hazardous substance into the "environment."[262]

The crux of CERCLA's reporting requirements is the concept of "reportable quantities." Simply stated, a reportable quantity is the amount of a substance which must be reported if released. Reportable quantities for hazardous substances are established by EPA pursuant to section 102. Where EPA has not indicated a listed substance's reportable quantity, section 102 further specifies that the quantity shall be one pound, unless the hazardous substance has a reportable quantity under the Clean Water Act, in which case the latter will be used.

EPA has promulgated regulations listing the various hazardous substances regulated under CERCLA and specifying their reportable quantities.[263] These regulations should be consulted in detail when determining whether a release must be reported because the reportable quantities for

---

[260]United States Environmental Protection Agency, Office of Enforcement and Compliance Monitoring, *Guidance on the Use of Stipulated Penalties In Hazardous Waste Consent Decrees* (1987).

[261] *See* 33 U.S.C. § 1251 *et seq.*.

[262] *See supra* section 2.4 for definition of "environment."

[263]40 C.F.R. § 302.

hazardous substances vary significantly. The regulations also provide detailed guidance on assorted issues that arise in determining whether a report must be filed, including the calculations for a reportable release. As a general rule, to ascertain whether a substance's release has equalled or exceeded its reportable quantity, the person in charge of the facility or vessel must calculate the total amount released during any twenty-four hour period. If the total amount equals or exceeds the reportable quantity during that twenty-four hour period, it must be reported.[264]

Failure to report a release involving a reportable quantity of a hazardous substance can result in both civil and criminal penalties. The maximum criminal penalty is three years in prison for a first conviction and five years for a subsequent conviction.[265] Fines may also be imposed. Civil penalties equal to $25,000 per day for failure to report may be assessed.[266]

Since there are more listed hazardous substances under CERCLA than under other environmental laws, it is important that parties do not assume a report need not be filed merely because it is not required under another statute.

Notwithstanding the above discussion, certain *types* of releases are exempted from CERCLA's notice requirements, irrespective of the quantity released. Pursuant to CERCLA section 103(a), the following types of releases need not be reported:

1. releases resulting from application, handling or storage of pesticides registered under the Federal Insecticide, Fungicide, and Rodenticide Act;[267]

2. federally permitted releases;[268]

3. releases regulated under subtitle C of RCRA which have been or need not be reported pursuant to RCRA;[269] and

4. continuous releases from a facility for which notification has been given previously.[270]

7.0 FEDERAL FACILITIES

As with the private sector, years of inattention to the environmental harm posed by certain activities have caused many federal facilities serious environmental problems. The greatest problems exist for facilities associated with the massive military-industrial complex—Department of Energy and Department of Defense facilities—which was constructed in

---

[264] 40 C.F.R. §§ 302.5, 302.6.
[265] 42 U.S.C. § 9603(b).
[266] 42 U.S.C. § 9609(b),(c).
[267] 42 U.S.C. § 9603(e).
[268] 42 U.S.C. § 9603(a).
[269] 42 U.S.C. § 9603(f)(1).
[270] 42 U.S.C. § 9603(f)(2).

response to World War II and the Cold War. Past disposal practices contributing to pollution at these facilities include the use of unlined pits, holding ponds, drying beds, landfills, discharge to the ground, and on-site burning of wastes. The estimated costs of cleanup are staggering. Citizens, states, and environmental groups have expressed outrage at the conditions of many of these facilities and have sought to inject themselves in determining appropriate cleanups.

CERCLA contains broad waivers of sovereign immunity which permit individuals and states to bring cost recovery actions against federal facilities,[271] and to bring "citizen suits" for the facilities' compliance with the statute.[272] The authority of citizens and states to bring action against these facilities has been a spur toward their cleanup.

The 1986 SARA amendments reflected Congress' great concern for federal facilities by creating an entire section—section 120—devoted to their cleanup. Section 120(a) provides for federal facility compliance, both substantively and procedurally, to the same extent as any private entity.[273] This compliance includes requirements related to listing on the NPL (for example, site assessments, hazardous ranking, and evaluation procedures).

Section 120 also addresses hazardous waste cleanup at federal facilities and establishes requirements that are unique to federal facilities. These requirements include the creation of a Federal Agency Hazardous Waste Compliance Docket listing facilities which manage hazardous waste or have potential hazardous waste problems. This list is then used to provide timetables for addressing the problems at each facility. A preliminary assessment and, as needed, site inspection are required within 18 months of a facility being listed. Subsequently, the facility is scored under the hazardous ranking system to determine whether it should be placed on the NPL. If listed on the NPL, the facility must begin an RI/FS within six months of its NPL listing. While performing the RI/FS, consultation with EPA and the state must occur. Within 180 days of EPA's review of the RI/FS, an interagency agreement must be entered into with EPA for the performance of the selected remedy.[274]

In response to the various hazardous waste problems at their facilities, both the Departments of Defense (DOD) and Energy (DOE) have formulated extensive long-term cleanup plans. DOD's plan—the Defense Environmental Restoration Program—is funded by monies set aside by Congress under the Defense Environmental Restoration Account (DERA). The 1984 Defense Appropriations Act created DERA as a set-aside fund to pay for DOD response actions under CERCLA and the NCP. The use of DERA funds

---

[271]42 U.S.C. § 9620(a).
[272]42 U.S.C. § 9659(a).
[273]42 U.S.C. § 9620(a).
[274]42 U.S.C. § 9620(c),(d),(e).

is limited to addressing past disposal problems, not correcting currently useable facilities. DOE announced in 1989 an Environmental Restoration and Waste Management Five-Year Plan. The Five-Year Plan addresses environmental restoration, corrective activities, and waste management.

For a more definitive discussion of this topic, the reader is referred to the Superfund Manual: Legal and Management Strategies *and related books and courses listed at the end of this book.*

Chapter 10

NATIONAL ENVIRONMENTAL POLICY ACT

James W. Spensley, Esq.
Holme Roberts & Owen
Denver, Colorado

1.0 OVERVIEW

The National Environmental Policy Act of 1969 (NEPA)[1] has been heralded as the Magna Carta of the country's environmental movement. It was signed into law on January 1, 1970 to address the need for a national environmental policy to guide the growing environmental consciousness and to shape a national response.

NEPA contains three important elements: (1) the declaration of national environmental policies and goals; (2) the establishment of "action-forcing" provisions for federal agencies to implement those policies and goals; and (3) the establishment of a Council on Environmental Quality (CEQ) in the Executive Office of the President. The essential purpose of NEPA is to insure that environmental factors are given the same consideration as other factors in decision-making by the federal agencies. The effectiveness of NEPA has stemmed from its environmental impact statement (EIS) requirement that federal agencies must consider the environmental effects of, and any alternatives to, all proposals for major federal actions that significantly affect the quality of the human environment.

Although CEQ published early guidelines for federal agencies to implement NEPA, it was the federal courts in the early 1970s that had the most influence on shaping NEPA's "action-forcing" provision, section 102(2)(C).[2] Because this provision was virtually ignored during its legislative formulation, judicial interpretations established the basic definitions for section 102(2)(C) concerning who must comply with NEPA, what level of federal involvement triggers an EIS, what constitutes a "major" action that "significantly affects" the environment, and other fundamental issues. This EIS requirement has become the heart of NEPA and has had a profound impact on federal agency decision-making.

During this early period, the threat of litigation over the EIS requirement caused many federal agencies to overreact by including in their statements every possible environmental reference that could be found. This

---

[1] 42 U.S.C. §§ 4321-4370c.

[2] 42 U.S.C. § 4332(2)(C); see also Frederick R. Anderson, *NEPA in the Courts: A Legal Analysis of the National Environmental Policy Act* (1973).

resulted in lengthy EIS's that neither decision-makers nor the public would read. Today, CEQ regulations emphasize the need to reduce excessive paperwork and focus on the essential information that is needed by decision-makers and the public. NEPA's emphasis and importance has evolved from a procedural lever used by project opponents to stop or delay proposed federal projects to a more comprehensive framework for documenting and integrating essential environmental information into the federal decision-making process.

The current trend in NEPA compliance has focused on the use of an environmental assessment (EA) to conduct a threshold analysis of whether a full EIS is required. CEQ is placing new emphasis on the use of the EA in order to avoid extensive and duplicative documentation while more effectively integrating key environmental factors in the federal decision-making process and opening up the process to outside parties.[3]

2.0 NEPA'S DEVELOPMENT

NEPA was enacted at a time when the Congress heard testimony from many quarters of society warning of impending environmental degradation and even disaster.[4] Members of the Congress competed for the popular leadership of this new environmental movement. More than 2,000 legislative proposals having a bearing on environmental matters were introduced into the 91st Congress that passed NEPA.[5] Few congressional members understood or expected that this brief, idealistic NEPA statute would be so successful in reforming federal agency decision-making and bringing the public into the process.

2.1 Legislative History

The legislative formulation of NEPA principles began years before the statute was enacted.[6] In 1959, Senator James E. Murray (D-Montana) attempted to legislate a national environmental policy when he introduced the Resources and Conservation Act of 1960, which included the creation of a high level council of environmental advisors.[7] However, it was not until the late 1960s that Senator Henry Jackson (D-Wash) and Congressman John Dingell (D-Mich) collaborated to enact the present statute. Early versions of the legislation contained neither policy and goals nor an "action-forcing" provision. It was not until the legislation had passed both houses of Congress and been amended by a House-Senate Conference Committee that

---

[3]Diana Bear, *NEPA at 19: A Primer on an "Old" Law with Solutions to New Problems*, 19 Envtl. L. Rep. (Envtl. L. Inst.) 10060 (1989).

[4]Environmental Quality: Hearings on H.R. 12143 Before the Subcommittee on Fisheries and Wildlife Conservation, Committee on Merchant Marine and Fisheries, 91st Cong., 1st Sess. (1969).

[5]Library of Congress, C.R.S., Env. Policy Div., Congress and the Nation's Environment and Environmental Affairs of the 91st Congress (1971).

[6]Anderson, *supra* note 2, at 4-14.

[7]S.2549, 86th Cong., 2d Sess. (1960).

the present policy and reporting provisions were included. Although the legislative history is unclear in many respects, Senator Jackson clearly felt that it was the federal government's failures and unresponsiveness that had lead to much of the country's environmental degradation. "The most important feature of the act," according to Senator Jackson, "is that it establishes new decision-making procedures for all agencies of the federal government."[8]

2.2 Policy and Goals

NEPA's policies are broad and general and its goals lofty. Indeed, section 101 of the act was written as if to inspire rather than to regulate. It emphasizes the need to recognize "the profound impact of man's activity on the interrelations of all components of the natural environment"[9] and to recognize that "each person should enjoy a healthful environment . . . and to contribute to the preservation and enhancement of the environment."[10] It recognizes the balancing of trade-offs that must occur in the decision-making process by promoting the "use [of] all practicable means and measures . . . [to] fulfill the social, economic, and other requirements of present and future generations of Americans."[11] It goes on to recognize six more specific goals as a guide to the federal government to implement this new policy.[12]

2.3 Council on Environmental Quality

The Council on Environmental Quality (CEQ) was created by Title II of NEPA[13] and modelled after the Council of Economic Advisors created by the Employment Act of 1946.[14] The CEQ was placed in the executive office of the president and composed of three members appointed by the president and confirmed by the Senate. Under the statute, CEQ is to assist and advise the president in the preparation of an annual environmental quality report, on the progress of federal agencies in implementing the act, on national policies to foster and promote the improvement of environmental quality, and on the state of the environment. Shortly after signing NEPA into law, President Nixon expanded CEQ's mandate by Executive Order No. 11514 directing it to issue guidelines to federal agencies for the preparation of EIS's and to coordinate federal programs related to environmental quality.[15]

---

[8]Henry Jackson, *Environmental Quality, the Courts and Congress*, 68 Mich. L. Rev. 1079 (1970).

[9]42 U.S.C. § 4331(a).

[10]*Id.* § 4331(c).

[11]*Id.* § 4331(a).

[12]*Id.* § 4331(b).

[13]*Id.* §§ 4341-4347.

[14]15 U.S.C. §§ 1021-1025.

[15]Exec. Order No. 11514, 3 C.F.R. 356 (1972).

This Executive Order further directed federal agencies to develop procedures to ensure timely dissemination of public information concerning federal plans and programs with environmental impacts in order to obtain the views of all interested parties. This public participation mandate, combined with the disclosure requirements of NEPA, has in large part been responsible for the significant and lasting effectiveness of NEPA.

CEQ has played a central role in the development of the EIS process. Its first guidelines were issued in April 1971, and required each department and agency of the federal government to adopt its own guidelines consistent with those from CEQ.[16] Although the guidelines did not have the status of formal agency regulations, the courts often recognized them with considerable deference.[17] Subsequently, President Carter by Executive Order 11991 authorized CEQ to adopt regulations rather than guidelines on EIS preparation.[18] In 1978, CEQ adopted regulations that reflected its earlier guidelines and the numerous court decisions that had created NEPA's early "common law."[19]

CEQ has no authority to enforce its regulations. However, it has played a major role in advising agencies on compliance matters. Federal agencies have not availed themselves of CEQ's advice as often as they should to avoid problems and litigation.

3.0 REQUIREMENTS FOR FEDERAL AGENCIES

The requirements of NEPA are mandatory for federal agencies and over the years have been a major force in reforming agency decision-making processes. NEPA contains largely "procedural" requirements that are supplemental to existing statutory responsibilities of the federal agencies.[20] In *Calvert Cliffs' Coordinating Comm. Inc. v. United States Atomic Energy Comm'n*,[21] Judge Skelly Wright writing for the court, notes:

NEPA, first of all, makes environmental protection a part of the mandate of every federal agency and department. . . . It [the agency] is not only permitted, but compelled, to take environmental values into account. Perhaps the greatest importance of NEPA is to require . . . agencies to *consider* environmental issues just as they consider other matters within their mandates.[22]

Although NEPA's provisions apply only to federal agencies, the pervasiveness of federal decisions affecting state and local matters as well as private actions makes NEPA an issue for many. An applicant should

---

[16]36 Fed. Reg. 7723 (Apr. 23, 1971).

[17]*See, e.g., Environmental Defense Fund, Inc. v. Hoffman*, 566 F.2d 1060 (8th Cir. 1977).

[18]Exec. Order No. 11991, 3 C.F.R., 1966-1970 Comp., p. 902 (1977).

[19]43 Fed. Reg. 55,978 (1978).

[20]*See Vermont Yankee Nuclear Power Corp. v. Natural Resources Defense Coun.*, 435 U.S. 519 (1978), *cert. granted*, 459 U.S. 1034 (1982), *rev'd on other grounds*, 462 U.S. 87 (1983).

[21]449 F.2d 1109 (D.C. Cir. 1971).

[22]*Id.* at 1112 (emphasis in original).

have a direct interest in the successful completion of an agency's EIS so as to avoid potential time-consuming and expensive litigation. Moreover, agencies increasingly are finding ways to shift the costs of NEPA compliance to those requesting some federal action or decision.[23] Therefore, an applicant will want to ensure that the environmental studies and documents are prepared in a cost-effective manner and in accordance with the procedural requirements of NEPA.

The only agency that the courts have recognized as having a limited exemption from NEPA is the Environmental Protection Agency (EPA). Although there is no reference to an exemption for EPA in the statute, EPA has argued that it should be exempt for the reason that it has statutory responsibility for protection of the environment. Some legislation has specifically exempted EPA from NEPA compliance. Under the Energy Supply and Environmental Coordination Act of 1974, an exemption is provided to EPA for its actions under the Clean Air Act.[24] Similarly, under the Clean Water Act, EPA is exempted from the obligation to prepare an EIS on some actions such as discharge permits for existing sources of water pollution.[25] Other EPA non-regulatory actions require NEPA compliance, such as the issuance of construction grants for water treatment facilities.

3.1 CEQ Regulations

The CEQ regulations begin by calling for agencies to integrate NEPA requirements with other planning requirements at the earliest possible time to ensure that plans and decisions reflect environmental values, avoid delays later in the process, and head off potential conflicts.[26] Agencies are to utilize a "systematic, interdisciplinary approach" as required by section 102(2)(A) and to study and develop appropriate alternatives to recommended courses of action for unresolved conflicts in the use of available resources as provided in section 102(2)(E).[27]

NEPA's action-forcing provision, section 102(2)(C), requires that an EIS shall be "include[d] in every recommendation or report on proposals for legislation and other major Federal actions significantly affecting the quality of the human environment. . . ."[28] The key terms in this statement are defined in the CEQ regulations and have been the most judicially interpreted words of NEPA.

CEQ states its intention that judicial review of agency compliance with these regulations should not occur before an agency has filed a final EIS or has made an appropriate finding of no significant impact, or takes action

---

[23] *See Alumet v. Andrus*, 607 F.2d 911 (10th Cir. 1979); *see also* David Sive and Frank Friedman, *A Practical Guide to Environmental Law* §§ 7.01(a), 7.02(k) (1987).

[24] 15 U.S.C. § 793(c)(1).

[25] 33 U.S.C. § 1371(c)(1).

[26] *Id.* § 1501.2.

[27] *Id.*

[28] 42 U.S.C. § 4332(2)(C).

that will result in irreparable injury.[29] Furthermore, CEQ suggests that a trivial violation of these regulations should not give rise to an independent cause of action.

The regulations require each agency to adopt procedures consistent with these regulations for implementing NEPA's provisions. Specifically, the agencies are to identify typical classes of action:

(i)   which normally require an EIS;
(ii) which normally do not require either an EIS or an environmental assessment (categorical exclusions (§ 1508.4)); and
(iii) which normally require environmental assessments but not necessarily an EIS.[30]

Agency procedures may provide specific criteria for limited exceptions to classified proposals.[31]

The first question is whether a federal agency must prepare an EIS. As noted earlier, each of the key words in section 102(2)(C) has been the subject of judicial interpretation in answering that question. Is there an agency "proposal" for an "action"? Is the action "federal"? Is it "major"? Is it "significant"? Does the action "affect the human environment"? The CEQ regulations define each of these statutory terms.[32]

The EIS requirement is not triggered unless there is a "proposal" for action by a federal agency.[33] Because agencies are constantly involved in planning and program formulation, it is not always easy to determine when a proposal has been made. If a proposal is made too early in the planning process, it will contain insufficient information to provide the necessary environmental disclosure.[34] On the other hand, if the agency prepares an EIS too late in the planning process, it becomes simply a post hoc justification for a decision already made. The regulations have addressed this timing question by defining the term "proposal" as that which:

> exists at the stage in the development of an action when an agency subject to the Act has a goal and is actively preparing to make a decision on one or more alternative means of accomplishing that goal and the effects can be meaningfully evaluated. Preparation of an environmental impact statement on a proposal should be timed (§ 1502.5) so that the final statement may be completed in time ... to be included in any recommendation or report on the proposal.[35]

---

[29] 40 C.F.R. § 1500.3 (1991).

[30] *Id.* § 1507.3(b)(2).

[31] *Id.* § 1507.3(c).

[32] *Id.* pt. 1508.

[33] *Id.* § 1502.5; *see also Kleppe v. Sierra Club*, 427 U.S. 390 (1976).

[34] *See Scientists' Inst. for Public Information, Inc. v. Atomic Energy Commission*, 481 F.2d 1079 (D.C. Cir. 1973) (for discussion of timing); *see also Aberdeen and Rockfish R.R. Co. v. Students Challenging Regulatory Agency Procedures (SCRAP)*, 422 U.S. 289 (1975).

[35] 40 C.F.R. § 1508.23 (1991).

If there is a proposal, it must be a "federal" proposal in order for an EIS to be required. Clearly, policies, plans, programs and projects proposed by federal agencies meet this definition.[36] CEQ regulations also address actions with "effects" that may be major and which are potentially subject to federal control and responsibility.[37] Further, private, state and local actions which have sufficient federal involvement may also require an EIS. Such non-federal actions that are regulated, licensed, permitted or approved by federal agencies generally are considered "federal" for NEPA purposes.[38] The need for federal permits, licenses and other approvals from a federal agency program are examples where seemingly non-federal actions have triggered NEPA compliance.

Federal assistance to a non-federal project or action may also trigger NEPA. The primary determinant in these cases is the extent to which the federal control is or may be exercised. Generally, there have been three forms of federal assistance: categorical grants, block grants and some form of revenue sharing. Federal categorical grants to non-federal projects usually require NEPA compliance. Block grants and revenue sharing arrangements are typically exempt from NEPA when there is limited federal involvement in these programs.[39]

There are two other key words that require definition in the threshold determination of NEPA application—one must determine whether the federal action is "major" and "significantly" affects the quality of the human environment. These two terms have been the subject of considerable judicial discussion without establishing a universally accepted definition. CEQ regulations provide that the term "major" reinforces but does not have a meaning independent of the term "significantly".[40] Agencies have defined "major actions" in their program-specific regulations. CEQ regulations have attempted to define "significantly" by suggesting consideration of both the "context" and the "intensity" of the specific circumstances.[41] The context refers to the surrounding circumstances where the action is proposed and its impact upon society as a whole, the affected region, the affected interests and the locality. The term "intensity" refers to the severity of the impact. The regulations refer to a list of considerations which an agency should take into account when weighing the significance of the impacts.[42]

The last key term is "quality of the human environment." At the time Congress enacted NEPA, primary attention was focused on improving and

---

[36]*Id.* § 1508.18.

[37]*Id.*

[38]*Id.; see generally* D. Mandelker, *NEPA Law and Litigation* § 8.16 (1984).

[39]*Carolina Action v. Simon*, 389 F. Supp. 1244 (M.D.N.C. 1975), *aff'd*, 522 F.2d 295 (4th Cir. 1975).

[40]40 C.F.R. § 1508.18 (1991).

[41]*Id.* § 1508.27.

[42]*Id.*

preserving the natural environment as reflected in the policies and goals section of NEPA. However, this phrase has been given broad definition.[43] In *Hanly v. Mitchell*,[44] where the plaintiffs were concerned about a detention center planned for downtown Manhattan, the court recognized that NEPA applied to protection of the urban quality of life as well. Although other cases have supported this broad definition of impacts upon the human environment, at least one case has concluded that "pure economic impacts" without other accompanying physical impacts do not trigger NEPA's application.[45] In one case, aesthetic impacts on the urban environment were sufficient to trigger a NEPA review.[46] The CEQ regulations advise that economic and social effects are not intended by themselves to require preparation of an EIS, but when they are interrelated with natural or physical environmental effects, then they must be discussed.[47]

3.2 Relationship to Other Federal Laws

NEPA is a policy and procedural statute that has been interpreted by the courts to make environmental protection a part of the mandate of every federal agency and department.[48] The court in *Calvert Cliffs* cites Senator Jackson, NEPA's principal sponsor, as stating that "no agency will be able to maintain that it has no mandate or no requirement to consider the environmental consequences of its actions."[49] Further, the court interpreted the congressional intent of NEPA to indicate that environmental factors must be considered throughout agency review processes. It went on to underscore the act's requirement that environmental consideration be given "to the fullest extent possible," finding that this language set a high standard for agencies to meet.

Courts have also recognized that in some limited circumstances federal actions may be wholly or partially exempt from compliance with NEPA due to statutory conflicts. These conflicts may arise from explicit statutory exemptions as well as implied conflicts. As noted previously, EPA has been expressly exempted from NEPA compliance for all of its actions under the Clean Air Act and specific actions under the Clean Water Act.[50] Congress has also expressly exempted specific agency projects or programs from NEPA compliance, such as the Alaskan Pipeline.[51]

---

[43]42 U.S.C. § 4331(a).

[44]460 F.2d 640 (2d Cir. 1972), *cert. denied*, 409 U.S. 990 (1972).

[45]*Breckinridge v. Rumsfeld*, 537 F.2d 864 (6th Cir. 1976), *cert. denied*, 429 U.S. 1061 (1977).

[46]*Save the Courthouse Comm. v. Lynn*, 408 F. Supp. 1323 (S.D.N.Y. 1975).

[47]40 C.F.R. § 1508.14 (1991).

[48]*Calvert Cliffs Coordinating Committee Inc.*, 449 F.2d at 1112.

[49]*Id.* at 1113.

[50]*See supra*, Section 3.0.

[51]15 U.S.C. § 719H(c)(3).

A more controversial situation arises where NEPA is determined to be inapplicable because of agency statutory duties that preclude compliance with NEPA's procedural requirements. In *Flint Ridge Dev. Co. v. Scenic Rivers Ass'n of Oklahoma*,[52] the Supreme Court held that an agency's specific statutory directive to review a matter within 30 days was mandatory and that compliance with NEPA would frustrate this legislative directive. However, the Court did not relieve the agency of all NEPA duties under this conflicting legislation. It specifically noted that the agency had the authority and obligation to require additional environmental information and to consider environmental factors in its decision-making process.

Some federal agencies have claimed an implied exemption from NEPA for actions taken under the cloak of national security or national defense. Although such an implied exemption has not been recognized, the Supreme Court has upheld a Freedom of Information Act exception to disclosure in the EIS process.[53] The Court specifically noted that public disclosure under NEPA is governed by the Freedom of Information Act while agencies must prepare NEPA documentation even for classified proposals. Agencies may include specific criteria for providing limited exceptions to the disclosure provisions of the CEQ regulations for classified proposals.[54]

Perhaps the most important relationship of NEPA to other environmental laws is the role the EIS plays as the public repository of the combined environmental assessment of all applicable environmental laws. Most agency regulations require the EIS to identify and discuss possible violations of the standards established by other more substantive environmental statutes.

3.3 Functional Equivalency

The courts have been asked in several cases to determine whether compliance with other environmental laws which require environmental analyses similar to NEPA constitutes the "functional equivalent" of the NEPA process. In a few cases, the courts have recognized such an exception to NEPA compliance for the EPA only.

For a court to apply the functional equivalency exception, it must find that the statute creating the agency, as well as the specific statute being applied, together provide sufficient substantive and procedural standards to ensure a full and adequate consideration of all pertinent environmental

---

[52] 426 U.S. 776 (1976); *see also cf. Jones v. Gordon*, 792 F.2d 821 (9th Cir. 1986).

[53] *Weinberger v. Catholic Action of Hawaii/Peace Education Project*, 454 U.S. 139 (1981); *see also*, F.L. McChesney, *Nuclear Weapons and "Secret" Impact Statements: High Court Applies FOIA Exemptions to EIS Disclosure Rules*, 12 Envtl. L. Rep. (Envtl. L. Inst.) 10007 (1982).

[54] 40 C.F.R. § 1507.3(c) (1991).

issues by the agency.[55] The key is the consideration of the issues by the *agency*; thus courts have rejected arguments for applying the exception where the environmental consequences of the actions were, or were not, considered by agency outsiders.

The functional equivalency exception is "not ... a broad exemption from NEPA for all environmental agencies or even for all environmentally protective regulatory actions of such agencies. Instead, [it is] a narrow exemption from the literal requirements for those actions which are undertaken pursuant to sufficient safeguards so that the purpose and policies behind NEPA will necessarily be fulfilled."[56]

Courts have held that the functional equivalency exception to NEPA has been met with respect to EPA actions under the Clean Air Act,[57] the Federal Insecticide, Fungicide and Rodenticide Act,[58] the Resource Conservation and Recovery Act,[59] the Toxic Substances Control Act,[60] the Safe Drinking Water Act,[61] and the Ocean Dumping Act.[62] Courts have not yet addressed whether EPA Superfund cleanup actions under the Comprehensive Environmental Response, Compensation and Liability Act (CERCLA) fall within the functional equivalency exception.

One of the primary arguments against applying the exception to CERCLA is that often the agency which caused the contamination is the one which is cleaning it up, albeit under EPA supervision. In such a case, the agency with primary responsibility does not have the mandate in its organic statute to protect the environment. Indeed, courts have not yet applied the exception to agencies other than EPA, even where the agency arguably has substantial environmental responsibilities,[63] and have rejected arguments to extend the exception to actions by the Forest Service,[64] the National Marine Fisheries Service,[65] the National

---

[55]*See, e.g., Alabama v. United States Environmental Protection Agency*, 911 F.2d 499 (11th Cir. 1990); *Environmental Defense Fund v. Environmental Protection Agency*, 489 F.2d 1247 (D.C. Cir. 1973).

[56]*EDF v. EPA*, 489 F.2d at 1257.

[57]*Portland Cement Ass'n v. Ruckelshaus*, 486 F.2d 375 (D.C. Cir. 1973), *cert. denied*, 417 U.S. 921 (1974).

[58]*EDF v. EPA*, 489 F.2d at 1256-57.

[59]*Alabama v. EPA*, 911 F.2d at 504.

[60]*Warren County v. State of North Carolina*, 528 F. Supp. 276, 286-87 (E.D.N.C. 1981).

[61]*Western Nebraska Resources Coun. v. United States Environmental Protection Agency*, 943 F.2d 867, 871-72 (8th Cir. 1991).

[62]*Maryland v. Train*, 415 F. Supp. 116, 121-22 (D. Md. 1976).

[63]*Compare Wyoming v. Hathaway*, 525 F.2d 66, 71-72 (10th Cir. 1975) *cert. denied, sub nom. Wyoming v. Kleppe*, 426 U.S. 906 (1976), *with Texas Comm. on Natural Resources v. Bergland*, 573 F.2d 201, 208 (5th Cir.)), *cert. denied*, 439 U.S. 966 (1978) *and Jones v. Gordon*, 621 F. Supp. 7, 13 (D. Alaska 1985)), *aff'd in part, rev'd in part*, 792 F.2d 821 (9th Cir. 1986).

[64]*Texas Committee on Natural Resources*, 573 F.2d at 208.

[65]*Jones*, 621 F. Supp. at 7.

Institutes of Health,[66] and the Bureau of Land Management,[67] among others.

However, it has been suggested that NEPA procedures could be easily melded with the early "remedial investigation and feasibility study" (RI/FS) required by CERCLA,[68] perhaps, in view of the importance CERCLA places on prompt remedial actions, by using the expedited process allowed by NEPA in cases of emergency.[69] Indeed, this is the approach taken by the Department of Energy, which has decided to prepare a programmatic EIS to address the agencywide implications of its CERCLA cleanup efforts, which can be tiered to "sitewide" EIS's which analyze the environmental impacts of treatment, storage and disposal facilities and the cumulative impacts of DOE clean-up actions.[70] NEPA compliance for individual DOE CERCLA projects will be accomplished through the use of categorical exclusions or EA/FONSIs[71] (FONSI: finding of no significant impact) drafted during the RI/FS process.[72]

4.0 STRATEGIC APPROACHES TO NEPA COMPLIANCE

The strategy for successful compliance with NEPA's provisions is achieved by integrating environmental awareness and environmental factors early in the planning and decision-making process. Recognizing that NEPA is largely a procedural statute, compliance with its provisions calls for planning and analysis which fully considers and documents on a timely basis the environmental considerations and alternatives to the proposed action. Sound environmental planning provides opportunities for the federal agency to design proposals early in the process that meet both the agency's programmatic and environmental objectives and help insure successful NEPA compliance.

4.1 Non-Major Actions

The first step in planning for an agency proposal or private action is to determine whether that proposal or action will be subject to NEPA. Agency regulations developed in accordance with CEQ directives should assist in defining those proposals or actions which may be excluded from NEPA documentation. The "categorical exclusion" is the method by which an agency identifies a category of actions which "do not individually or cumulatively have a significant effect on the human environment" and

---

[66]*Foundation on Economic Trends v. Heckler*, 587 F. Supp. 753, 765-66 (D.D.C. 1984), *aff'd in part, vacated in part on other grounds*, 756 F.2d 143 (D.C. Cir. 1985).

[67]*Sierra Club v. Hodel*, 848 F.2d 1068, 1094-95 (10th Cir. 1988).

[68]42 U.S.C. § 9620(e)(1).

[69]40 C.F.R. § 1506.11 (1991).

[70]Dept. of Energy, Guidance on Implementation of the DOE NEPA/CERCLA Integration Policy (Nov. 15, 1991).

[71]*See infra*, Section 4.4.

[72]*Id.* DOE expects only a relatively few projects will require the preparation of an EIS during the RI/FS for individual projects.

which have been found to have had no such effect in past instances.[73] Proposals or actions which fit these exclusion categories do not require an EA, an EIS or other documentation unless unique circumstances create the possibility that significant impacts could occur. However, categorical exclusion is not an exemption from compliance with NEPA, but merely an administrative tool to avoid paperwork for those actions without significant environmental effects.[74]

If a non-federal action has some "minor" federal involvement, a court may determine that the federal action is a minor action not subject to NEPA. To be subject to NEPA, the action must be one over which the federal agency has sufficient discretion and control to make NEPA application meaningful.[75]

4.2 Formulating the Proposal

It is important in the early planning stages to clearly define the "need" to be addressed by the proposed action. The definition of need is often closely aligned with the definition of the required "no-action" alternative which must be discussed in the EIS. If the need is ill-defined or vague, the proposed action and any alternatives may also suffer and will likely be difficult to assess. This result may weaken the proposal and increase its vulnerability to a potential challenge in the EIS process.

If early scoping and consultation with affected parties is accomplished, a notion of the environmental concerns will be known. To the extent that the proposed action can be designed or formulated to incorporate mitigation measures which address these concerns, it is more likely that the proposed action will have a sound footing for acceptance and will avoid significant impacts. This fulfills NEPA's intent.

In formulating the proposed action, the agency must be careful to include all of the actions related to the proposed action which constitute the proposal.[76] The problem of "segmentation" or "piece-mealing" has arisen in projects which involve various stages of development or where agencies have attempted in the past to avoid "major actions" by splitting up a proposed action. The proposed action must include all of these connected actions as part of the proposal. CEQ provides guidance in the definition of the "scope" of the EIS on such "connected actions" which are "closely related" and should be considered together in a single EIS.[77] The regulations state:

Actions are connected if they:

---

[73]40 C.F.R. § 1508.4 (1991).

[74]*See* Bear, *supra* note 3, at 10063.

[75]*See Macht v. Skinner*, 916 F.2d 13 (D.C. Cir. 1990); see also Daniel R. Mandelker, *NEPA Law and Litigation* § 8:16 (1984); *Winnebago Tribe of Nebraska v. Ray*, 621 F.2d 269, 272 (8th Cir.), *cert. denied*, 449 U.S. 836 (1980).

[76]40 C.F.R. § 1502.4(a) (1991).

[77]*Id.* § 1508.25(a).

(i)   automatically trigger other actions which may require EIS's.

(ii)   cannot or will not proceed unless other actions are taken previously or simultaneously.

(iii) are interdependent parts of a larger action and depend on the larger action for their justification.[78]

For example, in highway cases where this issue originally arose,[79] a project planned between two points may involve the construction of several highway segments over time. Under the Federal Highway Administration NEPA regulations, in order to avoid segmentation, a project must (1) connect logical termini; (2) have independent utility or independent significance; and (3) not restrict future transportation improvement alternatives.[80]

4.3 Tiering

There are various levels in the planning and decision-making process where an EIS may be required. Federal decisions made at the national level among competing programmatic alternatives and policies which affect the entire federal effort may require the preparation of a "programmatic" EIS (PEIS). Proposals for federal actions may also be made at a regional level requiring an EIS which is focused on regional considerations and which must be more specific than the national PEIS. Finally, a proposed project at a specific site may require an EIS more detailed than the regional EIS or national PEIS.

"Tiering" is an approach whereby the very site-specific project EIS can incorporate by reference and without repetition the broader considerations of a regionwide EIS, or even a national PEIS, if they are relevant. CEQ regulations note that tiering is appropriate when the sequence of EIS's is from a program, plan or policy EIS to a site-specific statement or from an EIS on a specific action at an early stage (such as a need and site selection) to a subsequent statement at a later stage. Tiering in such cases is appropriate when it helps the responsible federal agency focus on the issues which are ripe for discussion, and exclude from consideration issues already decided or not yet ripe.[81]

An example is the Federal Aviation Administration (FAA) which might prepare a programmatic EIS on its nationwide systems airport plan to evaluate choices and alternatives to providing national aviation services. On a regional or statewide basis, the FAA may focus on providing air service improvements within that region, utilizing a regionwide or statewide EIS. Finally, for a specific airport proposal, a project EIS would be developed which could incorporate by reference any relevant

---

[78]*Id.* § 1508.25(a)(1).

[79]*See Named Individual Members of the San Antonio Conservation Soc'y v. Texas Highway Dept.*, 446 F.2d 1013 (5th Cir. 1971), *cert. denied*, 406 U.S. 933 (1972).

[80]23 C.F.R. § 771.111(f)

[81]*Id.* § 1508.28.

information from the regionwide or statewide EIS, or information from the nationwide PEIS.

Tiering is a useful tool when new federal programs are initiated which must later be delegated to regional programs and finally become site-specific activities. Tiering can be used in the NEPA compliance process to avoid duplication and provide the appropriate detail required for the level of action under consideration. Using the tiered system, a project specific EA or EIS need only focus on potential environmental impacts of the project that are not covered by earlier, broader statements.

4.4 Environmental Assessments

An environmental assessment (EA) is used as a screening document to determine whether an agency must prepare an EIS or make a finding of no significant impact (FONSI). CEQ regulations describe an EA as a concise public document that also serves to aid an agency's compliance with NEPA when no EIS is necessary and to facilitate preparation of an EIS when one is necessary.[82] An EA should include a brief discussion of the need for the proposal, of alternatives as required by section 102(2)(E), of the environmental impacts of the proposed action and alternatives, and a listing of agencies and persons consulted.

Although most agency procedures do not require public involvement prior to finalizing an EA document, it is advisable for agencies to consider facilitating public comment at the draft EA stage. Early public input will help the agency prepare a final EA which addresses adequately and completely the environmental issues likely to be raised by opponents of an agency action. Moreover, it will assist the agency in preparing the FONSI, which becomes the record for review by a court if challenged.

A FONSI briefly presents the reasons why an action, not otherwise categorically excluded, will not have a significant effect on the human environment. It must include the EA or a summary of the EA in supporting the FONSI determination.[83] Although EAs and FONSIs are public documents, they are not filed in a central location like EIS's.

CEQ regulations require that in certain limited circumstances, the agency must make the FONSI determination available for public review by some means including state and areawide clearinghouses, for thirty days before the agency makes its final determination of whether to prepare an EIS, and before any action may begin.[84] Those circumstances are:

  (i) The proposed action is, or is closely similar to, one which normally requires the preparation of an EIS under the procedures adopted by the agency; or

  (ii) The nature of the proposed action is one without precedent.

---

[82]*Id.* § 1508.9.
[83]*Id.* § 1508.13.
[84]*Id.* § 1501.4(e)(2).

EAs need to be of sufficient length to insure that the underlying decision about whether to prepare an EIS is sound, but should not attempt to be a substitute for an EIS.[85] A thorough EA provides a good information base early in the process for both agency and public consideration.

5.0 EIS PREPARATION

If it is determined that a proposed federal action, or non-federal action having sufficient federal involvement, does not fall within a designated categorical exclusion or does not qualify for a FONSI, then the responsible federal agency or agencies must prepare an EIS.

5.1 Lead Agency

The proposed action may be one where several agencies have some responsibility and all must comply with NEPA. CEQ regulations provide for a "lead agency" to take primary responsibility for the preparation of the EIS and to supervise the process.[86] Other agencies which have a responsibility by law for the joint action then become "cooperating agencies."[87] If a disagreement should arise among the agencies as to who should be the lead, CEQ regulations provide guidance based upon the magnitude of the agency's involvement, their project approval authority, expertise, duration of involvement and sequence of agency's involvement.[88] If a determination cannot be made on these factors, the CEQ can be asked to make the necessary determination.

The lead agency concept avoids duplication and enhances cooperation among the agencies. In addition, where there are state or local environmental reporting requirements, the lead agency can team with state or local agencies in the preparation of one EIS or environmental document to satisfy all requirements, thereby reducing duplication.[89]

At this stage in the process, sufficient environmental planning should have been completed to clearly identify the proposed action and reasonable alternatives thereto. Further, if an EA has been prepared for this proposed action, some early coordination with affected agencies and interest groups will have already occurred. Thus, the agency should be prepared to publish a notice of intent to prepare an EIS and initiate the first step—the scoping process.[90]

---

[85] *See* Bear, *supra* note 3, at 10063.

[86] 40 C.F.R. § 1501.5 (1991).

[87] *Id.* § 1501.6.

[88] *Id.* § 1501.5(c).

[89] *Id.* § 1506.2.

[90] *Id.* § 1501.7. The "notice of intent" must (i) describe the proposed action and possible alternatives; (ii) describe the proposed scoping process; and (iii) provide the name and address of a person within the agency to contact concerning the EIS. *Id.* § 1508.22.

5.2 Scoping and Early Coordination

The scoping process is the first opportunity for the agency to involve the public by describing the agency's planning efforts to address the needs identified and to solicit comments on the scope of actions, alternatives and impacts which need to be considered. The CEQ regulations require that this be an early and open process conducted as soon as practicable after its decision to prepare an EIS.[91] The lead agency must invite the participation of affected federal, state and local agencies, any affected Indian tribes, the proponents of the action, and other interested persons (including those who might not be in accord with the action on environmental grounds).[92]

This scoping process is used to identify the significant issues requiring in-depth analysis in the EIS and to eliminate from detailed study those issues which are not significant or have been covered by prior environmental reviews. The scoping process is also used by the agency to make preliminary assignments between the lead agency and cooperating agencies concerning the EIS preparation, to identify other public EAs or EIS's which are being or will be prepared that are related to the EIS under consideration, to identify other environmental review and consultation requirements that need to be integrated into this process, and finally, to establish a schedule for the timing of the EIS and the ultimate decision on the proposed action.

The CEQ regulations allow the agencies flexibility in several other areas, such as setting page limits on environmental documents, setting time limits, adopting procedures to combine the EA process with the scoping process, and holding early scoping meetings or meetings which may be integrated with other early planning meetings.[93]

The scoping process is important because it sends a signal to the public about both the agency's attitude toward public involvement and its planning for the proposal at hand. It also provides an opportunity for the agency to set reasonable boundaries on the timing, content and process that will be used for the EIS. It may also be used to restrict new subjects from being introduced later to challenge the agency's decision.[94]

The scoping process also offers an opportunity for the agency to investigate the criteria which commenting agencies will use in determining the environmental factors that are important and what impacts are likely to be considered significant.

5.3 Use of the EA and Applicant's Information

After the scoping process is completed, the lead agency must begin to prepare for collecting and assimilating the environmental information

---

[91] *Id.* § 1501.7

[92] *Id.* § 1501.7(a).

[93] *Id.* § 1501.7(b).

[94] *See Vermont Yankee Nuclear Power Corp.*, 435 U.S. at 551-54.

needed for the EIS. A starting point for this process is to review the material prepared for the EA or supplied by the applicant.

CEQ regulations provide that an agency may require an applicant to submit environmental information for possible use by the agency in preparing an EIS. The agency must assist the applicant in outlining the types of information required and must independently evaluate the information submitted in order to take responsibility for its accuracy.[95] Similarly, if an agency permits an applicant to prepare an EA, the agency must undertake a similar evaluation of its own and assume responsibility for the scope and content of the EA.[96]

5.4 Delegation

The responsibility for preparing the EIS belongs to the lead federal agency pursuant to section 102(2)(C). Under many federal programs, delegation to the states has been a common practice, particularly where the state acts as an applicant for federal funding. The Federal Highway Administration is one agency that delegated to the states many of the responsibilities under the Federal Aid Highway program. In 1975, this practice was challenged by an environmental group in *Conservation Soc'y of S. Vermont v. Secretary of Transportation*.[97]

In holding that the Federal Highway Administration could not delegate its NEPA responsibility to the state, the court noted that:

> A state agency is established to pursue defined state goals. In attempting to serve federal approval of a project, "self-serving assumptions" may ineluctably color a state agency's presentation of the environmental data or influence its final recommendation. Transposing the federal duty to prepare the EIS to a state agency is thus unlikely to result in as dispassionate an appraisal of environmental considerations as the federal agency itself could produce.[98]

The surrounding states interpreted this decision to prohibit any delegation to state highway agencies and thus stopped all highway construction in the Northeast. Congress responded in 1975 with the only substantive amendment to NEPA since its enactment by adding a new section to address the delegation issue, section 102(2)(D).[99]

This section provides that an EIS may be prepared by a state agency having statewide jurisdiction so long as the responsible federal official furnishes guidance, participates in the preparation, and independently evaluates the EIS prior to its approval and adoption. Further, the amendment

---

[95] 40 C.F.R. § 1506.5 (1991).

[96] *Id.* § 1506.5(b).

[97] 508 F.2d 927 (2d Cir. 1974), *vacated*, 423 U.S. 809 (1975) (vacated as a result of subsequent legislation).

[98] *Id.* at 931.

[99] 42 U.S.C. § 4332(2)(D).

provides that if the proposed action has any impacts on an adjoining state or federal land management entity, the responsible federal official must solicit that state's or entity's views on potential impacts.[100]

An earlier court case had disapproved the preparation of an EIS by a private applicant on account of the potential self-serving interest of the applicant in receiving an approval from the agency.[101] However, this decision did not prevent an applicant from assisting the agency by submitting environmental information or by participating in environmental studies that form the basis for an EIS.[102]

Similarly, the use of consultants in the preparation of an EIS is a common practice and is acceptable so long as the federal agency retains sufficient control of their work product.[103] The CEQ regulations state that the agency should avoid conflicts of interest and require a disclosure statement from the contractor indicating that it has no financial or other interest in the project. Further, the federal agency is to provide guidance and participate in the preparation of the EIS, evaluate it independently, and take responsibility for its scope and content.[104]

5.5 Content of EIS

The purpose of an EIS is to help public officials make informed decisions that are based on an understanding of environmental consequences and the reasonable alternatives available to them. "[EIS's] shall be concise, clear, and to the point, and shall be supported by evidence that agencies have made the necessary environmental analyses."[105]

Section 102(2)(C) requires an EIS to describe: (i) the environmental impacts of the proposed action; (ii) any adverse environmental impacts which cannot be avoided should the proposal be implemented; (iii) the reasonable alternatives to the proposed action; (iv) the relationship between local short term uses of man's environment and the maintenance and enhancement of long term productivity; and (v) any irreversible and irretrievable commitments of resources which would be involved in the proposed action should it be implemented.

EIS's have evolved so that they place more emphasis on a description of the affected environment, the alternatives to the proposed action, and possible mitigation measures than on what is outlined in the statute. The CEQ regulations outline a recommended format for EIS preparation.[106]

---

[100]*Id.* § 4332(2)(D)(iv).

[101]*Green County Planning Bd. v. Federal Power Comm'n.*, 455 F.2d 412 (2d Cir.), *cert. denied*, 409 U.S. 849 (1972).

[102]*Sierra Club v. Lynn*, 502 F.2d 43 (5th Cir. 1974), *cert. denied*, 421 U.S. 994, 422 U.S. 1049 (1975).

[103]*Natural Resources Defense Coun. v. Callaway*, 524 F.2d 79 (2d Cir. 1975).

[104]40 C.F.R. § 1506.5(c) (1991).

[105]*Id.* § 1500.2(b).

[106]*Id.* § 1502.10.

The alternatives section of the EIS is the "heart" of the EIS.[107] Once the affected environment and environmental consequences are described, the discussion of the proposed action and alternatives should be presented in a comparative form in order to sharply define the issues and provide a clear basis for the choice among options by the decision-maker and the public. CEQ regulations require that all "reasonable" alternatives, within or outside the jurisdiction of the lead agency, including the no-action alternative, be discussed.[108] CEQ has provided guidance on the range of alternatives agencies must consider.[109] This discussion should also include appropriate mitigation measures not already included in the proposed action and alternatives.

The environmental consequences section of the EIS provides the scientific and analytic basis for the comparison of alternatives. It must include a discussion of direct effects of the proposed action and alternatives, indirect effects, possible conflicts with objectives of federal, regional, state, and local (including Indian tribes) land use plans, policies and controls of the area concerned, and other key areas outlined in the CEQ regulations.[110]

When evaluating reasonably foreseeable significant adverse effects in the EIS, if there is incomplete or unavailable information on account of the costs of obtaining such information, the agency is directed to include within the EIS a statement that such information is incomplete or unavailable, the relevance of such information, a summary of existing credible scientific evidence which is relevant to evaluating the reasonably foreseeable adverse impacts, and the agency's evaluation of such impacts based upon theoretical approaches or research methods generally accepted in the scientific community.[111] Earlier CEQ regulation had required a "worst case analysis" in such situations, but revoked this analyses requirement with a 1986 amendment to the regulations after considerable debate.[112] The Supreme Court later approved this revocation of the CEQ regulation noting that it was not a prior codification of any judicial determination and thus the Court should give substantial deference to CEQ's revocation amendment.[113]

The discussion of indirect effects or impacts has been the most vulnerable to challenge. Indirect effects include economic growth-inducing effects of the proposed action, changes in land use patterns induced by the action, anticipated changes in population density or growth areas, and

---

[107]*Id.* § 1502.14.

[108]*Id.* § 1502.14.

[109]46 *Fed. Reg.* 18026, 18027 (1981) (Council on Environmental Quality, Forty Most Asked Questions Concerning CEQ's National Environmental Policy Act Regulations, Question 1).

[110]40 C.F.R. § 1502.16 (1991).

[111]*Id.* § 1502.22.

[112]51 *Fed. Reg.* 15625 (1986).

[113]*Robertson v. Methow Valley Citizens*, 490 U.S. 332, 356 (1989).

related impacts on air, water and other natural systems, including ecosystems. Effects also include those resulting from actions which may have both beneficial and detrimental effects, even if on balance the agency believes that the effect will be beneficial.

Finally, "cumulative" impacts must also be covered in an EA or EIS which requires analysis of the "incremental impact of the action when added to other past, present, and reasonably foreseeable future actions regardless of what agency (federal or non-federal) or person undertakes such other actions. Cumulative impacts can result from individually minor but collectively significant actions taking place over a period of time."[114] This language from the CEQ regulations substantially expands the discussion of impacts in the EIS, but allows considerable discretion by the agency in defining some of the key terms in its definition. Further, the regulation defining "significantly" requires the federal agency to consider "actions related to other actions with individually insignificant, but cumulatively significant, impacts."[115] The courts have scrutinized closely cumulative impact analyses in EAs and EIS's and appear willing to find them inadequate on this basis.[116]

5.6 Commenting and Public Involvement

The NEPA statute makes public involvement in the process an essential element in ensuring informed decision-making at the federal level. Section 102(2)(C) requires that "[c]opies of [the EIS] and the comments and views of the appropriate Federal, state and local agencies, which are authorized to develop and enforce environmental standards, shall be made available to the President, the Council on Environmental Quality and *to the public* as provided by [the Freedom of Information Act]."[117] Further, section 102(2)(G) requires that the federal agencies must make available to the states, counties, municipalities, institutions, and *individuals*, advice and information useful in restoring, maintaining, and enhancing the quality of the environment.[118]

Public involvement was expanded by both Executive Order 11514[119] and the CEQ Guidelines[120] (now regulations). The CEQ regulations provide for involvement by requiring "public notice of NEPA-related hearings, public meetings, and the availability of environmental documents" so that interested persons and agencies can be informed.[121]

---

[114]40 C.F.R. § 1508.7 (1991).

[115]*Id.* § 1508.27(b)(7).

[116]*See Fritiofson v. Alexander,* 772 F.2d 1225 (5th Cir. 1985); *Thomas v. Peterson,* 753 F.2d 754 (9th Cir. 1985).

[117]42 U.S.C. § 4332(2)(C) (Emphasis added).

[118]*Id.* § 4332(2)(G) (Emphasis added).

[119]*See supra,* note 15.

[120]*See supra,* note 16.

[121]40 C.F.R. § 1506.6(b) (1991).

Public involvement can occur at three stages in the EIS process: initial scoping, commenting on the draft EIS, and commenting on the final EIS prior to a record of decision. At the scoping stage, public involvement is valuable to identify the potential environmental impacts, to judge the breadth of potential controversial issues, and to observe the public's reaction to the need for action and the alternatives that may exist to satisfy the need. Effective public involvement can also assist the agency in prioritizing the issues that need to be addressed in the EIS. At the draft EIS comment stage, the public can provide valuable feedback to the agency in identifying both the impacts which have not been adequately addressed and areas where gaps of information or analysis may exist. Comments regarding potential mitigation measures from the public may also be helpful to the agency at this juncture. Lastly, public comments on the final EIS assist the agency in making its final decision and preparing a formal record of decision. This is the last opportunity the public has to ensure that the agency has all the relevant information and analyses before it, and that significant issues have been properly addressed.

The CEQ regulations direct the agency, after preparing a draft EIS and before preparing a final EIS, to obtain the comments of any federal agency which has jurisdiction by law or special expertise with respect to environmental impacts involved or which is authorized to develop and enforce environmental standards.[122] Further, the agency must request the comments of appropriate state and local agencies which are authorized to develop and enforce environmental standards, Indian tribes, when effects may occur on a reservation, and any agency which has requested that it receive comments on actions of the kind proposed.[123] Finally, the agency must request comments from the applicant, if any, and from the public, affirmatively soliciting comments from those persons or organizations who may be interested or affected.[124]

The lead agency preparing the final EIS must then assess and consider the comments both individually and collectively and respond by making necessary changes in the EIS, making factual corrections or explaining why the comments do not warrant further agency response.[125] All of the substantive comments received on the draft EIS must be attached to the final EIS whether or not the comment is thought to merit individual discussion by the agency.

The CEQ regulations require agencies to make diligent efforts to involve the public in the NEPA process by providing public notice of NEPA-related hearings, public meetings and the availability of environmental documents, and holding or sponsoring public hearings or public meetings

---

[122]*Id.* § 1503.1.
[123]*Id.*
[124]*Id.*
[125]*Id.* § 1503.4.

whenever appropriate or in accordance with statutory requirements applicable to the agency.[126]

5.7 Mitigation of Impacts

Appropriate mitigation measures must be included in the EIS.[127] Once an agency decision is made, any mitigation measures or other conditions established in the EIS or during its review and committed as part of the decision must be implemented by the lead agency or other appropriate consenting agency.[128] CEQ lists five generic mitigation measures in their regulatory definition of "mitigation."[129]

Whether NEPA requires agencies to commit to mitigation measures in the first instance was addressed by the Supreme Court in *Robertson v. Methow Valley Citizens*.[130] The Court of Appeals had held that NEPA imposes a substantive duty on agencies to take action to mitigate the adverse effects of major federal actions, which entails the further duty to include in every EIS a detailed explanation of specific actions that will be employed to mitigate the adverse effects.[131] The Supreme Court reversed the finding, noting the difference between a requirement that mitigation be discussed and a substantive requirement that a complete mitigation plan be formulated and adopted. "[I]t would be inconsistent with NEPA's reliance on procedural mechanisms—as opposed to substantive, result-based standards—to demand the presence of a fully developed plan that will mitigate environmental harm before an agency can act."[132] The Court found no substantive requirement or duty to include in an EIS a detailed explanation of specific measures which will be employed to mitigate adverse impacts of a proposed action.

5.8 Proposals for Legislation

Section 102(2)(C) requires the preparation of an EIS for proposals for legislation as well as for major federal actions.[133] CEQ regulations require that a legislative EIS be transmitted to Congress within thirty days of the formal transmittal of a legislative proposal to Congress.[134] The intent is to provide a document that can serve as the basis for public and congressional debate. A scoping process is not required as part of a legislative EIS, and normally only a draft EIS will be required.[135]

---

[126]*Id.* § 1506.6.

[127]*Id.* § 1502.14(f).

[128]*Id.* § 1505.3.

[129]*Id.* § 1508.20.

[130]490 U.S. 332 (1989).

[131]*Methow Valley Citizens Coun. v. Regional Forester*, 833 F.2d 810 (9th Cir. 1987), *cert. granted*, 47 U.S. 1217 (1988), *rev'd*, 490 U.S. 332 (1989).

[132]*Robertson*, 490 U.S. at 353.

[133]42 U.S.C. § 4332(2)(C).

[134]40 C.F.R. § 1506.8 (1991).

[135]*Id.* § 1506.8(b).

Very little attention has been given to proposals for legislation under NEPA, primarily because most legislative proposals come from the president or the executive office of the president, which are not included in the definition of "federal agency."[136] Further, in the extensive communication which occurs between the Congress and the executive branch, it is often very difficult to determine when a "proposal" will trigger the need for an EIS.

The Supreme Court has addressed the question of whether an EIS is required for an appropriations request from an agency. In *Andrus v. Sierra Club*,[137] the Court held that an EIS was not required when the Office of Management and Budget proposed a significant reduction in the Fish and Wildlife Service appropriation for the operation of the National Wildlife Refuge System. The Court referenced CEQ regulations which defines "legislation" as "a bill or legislative proposal" and omits any reference to "appropriation requests."[138] Therefore, the Court held that an EIS was not required, and further, that requiring an EIS on appropriation proposals would circumvent and eliminate "the careful distinction Congress had maintained between appropriations and legislation."[139]

6.0 NEPA'S EXTRATERRITORIAL APPLICATION

International application of NEPA has been a matter of controversy since the statute does not explicitly indicate whether it applies outside the United States. Some agencies have argued that compliance with NEPA could present obstacles to meeting certain foreign policy objectives. While section 102(2)(F) requires that "all agencies of the federal government shall . . . recognize the worldwide and long-range character of environmental problems and . . . lend appropriate support . . . to maximize international cooperation," it appears to impose a duty on federal agencies only to "recognize" worldwide environmental problems. In a recent challenge to the operation of an incinerator in the Antarctica by the National Science Foundation, the court found that an EIS was not required because Congress had failed to "provide a clear expression of legislative intent through a plain statement of extraterritorial statutory effect."[140]

In 1979, President Carter issued Executive Order No. 12114 on the environmental effects abroad of major federal actions, based on his independent executive authority rather than on NEPA. Nevertheless, the objective of the Executive Order was to further the purposes of NEPA by providing procedures for ensuring that pertinent environmental considerations were given to actions having effects outside the geographical

---

[136]*Id.* § 1508.12. The presidential exemption applies only to the president and immediate staff, not to offices in the EOP like CEQ.

[137]442 U.S. 347 (1979).

[138]*Id.* at 357.

[139]*Id.* at 364.

[140]*Environmental Defense Fund v. Massey*, 772 F. Supp. 1296, 1297 (D.D.C. 1991).

boundaries of the United States.[141] Although it does not create a cause of action in the courts, it provides for environmental analysis and documentation for actions affecting the global commons or for actions in which foreign nations are not participating with the United States; and for certain actions which could create a serious public health risk.[142]

In February 1991, the United States signed a Convention on Environmental Impact Assessment with European countries obligating the signatories to consult when an activity is likely to cause adverse transboundary environmental impacts. The Department of State, EPA and CEQ are designing the implementation strategy for the convention.[143]

7.0 JUDICIAL REVIEW OF NEPA

The courts have played a crucial role in enforcing NEPA's environmental mandates. Judicial review is not expressly provided for in the statute, but federal agencies have held that judicial review of agency decisions is implied under NEPA.[144] Judicial review usually occurs when the agency either decides not to file an EIS or makes a final decision after completing the EIS process. Generally, the courts review an agency's EIS to determine whether it is "adequate" under NEPA's statutory provisions.

The court case most often cited in setting the standard of review for agency decisions under NEPA is *Citizens to Preserve Overton Park, Inc. v. Volpe.*[145] Although this case was not a NEPA case, the Supreme Court indicated that courts must conduct a "substantial inquiry" into agency decisions to determine whether the agency has taken a "hard look" at the issues. This "hard look" doctrine has become the hallmark of judicial review in environmental law.

However, this "hard look" does not mean that a court can substitute its own judgment for that of the agency. Under NEPA, as in administrative law generally, once a court is satisfied that the agency has given fair and adequate consideration to the relevant evidence, the agency decision will not be set aside absent a finding that the decision was "arbitrary, capricious, an abuse of discretion, or otherwise not in accordance with law."[146] In essence, this means that the agency decision will not be set aside unless the court is convinced there has been "a clear error of judgment" by the agency.[147] The reason for this deferential standard of review is that the agency's decision turns on the resolution of factual disputes—an inquiry

---

[141]Executive Order No. 12114, 3 C.F.R. 356 (1980).

[142]*Id.* §§ 2-3.

[143]Council on Environmental Quality 22nd Annual Report, p.136 (1992).

[144]*Calvert Cliffs Coordinating Committee, Inc.*, 449 F.2d at 1115; *see also Environmental Defense Fund v. Corps of Engineers of the United States Army*, 470 F.2d 289 (8th Cir. 1972), *cert. denied*, 412 U.S. 931 (1973).

[145]401 U.S. 402 (1971).

[146]5 U.S.C. § 706(2); *Marsh v. Oregon Natural Resources Coun.*, 490 U.S. 360 (1989).

[147]*Marsh*, 490 U.S. at 377-78, 385.

which the agency, by virtue of its substantial technical expertise, is more qualified to conduct than the court. Thus, the Supreme Court in 1989 held that an agency's decision not to prepare a supplemental EIS based on new information was not a clear error of judgment, inasmuch as there were conflicting views in the scientific community with respect to the significance of that information and the agency could only decide which side to believe based on its own scientific expertise.[148]

By contrast, where the outcome of the dispute turns on the agency's *legal* interpretation of applicable statutes or regulations, a court will conduct a less-deferential review, and may substitute its own judgment for that of the agency. The reason for this is clear—in matters of legal interpretation, as opposed to matters of fact, the agency has no special expertise that makes its decision preferable to that of a court. There is one important qualification to this rule, however. A court will give effect to an agency's interpretation of its *own* organic statute or regulations, as long as that interpretation is a "reasonable" one.[149] In addition, the courts have accorded "substantial deference" to CEQ's regulations regarding the implementation of NEPA.

An important issue in obtaining judicial review is "standing." Most environmental challenges under NEPA are brought by environmental organizations or third parties who may not have participated in the agency decision that is the subject of litigation. Their standing or access to the courts has been routinely granted under NEPA, although it may become more difficult in the future.

While the courts apply the basic "significant injury" test for standing under the Constitution and the Administrative Procedures Act (APA),[150] at least one court has suggested that when this test is applied to NEPA litigation, there is perhaps a lower threshold for standing than is typically required.[151] This is because the nature of rights created by NEPA may compel an unusually broad definition of the act's zone of interest, thus making it easier to obtain standing under NEPA than under most statutes.

In general, plaintiffs have successfully maintained standing by alleging their use of areas that may be affected by an agency's failure to prepare an EIS, or areas in close proximity to those areas.

In 1990, however, the Supreme Court held that plaintiffs failed to satisfy the specific injury requirement if they could only allege that they use certain lands "in the vicinity of" the potentially affected areas.[152] The Supreme Court acknowledged that NEPA does not provide a private right

---

[148]*Id.*

[149]*Robertson v. Methow Valley Citizens Council*, 490 U.S. at 358- 59.

[150]5 U.S.C. §§ 551-559.

[151]*Public Citizen v. Nat'l Highway Traffic Safety Admin.*, 848 F.2d 256, 261 (D.C. Cir. 1988).

[152]*Lujan v. National Wildlife Federation*, 487 U.S. 871 (1990).

of action for violations of its provisions, but rather that an injured party must seek relief under the APA.

To demonstrate standing under the APA, a plaintiff must identify some final agency action that affects him or her and must show that he or she has suffered a legal wrong because of the agency action or has been adversely affected by that action within the meaning of the relevant statute. To be "adversely affected within the meaning of the statute," a plaintiff must be within a "zone of interest" sought to be protected by the statutory provision that forms the basis of the complaint. Using this test of standing, the court found that the plaintiffs' interests were within the zone of interest to be protected by NEPA, but that the plaintiffs' claiming use "in the vicinity" of the agency action was not enough to render them "adversely affected." Given these findings, the court ruled that the plaintiffs had not set forth "specific facts" in their affidavit sufficient to survive the agency's motion for summary judgment.

While proving significant injury is certainly the most difficult part of establishing standing, a plaintiff must also show that the alleged significant injury will occur as a result of the agency's action. By characterizing the threatened injury as a chance that the agency, by failing to comply with NEPA, would overlook serious environmental harm, courts have found the causation element to be easily met. For example, in *City of Los Angeles v. Nat'l Highway Traffic Safety Admin.*,[153] the federal Court of Appeals for the District of Columbia granted standing to an environmental group that claimed the government, by failing to prepare an EIS, risked overlooking the impact of proposed federal fuel economy standards on global warming. The court held that as long as there is a "real possibility" that the agency would have reached a different decision if it had complied with the requirements of NEPA, standing should be granted. One judge disagreed, focusing instead on the alleged injury in the form of the "environmental nightmare" that would result from global warming. Because the agency's activity would, at most, have only an insignificant impact on global warming, the judge would have denied standing on the grounds that the agency's failure to prepare an EIS "appears to be but an insignificant tributary to the causal stream leading to the overall harm that petitioners have alleged."[154]

8.0 CONCLUSION

As NEPA enters its third decade, it continues to serve as the cornerstone environmental law whose mandates have been more fully integrated into the decision-making process of federal agencies. Environmental concerns have shifted from agency implementation issues to use NEPA to address global problems of biodiversity, pollution prevention, global warming, stratospheric ozone depletion and sustainable growth. Congressional

---

[153] 912 F.2d 478, 498 (D.C. Cir. 1990).
[154] *Id.* at 483-84.

legislation recently introduced could strengthen NEPA by extending its application to extraterritoral actions, requiring agencies to review the effectiveness of mitigation measures committed to in the EIS or record of decision, and eliminating two Council seats on the CEQ and vesting all functions and powers in the CEQ Chairman.

For a more definitive discussion of this topic, the reader is referred to the N E P A Compliance Manual *and related books and courses listed at the end of this book.*

Chapter 11

TOXIC SUBSTANCES CONTROL ACT

Stanley W. Landfair[1]
McKenna & Cuneo
Washington, D.C.

1.0 OVERVIEW

The Toxic Substances Control Act ("TSCA" or "the act"), 15 U.S.C. §§ 2601-2629, was enacted on October 11, 1976. The act has been amended three times, each amendment resulting in an additional title, so that TSCA now contains four titles: Title I—the Control of Toxic Substances; Title II—the Asbestos Hazard Emergency Response Act; Title III—the Indoor Radon Abatement Act; and Title IV—the Lead-Based Paint Exposure Reduction Act. Since Title IV was added so recently (it was signed into law by President Bush on October 29, 1992), it is worth noting that the new title will require EPA and the Occupational Safety and Health Administration to develop lead paint abatement training and certification programs for contractors who engage in lead-based paint activities, to identify lead-based paint hazards, and to define safe levels of lead in various media. The scope of this chapter, however, is limited to Title I of the act, the Control of Toxic Substances.

TSCA places on manufacturers the responsibility to provide data on the health and environmental effects of chemical substances and mixtures, and gives EPA comprehensive authority to regulate the manufacture, use, distribution in commerce, and disposal of chemical substances. To implement this authority, TSCA affords EPA the following regulatory tools:

- **Authority to require testing** of chemicals which may present a significant risk or which are produced in substantial quantities and result in substantial human or environmental exposure. (TSCA § 4)

- **Premanufacture review** of new chemical substances prior to their commercial production and introduction into the marketplace. (TSCA § 5)

- **Authority to limit or prohibit** the manufacture, use, distribution, and disposal of existing chemical substances. (TSCA §6)

---

[1] This chapter is condensed from the *TSCA Handbook* (Government Institutes 1989, 2d Ed.), of which Mr. Landfair is a co-author. Mr. Landfair acknowledges the assistance of Tyson E. Branyan, Carol R. Brophy and Elizabeth T. Coppage (associates, McKenna & Cuneo) and Dr. Joseph E. Plamondon (Technology Sciences Group, Inc.), in editing and updating this material, and to the many McKenna & Cuneo partners and associates who co-authored the *TSCA Handbook*.

- **Recordkeeping and reporting** requirements to ensure that the EPA administrator would continually have access to new information developed regarding adverse health or environmental effects associated with chemical substances. (TSCA § 8)
- **Export notice** requirements that allow EPA to inform foreign governments of shipments of chemical substances into their countries. (TSCA § 12)
- **Import certification** requirement to ensure that all chemical substances imported into the United States comply with the act. (TSCA §13)

Unlike other federal statutes that regulate chemical risks after a substance has been introduced into commerce, the major objective of TSCA is to characterize and understand the risks that a chemical poses to humans and the environment before it is introduced into commerce. Before undertaking regulatory action, however, TSCA requires that EPA balance the economic and social benefits derived from the use of a chemical against that chemical's identified risks. Thus, the goal of TSCA is not to regulate all chemicals which present a risk, but only those which present an "unreasonable" risk of harm to human health or the environment.

2.0 ACTIVITIES SUBJECT TO TSCA

The varied requirements of TSCA apply to persons and companies that manufacture, process, distribute, use, or dispose of TSCA-regulated chemicals. Thus, it is necessary to determine case-by-case whether a particular activity constitutes regulated conduct. Unfortunately, TSCA defines neither "use" nor "dispose," and the definitions of "manufacture," "process," and "distribute" are worded too broadly to provide meaningful guidance. Moreover, EPA's implementing regulations generally define these terms more narrowly than the statute. Consequently, the scope of TSCA jurisdiction often remains unclear. The definition of these important jurisdictional terms and the duties of those who fall within them are discussed below.

2.1 Manufacture

TSCA § 3(7) defines "manufacture" to include not only the traditional notions of manufacture and production, but also the importation of TSCA-regulated chemical substances or mixtures. Under TSCA, manufacturers of chemical substances generally must: (1) sponsor tests and submit data to EPA regarding chemicals they manufacture; (2) submit a premanufacture notice (PMN) before manufacturing a chemical substance not on the TSCA Inventory or before manufacturing a chemical for a significant new use; (3) avoid manufacture of PCBs; (4) maintain records and submit reports as required by § 8; (5) submit to EPA inspections and subpoenas as authorized by § 11; and (6) certify compliance with TSCA upon importation as required by § 13.

EPA regulations implementing TSCA § 5 (Premanufacture Notification) and § 8 (Reporting and Recordkeeping) limit jurisdiction to persons who "manufacture for commercial purposes" and define "commercial purposes" as:

> the purpose of obtaining an immediate or eventual commercial advantage for the manufacturer, and includes, among other things, . . .
>
> (i)   for distribution in commerce, including for test marketing.
>
> (ii)   for use by the manufacturer, including use for product research and development, or as an intermediate.
>
> [Further, this definition] applies to substances that are produced coincidentally during the manufacture, processing, use, or disposal of another substance or mixture, including both by-products that are separated from that other substance or mixture and impurities that remain in that substance or mixture.[2]

EPA has expanded the statutory definition of "manufacture" by including the act of "extracting" a chemical from another chemical substance or mixture of substances.[3] Importantly, a toll manufacturer—that is, an independent business which manufactures a chemical substance for another business—also is considered a manufacturer under the premanufacture and significant new use notification regulations. The purchasing or contracting company also may be considered a manufacturer, however, if: (1) the toll manufacturer produces the substance exclusively for that purchasing company; and (2) the purchasing company specifies the identity of the substance and controls the amount produced and the basic technology for the plant processes.[4]

2.2 Process

TSCA § 3(10) defines "process" to mean:

> the preparation of a chemical substance or mixture, after its manufacture, for distribution in commerce
>
> (A)   in the same form or physical state as, or in a different form or physical state from, that in which it was received by the persons so preparing such substance or mixture, or
>
> (B)   as part of an article containing the chemical substance or mixture.

TSCA § 3(11) further defines the term "processor" as "any person who processes a chemical substance or mixture."

Processors of chemical substances must: (1) provide EPA with data under test rules, in some circumstances; (2) notify EPA prior to processing a

---

[2]40 C.F.R. §§ 717.3(e), 712.3(h), 704.3, 716.3, and 720.3(r).

[3]40 C.F.R. §§ 704.3, 716.3 and 720.3(t).

[4]40 C.F.R. § 720.3(t).

chemical for a significant new use; (3) comply with EPA orders issued under §§ 5(e), 5(f) or 6(b) or rules promulgated under § 6(a); (4) avoid processing PCBs except as permitted by EPA; (5) comply with the reporting requirements of the Comprehensive Assessment Information Rule (CAIR) under § 8(a), and the recordkeeping and reporting requirements of §§ 8(c), 8(d) and 8(e); and (6) submit to EPA inspections and subpoenas, as authorized by § 11.

If EPA's regulations implementing the various subsections of TSCA applied to everyone who fell within the literal language of these broad definitions, TSCA requirements would be imposed on thousands of businesses that Congress never intended the law to touch. To avoid such problems for some reporting requirements under TSCA § 8, EPA has passed implementing rules that apply only to some processors.

Recognizing the need to address this issue in a comprehensive and organized manner, EPA recently announced the availability of a package of all EPA guidance documents that address the definitions of "process" or "processor."[5] EPA also solicited written comments and held a one-day public meeting to allow interested persons an opportunity to present their views on EPA's interpretation of "process" under TSCA. Several commentors urged EPA to begin formal rulemaking to modify the definition of "processor" and to limit or eliminate application of the term to basic manufacturers and other companies that traditionally have not considered themselves chemical processors. EPA indicates that the agency plans to review all written and oral comments received and address, as appropriate, the issues identified, starting with those that seem to be of the greatest concern to the regulated community and others.

2.3 Use

TSCA does not provide a definition of "use," nor has EPA issued comprehensive guidance on the distinction between "use" and "process." Nonetheless, users of chemical substances (who are not also manufacturers, processors, or distributors) must: (1) comply with regulations issued under § 6(a); (2) refrain from using PCBs, except as permitted by EPA; (3) refrain from using any chemical substance they know or have reason to know has been manufactured, produced, or distributed in violation of TSCA, as required under TSCA § 15(2); and (4) submit to EPA inspections and subpoenas, as authorized by § 11.

2.4 Distribution

Under TSCA § 3(4), the terms "distribute in commerce" and "distribution in commerce" mean to sell, to introduce, or to deliver a chemical substance into commerce or to hold the mixture or article after its introduction into commerce. The term "commerce" is defined in TSCA § 3(3) to mean

---

[5]*57 Fed. Reg.* 38,832 (1992).

interstate trade, traffic, transportation, or other activity which affects interstate trade, traffic, transportation, or commerce.

The TSCA definition of "distribution" thus encompasses more than the usual concept of sales or transportation, but its scope is not clear. For example, if applied literally, the portion that defines "holding" a chemical after its introduction in commerce as "distribution" would make any purchaser of a chemical a distributor since the person would necessarily hold the substance briefly before using it. In practice, EPA interprets the term to apply to persons who purchase a chemical and hold it for purposes of later distribution.

Distributors of chemical substances (who are not also manufacturers or processors) must: (1) comply with rules issued under § 6(a); (2) refrain from distributing PCBs except as permitted by EPA; (3) report "substantial risk information" to EPA under § 8(e); and (4) submit to EPA inspections and subpoenas, as authorized by § 11.

2.5 Disposal

Disposal is another activity not defined in TSCA. As a result, TSCA imposes no direct obligation on disposers of chemicals, but they may be subject to several types of rules or orders issued pursuant to the act. Disposers of chemical substances (who are not also manufacturers, processors, distributors, or users) must: (1) comply with regulations issued under § 6(a); (2) dispose of PCBs according to requirements of the PCB disposal regulations; and (3) submit to EPA inspections and subpoenas, as authorized by § 11.

3.0 THE TSCA INVENTORY

TSCA § 8(b) requires EPA to compile, keep current, and publish a list of chemical substances manufactured or processed for commercial purposes in the United States. This "list," known as the TSCA Inventory, forms the basis for distinguishing between "existing" chemicals (those included on the TSCA Inventory) and "new" chemicals (substances that require premanufacture notification under TSCA § 5). Thus, it is critically important to understand the TSCA Inventory and how it is compiled, kept current, and used.

3.1 Initial Compilation of the Inventory

The inventory was developed pursuant to EPA's inventory reporting regulations in December 1977. To be eligible for inclusion in the inventory, a substance had to be a "reportable chemical substance," defined under the regulations as: (1) a chemical substance; (2) manufactured, imported, or processed for a commercial purpose in the United States between January 1, 1975 and the date of publication of the Initial Inventory (June 1, 1979); and (3) not specifically excluded from the inventory.[6] These three criteria are discussed below.

---

[6] 40 C.F.R. § 710.4.

3.1.1 Chemical Substance

The statutory definition of the term "chemical substance" was incorporated directly into the inventory reporting regulation, and includes:

> any organic or inorganic substance of a particular molecular identity, including (i) any combination of such substances occurring in whole or in part as a result of a chemical reaction or occurring in nature and (ii) any element or uncombined radical.[7]

The regulations also incorporate the statutory exclusions from the definition of "chemical substance" for: (1) any mixture; (2) any commercial pesticide; (3) tobacco and certain tobacco products; (4) any nuclear source material or by-product; (5) any pistol, firearm, revolver, shells, and cartridges; and (6) any commercial food, food additive, drug, cosmetic, or device.[8]

3.1.2 Manufactured or Imported for a "Commercial Purpose"

A chemical substance manufactured or imported "for a commercial purpose" is one manufactured or imported for distribution in commerce (including test marketing) or for use by the manufacturer or importer, including use as an intermediate.[9]

3.1.3 Specifically Excluded Substances

"Mixtures" and "chemicals manufactured for a non-commercial purpose" are explicitly excluded from the inventory by virtue of the definition of "chemical substance" under TSCA § 3(2)(B). The following also are excluded pursuant to § 8(b) and implementing regulations.

Research and Development. Any chemical substance manufactured or processed only in small quantities for research and development (R&D) is excluded from the inventory under TSCA § 8(b)(1). The R&D exemption is discussed in further detail *infra* at Section 4.3.2.

Pesticides. Because pesticides, as defined in the Federal Insecticide, Fungicide, and Rodenticide Act (FIFRA) are specifically excluded from the definition of chemical substances under TSCA § 3(2)(B)(ii), such substances are excluded from the inventory. If a substance has multiple uses, those uses which are not subject to FIFRA are subject to TSCA, and thus must be included on the inventory.

Articles. EPA defines an "article" for TSCA purposes as a manufactured item formed into a specific shape or design during manufacture which has an end-use function dependent upon its shape or design during end-use and which has no change of chemical composition during its end-use separate from the purpose of the article.[10] Articles were excluded from inventory reporting.

---

[7]TSCA §3(2)(A). *See also*, 40 C.F.R. § 710.2(h).

[8]*See* TSCA § 3(2)(A); 40 C.F.R. § 710.2(h).

[9]40 C.F.R. § 710.2(p).

[10]40 C.F.R. § 710.2(f).

Impurities. An impurity is defined as "a chemical substance which is unintentionally present in another chemical substance."[11] Impurities are specifically excluded from the inventory by regulation.[12]

By-products. A by-product is a chemical substance produced without a specific commercial intent during the manufacture or processing of another chemical substance(s) or mixture(s).[13] EPA excluded from the inventory by-products which have no commercial purpose.[14]

Chemicals Produced from Incidental Reactions. Chemical substances produced as a result of incidental reactions were excluded from the inventory because they were not intentionally produced for commercial purposes.[15]

Non-isolated Intermediates. Intermediates, defined as chemicals that are both manufactured and partially or totally consumed in the chemical reaction process, or are intentionally present in order to affect the rate of chemical reactions by which other chemical substances or mixtures are being manufactured, are subject to inventory reporting. Non-isolated intermediates, however, defined as those intermediates that are not intentionally removed from the equipment in which they are manufactured, are excluded from reporting.[16]

3.2 Inventory Corrections

Recognizing that companies sometimes make errors in reporting substances and that often these errors are not discovered for many years, EPA in 1980 began to accept corrections to inventory submissions under the following limited circumstances. Corrections must be submitted by the company that currently owns the rights to the chemical, be accompanied by adequate documentation, and fall into one of the following three categories: (1) corrections of the chemical identity of previously reported materials; (2) corrections to identify previously unrecognized isolated intermediates; and (3) corrections made in response to communications from EPA which identify reporting errors.[17]

3.3 Maintaining and Updating the Inventory Data Base

EPA continuously adds to the inventory new chemicals that have cleared TSCA § 5 PMN review and for which Notices of Commencement of Manufacture have been filed. The agency also periodically removes, or "delists," from the inventory "orphan chemicals" that are not currently being manufactured or imported for commercial purposes.

---

[11] 40 C.F.R. § 710.2(m).
[12] 40 C.F.R. § 710.4(d)(1).
[13] 40 C.F.R. § 710.2(g).
[14] 40 C.F.R. § 710.4(d)(2).
[15] 40 C.F.R. § 710.4(d)(3)-(7).
[16] 40 C.F.R. § 710.4(d)(8).
[17] 45 *Fed. Reg.* 50,544 (1980).

Prior to delisting, the agency publishes a notice of its intent to delist in the *Federal Register* and in its quarterly "Chemicals in Progress Bulletin." As a result of this process, the inventory is maintained as a list of chemicals currently in commerce, not just those which were in commercial use during the 1975-1979 reporting period for the initial inventory.

In June 1986, EPA issued an Inventory Update Rule requiring manufacturers and importers of certain chemicals listed on the inventory to report current data on production volume, plant site, and site-limited status.[18] Such reporting is required every four years for all chemical substances listed on the inventory, except for the following: (1) polymers; (2) micro-organisms; (3) naturally occurring substances; and (4) inorganics.[19]

Under the rule, any company that manufactures or imports any "reportable substance" for commercial purposes in amounts of 10,000 pounds or more at any time during the most recent complete corporate fiscal year immediately preceding the reporting year is obligated to file the report.[20] Exceptions to the rule are available to small manufacturers and for certain chemicals exempt from premanufacture notification requirements.

The Update Rule requires each manufacturer or importer subject to the rule to maintain specific records documenting the information submitted to EPA.[21] Importantly, production records for substances manufactured at less than 10,000 pounds must be maintained to justify a decision not to report.

3.4 How To Use the Inventory

The 1985 edition of the inventory is the most current and consists of non-confidential identities and generic names for confidential substances. EPA maintains the master file that contains both the confidential and the non-confidential identities.

There are five volumes in the TSCA Inventory, each indexed to categorize the TSCA list of chemical substances in different ways. Volume One lists chemical substances in ascending order by CAS Registry Number, the CAS Index, or by preferred names. Volumes Two and Three are an alphabetically ordered listing of all CAS Index or Preferred Names, EPA submitter names, and CAS synonyms for the substances in the Chemical Substance Identity section. Volume Four lists all substances appearing in the Chemical Substance Identity section which have determinable molecular formulas. Volume Five lists substances of unknown or variable composition, complex reaction products, and biological materials (UVCB) substances.

3.4.1 Searching the Inventory

Volume One of the 1985 inventory contains instructions on how to use the inventory. The appropriate procedure for searching the inventory

---

[18] 51 *Fed. Reg.* 21,438 (1986).
[19] 40 C.F.R. § 710.26.
[20] 40 C.F.R. § 710.28.
[21] 40 C.F.R. § 710.37.

depends upon the amount of information known about the substance in question. The easiest way to determine if a substance is listed in the printed inventory is to search for its CAS registry number in Volume One. If the CAS Registry Number for the substance is already known, then it is necessary only to determine if the substance was included in the Chemical Substance Identities section. If the CAS Registry Number is not known, indices such as the Molecular Formula Index can assist in determining whether the chemical appears on the inventory.

3.4.2 Searches for Confidential Identities: Bona Fide Request

Because confidential chemicals are not listed by specific chemical identity and new confidential chemicals are continually being added, the only way to determine if a substance is or is not on the inventory is to search the master file version of the inventory. This version includes both confidential and non-confidential chemical identities and is kept current by EPA. EPA will search the confidential inventory only if the person requesting the search can demonstrate a *bona fide* intent to manufacture or import the substance for a commercial purpose.[22]

A notice of *bona fide* intent to manufacture or import must be submitted in writing and include the following information: (1) the specific chemical identity; (2) a signed statement of intent to manufacture or import for a commercial purpose; (3) a description of the research and development activities conducted; (4) the purpose of the manufacture or import; (5) an elemental analysis; and (6) either an x-ray diffraction pattern (for inorganic substances), a mass spectrum, or an infrared spectrum.[23]

4.0 NEW CHEMICAL REVIEW

Under TSCA § 5, any person intending to manufacture or import a chemical substance first must determine whether it is listed on the TSCA Inventory. If it is listed, then manufacture or importation may commence immediately. If the chemical substance is not listed on the inventory, then the manufacturer or importer must determine whether the chemical substance is excluded altogether from regulation under TSCA or whether it is exempt from the requirements. If the chemical substance is neither excluded nor exempted, the prospective manufacturer or importer must comply with the PMN requirements before commencing those activities.

4.1. PMN Requirements

The PMN must contain: (1) information such as the identity of the chemical, categories of use, amounts manufactured, by-products, employees exposed and the manner or method of disposal to the extent known or "reasonably ascertainable"; (2) any test data related to the chemical's effects on health or the environment in the submitter's possession or control; and

---

[22]40 C.F.R. § 720.25(b)(1).
[23]40 C.F.R. § 720.25(b)(2).

(3) a description of any other data concerning the health and environmental effects of the chemical, insofar as they are known to or "reasonably ascertainable" by the submitter.[24]

The policy underlying TSCA is that manufacturers and processors of chemical substances should bear the responsibility for developing adequate data regarding their effects on health and the environment. It is noteworthy that § 5 does not expressly authorize the administrator to require or obligate the PMN submitter to produce specific tests with a PMN, except where a chemical substance is subject to a rule promulgated under § 4. Thus, unlike comparable laws outside the United States, TSCA does not require a bare set of premarket data on a new chemical.

Under § 5(a), EPA must review the PMN within ninety days of its submission. During its PMN review, EPA must assess the potential risks associated with the manufacture, processing, distribution, use, and disposal of the new substance based upon information supplied by the PMN submitter and available from various agency data bases and the scientific literature, and, ultimately, based upon the agency's own professional judgment. If EPA takes no regulatory action on the PMN within the ninety-day review period, the submitter may commence commercial manufacture or importation forthwith and without the need for prior agency approval. Within thirty days of commencing manufacture or importation, the manufacturer or importer must file a Notice of Commencement (NOC) of Manufacture or Import.[25] The NOC certifies that commercial manufacture or importation actually has occurred. After receiving an NOC, EPA will add the PMN substance to the inventory, and the new chemical will then become an "existing" chemical under TSCA.

The statute provides EPA with three means to prevent, delay or limit manufacture after the ninety-day review period expires. First, under § 5(c), the agency may delay manufacture up to an additional ninety days for "good cause." Second, under § 5(e)(1)(A)(i), EPA may issue a proposed order to limit or prohibit manufacture if the agency determines that available information is "insufficient to permit a reasoned evaluation" of the health and environmental effects of the new chemical substance. Third, under § 5(f)(2) EPA may propose a § 6(a) rule limiting or conditioning manufacture or under § 5(f)(3)(B) may issue a proposed order totally banning manufacture, if there is a "reasonable basis to conclude that the manufacture . . . presents or will present an unreasonable risk of injury to health or the environment." Each of these agency actions is subject to judicial review, although the scope of review varies under each provision.

4.2 Exclusions from PMN Requirements

The PMN requirements apply to a "new chemical substance" and, once an applicable rule is promulgated, to a "significant new use" of an existing

---

[24]TSCA § 5(d).
[25]40 C.F.R. § 720.102.

chemical substance. The statutory definition of "chemical substance" excludes any mixture, any pesticide as defined by the Federal Insecticide, Fungicide and Rodenticide Act, and any food, food additive, drug, cosmetic, or device as defined by the Federal Food, Drug and Cosmetic Act, various nuclear materials regulated under the Atomic Energy Act, and any tobacco or tobacco product.[26] Thus, by definition, these substances are excluded from TSCA jurisdiction and, as such, are not subject to the PMN requirements. The PMN requirements nevertheless may apply to such "excluded" substances, if they also are intended for a "TSCA use."

4.3 Exemptions from PMN Requirements

TSCA establishes two exemptions from the PMN requirements—for test marketing and R & D—and grants EPA authority to establish additional exemptions by regulation where the agency determines that the manufacture, processing, distribution, or use of a chemical substance will not present an unreasonable risk to health or the environment. Pursuant to this authority, EPA has prescribed fifteen exemptions to the PMN requirements, some of which are discussed below.

4.3.1 Test Market Exemption

TSCA § 5(h)(1) authorizes the administrator to exempt a new chemical substance from the PMN requirements when it is manufactured for test marketing purposes if the administrator determines that the proposed test marketing activity will not present an unreasonable risk to human health or the environment. The Test Market Exemption (TME) permits a company to assess the commercial viability of a new chemical and to receive customer feedback on product performance before filing a PMN. Under TSCA § 5(h)(1), the test marketer must apply for this exemption and must demonstrate that the proposed activity is legitimate test marketing which will not present an unreasonable risk.

EPA reviews a TME application in essentially the same manner as it does a PMN. Yet, under TSCA § 5(h)(6), EPA must review a TME application within forty-five days of its receipt. According to EPA, however, the agency's failure to complete its review of a TME application within forty-five days does not constitute an automatic approval. Rather, unlike a PMN submitter, a TME applicant must await EPA approval prior to initiating activity.

4.3.2 Research and Development Exemption

TSCA § 5(h)(3) exempts from the PMN and "significant new use rule" (SNUR) requirements small quantities of new chemicals used solely for R&D under the supervision of a technically qualified individual, if the manufacturer or importer notifies persons engaged in R&D of any health risks associated with the substance. Unlike the other exemptions under § 5(h), the manufacturer or importer need not apply for the R&D exemption. EPA regulations establishing requirements for the R&D exemption appear at 40

---

[26]*See* TSCA § 3(2)(B).

C.F.R. § 720.36. EPA requires that a technically qualified individual supervise the R&D activities and that the manufacturer or importer evaluate any potential risks associated with the R&D substance, notify persons involved in the R&D of those risks, and maintain certain records of their R&D activity. In evaluating risks, the manufacturer or importer must consider all health and environmental effects data in its "possession or control." This includes information in the files of agents and employees engaged in the R&D and marketing of the new chemical. When R&D activity is conducted in laboratories using prudent laboratory conditions, however, this risk assessment need not be performed.

4.3.3 Low Volume Exemption

Under TSCA § 5(h)(4), EPA has exempted certain low volume chemicals from the full PMN requirements by providing an expedited twenty-one-day review.[27] A manufacturer or importer who intends to produce or import a new chemical substance in quantities of 1,000 kilograms or less per year may apply for the low volume exemption (LVE). This LVE is available to only one manufacturer for each new chemical. Therefore, once EPA has granted an LVE for a chemical, no other manufacturer can qualify for an LVE for that same chemical. A second manufacturer must submit a PMN. In order to grant an LVE, EPA must determine that the chemical substance will "not present an unreasonable risk of injury to health or the environment."[28]

EPA publishes in the *Federal Register* a notice listing each LVE granted. In addition, EPA adds the low volume chemical to a "low volume" list maintained by the agency. When a new LVE application is submitted, EPA searches this list. If EPA has already granted an LVE for that chemical, the subsequent application for an LVE is denied and the LVE applicant is required to file a PMN before beginning commercial manufacture. EPA does not require the filing of an NOC for an LVE chemical and does not place it on the TSCA Inventory. Hence, LVE chemicals remain "new" chemical substances under § 5.

If new information causes the LVE chemical to become ineligible for the LVE, EPA will revoke the exemption. Before revoking the LVE, however, EPA will notify the manufacturer or importer in writing of the agency's intent to revoke. After receiving notice of EPA's intent to revoke, the manufacturer or importer within fifteen days may file objections or an explanation of its "diligence and good faith" in attempting to comply with the terms of the exemption.[29] Within fifteen days of receiving the objections or explanation, EPA will make a final determination whether the chemical remains eligible for the LVE. If so, EPA will leave the LVE in effect. If not, then within twenty-four hours of notification by EPA, manufacture must cease.

---

[27] 40 C.F.R. § 723.50.
[28] TSCA § 5(h)(4).
[29] 40 C.F.R. § 723.50(g)(2).

4.3.4 Polymer Exemption

Under TSCA § 5(h)(4), EPA also provides for an expedited twenty-one-day review for certain polymers. In order to be eligible for the polymer exemption, applicants must meet three criteria: (1) the chemical must be a "polymer" as defined in 40 C.F.R. § 723.250(b)(12); (2) it must not be specifically excluded by 40 C.F.R. § 723.250(d); and (3) it must have a certain number-average molecular weight or be a polyester of a certain type as set forth in 40 C.F.R. § 723.250(e).

As with all exemptions under § 5(h)(4), including the LVE, EPA must find "no unreasonable risk" in order to grant a polymer exemption. If it makes this finding, EPA will publish a notice in the *Federal Register* that the twenty-one-day review period has expired.

If EPA cannot make this "no unreasonable risk" finding, it will notify the submitter that the substance is ineligible for expedited review. Under those circumstances, EPA automatically will extend the review period to ninety days. If EPA does extend the review period, the manufacturer either must withdraw the polymer exemption application or agree to suspend the review period and within sixty days to submit the additional information necessary to constitute a full PMN. Thereafter, EPA will review the polymer under EPA's standard PMN review procedures.

4.3.5 "Polaroid" Exemption

In response to a petition from the Polaroid Corporation, EPA exempted new chemical substances used in or for instant photographic and "peel-apart" film articles.[30] Under the terms of the so-called "Polaroid" exemption, manufacturers of instant photographic materials may commence manufacture of new chemical substances for these products immediately upon submitting an exemption notice pursuant to 40 C.F.R. § 723.175. These new chemical substances, however, cannot be distributed in commerce until a PMN is filed and the review period has ended.

4.3.6 New Chemicals Imported in Articles

Under 40 C.F.R. § 720.22(b)(1), a manufacturer must file a PMN on any new chemical substances imported into the United States for commercial purposes "unless the substance is imported as part of an article." The term "article" is defined at 40 C.F.R. § 720.3(c). Although EPA's definition of article specifically excludes "fluids and particles . . . regardless of shape or design," importers of articles that contain fluids or particles that are not intended to be removed and that have no separate commercial purpose are excluded from the PMN requirements. Conversely, EPA considers that a substance cannot be "a part" of an article if it is released and, upon release, has a commercial purpose. Thus, according to EPA, articles that contain fluids designed to be used or released in order for the article to function, like ink in pens or gasoline in cars, are not encompassed by this exemption.

---

[30]40 C.F.R. § 723.175.

4.3.7 Impurities, By-products, Non-Isolated Intermediates

EPA has excluded from the PMN requirements impurities, by-products, non-isolated intermediates, and chemicals formed incidentally when exposed to the environment or to other chemicals.[31] These exemptions are essentially identical to exemptions from the initial inventory which are found at 40 C.F.R. § 710.4. In fact, EPA often uses its discussion of these exemptions in the preamble and response to comments in its initial inventory reporting rule to clarify the scope and applicability of these same exemptions from the PMN requirements.

4.3.8 Chemicals Formed During the Manufacture of an Article

EPA also exempts from the PMN requirements "any other chemical substance formed during the manufacture of an article destined for the marketplace without further chemical change of the chemical substance except for those chemical changes that occur as described elsewhere in this paragraph."[32] Thus, for example, EPA exempts new chemicals formed upon use of rubber molding or curable plastic compounds, inks, drying oils, adhesives or paints, and metal finishing compounds.[33]

4.3.9 Chemicals Formed Incidental to the Use of Certain Additives

Under 40 C.F.R. § 720.30(h)(7), EPA exempts from the PMN requirements new chemicals formed incidental to the use of certain additives intended solely to impart specific physiochemical characteristics when these additives function as intended. Thus, the agency exempts new chemical substances formed incidental to use of a specific additive—such as a pH neutralizer, stabilizer, or binder—if the additive is used only for the purposes of achieving a specific physiochemical characteristic, and it functions solely to achieve that characteristic. For example, EPA excludes a new chemical substance formed incidental to the addition of bleach to cotton if the manufacturer adds the bleach only to change a specific physiochemical characteristic of the cotton and not to make a major compositional change.[34]

5.0 PREPARING THE PMN AND SEEING IT THROUGH EPA

Although more than 20,000 new chemical substances have been reviewed through the PMN process and the process has become routine from EPA's perspective, the PMN remains a substantial hurdle to overcome for the manufacturer who wants to market a new chemical quickly and efficiently. The unwary manufacturer may encounter such problems as delays in the review process, or unexpected and costly restrictions on manufacture (which EPA may impose under TSCA § 5(e) or § 5(f)). As discussed below, a manufacturer can minimize many of these potential problems by recognizing

---

[31] 40 C.F.R. § 720.30(h).
[32] 40 C.F.R. § 720.36(h)(6).
[33] *Id.*
[34] 43 *Fed. Reg.* 9256 (1978).

them in advance and planning a PMN strategy that is specific to the chemical substance.

5.1 Manufacturer's PMN Selection Strategy

For purposes of this discussion, there are four types of PMN: (1) the "standard" PMN for a single chemical substance; (2) the "consolidated" PMN for two or more substances sharing similar molecular structures and use patterns; (3) the "joint" PMN, for use when two companies must jointly submit data; and (4) the "exemption" PMN for substances that are polymers or are manufactured in low volumes. Each of the four types of PMN offers specific advantages and poses special problems to the PMN submitter.

The standard PMN is used in over seventy-five percent of all submissions. It is appropriate where the PMN substance has a distinct molecular structure, and the necessary data can be provided by a single company.

A consolidated PMN is appropriate where a company wishes to manufacture several chemicals that are similar in molecular structure and similar in use. A consolidated PMN reduces the need for repetitive filing and requires only a single $2,500 filing fee. Prior to its submission, however, EPA must confirm that the agency will treat the new chemicals as similar in structure for PMN purposes. The manufacturer must be aware that each chemical so noticed will receive a separate PMN number and that the manufacturer must file a separate Notice of Commencement for each chemical substance subsequently manufactured. Historically, consolidated PMNs are filed most often for certain sodium, lithium, and potassium salts of the same acid.

A joint PMN may be filed by two or more companies where one manufacturer does not possess all the information necessary to complete the PMN form. Such a situation commonly arises in cases where one company develops a new chemical substance that incorporates a second company's proprietary product. Manufacturers also may find joint PMNs useful as a means of sharing or reducing administrative costs and filing fees.

An exemption PMN is appropriate where a chemical substance meets either the low volume or polymer exemption criteria set forth at 40 C.F.R. §§ 723.50 and 723.250, respectively. The principal advantage of an exemption PMN is a shortened review period of twenty-one days. A manufacturer who relies upon an exemption PMN, however, is bound to its restrictions, primarily a volume limitation for the low volume PMN and limitations on the permissible amount of residual monomer and low molecular weight fractions for the polymer PMN. Because these limitations are targets of EPA inspection and enforcement activities, exemption PMNs generally are recommended only where time considerations make them especially attractive.

5.2 Minimizing Delays

The best way to avoid a delay in manufacturing operations arising from the PMN process is to submit the PMN far in advance of the production schedule. Although such a strategy can reduce production delays, it requires the manufacturer to initiate the PMN process rather early in the product development process. This presents a risk, of course, that some PMNs may be submitted for products that are not produced for intervening reasons.

Manufacturers frequently encounter delays in the PMN process due to the failure to submit required information. If any required information is missing or incomplete, EPA will return the PMN to the submitter. Delays also may result from the inconsistency of information from one section of the PMN to another. Another frequent source of delays arises when a submitter, in attempting to protect confidential business information, fails to supply a generic name for the new chemical or a generic description of its use. Such delays may be avoided only through coordination, planning, and experience.

5.3 Avoiding Unnecessary Regulation under Premanufacture Notification Provisions

New chemicals that are delayed during the PMN process or become subject to TSCA § 5(e) Consent Agreements and corresponding SNURs often lose much market value. It is most often the uncertainty arising from insufficient risk assessment data in the PMN that causes EPA to impose such restrictions.

If such restrictions are to be avoided, the PMN submitter must provide a risk assessment that is as comprehensive as possible. Risk is commonly derived by the simple equation: Risk = f (Hazard x Exposure). A manufacturer can demonstrate that the Risk is low by furnishing information sufficient to show that either the Hazard or Exposure component of the equation is low.

Hazard information for a new chemical is best supplied as actual human and environmental toxicity information on the specific chemical. Exposure information, although more difficult to quantify, typically includes the expected production volume and uses of the new substance and, when available: (1) certain of the substance's physical properties that impact exposure potential; (2) the numbers and types of human exposure; and (3) the types of release.

Once hazard and exposure information are known, a risk assessment should be developed and included in the PMN. The manufacturer must follow up the risk assessment with a discussion in the PMN of a risk management program, the most common elements of which include routine hazard communication techniques such as appropriate labels and Material Safety Data Sheets.

5.4 EPA'S Review of the PMN and Use of Checklists

EPA's PMN review process includes not only the elements of risk assessment, but also includes many technical and administrative details. A submitter thus is well-advised to develop a series of checklists for filing PMNs. These checklists should: (1) ensure that all requested information is included and is consistent throughout the PMN; (2) mirror the items on

EPA's own checklist, most of which can be obtained from EPA; and (3) address issues that continue after the PMN is submitted, including the obligation to file an NOC within thirty days after commercial manufacture begins, to adhere to any limitations that may apply in the case of exemption PMNs, and to ensure compliance with any TSCA § 5(e) restrictions.

6.0 REGULATION OF NEW CHEMICALS AND USES

Under TSCA § 5, once a manufacturer has submitted a PMN, it may commence commercial operations without specific EPA approval after waiting ninety days, unless the agency exercises one of three statutory options described below. First, under TSCA § 5(a) EPA may delay manufacture for one additional ninety-day review period for "good cause." Second, under TSCA § 5(e), EPA may issue a proposed order limiting or prohibiting manufacture if the agency makes statutorily prescribed findings regarding risk. Third, under TSCA § 5(f), EPA may propose a § 6(a) rule which becomes immediately effective to limit or condition manufacture, or issue a proposed order totally banning manufacture, if the agency concludes that manufacture "presents or will present an unreasonable risk of injury to health or [the] environment."

6.1 EPA Regulation of Premanufacture Notification

TSCA § 5(e) grants EPA authority to issue an administrative order regulating a new chemical substance if the agency finds that: (1) there is insufficient information to evaluate the risk reasonably; and (2) either the chemical may present an unreasonable risk to health and the environment, or it will be produced in such relatively large quantities that either substantial quantities will enter the environment or there will be substantial or significant human exposure to the substance. The purpose of a TSCA § 5(e) order is to ban or limit manufacture, distribution, use, or disposal of a chemical pending development of sufficient data for EPA to evaluate the risks the chemical poses to human health or the environment. Where EPA acts unilaterally to issue a § 5(e) order, it must be proposed at least forty-five days before the end of the PMN review period. Such unilateral orders become effective on the day the review period ends.

6.1.1 EPA's Standard § 5(e) Consent Order

TSCA § 5(e) does not provide explicit authority for EPA to enter into "consent" orders. EPA developed the consent order concept to permit the introduction of new chemicals into the market while controlling any potential risk during the time needed to develop the required data by agreement with the prospective manufacturer, thus avoiding an adversary procedure. Under a § 5(e) consent order, the manufacturer is usually permitted to proceed with commercial manufacture, and in return agrees to certain restrictions on the production, distribution, or disposal of the new chemical, pending development of information that EPA considers necessary to evaluate the potential hazards.

6.1.2 EPA Evaluation of § 5(e) Data

After receiving the required test data, EPA may determine that such data are: (1) invalid; (2) equivocal; (3) valid and positive (the chemical poses an unreasonable risk); or (4) valid and negative (the chemical poses no unreasonable risk). EPA interprets § 5 as enabling the agency to take further action under its standard consent order based on the submitted data without resorting to procedures required under TSCA §§ 4 or 6.

If EPA determines that the test results are scientifically invalid, the company must cease production or importation of the PMN substance when the aggregate volume reaches the production limit. The company may contest EPA's finding by submitting a report prepared by a "qualified person" (expert) explaining why the data are scientifically valid. If a specific event beyond the control of the company has prevented the development of scientifically valid data, the company may submit a report documenting this extenuating circumstance within several weeks of its occurrence. Upon EPA's concurrence, the company may continue to manufacture beyond the production limit provided a study is initiated, usually within three months, and that the data are submitted within a specified time.

Data are scientifically equivocal if insufficient for the agency to conduct a reasoned risk evaluation of the substance, when evaluated together with other available information. Upon a finding by EPA that the data are equivocal, a submitter has similar opportunities to refute the EPA finding or to negotiate for new conditions to allow for continued manufacture of the subject chemical.

A finding of valid, positive data indicates that the chemical poses an unreasonable risk. The company may challenge EPA's determination but may not manufacture the chemical until EPA is convinced that the chemical will not present an unreasonable risk, or a court reverses EPA's position.

EPA may determine that the data demonstrate the chemical will not present an unreasonable risk. Despite such negative data, however, the agency still may decline to modify or revoke the order if EPA finds that the risk may be unreasonable without continued use of engineering or other controls. Often the company must affirmatively petition for such a revocation of the consent order.

6.1.3 Preparation of the § 5(e) Consent Order

Because complex consent orders often take so long to negotiate and issue, EPA has created a "two track" system of consent order preparation. The "fast track" is used where the PMN submitter agrees to certain standard terms. Such "fast track" consent orders take an average of seventy working days, compared to 124 working days for a "standard" § 5(e) consent order.

A "standard" consent order is the product of several stages of draft, review, and comment. Once the consent order is signed by all parties, it becomes effective the day following the lapse of the PMN review period. If the review period has been suspended voluntarily beyond the statutory period, EPA and the submitter will revoke jointly any remaining time.

A party to a TSCA § 5(e) consent order may challenge an EPA decision that is based on the data submitted pursuant to the consent order. Companies that disagree with the agency's determination may challenge the decision by filing: (1) a petition under TSCA § 21 for the "issuance, amendment, or repeal" of the §5(e) order; (2) a petition under the terms of the consent order for modification or revocation of provisions of the consent order; or (3) an action for judicial review under the Administrative Procedure Act (APA).

6.1.4 Unilateral § 5(e) Orders

If EPA determines that the potential risk from a PMN substance cannot be reduced to acceptable levels through engineering controls or production limitations or that a mutually agreeable consent order cannot be negotiated, the agency will issue a proposed unilateral § 5(e) order. The agency generally uses these orders to ban a PMN substance outright. Because under § 5(e)(1)(B) a unilateral order must be issued no later than forty-five days before the end of the review period, EPA will give priority to its development and issuance.

If the PMN submitter files "objections specifying with peculiarity" the provisions of the order deemed objectionable and stating the grounds therefor, the proposed order will not take effect.[35] A company must address EPA's findings of fact with respect to the PMN chemical and the agency's resulting conclusion that the issuance of a § 5(e) order is required. In this instance, the administrator must apply to a federal district court for an injunction to prohibit or limit the commercial manufacture, processing, distribution, use, or disposal.[36] If, after evaluating the objections, the administrator determines there is no basis to limit or ban the PMN substance under § 5(e), he will not act to finalize the unilateral order.

6.2 EPA Regulations Limiting or Delaying Manufacture of a Chemical Substance

If EPA determines that a new chemical substance presents or will present an unreasonable risk before the agency can issue a rule under § 6 to protect against such risks, the administrator may act under § 5(f) to control that risk. Under § 5(f), the administrator may issue either a proposed rule to limit or delay manufacture, production, use, or disposal, or a proposed order to ban all use of the substance and apply for a federal injunction to prohibit the chemical from entering commerce.

6.2.1 Proposed § 5(f) Rules

TSCA § 5(f)(2) authorizes the administrator to issue an immediately effective proposed rule under § 6(a) that limits or delays manufacture of a chemical substance undergoing a PMN review. Under § 6(a), EPA has authority to: (1) limit the amount; (2) prohibit particular uses; (3) limit the

---

[35]TSCA § 5(e)(1)(C).
[36]TSCA § 5(e)(2)(A)(i).

amount or concentration for a particular use; (4) require specific labels; (5) require recordkeeping; (6) prohibit or regulate commercial use; (7) prohibit or regulate disposal; and (8) give notice of the risk. Such a rule is effective immediately upon publication in the *Federal Register*.

To date, EPA has proposed only three § 5(f) rules covering four chemicals. EPA has not yet "finalized" these proposed rules because the agency never contemplated rulemaking under TSCA § 6. Nevertheless, the rules were effective as of the date they were published. They were recorded in the *Code of Federal Regulations* and, for all intents and purposes, function as final rules.

Judicial relief from a § 5(f) rule is probably unavailable because TSCA § 6(d)(2)(A) provides that: "[s]uch a proposed rule which is made so effective shall not, for purposes of judicial review be considered final agency action." Presumably, an affected party could challenge EPA's failure to complete the rulemaking in an expeditious manner as directed by TSCA § 6(d)(2)(B). Any challenge to the merits of the rule, however, would have to wait until the final rule was issued.

6.2.2 Proposed Orders to Ban Chemicals

If EPA determines it necessary to ban a chemical from commercial manufacture, distribution, processing, use, and disposal, the agency must issue a proposed § 5(f) order and apply for an injunction. The proposed order takes effect upon the expiration of the review period unless the submitter files objections in accordance with TSCA § 5(e)(1)(C). If EPA issues a proposed order, the agency must apply to federal court for an injunction before the expiration of the review period, unless it determines on the basis of the objections filed that the substance does not or will not present an unreasonable risk.[37] To date, EPA has not proposed any orders under TSCA § 5(f).

6.3 Significant New Use Rules (SNUR)

Persons who submitted initial inventory notices were required to describe the uses to which their chemicals were being put. Similarly, a PMN submitter must describe the intended uses of his new chemical. If EPA determines that a particular use of a chemical already on the inventory constitutes a "significant new use," the agency can issue a Significant New Use Rule (SNUR). A SNUR requires anyone who wants to manufacture or process a chemical substance for a use that EPA has determined is a "significant new use" to give EPA ninety calendar days prior notice.[38] This notice is referred to as a "Significant New Use Notice" or SNUN.

If, after reviewing a SNUN, EPA fails to initiate any action under § 5, 6 or 7, then TSCA § 5(g) requires the administrator to publish a notice in the *Federal Register* giving EPA's reasons for not initiating any action. As is the case with a PMN, a SNUN submitter may manufacture, import, or process

---

[37]TSCA § 5(f)(3)(D).

[38]TSCA §§ 5(a)(1)(B) and 5(a)(2); 40 C.F.R. § 721.

the chemical for the "significant new use" without EPA approval or further notice to EPA upon expiration of the ninety-day review period.

6.3.1 SNUR Standard

TSCA does not set criteria for determining when EPA may deem a new use "significant," but EPA must consider "all relevant factors."[39] EPA generally defines a "significant new use" broadly as a use that will result in increased production volume, a different or greater extent of exposure, a different disposal method, or even a different manufacturing site.

6.3.2 Who Must Report

All persons who intend to manufacture, import, or process for commercial purposes a chemical substance identified at 40 C.F.R. § 721, subpart E are required to report. In addition, any person who intends to distribute the substance to others must submit a SNUN unless he can document that: (1) he has notified in writing each person who purchases or otherwise receives the chemical from him of the applicable SNUR; (2) each such recipient has knowledge of that specific section of subpart E; or (3) each recipient cannot undertake any significant new use described in the specific section of subpart E.[40] Finally, a person who processes a chemical substance listed in subpart E for a "significant new use" must submit a SNUN unless he can document that: (1) the person does not know the specific chemical identity of the chemical substance being processed; and (2) the person is processing the chemical substance without knowledge of the applicable SNUR.[41]

EPA recognizes certain exemptions from the requirement to make a SNUN report which are identical to those applied to PMNs.[42] EPA never has required manufacturers of non-isolated intermediates to apply for exemptions. Presumably manufacturers of SNUR-listed chemicals who produce them only as non-isolated intermediates are exempt from the SNUN requirements as well.

6.3.3 Alternative Measures to Control Exposure

EPA also has established a procedure whereby a manufacturer or processor may petition the agency to allow use of alternative measures to control exposure to or environmental release of a chemical substance without submitting a SNUN, if EPA determines that the alternative measure provides substantially the same degree of protection as the methods specified in the SNUR. Persons intending to employ alternative control measures must submit a request to EPA for a determination of equivalency before commencing manufacture, importation, or processing activities with the alternative controls. EPA has forty-five days to determine the equivalency of

---

[39]TSCA § 5(a)(2).
[40]40 C.F.R. § 721.5.
[41]*Id.*
[42]40 C.F.R. § 721.45.

the proposal and will mail a notice of the results to the submitter, who may commence manufacture upon receipt.[43]

6.3.4 Obligations of Distributors

If a manufacturer, importer, or processor of a chemical acknowledges that someone who purchases or otherwise obtains the chemical from him is engaged in a significant new use without submitting a SNUN, the distributor must stop supplying the chemical substance and must submit the SNUN, unless the distributor can document: (1) he has notified the recipient and the EPA Office of Compliance Monitoring (OCM) in writing within fifteen days of the first time he has knowledge; (2) within fifteen working days after notifying the recipient, the recipient has provided him with written assurance that the recipient is aware of the terms of subpart E and will not engage in the significant new use; and (3) he has promptly provided OCM with a copy of the recipient's written assurances.[44]

6.3.5 Determining Inventory Status

The chemicals listed in 40 C.F.R. § 721, subpart E are often listed by generic names because the manufacturers have claimed the specific chemical identities as confidential. In order to determine whether a specific chemical is subject to a SNUN, a *bona fide* request may be filed with the agency.[45]

6.3.6 Use of SNURs To Support § 5(e) Consent Orders

When EPA has concerns about a new chemical substance but does not want to prohibit its manufacture completely, the agency will enter into a consent order with the PMN submitter, allowing limited production under carefully controlled conditions. Once the chemical is placed on the inventory, however, other manufacturers can begin producing this substance without complying with the restrictions in the consent order, giving them a competitive advantage over the original manufacturer.

As a result, manufacturers subject to § 5(e) consent orders have urged EPA to designate as a "significant new use" any manufacture of such a substance that is not in compliance with the same restrictions placed upon the original manufacturers in the consent orders. Once EPA issues such a SNUR, any manufacturer who intends to depart from the conditions imposed under the SNUR must file a SNUN ninety days before doing so. Because development of even a relatively simple SNUR and its issuance concurrently with a § 5(e) consent order requires commitment of substantial agency resources, EPA rarely issues such SNURs.

6.3.7 Generic SNUR Rule

The agency's difficulties in developing SNURs to support the § 5(e) consent order program, prompted the agency to develop the "Generic SNUR

---

[43]40 C.F.R. § 721.30.
[44]40 C.F.R. § 721.5.
[45]40 C.F.R. § 721.11. *See supra* at Section 3.4.2.

Rule." This rule establishes standardized significant new uses, record-keeping requirements, and two procedures EPA can use to issue SNURs without the usual notice-and-comment rulemaking.[46] The Generic SNUR Rule has five subparts. Subpart A defines terms. Subpart B lists standardized significant new uses that EPA may, by rule, apply to any existing chemical. Subpart C establishes recordkeeping requirements which EPA may impose upon manufacturers, importers, or processors of any chemical subject to a SNUR. Subpart D establishes "expedited" rulemaking procedures that EPA may use to develop SNURs for chemical substances and creates a procedure by which persons affected by the SNUR may petition the agency to modify or revoke it. Subpart E is a list of chemicals subject to SNURs and their designated significant new uses. EPA may establish significant new uses other than those in subpart B and can impose recordkeeping requirements other than those in subpart C but only by notice-and-comment rulemaking.

The Generic SNUR Rule (subpart B) establishes five categories of standardized significant new uses. These are: (1) commercial activities where a program of appropriate protective equipment has not been established[47]; (2) commercial activities where a worker hazard communication program has not been established[48]; (3) disposal of a listed substance[49]; (4) release to water of a listed substance[50]; and (5) a broad "catch-all" section, designating over two dozen activities that taken collectively are so inclusive as to provide EPA the tools to regulate virtually any activity[51].

Section 721.160 (subpart D) establishes expedited procedures EPA can use to impose SNURs on chemicals that have been the subject of a final order issued under § 5(e). These procedures include: (1) direct final rulemaking; (2) interim final rulemaking; and (3) notice-and-comment rulemaking.

When EPA uses direct final rulemaking procedures to issue a § 5(e) consent order, it issues a final rule in the *Federal Register*. Unless EPA receives written notice within thirty days of publication that someone wishes to submit adverse or critical comments, the rule will be effective sixty days from the date of publication. If EPA receives such timely notice, however, the agency must provide for more formal rulemaking procedures.

EPA will use interim final rulemaking procedures when the agency believes that a significant new use is likely to take place before a direct final rule would become effective. In this case, the agency will issue an interim final rule in the final rule section of the *Federal Register*. The SNUR will take effect on the date of publication and persons will have thirty days to submit comments. However, such interim rules will cease to be effective 180 days

---

[46]*See* 40 C.F.R. § 721 *et. seq.*
[47]40 C.F.R. § 721.63.
[48]40 C.F.R. § 721.72.
[49]40 C.F.R. § 721.85.
[50]40 C.F.R. § 721.90.
[51]40 C.F.R. § 721.80.

after publication unless, within the 180-day period, EPA issues a final rule in the *Federal Register* that responds to any written comments received.

Although not an "expedited" procedure, EPA also may use traditional notice-and-comment procedures to issue a SNUR. In this case, EPA issues a proposal in the *Federal Register* and allows a thirty–day comment period. EPA generally uses notice-and-comment rulemaking where the agency anticipates adverse comments.

6.3.8 Expedited SNURs for New Chemical Substances Not Subject to § 5(e) Orders.

Section 721.170 of 40 C.F.R. establishes the procedures and criteria under which EPA may use expedited procedures to impose SNURs on a chemical that satisfied the PMN process but was not made subject to a § 5(e) consent order. EPA will promulgate a SNUR for such a chemical only if the substance meets one or more of the concern criteria listed in § 721.170(b). The concern criteria are basically the same criteria EPA uses when determining whether a new chemical substance should be subject to a § 5(e) consent order. Thus, the criteria call for a SNUR if exposure is likely to result from new uses not in the PMN or would have called for a § 5(e) order if they had been in the PMN.

Any person affected by a SNUR may request modification or revocation of any SNUR requirement that has been added to subpart E by using the expedited procedures. The request must be accompanied by information sufficient to support the request.[52]

7.0 BIOTECHNOLOGY

EPA's biotechnology policy under TSCA is developing amidst substantial controversy. The agency has asserted that it has broad authority under TSCA to regulate genetically engineered microorganisms. Because of the conflicting interests involved and the uncertainty surrounding biotechnology products, the agency has not yet proposed comprehensive biotechnology regulations. Until regulations are proposed, EPA is requiring certain researchers, manufacturers, processors, distributors, and importers to comply with selected TSCA reporting requirements.

7.1 1986 Framework for Regulation of Biotechnology Products

EPA first asserted TSCA authority over genetically engineered microorganisms in a 1984 proposed policy statement.[53] In 1986 EPA published the final version of the policy statement which established the reporting requirements that are currently in effect for genetically engineered microorganisms.[54] Pursuant to the policy statement, EPA requires compliance with PMN requirements for "new" microorganisms and § 8(e) reporting for all microorganisms. In addition, EPA requests voluntary

---

[52]40 C.F.R. § 721.185.

[53]49 *Fed. Reg.* 50,886 (1984).

[54]51 *Fed. Reg.* 23,324 (1986).

compliance with other § 8 reporting requirements. The agency has not provided clear guidance on reporting requirements, however, leaving submitters to rely largely on informal guidance.

7.2 Guidance Documents on PMN Submissions for Biotechnology Products

Several sources of information can provide guidance for PMN submitters. The basic reporting requirements for microorganisms are contained in EPA's 1986 policy statement. Also, to assist persons preparing PMNs for biotechnology products under the 1986 policy statement, EPA has prepared an information packet containing several draft guidelines. These guidelines are continuously evolving to reflect changes in policy and additional experience gained through reviewing PMNs on biotechnology products. Some of the guidelines are general and address the administrative details and informational requirements for completing a PMN. One deals with substantiation of confidentiality claims, another with *bona fide* submissions for a search of the Master Inventory File to determine if a microorganism is listed on the confidential portion of the inventory, and a third with preparing PMNs for closed system, large-scale fermentations. In addition, several 1986 and 1987 guidance documents address the full PMN submission, the sanitized version, and confidentiality claims.

7.3 EPA Biotechnology PMN Review Process

While its policies are still in gestation, EPA is addressing PMN submissions on biotechnology products on a case-by-case basis. Given the current state of uncertainty, the submitter should contact EPA as early as possible in the project development process for a pre-notice consultation. Nonetheless, EPA does have a process for reviewing these PMN submissions.

Following receipt of the PMN, EPA publishes an announcement in the *Federal Register* describing the submission.[55] EPA then develops hazard and exposure assessments based on information submitted in the PMN, other available scientific information, and consultation with non-agency experts. These assessments are then combined to form a risk assessment. At this point, EPA may ask for assistance from a Biotechnology Science Advisory Committee (BSAC) subcommittee containing scientists with expertise relevant to the PMN in question. At the conclusion of a PMN review the agency may reach one of three decisions: (a) there is sufficient information to determine that the risks are unreasonable; (b) there is sufficient information to determine that the risks are reasonable; or (c) there is insufficient information to make a reasoned evaluation of risk. Finally, the agency may issue a consent order under § 5(e) wherein it imposes certain restrictions on testing pending development by the PMN submitter of additional information.

---

[55] TSCA § 5(d)(2).

7.4 Future of EPA's Biotechnology Policy: Draft Proposed Rule

In 1988, EPA drafted a proposed biotechnology rule, but the White House Office of Management and Budget (OMB) returned it to EPA for reconsideration of several issues. In response to comments by OMB as well as other government agencies, industry, academia, and public interest groups, EPA continues to revise the draft. On June 21, 1991, EPA released yet another draft proposal but has not yet submitted it to OMB for review, nor has it been published in the *Federal Register*. Disagreement between EPA and the Bush administration over the scope of the pending biotechnology proposed rule stalled issuance of that rule. The change in administration may further complicate the process or relieve the log jam.

8.0 TESTING UNDER TSCA

One of Congress' objectives in enacting TSCA was to require chemical manufacturers and processors to develop data on the health and environmental effects of their products.[56] Under the act, EPA may require manufacturers and processors to develop safety and environmental data when: (1) the chemical may present an unreasonable risk of injury; or (2) substantial quantities of the chemical are produced with the potential for substantial environmental or human exposure.[57]

8.1 Selection of Chemicals for Testing

Congress created the Interagency Testing Committee (ITC) "to make recommendations to the Administrator respecting the chemical substances and mixtures to which the Administrator should give priority consideration."[58] The ITC consists of designees from eight agencies of the federal government. TSCA requires the ITC to give priority consideration to substances that are suspected of causing or contributing to cancer, gene mutations, or birth defects. Within twelve months after the ITC designates a chemical, the agency must initiate § 4 rulemaking or publish its reasons for not doing so.

In making its testing recommendations, the ITC must consider eight factors, including: the quantities in which the substance is manufactured or enters the environment; the extent and duration of human exposure; whether the substance is closely related to a chemical substance known to present an unreasonable risk of injury; the existence of data concerning the effects of the substance; and the extent to which testing may aid the agency to predict the effects of a substance on health or the environment.[59]

The addition of a chemical substance to the TSCA § 4(e) Priority List triggers reporting requirements under TSCA §§ 8(a) and 8(d). Under the § 8(a) Preliminary Assessment Information Rule (PAIR), manufacturers must

---

[56]TSCA § 2(b)(1).
[57]TSCA § 4(a)(1).
[58]TSCA § 4(e).
[59]TSCA § 4(e)(1)(A).

submit production and exposure data on ITC-listed chemicals within ninety days of publication in the *Federal Register* of the amendment adding the chemical. Under the § 8(d) Health and Safety Data Reporting Rule, manufacturers and processors must submit to EPA unpublished health and safety studies within ninety days of the agency's listing.[60]

8.2 Testing Triggers

Whether a test rule is risk-based or exposure-based will influence the type of testing required. The testing "triggers" are discussed below.

8.2.1 TSCA § 4(a)(1)(A): Risk Trigger

EPA may require testing if the agency finds that: (1) the chemical or mixture may present an unreasonable risk of injury to human health or the environment; (2) existing data on and experience with the chemical or mixture are insufficient to reasonably predict or determine the effects of the chemical substance; and (3) testing is necessary to obtain such data.[61] EPA's first step, therefore, is to make a risk determination. EPA must find that the chemical may present an unreasonable risk.

As EPA uses the term, "risk" is a function of both hazard (toxicity) and exposure. The agency considers several factors in assessing the possible unreasonable risk of a substance, including knowledge of a chemical's physical and chemical properties, structural relationships to other chemicals with demonstrated adverse effects, data from inconclusive tests, and case history data.[62] Moreover, EPA has advised manufacturers that risk may be significant, even when exposure is extremely low.

Even though a § 4(a)(1)(A) test rule is not exposure-based, the agency still must demonstrate some possibility of exposure before it may issue a test rule under the "unreasonable risk" rationale because exposure is a necessary component of risk analysis. In *CMA v. EPA*, however, the D.C. Circuit held that EPA could rely on inferences to establish exposure, "so long as all the evidence—including the industry evidence—indicates a more-than-theoretical probability of exposure."[63]

Not only must EPA determine that the chemical or mixture may present a risk, the agency also must find that the existing data and experience are insufficient to determine or predict the effects of concern.[64] Data may be insufficient if EPA determines that existing studies are too flawed to be relied upon or otherwise inadequate to determine risk. Additionally, the agency must affirm that testing is necessary to develop data under TSCA § 4(a)(1)(A)(iii). If the agency decides that ongoing studies will enable EPA to determine whether a substance presents an unreasonable risk, no further

---

[60]*See* 40 C.F.R. §§ 712, 716.

[61]TSCA § 4(a)(1)(A).

[62]*Id.*

[63]859 F.2d 977, 989 (D.C. Cir. 1988).

[64]TSCA § 4(a)(1)(A)(ii).

testing will be required. In addition, the agency will not require chemical testing if no testing methodology exists which would lead to the production of the necessary data.

8.2.2 TSCA § 4(a)(1)(B): Exposure Trigger

TSCA § 4(a)(1)(B) provides EPA with an alternative basis for requiring testing founded on an exposure trigger. Using an exposure trigger, EPA can require testing if: (1) a chemical substance is produced in substantial quantities; (2) a substance is reasonably expected to be released into the environment in substantial quantities, or there is or may be significant or substantial human exposure; (3) there are insufficient data or experience upon which to reasonably predict the effects on human health or the environment; and (4) testing is necessary to develop the data.

By its express terms, § 4(a)(1)(B) requires both substantial production and substantial or significant exposure. This trigger requires an exposure finding much higher than that required to satisfy the exposure trigger under § 4(a)(1)(A).[65] This difference is based on the fact that less exposure is necessary when EPA has a scientific basis for suspecting potential toxicity under § 4(a)(1)(A).

EPA, however, repeatedly has declined to quantify "substantial," contending that it is "neither feasible nor desirable to make strict numerical definitions of substantial exposure or release," and that production and exposure determinations should be made individually for each chemical.[66] In addition to making a finding of substantial production volume or exposure under TSCA § 4(a)(1)(B), EPA also must determine that there are insufficient data and that testing is necessary to develop the needed information. These required findings are identical to those in TSCA § 4(a)(1)(A), discussed above.

8.3 Tests and Studies of Chemicals Which May Present Significant Risks

After EPA determines that at least one of the regulatory triggers under TSCA § 4(a) has been met and after a public comment period, EPA publishes the test rule. A TSCA § 4 test rule must identify specifically the chemical substance or mixture to be tested, the standards for the development of test data and, for existing chemicals, the time period during which the test data must be submitted.[67]

TSCA § 4 grants EPA wide latitude in deciding the types and amount of testing it may require: "The health and environmental effects for which standards . . . may be prescribed include carcinogenesis, mutagenesis, teratogenesis, behavioral disorders, cumulative or synergistic effects, and any other effect which may present an unreasonable risk of injury to health

---

[65]45 *Fed. Reg.* 48,528 (1980).
[66]50 *Fed. Reg.* 20,664 (1985).
[67]TSCA § 4(b)(1).

or the environment."[68] Generally, EPA requires studies on acute, subchronic, and chronic toxicity; oncogenicity; reproduction; teratogenicity; mutagenicity; neurotoxicity; environmental effects; and chemical fate.

8.3.1 Good Laboratory Practice Standards

Any study whose purpose is to satisfy a TSCA test rule must meet EPA Good Laboratory Practice (GLP) standards. TSCA GLP standards are codified at 40 C.F.R. § 792. TSCA GLP standards prescribe minimum requirements that the laboratory and sponsor must fulfill in areas such as organization and personnel, equipment, test facility operations, and study protocol. Any person who submits to EPA a test required by a § 4 test rule must submit a statement, signed by the submitter and the study director, to the effect that: (1) the study complies with GLP requirements; or (2) describes the differences between the practices used in the study and TSCA GLP requirements; or (3) the person was not the sponsor of the study, did not conduct the study and does not know whether the study complies with TSCA GLP requirements.

8.3.2 Development and Implementation of Test Rules

EPA in 1985 issued guidelines and procedures for utilization of single-phase rulemaking and now uses this procedure almost exclusively.[69] In the single-phase test rule, EPA proposes the pertinent Office of Toxic Substances (now the Office of Pollution Prevention and Toxics (OPPT)) test guideline as the required test standard in the initial notice of proposed rulemaking. Other methodologies may be proposed during the public comment period. The final rule promulgates as the test standard either the OPPT test guideline or other suitable guidelines. The agency utilizes single-phase rulemaking for most TSCA § 4 rules, reserving two-phase rulemaking only for testing where there are no well-accepted test methodologies.

8.3.3 Letters of Intent

Within thirty days after the effective date of a test rule, each person subject to the rule must either notify EPA by letter of his intent to conduct testing or submit an application for exemption.[70] Manufacturers or processors who continue their activities and who do not submit a letter of intent to test or a request for an exemption will be considered in violation of the rule.[71] Typically, where both manufacturers and processors are subject to the test rule, processors will only participate if specifically directed to do so or if no manufacturer has made known its intent to test. If no manufacturer notifies EPA within thirty days of receipt of EPA's notification, all

---

[68]TSCA § 4(b)(2)(A).

[69]50 *Fed. Reg.* 20,652 (1985).

[70]40 C.F.R. § 790.45.

[71]40 C.F.R. § 790.45(e), (f).

manufacturers and processors will be in violation of the rule from the thirty-first day after receipt of notification.[72]

8.3.4 Test Standards

Each test rule must include standards that prescribe the manner in which data are to be developed and any test methodology or other requirements that are necessary to assure that the manufacturer produces reliable and adequate data.[73] EPA has codified guidelines that may be used to establish test standards in § 4 test rules.[74] These guidelines do not become mandatory test standards until they are promulgated as such in individual § 4 rulemakings.

8.4 Exemptions from Testing

Although TSCA § 4 requires any person who manufactures, imports, or processes a chemical subject to a test rule to conduct testing, such a person may seek an exemption. TSCA § 4(c)(2) authorizes EPA to exempt a manufacturer or processor from a test rule if it is determined that the applicant's substance "is equivalent to a chemical substance or mixture for which data has been submitted" or for which data are being developed in response to a test rule. Under the exemption, persons subject to a test rule have thirty days within which to either supply a letter of intent to comply or seek an exemption.[75]

EPA will conditionally grant an exemption if the agency has received and adopted a complete proposed study plan, has determined that the substance that is the subject of the exemption application is equivalent to the test substance for which the required data have been or will be submitted, and has concluded that submission of the required test data would be duplicative of data which have been or will be submitted under the test rule.[76]

EPA may deny an exemption application if: (1) the applicant fails to demonstrate data equivalency; (2) the applicant fails to submit the information required under 40 C.F.R. §§ 790.82 or 790.85; (3) the agency has not received an adequate study plan for the test rule for which the exemption is sought; or (4) the study sponsor fails to submit the required data.[77] Although an applicant whose exemption has been denied can appeal the denial, the appeal does not stay the applicant's obligations under TSCA § 4.[78] Moreover, an exemption is only conditional and may be terminated if the agency determines that equivalent testing has not been initiated in a

---

[72]40 C.F.R. § 790.48(a)(3).

[73]TSCA § 4(b)(1)(B).

[74]40 C.F.R. §§ 796 (Chemical Fate), 797 (Environmental Effects), and 798 (Health Effects).

[75]40 C.F.R. § 790.80(b)(1).

[76]40 C.F.R. § 790.87.

[77]40 C.F.R. § 790.88.

[78]40 C.F.R. § 790.90.

timely manner or the equivalent testing did not comply with the test rules or Good Laboratory Practices.[79]

Persons who manufacture less than 500 kilograms (1,100 pounds) of a chemical annually are exempt from the procedural requirements of a test rule unless the test rule directs them to comply with a rule's testing requirement.[80] As in the case of processors, such manufacturers still would be legally subject to test rules and would not be exempt from reimbursement claims.

8.5 Reimbursement Procedures

Any person receiving an exemption from a testing requirement must reimburse persons who perform required testing for a portion of costs expended in generating the data.[81] (Because processors are deemed to have fulfilled their testing and reimbursement obligation indirectly "through higher prices passed on by those directly responsible, the manufacturers," processors normally make no direct reimbursement payments.)[82] Although EPA strongly encourages the parties to reach a voluntary agreement on the amount of reimbursement, the administrator may issue a reimbursement order directing those who received an exemption "to provide fair and equitable reimbursement" to those who incurred the costs. Reimbursement Orders are developed in consultation with the Department of Justice and the Federal Trade Commission. The administrator must take into account all relevant factors, including competitive position and market share of the persons providing and receiving reimbursement.[83]

If the parties are unable to agree, they may submit their dispute to arbitration and may request a hearing with the American Arbitration Association (AAA).[84] A hearing notice will be published in the *Federal Register* after which any party may file a written answer in response or to set forth additional claims. However, once a hearing officer is appointed, no additional or different claims can be asserted without the consent of the hearing officer.

After the hearing, a proposed reimbursement order will be put forth which, based on a formula, provides that in general, each person's share of the test costs shall be in proportion to his share of the total production volume of the test chemical. EPA has recognized, however, that the allocation of test costs based on market share may not always be equitable. Therefore, any party may propose factors besides market share if their application produces a fair and equitable result.

---

[79] 40 C.F.R. § 790.93(a).
[80] 54 *Fed. Reg.* 21,237 (1989).
[81] TSCA § 4.
[82] 40 C.F.R. § 791.45(a).
[83] TSCA § 4(c)(4)(A).
[84] 40 C.F.R. § 791.20(a).

Cooperative testing reduces costs and avoids duplicative testing. The most frequent form of organization used to conduct cooperative testing is the joint venture, and these are being used with increasing frequency as a means to reduce the costs and risks of developing environmental and toxicological data required by a § 4 test rule. The joint venture is an unincorporated entity that operates much like a partnership but is limited to accomplishing the TSCA testing objectives of the group. Most joint ventures have a business group and a technical group. The latter develops protocols, monitors the studies, and reviews the results. The former typically decides when assessments will be made for expenses and decides if and when the scope of the testing program should be expanded beyond the original tests.

The most important provision in the agreement will be the terms of sharing the costs and testing. Generally the costs can be apportioned on the basis of the market share of each participant, on an equal basis, or on some variant of these two. The joint venture can test only one substance "representative" of all of the members' products and that substance must meet all the requirements of the test rule.

8.6 Judicial Review

TSCA § 19 provides for appellate review of EPA test rules that are contested. A court may review, however, only the record of the rulemaking proceeding before the agency, and the agency's findings are conclusive if supported by "substantial evidence."[85]

8.6.1 Jurisdiction, Standing and Venue

A petition for judicial review must be filed within sixty days of the final rule. The standing provision of § 19 indicates that "any person" may file a petition seeking review of a final rule. "Any person" would include any producer of a substance, any interested organization, such as a trade association or any environmental group; no injury need be shown. A petition may be filed in: (1) the District of Columbia; (2) the circuit in which the petitioner resides; or (3) the circuit in which the petitioner has its principal place of business.[86]

8.6.2 Rulemaking Record

TSCA test rules are promulgated on the basis of the rulemaking record, which the court of appeals will review to determine whether it is supported by substantial evidence. The court will not hold a new (*de novo*) hearing on whether and how a chemical substance or mixture should be tested. The reviewing court will consider only the evidence contained in the rulemaking record consisting of: (1) the final test rule; (2) the necessary findings; (3) transcripts of oral presentations; and (4) written submissions of interested parties. The rulemaking record also includes any other information which EPA considers relevant to the test rule and "which the administrator

---

[85]TSCA § 19(c)(1)(B)(i).
[86]*See* 28 U.S.C.A. § 1391(c).

identified, on or before the date of the promulgation of such rule, in a notice published in the *Federal Register*."[87]

8.6.3 Standard of Review: "Substantial Evidence"

TSCA § 19(c)(1)(B) also prescribes the standard of judicial review: "[T]he court shall hold unlawful and set aside such rule if the court finds that the rule is not supported by substantial evidence in the rulemaking record ... taken as a whole." In imposing the substantial evidence test, Congress cautioned that EPA need only demonstrate that the rule is "reasonably" supported.

In reviewing agency actions, however, courts give close scrutiny to the rulemaking record to assure that factual findings are supported by substantial evidence and that the rulemaking record adequately explains the agency's decisions. While a reviewing court may defer to EPA on scientific and policy issues, the court will examine the rulemaking record for a full explanation of the agency's rationale in its adopted approach. The courts agree that judicial review of § 4 test rules should be "demanding" and "fairly rigorous."[88]

8.7 TSCA § 4(f) Findings of Significant Risk

The agency's actions after receipt of test data that indicate a "significant risk" are governed by TSCA § 4(f). If the test data indicate to the administrator that there may be a "reasonable basis to conclude that a chemical substance or mixture presents or will present a significant risk of serious or widespread harm to human beings from cancer, gene mutations, or birth defects," the administrator must initiate appropriate rulemaking. If EPA chooses not to initiate rulemaking, the agency must publish in the *Federal Register* the reasons for not taking action.[89]

8.7.1 Criteria for Risk

Under TSCA § 4(f), EPA must take regulatory action when the chemical poses "a significant risk of serious or widespread harm to human beings." EPA considers this § 4(f) "significant risk" trigger to present a higher risk threshold than for those actions under TSCA § 6 which require a finding of "unreasonable risk."

EPA will determine that a significant risk of serious harm exists when there is a population whose members are at high individual risk from the substance. If the agency projects that humans will be exposed to doses that have produced an effect observed in animals or humans, the agency will make a § 4(f) finding. In addition, EPA will find a "significant risk of serious harm" where an exposed population does not enjoy an adequate margin of safety.

---

[87]TSCA § 19(a)(3)(E).

[88]*CMA v. EPA*, 859 F.2d 977, 992 (D.C. Cir. 1988); *Ausimont U.S.A. Inc. v. EPA*, 838 F.2d 93, 96 (3d Cir. 1988); *Shell Chemical Co. v. EPA*, 826 F.2d 295, 297 (5th Cir. 1987).

[89]TSCA § 4(f)(2).

Significant risk of widespread harm is determined to exist when a large number of persons are exposed to the substance at a level on which a significant aggregate population risk is predicated. Although the individual risk may not be as high as that needed under the previous criterion, the harm associated with the risk must be widespread.

8.7.2 Review Period

Once EPA determines that the § 4(f) criteria have been met, the agency has 180 days to decide whether to initiate regulatory action. This 180-day period can be extended for an additional ninety days for "good cause."[90] The agency will begin the 180-day review period when it receives sufficient information to make a § 4(f) finding. In general, EPA will not solicit public comments prior to making a § 4(f) finding and the final § 4(f) finding will be made by the administrator.

9.0 REPORTING AND RETENTION OF INFORMATION

TSCA § 8 establishes reporting and recordkeeping requirements to provide EPA with information on which to base regulatory and enforcement actions and to track patterns of adverse reactions to chemicals. EPA uses the information obtained under § 8 in other EPA programs to provide chemical information to industry and citizens, to evaluate existing data to determine their adequacy for risk assessment purposes, to identify data gaps, and to monitor ongoing activities with respect to specific chemicals.

9.1 TSCA § 8(a): Reports

Under TSCA § 8(a), EPA may require companies to maintain records and submit reports on their chemical manufacturing, importing, and processing activities. The agency has used its § 8(a) authority to impose recordkeeping and reporting requirements on specific chemicals, but its most significant use of § 8(a) has been the issuance of "model" rules that apply to multiple chemicals. The first of these model rules, the Preliminary Assessment Information Rule (PAIR), was issued in June 1982 and continues in effect.[91] The second, the Comprehensive Assessment Information Rule (CAIR), was issued on December 22, 1988 and eventually will replace the PAIR.[92]

9.2 TSCA § 8(b): Inventory Update Rule

In June 1986, EPA issued an Inventory Update Rule requiring manufacturers and importers of certain chemicals listed on the inventory to report current data on the production volume, plant site, and site-limited status of the substances.[93] The requirements under this rule are discussed above at Section 3.3, in conjunction with the TSCA Inventory.

---

[90]TSCA § 4(f)(2).
[91]40 C.F.R. § 712.
[92]40 C.F.R. §§ 704.1-.225.
[93]*See* 40 C.F.R. § 710.

9.3 TSCA § 8(c): Records of Significant Adverse Reactions

TSCA § 8(c) requires manufacturers, processors, and distributors to keep records of significant adverse reactions to health and the environment alleged to have been caused by a chemical substance or mixture they manufacture, process, or distribute. Allegations by employees must be kept on file for thirty years; allegations by others for five years. These allegations do not have to be reported to EPA unless the agency specifically requests them. EPA may require submission of copies of the § 8(c) records to the agency, however, and employees can petition the agency to collect and release § 8(c) information.

EPA has defined "significant adverse reaction" to mean a reaction that may indicate a substantial impairment of normal activities, or long-lasting or irreversible damage to health or the environment.[94] In order to place some limitation on an otherwise open-ended recording obligation, EPA has provided a narrow exemption for known human health effects.[95] Those environmental reactions which must be recorded include gradual or sudden changes in the composition of animal life or plant life, abnormal numbers of deaths of organisms, reduction of the reproductive success of a species, reduction in agricultural productivity, and alterations in the behavior or distribution of a species.[96]

In order to constitute a recordable allegation under § 8(c), the statement must state clearly the alleged cause of the adverse reaction.[97] An "allegation" is defined as a statement, made without formal proof or regard for evidence, that a chemical substance or mixture has caused a significant adverse reaction to health or the environment. It is important to remember that a series of identical or very similar allegations about a particular substance may indicate a significant risk, which can trigger reporting requirements under § 8(e).

9.4 TSCA §8(d): Health and Safety Studies

Section 8(d) requires that upon request a person who manufactures, processes, or distributes in commerce any chemical substance or mixture, must submit to the administrator lists and copies of health and safety studies conducted by, known to, or ascertainable by that person.

Under the § 8(d) Model Reporting Rule, submission of unpublished health and safety studies is required on certain specifically listed chemicals or mixtures. Persons who currently manufacture, import, or process a chemical substance or a mixture listed at 40 C.F.R. § 716.120 (or propose to do so) or who manufactured, imported, or processed (or proposed to do so) within the ten years preceding the effective date of the listing of the chemical are subject to the provisions of the Model Reporting Rule. There are two

---

[94] 40 C.F.R. § 717.3(i).
[95] 40 C.F.R. § 717.12(b).
[96] 40 C.F.R. § 717.12(c).
[97] 40 C.F.R. § 717.10(b)(2).

phases to § 8(d) reporting. First, persons are required to submit copies of all non-exempt studies in their possession at the time they become subject to the rule. Second, EPA must be informed within thirty days of any study on a subject chemical initiated by or for such manufacturer or processor.[98]

9.5 Section 8(e): Substantial Risk Information

Section 8(e) requires the manufacturer, processor, or distributor of a chemical substance to report to EPA any information concerning the substance that "reasonably supports the conclusion that the chemical substance or mixture presents a substantial risk of injury to health or the environment." EPA has not issued regulations implementing § 8(e). The agency has issued other types of formal guidance, however.[99] EPA also provides some limited policy guidance through § 8(e) Status Reports, and from time to time through its monthly publication, "TSCA Chemicals in Progress." The Status Reports are a summary of EPA's initial review of submitted § 8(e) and "For Your Information" reports and are available for public viewing in the OTS Public Reading Room at EPA Headquarters in Washington, D.C. Moreover, in the course of the recent TSCA § 8(e) Compliance Audit Program (CAP), EPA has issued publicly a number of responses to inquiries from CAP participants and trade associations. The 1978 Policy Statement remains the fundamental source of specific guidance.

10.0 EXISTING CHEMICAL REGULATION

TSCA § 6 grants EPA full authority to regulate existing chemicals that present unreasonable risks to health or the environment. Under TSCA § 6, EPA must place controls and restrictions, including outright bans if necessary, upon the manufacture, use, processing, disposal, or distribution of such chemicals. This is EPA's most extreme regulatory power.

10.1 Procedures and Standards for TSCA § 6 Regulation

EPA must initiate § 6 rulemaking to regulate a chemical substance when the agency finds "a reasonable basis to conclude that the manufacture . . . use, or disposal of a chemical . . . will present an unreasonable risk of injury to health or the environment" and that the risks cannot be addressed by EPA or any other agency under another statute.[100] In determining whether a perceived risk is "unreasonable," the agency must conduct a risk assessment of the chemical substance. The risk/benefit comparison required by § 6 must consider: (1) the effects on health and the environment; (2) the magnitude of exposure to humans and the environment; (3) the benefits of the substance and the availability of substitutes; and (4) the reasonably ascertainable

---

[98]40 C.F.R. §§ 716.60, 716.65.

[99]Statement of Interpretation and Enforcement Policy, 43 *Fed. Reg.* 11,110 (1978) ("1978 Policy Statement").

[100]TSCA § 6(a).

economic consequences of the rule.[101] Once having found an unreasonable risk, EPA must choose the least burdensome restrictions adequate to protect against the identified risk.[102] In addition to controls on the chemical itself, EPA can order a manufacturer or processor to use approved quality control procedures if EPA determines the chemical substance is manufactured or processed in a manner "which unintentionally causes" it to present an unreasonable risk.

10.2 Chemical Specific Regulations

EPA has regulated only six chemical substances under this section since TSCA's inception: asbestos; chloroflourocarbon; dioxins; hexavalent chromium; certain metal-working fluids; and polychlorinated biphenyls. In the case of asbestos the regulations were ultimately overturned. In the case of polychlorinated biphenyls (PCBs), the regulations may be the most widely applicable and best known of any TSCA regulations.

10.2.1 Asbestos

EPA's asbestos regulations serve to illustrate some of the difficulties the agency has experienced implementing TSCA § 6 controls. After more than ten years of effort, EPA in 1989 issued a final rule to ban the manufacture, import, processing, and distribution of virtually all asbestos products. EPA issued the regulations because exposure to asbestos fibers is associated with pulmonary fibrosis (asbestosis), lung cancer, and other cancers and diseases both inside and outside the lungs, and because millions of people are exposed to airborne asbestos fibers.[103]

After a bitterly fought challenge to the asbestos regulations brought by industry, the U.S. Court of Appeals for the Fifth Circuit overturned EPA's ban.[104] The court held that EPA failed to justify use of the ban. EPA did not demonstrate that some intermediate alternative action would not be adequate. Nor did the agency give notice that it intended to predict exposure by use of data on "analogous" substances. Moreover, said the court, EPA failed to consider evidence that available substitutes were toxic also. This failure demonstrates the regulatory hurdles facing EPA under § 6 and suggests why so few TSCA § 6 actions have been initiated.

10.2.2 Chlorofluorocarbons (CFCs)

Chlorofluorocarbons (CFCs) had been earmarked for regulation prior to the effective date of TSCA. In 1978, EPA promulgated final regulations prohibiting almost all propellant uses of chlorofluorocarbons (for example, in aerosol sprays).[105] Under the regulations, the manufacturing, processing, or

---

[101]TSCA §§ 6(c)(1)(A)–(D).
[102]TSCA § 6(a).
[103]40 C.F.R. § 763.
[104]*Corrosion Proof Fittings v. EPA*, 987 F.2d 1201 (5th Cir. 1991).
[105]40 C.F.R. § 762.

distribution of fully halogenated chlorofluoroalkanes for aerosol propellant use is prohibited, except for enumerated "essential" uses.[106]

EPA also has issued a rule to implement the Montreal Protocol on Substances That Deplete the Ozone Layer. This international agreement calls for a fifty percent reduction in production and consumption of CFCs. However, EPA did not issue this rule under TSCA, but rather under its Clean Air Act Authority.[107] Although the rule regulates production and consumption of CFCs through an allotment system, it does not modify or rescind the TSCA CFC regulations regarding CFC use as a propellant.

10.2.3 Hexavalent Chromium

EPA prohibits use of hexavalent chromium as a corrosion inhibitor in comfort cooling towers (CCTs) as part of air conditioning and refrigeration systems.[108] EPA determined that hexavalent chromium compounds are human carcinogens and that continued use in CCTs would pose an unreasonable risk to human health. Because the risk of human exposure posed by the use of hexavalent chromium chemicals in industrial cooling towers is low, the rule does not ban such use. To eliminate misuse, distributors of hexavalent chromium-based water treatment chemicals are required to place warning labels on containers and retain records of all shipments of hexavalent chromium-based chemicals intended for use in industrial cooling towers.

10.2.4 Metalworking Fluids

On three occasions EPA has used its § 6(a) authority to address potential hazards that could arise from mixing nitrosating agents with certain amides and salts. The three rules involved PMN substances that were intended for use in metalworking fluids. In each case, EPA determined that under common metalworking industry practices, use of the new substance would expose employees to incidentally created N-nitrosodiethanolamine. The rules EPA promulgated prohibit mixing nitrosating agents with metalworking fluids that contain the specific PMN substances and require distributors of the PMN substances to affix warning labels to containers of the substances and to send advance warning letters and copies of the regulations to customers.

10.2.5 Polychlorinated Biphenyls

TSCA § 6 specifically required EPA to regulate PCBs by establishing a legal presumption under § 6(e) that PCBs pose an unreasonable risk. In general, EPA's PCB regulations, set forth at 40 C.F.R. § 761, cover the following areas: (1) prohibited and authorized commercial activities; (2) marking requirements; (3) storage and disposal requirements; (4) exemptions from the general prohibitions; (5) spill cleanup policy; and

---

[106] 40 C.F.R. § 762.58.
[107] 53 *Fed. Reg.* 30,566 (1988).
[108] 40 C.F.R. § 749.68.

(6) recordkeeping requirements. These widely applicable regulations are discussed briefly below.

The manufacture, processing, or distribution of PCBs in commerce for use in the United States is prohibited unless conducted in a manner that EPA has determined is "totally enclosed" or has otherwise specifically authorized. A "totally enclosed" manner is defined as any manner which will ensure that exposure of human beings or the environment to PCBs as a result of the activity will be insignificant.[109]

Standardized PCB warning labels must be affixed to specific types of items such as electrical, hydraulic, and heat transfer equipment, containers, and vehicles.[110] There are formats for large and small PCB labels, and these labels must be used whenever PCB warning marks are required. Marking requirements extend to storage areas, as well as particular PCB articles.

Existing PCBs and PCB articles are to be disposed of gradually through methods by which exposure is virtually eliminated. The regulations define "disposal" so that virtually any release of PCBs to the environment in concentrations of fifty ppm or greater is considered a prohibited act of disposal. Disposal standards exist that encompass the diversity of PCB contaminated waste, including: liquids; electrical equipment; hydraulic machinery; other contaminated articles; dredge and sludge; as well as containers that once held PCBs.

When PCBs and PCB-containing items are removed from use, they may be stored for up to one year while awaiting disposal. All items stored must be marked to indicate the date the item was removed from service, and the storage facility must be constructed to contain spills. In addition, operators must inspect the stored PCBs every thirty days and follow specific recordkeeping requirements.

EPA has issued a policy governing the reporting and cleanup of all spills resulting from the release of materials containing PCBs in concentrations greater than fifty ppm.[111] The policy classifies PCB spills as either low concentration spills or high concentration spills. Low concentration spills have a PCB concentration less than 500 ppm and involve less than one pound of PCBs. High concentration spills have a PCB concentration greater than 500 ppm or are low concentration spills that either involve one pound or more of PCBs or 270 gallons or more of untested mineral oil.[112] Any spill that involves a release of more than ten pounds of PCBs must be reported immediately to the appropriate EPA Regional Office. (CERCLA also requires reporting to the National Response Center.)

The level of cleanup required under the PCB cleanup policy is determined by the following facts: (1) the spill location; (2) the potential for exposure to residual PCBs remaining after the cleanup; (3) the concentration

---

[109]TSCA § 6(e)(2).

[110]40 C.F.R. § 761.

[111]40 C.F.R. §§ 761.120-135.

[112]52 *Fed. Reg.* 10,692 (1987).

of PCBs initially spilled; and (4) the nature and size of the population potentially at risk from exposure.[113] In general, the greater the potential human exposure, the more stringent the cleanup standard.

Compliance with the PCB cleanup policy will "create a presumption against both enforcement action for penalties and the need for further cleanup under TSCA."[114] However, when cleanups are required under RCRA, CERCLA, or other statutes, they may have to meet standards different from those imposed by TSCA.

Operators of a facility must prepare and keep at hand an annual report for the previous calendar year if their facility contains forty-five kilograms or more of PCBs in PCB containers, one or more PCB transformers, fifty or more large PCB capacitors, or is used for PCB storage or disposal.[115] Other records described specifically in part 761 must be maintained by persons engaged in activities involving PCBs.

EPA has promulgated a rule that creates a nationwide PCB manifesting system under TSCA.[116] The rule requires all PCB disposal companies, transporters, commercial storers, and generators of PCB wastes who store their own wastes to notify EPA of their activities and identify their facilities. All companies that notify EPA receive an EPA registration number. EPA has attempted to use the least burdensome restrictions by integrating its federal PCB regulations with state regulations under RCRA and by allowing PCB operators to utilize the RCRA Uniform Manifest, which has space designated for additional information required under various state RCRA programs.

11.0 RELATIONSHIP BETWEEN TSCA AND OTHER LAWS

Pesticides regulated under the Federal Insecticide, Fungicide, and Rodenticide Act and substances regulated under the Federal Food, Drug, and Cosmetic Act are excluded from jurisdiction under TSCA. Moreover, other statutes administered by EPA, statutes administered by other federal agencies such as the Occupational Safety and Health Act and Consumer Product Safety Act, and toxic substances laws adopted by states or their political subdivisions also regulate chemical risks. The relationship between TSCA and these statutes is discussed below.

11.1 Federal Insecticide, Fungicide, and Rodenticide Act (FIFRA)

A chemical must satisfy a two-pronged test to meet the TSCA pesticide exclusion. First, the chemical must fall within the FIFRA definition of a "pesticide." Second, the chemical must be "manufactured, processed, or distributed in commerce for use as a pesticide."[117] Accordingly, EPA

---

[113]*Id.* at 10,688-90.

[114]*Id.* at 10,694.

[115]40 C.F.R. § 761.180.

[116]Polychlorinated Biphenyls: Notification and Manifesting for PCB Waste Activities, 53 *Fed. Reg.* 37,436 (1988).

[117]TSCA § 3(2)(B)(ii).

considers raw materials and inert ingredients to be subject to TSCA until they become components of a pesticide product, at which time the agency considers them to be subject to FIFRA.[118] EPA also contends that TSCA's provisions, including the TSCA § 8(e) notification of substantial risk requirements, apply to R&D candidate pesticides prior to the submission of an application for an Experimental Use Permit or a FIFRA § 3 registration because under FIFRA these chemicals are not yet considered pesticides.[119] EPA also takes the position that a pesticide does not fall within the TSCA § 3(2)(B)(ii) pesticide exclusion during disposal because the chemical is not being "manufactured, processed, or distributed in commerce for use as a pesticide" during the disposal process.

11.2 Federal Food, Drug, and Cosmetic Act (FDCA)

TSCA § 3 also excludes foods, food additives, drugs, devices, and cosmetics subject to the FDCA from the TSCA definition of "chemical substance."[120] EPA's position is that a substance should be exempt from TSCA regulation at the point that the Food and Drug Administration (FDA) regulates the substance.[121]

11.3 TSCA'S Relationship to Other Federal Laws

TSCA § 9 addresses EPA's authority to regulate those chemicals which fall within the purview of both TSCA and other federal statutes. Commonly called TSCA's "referral" provision, § 9 establishes procedures by which EPA can refer regulation of chemical risks to other agencies that have adequate statutory authority to regulate the risks. Referral is accomplished by means of a detailed report which describes EPA's findings. If the referral agency either issues an order declaring that the activities described in EPA's report "do not present the risk" that the administrator alleged, or initiates within ninety days of its response to EPA "action to protect against such risk," EPA is barred from using TSCA §§ 6 or 7 to regulate the risk.[122] If the referral agency determines, however, that it lacks adequate authority to regulate the risk "to a sufficient extent," explicitly defers the regulatory prerogative back to EPA, or fails to respond within the deadline set by EPA, then EPA remains free to act under TSCA to regulate the risk.

TSCA § 9(b), the intra-agency counterpart of § 9(a), requires the administrator to "coordinate" actions taken under TSCA with actions taken under other statutes administered "in whole or part" by EPA. If the administrator determines that a chemical risk "could be eliminated or reduced to a sufficient extent by actions taken under the authorities contained in such other Federal laws, the Administrator shall use such

---

[118]42 *Fed. Reg.* 64,586 (1977).
[119]51 *Fed. Reg.* 15,098 (1986).
[120]TSCA § 3(2)(B)(vi).
[121]42 *Fed. Reg.* 64,586 (1977).
[122]TSCA § 9(a)(2).

authorities to protect against such risk."[123] If, however, the administrator in his discretion determines that "it is in the public interest to protect against such risk" by actions taken under TSCA, he is not required to regulate the risk under the other statute.[124]

11.4 TSCA Preemption of State and Local Laws

TSCA § 18 governs the relationship between TSCA and state and local laws which regulate chemical risks. Section 18 states that TSCA does not "affect [that is, preempt] the authority" of states or their political subdivisions to regulate the same chemicals covered by TSCA, subject to two exceptions. First, if EPA adopts a testing rule under TSCA § 4, state and local requirements for testing the same chemical are prohibited.[125] Second, if EPA adopts a rule or order under TSCA §§ 5 or 6, state and local regulations on the same chemical (other than disposal regulations) are prohibited, unless such regulations are identical to EPA's, carry out a federal law (such as the Clean Air Act), or ban the use of the chemical (other than its use in manufacturing or processing of other chemicals).[126]

Despite the foregoing, § 18(b) gives the administrator authority to allow (by rule) otherwise preempted state or local laws to be adopted or to continue in effect if they are consistent with EPA's actions under TSCA, afford a higher degree of protection than actions taken by EPA under TSCA, and do not unduly burden interstate commerce.

12.0 TSCA INSPECTIONS AND ENFORCEMENT

TSCA §§ 11 and 16 authorize EPA to conduct inspections and subpoena documents to monitor for compliance with the act and provide for the imposition of both civil and criminal penalties for TSCA violations. In addition, EPA may seize products under the authority of §§ 7 or 17(b). The agency usually limits seizure actions to those instances where a civil penalty action is insufficient to protect human health or the environment. Under § 7, EPA may conduct an "imminent hazard" seizure even absent a violation of TSCA.

12.1 Inspections

Under TSCA § 11 an EPA agent may inspect: (1) any establishment in which chemical substances or mixtures are manufactured, processed, stored, or held before or after distribution in commerce; and (2) any conveyance being used to transport such materials in connection with distribution in commerce. An inspection may extend to all things within the premises or

---

[123]TSCA § 9(b).
[124]*Id.*
[125]TSCA § 18(a)(2)(A).
[126]TSCA § 18(a)(2)(B).

conveyances under inspection, including records, files, papers, processes, controls, and facilities, so long as they bear on compliance with the act.[127]

Although TSCA § 11 does not require EPA to obtain a search warrant prior to entry and inspection, independent constitutional considerations may make it necessary for EPA to obtain an administrative search warrant in order to enter the premises when permission is denied.[128] EPA policy presently calls for an inspector to obtain a warrant when lawful entry has been denied.

12.1.1 Types of Inspections

A company may undergo any of several "types" of inspections. For example, an inspection may be conducted for § 5 new chemical activity, for § 6(e) PCB violations, for § 8 reporting and recordkeeping compliance, or for any combination of the above. In addition, an inspection may be either "specific" (that is, targeting specific chemicals or regulations) or "general" (that is, assessing overall compliance).

Often the most extensive inspections are § 8 "verification" inspections. EPA will check to see if the targeted company has set up a centralized system for tracking allegations of adverse effects concerning chemicals under § 8(c) and a well-publicized procedure for its employees to report significant risk information under § 8(e). The absence of such systems and procedures would raise suspicions about a company's TSCA compliance.

12.1.2 EPA Inspection Procedures

Inspection procedures fall into the following categories: (1) pre-inspection preparation; (2) notification and entry; (3) opening conference; (4) sampling and documentation; (5) closing conference; and (6) report preparation and follow-up.[129]

Pre-inspection Preparation. EPA's appropriate regional office will usually provide written notification to a facility several weeks prior to an actual inspection. The notice will specify the authority for the inspection and discuss what will be covered by the inspection. The inspector also will provide a declaration of confidential business information (CBI) form that the company must use to declare that certain information requested is CBI.

Notification and Entry. At the inspection, the investigator will identify himself and present official agency credentials. If the inspector does not have a search warrant he must obtain the consent of the facility officials. Although the company may at any time revoke its permission to enter, all information collected before permission is revoked remains in the possession of the inspector.

Opening Conference. The inspector will conduct an opening conference with facility officials where the purpose of the inspection, the parameters of

---

[127]TSCA § 11(b).

[128]*See Marshall v. Barlow's, Inc.*, 436 U.S. 307, 325 (1978).

[129]EPA, TSCA Inspection Manual 3-1 to 3-62 (1980).

the inspection, and the procedures to be followed are outlined. He will discuss how questions will be handled during the inspection and at the closing conference, and should inform facility officials of their legal rights. If the facility officials have any objections as to how the inspection will be carried out, they should raise them during the opening conference.

Sampling and Documentation. In most cases, the inspector will know from pre-inspection preparation which records will be reviewed during the inspection. The investigator will always examine facility records and, when deemed necessary, will take physical samples in order to obtain documentation in support of any contemplated enforcement action.

Closing Conference. At the conclusion of the inspection, the EPA inspector will present the facility with a receipt itemizing all samples and documents taken during the inspection. Inspectors will not make statements as to the ultimate status of the facility or discuss the legal consequence of potential non-compliance. However, an inspector may discuss observed deviations from recommended procedures and inform facility personnel of problems that might require immediate attention. Inspectors may offer suggestions based on their preliminary findings. Inspectors also may request additional data and ask follow-up questions regarding their observations and measurements.

Report Preparation and Follow-up. The inspection report is the compilation of factual information gathered at the compliance inspection. A copy of the final audit report may be obtained through the EPA office that initiated the audit. The regional office will use this report to determine whether follow-up action is appropriate and whether it should pursue criminal charges or civil enforcement.

12.1.3 EPA Authority to Issue Subpoenas

TSCA § 11(c) authorizes EPA to issue administrative subpoenas to require the attendance and testimony of witnesses, the production of reports, papers, documents, answers to questions and such other information "that the administrator deems necessary."[130] Moreover, EPA interprets its § 11(c) power as an omnibus subpoena authority to support its regulatory activities under other statutes which do not provide subpoena authority so long as a "chemical substance" is involved.

12.2 Civil Penalties

In determining an appropriate civil penalty for a TSCA violation, the administrator must take into account nine specific factors that pertain to the nature, circumstances, extent, and gravity of the violation and also pertain to the violator's culpability, compliance history, financial position, and "other

---

[130]*See EPA v. Alyeska Pipeline Service Co.*, 836 F.2d 443 (9th Cir. 1988) (holding that EPA is required only to show that the documents or testimony sought by the subpoena are relevant to determining whether there is a problem that may be remedied under TSCA).

matters" as justice requires.[131] The agency's treatment of these factors is set forth in EPA's Guidelines for the Assessment of Civil Penalties Under Section 16 of the Control Act[132,] and other more specific policies, as discussed below.

12.2.1 TSCA Civil Penalty Policy

The TSCA Civil Penalty Policy requires a two-stage determination of a proposed civil penalty. First, a penalty matrix is used to calculate a Gravity Based Penalty (GBP). The GBP is based on the nature, extent, and circumstances of the violation. Second, the GBP may be adjusted upward or downward, taking into account several additional factors, including ability to pay, effect on ability to conduct business, any history of prior violations, culpability, and such other factors "as justice may require."

EPA considers two principal criteria for assessing a violator's culpability: (1) the person's knowledge of the TSCA requirement; and (2) the person's degree of control over the violation.[133] Where the violation is "willful" (that is, the violator intentionally committed an act which he knew was a violation), the TSCA Civil Penalty Policy calls for a twenty-five percent increase in the civil penalty.[134] Criminal penalties may apply as well.[135] EPA considers the culpability of a violator to include the violator's "attitude" after the violation is discovered. Accordingly, the agency will adjust a proposed penalty upward or downward by up to fifteen percent, depending on whether the violator is making "good faith" efforts to comply with the appropriate regulations, the promptness of the violator's corrective actions and any assistance the violator gives EPA to minimize any harm to the environment that was caused by the violation.

The TSCA Civil Penalty Policy lists nine additional matters EPA will consider under its statutory mandate to consider "such other matters as justice may require." EPA takes the position that, regardless of other factors, proposed penalties should be increased when necessary to pay for government investigative and clean-up costs and, in appropriate cases, to ensure that the violator does not profit from noncompliance.[136] On the other hand, EPA will consider reducing proposed penalties where: (1) the violator's cost of cleanup plus penalty seem excessive; (2) there is conflict or ambiguity *vis-a-vis* other federal regulations; (3) the violator makes voluntary environmentally beneficial expenditures above and beyond those required by law; (4) national defense or foreign policy issues intervene; (5) new owners are burdened with a prior owner's history of violations; and (6) the "extent" of the violation falls very close to the borderline between a

---

[131]TSCA § 16(a)(2)(B).

[132]45 *Fed. Reg.* 59,770 (1980).

[133]45 *Fed. Reg.* 59,773 (1980).

[134]*Id.*

[135]*See* Criminal Liability section below.

[136]45 *Fed. Reg.* 59,774 (1980).

significant or a minor violation, and as a result the penalty calculated seems disproportionately high.

12.2.2 Regulation-Specific Penalty Policies

The TSCA § 5 Penalty Policy prescribes administrative penalties for noncompliance with TSCA § 5(e) or 5(f) orders, rules, or injunctions, and significant new use rules; for failure to submit PMNs; for submission of false or misleading information; and for commercial use of a substance that was produced without a PMN or valid exemption. The § 5 Policy also addresses violations of the regulations governing NOCs, although those regulations were promulgated under § 8.

The TSCA § 5 Penalty Policy assigns each type of potential violation to one of the three categories, as follows: (1) Chemical Control Violations; (2) Control-Associated Data-Gathering Violations; and (3) Hazard Assessment Violations.[137] These categories are then used in conjunction with facts pertaining to the specific case to calculate the GBP. After the GBP is calculated, the penalty may be increased or decreased due to the various factors listed in the TSCA Civil Penalty Policy. In a like manner, the TSCA §§ 8, 12 and 13 Penalty Policy addresses § 8 reporting and recordkeeping violations; § 12(b) export notification violations; and §13 import certification violations.

Both the TSCA § 5 Penalty Policy and the TSCA §§ 8, 12 and 13 Penalty Policy allow violators to reduce penalties by up to eighty percent as a result of confessing and cooperating. The agency has shown great reluctance, however, to reduce the base penalty by more than eighty percent, even if the self-confessor can show the best of attitudes and substantial steps taken to rectify the violation and to bring itself into full compliance with TSCA. A strict application by EPA of the Civil Penalty Policy is not appropriate in every instance, however. Recently, in an appeal before EPA's chief judicial officer, a company prevailed against the agency's position that the civil penalty to be assessed must be determined by strict adherence to the penalty policy.[138] On appeal by EPA, the hearing officer's downward adjustment of the penalty for "good attitude" and appropriate mitigating steps taken by 3M was upheld. More importantly, however, the appeals officer departed entirely from the civil penalty policy and reduced the penalty by an additional fifteen percent pursuant to TSCA § 16(a)(2)(B), which allows for an increase in the downward adjustment to account for "such other matters as justice may require." The total penalty was thereby reduced ninety-five percent from that originally proposed. This aspect of the 3M case has since been utilized successfully by other companies seeking reduced penalties.

Before initiating civil penalty procedures under TSCA, the agency sometimes will issue a notice of noncompliance (NON), advising a company

---

[137]TSCA § 5 Penalty Policy at 7.

[138]*In the Matter of 3M Company (Minnesota Mining and Mfg.)*, Docket No. TSCA-88-H-06, TSCA Appeal No. 90-3, (Feb. 28, 1992).

that a violation of TSCA has been detected or that the agency is keeping track of the company's actions with respect to correcting a violation. The issuance of a NON is discretionary and may occur when the violation is a minor one not posing a significant threat to human health and other positive factors are present.[139]

12.3 Settlement Procedures

EPA encourages negotiated settlements of civil penalty proceedings.[140] Thus, a settlement conference may be requested at any time during civil enforcement proceedings. A negotiated settlement agreement often will provide for two types of activities. First, it might include a mandatory audit provision, requiring the violator to conduct a self-audit to uncover and report additional TSCA violations and to initiate remedial measures. Second, a negotiated settlement may provide for additional compliance measures designed to further the agency's policies, for example, a commitment by the defendant to conduct a series of TSCA educational seminars or to prepare a TSCA guidance manual for employees. Generally, a provision is included which places a cap on the total amount of fines.

In certain circumstances, a settlement in an administrative action may be reached that assesses a civil penalty but also provides for the respondent to undertake remedial action as a means of remitting all the assessed penalty. Such a settlement is referred to as a Settlement with Conditions (SWC). The purpose of an SWC is to enhance the level of compliance where violations require complex remedies.

12.4 Administrative Hearings

If the agency considers a violation serious enough or if settlement negotiations are unsuccessful, EPA will institute civil penalty actions leading to an administrative hearing. During the action, EPA will follow the procedures set forth in the Consolidated Rules of Practice (CROP) which govern these administrative actions.[141] Usually a pre-hearing conference intended to facilitate and expedite the proceedings is held where the parties discuss settlement of the case, consolidation of issues, evidence and witnesses to be presented, and any potential method to expedite the hearing.[142]

The administrative hearing is a full evidentiary hearing conducted under the CROP and the Administrative Procedure Act. Witnesses usually are examined orally under oath, but may submit a written statement if the testimony is complicated.[143] The presiding officer may issue a subpoena to

---

[139]EPA, TSCA Compliance/Enforcement Guidance Manual at 6-3 (July 21, 1984).
[140]40 C.F.R. § 22.18(a).
[141]40 C.F.R. § 22.
[142]40 C.F.R. § 22.19(a).
[143]40 C.F.R. § 22.22(b).

compel the attendance of witnesses or the production of documentary evidence.[144]

At the conclusion of the hearing, the parties may detail their position in proposed findings of fact and law, and proposed orders submitted to the presiding officer for consideration in issuing the initial decision. The initial decision becomes a final order within forty-five days unless an adversely affected party makes an appeal to the administrator, the administrator determines *sua sponte* that a review of the initial decision is appropriate, or the party files within twenty days a motion to reopen the hearing.[145]

TSCA § 19(a)(1)(A) provides that any person may seek judicial review in the court of appeals of a rule or order under §§ 4(a), 5(a)(2), 5(b)(4), 6(a), 6(e), 8, or Title II (AHERA). Judicial review under TSCA § 19 is appellate review; that is, the court reviews the record of the civil penalty proceeding before the agency, and the agency's findings of fact are conclusive if supported by "substantial evidence."

12.5 Criminal Liability

It is a misdemeanor punishable by up to one year's imprisonment and up to $25,000 for each day of violation for any person "knowingly or willfully" to violate any provision of § 15.[146] To obtain a conviction against a company or an individual under § 16(b), the government must prove beyond a reasonable doubt that the defendant violated a requirement of TSCA and that the violation was committed "knowingly or willfully."

Case law indicates that specific knowledge of a TSCA requirement may not be necessary to establish a "knowing and willful" violation when the probability of regulation is so great that anyone handling the substance should be presumed to be aware that it is regulated.[147]

A corporation generally may be found liable for violations of regulations and statutes such as TSCA when such violations are committed by any of its employees, regardless of their position within the company, so long as those employees are acting within the scope of their authority and for the benefit of the corporation. In addition, courts generally will not permit a corporation to assert lack of corporate knowledge as a defense when information was obtained by any one individual who comprehended its full import: a corporation is considered to have acquired the collective knowledge of its employees. Moreover, it makes no difference whether a corporation has instructed its lower level employees to obey the law in performance of their

---

[144]40 C.F.R. § 22.33(b).

[145]40 C.F.R. §§ 22.27, 22.28.

[146]TSCA § 16(b).

[147]*See United States v. International Minerals & Chemical Corp.*, 402 U.S. 558 (1971) (concluding that no actual knowledge of a restrictive shipping regulation was necessary when the shipper was aware that he was shipping sulfuric acid).

duties. If such an employee disobeys company instructions and violates the law, the corporation is not shielded from criminal liability.[148]

12.6 Citizen Actions and Petitions

TSCA contains "private attorney general" provisions, whereby any person may commence a civil action against any other person who is alleged to be in violation of TSCA. In addition, any person may sue to force the administrator to compel the performance of any non-discretionary act under TSCA.[149] Attorneys fees and other court costs may be awarded if a court determines that such an award is appropriate.

TSCA § 21 likewise permits any person to petition the administrator to initiate proceedings for the issuance, amendment, or repeal of certain rules.[150] EPA may hold a public proceeding in order to determine the merit of a citizen's petition but must act on the petition within ninety days of its filing.[151] If the petition is granted, the administrator must promptly commence an appropriate proceeding under §§ 4, 5, 6, or 8.[152] If the petition is denied, the administrator must publish the reasons for such denial in the *Federal Register*.[153]

An unsuccessful petitioner may seek judicial review by filing an action in a United States district court.[154] The type of agency action sought in the citizen's petition will determine the legal standard a court will apply to EPA's petition denial. If the subject petition sought the initiation of rulemaking, the petitioner is entitled to *de novo* review.[155] By contrast, if the administrator denies or fails to act upon a § 21 petition to amend or repeal an existing rule the court will apply the APA's arbitrary and capricious standard.

EPA has issued guidance, including a TSCA checklist for preparing citizen petitions under TSCA § 21.[156] With this guidance petitioners should be able to present their requests in a comprehensive and persuasive manner and to facilitate the agency's review and response.

13.0 IMPORTATION AND EXPORTATION

Importers of any chemical substance must comply not only with the same obligations imposed on domestic manufacturers, but also with a

---

[148]*See, e.g., Hilton Hotels Corp.,* 467 F.2d 1000 (9th Cir. 1972), *cert. denied,* 409 U.S. 1125 (1973); *but cf. United States v. Beusch,* 596 F.2d 871 (9th Cir. 1979) (existence of company instructions and policies may be considered by the jury in determining whether the employee in fact acted to benefit the corporation).

[149]TSCA § 20.

[150]*See* 40 C.F.R. § 702.

[151]*See* TSCA § 21(b)(2) and (3).

[152]TSCA § 21(b)(3).

[153]*Id.*

[154]TSCA § 21(b)(4)(A).

[155]TSCA § 21(b)(4)(B).

[156]*See* 50 *Fed. Reg.* 46,825 (1985).

certification requirement pursuant to TSCA § 13. Similarly, exporters of chemicals may be subject to export notification obligations pursuant to TSCA § 12.

13.1 Import Regulation: TSCA § 13

TSCA § 13 requires the Secretary of the Treasury (the executive branch with authority over the U.S. Customs Service) to refuse entry into U.S. customs territory for a shipment of any chemical substance or mixture, if: (1) it fails to comply with any TSCA rule or regulation; or (2) it is offered for entry in violation of a section 5, 6, or 7 rule order, or action.[157] The U.S. customs territory includes the fifty states, the District of Columbia and Puerto Rico.[158] Thus, Customs Service regulations require an importer to certify at the port of entry that either: (1) any chemical substance in the shipment is subject to TSCA and complies with all applicable rules and orders thereunder; or (2) is not subject to TSCA.[159] Customs has established approximately ninety ports where entry documents may be filed.[160]

Customs Service regulations establish precise requirements regarding the form of the required certification, including sample statements. According to the regulations, the importer must use one of the statements as worded; no other language may be substituted. The certification may appear either on the appropriate entry document or commercial invoice, or on an attachment to the entry document or invoice. The importer, or its agent, must keep a copy of the import certification along with other customs entry documentation for five years.[161]

13.1.1 Importer Defined

Under customs regulations, an "importer" is the "person primarily liable for the payment of any duties on the merchandise, or an authorized agent acting on his behalf." Thus, the importer may be a consignee, the importer of record, or the actual owner of the merchandise.[162] Generally, the consignee will make the certification.

13.1.2 Determining TSCA Status of Imported Substance

The importer is responsible for determining whether a chemical substance is on the TSCA Inventory. If the importer does not know whether the chemical substance to be imported is on the inventory, the importer can file a *bona fide* intent to import request in order to have EPA search the master inventory.[163]

---

[157] TSCA § 13(a)(1).
[158] 19 C.F.R. § 101.1(e).
[159] 19 C.F.R. § 12.121(a).
[160] 19 C.F.R. § 101.3(b).
[161] 19 C.F.R. §§ 162.1a(a)(2), .1b, .1c.
[162] *See* 19 C.F.R. § 101.1(1).
[163] 40 C.F.R. § 720.25(b).

If the chemical is not on the inventory and is being imported for a commercial purpose, the importer must comply with the TSCA § 5 premanufacture notification requirements before importation. If the chemical product is not on the inventory but is being imported solely for research and development purposes governed by TSCA, the importer still must make a positive certification that the chemical substance is imported in compliance with TSCA.

13.1.3 Exclusions

If a chemical substance is excluded from TSCA jurisdiction under TSCA § 3(2)(B), it is subject to a negative certification or to no certification at all, depending on which exclusion applies. EPA takes the position that in order to be excluded from all certification requirements, a chemical substance must be imported solely for an excluded purpose. If, subsequent to importation, a substance is used by the importer for a TSCA purpose, then such use could constitute a TSCA violation. If a shipment is being imported for both a non-TSCA and a TSCA purpose, the importer must identify that portion of the shipment which is subject to TSCA and that which is not. For the former, the importer must certify that it complies with TSCA and for the latter the importer must certify that it is not subject to TSCA.

13.1.4 Articles, Samples, and Wastes

A manufacturer of any new chemical substance imported into the United States for commercial purposes must file a PMN "unless the substance is imported as part of an article."[164] EPA interprets this to exempt from the PMN requirement articles containing chemical substances that: (1) are not intended to be removed from the article; and (2) have no separate commercial purpose. Articles containing chemical substances intended to be used or released, such as ink in pens or gasoline in cars, are not encompassed by this exemption.

Companies occasionally receive unsolicited free samples of chemicals from offshore vendors for R&D purposes. Such samples are subject to TSCA § 13, as well as other TSCA provisions, such as § 5, even though they are unsolicited. To avoid potential liability, many companies refuse to accept such samples and return them to the shipper.

Imported wastes, both hazardous and non-hazardous, are also subject to TSCA because they are "chemical substances" within the meaning of the act. As such, they require a positive certification, even if accompanied by a hazardous waste manifest pursuant to the Resource Conservation and Recovery Act of 1976 (RCRA).[165]

13.1.5 Detention of Shipments by Customs

A shipment may be detained by customs whenever there exists a reasonable belief that the shipment is not in compliance with TSCA or no

---

[164] 40 C.F.R. § 720.22(b)(1).
[165] 42 U.S.C. §§ 6901-6992k.

certification is filed. When customs detains a shipment, it must give prompt notice of the detention and specify the reasons therefor to both EPA and the importer.[166] If reasonable grounds exist to believe that the shipment may be brought into compliance with TSCA, the shipment may be released under bond. If released under bond, the shipment must not be used or disposed of until EPA makes a final determination on its entry into the United States.[167]

An importer whose shipment has been detained may submit a written explanation to EPA as to why the shipment should be permitted entry. EPA then, within thirty days of the date of notice of detention, will make a decision on whether to allow entry.[168] Only if EPA determines that the shipment is in compliance with TSCA will it be released.[169] If the shipment is not in compliance, however, entry will be refused, or if the shipment has been released on bond, its redelivery will be demanded.[170] Under such circumstances, the importer must bring the shipment into compliance or export the shipment.[171] If the importer decides to export the non-complying shipment the importer must provide written notice of the exportation.[172]

13.2 Export Regulation: TSCA § 12

TSCA § 12(a) exempts from most provisions of the act any chemical substance, mixture, or article manufactured, processed, or distributed solely for export from the United States.[173] In order to qualify for this export exemption, the substance, mixture, or article must bear a stamp or label stating that it is intended solely for export.[174] The recordkeeping and reporting requirements of TSCA § 8, however, continue to apply to such chemical exports.

TSCA § 12(b) requires exporters to notify EPA before exporting any substance for which test data are required under §§ 4 or 5(b), regulatory action has been proposed or taken under §§ 5 or 6, or an action is pending or relief has been granted under §§ 5 or 7. Export notification is required regardless of the intended foreign use of the regulated chemical. EPA does not consider it relevant that the chemical is being exported for use in a manner that is not regulated domestically under an action, rule, or order.[175] In addition to the export notices required under § 12(b), special notices are required in the case of PCBs.[176]

---

[166]19 C.F.R. § 12.122(c).
[167]19 C.F.R. § 12.123(b).
[168]19 C.F.R. § 12.123(a).
[169]19 C.F.R. § 12.123(c).
[170]*Id.*
[171]19 C.F.R. § 12.124(a).
[172]19 C.F.R. § 12.125.
[173]TSCA § 12(a)(1).
[174]TSCA § 12(a)(1)(B).
[175]*45 Fed. Reg.* 82,844 (1980).
[176]*See* 40 C.F.R. § 70760(c).

13.2.1 Export Notification Requirement

An exporter of a chemical substance subject to TSCA § 12(b) must submit notice of the first export to each country into which the product is exported in a calendar year. The notice must be postmarked on the date of export or within seven days of forming the "intent to export," whichever is earlier.[177] Intent to export regulated substances "must be based on a definite contractual obligation, or an equivalent intra-company agreement, to export the regulated chemical."[178]

EPA's Export Notification Rule defines an "exporter" as the "person who, as the principal party in interest in the export transaction, has the power and responsibility for determining and controlling the sending of the chemical substance or mixture to a destination out of the customs territory of the United States."[179]

Within five days of receiving a TSCA § 12(b) export notice, EPA must transmit the following information to the importing country: (1) the name of the regulated chemical; (2) a summary of the regulatory action the agency has taken; (3) the name of an EPA official to contact for further information; and (4) a copy of the relevant *Federal Register* notice.[180]

13.2.2 New Chemicals

A new chemical substance is subject to export notification only if it is subject to a § 4 test rule; is included on the § 5(b)(4) "risk" list; is subject to an order under § 5(e) or 5(f); or is subject to a proposed or final significant new use rule.[181] In the absence of such specific action, the export notification provisions do not apply to new chemical substances intended solely for export. Moreover, export notification need not accompany export of a chemical substance contained in an article, unless the agency specifically requires export notification for such articles in the context of individual rulemakings.[182]

13.2.3 Confidentiality

Exporters may assert confidentiality claims for any information contained in export notices at the time such notices are submitted.[183] No proof of the confidentiality claim is required at the time of submission, but each page must be marked "confidential business information," "proprietary," or "trade secret."[184] Such information is treated by EPA as

---

[177] 40 C.F.R. § 707.65(a)(1)-(3).

[178] 40 C.F.R. § 707.65(a)(3).

[179] 40 C.F.R. § 707.63(b).

[180] 40 C.F.R. § 707.70(a), (b).

[181] 45 *Fed. Reg.* 82,844 (1980).

[182] 40 C.F.R. § 707.60(b).

[183] 40 C.F.R. § 707.75(a), (b).

[184] 40 C.F.R. § 707.75(b).

prietary," or "trade secret."[184] Such information is treated by EPA as confidential and may be disclosed to the public only through the procedures set forth at 40 C.F.R. § 2.[185]

For a more definitive discussion of this topic, the reader is referred to the TSCA Handbook *and related books and courses listed at the end of this book.*

---

[184]40 C.F.R. § 707.75(b).
[185]40 C.F.R. § 707.75(c).

Chapter 12

ASBESTOS

Daniel M. Steinway
Anderson, Kill, Olick & Oshinsky
Washington, DC

1.0 ASBESTOS: A CLOSELY REGULATED SUBSTANCE

Asbestos is currently one of the major environmental issues in the U.S. because the material was so widely used in building construction up to the mid-1970s.

Asbestos is a naturally occurring mineral. Because of its properties of incombustibility, noise absorption, and resistance to electrical current, corrosive and bacterial attack, asbestos was used in a large number of building products intended for fireproofing, acoustical sound-proofing, and heating and cooling system insulation.

Exposure to airborne asbestos fibers during the manufacturing process has been known to present hazards requiring special care. Recently, however, there have been potential health concerns raised regarding the exposure of individuals to materials containing asbestos in buildings where such materials have been installed, and various studies have been conducted to determine its health affects in such installations.

Asbestos fibers are small enough to penetrate deeply into the lungs if they become airborne, and have been associated with three major forms of disease in humans:

1. **Asbestosis,** a scarring of the inner tissue of the lung which stiffens the tissues and interferes with oxygen exchange. It decreases the lung volume and increases resistance in the lung to the passage of air. Asbestosis generally has a latency period of at least 15 to 20 years and can become progressively worse with time.

2. **Lung cancer,** a malignant tumor of the lungs. It generally has a latency period of 20 to 30 years.

3. **Mesothelioma,** a cancer of the mesothelium or pleural linings of the lungs. It generally has a latency period of 30 to 40 years.

The U.S. Environmental Protection Agency (EPA) has instituted a number of regulatory actions under various statutory authorities regarding asbestos materials. In 1973, EPA banned the use of asbestos-containing sprayed-on or trowelled-on friable material for all but decorative purposes. EPA has subsequently called for a "phased-in" ban for asbestos materials under the Toxic Substances Control Act (TSCA), **but this ban** was overturned by the Fifth Circuit in *Corrosion Proof Fittings*.[1]

Asbestos concerns have resulted in extensive litigation with literally thousands of lawsuits filed. Typically, these suits involve claims for personal injuries, property damage, costs of removal or insurance coverage.

In response, the federal, state and local governments have been focusing ever-increasing attention on the presence of asbestos-containing materials in buildings. As a result, a maze of overlapping statutes, ordinances and regulations have been adopted governing the use, handling, treatment, removal and disposal of asbestos-containing materials. The federal government has specifically established several regulatory programs in the EPA, the U.S. Occupational Safety and Health Administration (OSHA) and the Department of Transportation (DOT). In addition, many states have enacted laws to regulate hazardous substances generally and in some cases asbestos specifically. This chapter will briefly describe the current asbestos regulatory programs at both the federal and state levels.

2.0 EPA REGULATION OF ASBESTOS

EPA currently regulates asbestos under several federal environmental statutes:

- Under the Clean Air Act, Congress created a comprehensive regulatory system aimed at reducing and, when feasible, eliminating air pollution. Pursuant to the National Emission Standard for Hazardous Air Pollutants (NESHAP) program, EPA has promulgated regulations specifically addressing asbestos emissions from manufacturing operations, building demolition/renovation operations, and waste disposal.[2]

  The NESHAP standard does not set a numerical threshold for asbestos fiber emissions; instead, it requires persons conducting asbestos-related activities, such as demolition and renovation operations, to notify EPA and to follow certain procedures relating to the stripping and removing of asbestos materials, and to adopt specific work practices to prevent the release of asbestos fibers into the air. Persons involved in these activities must deposit all asbestos-containing material at a waste disposal site meeting specified guidelines.

- Under the Clean Water Act, EPA has set specific effluent limits for discharges of asbestos fibers into navigable waters by facilities such

---

[1] *Corrosion Proof Fittings v. U.S. EPA*, 947 F.2d 1201 (5th Cir. 1991) ("Corrosion Proof Fittings").

[2] 40 C.F.R. Part 61, Subpart M. EPA has proposed a draft schedule for issuance of a revised NESHAP standard for asbestos milling, manufacturing and fabricating activities in response to the 1990 Clean Air Act Amendments. 57 *Fed. Reg.* 44, 147 (Sept. 24, 1992). According to its proposed schedule, EPA is planning to issue a revised standard by November 15, 1994.

as asbestos roofing and floor tile manufacturers.[3] EPA also has set performance and pretreatment standards for those facilities which discharge asbestos fibers to public sewer systems.[4]

- Under TSCA, EPA has promulgated regulations requiring all persons who manufacture, import or process asbestos to meet certain reporting requirements.[5] Pursuant to section 6 of TSCA, EPA has, by regulatory action, proposed to phase out and/or ban nearly all uses of asbestos in new products over the next seven years.[6] Exemptions from this ban would have been granted on a case-by-case basis. However, this ban was overturned in *Corrosion Proof Fittings*. Other EPA regulation of asbestos under TSCA pertaining to schools and other buildings is discussed below.

- EPA has not listed asbestos-containing material as hazardous waste under the Resource Conservation and Recovery Act (RCRA); however, asbestos wastes are treated as solid wastes for purposes of RCRA regulation, and EPA has listed asbestos as a hazardous substance covered by the Comprehensive Environmental Response, Compensation and Liability Act (CERCLA/Superfund).[7]

3.0 ASBESTOS HAZARD EMERGENCY RESPONSE ACT OF 1986 (AHERA)

Because of the potential for serious health hazards associated with asbestos, Congress amended TSCA in 1986 by adding a new Title III, the Asbestos Hazard Emergency Response Act of 1986 or "AHERA."[8] AHERA requires the EPA to establish a comprehensive regulatory framework of inspection, management, planning, operations and maintenance activities, and appropriate abatement responses for controlling asbestos-containing materials in schools. Under AHERA, EPA promulgated its "AHERA-in-Schools Rule" on October 17, 1987. Because of severe time constraints, the 1988 AHERA amendments provided additional time for local educational agencies to submit asbestos management plans to the state governors and to begin the implementation of these plans.

AHERA also required that EPA conduct a study, discussed below, to determine the extent of danger to human health posed by asbestos in public and commercial buildings and the means to respond to such danger. This study has now been submitted to Congress.

---

[3] 40 C.F.R. Part 427.
[4] 40 C.F.R. Part 427.
[5] 40 C.F.R. § 763.60.
[6] *See* 54 *Fed. Reg.* 29,461 (July 12, 1989).
[7] *See* 40 C.F.R. § 302.4.
[8] Pub. L. No. 99-579 (1986).

3.1 Asbestos In Schools and the Asbestos School Hazard Abatement Act

AHERA requires school systems to identify and abate asbestos hazards in school buildings. Previously, school districts were required to inspect school facilities for asbestos-containing materials and to inform teachers and parents of the inspection results, but they were not required to take any abatement action.

Under the current law, EPA distributes loan and grant money to financially needy schools to help pay for abatement costs. The 1984 Asbestos School Hazard Abatement Act establishes an "Asbestos Trust Fund" where funds appropriated for schools' use in the loan program are to be deposited.[9]

At the present time, AHERA's abatement provisions affect only schools, but as noted above, there has been considerable attention directed toward possible regulation of public and commercial buildings in the future.

3.2 Asbestos in Public and Commercial Buildings

In February 1988, as required by AHERA, EPA sent Congress a study on asbestos-containing materials in public buildings. This report recommended a four-part program to address existing asbestos hazards in public and commercial buildings. The recommended program would:

1. increase the availability of accredited asbestos inspectors and abatement professionals,
2. develop procedures for dealing with thermal system insulation,
3. improve the enforcement of existing asbestos regulations, and
4. assess the effectiveness of the AHERA school program.

EPA at the present time does not recommend a regulatory program modeled on AHERA for public and commercial buildings. However, in its *Green Book*, EPA has published guidance for building owners on how to manage asbestos-containing materials in buildings. Possible future activities in Congress are discussed below.

4.0 STATE REGULATORY ACTIVITIES

Almost all states have enacted some form of asbestos-related legislation. In contrast to AHERA, which applies only to schools, state asbestos laws generally apply to all types of buildings.

The scope and/or status of individual state laws can vary from the federal laws, and from each other, in many areas, including:

- State accreditation plans for the training and certification of inspectors, abatement project designers, contractors, workers and others involved in asbestos work.
- Performance standards and disposal methods.

---

[9] 20 U.S.C. §§ 4011 et seq.

- Asbestos control measures required for issuance of building permits for demolition or renovation, or as a condition of license renewal (for example, for state-licensed hospitals), condominium conversion, etc.
- The liability of abatement project contractors, including fines for improper removal.

In addition, many local governments have adopted laws governing asbestos abatement actions. For example, New York City has developed a comprehensive asbestos control program, which became effective in 1987 under its Local Laws 76 and 80. These laws, which amended the local building codes, are enforced jointly by the New York City Department of Environmental Protection (DEP) and the Department of Buildings. The laws require that any renovation or demolition projects which disturb asbestos be conducted in accordance with certain procedures, and that workers who handle asbestos-containing materials receive proper training.[10] Local Law No. 76 also requires DEP to establish criteria for certifying persons eligible to obtain an asbestos handling certificate or become asbestos investigators.[11]

4.1 National Implications of California's Proposition 65

In California, Proposition 65, the Safe Drinking Water and Toxics Enforcement Act of 1986, was adopted to protect citizens and drinking water from exposure to toxic chemicals. Toxic chemicals covered by Proposition 65 include those chemicals and materials such as asbestos which are known to cause cancer or to be associated with reproductive toxicity, and which have been specifically listed by the Governor as required under the law. The first list of 29 chemicals was published in February 1987 and included asbestos.

Several broad regulatory programs are established under Proposition 65, including a prohibition against knowingly discharging or releasing toxic chemicals into the water or onto land where the chemical will pass into the drinking water. There is also a prohibition against knowingly and intentionally exposing any individual to a chemical known to cause cancer, such as asbestos, without first giving a clear and reasonable warning of this exposure.[12]

Legislation similar to Proposition 65 has been introduced in more than 20 states but as of this writing, none has passed yet.

5.0 OSHA REGULATIONS

Several regulatory actions have previously been taken by OSHA. OSHA also has recently proposed certain new regulatory requirements for asbestos, but it is unclear when these new regulations will, in fact, be promulgated.

---

[10] N.Y.C. Local Law No. 76, & 1.

[11] N.Y.C. Admin. Code § 24-146.1(d).

[12] Cal. Health & Safety Code § 25249.6.

5.1 OSHA Asbestos Standard

OSHA's asbestos regulations, which took effect on July 21, 1986, established a permissible exposure limit (PEL) of 0.2 fibers per cubic centimeter for employees who may be exposed to asbestos-containing material (ACM) in the workplace.

OSHA's regulations governing asbestos in the workplace are contained in the general industry standards[13] and construction standards.[14] Both standards require an employer to ensure that no employee "is exposed to an airborne concentration of asbestos in excess of 0.2 fibers per cubic centimeter of air as an eight (8)-hour time-weighted average (TWA)."[15] These standards also establish an "action level" defined as an airborne concentration of asbestos "of 0.1 fibers per cubic centimeter of air calculated as an eight (8)-hour time weighted average."[16] Under both regulations, if employees are exposed at or above the action level, the employer must initiate specific compliance activities, that is, air monitoring, employee training and medical surveillance.

This exposure limit was challenged by the Asbestos Information Association/North America and several other industrial and labor organizations,[17] but the U.S. Court of Appeals for the District of Columbia Circuit upheld the exposure limit. Even though the Circuit Court upheld the exposure limit, it directed OSHA to re-examine certain other aspects of its regulations. Specifically, the Court directed OSHA to:

- determine whether a 0.1 fiber per cubic centimeter permissible exposure limit is feasible for the automotive brake and repair industry,
- review its respirator policy and re-examine more vigorous measures to reduce smoking-related asbestos risks among workers,
- clarify that a construction industry employer must monitor air when a change in workplace conditions could result in exposure to asbestos above the permissible limit,
- consider whether bilingual warnings or universal warning signals are necessary,
- clarify the small-scale, short-duration exception under the present asbestos regulations, and
- decide whether to require all construction industry employers to file reports prior to undertaking an asbestos abatement project.

---

[13] 29 C.F.R. § 1910.1001.

[14] 29 C.F.R. § 1926.58.

[15] 29 C.F.R. 1910.1001(c) (general industry); 29 C.F.R. 1926.58(c) (construction industry).

[16] 29 C.F.R. 1910.1001(b) (general industry); 29 C.F.R. 1926.58(b) (construction industry).

[17] *Building and Construction Trades Department, AFL-CIO v. Secretary of Labor* (C.A. No 86-1359) (February 2, 1988); *AFL-CIO v. Department of Labor* (C.A. No. 86-1360) (February 2, 1988).

In response to the court's directions, OSHA has issued a new short-term exposure limit (STEL) for asbestos exposures.[18] The STEL for asbestos is one fiber per cubic centimeter averaged over a sampling period of 30 minutes. OSHA also expanded the ban on smoking in the workplace during asbestos removal operations, and suggested that employers use warning signs with universal symbols, graphics, or foreign languages. OSHA has recently proposed new asbestos regulations which, among other things, reduce the PEL to 0.1 fibers per cubic centimeter and eliminate the existing action level standard, clarify the use of glove-bagging operations, require oversight of all construction operations by a competent person, and impose a project reporting requirement.[19] OSHA has recently requested additional comments on its workplace standard for exposure to asbestos, specifically asking for information on asbestos in public and commercial buildings and employee notification regarding the presence of asbestos-containing materials.

5.2 OSHA Federal Hazard Communication Standard

OSHA has promulgated a revised federal hazard communication standard which would cover all employees exposed to hazardous chemicals including asbestos in the workplace.[20] This standard requires both manufacturing and non-manufacturing employers to establish written hazard communication programs that provide information about these chemicals. This information must be conveyed by means of labels (or other forms of warning) on containers, the preparation and distribution of material safety data sheets, and the development and implementation of employee training programs.[21]

5.3 Use of Respirators

Whenever feasible engineering controls and work practices are not sufficient to reduce employee exposures to or below the PEL limit, employers still must utilize these practices and, additionally, provide for the use of respiratory protection equipment.[22] Employers also must provide respirator equipment in emergency cases.[23] The OSHA regulations impose specific respirator requirements depending on the levels of airborne asbestos

---

[18] 53 *Fed. Reg.* 35,610 (September 14, 1988).

[19] 55 *Fed. Reg.* 29,712 (July 20, 1990). The U.S. Coast Guard also has proposed regulations recently to limit industrial maritime workers' exposure to asbestos fibers. 57 *Fed. Reg.* 46, 126 (Oct. 7, 1992). Under its proposed regulations, the PEL would be reduced to 0.05 fibers per cubic centimeter, and the action level dropped to 0.03 fibers per cubic centimeter.

[20] 52 *Fed. Reg.* 31,852 (August 24, 1987).

[21] 29 C.F.R. § 1910.1200.

[22] *See* 29 C.F.R. § 1910.1001(g) (general industry); 29 C.F.R. § 1926.58(h) (construction industry).

[23] Id.

fibers.[24] Under its asbestos regulations, OSHA also has promulgated regulations clarifying the use of certain types of respirators.[25]

6.0 DOT REGULATIONS

DOT regulates the transport of asbestos in accordance with the provisions of the Hazardous Materials Transportation Act of 1975 (HMTA).[26] Pursuant to its authority under HMTA, DOT has designated asbestos as a hazardous material for purposes of transportation and has prescribed requirements for shipping papers, packaging, marking, labeling and transport vehicle placarding relating to the shipment and transportation of asbestos materials.[27] In accordance with these requirements, commercial asbestos must be transported in (1) rigid, leaktight packagings, (2) bags or other non-rigid packagings in closed freight containers, motor vehicles, or rail cars that are loaded by and for the exclusive use of the consignor and unloaded by the consignor, or (3) bags or other nonrigid packagings which are dust- and sift-proof in strong outside fiberboard or wooden boxes.[28] Specific regulations have been promulgated for the transport of asbestos materials by highway. Under these regulations, asbestos must be loaded, handled and unloaded in a manner that will minimize occupational exposure to airborne asbestos particles released incident to transportation, and any asbestos contamination of transport vehicles removed.[29]

7.0 FUTURE ACTIONS

Several laws have been recently passed which impose new regulatory requirements relating to asbestos materials. For example, the Asbestos Information Act of 1988 (Pub.L. 100-577), was enacted during the waning moments of the 100th Congress. This law requires asbestos product manufacturers to provide EPA with information on the years of manufacture, types and classes, and other identifying characteristics of their asbestos products.

In addition, the Congress has specifically designated asbestos as a hazardous air pollutant for purposes of regulation under the Clean Air Act Amendments of 1990. The Congress also has enacted the Sanitary Food Transportation Act of 1990, which prohibits the transportation of asbestos in motor vehicles or rail vehicles that were used to transport food and other consumer products. Under this law, DOT is required to issue new regulations prohibiting the use of motor or rail vehicles for other purposes if these

---

[24] Id.
[25] 52 *Fed. Reg.* 17,752 (May 12, 1987).
[26] 49 U.S.C. § 1801 *et seq.*
[27] 49 C.F.R. § 172.101.
[28] 49 C.F.R. § 173.1090.
[29] 49 C.F.R. § 177.844.

vehicles provide transportation for asbestos wastes, extremely hazardous substances, or refuse. Finally, the Asbestos School Hazard Abatement Reauthorization Act of 1989 extends AHERA training and accreditation requirements to contractors involved in asbestos projects in public and commercial buildings. It also requires EPA to issue an advisory notice to all local educational agencies and state governors on the risks associated with "in-place management of asbestos-containing building materials and removals" and methods to "promote the least burdensome response actions necessary to protect human health, safety, and the environment."

Finally, EPA has promulgated certain Phase I changes to the current requirements regarding asbestos contained in the National Emission Standard for Hazardous Air Pollutants (NESHAP) under the Clean Air Act. Most of these changes relate to asbestos notification, work practice and disposal requirements, including project specific work practices for approved facilities, and various recordkeeping requirements. These changes will make both the landfill owner/operator and the generator liable for violations under the NESHAP requirements. In addition, EPA has indicated that it would propose additional Phase II asbestos NESHAP regulations imposing more stringent demolition and renovation requirements at some point in the future. As part of this action, EPA is expected to propose new standards based on maximum or generally achievable control technology.

Moreover, as noted above, EPA has issued regulatory guidance in the form of the "Green Book" to guide building owners on the use of acceptable operations and maintenance programs to control asbestos materials in place.

Finally, in an effort to signal improved enforcement of the NESHAP regulations, EPA has announced a more stringent civil penalty policy for violations of these regulations. EPA has stressed that separate penalties will be imposed for each specific violation of NESHAP requirements. Current law authorizes EPA to impose civil penalties of up to $25,000 per day for non-compliance.

8.0 CONCLUSION

The ever-expanding regulation of asbestos materials has broad implications for the employers, workers, and owners and occupiers of buildings containing or suspected of containing asbestos materials. Generally speaking, given building industry practices prior to the mid-1970s, buildings constructed prior to that point in time are likely to contain asbestos fireproofing and insulating materials. Asbestos may also be found in wallboard and wall finishes, floor tiles, ceiling tiles and other building components.

A facility survey for the presence of asbestos-containing material may be a worthwhile endeavor. However, to avoid potential liability, asbestos inspection testing, analysis and abatement activities are best conducted with the assistance of environmental consultants and legal counsel who are qualified to address properly the technical and legal/regulatory compliance issues.

For additional information on this topic, the reader is referred to the related books and courses listed at the end of this book.

Chapter 13

FEDERAL REGULATION OF PESTICIDES

Marshall Lee Miller, Esq.
Baker & Hostetler
Washington, D.C.

1.0 OVERVIEW

The benefits of pesticides, herbicides, rodenticides, and other economic poisons are well known. They have done much to spare us from the ravages of disease, crop infestations, noxious animals, and choking weeds. Over the past several decades, however, beginning with Rachel Carson's book *Silent Spring*[1] in 1962, there has been a growing awareness of the hazards as well as the benefits of these chemicals, which may be harmful to man and the balance of nature. The ability to balance these often conflicting effects is hampered by continuing scientific uncertainties. We still lack full understanding of environmental side effects, the sub-cellular mechanism of human carcinogens, and a host of other factors that are important for a proper evaluation of pesticide suitability. The dilemma will become increasingly acute during the next few years as the agency attempts to conduct accelerated reviews of hundreds of chemicals registered earlier under less strict standards.

1.1 Background

Public concern regarding pesticides was a principal cause of the rise of the environmental movement in the U.S. in the late sixties and early seventies and therefore was perhaps the single most important reason for the creation of the EPA. While public attention since then has shifted to various other environmental media, the pesticide issue—with its implications for the safety of food supply and of people in the agricultural area—is still central to the public's notion of environmental protection. Indeed, interest in this topic is often an accurate barometer of public distrust in the official environmental agencies.

For that reason, the recent renewed interest in pesticides, on matters ranging from the Alar pesticide scare on apples to the sweeping provisions in California's (unsuccessful but hotly-contested) environmentally sweeping Proposition 128, is a signal of alarm. The public perceptions may be due to a time lag, for the situation in pesticide regulation is not worse now than in the past; quite the contrary. But this could mean increased media and environmental organization attention to pesticides in the coming few years.

---

[1]Rachel Carson, *Silent Spring* (New York, 1962).

412

1.2 Early Efforts at Pesticide Regulations

Chemical pesticides have been subject to some degree of federal control since the Insecticide Act of 1910.[2] This act was primarily concerned with protecting consumers, usually farmers, from ineffective products or deceptive labeling, and it contained neither a federal registration requirement nor any significant safety standards. The relatively insignificant usage of pesticides before World War II made regulation a matter of low priority.

The war enormously stimulated the development and use of pesticides. The resulting effects on public health and farm production made pesticides a virtual necessity. The agricultural chemical industry became an influential sector of the economy. In 1947 Congress enacted the more comprehensive statute, the Federal Insecticide, Fungicide, and Rodenticide Act (FIFRA).[3] It required that pesticides distributed in interstate commerce be registered with the United States Department of Agriculture (USDA). It also established a rudimentary labeling provision. This act, like its predecessor, was more concerned with product effectiveness, but the statute did declare pesticides "misbranded" if they were necessarily harmful to man, animals, or vegetation (except weeds) even when properly used.[4]

Three major defects in the new law soon became evident. First, the registration process was largely an empty formality since the Secretary of Agriculture could not refuse registration even to a chemical he deemed highly dangerous. He could register "under protest," but this had no legal effect on the registrant's ability to manufacture or distribute the product. Second, there was no regulatory control over the use of a pesticide contrary to its label, as long as the label itself complied with the statutory requirements.[5] Third, the secretary's only remedy against a hazardous product was a legal action for misbranding or adulteration, and—this was crucial—the difficult burden of proof was on the government.

The statute nevertheless remained unchanged for almost two decades. Pesticides were not then a matter of public concern, and the Department of Agriculture (USDA) was under little pressure to tighten regulatory control. Only a handful of registrations under protest were made during that period, and virtually all these actions involved minor companies with ineffective products. The one notable lawsuit involving a fraudulently ineffective product was lost by the USDA at the district court level and mooted by the court of appeals.[6]

---

[2]36 Stat. 331 (1910).

[3]61 Stat. 190 (1947). The present act is still known by this name, although there have been major changes, especially in 1972, in the law since then. For convenience, we will refer to the pre-1972 version as the "Old FIFRA."

[4]Old FIFRA (pre-1972) § 2(z)(2)(d). See H. Rep. 313 (80th Cong., 1st Sess.). 1947 U.S. Code Cong. Serv. 1200, 1201.

[5]Under FDA practice, doctors may prescribe pharmaceuticals for "off indication" purposes not mentioned on the labels.

[6]*Victrylite Candle Co. v. Brannan*, 201 F.2d 206 (D.C. Cir., 1952).

In 1964 the USDA persuaded Congress to remedy two of these three perceived defects: the registration system was revised to permit the secretary to refuse to register a new product or to cancel an existing registration, and the burden of proof for safety and effectiveness was placed on the registrant.[7] These changes considerably strengthened the act in theory, but made little difference in practice. The Pesticide Registration Division, a section of USDA's Agricultural Research Service, was understaffed—in 1966 the only toxicologist on the staff was the division's director—and the division was buried deep in a bureaucracy primarily concerned with promoting agriculture and facilitating the registration of pesticides. The cancellation procedure was seldom, if ever, used,[8] and there was still no legal sanction against a consumer's applying the chemical for a delisted use.

The growth of the environmental movement in the late 1960s, with its concern about the widespread use of agricultural chemicals, overwhelmed the meager resources of the Pesticide Division. Environmental groups filed a barrage of law suits demanding the cancellation or suspension of a host of major pesticides such as DDT, Aldrin-Dieldrin, and the herbicide 2,4,5-T. This demanding situation required a new approach to pesticide regulations.

1.3 Pesticide Regulation Transferred to the Environmental Protection Agency

On December 2, 1970, former president Richard Nixon signed Reorganization Order No. 3[9] creating the Environmental Protection Agency (EPA) and assigned to it the functions of, and many personnel formerly belonging to, Interior, Agriculture, and other government departments. EPA inherited from USDA not only the Pesticides Division but also the environmental law suits against the Secretary of Agriculture.

Thus, within the first two or three months, the new agency was compelled to make a number of tough regulatory decisions. The EPA's outlook was influenced considerably by judicial decisions in several of the cases it had inherited from USDA.[10] These court decisions consistently held that the responsible federal agencies had not sufficiently examined the health and environmental problems associated with pesticide use. They have helped to shape, indeed force, EPA's pesticide policy during its formative period and ever since.[11]

---

[7]Act of May 12, 1964, Pub. L. No. 88-30S, 78 Stat. 190. There were other, less significant, amendments in 1959 (73 Stat. 286) and 1961 (75 Stat. 18, 42).

[8]Instead, a Pesticide Registration Notice would be sent ordering the removal of one or more listed uses from the registration.

[9]Reorganization Order No. 3 of 1970, §2(a)(1), 1970 U.S. Code Cong. Ad. News 2996, 2998, 91st Cong. 2nd Sess.

[10]It also inherited cases concerning pesticide residues from the Food and Drug Administration (FDA) of the Department of Health, Education, and Welfare (HEW), now the Department of Health and Human Services (HHS).

[11]These cases will be discussed in a later section.

2.0 FEDERAL INSECTICIDE, FUNGICIDE AND RODENTICIDE ACT (FIFRA) AND AMENDMENTS

2.1 Background to FIFRA and the 1972 Amendments

The Federal Insecticide, Fungicide, and Rodenticide Act (FIFRA)[12], as amended by the Federal Environmental Pesticide Control Act (FEPCA)[13] of October 1972 and the FIFRA amendments of 1975, 1978, 1980, and 1988,[14] is a complex statute. Terms sometimes have a meaning different from, or even directly contrary to, normal English usage. For example, the term "suspension" really means an immediate ban on a pesticide, while the harsher-sounding term "cancellation" indicates only the initiation of administrative proceedings which can drag on for years. The repeated amending of FIFRA reflects congressional, industry, and environmentalist concern about the federal control of pesticide distribution, sale, and use.

The amendments to FIFRA in 1972, known as the Federal Environmental Pesticides Control Act (FEPCA), amounted to a virtual rewriting of the law. FEPCA, not the 1947 FIFRA, is the contemporary pesticide law. The changes were considered necessary to (1) strengthen the enforcement provisions of FIFRA, (2) shift the legal emphasis from labeling and efficacy to health and environment, (3) provide for greater flexibility in controlling dangerous chemicals, (4) extend the scope of federal law to cover intrastate registrations and the specific uses of a given pesticide, and (5) streamline the administrative appeals process.

EPA was given expanded authority over the field use of pesticides, and several categories of registration were created which give EPA more flexibility in fashioning appropriate control over pesticides.

2.2 Need for FIFRA Renewal

The authorization for FIFRA under the 1972 act was limited to three years.[15] Congress was therefore provided the opportunity in 1975 and periodically thereafter to review the strengths and shortcomings of the 1972 legislation, even though some portions of that law were not scheduled to go into effect until four years after enactment.[16] This review, however, also provided a chance to redress the balance for those, both within and without Congress, who believed that EPA had been given too much authority.[17]

---

[12]7 U.S.C. § 135, *et seq.*

[13]Pub. L. No. 92-516, 86 Stat. 973, October 21, 1972.

[14]Pub. L. No. 96-516, 86 Stat. 973, October 1972; Pub. L. No. 94-140, November 28, 1975; Pub. L. No. 95-396, 92 Stat. 819, September 30, 1978; Pub. L. No. 96-539, 94 Stat. 3194; December 17, 1980.

[15]FIFRA § 27. Actually the term for the act was less than three years since the act finally went into effect in October 1972 and the authorization expired June 30, 1975.

[16]One such example is EPA's authority under § 27 to require that a pesticide be registered for use only by a certified applicator.

[17]House Report No. 94-497, "Extension and Amendment of the FIFRA, as Amended," September 19, 1975, for H.R. 8841, p. 5.

2.3 1975 Amendments to FIFRA

Congress' 1975 amendments to the FIFRA were significant not for what they actually changed but because of the motivations that prompted them. The amendments themselves were viewed by many as, at best, unnecessary and, at worst, a further encumbrance upon an already complicated administrative procedure.

They did, however, reflect a strong desire on the part of Congress—or at least the respective agriculture committees of the House and Senate—to restrict EPA's authority to regulate pesticides. EPA was required to consult with the Department of Agriculture and Agricultural Committees of Congress before issuing proposed or final standards regarding pesticides. EPA also got the authority to require that farmers take exams before being certified as applicators. The situation was summarized by an editorial in a Washington, D.C., newspaper captioned, "Trying to Hogtie the EPA."[18]

2.4 1978 Amendments to FIFRA

The 1978 amendments reflected the near-collapse of EPA's pesticide registration program. EPA was given the authority to conditionally register a pesticide pending study of the product's safety and was authorized to perform generic reviews without requiring compensation for use of a company's data.

In addition, studies showing pesticide efficacy were made optional, relieving EPA of the chore of determining whether a pesticide actually worked for the purposes claimed.

2.5 1980 Amendments to FIFRA

The 1980 amendments provided for a two-house veto over EPA rules and regulations, and they required the administrator to obtain Scientific Advisory Review (SAR) of suspension actions after they were initiated. The 1988 legislation provided for accelerated review of pre-1970 registrations and removed most of the indemnification requirements for canceled pesticides.

2.6 1988 Amendments to FIFRA

FIFRA was amended again in 1988.[19] Dubbed "FIFRA lite," the amendments were notable mostly for what they did not contain, namely, the hotly-debated provisions sought by environmentalists for protection of the nation's groundwater supplies from contamination by pesticides. The bill also lacked the section sought by the grocery manufacturers to preempt stricter state standards like those under California's Proposition 65 right-to-know law. The legislation did correct a long-standing flaw in the act involving compensation for canceled pesticides, and it streamlined the pesticide reregistration process but imposed a substantial fee.

---

[18]*The Washington Star*, October 8, 1975.

[19]The 1988 amendments to FIFRA were signed into law by President Reagan on October 25, 1988.

3.0 PESTICIDE REGISTRATION

3.1 Pesticide Registration Procedures

All new pesticide products used in the United States, with minor exceptions, must first be registered with EPA. This involves the submittal of the complete formula, a proposed label, and "full description of the tests made and the results thereof upon which the claims are based." The administrator must approve the registration if the following conditions are met:

(A)   its composition is such as to warrant the proposed claim for it;

(B)   its labeling and other materials required to be submitted comply with the requirements of this act;

(C)   it will perform its intended function without unreasonable adverse effects on the environment; and

(D)   when used in accordance with widespread and commonly recognized practice it will not generally cause unreasonable adverse effects on the environment.

The operative phrase in the above criteria is "unreasonable adverse effects on the environment," which was added to the act in 1972. This phrase is defined elsewhere in FIFRA as meaning "any unreasonable risk to man or the environment, taking into account the economic, social, and environmental costs and benefits of the use of the pesticide."[20]

This controversial expression, which appears also in the cancellation-suspension section of the act,[21] disturbed some environmentalists who feared that the word "unreasonable" along with the consideration of social and economic factors would undermine the effectiveness of the cancellation procedure, but experience to date has not indicated that this is really a problem.

The registration is very specific; it is not valid for all uses of a particular chemical. Each registration specifies the crops and insects on which it may be applied, and each use must be supported by research data on safety and efficacy. Registrations are for a limited, five-year period; thereafter they automatically expire unless an interested party petitions for renewal and, if requested by EPA, provides additional data indicating the safety of the product.[22] For the past few years, pre-EPA registrations have been coming up for renewal under much stricter standards than when originally issued. The agricultural chemical companies have justifiably complained that the increased burden of registration is discouraging the development of new pesticides, but there seems no responsible alternative.

---

[20]FIFRA § 2(bb), 7 U.S.C. § U.S.C. § 136(bb). The 1975 amendments, as will be discussed, added the specific requirement that decisions also include consideration of their impact on various aspects of the agricultural economy.

[21]FIFRA § 6, 7 U.S.C. § 136d.

[22]FIFRA § 6(a), 7 U.S.C. § 136d(a).

3.2 Trade Secrets

Surprisingly, the issue in FIFRA that has generated more controversy than any other over the past decade involves the treatment of the trade secrets in data submitted to EPA for registration.[23] The judicial protection of commercial trade secrets has gradually eroded during the past few years. Many so-called trade secrets were in fact widely known throughout the industry and did not merit confidential status. Section 10 of FIFRA, added in the 1972 amendments, provides that trade secrets should not be released but, if the administrator proposes to release them, he should provide notice to the company to enable it to seek a declaratory judgment, ruling on the matter, in the appropriate district court.

Section 10 provides that "when necessary to carry out the provisions of this act, information relating to formulas of products acquired by authorization of this act may be revealed to any federal agency consulted and may be revealed at a public hearing or in findings of fact issued by the administrator."[24] Consequently, if the public interest requires, a registrant must assume that the formula for his product can be made available, although in practice this may not occur very often.

It is, of course, desirable that scientists and others outside industry and government should be able to conduct tests on the effects of various pesticides. In one case debated by the agency for several years, a professor needed to know the chemical composition of a particular pesticide to conduct certain medical experiments. The question of whether EPA or a court should furnish this information to a bona fide researcher, with or without appropriate safeguards to preserve confidentiality, was resolved in the experimenter's favor after an investigation revealed that the chemical composition in fact was not a trade secret within the industry.[25]

Because of the controversy surrounding the disclosure of trade secrets, Congress amended FIFRA in 1975 and 1978. The 1975 amendments[26] cleared up an ambiguity created by the 1972 amendments by specifying that the new use restrictions applied only to data submitted on or after January 1, 1970. The definition of trade secrets was left to the administrator.

EPA took the position that the 1972 and 1975 amendments restricted use and disclosure of only a narrow range of data, such as formulas and manufacturing processes, but not hazard and efficacy data. However, the

---

[23]FIFRA § 10, 7 U.S.C. § 136h. Trade secrets are also becoming a source of contention in the implementation of the Toxic Substances Control Act.

[24]FIFRA § 10(b), 7 U.S.C. § 136h(b). Note that state agencies are not mentioned.

[25]The reverse situation, where a chemical company sought an administrative subpoena of the testing files of two university researchers on pesticides, was raised in *Dow Chemical Co. v. Allen*, 672 F.2d. 1262, 17 ERC 1013 (7th Cir., 1982). The request was rejected as unduly burdensome and not particularly probative, since the EPA had not relied on their data in studies still uncompleted.

[26]Pub. L. No. 94-140, 89 Stat. 75 (1975).

industry challenged this view with some initial success.[27] In 1978, Congress again amended Section 10 to limit trade secrets protection to formulas and manufacturing processes, thus reflecting EPA's position. This was a significant change and has spawned a host of litigation.[28]

In *Ruckelshaus v. Monsanto*,[29] the Supreme Court held almost unanimously (7-1/2 to 1/2) that while a company did have a property right to the data under state law, the key question was whether it "could reasonably expect" that secrets would not be disclosed or used by other companies, even with adequate compensation. This expectation, the court found, could only be for the period between the 1972 FIFRA amendments and the 1978 amendments, when the interim change in Section 10 of the act first promised strict confidentiality.[30] For this period, compensation is available through the federal Tucker Act, and probably through the statutory arbitration process, too. For the periods on either side of those dates, there need be no compensation.

3.3 "Featherbedding" or "Me-Too" Registrants

The second most contested provision in FEPCA, after the question of indemnities, dealt with the issue of "featherbedding" on registration. The original version in the House stated that "data submitted in support of an application shall not, without permission of the applicant, be considered by the administrator in the support of any other application for registration."[31] Supporters of the provision, basically the larger manufacturers, claimed that it prevented one company from "free-loading" on the expensive scientific data produced by another company; environmentalists dubbed this the "mice extermination amendment" for requiring subsequent registrants to needlessly duplicate the laboratory experiments of the first registrant.

The groups finally found an acceptable compromise allowing subsequent registrants to reimburse the initial registrant for reliance on its data, adding to the above language the words: "unless such other applicant shall first offer to pay reasonable compensation for producing the test data to be relied upon."

The section originally provides that disputes over the amount of compensation should be decided by the administrator. The 1975 amendments deleted the unfortunate clause which ensured that the original registrant should have nothing to lose by appealing to a district court since "in no event shall the amount of payment determined by the court be less than that determined by the Administrator." The 1978 amendments entirely

---

[27]*Mobay Chemical Corp. v. Costle*, 447 F.Supp 811, 12 ERC 1228 (W.D. Mo. 1978), appeal dismissed 439 U.S. 320, reh. denied 440 U.S. 940 (1979); *Chevron Chemical Co. v. Costle*, 443 F.Supp 1024 (N.D. Cal. 1978).

[28]Pub. L. No. 95-396, 92 Stat. 812.

[29]104 S. Ct. 2862, 21 ERC 1062 (1984).

[30]28 U.S.C. §1491.

[31]FIFRA, § 3(C)(1)(D), 9 U.S.C. § 136a(C)(1)(D).

removed the unwelcome task from the administrator by providing for mediation by the Federal Mediation & Conciliation Service.[32] The 1975 amendments also pushed back the effective date of the compensation provision from October 1972, the date of the enactment of the FEPCA amendments, to January 1, 1970.[33]

The data compensation provision has created many problems in the registration process. Pesticide manufacturers brought several lawsuits to determine the breadth of this provision, the proper use of the data, and the amount of compensation that a manufacturer is entitled to for use of its data.[34]

In the case *In re Ciba-Geigy Corp. v. Farmland Industries, Inc.*,[35] EPA set out criteria to be applied in determining what constitutes reasonable compensation under Section 3(c). Plaintiff Ciba-Geigy claimed that it was entitled to $8.11 million in compensation from Farmland Industries for the latter's use of test data to register three pesticides. The defendant argued that it should pay only a proportional share of the actual cost of producing the data based on its share of the market for the products, approximately $49,000. The plaintiff contended that reasonable compensation should be based on the standards used in licensing technical knowledge: an amount equal to the cost of reproducing the data plus a royalty on gross sales for three years.

The administrative law judge hearing the case ruled that the latter, cost-royalty formula was closer to Congress' intent to avoid unnecessary testing costs. He concluded that the reasonable compensation provision was not intended to provide reward for research and development as the plaintiff's formula would do. The fairest compensatory formula, according to the judge, was using the data producer's cost adjusted for inflation and the defendant's market share two or three years after initial registration. Although no reward for research and development was created, this compensation formula does create an incentive to research because the benefits gained from decreased costs of subsequent registrants outweighs the disadvantages of decreasing the original data producer's projects.

In 1984, the United States Supreme Court ruled in *Ruckelshaus v. Monsanto Co.*[36] that pesticide health and safety data was property under Missouri law and thus was protected under the Fifth Amendment of the Constitution. However, as noted above, this was the case where the court overruled a lower court in finding that data submitted prior to 1972 and after 1978 was

---

[32]Pub. L. No. 95-396 § 2(2), 92 Stat. 819.

[33]Pub. L. No. 94-140, §12, amending FIFRA §3(c)(1)(D). The 1972 amendments had not actually specified an effective date but most authorities assumed it was the date of enactment.

[34]*See Amchem Products Inc. v. GAF Corp.*, 594 F.2d 470 (5th Cir., 1979), reh. den. 602 F.2d 724 (5th Cir. 1979); *Mobay Chemical v. EPA*, 447 F.Supp. 811, 12 ERC 1572 (W.D. Mo., 1975), 439 U.S. 320, 12 ERC 1581 (per curiam) (1979).

[35]Initial Decision, FIFRA Comp. Dockets Nos. 33, 34 and 41 (August 19, 1980).

[36]*Ruckelshaus v. Monsanto Co.*, 104 S.Ct. 2862 (1984).

not a "taking" since the registrant had no expectation of confidentiality, except for the ambiguous period between the 1972 and 1978 amendments. The Supreme Court decided the remedy was not to find FIFRA unconstitutional, as the lower court had done, but to allow a claim against the government for compensation under the Tucker Act, 28 U.S.C. Section 1491.

3.4 Essentiality in Registration

Another registration change strongly supported by the pesticide industry was that EPA was prohibited from refusing to register a substance because it served no useful or necessary purpose. This is not the same issue as efficacy, above, nor was this a dispute as to whether, under both the old and new FIFRA, a registration application must demonstrate that a product would "perform its intended function." The agricultural chemical companies, however, had been concerned that EPA might refuse to register a new product because an old one satisfactorily performed its intended function. These fears seem misplaced; EPA's best interest, and that of the public, lies in having as much duplication of pesticide applications as reasonably possible, since the existence of a similar but safer chemical facilitates the removal of a hazardous pesticide from the market.

3.5 Intrastate Registrations

Under the old FIFRA[37] federal authority did not extend to intrastate use and shipment of pesticides with state registrations. This meant that federal authority could be avoided simply by having manufacturing plants in the principal agricultural states. The FEPCA amendments broadened the registration requirement to include any person in any state who sells or distributes pesticides.

The states do retain some authority under Section 24 "to regulate the sale or use of any pesticide or device in the state, but only if and to the extent the regulation does not permit any sale or use prohibited by this Act." States, furthermore, cannot have labeling and packaging requirements different from those required by the act, a measure which was popular among some chemical manufacturers who feared that each state might have different labeling requirements. It also seems to exclude a feature common to several of the other environmental laws whereby states may impose stricter requirements than the federal ones on pesticide use within their jurisdiction.

Finally, the section gives a state the authority, subject to certification by EPA, to register pesticides for limited local use in treating sudden and limited pest infestations, without the time and administrative burden required by a full EPA certification.

The fears of pesticide manufacturers that the states would impose more stringent labeling requirements were justified in spite of the FEPCA amendments. California imposed additional data requirements under its restricted-

---

[37]Old FIFRA § 4(a).

use registration. In *National Agricultural Chemicals Association v. Rominger*,[38] a federal district court declined to issue a preliminary injunction against the state's regulations. The judge decided that there had been no congressional mandate to occupy the field when Section 24 was enacted, and thus there was no federal preemption of restricted-use registrations.[39]

3.6 Conditional Registration

The near-collapse of EPA's pesticide registration process in the mid-1970s prompted creation of a system of *conditional* registration or reregistration. This could be applied when certain data on a product's safety had either not yet been supplied to EPA or had not yet been analyzed to ensure, according to FIFRA Section 3(a)(5)(D), that "it will perform its intended function without unreasonable adverse effects on the environment."

Three kinds of conditional registrations are authorized by Section 6 of the 1978 law which amended FIFRA Section 3(c) with a new section, entitled "Registration Under Special Circumstances": (1) pesticides identical or very similar to currently registered products; (2) new uses to existing pesticide registrations; and (3) pesticides containing active ingredients not contained in any currently registered pesticide for which data need be obtained for registration. These conditional registrations must be conducted on a case-by-case basis, with the last type of conditional registration further limited both by duration and by the requirement that the "use of the pesticide is in the public interest." Conditional registration is prohibited if a Notice of Rebuttable Presumption Against Registration (RPAR) has been issued for the pesticide, and if the proposed new use involves use on a minor food or feed crop for which there is an effective registered pesticide not subject to a RPAR proceeding.

Cancellation of conditional registrations must be followed by a public hearing, if requested, within seventy-five days of the request, but must be limited to the issue of whether the registrant has fulfilled its conditions for the registration.[40]

EPA published final regulations implementing conditional registration on May 11, 1979.[41]

3.7 Streamlining of Registration

EPA's reregistration of pesticides, required every five years, has always been plagued by both a slow regulatory pace and the feeling that much of the safety data underlying the registrations was inadequate by contemporary scientific standards. The 1988 amendments added an entire section,

---

[38]500 F. Supp 465, 15 ERC 1039 (E.D. Cal. 1980).

[39]The court also dismissed challenges to two other provisions of the California laws for lack of ripeness. These challenges were claims that the statute improperly allowed the state to set residue tolerances different from EPA tolerances and that certain labeling requirements for insecticides were improperly imposed.

[40]§ 12 of 1978 act, amending FIFRA § 6.

[41]44 Fed. Reg. 27932 (May 11, 1979).

renumbered as FIFRA Section 4, covering this topic.[42] This section provided that the data submitted in support of registrations before EPA's creation in 1970 would no longer be considered adequate for reregistration, unless the applicant bears the burden of proof otherwise.[43]

The new section set a 48-month timetable for the completion of the studies needed for reregistration. These deadlines are to parallel the time requirements currently in FIFRA Section 3(c)(2)(B), entitled "Additional Data to Support Existing Registration." These timetables are to be virtually absolute; they may be extended only in such extraordinary circumstances as a major animal loss, the unintentional loss of laboratory results, or the destruction of laboratory equipment and facilities.

After the administrator's review is completed, EPA may ask for additional data to support the reregistration or may declare the pesticide canceled or suspended. Otherwise, EPA is to approve the reregistration. Under the previous version of FIFRA, no consequences were set for failure of a registrant to provide compensation to the original provider of any data relied upon or share in the payments. The 1988 amendments specified that the administrator, in such a case, must issue a notice of intent to suspend that registrant's registration.

The reregistration continues to lag, despite years of criticism from Congress and environmentalists, and one can safely anticipate these complaints will persist for years to come.

3.8 Registration of "Me-Too" Pesticides

For those pesticides which are identical or very similar to other registered products, akin to "me-too" generic drugs, the 1988 amendments provide that EPA should expedite approvals of these registrations.[44] To assist this process, the administrator is to utilize up to $2 million of the fees collected (see below).[45]

3.9 Registration Fees

A one-time registration fee per active ingredient is authorized by the 1988 amendments.[46] In addition, registrants must pay an annual fee through 1997 to supplement EPA's pesticide reregistration budget. The legislation emphasizes, however, that no other fee can be imposed by EPA other than the above. Moreover, the administrator is empowered to reduce or waive the fees for minor use pesticides where their availability would otherwise be in question. EPA is to report annually to Congress on the application of this authority.

---

[42]Section 102 of the 1988 amendments, redesignated as Section 4 of FIFRA by Section 801(q) of the 1988 law.

[43]The actual cut-off date is given as January 1, 1970; the EPA was not created until December 2, 1970.

[44]FIFRA, Section 3(c) (3).

[45]FIFRA, Section 4(k) (3).

[46]FIFRA, Section 4(i).

3.10 Generic Pesticide Review

EPA has long complained that registration, and especially reregistration reviews, should be conducted for entire classes of chemicals rather than be limited to examining each particular registration as it comes up for five-year renewal. This authority has always existed under FIFRA, but a district court decision in 1975[47] on compensation for data made this so complicated that the plan was dropped pending a legislative solution.

The amendment that finally emerged under this label in Section 4 of the 1978 act, however, was considerably different in scope: "No applicant for registration of a pesticide who proposes to purchase a registered pesticide from another producer in order to formulate such purchased pesticide into an end-use product shall be required to (i) submit or cite data pertaining to the safety of such purchased product; or (ii) offer to pay reasonable compensation . . . for the use of any such data."[48]

3.11 Efficacy

The requirements for test data on a pesticide's efficacy are now made discretionary for EPA. This does not change the present practice very much, because efficacy information has been increasingly less important over the past few years. But the provision is interesting because it marks a complete reversal from the original purpose of federal pesticide legislation earlier in this century, which was to protect farmers from "snake oil" pesticide claims.

4.0 CONTROL OVER PESTICIDE USAGE

4.1 Statutory Basis for Control over Pesticide Usage

Until the 1972 FEPCA reforms, the government had no control over the actual use of a pesticide once it had left a manufacturer or distributor properly labeled. Thus, for example, a chemical which would be perfectly safe for use on a dry field might be environmentally hazardous if applied in a marshy area, and a chemical acceptable for use on one crop might leave dangerous residues on another. EPA's only recourse (other than occasional subtle hints to the producer) was to cancel the entire registration—obviously too unwieldy a weapon to constitute a normal means of enforcement. A second problem was that a potential chemical might be too dangerous for general use but could be used safely by trained personnel. There was, however, no legal mechanism for limiting its use only to qualified individuals.

Because of these problems, both environmentalists and the industry agreed that EPA should be given more flexibility than merely choosing between canceling or approving a pesticide. Congress therefore provided for the classification of pesticides into general and restricted categories, with the latter group available only to "certified applicators." There are several

---

[47]*Mobay Chemical Corp. v. Train*, 392 F. Supp. 1342, 8 ERC 1227 (W.D. Mo. 1975).
[48]1978 act, amending FIFRA § 3(c)(2).

categories of applicators, including private applicators and commercial applicators, who use or supervise the application of pesticides on property other than their own. A pesticide label permitting use only "under the direct supervision of a Certified Applicator" means of course that the chemical is to be applied under the instructions and control of a Certified Applicator who, however, curiously is not required to be physically present when and where the pesticide is applied.

The additional flexibility of the certification program was a principal reason the agro-chemical industry eventually supported the 1972 amendments to FIFRA, but some environmentalists were concerned that the program might become a farce, especially when administered by certain states. Certification standards are prescribed by EPA, but any state desiring to establish its own certification program may do so if the administrator determines that it satisfies the guidelines and statutory criteria. (See further, in Section 4.3, below.)

Since 1972 it has been unlawful either "to make available for use, or to use, any registered pesticide classified for restricted use for some or all purposes other than in accordance with" the registration and applicable regulations. Stiff penalties for violations of these restrictions include fines of up to $25,000 and imprisonment for up to a year.

The validity of the certification program, however, was considerably undermined by the 1975 amendments to FIFRA. The amendments considerably relaxed the procedures for certification by forbidding EPA to demand any examinations of an applicant's knowledge.[49] Some states may license anyone who applies, but EPA requirements for periodic reporting and inspection provide some degree of control. There would be no objection to every farmer becoming a Certified Applicator if he so desired, provided that he was seriously willing to undergo training.

4.2 Experimental Use Permits

FIFRA provides for experimental use permits for registered pesticides.[50] The purpose of this seemingly innocuous section is to permit a registration applicant to conduct tests and "accumulate information necessary to register a pesticide under Section 3."[51] This provision, however, has already been used in at least one successful effort to evade a FIFRA cancellation-suspension order. Under strong political pressure from western sheep interests and their congressional spokesmen, EPA granted a Section 5 permit for the limited use of certain banned predacides and devices including the "coyote getter," a poison-rigged trap for wild animals.

---

[49]Pub. L. No. 94-140 § 5, amending FIFRA § 4(a)(1).

[50]FIFRA § 5, 7 U.S.C. § 136c. The 1975 amendments added a specific provision for agricultural research agencies, public or private.

[51]FIFRA § 5(a), 7 U.S.C. § 136c(a).

On July 18, 1979, EPA issued final regulations under which a state may develop its own experimental permits program.[52] A state, by submitting a plan which meets the requirements of EPA's regulations, may receive authorization to issue experimental use permits to potential registrants under 24(c) of FIFRA (restricted use registration), agricultural or educational research agencies, and certified applicators for use of a restricted use pesticide.

Permits cannot be issued by a state for a pesticide containing ingredients subject to an EPA cancellation or suspension order, or a notice of intent to cancel or suspend, or which are not found in any EPA registered product.[53] The regulations also contain strict limitations on the production and use of a pesticide. Periodic reports must be submitted by the permittee to the state detailing the progress of the research or restricted use. In addition, permits cannot be issued for more than three years.

4.3 Self-Certification of Private Applicators

The clearest illustration of Congress' altered view toward FIFRA is their treatment of the certification program which had been a major reason for the enactment of the FIFRA overhaul in 1972. The amendments provided that the pesticides which might be too harmful to the applicators or to the environment if indiscriminately used could continue to be applied by farmers and pesticide operators who had received special training in avoiding these problems.

The program had run into resistance from the beginning from farmers who resented the requirement that they be trained to use chemicals on their own property. The changed law does not remove the examination requirement from commercial applicators, who apply pesticides to property other than their own.[54] It does create an exemption, however, which covers not only the farmer who is applying pesticides to his own land but also his employees. And it must be remembered that the hazards are not necessarily limited to the applicator; organophosphates, which are nerve gases, may be highly toxic to the applicators, but many other substances if improperly used may run off to threaten neighboring farms or the environment in general. The amended law does not seem to recognize this latter problem.

The 1975 amendments also removed the authority of the administrator to require, under state plans submitted for his approval, that farmers take exams before being certified. In other words, EPA may require a training program but may not require any examination to determine if the information has been learned.[55] In the opinion of the House Agriculture

---

[52]44 Fed. Reg. at 41783 (July 18, 1978); 40 C.F.R. § 172.20.

[53]44 Fed. Reg. at 41788. States may, however, issue permits for products containing ingredients subject to the Rebuttable Presumption Against Review process (RPAR).

[54]See the definition of commercial applicator in FIFRA § 2(e).

[55]States may themselves require an examination of certified applicators but, under the amended FIFRA, EPA could not make this a prerequisite for state plan approval. See Pub. L. 94-140 § 5, amending FIFRA § 4, 7 U.S.C. 136b. See also Senate Report No. 94-452, pp. 7-8.

Committee, "The farmer would be more aware of the dangers of restricted use pesticides if each time he makes a purchase he is given a self-certification form to read and sign." One wonders if a similar arrangement for airline pilot certification would be considered acceptable.[56]

4.4 Greater State Authority

Several sections of the 1978 amendments reflect Congress' intent to give the states greater responsibility in regulating pesticides. This includes not only training and cooperative agreements, but also increasing federal delegation over such matters as intra-state registrations and enforcement. The EPA administrator, however, retains overall supervisory responsibility and ultimate veto authority.

Because some states, such as California, have promulgated stringent guidelines for pesticide regulations, there has been proposed legislation to limit state authority under Section 24 to gather data about a pesticide for state registration.[57] Pesticide manufacturers have complained for several years that state registration procedures, which may require additional studies and data gathering, are time-consuming and costly. There have been no changes in Section 24 yet; however, Congress may limit the regulatory authority of the states in future legislation.

4.5 Two-House Congressional Veto Over EPA Regulations

The 1980 amendments amended Section 25(a) to provide a two-house congressional veto over EPA rules or regulations.[58] Under the amendments, the administrator is required to submit to each house of Congress new FIFRA regulations. If Congress adopts a concurrent resolution disapproving the new regulation within ninety days of its promulgation it will not become effective. However, if neither house disapproves the regulation after sixty days and the appropriate committee of neither house has voted for a resolution of disapproval, the regulation becomes effective.[59]

5.0 REMOVAL OF PESTICIDES FROM THE MARKET

FIFRA is not merely concerned with the registration, or reregistration, of pesticides coming on the market. It also has mechanisms for taking action against products considered to pose a risk to man and the environment.

---

[56]House Report No. 94-497, p. 9.

[57]See "Hearings Before the House Agricultural Committee, Federal Insecticide, Fungicide, and Rodenticide Act Amendments," H.R. 5203, Serial No. 97-R, (1982).

[58]Pub. L. No. 96-539, 94 Stat. 3194, 3195 amending 7 U.S.C. § 136w(4).

[59]The constitutionality of congressional vetoes of administrative rules is unsettled. The Supreme Court in 1983 held that one-house vetoes are unconstitutional, and since then legislation has had to be revised to conform to the legislative mode: *both* houses must pass legislation which is then presented to the president for his approval or disapproval. *Immigration & Naturalization Service v. Chadha*, 462 U.S. 919, 103 S.Ct. 2764 (1983), affirming 64 F.d 408 (9th Cir., 1980).

5.1 Cancellation

While the registration process may be the heart of FIFRA, cancellation represents the cutting edge of the law and attracts the most public attention. Cancellation is used to initiate review of a substance suspected of posing a "substantial question of safety" to man or the environment.[60] Contrary to public assumptions, during the pendency of the proceedings the product may be freely manufactured and shipped in commerce. A cancellation order, although final if not challenged within thirty days, usually leads to a public hearing or scientific review committee, or both, and can be quite protracted; this can last a matter of months or years. A recommended decision from the agency hearing examiner (now called the administrative law judge) goes to the administrator or to his delegated representative, the chief agency judicial officer, for a final determination on the cancellation. If the decision is upheld, the product would be banned from shipment or use in the United States.[61]

There are several quite different types of action covered under the single term "cancellation."[62] First, there is a cancellation when EPA believes a substance is a highly probable threat to man or the environment but there is not yet sufficient evidence to warrant its immediate suspension. This is the usual meaning. Second, there can be a cancellation when scientific tests indicate some cause for concern, and a public hearing or scientific advisory committee is desired to explore the issue more thoroughly. And third, there could be a cancellation issued in response to a citizens' suit to enable both critics and defenders of the pesticide to present their arguments. These distinctions, although not found in the statute, are nevertheless quite important. State authorities, for example, often recommend that farmers cease using a canceled product which they thought had been declared unsafe, although EPA may have considered the action in category two or three above. Conversely, there were occasions when EPA wanted to communicate its great concern over the continued use of a product without resorting to the more immediate and drastic remedy of suspension.

This problem is not resolved completely by the amended FIFRA, but two levels of action are distinguished. The administrator may issue a notice of his intent either (1) to cancel its registration or change its classification together with the reasons (including the factual basis) for his action, or (2) to hold a hearing to determine whether or not its registration should be canceled or its classification changed.[63] This revision of the law may not have solved EPA's communications problem with local officials, but it does provide a basis for a distinction which EPA sometimes needed to make.

---

[60]*EDF v. Ruckelshaus*, 439 F.2d 584, 591-92, 2 ERC 1114, 1119 (D.C. Cir., 1971).

[61]The scientific review committee and other features of this process will be discussed later in more detail.

[62]The cancellation-suspension section of the old act was § 4(c); it is § 6 of the post-1972 FIFRA.

[63]FIFRA § 6(b), 7 U.S.C. § 136d(b). Note that the administrator himself may request a hearing, a power which he did not have under the old FIFRA, although in fact he assumed this authority in his August 1971 cancellation order on 2,4,5-T.

5.2 Suspension

A suspension order, despite its misleading name, is an immediate ban on the production and distribution of a pesticide. It is mandated when a product constitutes an "imminent hazard" to man or the environment and it may be invoked at any stage of the cancellation proceeding or even before a cancellation procedure has been initiated. According to the 18th of March Statement, a seminal 1971 EPA pronouncement, "an imminent hazard may be declared at any point in the chain of events which may ultimately result in harm to the public."[64] A suspension order must be accompanied by a cancellation order if one is not then outstanding.

5.2.1 Ordinary Suspension

The purpose of an ordinary suspension is to prevent an imminent hazard during the time required for cancellation or change in classification proceedings. An ordinary suspension proceeding is initiated when the administrator issues notice to the registrant that he is suspending use of the pesticide and includes the requisite findings as to imminent hazards. The registrant may request an expedited hearing within five days of receipt of the administrator's notice. If no hearing is requested, the suspension order can take effect immediately thereafter and the order is not reviewable by a court.

The original notion was that suspension procedurally "resembles . . . the judicial proceedings on a contested motion for a preliminary injunction,"[65] and that it remains in effect until the cancellation hearing is completed and a final decision is issued by the administrator.[66] This connotation of temporariness does not actually accord with reality but has been the consistent theme of judicial decisions since the agency's inception. According to this view, the function of a suspension order is not to reach a definitive decision on the registration of a pesticide but to grant temporary, interim relief.[67] The Circuit Court of Appeals for the District of Columbia has repeatedly stated this view: "The function of the suspension decision is to make a preliminary assessment of evidence and probabilities, not an ultimate resolution of difficult issues,"[68] and "the suspension order thus operates to afford interim relief during the course of the lengthy administrative proceedings."[69]

The court of appeals has specifically noted that "imminent hazard" does not refer only to the danger of an immediate disaster: "We must caution against any approach to the term 'imminent hazard' used in the statute, that

---

[64]*See* EPA's March 18, 1971, Statement, p. 6.

[65]*EDF v. EPA* 465 F. 2d 538, 4 ERC 1523, 1530 (D.C. Cir., 1972).

[66]*Nor-Am v. Hardin*, 435 F. 2d 1151, 2 ERC 1016 (7th Cir., 1970), *cert. denied* 402 U.S. 935 (1971).

[67]*See, In re Shell Chemical*, Opinion of the administrator, pp. 8-11, 6 ERC 2047 at 2050 (1974).

[68]*EDF v. EPA, supra*, 465 F. 2d at 537, 4 ERC at 1529.

[69]*EDF v. Ruckelshaus, supra*, 439 F. 2d at 589, 2 ERC at 1115.

restricts it to a concept of crises."[70] In another case, the court declared that the secretary of agriculture concluded that the most important element of an "imminent hazard to the public" is a serious threat to public health, that a hazard may be "imminent" even if its impact will not be apparent for many years, and that the "public" protected by the suspension provision includes fish and wildlife. These interpretations all seem consistent with the statutory language and purpose.[71]

5.2.2 Emergency Suspension

The emergency suspension is the strongest environmental action EPA can take under FIFRA and immediately halts all uses, sales, and distribution of a pesticide.[72] An emergency suspension differs from an ordinary suspension in that the registrant is given neither notice nor the opportunity for an expedited hearing prior to the suspension order's taking effect. The registrant is, however, entitled to an expedited hearing to determine the propriety of the emergency suspension. The administrator can only use this procedure when he determines that an emergency exists which does not allow him to hold a hearing before suspending use of a pesticide. This authority has only rarely been invoked.

EPA first used the emergency suspension procedure in 1979 when it suspended the sale and use of 2,4,5-T and Silvex for specified uses. EPA issued the suspension orders based on its judgment that exposure to the pesticides created an immediate and unreasonable risk to human health. EPA's action was reviewed by a Michigan district court in *Dow Chemical Co. v. Blum*,[73] where the plaintiffs petitioned for judicial review of EPA's decision and a stay of the emergency suspension orders. In upholding EPA's order, the court analogized the emergency suspension order to a temporary restraining order and defined the term emergency as a "substantial likelihood that serious harm will be experienced during the three or four months required in any realistic projection of the administrative suspension process."[74]

The court held that this standard required the administrator to examine five factors: (1) the seriousness of the threatened harm; (2) the immediacy of the threatened harm; (3) the probability that the threatened harm would result; (4) the benefits to the public of the continued use of the pesticides in question during the suspension process; and (5) the nature and extent of the information before the administrator at the time he makes his decision. The court also held that an emergency suspension order may be overturned only

---

[70]*EDF v. EPA, supra,* 465 F. 2d at 540, 4 ERC at 1531.

[71]*EDF v. Ruckelshaus, supra,* 439 F.2d at 597, 2 ERC at 1121-22.

[72]Its counterpart in the Toxic Substances Control Act, TSCA, is Section 7, but that provision has remained virtually unused over the past decade.

[73]469 F. Supp. 892, 13 ERC 1129 (E.D. Mich., 1979).

[74]*Ibid.* at 902, 13 ERC at 1135.

if it was arbitrary, capricious, or an abuse of discretion or if it was not "issued in accordance with the procedures established by law."[75]

5.3 Misbranding and Stop-Sale Orders

EPA has traditionally used the bare charge of "misbranding" for certain unambiguous offenses, notably instances where the pesticide made claims unsupported by the registration. The violation was usually obvious, the appeals uncommon, and the remedy simple—namely, to order the sales halted.

In the early 1990s, however, EPA began for the first time to use the charge of misbranding in cases where the agency questioned the effectiveness of the registered formulation. If the product does not work, it should not be re-registered, or it should be cancelled under Section 6. By using misbranding rather than cancellation, the agency circumvents the procedural safeguards, including the public hearings and scientific advisory committees provided in the statute. For that very reason, this approach should be disfavored.[76]

Ironically, while less procedural protection is afforded by the misbranding approach, the legal consequences can be more severe; unlike cancelled or even suspended products, a misbranded product can be prohibited by EPA from export or sale abroad.

5.4 International Effect of EPA Cancellations

EPA cancellation and suspension decisions, as agency administrators have repeatedly noted, are meant to apply only to the United States. The reason is that the risk-benefit calculations applied to challenged pesticides are based on conditions in this country and would not necessarily be valid for different risks and different benefits abroad.

This interpretation has not been without its critics. Because of its potential significance, an entire separate part of this chapter (Part 8.0, below) is devoted to this topic.

5.5 Disposal and Recall

An important question following a cancellation or suspension action is whether to recall those products already in commerce.[77] "Misbranded" pesticides may be confiscated, and on several occasions EPA has ordered manufacturers to recall a pesticide when the hazard so warranted, but for both practical and administrative reasons cancellation-suspension orders

---

[75]*Ibid.* The court stated that it arrived at its decision to uphold EPA's order "with great reluctance" and would not have ordered the emergency suspension on the basis of the information before EPA, but was not empowered to substitute its judgment for that of EPA's. 469 F. Supp. at 907, 13 ERC at 1140.

[76]The agency suffered a setback in the first case in federal court utilizing this theory, *Metrex v. EPA,* (unreported) although on the narrower grounds that EPA's test data was invalid. A second case, involving another disinfectant producer, Sporicidin International, is pending.

[77]FIFRA §§ 19 and 25, 7 U.S.C. §§ 136q and 136w. See also the previous discussion of indemnities.

have generally provided that banned pesticides may be used until supplies are exhausted, without being subject to recall.[78] It may seem inconsistent to ban a substance as an imminent hazard and yet allow quantities already on the market to be sold, but repeated challenges by environmentalist groups have been unsuccessful.[79]

This policy was thought necessary, for example, in the mercury pesticides case when EPA scientists concluded that the recall of certain mercuric compounds would result in a concentration more harmful to the environment than permitting the remaining supplies to be thinly spread around the country. In the DDT case the administrator decided that his final cancellation order would not go into effect for six months to ensure the availability of adequate supplies of alternative pesticides (namely, organophosphates which can be very hazardous to untrained applicators) and to allow time for training and educational programs to prevent misuse of the new chemicals.

EPA promulgated regulations for the storage and disposal of pesticides in May 1974.[80] These detailed the appropriate conditions for incinerations, soil injection, and other means of disposal, established procedures for shipment back to the manufacturers or to the federal government, directed that transportation costs should be borne by the owner of the pesticide, and provided standards for storage. The regulations devote considerable attention to the disposal problem of pesticide containers, which have caused a significant proportion of accidental poisonings.

5.6 Compensation for Canceled Pesticides

Section 15 provides financial compensation to registrants and applicators owning quantities of pesticides who are unable to use them because of cancellation or suspension. This section was the most controversial in the entire act; the amendment's industry supporters threatened to block passage of the entire 1972 legislation if this section were not attached. Public interest groups complained that it would force taxpayers to indemnify manufacturers for inadequate testing and would encourage the production of unsafe chemicals.[81] To the extent that this provision was intended not so much for indemnification as to deter EPA cancellations,[82] it served to undermine the purposes of this act.

As a partial compromise, a clause was added to bar indemnification to any person who "had knowledge of facts which, in themselves, would have shown that such pesticide did not meet the requirements" for registration,

---

[78]Compare the recall authority of the Consumer Product Safety Commission under Section 15 of its Hazardous Substance Act, 15 U.S.C. §1274, Pub. L. No. 91-113, which makes recall almost mandatory. The Consumer Product Safety Act, Section 15, on the other hand, provides several options, 15 U.S.C. 2064, Pub. L. No. 92-573.

[79]*See*, e.g., *EDF v. EPA* 510 F. 2d 1292, 7 ERC 1689 (D.C. Cir., 1975).

[80]39 *Fed. Reg.* 15236, (May 1, 1974), 40 C.F.R. § 165.

[81]FIFRA § 15, Pub. L. No. 92-516.

[82]See section 4.1 "Indemnities" in this chapter.

and continued thereafter to produce such pesticide without giving notice of such facts to the administrator. If properly applied, even under the most expedited agency procedures, that saving clause could have disqualified registrants and manufacturers from compensation in virtually all cancellation and suspension actions.

Under this provision, the EPA has paid out $20 million to manufacturers of the two pesticides 2,4,5-T and ethylene dibromide (EDB). An additional $40 million indemnification is estimated for a third canceled pesticide, dinoseb. These sums come directly from the budget of EPA's Pesticide Office, which last year totaled only $40 million, and thus would require that the agency cut back on other activities.[83]

This indemnities provision is now generally regarded as a mistake. In the 1988 legislation on FIFRA, the House and Senate both voted to remove the section, except for the indemnification of end users (that is, farmers and applicators), so chemical manufacturers would no longer be covered.[84] Farmers and other users would still be eligible for compensation through the federal government's regular Judgment Fund.[85] This reflects the philosophy of an earlier congressional prohibition, contained in the Appropriations Bill for fiscal year 1988, which provided that any sums should be paid from the general U.S. Treasury, not from EPA's budget, so the agency would not be penalized for taking measures it deemed proper.[86]

5.7 Balancing Test in FIFRA

The balancing of risks versus benefits is mandated by FIFRA, and its importance warrants a separate discussion. There are some who feel that certain types of pesticides, particularly carcinogens, should be forbidden *per se* as under the Delaney Amendment to the Food, Drug, and Cosmetics Act.[87] FIFRA does not require this inflexibility, although the courts have cautioned that the law "places a heavy burden on any administrative officer to explain the basis for his decision to permit the continued use of a chemical known to produce cancer in experimental animals."[88]

The balancing that is applied during the registration process and, more formally, during the cancellation proceedings is to determine whether there are "unreasonable adverse effects on the environment," taking into consideration the "economic, social, and environmental costs and benefits of the use of any pesticide."

In a suspension proceeding, however, FIFRA does not require a balancing of environmental risks and benefits. It has nevertheless been EPA's

---

[83] *Washington Post*, September 15, 1988.

[84] See the fuller discussion of the FIFRA Amendments of 1988, *infra*.

[85] Section 501 of the 1988 amendments.

[86] FY 1988 Continuing Appropriation Act, Pub. L. No. 100-202.

[87] FDCA § 409(c)(3)(A), 21 U.S.C. § 348(c)(3)(A). The relationship between the FIFRA and the FDCA will be discussed later in more detail.

[88] *EDF v. Ruckelshaus, supra*, 439 F. 2d at 596, 2 ERC at 1121.

policy since its inception to conduct such an analysis, although in practice the benefits would obviously need to be considerable to balance a finding of "imminent hazard." One administrator noted that "the Agency traditionally has considered benefits as well as risks . . . and, in his opinion, should continue to do so."[89]

5.8 Requirements of Consultation by EPA with USDA

Congress decided in the 1975 amendments to require that EPA engage in formal consultation with USDA and with the Agriculture Committees of the House and Senate before issuing proposals or final standards regarding pesticides. This amended Section 6(b) of the FIFRA to provide that EPA should give 60 days' notice to the Secretary of Agriculture before a notice is made public. The Secretary then must respond within 30 days, and these comments, along with the response of the EPA administrator, are published in the *Federal Register*.[90] These consultations, however, are not required in the event of an imminent hazard to human health for which a suspension order under Section 6(c) is warranted.

At the same time that the administrator provides a copy of any proposed regulations to the Secretary of Agriculture, he is also required to provide copies to the respective House and Senate Agricultural Committees. The practical impact of this requirement is that Congress is provided an opportunity to communicate displeasure to the administrator before a proposal is issued without necessarily having to subject these comments to scrutiny in the public record.[91]

5.9 Economic Impact On Agriculture Statement

The 1975 amendments also reflected the increasing trend in government toward requiring impact statements before regulations can be issued. Congress, borrowing from the environmental impact statement process[92] and the economic impact statement requirements,[93] mandated that the administrator, when deciding to issue a proposal, "shall include among those factors to be taken into account the impact of the action proposed in such notice on production and prices of agricultural commodities, retail food prices, and otherwise on the agricultural economy."[94]

---

[89]*In re Shell Chemical, supra.*, p. 11, 6 ERC at 2050-51, upheld unanimously by the D.C. Court of Appeals in *EDF v. EPA*, 510 F. 2d 1292, 7 ERC 1689 (April 4, 1975).

[90]These time deadlines may be by agreement between the administrator and the secretary, Pub. L. No. 94-140, § 1.

[91]EPA has often required that congressional communications after the issuance of a proposal be placed on the public record; and where this was not done, as in the DDT proceedings, environmental groups successfully sued to ensure that these contacts and written comments were made public.

[92]National Environmental Policy Act, § 102(2)(c), U.S.C. §§ 4321 *et seq.*, (1969); see also 36 *Fed. Reg.* 7724 (1971) and 38 Fed. Reg. 20549 (1973).

[93]Presidential Executive Order No. 11821, November 29, 1974.

[94]Pub. L. No. 94-104, § 1, amending FIFRA § 6(b), 7 U.S.C. § 136d.

The necessity for this legal provision is questionable since the balancing of risks and benefits is at the heart of FIFRA. No one at EPA or anywhere else has contended that the agricultural benefits of pesticides should not be taken into consideration in this balancing equation. In fact, although the courts have stated that EPA legally need not consider benefits in suspension actions involving an imminent hazard to human health and the environment, EPA from the beginning has always made the agricultural factor an essential element in its determinations. The committees themselves were vague about the actual need for this legislation. (The Senate stated, "The Committee concurs in the House position that EPA has not always given adequate consideration to agriculture in its decisions. This concern was also expressed by many witnesses appearing before the Committee.")[95]

5.10 Scientific Advisory Committees

Because the Scientific Advisory Committees play such an important role in the cancellation-suspension process, they deserve special attention in this section.

According to the old FIFRA, prior to 1972, a registrant challenging a cancellation order could request either a public hearing or a scientific advisory committee; and in practice, cases involving several registrants usually resulted in both. EPA was also strongly dissatisfied with the vague and often contradictory reports of the advisory committees.

In the 1972 amendments to FIFRA, the advisory committee was transformed into an adjunct of the hearing process, resolving those scientific questions which the administrative law judge or the parties determined were essential to the final decision by the administrator. The amendments streamlined the process so that Committee deliberations could proceed simultaneously with the administrative hearings, thereby saving time and making them a part of the fact-finding and evaluation system, rather than in a separate proceeding with long delays and divisions of responsibility. By meeting outside of the public hearing, the scientists can also avoid being subject to cross examination and other legal burdens they consider unappealing.

The advisory process, however, was again made more formalistic by the 1975 amendments. The use of a scientific advisory committee was mandated both for cancellation actions (where they are usually requested anyway) and for any general pesticide regulations.[96] The amendments required that the administrator submit proposed and final regulations to a specially constituted scientific advisory panel, separate from the regular Scientific Advisory Committees, at the same time that he provides copies to the Secretary of Agriculture and to the two agricultural committees of Congress. The advisory committee then has 30 days in which to respond. Membership on this committee is prescribed in unusual detail. The administrator can select seven members from a group of twelve nominees, six nominated by

---

[95]Senate Report No. 94-452, p. 9.
[96]Pub. L. No. 94-140, § 7, amending FIFRA § 25.

the National Science Foundation, and six by the National Institutes of Health.[97]

In 1980, Section 25(d) was amended to allow the chairman of a Scientific Advisory Committee to create temporary subpanels on specific projects.[98] Section 25(d) was also amended to require the administrator to submit any decision to suspend the registration of a pesticide to a scientific advisory panel (SAP) for its comment.[99] The amendment does not alter the administrator's authority to issue a suspension notice prior to the SAP review; it only requires him to obtain SAP review after the suspension is initiated. The 1980 amendments also require the administrator to issue written procedures for independent peer review of the design, protocol and conduct of major studies conducted under FIFRA.[100]

One might question the value of ever more advisory committees when, as EPA administrator Russell Train pointed out years ago, "EPA is already awash in scientific advisory panels."[101]

6.0 ADMINISTRATIVE AND JUDICIAL REVIEW

6.1 Scope of the Administrator's Flexibility

The EPA administrator renders the final agency judgment on administrative actions and appeals.[102] Since issues reach him only after passing through a series of committees, lower level enforcement officials, and administrative law judges, the question is how much discretion he has to come to a decision at variance with those rendered below?

6.1.1 Concerning the Scientific Advisory Committee

In emphasizing the administrator's regulatory flexibility, the courts have rejected the contention that he must "rubber stamp" the findings of the Scientific Advisory Committee or the administrative law judge. This is illustrated by *Dow Chemical v. Ruckelshaus*[103] concerning the herbicide 2,4,5-T. In 1970 the USDA suspended some uses of the chemical and canceled others because of the high risk that it, or a dioxin contaminant known as TCDD, had proved a potent teratogen in laboratory tests. Most of these uses were not challenged, but Dow did contest the cancellation on rice. A Scientific Advisory Committee convoked by EPA concluded that the "confused aggregate of observations indicated registrations should be maintained" but that there remained serious questions needing further

---

[97]Pub. L. No. 94-140, § 7, amending FIFRA § 25(d), 7 U.S.C. § 136w.

[98]Pub. L. No. 96-539, 94 Stat. 3195.

[99]*Id.*

[100]No. 96-1020, 96th Cong., 2d Sess. (1980) p. 4.

[101]Statement of EPA administrator Russell Train to the Senate Agricultural Committee, reprinted in Senate Report No. 94-452, p. 18.

[102]In practice, most appeals to the administrator are handled and decided by the Chief Judicial Officer, in the office of the administrator.

[103]477 F.2d 1317, 5 ERC 1244 (8th Cir., 1973).

extensive research. The administrator reviewed the report in considerable detail and concluded that a "substantial question of safety" existed sufficient to justify an administrative hearing; in the meantime, the cancellation was maintained.[104] Dow appealed, but the court of Appeals for the Eighth Circuit held that the administrator was not compelled to follow the recommendations of the advisory committee if—and this is, of course, crucial—he had a justifiable basis for doing otherwise.[105]

6.1.2 Concerning the Administrative Law Judge

The administrator is not bound by findings of the administrative law judges, either. This conclusion follows the general principle of administrative law that a hearing examiner's decision should be accorded only the deference it merits. As the Supreme Court said long ago in *Universal Camera*, "we do not require that the examiner's findings be given more weight than in reason and in light of judicial experience they deserve."[106] Only if the decision-maker arbitrarily and capriciously ignored the findings of an examiner, or if the credibility of witnesses was crucial to the case—a situation that rarely exists in an administrative hearing—would a different conclusion be indicated.

6.2 Standing for Registration, Appeals and Subpoenas

FIFRA originally assumed that only registrants would be interested in the continuation of a product's registration or the setting of public hearings and scientific advisory committees. It was increasingly evident, however, that this unintended exclusion of both users and environmentalists needed revision. Whereas a registrant, when faced with cancellation, might prefer not to contest those minor categories of use which it regarded as financially insignificant, a user might regard them as essential for the protection of his crops. The law was therefore amended by FEPCA to allow not only registrants but any "other interested person with the concurrence of the registrant" to request continuation of the registration.[107] While this amendment remedies the problem of legal standing, it does not provide the resources and

---

[104]The deficiencies in the advisory report, which was poorly reasoned and internally inconsistent, contributed to the agency's skepticism towards this system of information collection and analysis.

[105]This case is better remembered for its unconscionable delay of the administrative process. Dow appealed first to a district court in Arkansas and obtained an injunction against further EPA action on 2,4,5-T, although the statute explicitly excluded district courts from jurisdiction. The Eighth Circuit reversed, noting that the court below lacked jurisdiction and that, in any case, Dow was not entitled to an injunction during a period when "the cancellation orders have no effect on Dow's right to ship and market its product until the administration cancellation process has been completed." *Ibid.*, at 1326, 5 ERC at 1250.

[106]*Universal Camera Corp. v. NLRB*, 340 U.S. 474 (1951).

[107]FIFRA § 6(a)(1), 7 U.S.C. § 136d(a)(1). See also *McGill v. EPA*, 593 F. 2d 631, 13 ERC 1156 (5th Cir., 1979).

data which users, particularly small farmers or organizations, would need to support a renewal application.[108]

Another problem of standing relates to the right of environmental and consumer groups to utilize the administrative procedures under cancellation-suspension. The act does not specifically give citizens' groups the right to request a public hearing but the administrator himself is now empowered to call a hearing which he might do at the request of such a group. Furthermore, as already discussed, all interested parties may request consent of the administrative law judge to refer scientific questions to a special committee of the National Academy of Sciences for determination, a right which did not exist before.

The issue of standing came up in *Environmental Defense Fund v. Costle*[109] when the D.C. Circuit upheld EPA's denial of standing for an environmental group which requested a Section 6(d) cancellation hearing for the continued use of chlorobenzilate in four states. The Environmental Defense Fund (EDF) requested the hearing after the administrator issued a Notice of Intent to Cancel the registration of chlorobenzilate for all uses other than citrus spraying in four states. The administrator denied the hearing holding that FIFRA was not structured for the purpose of entertaining objections by persons having no real interest in stopping the cancellation from going into effect, but who object to the agency's refusal to propose actions.[110]

The D.C. Circuit upheld the administrator's decision that EDF was not an "adversely affected" party under Section 6(d), stating that a 6(d) hearing may be used only to stop a cancellation proceeding, not initiate one. The proper procedure for EDF in seeking review of EPA's decision to retain the registration for citrus users was to challenge the notice provisions permitting the limited use in district court under Section 16(a) of FIFRA.[111]

6.3 Judicial Appeals

Under the old version of FIFRA,[112] appeals from decisions of the administrator went to the United States court of appeals. According to Section 16 of the amended FIFRA, however, appeals under some circumstances may go to a federal district court.[113] Other appeals go to the court of appeals.

---

[108]A good example is the Aldrin-Dieldrin suspension proceeding, in which the registrant was almost solely interested in the use for crops, while the USDA had to join the proceeding to insure that other registrations were properly represented. This USDA action under the new FIFRA, however, was necessary not because the users now lacked legal standing, but presumably because they lacked adequate resources. *In re Shell Chemical, supra.*, 6 ERC 2047.

[109]631 F.2d 922, 15 ERC 1217 (D.C. Cir., 1980), *cert. denied* 449 U.S. 1112.

[110]Final Decision, FIFRA Docket No. 411 (August 20, 1979) at 12-22.

[111]631 F. 2d at 935, 15 ERC at 1229. This case is also noteworthy for its treatment of judicial review under Section 16(b): See discussion of Judicial Review in 4.2.

[112]Old FIFRA § 4(d).

[113]FIFRA § 16(a)-(c), 7 U.S.C. § 136n(a)-(c).

This change provoked considerable controversy in EPA during the legislative process. The rationale for change was that courts of appeals are not designed to develop a record if none existed from the proceeding below. It thus seemed logical that in those instances where a record was developed, after public hearing or otherwise, the appeal should be to the court of appeals, whereas in cases where there was no record for the court to review, the matter should go to a district court for findings of fact.

Section 16 has been the focus of two courts of appeals decisions which reached contrary holdings on the issue of whether the federal courts or the courts of appeals have jurisdiction to review the denial of a request for a FIFRA Section 6(d) hearing on a notice of cancellation. In *Environmental Defense Fund v. Costle,*[114] the D.C. Circuit Court held that if an administrative record exists in support of a denial of a hearing request, jurisdiction lies exclusively with the courts of appeals. In *AMVAC Chemical Corp. v. EPA,*[115] a divided Ninth Circuit rejected the D.C. Circuit's analysis and held that a denial of a hearing was a procedural action and not an "order" following a "public hearing" within the meaning of Section 16(b). Hence, the court held that judicial review of hearing request denials lies in the district courts.

7.0 LITIGATION ISSUES

The litigation over FIFRA for the last decade has shifted from being concerned with product safety to focusing on data confidentiality and the financial compensation for its use by other companies. That does not necessarily mean that safety is ignored or that all sides have reached consensus on what constitutes a health risk, but that the environmental safety issue is now contested more at the staff level within EPA's Pesticide Office than at the administrator's level or in the courts.

The pesticide industry has focused instead on allocating the tremendously expensive costs of developing and registering the few products that survive the testing process and can be marketed. But for that reason, the judicial doctrines set forth in EPA's first half dozen years remain the basis for pesticide regulation.

7.1 Basic Cases

The early pesticides cases, originating in the period before EPA's creation, generally resulted in court determinations that the responsible federal agency had not sufficiently examined the health and environmental problems.

A leading case in this respect is the landmark 1970 court of appeals decision by Judge Bazelon in *Environmental Defense Fund v. Hardin,*[116] which

---

[114]631 F. 2d 922, 15 ERC 1217 (D.C. Cir., 1980) *cert. denied* 449 U.S. 1112. This case is also important for its treatment of standing, discussed in the previous subsection.

[115]653 F. 2d 1260, 15 ERC 1467 (9th Cir., 1980) as amended February 5, 1981, *reh. denied,* April 10, 1981.

[116]428 F. 2d 1083, 1 ERC 1347 (D.C. Cir., 1970).

not only gave legal standing to environmental groups under the FIFRA but also determined that the Secretary of Agriculture's failure to take prompt action on a request for suspension of the registration of DDT was tantamount to a denial of suspension and therefore was suitable for judicial review.[117]

That same year the Seventh Circuit Court of Appeals held en banc in *Nor-Am v. Hardin*[118] that a pesticide registrant could not enjoin a suspension order by the Secretary of Agriculture, since the administrative remedies, namely the full cancellation proceedings, had not been exhausted: "The emergency suspension becomes final only if unopposed or affirmed in whole or in part, by subsequent decisions based upon a full and formal consideration."[119]

An underlying reason for the court's action, which reversed a three-judge court of appeals panel in the same circuit,[120] was the realization that the suspension procedure, which had been designed to deal with imminent hazards to the public, could effectively be short-circuited by injunctions. In the court's view, therefore, a suspension decision is only equivalent to a temporary injunction which shall hold until the full cancellation proceedings are completed.[121]

One of the most important of the earlier cases was *EDF v. Ruckelshaus*.[122] The court in another opinion by Judge Bazelon found that the Secretary of Agriculture failed to take prompt action on a request for the interim suspension of DDT registration but that the secretary's findings of fact, such as the risk of cancer and its toxic effect on certain animals, implicitly constituted a finding of "substantial question concerning the safety of DDT" which the court declared warranted a cancellation decision. The suspension issue was remanded once again for further consideration.

The decision is worthy of attention on two additional points. First, Judge Bazelon made the sweeping statement that "the FIFRA requires the secretary to issue notices and thereby initiate the administrative process whenever there is a substantial question about the safety of the registered pesticide, . . . The statutory scheme contemplates that these questions will be explored in

---

[117]As there was no administrative record underlying the secretary's inaction, however, the court remanded the issue to the Department of Agriculture "to provide the court with a record necessary for meaningful appellate review."

[118]435 F. 2d 1151, 2 ERC 1016 (7th Cir., en banc, 1970).

[119]*Ibid.*, at 1157, 2 ERC at 1019.

[120]435 F. 2d 1133, 1 ERC 1460 (7th Cir., 1970).

[121]435 F. 2d at 1160-1161.

[122]*EDF v. Ruckelshaus*, 439 F.2d 584, 2 ERC 1114 (D.C. Cir., 1971). This was a sequel to the earlier *EDF v. Hardin* case, supra, but the name of the administrator of EPA was substituted for the Secretary of Agriculture since the authority of USDA had been transferred to the EPA the month before.

the full light of a public hearing and not resolved behind the closed doors of the secretary."[123]

Second, the court approved the findings of the secretary that a hazard may be "imminent" even if its effect would not become realized for many years, as is the case with most carcinogens, and that the "public" protected by the suspension provision includes fish and wildlife in the environment as well as humans.

Wellford v. Ruckelshaus,[124] another case inherited by EPA from USDA, involved a partial remand of the Secretary of Agriculture's decision concerning suspension and cancellation of certain uses of the herbicide 2,4,5-T for use around the home, in aquatic areas, and on food crops. This case is primarily important for its articulation of certain procedural grounds. It agreed with the contention that suspension is only "a matter of interim relief," and stated that the criteria for suspension during an administrative process involved the secretary's first determining "what harm, if any, is likely to flow from the use of the product during the course of administrative proceedings. He must consider both the magnitude of the anticipated harm and the likelihood that it would occur. On the basis of that factual determination, he must decide whether anticipated harm amounts to an 'imminent hazard to the public.' "

7.2 Label Restrictions: Theory and Practice

One of the most interesting pesticide cases, *In re Stearns*,[125] raised the question whether a chemical could be banned that was too toxic to be safely used around the home but which nevertheless was labeled properly with cautionary statements and symbols such as the skull and crossbones. "Stearn's Electric Paste," a phosphorous rat and roach killer, was so potent that even a small portion of a tube could kill a child and a larger dose would be fatal to an adult. There was no known antidote. An incomplete survey conducted by state health officials indicated several dozen deaths and many serious accidents, most involving young children.

Because of this hazard and the existence of safer substitutes, the USDA canceled the registration of the paste in May 1969, before the creation of EPA, and a USDA judicial officer upheld this action in January 1971 by relying on the provision in the old FIFRA that "the term misbranded shall apply. . .to any economic poison. . .if the labeling accompanying it does not contain directions for use which are necessary and, if complied with, adequate for the protection of the public."[126]

---

[123]*Ibid.*, at 594, 2 ERC at 1119. Because there may be a "substantial question of safety" about most pesticides, administrative necessity has forced EPA to interpret this as requiring cancellation of only the most harmful chemicals.

[124]439 F. 2d 598, 2 ERC 1123 (D.C. Cir., 1971).

[125]2 ERC 1364 (Opinion of Judicial Officer, USDA, 1971); *Stearns Electric Paste Company v. EPA*, 461 F. 2d 293, 4 ERC 1164 (7th Cir., 1972).

[126]Old FIFRA § 2(z)2(c).

A year and a half later, however, the Seventh Circuit Court of Appeals concluded that the statutory test for misbranding was whether a product was safe when used in conformity with the label directions, not whether abuse or misuse was inevitable. The court was impressed with the conspicuous "poison" markings and contended that "disregard of such a simple warning would constitute gross negligence."[127] The hazard to young children left the court unmoved: "such tragedies are a common occurrence in today's complex society and must be appraised as discompassionately as possible." The cancellation order was set aside. To put it bluntly, this decision placed much too much emphasis on the label and not on the environmental safety of the product.

The issue was confronted more decisively by the Eighth Circuit a year later in another Lindane case, *Southern National v. EPA.*[128] The registrants challenged a proposed EPA label reading in part, "Not for use or sale to drug stores, supermarkets, or hardware stores or other establishments that sell insecticides to consumers. Not for sale to or use in food handling, processing or serving establishments." In EPA's opinion, acceptance of such a label would avoid the necessity of canceling the entire registration. The court questioned whether EPA was within the scope of its powers under the (old) FIFRA in placing the burden on the manufacturer to discourage distribution to homes, but nevertheless sustained the agency action in all respects.

EPA's policy position, both then and now, is that if there are safer alternatives to a product which arguably gives rise to a substantial question of safety, the hazardous product should be removed from the market.[129]

7.3 Federal Preemption and State Authority

As the name implies, FIFRA is a federal statute. For all pesticides, nationwide, it is EPA that controls registration, labeling, cancellation proceedings, and other regulatory activities. States and local communities, however, are often under strong political pressure from constituents who wish to feel EPA's regulation is adequate. This feeling may be the result of either skepticism about the agency's motives or competence, or of a belief that specific local conditions exist beyond the scope of federal interest.

On the other hand, pesticide manufacturers and applicators fear that hundreds of conflicting local pesticide ordinances will create a regulatory nightmare. Resolution of this conflict requires a political determination by Congress. Unfortunately, Congress has largely avoided the issue; without adequate guidance, therefore, the courts have had to struggle to guess from existing legislation what Congress intended. For that reason, the various inconsistent judicial decisions have created more confusion than they have cleared up.

---

[127]*Stearns Electric Paste, supra.*, 461 F.2d at 310, 4 ERC at 1175.

[128]470 F. 2d 194, 4 ERC 1881 (8th Cir., 1972). This case was decided about a month after the enactment of the new FIFRA on October 21, 1972, but that law was not applied here.

[129]See *In re King Paint*, 2 ERC 1819 (Opinion of EPA Judicial Officer, 1971).

The U.S. Supreme Court has attempted to clarify this muddle. In *Wisconsin Public Intervenor v. Mortier*[130] the court considered a small town ordinance requiring 60 days notice and a permit for applying pesticides on public and some private lands. Warning signs were required to be set up 24 hours before spraying. A pesticide sprayer who was denied a permit sued, contending that the ordinance violated federal and state laws regulating pesticides. The Wisconsin Supreme Court agreed.

The U.S. Supreme Court held unanimously, however, that the local ordinance was not preempted by federal law. States were authorized by FIFRA to regulate certain aspects of pesticide use, said the court, and states may delegate this to their political subdivisions, towns, and municipalities. EPA and the Justice Department, which had traditionally opposed a multiplicity of local regulations on pesticides, altered their positions to support this limitation of preemption.

That case was simple, however, compared to the controversy over the tort consequences of pesticide labels. In short, the question was whether state courts could decide that EPA-approved labels provided the public with inadequate warning of pesticide hazards. After all, states don't have the authority to order labels changes; why should they be allowed to do so indirectly by the threat of tort litigation? The 11th Circuit Court of Appeals held in *Papas*[131] that the states were preempted; the D.C. Court of Appeals in *Ferebee*[132] held that they were not.

The argument in favor of preemption was superior. The Supreme Court, however, had ruled against preemption in a seemingly similar case involving health warnings on cigarette packs.[133] Consequently, when the *Papas* case favoring preemption reached the high court, the justices unanimously overturned the lower court's judgment and remanded the case to the Eleventh Circuit to decide in light of *Cipollone*.[134]

8.0 EXPORTS AND IMPORTS

Section 17 of FIFRA, in addition to maintaining the provision that imports should be subject to the same requirements of testing and registration as domestic products, also retained the controversial provision excluding U.S. exports from coverage under the act other than for certain recordkeeping requirements.[135] The treatment of manufacturing and imports is logical, since potential harm to the environment is not dependent on the origin of the pesticides. The exemption of exports is more

---

[130]111 S.Ct. 2476 (1991).

[131]*Papas v. The Upjohn Company*, 926 F.2d 1819 (11th Cir. 1991).

[132]*Ferebee v. Chevron Chemical Company*, 786 F.2d 1529 (D.C. Cir. 1984), *cert. denied*, 469 U.S. 1062 (1984).

[133]*Cipollone v. Riggett Group*, 112 S.Ct. 2608 (1992).

[134]*Papas v. Zoecon Corporation*, 112 S.Ct. 3020 (1992).

[135]FIFRA § 8, 17(c), 7 U.S.C. § 1360(c). The old FIFRA provisions on exports is § 3(a)(5)(b); FIFRA § 8, 7 U.S.C. § 136 f.

controversial. There were two reasons for this treatment of exports. First, the agricultural chemical producers, seeing the market for some of their products such as the chlorinated hydrocarbons drying up in this country, wished to continue exporting the products abroad. They argued that foreign producers would not be stopped from manufacturing these chemicals and they wished to continue to compete, as well as to keep in operation profitable product lines.

A secondary but more compelling reason was that cancellation decisions made in the United States are based upon a risk-benefit analysis that might have little relevance to conditions abroad. For example, DDT is neither needed nor, because of insect resistance, very useful for the control of malaria in the United States. However, the situation in, say, Ceylon, may be quite different (although resistance is becoming an increasing problem there as well) and should be considered differently.

One objection to this approach is that persistent pesticides may be distributed by oceans and the atmosphere in a worldwide circulation pattern that does not stop at national boundaries. A second problem is that there is no requirement that foreign purchasers relying on EPA registration as proof of a product's safety be notified of cancellation-suspension proceedings. Only after a final agency decision—which may take years—is the State Department legally required to inform foreign governments. The 1978 amendments did add a requirement that such exports be labeled that they are "not registered for use in the U.S."[136]

In 1980, EPA issued a final policy statement on labeling requirements.[137] Under the 1978 amendments, pesticides which are manufactured for export must have bilingual labeling which identifies the product and protects the persons who come into contact with it. If the pesticide is not registered for use in the United States, the exporter must obtain a statement from the foreign purchaser acknowledging its unregistered status.[138]

The policy statement implements these new requirements by requiring exported products to bear labels containing an EPA establishment number, a use classification statement, the identity of the producer, as well as information about whether the pesticide is registered for use in the United States. In the case of highly toxic pesticides, a skull and crossbones must appear and the word "poison" along with a statement of practical treatment written bilingually.[139]

The policy statement also requires that a foreign purchaser of an unregistered pesticide sign a statement showing that he understands that the pesticide is not registered for use in the United States. The exporter must receive the acknowledgment before the product is released for shipment and submit it to EPA within seven days of receipt. EPA then transmits the acknowledg-

---

[136]FIFRA § 17(a)(2), 7 U.S.C. § 136o(e)(f). See also 44 Fed. Reg. 4358 (January 19, 1979).

[137]45 Fed. Reg. 50274 (July 28, 1980).

[138]Pub. L. No. 95-396, 92 Stat 833; codified at 7 U.S.C. § 136(o).

[139]45 Fed. Reg. at 50274, 50278 (July 28, 1980).

ments to the appropriate foreign officials via the State Department. The acknowledgement procedure applies only to the first annual shipment of an unregistered pesticide to a producer; subsequent shipments of the product to the same producer need not comply with the acknowledgment process.[140]

During the FIFRA amendment and farm bill debates in the early 1990s, there was considerable congressional support for much stricter controls on the export of American pesticides which have been banned in the United States or have been rejected or never approved for registration. There are only two in the first category, the related pesticides: termiticides heptachlor and chloradane; reportedly, there are currently about eight chemicals in the second category.

9.0 PESTICIDE REGULATION UNDER OTHER FEDERAL STATUTES

Pesticides are not regulated solely under the FIFRA. They may also involve regulatory authority under the Food, Drug and Cosmetic Act (FDCA), under the statutes of several other federal agencies, and under other environmental laws administered by EPA.

9.1 Pesticides Under the Food, Drug & Cosmetics Act

One important function of EPA regarding pesticides is not derived from the FIFRA—the setting of tolerances for pesticide residues in food. This authority, originally granted to the Food and Drug Administration (FDA) under the Food, Drug and Cosmetic Act (FDCA),[141] was transferred to EPA by the 1970 Reorganization Plan establishing the agency and, more specifically, by subsequent detailed memos of agreement between EPA and FDA.

The reorganization plan provided that EPA should set tolerances and "monitor compliance," while the Secretary of HEW (now HHS) would continue to enforce compliance. The amendments to FIFRA in 1972 also vested EPA with authority to prevent misuse of registered pesticides. Under Section 408 of the FDCA, the administrator issues regulations exempting any pesticides for which a tolerance is unnecessary to protect the public health. Otherwise, he "shall promulgate regulations establishing tolerances with respect to . . . pesticide chemicals which are not generally recognized among experts . . . as safe for use . . . to the extent necessary to protect the public health."

Pesticide residues are present in (mostly) negligible levels in most meats, fruits, and vegetables whether or not chemicals are applied to them. DDT, for example, has been detected in most foods, even in mothers' milk. As analytical chemical methods continue to improve, detection of pesticides in any substance is possible. Before registration of a pesticide, a residue tolerance must be set for the maximum level at which that chemical can be safely ingested. Tolerances are usually set at two orders of magnitude (one hundredth) below the level at which the pesticide has demonstrated an effect

---

[140]*Ibid.*, at 50276-77.

[141]FDCA § 408, 21 U.S.C. § 346a, *et seq.*

on experimental animals.[142] Some particularly hazardous chemicals are set at "zero residue," but this is causing an increasing problem as the detection capability of analytical equipment is improved.

EPA's pesticide jurisdiction is supposed to cover only residues resulting from a chemical's use as a pesticide but not exposure resulting from, say, dust blowing from a factory (this may be covered by EPA's Clean Air Act) or a truck carrying the chemicals. In two major cases involving HCB (hexachlorobenzene) contamination of cattle in Louisiana and sheep in the Rocky Mountains, the HCB was blown from open trucks onto pasture land while being transported from one point to another. EPA assumed responsibility for these cases because the tolerance problems regarding health are really the same whether the chemical entered the food as a result of agricultural use or for some other reason, and FDA was only too glad to oblige.

The question of whether DDT was a food "additive" in fish within the meaning of the FDCA was raised again in *U.S. v. Ewing Bros.*[143] The Seventh Circuit explained that prior to the Delaney Amendment, which banned all additives "found to induce cancer when ingested by man or animal," the term did not cover substances present in the raw product and unchanged by processing, but after 1958 the definition was expanded so a single tolerance could cover both raw and processed foods. Since DDT was an additive and EPA had not issued a tolerance, DDT was theoretically a food adulterant and contaminated items were liable to seizure.[144] This could mean, however, that most foods could be seized as adulterated, including the Great Lakes fish at issue in *Ewing*. Realizing this in 1969, the FDA had established an interim action level of 5 ppm DDT in fish, thereby excluding all but the most contaminated samples.[145] This procedure was approved by the Seventh Circuit Court of Appeals in *U.S. v. Goodman*,[146] which held that the Commissioner of FDA had "specific statutory authority in the Act empowering him to refrain from prosecuting minor violations,"[147] and that this permitted him to set and enforce action levels in lieu of totally prohibiting the distribution of any food containing DDT at any level.

EPA has tried to follow a more reasonable approach than the rigid Delaney Clause requirements of FDA. Indeed, in October 1988, in a new

---

[142]This is an oversimplification. The tolerance margin depends on the particular effects of the chemical.

[143]502 F.2d 715, 6 ERC 2073 (7th Cir., 1974).

[144]Under FDCA § 402(a)(2)(C), 21 U.S.C. § 342(a)(2)(C), this affects only a substance that "is not generally recognized among experts . . . as having been adequately shown . . . to be safe under the conditions of its intended use . . . ." See FDCA § 201(s), 21 U.S.C. § 321(s). Without a tolerance, "the presence of the DDT causes fish to be adulterated without any proof that it is actually unfit as food." 6 ERC 2073, 2077.

[145]Action levels and enforcement, unlike tolerance setting, remain a prerogative of FDA under Section 306 of the FDCA, 21 U.S.C. § 336.

[146]486 F.2d 847, 5 ERC 1969 (7th Cir., 1973).

[147]*Ibid.*, at 855, 5 ERC at 1974; FDCA §306, 21 U.S.C. §336, *U.S. v. 1500 Cases*, 245 F.2d 208, 210-11 (7th Cir., 1956); *U.S. v. 484 Bags*, 423 F.2d 839, 841 (5th Cir., 1970).

interpretation of the Delaney Clause, the EPA issued regulations permitting use of four pesticides which were known carcinogens—benomyl, mancozeb, phosmet and trifluralin—under circumstances which the agency concluded would pose only only a *de minimis* risk of causing cancer.[148] However, a federal appellate court held in *Les v. Reilly*[149] that EPA has no discretion to permit use of food additives, including pesticides, if those additives are known to be carcinogenic, regardless of the degree of risk. The court explained that "once the finding of carcinogenicity is made, the EPA has no discretion."[150] This decision insured that a pesticide that has been found to cause cancer may not be approved for use in food for any purpose. It is true that the decision is faithful to the legislative history of the Delaney Clause. But that 1958 provision is now a regulatory dinosaur. Congress is fearful of changing it without seeming soft on cancer, but the result will be more harsh cases like *Les*.

Recently, the FDA has decided to expand the presumed scope of its authority under the Medical Devices Act of 1976 so as to include disinfectants under "medical devices." These pesticides, which have always been regulated as registered pesticides under FIFRA, have now been subjected to dual jurisdiction. In fact, EPA seems to be uncharacteristically disinterested in retaining authority over this field, even for biocides which have only the faintest connection to medical uses.

9.2 Clean Air Act of 1970

Pesticides in the air may be regulated under Section 112 of the Clean Air Act pertaining to hazardous air pollutants. A hazardous pollutant is defined as one for which "no ambient air quality standard is applicable and which in the judgment of the Administrator may cause, or contribute to, an increase in mortality or an increase in severe irreversible, or incapacitating reversible illness."[151] EPA publishes a list of hazardous air pollutants from time to time, and once a pollutant is listed, proposed regulations establishing stationary source emission standards must be issued unless the substance is conclusively shown to be safe. This section has so far not been applied to pesticides but could acquire more significance in the future.

9.3 Federal Water Pollution Control Act of 1972

The Federal Water Pollution Control Act as amended in 1972 has at least three provisions applicable to pesticides. Under Section 301, pesticide manufacturers and formulators, as with all other industrial enterprises, must apply for discharge permits if they release effluent into any body of water. These point sources of pollution must apply the "best practicable control

---

[148]53 *Fed. Reg.* 41110.
[149]968 F.2d 985 (9th Cir. 1992).
[150]*Ibid*, 988.
[151]Clean Air Act, § 112(a)(1), 42 U.S.C. § 1857c-7(a)(1) (1970).

technology" by 1977 and by 1983 must use "the best available control technology."[152]

Hazardous and ubiquitous pesticides may be controlled under Section 307 governing "toxic substances."[153] Within one year of the listing of a chemical as a "toxic substance," the special discharge standards set for it must be achieved. There was originally some dispute whether pesticides should be regulated under this section, because, unless they are part of a discharge from an industrial concern, they generally derive from non-point sources such as runoff from fields and therefore could be controlled under a third provision, Section 208, which is largely under the jurisdiction of the states.[154]

EPA's principal function under Section 208 is to identify and oversee problems of agricultural pollution regulated at the state and local level. By 1977, according to the statute, state authorities were to have formulated control programs for the protection of water quality, pesticides and other agricultural pollutants such as feed-lots.

The reportedly serious problem of pesticide contamination of groundwater has been hotly debated. Legislation intended to address this issue was considered in the 1988 amendments to FIFRA but deferred to allow the passage of the other portions of that bill.

In January 1991, EPA issued regulations requiring operators of 80,000 drinking water systems to monitor for the presence of 60 contaminants, including a number of pesticides, and remove those in excess of permitted levels.

9.4 Solid Waste Disposal Acts

The EPA had very limited authority under Section 204 of the Solid Waste Disposal Act (SWDA), as amended by the Resource Recovery Act of 1970,[155] to conduct research, training, demonstrations and other activities regarding pesticide storage and disposal.[156] Enactment of the Resource Conservation and Recovery Act (RCRA) in October 1976 gave EPA an important tool for controlling the disposal of pesticides, particularly the waste from pesticide manufacture.

9.5 Occupational Safety and Health Act

The EPA and the Department of Labor share somewhat overlapping authority under FIFRA and the Occupational Safety and Health Act (OSHA) for the protection of agricultural workers from pesticide hazards. This

---

[152]FWPCA § 301, 33 U.S.C. § 1311.

[153]FWPCA § 307, 33 U.S.C. § 1317. The criteria for this list are given in 38 *Fed. Reg.* 18044 (1973).

[154]EPA, however, has not followed this reasoning. The present § 307 list of 299 toxic pollutants contains many of the major pesticides. See *NRDC v. Train* (D.C. Cir., 1976) 8 ERC 2120.

[155]42 U.S.C. § 3251 *et seq.*, 79 Stat. 997 (1965), 84 Stat. 1227 (1970); RCRA § 204, 42 U.S.C. § 3253.

[156]RCRA § 212, 42 U.S.C. 3241. See also RCRA § 209, 42 U.S.C. § 3254c.

produced a heated inter-agency conflict during the first half of 1973, although the FIFRA and its legislative history clearly indicated that EPA had primary responsibility for promulgating "re-entry"[157] and other protective standards in this area, and that OSHA specifically yielded to existing standards by other federal agencies.[158] The question was finally settled by the White House in EPA's favor after a court had enjoined Labor's own proposed standards.[159]

Since then, the two agencies have cooperated on development of the federal cancer policy in the late 1970s, which grew out of EPA's suspension of the pesticides aldrin and dieldrin. Most recently, in 1990, they concluded a memorandum of understanding (MOU) to facilitate joint enforcement of their laws.

9.6 Federal Hazardous Substances Act

The Federal Hazardous Substances Act of 1970 regulates hazardous substances in interstate commerce. However, pesticides subject to the FIFRA and the FDCA have been specifically exempted by regulation[160] from the definition of the term "hazardous substance." This statute is administered by the Consumer Product Safety Commission (CPSC) which also administers the Poison Prevention Packaging Control Act of 1970, designed to protect children from pesticides and other harmful substances. It is not yet clear how EPA and the CPSC will divide their overlapping authority in this area. EPA might welcome the involvement of CPSC in this limited portion of the pesticide area to the extent that its own hands are tied by the court of Appeals decision in the *Stearns Paste* case.[161]

9.7 Federal Pesticide Monitoring Programs

The FDA and USDA assist EPA in monitoring pesticide residues in food. The FDA conducts frequent spot checks and an annual Market Basket Survey in which pesticide residues in a representative sampling of grocery items are analyzed. The FDA's Poison Control Center also compiles current statistics on chemical poisoning. The USDA's Animal and Plant Health Inspection Service conducts spot checks on pesticides in meats and poultry based on samples taken at slaughter houses throughout the country.

The Department of Interior samples pesticide residues in fish and performs experiments to determine the effects of pesticides which may be introduced into the aquatic environment. The Geological Survey Division of Interior also conducts periodic nationwide water sampling for pesticides and other contaminants. The National Oceanic and Atmospheric Administration

---

[157]Re-entry is the required period after pesticide spraying when workers are not allowed to enter the fields.

[158]OSHA § 6, 29 U.S.C. § 655.

[159]*Florida Peach Growers Assn. v. Dept. of Labor*, 489 F. 2d 120, (5th Cir., 1974).

[160]16 C.F.R. § 1500 3(b)(4)(ii).

[161]*U.S. v. Stearns Electric Paste, supra.*

(NOAA) under the Department of Commerce monitors aquatic areas for pesticide levels, and the Department of Transportation's Office of Hazardous Substances records accidents involving pesticides in shipment and distribution.

Several of the FIFRA amendments considered in the early 1990s have been directed toward remedying perceived shortcomings in the pesticide residue system. (See "Legislative Developments" section at end of this chapter.) Unless there is some new evidence of a real need for such legislative protection, this seems to be a solution looking for a problem.

9.8 National Environmental Policy Act

The EPA is not bound by the National Environmental Policy Act (NEPA) to file environmental impact statements on its pesticide decisions. The procedures under the FIFRA are an adequate substitute. Although the strict language of NEPA states that *all* agencies of the federal government should file impact statements, this law was enacted before EPA existed. The courts almost unanimously have found that there is little logic in requiring an agency whose sole function is protection of environment to file a statement obliging it to take into consideration environmental factors.[162] Courts nevertheless hesitated to grant a blanket exemption to EPA, preferring to stress that EPA actions are mandated by a given statute, although this justification has not exempted certain non-environmental agencies; or they have noted that Environmental Protection Agency procedures for articulating its position and providing for public comment were an adequate substitute for the same procedures under NEPA.[163]

10.0 BIOTECHNOLOGY

The field of biotechnology promises great advances in human well being, such as the creation of industrial enzymes which would be capable of, among other things, purifying water and degrading toxic chemical wastes. However, because genetic engineering is so new, still being developed, and little understood, it has been surrounded by controversy over both its safeness and who should regulate it.

On June 18, 1986, former president Reagan signed the Coordinated Framework for Regulation of Biotechnology, which sets out specific agency roles and statutory authority and ensures the industry's environmental safety and economic viability. Legislation has also been proposed in Congress to set up a regulatory structure for reviewing the safety of genetically engineered products under TSCA.

There are some who are not satisfied that the efforts have regulated the biotechnology industry enough. Jeremy Rifkin, who heads the environmental group called Foundation for Economic Trends, is one of the most determined

---

[162]For example, *Essex Chemical Corp. v. Ruckelshaus*, 486 F.2d 427, 5 ERC 1820 (D.C. Cir., 1973), *Portland Cement Assn. v. Ruckelshaus*, 486 F.2d at 375, 5 ERC 1593 (D.C. Cir., 1973).

[163]*EDF v. EPA*, 489 F.2d at 1257, 6 ERC at 1119.

opponents. In fact, he believes that biotechnology should be banned altogether. Most of his attention has focused on biotechnology developments and efforts in the pesticides field.

For example, on September 2, 1986, Rifkin filed suit in the U.S. District Court for the District of Columbia against the Department of Defense (DOD) to enjoin the U.S. military from testing, developing and producing toxic biological warfare materials until the military prepares environmental impact statements. The foundation first sued DOD in November 1984 to prohibit the military from building a proposed biological warfare testing facility in Utah. An injunction was granted in May 1985 and is still in effect.

A landmark case was decided in 1980, which Rifkin lost and which should be mentioned here. In *Diamond v. Chakrobatry*[164] the Supreme Court ruled in June 1980 that genetically altered organisms may be patented. Now when individuals and firms put time and money into biotechnology research they can be assured of earning economic rewards. Rifkin's foundation has filed a "friend of the court" brief supporting the U.S. Attorney General's office in its contention that the federal patent laws should not cover such organisms.

In May 1986, EPA authorized the first permits for the release of a genetically engineered pesticide to a professor from the University of California at Berkeley. The genetically altered bacteria strain, known as "ice-minus" or "Frostban," was developed by the university and licensed by Advanced Genetic Sciences, Inc. (AGS).[165]

The court held that this standard required the administrator to examine five factors: (1) the seriousness of the threatened harm; (2) the immediacy of the threatened harm; (3) the probability that the threatened harm would result; (4) the benefits to the public of the continued use of the pesticides in question during the suspension process; and (5) the nature and extent of the information before the administrator at the time he makes his decision. The court also held that an emergency suspension order might be overturned only if it was arbitrary, capricious, or an abuse of discretion or if it was not "issued in accordance with the procedures established by law."[166]

In August 1990 a blue-ribbon panel under the direction of Vice President Dan Quayle concluded that biotech products should be treated no differently from those produced by conventional chemical methods. These risk-based principles, for use by EPA, USDA, FDA, and others, were not much different from those currently in use for FIFRA. In other words, only the end-product is relevant; how it was produced, whether by biochemists or by bacteria, should be irrelevant.

---

[164]100 S.Ct. 2204, 447 U.S. 303.

[165]*Ibid.* at 902, 13 ERC at 1135.

[166]*Ibid.* The court stated that it arrived at its decision to uphold EPA's order "with great reluctance" and would not have ordered the emergency suspension on the basis of the information before EPA, but was not empowered to substitute its judgment for that of EPA's. 469 F. Supp. at 907, 13 ERC at 1140.

The principles are as follows:

1. Federal government regulatory oversight should focus on the characteristics and risks of the biotechnology product not the process by which it is created.

2. For biotechnology products that require review, regulatory review should be designed to minimize regulatory burden while assuring protection of public health and welfare.

3. Regulatory programs should be designed to accommodate the rapid advances in biotechnology. Performance-based standards are, therefore, generally preferred over design standards.

4. In order to create opportunities for the application of innovative new biotechnology products, all regulation in environmental and health areas, whether or not they address biotechnology, should use performance standards rather than specifying rigid controls or specific designs for compliance.[167]

11.0 CONCLUSION

Two decades of amendments to FIFRA have produced no coherent pattern of improvements to the basic statute. Unlike most other environmental statutes, there has been no clear progress towards greater protection (some amendments, in the 1970s, even went the other way). Those that were more protective in theory have not proved very effective.

That record has not discouraged a host of senators and congressmen from offering amendments to the stalled FIFRA reauthorization bill. Two influential members, Sen. Ted Kennedy (D-Mass.) and Rep. Henry Waxman (D-Calif.), have offered legislation to tighten the pesticide residue portion of the Food, Drug and Cosmetic Act (FDA Act). Reviving the issue of efficacy which EPA has minimized until recently, Sen. Paul Sarbanes (D-Maryland) wants to require that EPA test pesticides to verify the claims in their registration applications.

Rep. Terry Bruce (D-Ill.) has also focused on pesticide tolerances, but he also sought to truncate the cancellation process. Rep. Charles Rose (D-N.C.) has offered his own bill to ease cancellation, but he also has favored speeding up the pokey registration process. Sen. Joseph Lieberman (D-Conn.) has offered a bill requiring that the cancellation process be completed within two years.

The major policy issues in FIFRA have not been entirely neglected. To change the present provisions allowing export of cancelled pesticides, Sen. Patrick Leahy (D-Vt.) submitted an amendment in the last Congress. Rep. Rose, mentioned above, has sought to limit local regulation of pesticides to those on the state-wide level.

---

[167]BNA Chemical Reporter, 17 August 1990, 788.

Not one of these bills amending FIFRA was offered by a Republican. With a Democratic president and a Democratic-controlled Congress, the prospects for a significant revision of FIFRA, for good or ill, have increased.

For a more definitive discussion of this topic, the reader is referred to the related books and courses listed at the end of this book.

Chapter 14

EMERGENCY PLANNING AND
COMMUNITY RIGHT-TO-KNOW ACT

Wayne T. Halbleib
Mays & Valentine
Richmond, Virginia

1.0 OVERVIEW

On October 17, 1986, the Superfund Amendments and Reauthorization Act of 1986 (SARA) was signed into law. One part of the SARA legislation is Title III, otherwise known as the "Emergency Planning and Community Right-To-Know Act of 1986" (EPCRA). EPCRA requires states to establish a process for developing local chemical emergency preparedness programs and to receive and disseminate information on hazardous chemicals present at facilities within local communities.

EPCRA has four major components: (1) emergency planning (Sections 301-303); (2) emergency release notification (Section 304); (3) community right-to-know reporting (Sections 311-312); and (4) toxic chemical release inventory reporting (Section 313). Each component has its own facility and chemical substance reporting requirements. The information submitted by facilities under these four reporting requirements allows states and local communities to develop a broad perspective of chemical hazards for the entire community as well as for individual facilities.

2.0 EMERGENCY PLANNING

Section 301 of EPCRA requires the governor of each state to designate a State Emergency Response Commission (SERC). The SERC is required to designate emergency planning districts within each state to facilitate the preparation and implementation of the emergency plans required under Section 303. In addition, Section 301 requires the SERC to appoint a local emergency planning committee (LEPC) in each of those districts.[1]

2.1 Covered Facilities and Substances

Section 302 of EPCRA requires any facility that produces, uses or stores any of the substances on the U.S. Environmental Protection Agency's (EPA) List of Extremely Hazardous Substances in quantities equal to or greater than the threshold planning quantity established for each substance to notify the

---

[1] *See*, 42 U.S.C.A. § 11001(a)-(c).

SERC.[2] A list of the extremely hazardous substances and their threshold planning quantities is contained in the EPA's *Title III List of Lists*. [3]

If a facility is covered by Section 302, the owner or operator of the facility should have notified the SERC by May 17, 1987, that the facility is subject to the emergency planning requirements. After May 17, 1987, the owner or operator must notify the SERC and the LEPC, within 60 days, if an extremely hazardous substance (EHS) becomes present at the facility in a quantity that equals or exceeds the established threshold planning quantity.[4]

A covered facility must designate a facility representative who will participate in the local emergency planning process as a facility emergency response coordinator. In addition, the facility owner or operator must submit additional information to the LEPC upon request and notify the LEPC of any changes occurring at the facility which may be relevant to emergency planning (for example, change in person designated as facility emergency response coordinator; any material change in the inventory of EHS's maintained by the facility).[5]

2.2 Comprehensive Emergency Response Plans

Each LEPC is responsible for reviewing the information submitted by facilities covered by the emergency planning requirements and developing a plan to respond to local hazardous chemical emergency releases.[6] The local emergency response plan must address the following:[7]

1. Identify all the facilities subject to the emergency planning requirements within the emergency planning district;
2. Identify all routes within the emergency planning district used to transport extremely hazardous substances;
3. Identify all risk-related facilities near covered facilities, such as natural gas facilities, power stations/high transmission towers, or schools or hospitals, within the emergency planning district;
4. Describe the methods and procedures that will be followed by emergency response personnel to respond to a chemical release within the emergency planning district;
5. Designate the community emergency response coordinator and identify all the facility emergency response coordinators within the emergency planning district;
6. Describe the emergency notification procedures to be used to notify the public of a chemical release and the evacuation plans to be implemented in the event a chemical emergency requires an evacuation;

---

[2] *See*, 42 U.S.C.A. § 11002(b)-(c); 40 C.F.R. § 355.30.

[3] *See*, EPA's Title III List of Lists, Document No. EPA 560/4-92-011 or Appendix A or Appendix B to 40 C.F.R. Part 355.

[4] *See*, 42 U.S.C.A. § 11002(c); 40 C.F.R. § 355.30(b).

[5] *See*, 42 U.S.C.A. § 11003(d); 40 C.F.R. § 355.30(c) and (d).

[6] *See*, 42 U.S.C.A. § 11003.

[7] *See*, 42 U.S.C.A. § 11003(c).

7. Specify the methods for determining whether a chemical release has occurred and the probable affected area and population;

8. List all community and facility emergency equipment or facilities available and their location as well as the persons responsible for them; and

9. Describe the training program used to train emergency response personnel for chemical emergencies and list a schedule for exercising the emergency response plan within the emergency planning district.

Although the primary responsibility for emergency planning rests with the LEPC, the SERC must review each local chemical emergency response plan. The SERC must review each plan to determine whether all required plan elements have been included. In addition, the SERC's review will include recommendations to the LEPC on revisions to the plan that may be necessary to ensure coordination of the plan with the emergency response plans of other emergency planning districts.[8]

3.0 EMERGENCY RELEASE NOTIFICATION

3.1 Covered Releases

Under Section 304 of EPCRA, the owner or operator of a facility which either produces, uses or stores a hazardous chemical must immediately notify the SERC and the LEPC if there is a release of a listed hazardous substance that is not federally permitted and which exceeds the reportable quantity (RQ) established for that substance and results in exposure to persons off-site.[9] Substances subject to this notification requirement include substances on the EPA's List of EHS's and hazardous substances subject to the emergency notification requirements under Section 103(a) of the Comprehensive Environmental Response, Compensation and Liability Act of 1980 (CERCLA).[10]

3.2 Notification Requirements

The initial notification of a release can be made by telephone, radio or in person. The owner or operator of a covered facility must immediately notify the community emergency coordinator for the LEPC of any area likely to be affected by the release and the SERC of any state likely to be affected by the release.[11] In addition, when there is a reportable release of a CERCLA-listed hazardous substance, notification must be given to the National Response Center (NRC) in Washington, D.C. at 1-800-424-8802.[12] The notifications made under EPCRA are in addition to the notifications normally made to local emergency response or fire personnel.

---

[8] *See*, 42 U.S.C.A. § 11003(e).

[9] *See*, 40 C.F.R. § 355.40(a).

[10] *Ibid*.

[11] *See*, 40 C.F.R. § 355.40(b).

[12] *See*, 40 C.F.R. § 302.6(a).

3.3 Contents of Notice

The emergency notification must include the following information to the extent known at the time of the release:[13]

1. Chemical name of the substance involved;
2. Indication of whether it is an extremely hazardous substance;
3. Estimate of the amount released into the environment;
4. Time and duration of the release;
5. Environmental media into which the release occurred;
6. Known or anticipated acute or chronic health risks associated with the release and advice regarding medical attention necessary for exposed individuals;
7. Proper precautions to be taken as a result of the release, including evacuation; and
8. Name and telephone number of a person at the facility to be contacted for further information.

3.4 Written Follow-up Emergency Notice

Section 304 further requires that the owner or operator of a covered facility provide a written follow-up emergency notice as soon as possible after the release.[14] The notice must be sent to the appropriate SERC(s) and the appropriate LEPC(s). The follow-up notice must include the following information:[15]

1. An update of the information included in the initial release notification;
2. Information on actions taken to respond to and contain the release;
3. Any known or anticipated acute or chronic health risks associated with the release; and
4. Where appropriate, advice regarding medical attention for exposed individuals.

The written follow-up notice must be sent to the appropriate SERC(s) and the appropriate LEPC(s).

3.5 Transportation-Related Releases

The owner or operator of a facility from which there is a transportation-related release can satisfy the emergency release notification requirements under Section 304 by providing the above-mentioned information required during the initial notification to the 911 operator, or in the absence of a 911 emergency telephone, providing such information to the operator.[16] A "transportation-related release" includes a release during transportation, or

---

[13]*See,* 40 C.F.R. § 355.40(b)(2).
[14]*See,* 42 U.S.C.A. § 11004(c); 40 C.F.R. § 355.40(b)(3).
[15]*Ibid.*
[16]*See* 42 U.S.C.A. § 11004(b)(1); 40 C.F.R. § 355.40(b)(4)(ii).

storage incident to transportation if the stored substance is moving under active shipping papers and has not reached the ultimate consignee.[17]

3.6 Continuous Release Reporting

Reporting requirements for "continuous" releases of hazardous substances under CERCLA were issued by the EPA on July 24, 1990. Under the final rule, which became effective on September 24, 1990, releases that qualify as "continuous" and that are "stable in quantity and rate" are subject to reduced reporting under CERCLA § 103(f)(2).[18]

The final rule defines "continuous" broadly to include a "release that occurs without interruption or abatement or that is routine, anticipated, and intermittent and incidental to normal operations or treatment processes." The definition of "stable in quantity and rate" includes a "release that is predictable and regular in amount and rate of emission."[19]

3.7 Continuous Release Notification

The new rule requires a minimum of one telephone call to the NRC under CERCLA § 103(a) and to the appropriate SERC(s) and LEPC(s) under EPCRA § 304. In addition, within 30 days of the initial telephone notification, an initial written notification must be made to the appropriate EPA Regional Office, the appropriate SERC(s), and the appropriate LEPC(s).

3.8 Initial Telephone Notification

To satisfy the initial telephone notification requirement, the person in charge of a facility or vessel must identify the release in the telephone call to the NRC, the appropriate SERC(s), and the appropriate LEPC(s) as a report under CERCLA § 103(f)(2) of a continuous release above the RQ.[20] The following information must be provided for each release:[21]

1. The name and location of the facility or vessel; and
2. The name(s) and identity(ies) of the hazardous substance(s) being released.

3.9 Initial Written Report

The initial written report must include the following information:[22]

1. The name of the facility or vessel; the location, including the longitude and latitude; the case number assigned by the NRC or the EPA; the Dun & Bradstreet number of the facility, if available; the port of registration of the vessel; the name and telephone number of the person in charge of the facility or vessel.

---

[17]*See*, 40 C.F.R. § 355.40(b)(4)(ii).
[18]*See*, 55 Fed.Reg. 30185 (July 24, 1990); 40 C.F.R. § 302.8.
[19]*See*, 40 C.F.R. § 302.8(b).
[20]*See*, 40 C.F.R. § 302.8(d)(3).
[21]*See*, 40 C.F.R. § 302.8(d)(3)(i)-(ii).
[22]*See*, 40 C.F.R. § 302.8(e)(1).

2. The population density within a one-mile radius of the facility or vessel, described in terms of the following ranges: 0-50 persons; 51-100 persons; 101-500 persons; 501-1,000 persons; more than 1,000 persons.

3. The identity and location of sensitive populations and ecosystems within a one-mile radius of the facility or vessel (for example elementary schools, hospitals, retirement communities, or wetlands).

4. The name/identity of the hazardous substance; the Chemical Abstracts Service (CAS) Registry Number for the substance, if available. If the substance being released is a mixture, the components of the mixture and their approximate concentrations and quantities by weight.

5. The upper and lower bounds of the normal range of the release (in pounds or kilograms) over the previous year.

6. The source(s) of the release (for example, valves, pump seals, storage tank vents, stacks). If the source is a stack, the stack height (in feet or meters).

7. The frequency of the release and the fraction of the release from each release source and the specific period over which it occurs.

8. A brief statement describing the basis for stating that the release is continuous and stable in quantity and rate.

9. An estimate of the total annual amount of the hazardous substance that was released in the previous year (in pounds or kilograms).

10. The environmental media affected by the release:
    a. If surface water, the name of the surface water body.
    b. If a stream, the stream order or average flowrate (in cubic feet/second) and designated use.
    c. If a lake, the surface area (in acres) and average depth (in feet or meters).
    d. If on or under ground, the location of public water supply wells within two miles.

11. A signed statement that the hazardous substance release(s) described is(are) continuous and stable in quantity and rate and that all reported information is accurate and current to the best knowledge of the person in charge.

3.10 Follow-up Notification

Within 30 days of the first anniversary date of the initial written notification, the person in charge must evaluate the reported releases and submit a one-time follow-up report to the appropriate EPA Regional Office. The purpose of this report is to verify or update the information submitted in the initial written report.[23]

---

[23]*See*, 40 C.F.R. § 302.8(f).

3.11 Annual Evaluation of Continuous Releases

After the submission of the follow-up report, the person in charge must reevaluate annually each reported hazardous substance release within 30 days of the anniversary date of the initial written notification to determine whether there have been changes in the release that require modification of the information previously submitted.[24] Each annual evaluation must be documented, but no annual report or notification of the annual evaluation is required. Notification subsequent to the written follow-up report must be made to the appropriate EPA Regional Office only if there is a change in any of the information submitted previously.[25]

3.12 Change in the Composition or Source of the Release

If there is a change in the composition or source(s) of the release, the release is considered a "new" release. To qualify a "new" release for reduced reporting under CERCLA § 103(f)(2), both the initial telephone notification and the initial written notification must be made. The initial telephone notification should be made as soon as there is a sufficient basis for asserting that the "new" release is continuous and stable in quantity and rate.[26]

3.13 Notification of a Statistically Significant Increase

A "statistically significant increase" must be reported immediately by telephone to the NRC, the appropriate SERC(s) and the appropriate LEPC(s). A statistically significant increase in a release is defined as "an increase in the quantity of the hazardous substance released above the upper bound of the reported normal range of the release."[27] The normal range is defined to include all releases of a hazardous substance reported or occurring during any 24-hour period under normal operating conditions during the previous year.[28]

Because such a release is considered episodic, it must be reported under CERCLA § 103(a) and EPCRA § 304(b). The release must be identified by the person in charge as a statistically significant increase in a continuous release. The written follow-up emergency notice required under § 304 of EPCRA must also be made to the appropriate SERC(s) and LEPC(s) after the initial telephone notification of a statistically significant increase.[29]

3.14 Changes in Other Reported Information

If there is a change in any information submitted in the initial written notification or the follow-up notification other than a change in the source, composition, or quantity of the release, the person in charge of the facility or vessel must provide written notification of the change to the appropriate

---

[24] *See*, 40 C.F.R. § 302.8(i).
[25] *See*, 40 C.F.R. § 302.8(g).
[26] *See*, 40 C.F.R. § 302.8(g)(1).
[27] *See*, 40 C.F.R. § 302.8(b).
[28] *Ibid.*
[29] *See*, 40 C.F.R. § 355.40(b).

EPA Regional Office within 30 days of determining that the information submitted previously is no longer valid.[30]

3.15 Use of the EPCRA Section 313 Form

In lieu of an initial written report or a follow-up report on a continuous release, owners or operators of facilities subject to the EPCRA Section 313 reporting requirements can submit to the appropriate EPA Regional Office, a copy of the relevant Toxic Chemical Release Inventory Reporting Form submitted to EPA the previous July 1. If this option is selected, however, facility owners or operators must submit the following additional information:[31]

1. The population density within a one-mile radius of the facility or vessel, described in terms of the following ranges: 0-50 persons; 51-100 persons; 101-500 persons; 501-1,000 persons; more than 1,000 persons;

2. The identity and location of sensitive populations and ecosystems within a one-mile radius of the facility or vessel (for example, elementary schools, hospitals, retirement communities, or wetlands);

3. The upper and lower bounds of the normal range of the release (in pounds or kilograms) over the previous year;

4. The frequency of the release and the fraction of the release from each release source and the specific period over which it occurs;

5. A brief statement describing the basis for stating that the release is continuous and stable in quantity and rate; and

6. A signed statement that the hazardous substance release(s) is(are) continuous and stable in quantity and rate and that all reported information is accurate and current to the best knowledge of the person in charge.

The person in charge can rely on recent release data, engineering estimates, the operating history of the facility or vessel, or other relevant information, including best professional judgment, to support notification. All supporting documents, materials, and other information shall be kept on file at the facility, or in the case of a vessel, at an office within the United States in either a port of call, a place of regular berthing, or the headquarters of the business operating the vessel. Supporting materials must be kept on file for one year. These materials must be made available to the EPA upon request.[32]

4.0 COMMUNITY RIGHT-TO-KNOW REPORTING

There are two community right-to-know reporting requirements contained within Sections 311 and 312 of EPCRA. Facilities covered under Section 311 are covered also under Section 312.

---

[30]*See*, 40 C.F.R. § 302.8(g)(3).

[31]*See*, 40 C.F.R. § 302.8(j).

[32]*See*, 40 C.F.R. § 302.8(k).

4.1 MSDS/List of Hazardous Chemicals

Section 311 requires the owner/operator of a facility which must prepare or have available material safety data sheets (MSDS's) under OSHA's Hazard Communication Standard regulations to submit either copies of its MSDS's or a list of hazardous chemicals to the SERC, the LEPC and the local fire department (LFD) with jurisdiction over the facility.[33] Most SERCs either require or encourage owners or operators of covered facilities to submit a "list" of hazardous chemicals grouped by health and physical hazard categories as defined by EPA in lieu of submitting the MSDS on each hazardous chemical.

4.1.1 Submission of a List of Hazardous Chemicals

If the facility owner or operator elects to submit a list of hazardous chemicals, the list must include the chemical or common name of each substance and it must identify the applicable hazard categories. The hazard categories are as follows:

1. *Immediate (acute) health hazard* (which includes the OSHA health hazard categories: "highly toxic," "toxic," "corrosive," "irritant," and "sensitizer");

2. *Delayed (chronic) health hazard* (which includes the OSHA-defined "carcinogen");

3. *Fire hazard* (which includes the OSHA physical hazard categories: "combustible liquid," "flammable," "oxidizer," and "pyrophoric");

4. *Sudden release of pressure hazard* (which includes the OSHA physical hazard categories: "compressed gas," and "explosive"); and

5. *Reactive hazard* (which includes the OSHA physical hazard categories: "organic peroxide," "unstable reactive," and "water reactive"). [34]

If the facility elects to submit a list, it must submit a copy of the MSDS for any chemical on the list upon the request of the SERC or the LEPC within 30 days of the receipt of such request.[35] EPA has established minimum threshold quantities for reporting hazardous chemicals present at a facility. The threshold levels are as follows:

1. "Hazardous chemicals" present in amounts equal to or greater than 10,000 pounds; and

2. "Extremely hazardous substances" present in amounts equal to or greater than 500 pounds or the threshold planning quantity established for the substance, whichever is lower.

4.1.2 Reporting Requirements

The owners or operators of facilities subject to the reporting requirements under Section 311 had until October 17, 1990 to submit the

---

[33]*See, also,* 40 C.F.R. § 370.21.

[34]*See,* 40 C.F.R. § 370.2.

[35]*See,* 40 C.F.R. § 370.21(d).

required information. The owners or operators of new facilities (that is, those opening after October 17, 1990) that are covered by the OSHA regulations must submit MSDS's or a list of MSDS chemicals within three months after they first become subject to the OSHA regulations.[36]

The owner or operator of a covered facility must provide within three months either MSDS's or a revised list of MSDS chemicals when new hazardous chemicals become present at a facility in quantities at or above the established threshold levels after the deadline.[37] The owner or operator of a covered facility must provide a revised MSDS within three months after discovery of significant new information concerning the hazardous chemical.[38]

4.1.3 Mixture Reporting

The vast majority of chemicals subject to reporting under Section 311 will be mixtures. The owner or operator of a covered facility has two options with respect to reporting hazardous mixtures. The first option is to provide the required information on the mixture itself. The second option is to provide the required information on each component in the mixture which is a hazardous chemical.[39]

The above-mentioned threshold levels apply to the *total quantity* of either the hazardous mixture, or each hazardous component that is present, at the facility at any time during the preceding calendar year. A hazardous component of a mixture which is present in an amount greater than 1% of the mixture (or 0.1% if carcinogenic) must be included when calculating the total quantity of the chemical subject to reporting.

The regulations require the owner or operator of a covered facility to *aggregate* (that is, total) each extremely hazardous substance, whether it is present as a mixture component, or in its pure form, to determine whether the reporting threshold for an extremely hazardous substance has been met.[40] Aggregation of hazardous chemicals that are not extremely hazardous substances present in mixtures and in their pure form is not required, but may be done if a facility is reporting all hazardous chemicals in mixtures by component.

Once the determination is made that an extremely hazardous substance must be reported, the owner or operator of the facility has the option of reporting the extremely hazardous substance separately, as a component of one or several different mixtures, or reporting the mixture(s) as a whole.[41]

4.2 Tier One/Tier Two Reporting

Section 312 requires the owner or operator of a covered facility to submit an emergency and hazardous chemical inventory form to the VERC, the

---

[36]*See*, 55 Fed. Reg. 30646 (July 26, 1990); 40 C.F.R § 370.20(b)(1).

[37]*See*, 40 C.F.R. § 370.21(c)(2).

[38]*See*, 40 C.F.R. § 370.21(c)(1).

[39]*See*, 40 C.F.R. § 370.28(a).

[40]*See*, 55 Fed. Reg. 30646 (July 26, 1990); 40 C.F.R § 370.28(c)(1).

[41]*See*, 40 C.F.R. § 370.28(c)(2).

LEPC and the LFD. The hazardous chemicals covered by Section 312 are the same chemicals for which facilities are required to submit MSDS's or a list of MSDS chemicals under Section 311. In addition, the threshold levels established for reporting under Section 312 are the same as those established for reporting under Section 311.[42]

The inventory form incorporates a two-tier approach. Under Tier One, the owner or operator of a covered facility must submit for each health and physical hazard category the following aggregate information:

1. An estimate (in ranges) of the maximum amount of hazardous chemicals for each category present at the facility at any time during the preceding calendar year;
2. An estimate (in ranges) of the average daily amount of hazardous chemicals in each category; and
3. The general location of hazardous chemicals in each category.

Tier One information must be submitted on or before March 1st of the first year after a covered facility becomes subject to the reporting. The owner or operator of a covered facility is required to submit the Tier One information every year on or before March 1st.[43]

The public may also request additional information on specific facilities from the SERC or the LEPC. In addition, upon the request of the SERC, the LEPC or the LFD, the facility must provide for each substance covered by the request the following information:

1. The chemical name or the common name of the chemical and the CAS registry number as provided on the MSDS;
2. An indication of whether the hazardous chemical is an extremely hazardous substance;
3. An indication of whether the hazardous chemical is present at the facility in its pure state or in a mixture and whether it is a solid, liquid or gas;
4. The applicable health and physical hazard categories;
5. An estimate (in ranges) of the maximum amount of the hazardous chemical present at the facility at any time during the preceding calendar year;
6. An estimate (in ranges) of the average daily amount of the hazardous chemical present at the facility during the preceding calendar year;
7. The number of days the hazardous chemical was found on-site at the facility;
8. A brief description of the manner of storage of the hazardous chemical at the facility;
9. A brief description of the precise location of the hazardous chemical at the facility; and

---

[42]*See,* 40 C.F.R. § 370.20(b).
[43]*See,* 40 C.F.R. § 370.20(b)(2).

10. An indication of whether the owner or operator of the facility elects to withhold location information on a specific hazardous chemical from disclosure to the public.

This information is usually submitted as a Tier Two report. A covered facility may submit a Tier Two report to the SERC, the LEPC and the LFD in lieu of the Tier One report. EPA published a uniform format for the inventory forms on July 26, 1990.[44] The Tier Two report is preferred by most SERCs, LEPCs, and LFDs because of the chemical specific information it contains.

If the owner or operator of a covered facility elects to withhold location information on a specific chemical from disclosure to the public, the facility owner or operator must complete a separate Tier Two Confidential Location Information Sheet. When the Tier Two submissions are made, the Tier Two Confidential Location Information Sheet(s) must be attached to the Tier Two Inventory Form. The information contained on the Tier Two Confidential Location Information Sheet(s) is not subject to public disclosure.

5.0 TOXIC CHEMICAL RELEASE INVENTORY REPORTING

Section 313 of EPCRA requires the owners or operators of certain manufacturing facilities to submit annual reports on the amounts of listed "toxic chemicals" their facilities release into the environment, either routinely or as a result of an accident. The owners or operators of facilities subject to this reporting requirement must report releases to the air, water and land as well as discharges to publicly owned treatment works (POTWs) and transfers to off-site locations for proper treatment, storage, or disposal. The initial reports were required to be submitted to EPA and a designated state official on or before July 1, 1988, and annually thereafter on July 1st, reflecting releases during each preceding calendar year.

5.1 Reporting Requirements

The Section 313 reporting requirement applies to owners and operators of facilities that are in Standard Industrial Classification (SIC) Codes 20 through 39 (see Table 1 on the following page); that have ten or more full-time employees; and that manufacture, import, process or otherwise use a listed toxic chemical in excess of established threshold quantities.[45]

A "full-time employee," for purposes of Section 313 reporting, is defined as 2,000 hours per year of full-time equivalent employment. This definition is dependent *only* upon the number of hours worked by all employees at the facility during the calendar year and *not* the number of persons working. A facility must calculate the number of full-time employees by totaling the hours worked during the calendar year by all employees, including contract employees, and dividing that total by 2,000 hours.[46] If the total number of

---

[44]*See*, 55 *Fed. Reg*. 30632 (July 26, 1990); 40 C.F.R. §§ 370.40 and 370.41.

[45]*See*, 40 C.F.R. § 372.65(a) for a list of the chemicals subject to reporting under section 313.

[46]*See*, 40 C.F.R. § 372.3.

TABLE 1
TRI INDUSTRY CATEGORIES

SIC Code	Industry
20	Food and Kindred Products
21	Tobacco Products
22	Textile Mill Products
23	Apparel and Other Finished Products Made from Fabrics
24	Lumber and Wood Products
25	Furniture and Fixtures
26	Paper and Allied Products
27	Printing, Publishing and Allied Industries
28	Chemicals and Allied Products
29	Petroleum Refining and Related Industries
30	Rubber and Miscellaneous Plastic Products
31	Leather and Leather Products
32	Stone, Clay, Glass and Concrete Products
33	Primary Metal Industries
34	Fabricated Metal Products
35	Industrial and Commercial Machinery and Computer Equipment
36	Electronic and Other Electrical Equipment and Components
37	Transportation Equipment
38	Measuring, Analyzing, and Controlling Instruments; Photographic, Medical and Optical Goods; Watches and Clocks
39	Miscellaneous Manufacturing

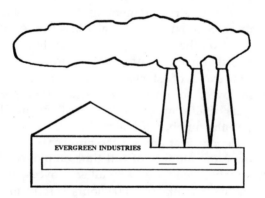

EVERGREEN INDUSTRIES

hours worked by *all* employees is 20,000 hours or more, the facility meets the ten employee threshold.

Section 313 requires that reports be filed by the owners or operators of "facilities" which are defined as "all buildings, equipment, structures, and other stationary items which are located on a single site or on contiguous or adjacent sites and which are owned or operated by the same person." The SIC code system, however, classifies business "establishments," which are defined as "distinct and separate economic activities [that] are performed at a single physical location." Many facilities may include multiple establishments that have different primary SIC codes. Such facilities should calculate the *value* of the products produced or shipped from each establishment within the facility and determine whether the facility meets the SIC code criteria by using the following rules:

1. If the total value of the products shipped from or produced at establishments with primary SIC codes between 20 and 39 is greater than 50 percent of the value of the entire facility's products and services, the entire facility meets the SIC code criteria; and

2. If any one establishment with a primary SIC code between 20 and 39 produces or ships products whose value exceeds the value of products and services produced or shipped by any other establishment within the facility, the facility meets the SIC code criteria.[47]

The term "manufacture" means to produce, prepare, compound, or import a listed toxic chemical. The term "manufacture" also includes coincidental production of a toxic chemical (for example, as a by-product or impurity) as a result of the manufacture, processing, use, or treatment of other chemical substances.[48] In the case of coincidental production of an *impurity* (that is, a chemical that remains in the product that is distributed in commerce), the *de minimis* limitation applies. Thus, if a listed toxic chemical is present as an impurity in a concentration of 1 percent (0.1% if the listed toxic chemical is a carcinogen) or less, the quantity of that chemical need not be considered for purposes of determining whether a reporting threshold has been met.[49]

The *de minimis* limitation does *not* apply to the coincidental production of a by-product (for example, a chemical that is separated from a process stream and further processed or disposed). Certain listed toxic chemicals may be manufactured as a result of wastewater treatment or other treatment processes. For example, neutralization of nitric acid wastewater with ammonia can result in the coincidental manufacture of ammonium nitrate solution as a by-product. Thus, if the ammonium nitrate solution is produced in a quantity that exceeds the applicable threshold, the facility must report for ammonium nitrate solution.

---

[47]*See*, 40 C.F.R. § 372.22.
[48]*See*, 40 C.F.R. § 372.3.
[49]*See*, 40 C.F.R. § 372.38.

The term "import" is defined as causing the listed toxic chemical to be imported into the customs territory of the United States.[50] When a facility orders a listed toxic chemical (or a mixture containing the chemical) from a foreign supplier, then the facility has imported the chemical when that shipment arrives at the facility directly from a source outside of the United States.

The term "process" means the preparation of a listed toxic chemical, after its manufacture, for distribution in commerce. Processing is usually the intentional incorporation of a toxic chemical into a product. Processing includes preparation of the chemical in the same physical state or chemical form as that received by the facility, or preparation that produces a change in physical state or chemical form. The term also applies to the processing of a mixture or other trade name product that contains a listed toxic chemical as one component.[51]

The term "process" would include use of the listed toxic chemical as (1) a reactant; (2) a formulation component; or (3) a component of an article distributed for industrial, trade, or consumer use. The term "process" also would include the repackaging of a listed toxic chemical for distribution in commerce in a different form, state, or quantity.

The term "otherwise use" encompasses any use of a listed toxic chemical at a facility that is not covered under the definitions of "manufacture" or "process."[52] A chemical that is otherwise used by a facility is *not* intentionally incorporated into a product distributed in commerce. The term "otherwise use" would include use of the listed toxic chemical as (1) a cleaner; (2) a degreaser; (3) a fuel; (4) a lubricant; (5) a chemical used for treating waste; (6) a chemical processing aid (for example, process solvents, catalysts, inhibitors, initiators, reaction terminators, and solution buffers); or (7) as a manufacturing aid (for example, process lubricants, metalworking fluids, coolants, refrigerants, and hydraulic fluids).

5.2 Exemptions

Certain uses of listed toxic chemicals are specifically exempted: (1) use as a structural component of the facility; (2) use of products for routine janitorial or facility grounds maintenance, provided the product is similar in type or concentration to consumer products; (3) personal uses by employees or other persons at the facility of foods, drugs, cosmetics, or other personal items containing listed toxic chemicals; (4) use of products containing toxic chemicals for the purpose of maintaining motor vehicles operated by the facility; and (5) use of listed toxic chemicals contained in intake water (used for processing or non-contact cooling) or in intake air (used either as compressed air or for combustion).[53]

---

[50]*See*, 40 C.F.R. § 372.3.

[51]*See*, 40 C.F.R. § 372.3.

[52]*See*, 40 C.F.R. § 372.3.

[53]*See*, 40 C.F.R. § 372.38.

The owner or operator of a covered facility does not have to factor into threshold or release determinations the quantities of a listed toxic chemical contained in an "article" when that article is processed or used at the facility. An "article" is defined as a manufactured item (1) which is formed to a specific shape or design during manufacture; (2) which has end use functions dependent in whole or in part upon its shape or design during end use; and (3) which does not release a toxic chemical under normal conditions of processing or use of that item at the facility or establishments.[54]

If the processing or otherwise use of similar articles results in a total release of less than 0.5 pound of a listed toxic chemical in a calendar year to any environmental media, EPA will allow this release quantity to be rounded to zero and the manufactured items remain exempt as articles. EPA requires the owners or operators of covered facilities to round off and report all estimates to the nearest whole number. The 0.5 pound limit does not apply to each individual article, but applies to the sum of all releases from processing or the otherwise use of like articles.

The article exemption applies to the normal processing or otherwise use of an article. It does not apply to the manufacture of an article. Listed toxic chemicals that are incorporated into articles produced at a facility must be factored into threshold and release determinations.[55] For example, if a facility services a transformer containing PCBs by replacing the PCBs, the PCBs added during the reporting year must be counted in making the threshold and release calculations.

The article exemption is not applicable when the processing or otherwise use of an item generates fumes, dust, filings, or grindings. The listed toxic chemicals in the item must be counted toward the appropriate threshold determination, and the fumes, dust, filings, and grindings reported as releases or wastes. In addition, scrap pieces of a manufactured item that are recognizable as an article do not constitute a release.

5.3 Threshold Levels

Section 313 reporting is required if established threshold quantities are exceeded. The threshold quantities vary depending upon the year for which the report is submitted and separate threshold quantities apply to the amount of the listed toxic chemical that is manufactured, imported, processed or otherwise used.[56]

The owner or operator of a facility that "otherwise used" any of the listed toxic chemicals in amounts equal to or in excess of 10,000 pounds in a calendar year is required to submit a toxic chemical release form on each listed chemical by July 1 of the following year. Such reporting began with the 1987 calendar year. Similarly, owners or operators of facilities that manufacture, import or process any of the listed toxic chemicals in amounts

---

[54]*See*, 40 C.F.R. § 372.3.
[55]*See*, 40 C.F.R. § 372.3.
[56]*See*, 42 U.S.C.A. § 11023(f).

equal to or in excess of 25,000 pounds in a calendar year are required to report by July 1 of the following year.[57]

5.4 Mixture Reporting

Listed toxic chemicals in mixtures and in trade name products must be factored into threshold and release determinations. If the owner or operator of a facility imported, processed, or otherwise used mixtures or trade name products during the preceding calendar year, the owner or operator is required to use the best information available at the facility to determine whether the components of a mixture are above the *de minimis* concentration. If the owner or operator knows that a mixture or trade name product contains a listed toxic chemical, the owner or operator must combine the amount of the listed chemical in the mixture or trade name product with the other amounts of the same chemical imported, processed or otherwise used at the facility for threshold and release determinations.[58]

If the owner or operator of a facility knows that a mixture contains a listed toxic chemical but no concentration information is provided by the supplier, then the facility does not have to consider the amount of the listed toxic chemical present in that mixture for purposes of threshold and release determinations.[59]

If the owner or operator of a facility only knows the lower bound concentration of a listed toxic chemical present in a mixture, the owner or operator should first subtract out the percentages of any other known components of the mixture to determine a reasonable "maximum" for the listed chemical. The owner or operator should assume the "maximum" is 100% if no other information is available. The owner or operator must then use the midpoint of the known "minimum" (the lower bound concentration) and the reasonable "maximum" for threshold determinations. The owner or operator should use an average of the low and high concentration numbers for threshold determinations if only a range of concentrations is available for a listed toxic chemical present in a mixture.

A listed toxic chemical does not have to be considered if it is present in a mixture at a concentration below the *de minimis* level.[60] If a mixture contains more than one member of a listed chemical category, the *de minimis* level applies to the aggregate concentration of all such members and not to each individually. In making threshold determinations, the *de minimis* limitation applies to the following:

1. A listed toxic chemical in a mixture or trade name product received by the facility; and

---

[57]*See*, 40 C.F.R. § 372.25.
[58]*See*, 40 C.F.R. § 372.30(b)(3)(i).
[59]*See*, 40 C.F.R. § 372.30(b)(3)(iii).
[60]*See*, 40 C.F.R. § 372.38(a).

2. A listed toxic chemical manufactured during a process where the chemical remains in a mixture or trade name product distributed by the facility.

The *de minimis* limitation does *not* apply to a listed toxic chemical manufactured at the facility that does not remain in a product distributed by the facility. A threshold determination must be made on the annual quantity of the listed chemical manufactured regardless of the concentration. For example, quantities of formaldehyde produced as a result of waste treatment must be applied toward the threshold for "manufacture" of this chemical, notwithstanding the concentration of this chemical in the wastestream.

5.5 Supplier Notification Requirement

EPA requires some suppliers of mixtures and trade name products containing one or more of the listed toxic chemicals to notify their customers. This requirement has been in effect since January 1, 1989. The supplier notification requirement applies to facilities in SIC codes 20 through 39 that manufacture, import, or process a listed toxic chemical which is *sold or otherwise distributed* in a mixture or trade name product containing the listed chemical to either a facility that must report under Section 313 or a facility that in turn sells the same mixture or trade name product to a firm in SIC codes 20 through 39.[61]

Supplier notification is required if a waste mixture containing a listed toxic chemical is sold to a recycling or recovery facility. If, however, the waste mixture containing a listed toxic chemical is sent off-site as a waste for treatment or disposal, no supplier notification is required.

The supplier notification must include the following information:

1. A statement that the mixture or trade name product contains a listed toxic chemical(s) subject to the reporting requirements of Section 313 and 40 C.F.R. Part 372;

2. The name of each listed toxic chemical(s) and its applicable CAS registry number; and

3. The percentage, by weight, of each listed toxic chemical(s) contained in the mixture or trade name product.[62]

The required notification must be provided at least *annually* in writing. Acceptable forms of notice are a letter, product labeling, and product literature distributed to customers. The owners and operators of facilities that are required to prepare and distribute a MSDS for the mixture under the OSHA Hazard Communication Standard must either attach their supplier notification to the MSDS or modify their MSDS to include the required information. Suppliers subject to the notification requirement must make it

---

[61] *See*, 40 C.F.R. § 372.45.
[62] *See*, 40 C.F.R. § 372.45(b).

clear to their customers that any copies or redistribution of the MSDS must include the Section 313 notice.[63]

Suppliers must notify each customer receiving a mixture or trade name product containing a listed toxic chemical with the *first shipment of each calendar year*. Once customers have been furnished with a MSDS containing the Section 313 information, a supplier may refer to the MSDS by a written letter in subsequent years if the MSDS is current.[64]

Whenever a supplier's products contain newly listed toxic chemicals, the supplier must notify customers with the *first shipment made during the next calendar year* following EPA's final decision to add the chemical to the list.[65] Suppliers must send a *new notice* to their customers *within 30 days* when they discover that their previous notification did not properly identify the listed toxic chemical(s) in the mixture or correctly indicate their percentage by weight. Suppliers must identify in the new notice the prior shipments of the mixture or product in that calendar year to which the new notification applies.[66]

Suppliers must send a *revised notice* to their customers when they change a mixture or trade name product by adding, removing, or changing the percentage by weight of a listed chemical. The revised notice must be sent with the *first shipment* of the changed mixture or trade name product to the customer.[67]

Supplier notification is *not* required for a "pure" listed toxic chemical unless a trade name is used. Supplier notification is also *not* required if the mixture or trade name product does not contain a listed toxic chemical in an amount greater than the applicable *de minimis* level established for that chemical. Likewise, supplier notification is *not* required if the mixture or trade name product is an "article"; food, drug, cosmetic, alcoholic beverage, tobacco, or a tobacco product packaged for distribution to the general public; or a "consumer product" as defined in the Consumer Product Safety Act packaged for distribution to the general public.[68]

If a supplier considers the specific identity of a listed toxic chemical in a mixture or trade name product to be a trade secret, the notice must contain a generic chemical name that is descriptive of the structure of that chemical (that is, halogenated aromatic).[69] Similarly, if a supplier considers the specific percent by weight composition of a toxic chemical in the mixture or trade name product to be a trade secret under the Restatement of Torts, the notice must contain a statement that the listed chemical is present at a

---

[63]*See*, 40 C.F.R. § 372.45(c)(5).
[64]*See*, 40 C.F.R. § 372.45(c)(1).
[65]*See*, 40 C.F.R. § 372.45(c)(2).
[66]*See*, 40 C.F.R. § 372.45(c)(4).
[67]*See*, 40 C.F.R. § 372.45(c)(3).
[68]*See*, 40 C.F.R. § 372.45(d).
[69]*See*, 40 C.F.R. § 372.45(e).

concentration that does not exceed a specified upper bound concentration value.[70]

Suppliers are required to retain for *three years* records of the following:

1. Copies of the notifications sent to customers;
2. All supporting materials and documentation used to determine whether a notice was required;
3. All supporting materials and documentation used to develop the notice;
4. All supporting materials and documentation which explain why a specific chemical identity is considered a trade secret and why the generic chemical name provided in the notification is appropriate; and
5. All supporting materials and documentation which explain why a specific concentration is considered a trade secret and the basis for the upper bound concentration limit.[71]

5.6 Reporting Form: Form R

Facilities covered by the Section 313 reporting requirements must use the Toxic Chemical Release Inventory Reporting Form (Form R) to report the following information:

1. The name, location and principal business activities at the facility;
2. Off-site locations to which any waste that contains the listed chemical is transferred;
3. Whether the listed chemical is manufactured, imported, processed, or otherwise used and the general use categories of the chemical;
4. An estimate (in ranges) of the maximum amounts of the listed chemical present at the facility at any time during the preceding year;
5. The quantity of the listed chemical entering each environmental medium—air, water and land—annually;
6. Waste treatment and disposal methods and the efficiency of such methods for each waste stream;
7. Information on source reduction and recycling or pollution prevention; and
8. A certification by a senior management official that the report is complete and accurate.

5.7 Mandatory Pollution Prevention Reporting on EPA Form R

The Pollution Prevention Act of 1990, passed in October 1990 as part of the Budget Reconciliation Act of 1990, requires the owners or operators of facilities that must report under Section 313 to provide information on source reduction and recycling activities with each annual toxic chemical release

---

[70]*See,* 40 C.F.R. § 372.45(f).
[71]*See,* 40 C.F.R. § 372.10(b).

inventory report beginning with the 1991 calendar year. These reports were due by July 1, 1992.[72]

The new pollution prevention report on each chemical reported includes the following information:

1. Amount entering the wastestreams before recycling, treatment, or disposal and the percentage change from the previous year;

2. Amount recycled, the percentage change from the previous year, and the recycling process used;

3. Amount treated on-site or off-site and the percentage change from the previous year;

4. Estimate of the amount that will be reported as entering any wastestream prior to recycling, treatment, or disposal for the next two years;

5. Estimate of the amount that will be reported as recycled for the next two years;

6. Specific source reduction practices used by the facility (for example, equipment, technology, process, or procedure modifications; reformulation or redesign of products; substitution of raw materials; improvement in management, training, inventory control, or materials handling;

7. Techniques used to identify source reduction opportunities (for example, employee recommendations, external and internal audits, participative team management, and material balance audits);

8. Ratio of production in the reporting year to production in the preceding year; and

9. Amount released because of accidents or other one-time events (for example, catastrophic event or remedial action) not associated with production processes.

The new data will facilitate a comparison between production levels and the amount of waste generated. The inclusion of this new data in the Toxics Release Inventory (TRI) will allow citizen groups, state and local governments, and EPA to see for the first time whether waste reduction is occurring at the source.

5.8 Recordkeeping Requirements

The owner or operator of a facility covered by the Section 313 reporting requirements (excluding the supplier notification requirements) must retain for *three years* records of the following:

1. A copy of each toxic chemical release inventory report;

---

[72]On May 27, 1992, EPA announced that because of delays in finalizing and distributing the approved 1991 Form R and in recognition of the importance to the public that facilities submit complete and accurate Form R reports, it will *not* initiate enforcement actions against facilities that file accurate Form R reports between July 1, 1992 and September 1, 1992. *See,* 57 *Fed.Reg.* 22330 (May 27, 1992).

2. All supporting materials and documentation used to make the compliance determination that the facility or establishments within the facility is a covered facility;

3. Documentation supporting any determination that a claimed allowable exemption applies;

4. Data supporting the determination of whether a reporting threshold applies for each reported chemical;

5. Documentation supporting the calculations of the quantity of each reported chemical released to the environment or transferred to an off-site location;

6. Documentation supporting the activities, use classifications, and quantity–on–site reported for each reported chemical, including the date of manufacture, processing, or use;

7. Documentation supporting the basis of estimate used in developing any release or off-site transfer estimates for each reported chemical;

8. Receipts or manifests associated with the transfer of each reported chemical in waste to off-site locations; and

9. Documentation supporting reported waste treatment methods, estimates of treatment efficiencies, ranges of influent concentration to such treatment, the sequential nature of treatment steps, if applicable, and the actual operating data, if applicable, to support the waste treatment efficiency estimate for each reported chemical.[73]

The records must be maintained at the facility for three years from the date each report was submitted and they must be readily available for inspection by EPA officials.[74]

In view of the new data requirements mandated by the Pollution Prevention Act of 1990, EPA has proposed that several new records be maintained under Section 313.[75] Those records include the following:

1. Documentation supporting the estimates of the amounts of the chemical entering any wastestream, recycled on-site, sent off-site for recycling or treatment, and entering any wastestream as a result of remedial actions, catastrophic, or one-time events;

2. Documentation supporting the estimates for the previous year and the first and second years following the reporting year of the amounts of the chemical entering any wastestream or otherwise released to the environment, recycled on-site, and recycled off-site;

3. Documentation supporting the estimates for the previous year of the amounts of the chemical entering treatment on-site and sent off-site for treatment;

4. Documentation supporting the validity of the method used to estimate the amount that would have been generated in waste if

---

[73]See, 40 C.F.R. § 372.10(a).

[74]See, 40 C.F.R. § 372.10(c).

[75]See, 56 Fed. Reg. 48475 (September 25, 1991).

source reduction had not been implemented, and the calculation of the estimate of that quantity, including index of production or activity level in the reporting year to the prior year level;

5. Documentation supporting the determination of whether changes in accounting practices, estimation methods, or point of measurement occurred in the reporting year versus the previous year;

6. Documentation supporting the type of recycling process used on-site and off-site;

7. Documentation of the implementation of source reduction and recycling activities, including receipts for new capital equipment; and

8. Documentation demonstrating how the production ratio or activity index was calculated.

6.0 TRADE SECRETS

Only the specific chemical identity of a covered chemical can be claimed as a trade secret in submissions to EPA, the SERC, the LEPC, or the LFD required under Sections 303, 311, 312, and 313. EPCRA provides no trade secret protection for Section 304 submissions. When claiming confidentiality, the owner or operator of a covered facility must submit all other required information, including a generic name for the chemical whose identity is claimed as a trade secret, on the MSDS (or list of MSDS chemicals) and the Tier Two report.[76]

6.1 Substantiation Required

Substantiation for the claim must be provided to EPA, in both sanitized and unsanitized form, at the same time the Section 303, 311, 312 or 313 submission is made to the SERC, the LEPC or the LFD. The substantiation must include the following information:

1. Specific measures taken to safeguard the confidentiality of the chemical identity claimed as a trade secret and whether these measures will continue in the future;

2. Whether the chemical identity claimed as a trade secret has been disclosed to any other person (other than a member of a LEPC, officer or employee of the U.S. or a state or local government, or an employee) who is not bound by a confidentiality agreement to refrain from disclosing this trade secret information to others;

3. All local, state and federal government entities to which the specific chemical identity claimed as a trade secret has been disclosed;

4. Indication of whether a confidentiality claim for the chemical identity was asserted at the time of disclosure to the local, state and federal government entities and whether the government entity denied that claim;

5. The specific use of the chemical claimed as a trade secret, including the product or process in which it is used;

---

[76]*See*, 42 U.S.C.A. § 11042(a); 40 C.F.R. § 350.5.

6. Whether the company's or the facility's identity has been linked to the specific chemical identity claimed as a trade secret in a patent, or in publications or other information sources available to the public or competitors;

7. Explanation of how competitors could deduce the use of the chemical claimed as a trade secret from disclosure of the chemical identity together with other information on the SARA Title III submission;

8. Explanation of why the use of the chemical claimed as a trade secret would be valuable information to competitors;

9. Indication of the nature of the harm to the company's competitive position that would likely result from disclosure of the specific chemical identity and why such harm would be substantial;

10. The extent to which the chemical claimed as a trade secret is available to the public or competitors in products, articles, or environmental releases; and

11. Whether the chemical claimed as a trade secret is in pure form or is mixed with other substances.[77]

6.2 Trade Secret Disclosure

All information for which a trade secrecy claim is not ultimately upheld is available to the public on request with one exception. Under Section 324, the SERC, the LEPC, and the LFD are required to withhold information regarding the location within a facility of any specific chemical contained in a Tier Two report if requested to do so by the owner or operator of a facility submitting the report.

Information concerning the specific chemical identity of a substance must be provided to health professionals upon request in the following situations:

1. The information is needed by a health professional for the purpose of diagnosis or treatment;

2. The information is needed by a health professional working for a local government to assess exposure; conduct sampling, periodic medical surveillance, or studies on the health effects of exposure; or provide medical treatment to exposed individuals or population groups; or

3. The information is needed by doctors or nurses in order to treat exposed individuals in a medical emergency.

The owner or operator of a covered facility is required to furnish the specific chemical identity in the first two situations described above only if the request for the information is *in writing* and is accompanied by a *written confidentiality agreement*. In a medical emergency, however, no written statement of need or written confidentiality agreement is required as a precondition to disclosure. The owner or operator of a covered facility may

---

[77]*See*, 40 C.F.R. § 350.7(a).

require a written statement of need and written confidentiality agreement as soon as circumstances permit.[78]

7.0 PUBLIC AVAILABILITY OF EPCRA INFORMATION

The information submitted by facilities under Sections 304, 311, 312 and 313 must generally be made available to the public by the SERC and the LEPCs during normal working hours.[79] Each SERC must have established written guidelines on receiving and processing requests for information under EPCRA.[80]

As a general policy, the SERCs and LEPCs will make the fullest possible disclosure of records to the public consistent with the provisions of EPCRA and their State Freedom of Information Act. All SERC and LEPC records are available to the public unless they are specifically exempt from the disclosure requirements.

8.0 ENFORCEMENT AUTHORITIES AND PENALTIES

EPCRA contains a complex set of administrative, civil and criminal penalties for violations of its various provisions. Sections 325 and 326 authorize the EPA, the SERCs, the LEPCs, and citizens to take legal action against owners or operators of facilities who fail to comply with the law.

The enforcement authorities vary for each requirement in EPCRA. In some instances, federal authority is primarily administrative; in other instances it is judicial. For some requirements, but not all, there is express authority for state and local suits. Similarly, for some requirements, but not all, there are citizen suits.

Congress intended that the implementation of EPCRA be mainly a state and local function with the notable exception of Section 313 pertaining to toxic chemical release inventory reporting. The EPCRA enforcement authorities are summarized below.

8.1 Violations of Sections 302 and 303

Section 325 of EPCRA authorizes the administrator of the EPA to order the owner or operator of a covered facility to comply with Sections 302 and 303. The local U.S. district court has jurisdiction to enforce the order and impose a penalty.[81]

Under Section 326, the SERC and the LEPC can bring a civil action against the owner or operator of a covered facility for failing to report that the facility is covered by the emergency planning requirements.[82] The SERC and the LEPC can bring a civil action against the owner or operator of a covered facility for failing to notify the LEPC of a facility representative who

---

[78] *See*, 40 C.F.R. § 350.40.

[79] *See*, 42 U.S.C.A. § 11044(a).

[80] *See*, 42 U.S.C.A. § 11001(a).

[81] *See*, 42 U.S.C.A. § 11045(a).

[82] *See*, 42 U.S.C.A. § 11046(a)(2)(A).

will participate in the emergency planning process or for failing to provide information promptly upon request by the LEPC.[83] The local U.S. district court has the authority to impose civil penalties provided by EPCRA in such suits.[84]

Violations of Sections 302 and 303 subject the violator to civil penalties of up to $25,000 per day for each day the violation or failure to comply with the order continues.[85]

8.2 Violations of Section 304

The CERCLA Section 109 and EPCRA Section 325 enforcement provisions for emergency notification are very similar. Both establish administrative penalties and the authority to bring actions judicially to assess penalties for failing to notify the proper authorities at the time of an emergency release of a listed hazardous substance subject to reporting.[86]

CERCLA and EPCRA both provide criminal fines for knowingly failing to provide notice of a reportable release or providing false or misleading information.[87] Section 326(a) of EPCRA authorizes any citizen to file a civil action in the local U.S. district court for failure to submit a written follow-up report of a release required to be reported to the SERC and the LEPC under Section 304(c).[88] The SERC and the LEPC may bring a civil action under the citizen suit provisions for Section 304 violations.[89]

Under Section 325 of EPCRA and CERCLA Section 109, a Class I administrative penalty of up to $25,000 per violation and a Class II administrative penalty of up to $25,000 per day for each day during which the violation continues may be assessed for each violation of Section 304.[90] This penalty also may be assessed judicially.[91]

In the case of a second or subsequent violation of Section 304, civil penalties of up to $75,000 per day for each day during which the violation continues may be assessed.[92] Both penalties also may be assessed judicially.[93]

Any person who knowingly and willfully fails to provide notice in accordance with EPCRA Section 304 can, upon conviction, be fined up to

---

[83]See, 42 U.S.C.A. § 11046(a)(2)(B).

[84]See, 42 U.S.C.A. § 11046(b)(1).

[85]See, 42 U.S.C.A. § 11045(a).

[86]See, 42 U.S.C.A. § 9609 and 42 U.S.C.A. § 11045.

[87]See, 42 U.S.C.A. § 9603(b) and 42 U.S.C.A. § 11045(b)(4).

[88]See, 42 U.S.C.A. § 11046(a)(1)(A)(i).

[89]See, 42 U.S.C.A. § 11049(7) and 42 U.S.C.A. § 11046(a). The term "person" used in Section 326 of EPCRA is defined to include, among others, "any ... State, municipality, commission, political subdivision of a State, or interstate body."

[90]See, 42 U.S.C.A. § 11045(b)(1) and (2); and 42 U.S.C.A. § 9609(a) and (b).

[91]See, 42 U.S.C.A. § 11045(b)(3) and 42 U.S.C.A. § 9609(c).

[92]See, 42 U.S.C.A. § 11045(b)(2) and 42 U.S.C.A. § 9609(b).

[93]See, 42 U.S.C.A. § 11045(b)(3) and 42 U.S.C.A. § 9609(c).

$25,000 or imprisoned for up to two years, or both.[94] In the case of a second or subsequent conviction, the violator is subject to a fine of up to $50,000 or imprisonment for up to five years, or both.[95]

8.3 Violations of Sections 311–313

Under Section 325 of EPCRA, the Administrator of the EPA can assess civil penalties for violations of Sections 311, 312, and 313 through the issuance of administrative orders or bring actions to enforce compliance and assess penalties in the local U.S. district court.[96]

Under Section 326 of EPCRA, the SERC and the LEPC can bring civil actions for failing to submit MSDS's or Tier One/Tier Two Inventory Reports under Sections 311 and 312.[97] Under the citizen suit provisions of Section 326, the SERC and the LEPC can bring a civil action for failing to submit toxic chemical release inventory reports under Section 313.[98]

Section 326 gives citizens the authority to bring a civil action against an owner or operator of a covered facility for violations of Sections 311, 312, and 313.[99] The local U.S. district court has the authority to enforce the reporting requirements and to impose any civil penalty provided for violation of the requirements.[100]

A violation of Section 311 subjects the violator to a civil penalty of up to $10,000 per day for each such violation.[101] Each day a violation continues constitutes a separate violation.[102]

A violation of Sections 312 or 313 subjects the violator to a civil penalty of up to $25,000 per day for each such violation.[103] Each day a violation continues constitutes a separate violation.[104]

9.0 CONCLUSION

Compliance with EPCRA presents a continuing challenge to those facilities subject to its planning and reporting requirements. Facilities subject to the emergency planning provisions should participate actively in the local planning process as a matter of good community relations and to provide the technical expertise needed by the LEPCs. Facilities subject to the reporting requirements need clearly written and rigorously implemented compliance

---

[94]*See,* 42 U.S.C.A. § 11045(b)(4).
[95]*Ibid.*
[96]*See,* 42 U.S.C.A. § 11045(c).
[97]*See,* 42 U.S.C.A. § 11046(a)(2).
[98]*See,* 42 U.S.C.A. § 11046(a)(1)(A)(iv).
[99]*See,* 42 U.S.C.A. § 11046(a)(1).
[100]*See,* 42 U.S.C.A. § 11046(c).
[101]*See,* 42 U.S.C.A. § 11045(c)(2).
[102]*See,* 42 U.S.C.A. § 11045(c)(3).
[103]*See,* 42 U.S.C.A. § 11045(c)(1).
[104]*See,* 42 U.S.C.A. § 11045(c)(3).

plans and information management programs to avoid enforcement actions for noncompliance.

For a more definitive discussion of this topic, the reader is referred to the EPCRA Handbook, 4th Edition *and related books and courses listed at the end of this book.*

Chapter 15

OCCUPATIONAL SAFETY AND HEALTH ACT[1]

David G. Sarvadi
Keller and Heckman
Washington, D.C.

1.0 OVERVIEW: TWENTY YEARS OF THE OCCUPATIONAL SAFETY AND HEALTH ACT

Familiarity with the Occupational Safety and Health Act (OSH Act) is increasingly important for anyone involved in the environmental law field. Three examples of the relationship between the Occupational Safety and Health Administration (OSHA) and the Environmental Protection Agency (EPA) may illustrate why. First, Congress relied on the Occupational Safety and Health Administration's Hazard Communication Standard in defining company obligations under the Emergency Planning Community Right-to-Know Act.[2] Second, in reviewing premanufacture notifications for new chemicals under the Toxic Substances Control Act,[3] the EPA staff considers worker safety and has required specific warning statements or labeling language under TSCA Section 5(e)[4] orders. Third, OSHA and EPA have agreed to cross-train inspectors so that OSHA inspectors will be alert for obvious environmental violations, while EPA inspectors will be alert for potential OSHA violations. Under this cooperative agreement, inspectors from one agency will notify the other agency of potential violations.

1.1 OSHA Achievements

There were an estimated 10,000 workers who died from job-related causes in 1991, according to the National Safety Council. When the Occupational Safety and Health Act (OSH Act) was passed in 1970, the NSC estimated that there were some 14,400 such fatalities. While even one lost life is unacceptable if preventable, these figures represent dramatic progress in controlling workplace health and safety hazards. The significance of this accomplishment is brought home when the increase in the private sector

---

[1]The author gratefully acknowledges the assistance and contributions of the members of the Occupational Safety and Health practice group at Keller and Heckman, including Lawrence P. Halprin, Patrick J. Hurd, Garen E. Dodge, Peter A. Susser, David B. Berry, and Martha E. Pelligrini. The author is especially grateful for the patient assistance of Peter L. de la Cruz for his assistance in editing and reviewing the final manuscript.

[2]See, e.g., sections 311 and 312 of the Emergency Planning and Community-Right-to-Know Act of 1986, 42 U.S.C. Sections 11021 and 11022.

[3]15 U.S.C. §§ 2601 to 2671.

[4]15 U.S.C. § 2604(e).

workforce—from 70 million to over 125 million[5]—is taken into account. The incidence rate—the number of fatalities per 10,000 workers—has dropped dramatically from approximately 2.1 to 0.8. In other words, the rate has dropped by more than half while the number of covered employees has nearly doubled. In fact, nearly 18,000 additional fatalities would have been expected in 1990 if the current fatality rate was equal to that of 1970. In other words, with the present workforce, nearly three times as many American workers would have died.

From these figures, we might agree that the Occupational Safety and Health Act has been a success.[6] This performance appears even better, given competing messages from Congress which limited OSHA's resources at the same time it was setting standards for the nation's employers to achieve the highest degree of safety in the workplace. Moreover, this progress has been accomplished largely through a system of civil enforcement coupled with voluntary compliance by employers. This supports the view that the vast majority of employers still believe in the national goal of providing a safe workplace for all, even in the face of unceasingly greater regulatory demands (especially in the environmental arena) and worldwide competitive pressures.

This chapter will introduce the regulatory program administered by OSHA, including the scope and enforcement of OSHA regulations and recordkeeping requirements. Our review will include discussions of the standards-setting process; inspection, citations, and the process of challenging OSHA's citations; some of OSHA's administrative activities that affect employer's duties; and one of the more important so-called generic standards, the Hazard Communication Standard, because of its special relation to the environmental field. Finally, legislative changes expected in the near future are highlighted, and some brief guidance on compliance is provided.

1.2 History

The passage of the OSH Act in 1970 was part of a flurry of social and environmental legislation that resulted from the desire to correct what were considered to be failures of the market—to "engineer" social change through legislation. The lofty goal of the act was "to assure so far as possible every

---

[5]Total employment, private and public sector, 1970 and 1990. *Source:* Bureau of Labor Statistics.

[6]There are some who argue that the current statistics on workplace fatalities, illnesses, and injuries understate by a significant amount the true cost of workplace accidents and exposures. Even if this is true, it doesn't change, and may even enhance, the conclusion that significant strides in workplace health and safety have occurred. For example, it is more likely than not, given the amount of emphasis on workplace health and safety issues and on reporting cases—especially in recent years—that the statistics of 20 years ago understated the true rate to a greater degree than the current data. If this is true, the improvement in both the rate and the absolute numbers is even greater and thus even more significant. And while the absolute number of reported injuries and illnesses has not decreased significantly (it may have even increased slightly), the *rate* has declined significantly from more than 13 to less than 9 reported cases per 100 full time employees over the same period.

working man and woman in the nation safe and healthful working conditions and to preserve our human resources." In 1971, there were 4.2 million establishments and over 57 million employees covered by the act. By 1990, more than 6 million workplaces and over 90 million[7] employees in those workplaces were covered.

1.3 Scope of OSHA Coverage

The OSH Act applies to private sector employers. For nearly the entire history of the act, Congress has in effect exempted from inspection employers with 10 or fewer employees, except in cases of complaints or accident investigations. These same employers are exempt from certain recordkeeping requirements (discussed below) by regulation. Small employers can still be cited for violations of substantive standards, including the Hazard Communication Standard (HCS).

Notable statutory exceptions to OSHA coverage have included federal, state, and local employees. Protection for federal employees was adopted by Executive Order 12196 in February 1980[8] under which all federal agencies were ordered to develop health and safety programs and to comply with OSHA standards.

All of the 23 state plans presently approved by OSHA provide coverage for state and local government employees, including several that provide for monetary penalties where the agencies fail to comply with state standards, as required by the OSHA regulations for approval of state plans. At the time of passage, Congress recognized the states' interest in workplace health and safety and devised a system under which the federal agency would set minimum standards, allowing the states, if they so chose, to play a significant role. Direct coverage of state and local government employees was not included in the original act because of the belief that Congress had no power to regulate the conditions of employment between the state governments and their employees. Some believe that Supreme Court decisions over the last twenty years have modified that conclusion.

Other employment sectors that are not directly subject to OSHA standards include certain segments of the transportation industry (railroads and the trucking industry), aspects of the atomic energy industry subject to Nuclear Regulatory Agency Standards, and the mining industry. The transportation sectors are covered by specific Department of Transportation regulations under other statutes, while the mining industry is regulated by the Mine Safety and Health Administration, a comparable sister agency in the Department of Labor. The Coast Guard also regulates some aspects of shipboard health and safety. Finally, the manufacture, transportation, and

---

[7]Because the act does not cover all employed persons, the number covered is less than total employment.

[8]Congressional employees remain excluded from coverage. Because they are not executive branch employees, the Executive Order does not apply to Congressional workers.

storage of explosives is regulated by the Bureau of Alcohol, Tobacco, and Firearms in the Department of the Treasury.

These agencies exercise only partial authority in their respective industries. Where an OSHA standard exists, and the primary agency has not regulated the subject matter, OSHA is permitted to regulate the employers. In recent years, courts have been increasingly reluctant to prohibit OSHA from exercising its authority to protect employees in arguably exempt industries or occupations.

1.4 State Plans

Congress recognized that many states had effective programs of worker protection. As with air, water, and hazardous waste regulatory plans, Congress included provisions in the OSH Act permitting states (1) to exercise jurisdiction over any occupational safety and health issue where no federal standard exists; (2) to assume responsibility for development and enforcement of state rules equivalent to federal standards; (3) to operate an occupational health and safety program comparable in funding, authority, and staffing to the federal program; and (4) to enforce more stringent standards where they are compelled by local conditions and do not unduly burden interstate commerce.

Section 18 requires a state to submit a plan to OSHA if the state desires to assume responsibility for the development and enforcement of standards "relating to" any occupational safety or health issue with respect to which a federal standard has been issued. Congress provided for funding of up to 50 percent of the cost of administering and enforcing programs in the states, and up to 90 percent to improve state capabilities in this area.

Twenty-one states and two territories[9] have state plans approved by the Secretary of Labor under this provision of the act. Although the law provides for withdrawal of approval by the secretary after notice and hearing, no state plans have had their approval involuntarily withdrawn. In 1991, as a result of allegations of ineffective operation of the state's plan, OSHA proposed to withdraw approval of North Carolina's program. The state vigorously opposed OSHA's action, and succeeded in retaining jurisdiction after making significant changes in funding, resources, and enforcement.

The states with approved state plans promulgate and enforce their own standards. Generally, the states have six months after promulgation of a new federal standard to adopt an equivalent standard under their own rules. The majority of states simply adopt the federal standard. In some cases, the states have acted in advance of the federal government because of perceived needs that have not been addressed; in several cases, the states have adopted standards which are significantly different from the federal rule. For example, Maryland has had provisions limiting exposure to lead in the construction industry for more than ten years, while the federal standard has yet to be adopted. More recently, California has adopted a standard

---

[9]Puerto Rico and the Virgin Islands.

addressing Process Safety Management that applies to a smaller group of industries than does the federal rule, while covering a larger list of chemicals at lower quantities.[10]

Approximately 10 of the states with state plans have adopted or retained state standards which are more restrictive than the federal rules, or which address areas in which there are no comparable federal standards. Many of these standards were carried over from state health and safety programs that existed prior to the passage of the OSH act. Some examples include standards on elevators, boiler and pressure vessels, confined spaces, and exterior window cleaning on skyscrapers. A number of the states have more expansive hazard communication standards as well.

Approximately five states have laws providing for misdemeanor criminal penalties where willful or knowing violations can be proven. Sanctions range from several thousands of dollars up to $100,000. In some cases, the criminal sanctions provided under state law can be assessed for violating "general responsibilities" under state law as well as for violation of individual rules.

1.5 Preemption

The state plan provisions of the OSH Act and the federal rules were given new vitality in 1992 in a U.S. Supreme Court decision which invalidated a state law requiring heavy equipment operators on hazardous waste sites to have additional training and qualifications in excess of OSHA requirements. In *Gade v. National Solid Wastes Management Association*,[11] the Court held that the OSH Act and the Hazardous Waste Operations and Emergency Response regulations (HAZWOPER)[12] preempt a state occupational safety and health law even though the state law purports to have a "dual" purpose or impact; that is, that it protects public as well as worker safety or health. Such a dual purpose state law may stand only if OSHA has explicitly approved it as part of a state plan established pursuant to Section 18 of the OSH Act.

Four justices found that the OSH Act "impliedly" preempted the state law because the state law stands as an obstacle to the accomplishment and execution of the OSH Act's full purposes, while the fifth justice found "express" preemption. The *Gade* plurality found that state occupational safety and health standards regulating an issue on which a federal standard exists conflict with Congress's intent to subject employers and employees to only one set of regulations. Laws which regulate workers simply as members of the general public, the court cautioned, cannot fairly be characterized as occupational standards. The Illinois statute under challenge in *Gade*, however, was found to be directed at workplace safety, and thus not saved from preemption by its dual purpose.

---

[10]29 C.F.R. § 1910.119.

[11]*Gade v. National Solid Wastes Management Ass'n*, 505 U.S.—, 112 S. Ct. 2374 (1992).

[12]29 C.F.R. § 1910.120

The decision has important implications for other state laws that have been enacted ostensibly to protect the public, but which also have an effect on worker health and safety. Prior to *Gade*, three federal circuits had ruled that state statutes which impact public safety as well as worker safety are not necessarily preempted by the OSH Act. The Court's decision in *Gade* calls into question the continuing force of these decisions. In particular, state statutes that regulate Right-to-Know through labeling and hazard communication are suspect under the *Gade* decision rationale.

2.0 OSHA RULEMAKING PROCESS

When Congress passed the Occupational Safety and Health Act, it provided the Secretary of Labor with the authority to promulgate rules regulating an employer's conduct in the operation of his business. Section 6 of the act gave the secretary general rulemaking authority with specific procedural guidelines, as well as guidelines on the content of the rules the Occupational Safety and Health Administration (OSHA) could impose. Section 6 also defines the rulemaking process to be followed, paralleling most of the provisions of the Administrative Procedure Act, but incorporating specific timetables and providing supplementary authority to convene advisory committees.

Under the statute, any person may petition for a rule, or the secretary may act on his own initiative or at the recommendation of the National Institute for Occupational Safety and Health (NIOSH). If the secretary feels it useful, he may convene at his discretion advisory committees to assess the potential hazard and to develop a proposal for a standard. Within 90 days of its appointment, an advisory committee must send recommendations to the secretary; the secretary can permit a delay in the report of the advisory committee, but in any event it may be delayed for no more than 270 days.

However if the secretary decides to propose a rule, he must publish it in the *Federal Register*. If the proposal is based on an advisory committee recommendation, the proposal must be published within 60 days. Thirty days are provided for public comment. Within 30 days after the end of the comment period, the secretary must publish a hearing notice if one is requested by any interested person. Currently, OSHA nearly always schedules a public hearing in anticipation of public participation and interest.

Hearings are held under the auspices of an Administrative Law Judge (ALJ), and witnesses may be cross-examined. After the hearing is complete, the ALJ will normally permit submission of post-hearing comments for a period of thirty to sixty days to rebut opposing testimony or to illuminate points made during the hearing. Although the statute provides a stringent timetable for completing the rulemaking, requiring publication of the final rule within 60 days of the end of the comment period, in practice no standard has ever beenissued within that time frame. Court decisions beginning in the 1970's clarified OSHA's obligation to provide a statement of reasons as required by the statute.

3.0 DEVELOPMENT OF OSHA HEALTH AND SAFETY STANDARDS

The general standard to which all specific OSHA standards are compared is found in Section 2(b) of the act. In noble language, Congress set the guideline at a high mark:

> to assure so far as possible every working man and woman in the Nation safe and healthful working conditions.

A standard is defined in Section 3(8) as one "which requires conditions or the adoption or use of one or more practices, means, methods, operations, or processes reasonably necessary or appropriate to provide safe and healthful employment and places of employment."

Safety standards—those affecting conditions which can lead to traumatic injury—must meet this requirement, viewed by the Court as a less demanding one than that for health standards. Safety standards are subject to a limited cost-benefit requirement: OSHA must show that the requirements produce measurable benefits in mitigating the risk of injury and that the costs of achieving them on an industry-wide scale do not threaten the economic viability of the whole industry, even though individual companies may not be able to compete with the additional costs.

Health standards, on the other hand, require no such balancing of costs, requiring only a showing that the proposed standard is technically feasible, that a substantial risk exists, and that the industry will not be wiped out by the additional costs. Under Section 6(b)(5), standards for toxic substances and physical agents must be developed which

> most adequately assures, to the extent feasible, on the basis of the best available evidence, that no employee will suffer material impairment of health or functional capacity even if exposed for their working life....

The court has interpreted this passage to mean that Congress has already made the cost-benefit calculation and decided that the agency is to err on the side of safety. Moreover, the act is viewed as technology-forcing, requiring employers to attempt that for which success is uncertain and to adopt the most current and effective measures feasible. Cost is not a determinative factor until the health of the entire industry is at stake.

Feasibility is determined solely on the basis of technical capability—whether there are methods and means to accomplish the objective desired. It is intended to push the capability of employers to the limits of their imagination. And in a number of significant cases, OSHA has been successful. For example, when the vinyl chloride standard was proposed, manufacturers of vinyl resins (with perhaps one exception) had exposures to their employees in the hundreds of parts per million (ppm) range. A standard of 1 ppm was considered impossible to meet. Yet shortly after the standard went into effect, B.F. Goodrich, a major producer, announced technology that allowed them to meet and even exceed the new standard.

OSHA has the authority to adopt three types of regulations governing workplace safety and health standards. (1) For a two year period from 1970-

1972, under Section 6(a), OSHA was permitted to adopt consensus standards—those developed and adopted through a system of voting open to interested persons. (2) Section 6(b) outlines procedures for OSHA to follow in adopting permanent standards. (3) Section 6(c) allows OSHA in extraordinary circumstances to adopt Emergency Temporary Standards effective for a six month period without comment.

3.1 Permanent Standards

Under Section 6(b), OSHA is authorized to establish standards limiting employee exposure to hazardous substances, physical agents, and safety hazards. The standards must, wherever practicable, be based on objective criteria describing the performance desired.

OSHA is required to identify whether a risk of illness or injury exists, whether and to what degree the proposed rule will mitigate that risk, and whether the particular standard is feasible both technically and economically for covered industry sectors. OSHA's standards in the recent Lockout/-Tagout and the PEL decisions[13] were rejected based on inadequate statements of reasons published by the agency. However, contrary to numerous commentators' conclusions that OSHA has much difficulty in satisfying court mandates for sound reasons for its regulatory decisions, OSHA has been able to provide adequate justification for its rules in many cases. In the Lockout/Tagout and PEL decisions, OSHA simply failed to do what courts required of it in earlier cases.

Under the statute, the final rule may include, as appropriate, requirements for labels, medical examinations, protective equipment, and engineering controls, and such provisions as are necessary and feasible to reduce to acceptable levels the risk of injury or illness of exposed employees. A major point of contention in the development of standards, and the principal source of litigation of them, is always the pressure from the labor movement for zero risk and the resistance of employers to additional costs.

The Secretary of Labor may delay the effective date of a standard for 90 days (or longer if justified). Any person who may be affected can appeal within 60 days to a Circuit Court of Appeals. A request for an administrative stay of the regulations pending court appeal is often filed, and the court will frequently grant a judicial stay if the administrative stay is not forthcoming.

3.2 Emergency Temporary Standards

The third kind of standard that may be issued by OSHA is the Emergency Temporary Standard (ETS). In all, nine have been issued since 1970. Three were not challenged—vinyl chloride monomer, asbestos (1972), and dibromochloropropane (DBCP). Six were vacated and remanded: one—benzene—on procedural grounds; the remainder on substantive grounds—

---

[13]*International Union, UAW v. Occupational Safety and Health Administration, U.S. Department of Labor*, 938 F.2d 1310 (D.C. Cir. 1991) (Lockout/Tagout).
AFL-CIO v. Secretary of Labor, 965 F.2d 962 (11th Cir. 1992). (PEL).

asbestos (1983), 14 carcinogens, field reentry (pesticides), acrylonitrile, and commercial diving.

OSHA has largely abandoned the use of the ETS as a regulatory vehicle because of the high standard set by the courts that OSHA must meet to justify the *ex parte* nature of the process. Secondarily, an ETS sets in motion a timetable for publishing a permanent standard that OSHA has extraordinary difficulty meeting. As a result, the ETS is not viewed as a viable alternative to the normal rulemaking process and the judicious use of the General Duty Clause (GDC, described further on) to address pressing issues has been used instead. By employing the GDC, coupled with the so-called egregious violations policy,[14] OSHA has successfully caused large segments of industry to change its approach to safety and health while avoiding what has become a somewhat tedious standards setting process.

3.3 Variances

Congress provided that employers who were unable to meet specific standards or could show by a preponderance of the evidence that their practices and facilities provide equivalent protection for their employees could obtain a variance from the standard. Under OSHA's regulations, both a temporary variance and a permanent variance may be obtained. A temporary variance is permitted when the employer can comply with the standard but is unable to meet the regulatory compliance deadline; permanent variances are provided where compliance by the method specified is not feasible and employees are protected from the hazard.

3.3.1 Temporary Variances

A temporary variance may be obtained where the employer can show that he (1) is unable to comply; (2) is taking all steps to safeguard employees; and (3) has an effective program to comply as soon as possible. Temporary variances must prescribe methods the employer will follow to comply and state the employer's compliance plan in detail. The temporary variance is initially effective for one year. Employees must be notified and have an opportunity for a hearing before the variance is granted. Temporary variances are renewable not more than twice, based on an application filed at least 90 days in advance of expiration of the current order; each interim order may not be effective for more than 180 days.

3.3.2 Permanent Variances

Permanent variances address situations where compliance with the specific method required by the standard is obviated by the existence of alternative means of protection. The critical showing is that the employer's controls are equivalent in terms of employee protection to those specified in

---

[14]Under the egregious violations policy, OSHA issues separate citations (and separate penalties) for each instance of a violation of a particular standard. Under normal circumstances, similar occurrences—a number of machines missing guards, for instance—are grouped as a single violation. The effect is to multiply potential penalties substantially, from a few tens of thousands of dollars to millions in many cases. See paragraph 5.8.

the standard. These procedures and methods must be adopted into the order, after notice to affected employees and an opportunity for comment, and may be modified or revoked any time after they have been in effect for six months. The result is a mini-rulemaking for the individual employer. Relatively few permanent variances have been issued in OSHA's twenty year history, and most have been issued for situations related to traditional safety problems as opposed to health standards.

4.0 INSPECTION AND ENFORCEMENT OF OSHA STANDARDS

4.1 Inspection Authority

Inspections are authorized under the act. OSHA's Compliance Safety and Health Officers (CSHO) are authorized to enter without delay and at reasonable times the premises of any covered employer. In the mid-1970s, the inspection authority was limited, but only to what may be an insignificant degree. The Supreme Court held in the *Barlow's* case[15] that employers may refuse entry to an inspector who appears without a search warrant under the Fifth Amendment. However, the application of the principle to the real world has left employers with something less than they expected. OSHA may obtain a warrant on very limited grounds in an *ex parte* proceeding before a magistrate. As a result, most employers have foregone the right to insist on a warrant prior to inspection for fear of antagonizing the government's agent.

4.1.1 Inspections Triggered by Complaints

The OSH Act provides a mechanism for employees to register complaints with the agency, following which OSHA may inspect the employer's facility. Presently, fewer than one in ten of the complaints OSHA receives result in a physical inspection of the employer. The normal process is for the area director to send a letter to the employer identifying the alleged violative condition and requesting the employer's investigation and response. If the response is not forthcoming, or is unsatisfactory, the agency may then inspect.

A major deficiency in the system is that often OSHA complaints are used as a bargaining tool in labor management disputes. This occurs whether the employees are organized or not. Often, the complaint is a vendetta by a disgruntled employee; occasionally, the complaint is a plea for assistance in an untenable situation. OSHA's difficult task, and the one most politically charged, is to distinguish between the two when, in the usual case, a verbal complaint and a description of the problem is all the agency has. If the agency responds to an unjustified complaint, it is wasting both its and the employer's resources. But, if OSHA fails to inspect, a disaster may broadcast its failure to the world. In light of the competing demands for its resources,

---

[15]*Marshall, Secretary of Labor, et al. v. Barlow's, Inc.* 436 U.S. 307, 98 S.G. 1816, 56 L.Ed. 2d 305 (1978).

the agency has had remarkably few major failures in responding to complaints.

4.2 Scope of Inspection

The scope of the inspection depends principally on the reason the inspection is initially scheduled. Complaint inspections are frequently limited to the specific conditions identified in the complaint. On the other hand, general schedule inspections are planned using a weighted method of identifying target employers. A larger proportion of inspections are conducted in high hazard industries—those with injury and illness rates above the national average.

In the course of a general schedule inspection, the CSHO may investigate any and all situations. In every case, he/she is instructed by the Field Operations Manual (FOM)—OSHA's policy and procedures manual for CSHO—to review all of the illness and injury logs the employer is required to maintain, the written Hazard Communication program and the lockout/tagout program. Other written procedures and documents that the CSHO may review include fire and emergency plans; programs for Bloodborne Pathogens, Process Safety Management, and Respiratory Protection; company safety inspections; safety committee minutes; and checklists. Written programs that are not adequately implemented may prompt a more meticulous review of the employer's facility. On the other hand, employers whose programs are adequately documented and followed will be less susceptible to citation for willful or repeat violations.

4.3 Closing Conferences

The Occupational Safety and Health Act includes comprehensive guidance governing post-inspection procedures, such as the issuance of citations and employer contests of OSHA citations. The citation process begins at the closing conference following the inspection, and citations become final orders of the Occupational Safety and Health Review Commission unless the employer initiates a notice of contest.

Generally, at the conclusion of an inspection, a closing conference is held between the inspector and employer and employee representatives. The inspector is expected to describe apparent violations discovered during the inspection, and must inform the employer that (1) citations may be issued and monetary penalties imposed; (2) appeal and contest procedures exist; (3) follow-up inspections may be held to verify compliance; (4) and if he receives a citation, a follow-up inspection may be conducted to ensure that the citation has been posted and employees will be protected during abatement period. A copy of "Employer Rights and Responsibilities Following an OSHA Inspection" (Form OSHA-3000) must be left with the employer.

If no closing conference is held, citations will not be vacated unless the employer can show that "actual prejudice" resulted. The timing of the closing conference is not critical. A delay of days or weeks between the inspection and the closing conference can occur when, for example, air samples are taken which must first be analyzed, or certain citations (for example, "willful" citations) are to be issued which require higher-level approval.

During the closing conference, employer representatives should not engage in debate with the inspector over his observations. The way certain conditions or practices are characterized can be very subjective, and the employer representative can influence the penalties being recommended. Thus, the employer representative should have good "people handling" and negotiation skills.

4.4 Citations

4.4.1 General Duty Clause and Citations

Under the statute, OSHA may issue a citation to an employer for failure to comply with a particular health or safety standard, or in the case of serious health or safety hazards for which there is no specific standard, a violation of the General Duty Clause (GDC). The General Duty Clause of the statute, Section 5(a), requires the employer to

> furnish to each of his employees employment and a place of employment which are free from recognized hazards that are causing or likely to cause death or serious physical harm to his employees.

Thus, by statute, before OSHA can cite an employer under the GDC, there must be a danger threatening physical harm to those employees who are exposed to it. The lack of a particular abatement method or the occurrence of an accident are *not* violations of the GDC; they may be evidence of such a violation, but additional elements must be proven.

First, the hazard must be recognized, either by the employer specifically, generally by the industry of which the employer is a part, or by "common sense." In its Field Operations Manual, OSHA identifies nine different ways to establish that a hazard is recognized by an industry. Among them are statements by health and safety experts familiar with the industry; implementation of abatement method; warning labels on equipment; studies conducted by employers; unions, or trade associations; state or local laws; and consensus standards from organizations such as NFPA and ANSI.

Similar sources may be used to demonstrate that the individual employer recognizes the hazard. Company memoranda, safety rules, inspections, operating manuals, safety audits, or accident reports are but a few examples of the kinds of documents that can be used. Employee complaints and half-hearted or ill-maintained corrective actions also may show that the employer was aware of the hazards. Finally, where any reasonable person would recognize the hazard, OSHA may cite under the GDC.

The second element of the GDC violation is that the hazard must be likely to cause death or serious physical harm, defined by OSHA as

> impairment of the body in which part of the body is made functionally useless or is substantially reduced in efficiency, and

which may be temporary or permanent, chronic or acute, usually requiring treatment by a physical.

Cuts, lacerations, or punctures involving significant bleeding and/or requiring sutures are considered by OSHA to be serious physical harm, but abrasions, bruises, or contusions generally would not be.

Finally, OSHA must be able to show that the hazard may be abated by a feasible and useful method. The focus is on whether the recognized hazard is preventable, consistent with the Congressional purpose. Legal precedent requires that the GDC may be used only where a specific standard is not available, unless the employer knows the particular standard is inadequate to protect his employers from the hazard.

4.4.1.1 Repetitive Motion Injury

Most recently, OSHA has used the GDC to cite employers where a substantial number of employees suffer from repetitive motion injury, sometimes called Cumulative Trauma Disorders (CTD). In the meat packing and poultry industries, in automotive and food processing, and in a number of other cases, OSHA has shown that employers failed to take necessary steps to prevent the occurrence of conditions such as carpal tunnel syndrome. In settlements involving millions of dollars in fines, OSHA has imposed extensive programs of investigation, education, engineering and medical surveillance. Some believe that OSHA has followed this path because of frustration with the standards setting process, or because the agency is unable to articulate a scientifically defensible and ultimately enforceable standard. Arguably, establishment of a standard of care, under which employers are liable for citation and imposition of the full force of OSHA's enforcement authority, in this manner fails to provide adequate notice to the regulated community and opportunity for comment as required by the standards setting authority of the statute. This process of stealth rulemaking ultimately undermines OSHA's persuasive authority.

4.4.2 Timing of Citations

Citations must be issued within 6 months of the date of inspection. The six month period begins to run on the first date of inspection, not when the OSHA investigation is completed. When OSHA amends the original citation, the amendment relates back to the original citation date and is not barred by the fact that more than 6 months have passed between inspection and amendment.

Certain citations may be issued immediately at the discretion of the inspector, although the CSHO has no authority to issue proposed penalties at the worksite. Factors which the CSHO must consider include: whether laboratory analysis is required; whether the advice of specialists or legal counsel is needed; and whether OSHA's jurisdiction is in question. The CSHO must discuss his or her findings with the OSHA area director before issuing worksite citations.

Citations issued after the closing conference must be issued "with reasonable promptness after termination of the inspection." The Occupational Safety and Health Review Commission (OSHRC) has rarely vacated a citation because of delay in issuance as long as it is issued within the six-month statute of limitations, unless actual prejudice to the employer's preparation of a defense against the citation could be shown. A lack of "reasonable promptness" is a defense that must be pleaded and proved by the employer. Citations are mailed by certified mail, return receipt requested. The date of the return receipt defines the contest period. Notice of the proposed penalty must be given to someone who has authority to pay the violation or contest the citation. Service of process must be made on a corporate official, not on an employee at the worksite. The Review Commission will normally find that the service of process was adequate when it can be reasonably calculated that the employer was actually given notice, even if the citations were not given to the proper person.

4.4.3 Content of Citations

The citation must "describe with particularity the nature of the alleged violation, including a reference to the provision(s) of the act, standard, rule, regulation, or order alleged to have been violated." The employer must be able to identify the violation although the citation does not have to state all details of the alleged violation. Lack of particularity is an affirmative defense to be pleaded and proved by the employer. The citation must include a proposed penalty and must fix a reasonable time for abatement: it may be amended before or after filing a notice of contest if additional facts establish a need for revision.

The employer must post the citation or a copy at or near each place an alleged violation occurred or in a prominent place for affected employees to see. The citation must remain posted until the violation abated, or for 3 working days, whichever is later.

4.4.4 Penalties

Citations are classified by OSHA according to their seriousness. *De minimis* violations are those involving a technical violation of the standard which does not result in a hazard to health or safety. An example of such a violation might be the installation of a stair rail at a height slightly above the maximum permitted under the standard, or the use of a nuisance dust respirator without a respiratory protection program against a non-toxic dust. Such violations are noted, but carry no precedential value, including the fact that they cannot be used as the basis for a repeat violation. No abatement period is fixed for correction of the condition, and no penalties are assessed.

Other-than-serious violations are those for which the risk of serious physical harm is small or the likelihood of injury is so remote as to be a nearly impossible occurrence. Serious violations are those which involve the potential for real harm to employees. The penalty for serious violations can be as much as $7000, while willful or repeated violations carry potential fines of up to $70,000 per violation.

Between 1988 and 1990, citations issued for serious violations of this standard increased by a factor of six, from 1,700 to over 10,000. Other-than-serious citations dropped from nearly 14,000 to approximately 6,000. While OSHA surely would argue that the standard has not changed, it is clear that the Agency's interpretation of the standard has changed, at least with respect to severity. This is amply demonstrated by the fact that over 60% of the violations in 1990 were categorized as serious, as compared to less than 10% two years earlier.

During the 1990 budget negotiations, Congress, in its search for new sources of money, changed the OSHA penalty structure, partly in response to a small but vocal minority that wanted to increase OSHA's enforcement penalties to create more pressure on business. Congress included an amendment in the budget package which increased OSHA's penalty structure by a factor of seven, probably a needed change. However, Congress also turned the agency into a revenue source, charging it with increasing its revenues from penalties from its then current level of $40 million per year to a total of $900 million over 5 years. In the 20 years of OSHA's existence, the total amount of fines assessed has been less than $4 billion, with approximately $90 million in the last fiscal year.

4.5 Appeals

Employers are permitted an initial appeal under the OSHA statute following an administrative process within the Department of Labor. An employer, or employee representatives, may request an informal conference upon receipt of a citation and notice of proposed penalty. Requests for these conferences are granted as a matter of routine before the end of the 15-working-day contest period. The conference is held with the OSHA Area Director or his representative who has authority to negotiate an agreement to settle the citation without litigation. Area directors are authorized to enter into informal settlement agreements only before the employer files a written Notice of Contest (NOC)(see below). The informal conference provides an opportunity (1) for resolving disputed citations and penalties without resorting to litigation; (2) to improve understanding of specific safety or health standards which apply; (3) to discuss ways to correct violations; and (4) to discuss problems with proposed abatement dates.

The benefits of an informal conference include rapid settlement of the citation; and the opportunity for the employer to obtain a reduction in the penalty or a modification of the abatement date. Neither the informal conference nor the request for a conference stays the 15-working-day period within which the employer must file a Notice of Contest (NOC) or a notice alleging that the time fixed for abatement is unreasonable. Employers should consider filing the NOC as a contingency even if they choose to attempt to negotiate a settlement.

4.5.1 Notices of Contest

A Notice of Contest (NOC) is the beginning of the formal appeals process. The procedure is governed by regulation and is conducted before the Occupational Safety and Health Review Commission (OSHRC). The benefits of contesting a citation include: possible dismissal or modification of the violation; possible reduction of proposed fines; and possible modification of required abatement. The employer should be aware that acceptance of certain citations (for example, willful citations) may support criminal charges. The main disadvantage of contesting a citation is the substantial cost involved in litigation.

While the act itself does not specify the procedures for initiating the NOC, the implementing regulations state that the employer must notify the area director "in writing." The Review Commission has found an oral Notice of Contest to be valid in some very limited cases; however, the general rule is that the NOC must be in writing. No particular form is required for the NOC, and the Review Commission is liberal in its interpretation of documents that satisfy the requirement for giving notice. However, the thoughtful employer will prepare the NOC carefully so that it makes clear which items of the citation are being contested (for example, if OSHA finds that only the amount of the penalty is contested, the employer will not be allowed later to contest the citation itself). A copy of both the citation and the NOC must be posted at the worksite where it is accessible to affected employees, allowing employee representatives to file a NOC to challenge the reasonableness of an abatement date. A Notice of Contest may be withdrawn at any stage of the proceedings.

The NOC must be postmarked within 15 working days of receipt of a citation. Employers are nearly always unsuccessful in seeking an extension of the 15-day period. An employer may be excused for not filing within the 15-day period if the delay was caused by reliance on erroneous representations, deception, or failure by OSHA to follow proper procedure; however, except in the most unusual cases, his own delays will not relieve the employer of filing the NOC within the statutory period. A failure to file a timely NOC will convert the citation into a final order not subject to review and will subject the employer to a follow-up inspection to determine whether the violation has been corrected.

4.5.1.1 *Extending the Abatement Period*

The burden of showing reasonableness of the abatement period is on OSHA. A Petition for Modification of Abatement (PMA) may be filed when an employer has made a good faith effort to comply, but abatement has not been completed due to factors beyond his control, or when abatement would cause a significant financial hardship to the employer. The PMA must be filed no later than the next working day following the date on which abatement was originally required. The PMA must be in writing and include the following: (1) steps already taken in an effort to comply and the dates those steps were taken; (2) the amount of additional time needed to comply; (3) the reasons the additional time is needed; (4) interim steps being taken to protect employees; and (5) certification that the petition has been posted in a conspicuous place in the worksite. If uncontrollable circumstances prevent the employer from meeting the abatement date and the 15-working-day contest period has expired, a PMA may be filed if accompanied by a statement explaining the circumstances.

Once an NOC is filed, the abatement period does not begin to run until the entry of the final order by the Review Commission. If the Review Commission finds that the only purpose of the employer's Notice of Contest is to delay or avoid the abatement period, the abatement period begins to run from the date of receipt of the citation.

4.5.2 Opportunity for Settlement after Filing Notice of Contest

Settlement is encouraged at all stages of the proceeding as long as it is consistent with provisions and objectives of the act. However, the employer may not withdraw his Notice of Contest in favor of settlement unless there is certification of the date on which the violations have been or will be abated. Settlement is treated as an admission of liability for the original citation unless a settlement clause provides otherwise. In addition, the settlement agreement may be used in future proceedings concerning subsequent violations to show knowledge of a condition or practice.

Under the rules governing settlements, an administrative law judge (ALJ) is assigned when "there is a reasonable prospect of substantial settlement with assistance of mediation by a Settlement Judge." Affected employees who have party status must receive written notice of a proposed settlement (either by personal service or posting) so they can file objections with the ALJ within 10 days.

4.6 Appeals Process

From the OSHRC, employers or OSHA may appeal to a Circuit Court of Appeals. The process beyond the Review Commission is identical to any other appeal of a judicial proceeding. Substantively, however, the standard of review is a more lenient one. Unless unreasonable or inconsistent with the standard or the statute, the interpretation of the Secretary of Labor is controlling. There must be substantial evidence in the record taken as a whole to support the secretary's interpretation, and the factual determinations of the OSHRC are final.

5.0 RECORDS UNDER OSHA

One of the major reasons that Congress enacted the OSH Act was the recognition that some kinds of work-related illnesses develop after exposure over long periods of time, and that little information was available in 1970 to define, on the basis of objective science, "safe" working conditions. Thus, the Secretary of Labor, through the efforts of the Occupational Safety and Health Administration (OSHA or the agency) and the Bureau of Labor Statistics (BLS), develops statistical data under the provision requiring the Secretary of Labor to issue regulations "requiring employers to maintain accurate records of, and make periodic reports on, work-related deaths, injuries and illnesses..." The secretary was further ordered to "develop and maintain an effective program of collection, compilation and analysis of occupational safety and health statistics." This information is used to prioritize enforcement goals and regulatory efforts.

Another reason for the requirement to keep records, which also explains the tendency of OSHA to increase these requirements continually, is the need for the agency in its enforcement posture to document the existence of violations of the rules it issues. It is not possible for OSHA inspectors to be present on the job site every day, or even to inspect each workplace each year. It thus falls to the inspector to ascertain the compliance status of the employer through other means. Principal among these is the inspection of the records kept in the ordinary course of business. This is the classic approach of the government lawyer in searching the "paper trail" for evidence of wrongdoing.

5.0.1 Implications for Employers

While Congress' intent and the regulations seem clear, the actual enforcement by OSHA has substantially broadened employer's duties under the statute. This process of "stealth rulemaking" is illustrated by OSHA's position on recording of "illnesses."

Congress concluded that the government needed injury and illness information to administer effectively the nation's workplace safety and health programs by ensuring that full and accurate information would be available. Moreover, as indicated by the statute's language on injury and illness reporting, Congress intended that the scope of injuries and illnesses covered by the act should be quite broad, but at the same time recognized that some conditions are so trivial that no public health purpose would be served by recording them. In both of the provisions noted above, Congress limited the authority of the secretary by excluding "minor injuries requiring only first aid treatment and which do not involve medical treatment, loss of consciousness, restriction of work or motion, or transfer to another job."

Many private entities—as well as OSHA—interpret these words to mean that *all* illnesses need to be reported, but that only some, albeit a large majority of, injuries qualify as recordable cases. It is not clear that Congress intended that all illnesses be recorded. The legislative history clearly shows that Congress considered that injuries and illnesses involving "only a minimal loss of work time or perhaps none at all may not be of sufficient significance to the Government to require their being recorded..."[16] Further, in authorizing the Secretary to compile statistics on workplace injuries and illnesses, Congress specifically limited the secretary's authority to "all *disabling, serious, or significant* injuries and illnesses..." [emphasis added]. Moreover, in directing the secretary to establish standards, Congress clearly

---

[16]Senate Report, p. 16. The House bill mandated reporting of all cases. However, the House receded in conference and the final bill exempted minor cases.

focused the secretary's attention on those working conditions which threaten workers with material impairment of health or functional capacity. Case law also supports the notion that some "ailments," as well as some minor injuries, are not reportable.

A series of publications from the Bureau of Labor Statistics (BLS) has provided guidance to employers in completing the forms. The most recent, published in April 1986, included answers to questions commonly asked by employers. OSHA has attempted—through its current enforcement initiative—to give those guidelines binding effect. Employers fined hundreds of thousands of dollars for their failure to follow the BLS guidelines will find little comfort in the OMB-OSHA position that the guidelines are merely supplemental instructions. As shown below, OSHA is continually expanding the definition of illness through its enforcement process, and is now well beyond the classical dictionary definition of "a sickness of body or mind, ailment" to include minor deviations from normal response without regard for the establishment of a specific medical diagnosis, even though the case law leads to a contrary conclusion.[17]

Over the last two years, however, two cases have strengthened OSHA's authority to issue and interpret regulations. In the most recent case, *Martin v. Occupational Safety and Health Review Commission*, 59 U.S.L.W. 4197 (1991), the U.S. Supreme Court held that courts must defer to the secretary's interpretation of OSHA regulations so long as they are reasonable in the context of the statute and the regulations themselves. The case of *Dole, Secretary of Labor, et al. v. United Steelworkers of America, et al.*, 110 S. Ct. 929 (1990) addressed the authority of the Office of Management and Budget (OMB) to influence OSHA's regulatory approach through OMB's responsibility for implementing the Paperwork Reduction Act and subsequent legislation. OMB must approve forms and data-gathering requirements of federal agencies. However, OMB's authority is limited under the *Steelworkers* case to a review of those requirements which relate to information required to be sent or made available to federal agencies. OMB has concluded that the BLS guidelines are not regulations but rather are "supplemental instructions" to the required OSHA recordkeeping forms. Since the rules in question are clearly within the scope of OMB's authority as defined by the *Steelworkers* case, OMB's conclusion lends support to OSHA's position.

5.1 General Recordkeeping Requirements

Specifically, three general types of records are authorized:

Each employer shall make, keep, and preserve, and make available to the Secretary...such records regarding his activities relating to this Act as the Secretary...may prescribe....

---

[17]OSHA's position that the guidelines merely interpret the rules, supported by OMB's conclusion, reduces the argument to a challenge on the basis of a procedural defect: the guidelines are a substantive versus a procedural change in the Agency's position which must be adopted through rulemaking under OSHA's enabling legislation.

The Secretary...shall prescribe regulations requiring employers to maintain accurate records of, and to make periodic reports on, work-related deaths, injuries and illnesses....

The Secretary...shall issue regulations requiring employers to maintain accurate records of employee exposures to potentially toxic materials or harmful physical agents....[18]

The kinds of records kept generally fall into four classes. First, there are the usual kinds of communications between individuals, both within the organization and with those outside the organization. Such communications document the steps the responsible manager takes to carry out company policies and activities.

The second type of records kept includes the written expressions of company policies, procedures and instructions. These document the specific actions that the company takes to implement both mandated and voluntary programs. In some cases, the statutes or regulations require that a written program be developed; in others, it is simply good management practice to prepare such documents in order to consolidate instructions to company personnel.

The third kind of records comprises those documents that describe the specific day-to-day activities of company employees in carrying out the mandates of company programs and policies. These include daily, weekday or monthly inspection reports, summary management reports, records of training and discipline, and similar documents.

The last category of records involves those mandated by government at all levels. In many instances, they are the same as those that are kept for other purposes. But often, they are discarded quickly and are unavailable for governmental purposes because they lose their business utility as more current data develop. Government, on the other hand, wants the paper trail to remain, at least until the statute of limitations runs out in order to facilitate its functions.

Records of activities and programs are always a double-edged sword. On the one hand, they document the reasonable and prudent actions of company officials and employees in conducting the business lawfully. They also often document the failure of company personnel to perform specific tasks, or of the corporate organization to respond adequately to problems. This tension between the utility of records and the risks inherent in keeping them has created a significant dilemma for many people. Nevertheless, the maintenance of good records is always, on balance, positive.

5.1.1 Standard Specific Records

A discussion of the requirements of the Hazard Communication Standard (HCS) (discussed in detail below) illustrates the variety and types of records required. The HCS covers virtually all employers in the private sector in the U.S. with the exception of the mining industry. The standard

---

[18]29 U.S.C. 657 § (c)(1), (2), and (3).

requires employers to address all hazardous chemicals to which employees may be exposed. All employers are required to communicate to their employees information about hazardous substances which are known to be present at the worksite. This requirement applies regardless of whether the employer created the exposure; a primary issue for all employers is whether they "know" that their employees are exposed.

There are four specific kinds of records that must be kept under the HCS. First, there is the written program which must contain sections addressing specific subjects listed in the standard. Secondly, every employer must have a list of hazardous chemicals to which employees may be exposed. This list must contain the names of the products that are used on the label and Material Safety Data Sheets (MSDS). The user must be able to find the appropriate MSDS from the name on the label. Consequently, the OSHA standard does not require the inclusion of component chemical names on the list of hazardous chemicals. This is a common misconception.

The third kind of record that must be kept is the MSDS. The ostensible purpose of the MSDS is to provide information to employees about the hazardous chemicals to which they are exposed. However, OSHA attributes a secondary purpose to both the list and the MSDS: to document the exposures of employees over time for use as a tool in conducting epidemiological studies. Thus, these records may be considered records of exposure which are subject to the 30 year record retention provisions of 1910.20(d)(1)(ii).

Labels may also be considered records, although they are arguably not exposure records. Certainly companies will want to keep records of what label statements were used and, in particular, the reasons for making the choices. The standard requires that "appropriate hazard warnings" be used on labels on all containers in the workplace. OSHA recognizes that appropriate labels need not include warnings about every toxic effect of every component in a product.[19] Therefore, where labels evolve as manufacturers learn more about their products—both the inherent dangers and the usage characteristics of customer's operations—the "appropriate" warnings will change. It is important to document this evolution, both for OSHA as well as for other legal purposes, and such records will thus become part of the business' ordinary records system.

These are all the records that are explicitly mandated by the HCS, and not all of them are subject to any particular retention policy. However, implicit in the requirements of the standard, such as training, hazard communication and others, is the need to document compliance activities.

For instance, implementation of the written program necessitates the generation of additional records, such as historical records of program reviews, notes on hazard determinations, drafts of labels and material safety

---

[19]OSHA Compliance Instruction (CPL) CPL 2-2.38C, *Inspection Procedures for the Hazard Communication Standard*, 29 C.F.R. 1910.1200, 1915.99, 1917.28, 1918.90, 1926.59, 1928.21, October 1990.

data sheets and training records. These records are almost always necessary to document that the program in fact is implemented. For example, only in the case of the employer who relies solely on his suppliers for MSDS's and labels will there be no hazard determinations. And unless an employer can demonstrate that employees are well trained by other means, records of training will be necessary.

The last kind of record the HCS *implicitly* requires is the response of the employer to requests for copies of MSDS's or other information by medical specialists in an emergency. Under the standard, manufacturers may withhold chemical composition information from labels and MSDS's, but must disclose the information when a *bona fide* request is received from a physician or other health care professional. These requests must be in writing and must contain specific information, and the responses must be prepared accordingly. Of course, such correspondence inevitably creates a record of the transaction which then must be maintained.

It is not always obvious that records are being developed when managers perform their jobs. The process of requesting material safety data sheets generates additional records that OSHA inspectors wish to see. These documents are evidence of good faith in carrying out an employer's responsibilities under the HCS. In addition, they leave an audit trail for in-house verifications that compliance programs are effective.

Audits generate additional records that demonstrate both compliance and corporate commitment. These documents are not primary sources of compliance information, but rather document the internal feedback systems necessary for management to assure that company policies and programs are effectively implemented.

In developing records under the HCS, it becomes important to consider what information must be kept. With regard to hazard determinations, chemical manufacturers should document the decision-making process they follow to prepare MSDS's and labels. The record should reflect the specific sources of information considered, the issues related to selection of hazard warning statements, and considerations of normal use or foreseeable emergency.

The importance of these documents is that they establish both the employer's good faith efforts to evaluate the hazard as well as the rationale for selecting the particular content and wording of labels and MSDS's. In an inspection situation, the compliance officer is at a distinct disadvantage because he does not have reference sources available. Where the procedures and decisions are adequately documented, he is not in a position to question them unless he is willing to spend a significant amount of time researching the issues. Moreover, the judgement of hazard is the employer's, which, of course, can be subject to review by OSHA, but the burden is then on OSHA to demonstrate that the employer's determination is incorrect.

5.1.2 Recordkeeping and Other OSHA Standards

The broad scope of OSHA's standards is illustrated by the index of standards.[20] The chemical specific standards often include requirements for the development of specific exposure and medical records, administrative memoranda, reports, and certifications. The lead standard, for example, requires that employers address a large number and variety of specific requirements, each of which requires or implies that the employer maintain some form of record. The recordkeeping is, of course, an enormous burden, but more importantly, creates a significant problem for assuring compliance. Not only do the records have to be kept, they must be maintained. This is interpreted by OSHA to mean that the information in the records must be updated every time it changes.

Some of the OSHA standards which imply significant recordkeeping requirements do so because they require some kind of periodic inspection. For example, the standard on *Portable Wood Ladders* requires that

> ladders shall be inspected frequently and those which have developed defects shall be withdrawn from service...."[21]

The defense to a citation would likely be the defense of "employee misconduct," that the employee failed to perform his job properly. The employer would have to show that he had a policy requiring employees to inspect the ladders "frequently," that the employee had been told of the policy, and that the policy was actively enforced. Without contemporaneous records to show that (1) there was a policy, (2) the employee had been trained, (3) inspections had been conducted regularly by others, and (4) that supervisors had enforced the requirement, the employer will be held liable for the violation. This last element would likely be shown through evidence that employees had been disciplined for failure to perform the required acts.

This provision does not explicitly require records. However, most employers would find them useful if an inspector found an employee using a ladder that had a defect. Thus, the rule could be interpreted as requiring that at least four types of records would have to be kept to demonstrate employer compliance with the inspection requirement. Of course, not all employers will have such records, and in fact, many do not keep them. Nevertheless, because the burden is on the employer to demonstrate compliance with the standard when the *prima facie* case is made in the agency's complaint, records of such kinds of activities are always desirable.

Table 1 is a listing, by no means complete, of other OSHA standards that have either written program, training or inspection requirements. Nearly every standard that is proposed by OSHA today has significant recordkeeping provisions. We can anticipate that all future standards will be equally designed to provide adequate records for inspectors to use in evaluating compliance. The challenge for employers today is to assure that

---

[20] 29 C.F.R. Part 1910. Index of OSHA Standards.
[21] 29 C.F.R. 1910.25(x).

Table 1
Current Requirements for
Health and Safety Records in the Workplace

	Written Program	Specific Training	Routine Inspections	1910 Section
Portable Ladders	N	N	Y	25
Emergency Response	Y	Y	N	38
Walking Working Surfaces	N	N	Y	68
Ventilation Systems	N	N	Y	94
Noise	N	Y	Y	95
Ionizing Radiation	N	Y	Y	96
Flammable/Combustible Liquids	N	N	N	106
Hazardous Waste	Y	Y	N	120
Personal Protective Equipment	Y	Y	N	134
Lockout/Tagout	Y	Y	Y	147
Medical Services and First Aid	N	Y	N	151
Fire Brigades	Y	Y	Y	156
Fire Extinguisher	Y	Y	Y	157
Sprinklers/Hoses Standpipes	Y?	Y?	Y	158
Employee Alarms	Y	Y	Y	165
Servicing Truck Tires	N	Y	N	177
Powered Industrial Trucks	N	Y	Y	178
Cranes	N	N	Y	178,179
Derricks	N	Y	Y	181
Slings	N	N	Y	184
Machine Guarding	N	N	Y	217
Mechanical Power Presses	N	Y	Y	217
Portable Power Tools	N	N	Y?	241-244
Welding	N	Y	N	252
Electrical Systems	N	Y	N	301-399
Hazard Communication	Y	Y	Y	1200
Laboratories (Non-production)	Y	Y	N	1450
Bloodborne Pathogens	Y	Y	Y	1030
Process Safety Management	Y	Y	Y	119

? = Implied by the language of the standard.

the appropriate records are being kept and that they are accurate, and it is by no means an easy task.

5.2 OSHA Illness and Injury Recordkeeping—Three Types of Records

The recordkeeping regulations promulgated by the Department of Labor impose three basic obligations on employers. First, employers must maintain a Log and Summary of Recordable Occupational Injuries and Illnesses (OSHA No. 200) for each business establishment. OSHA regulations define "establishment" as a "single physical location where business is conducted or where services or industrial operations are performed."[22] However, if distinctly separate activities are performed at a single physical location, each activity should be considered a separate establishment and OSHA records should be maintained separately.

Second, employers must prepare a supplementary, detailed record, the OSHA Form No. 101, *Supplementary Record of Occupational Injuries and Illnesses*, for each recordable occupational injury or illness. The employer may keep the required information on other forms, such as workers compensation forms, Supervisor's First Report of Accident forms, or other insurance forms, so long as all the necessary information is present.

Finally, employers must post in the month of February a signed copy of the prior year's annual summary (Form 200) for each establishment which describes that facility's recordable occupational injuries and illnesses for the past calendar year. Occasionally, an employer may also be requested to complete a statistical survey form containing occupational injuries and illnesses and return it to the BLS.

5.2.1 Recordkeeping Exemptions

The standard generally applies to all employers to whom the OSH Act applies. However, the regulations provide exceptions for small employers and employers classified in certain industries. Employers who have fewer than 11 employees at all times during a calendar year are required only to log all cases, to report fatalities and multiple hospitalizations and to complete the BLS statistical survey if requested. Small employers do not have to complete the OSHA No. 101 form for each occupational injury or illness, nor do they have to compile and post an annual summary of recordable injuries and illnesses.

OSHA exempts employers in certain industries because they are considered low hazard industries. Generally, the exempted industries include employers in certain retail trades, financial services, insurance, real estate, and other service-based industries. For employers whose establishments are mixed use, the predominant classification by the largest share of production, sales, or revenue controls the classification of the establishment, although payroll or employment may be used where the primary economic activity is not accurately measured by revenue measures. The exempted industries

---

[22] 29 C.F.R. § 1904.12(g)(1).

include most but not all classifications in Standard Industrial Classification Codes 52-89.

5.3 Recording Occupational Injuries or Illnesses

For each recordable occupational injury or illness, there must be a separate entry in the Log and Summary (OSHA No. 200) which identifies the employee and briefly describes the injury or illness. The employer is required to record this information as soon as possible, but no later than six working days after learning that such a recordable occupational injury or illness has occurred.

The OSHA position is that this obligation to record an injury or illness extends for the five-year period that the employer is required to retain its log. For example, an employer may discover some time after the fact that a former employee was injured or became ill due to a work-related event while still employed by the employer. If this discovery is made within the five-year record retention period, OSHA contends that the employer must generally record that injury or illness on the log for the year in which the case occurred, even though the involved employee may have not worked at the facility for several years.

However, the regulations state that the records which employers are required to keep must be "retained" for five years after the end of the reporting year. It is not clear how OSHA can interpret the present rule to retain a record to mean that the records have to be "maintained," that is, updated, after the close of the reporting year. Nor is it clear what purpose is served by updating what is essentially historical data. The BLS annual survey of employers is used to develop the statistical data reported in the annual *Survey of Occupational Injuries and Illnesses in the United States by Industry*. These data are collected once a year by mail from selected employers. Any further use of the records kept by employers, aside from their own internal use, apparently is limited to determining whether employers comply with the recordkeeping requirements during OSHA inspections. It would seem somewhat inconsistent with the statutory mandate to obtain information "with a minimum burden on employers" to interpret the word "retain" in the manner in which OSHA presently enforces the rule. In the recent case of *Secretary of Labor v. General Dynamics Corp. Electric Boat Division Quonset Point Facility,*[23] the Administrative Law Judge (ALJ) rejected OSHA's interpretation. The case has been directed for review on this and several other issues.

In this case, the ALJ held that the regulation on retention of records "may not properly be read to require the accuracy of the logs....Maintenance of proper logs is governed by § 1904.2." According to this decision, a misrecorded case is not a continuing violation for the five-year retention period. The issue typically arises in the context of a citation issued more than six months after the date of the alleged violation. OSHA most often argues

---

[23]1990 W.L. 122615 (O.S.H.R.C.), 1990 OSHD (CCH) ¶ 29,000.

that the five-year requirement mandates maintenance rather than mere retention because it often is attempting to hold employers responsible for events which occurred years after the act of recording the case. The six-month statute of limitations is found in Section 9(c) of the OSH Act. While a purely technical legal argument regarding the statute of limitations may occasionally provide an advantage to employers, it is clear that intentional falsification of the records is risky business. The penalty provisions of § 17(g) of the act make knowing false representation of any "statement, representation, or certification in any application, *record, report*, plan or other document filed or required to be maintained..." a misdemeanor. Responsible employees are therefore subject to criminal prosecution under OSHA's interpretations of these rules.

Interestingly, when there is a change in ownership of an establishment, OSHA interprets the retention requirement to relieve the new owner of the obligation to update the records. The regulations only require the new owner to preserve the records of the prior owner, and to record cases for that portion of the year in which he owns the establishment.

5.3.2 Annual Summary

By February 1 of each year, an employer must post in each of its establishments a copy of the summary of the establishment's recordable occupational injuries and illnesses for the previous year. The summary must be presented on the right-hand portion of the OSHA No. 200 form, which is designed to remove personal identifiers and the specific description of the illness or injury. It must include the calendar year covered, the company's name, the facility's address, a signature certifying that the information contained on the annual report is correct, the title of the person signing, and the date of the certification. This summary must be posted throughout the month of February in a conspicuous place or places where notices to employees are customarily posted. If an employer has employees who do not regularly report to or work at a single facility, the employer must mail or present a copy of the summary to those employees at the appointed time. Note that the person signing the summary is specifically subject to the Section 17(g) sanctions under § 1904.5 (d)(2).

5.4 Retention of and Access to Records

OSHA does not have a generic recordkeeping standard mandating the kinds of records to be kept. Section 1910.20 of the regulations addresses retention periods and authorized access to medical records. The retention provisions require employers to maintain medical and exposure records for 30 years, and provide for the transfer of records to the National Institute for Occupational Safety and Health (NIOSH) in the event the employer intends to dispose of them or ceases to do business. The definitions of medical records exempts health insurance claims records, first aid records of one-time treatment and subsequent observation of cases not involving medical treatment, and records of employees employed for less than one year who are given the records on termination of employment. The exemption for first aid records applies essentially to those cases which would otherwise not be recordable on the OSHA Form 200.

Paragraph (e) of this section establishes the right of employees and their designated representatives to obtain access to and copies of medical and exposure records. Employers may not charge for initial copies of records, and must provide access within 15 working days of a request. Employee medical records are subject to a provision that can limit the employee's access to them if, in the opinion of an employer's physician, there is information regarding a terminal illness or psychiatric condition that could be detrimental to the employee's health. In such cases, the employer may provide the information to another physician of the employee's choosing after denying, in writing, the employee's access to the detrimental information. Confidential information identifying persons who have provided information about the employee may be excised from the record provided to the employee.

Former employees are specifically included among those who are to be provided access to the records kept pursuant to § 1904. It has been held that the disclosure of these records does not violate the Fourth Amendment right against unreasonable search and seizure because it authorized the access without a warrant. When the Form 200 is posted, whatever reasonable expectation of privacy the employer might have had in the information is lost, and lacking this element, the access requirement under the rule did not violate the Constitution.

A separate provision of the standard describes OSHA procedure for gaining access to personally identifiable medical records.[24] The rules, issued to satisfy privacy concerns, limit the types of requests that may be made, the agency personnel who may be granted authority to access the records, and the uses to which the records may be put. The regulations require that mandated records be provided, upon request, for the purpose of inspection or copying, to OSHA inspectors as well as representatives of the Secretary of the Department of Health and Human Services.

5.4.1 Access by OSHA Inspectors

Despite an ongoing legal debate over an employer's rights to withhold required data in the absence of a warrant or subpoena, many employers have long made such information available for review by OSHA inspectors. Depending on the circumstances, firms often conclude that it is more beneficial to be cooperative than confrontational, reasoning that an evaluation of injury and illness records might limit the scope of an inspection. This judgment may be based in part on the relative ease with which the health and safety agency might obtain a warrant or subpoena. Nevertheless, OSHA citations are occasionally vacated when challenged on the grounds of employer objections to the lack of a warrant, and the

---

[24]29 C.F.R. § 1910.20

employer's right to require a warrant is firmly established even for the most unobtrusive request by OSHA inspectors.

5.5 Recordable Cases

As suggested by the statutory language described above, the following injuries and illnesses come within OSHA's recordkeeping obligations:

1. Occupational fatalities, regardless of the time between the injury and death or the length of the illness;

2. Occupational injuries and illnesses, other than fatalities, that result in lost workdays; and

3. Non-fatal occupational injuries or illnesses that do not involve lost workdays but result in the transfer of the employee to another job or termination of employment, require medical treatment (other than first aid)[25], or involve loss of consciousness or restriction of work or motion.

Also included in this last category are diagnosed occupational illnesses that are reported to the employer (but are properly not classified as fatalities or lost workday cases.)

To help an employer decide whether a particular case needs to be recorded, the BLS suggests the following five-step analysis:

1. Determine whether a case occurred (that is, whether there was a death, injury, or illness);

2. Determine whether the case was work-related (whether it was caused, contributed to, or aggravated by an event or exposure in the work environment);

3. Decide whether the case is an injury or an illness; and

4. If the case is an illness, record it and check the appropriate illness category on the log; or

5. If the case is an injury, decide if it is recordable based on a finding of medical treatment, loss of consciousness, restriction of work or motion, or transfer to another job.[26]

One serious problem with the BLS guidelines is that the definition of the term "illnesses" on the back of the Form 200 appears to be over-inclusive when compared to the regulation's language and to OSHA's statutory au-

---

[25]OSHA's regulations define "medical treatment" as treatment administered by a physician or by a registered health professional under the standing orders of a physician. Medical treatment does not include first-aid assistance, regardless of who provides this service. "First aid" is defined as any one-time treatment of minor scratches, cuts, burns, splinters, and comparable conditions which ordinarily do not require medical care, even though provided by a physician or other registered health professional. Follow-up visits for observation are also classified as first-aid assistance. 29 C.F.R. § 1904.12(d), (e).

[26]Bureau of Labor Statistics, *Recordkeeping Guidelines for Occupational Injuries and Illnesses* (U.S. Department of Labor, 1986), p. 28.

thority. The regulation defines non-fatal cases to include "any *diagnosed* occupational illnesses..." An "occupational illness" is any abnormal condition or disorder (other than one resulting from an occupational injury) caused by exposure to environmental factors associated with employment. It includes acute and chronic illnesses or diseases that may be caused by inhalation, absorption, ingestion, or direct contact.[27] The example given by BLS is that of an abnormal chest x-ray, which the agency considers recordable. However, in the case of *Amoco Chemicals Corp.*,[28] this interpretation was rejected.

In *Amoco Chemical*, the Occupational Safety and Health Review Commission (OSHRC) held that the employer need record only diagnosed occupationally-related illnesses. The OSHRC specifically rejected the secretary's position that: (1) it was irrelevant what the employer called the condition or whether the condition was diagnosed as a particular illness, and (2) the secretary need only show that employees experienced lost workdays or were placed on work restriction as a result of "work-related conditions."[29]

Amoco had hired an outside physician to evaluate the company's employees. Several employees were identified by the physician as having abnormal pulmonary function tests which were consistent with asbestosis; however, no medical diagnosis of asbestosis was made by this physician. Diagnoses of asbestosis were subsequently made by physicians retained by Amoco employees, but these diagnoses were not provided to Amoco.

The OSHRC rejected OSHA's position that these "conditions" were recordable. The OSHRC distinguished between "conditions" which differ from expected norms, and "illnesses" which must be recorded. The secretary's contention that he only need prove that an employee was suffering from an "occupationally-related condition" was rejected. Following *Ohio Edison*,[30] the Commission held that a medical diagnosis of an illness was required before the illness need be recorded. An abnormal condition identified in a diagnostic test is not an illness.

Further discussion of Amoco's determination that the employees were not suffering from diagnosed illnesses turned on the basis of the judgment made by Amoco. The Commission concluded that there was "no clear indication of what kind of medical review the standard require[d]." In the absence of clear regulatory guidance, the OSHRC held that the employer must make a reasonable judgment based on the information at hand.[31]

---

[27]Log and Summary of Occupational Injuries and Illnesses, OSHA No. 200.

[28]12 OSHC 1849, OSHD ¶ 27,621 (OSHRC 1986).

[29]*Amoco Chemical* at 1852.

[30]*Ohio Edison*, 9 OSHC 1450, OSHD ¶ 25,272 (1981). Ohio Edison did not record four cases of skin irritation resulting from exposure to creosote in which there was no medical treatment, no medical evaluation, no lost time, and no restriction of work activity.

[31]"To find Amoco in violation of the standard on these facts would mean that every employer must exercise the same medical judgment as the best qualified experts in the nation....In the absence of what kind of medical review the standard requires, the standard cannot be read to require an employer to do more that make a reasonable judgment based on the information and expertise available to it." *Amoco Chemical* at 1855.

OSHA had the burden of proving that the employer's decision was unreasonable.

In the case of *Ohio Edison Co.*, a citation for failure to record a skin rash that was presumed to be caused by exposure to creosote, a potent skin irritant, was vacated. The administrative law judge (ALJ) concluded that the conditions did not rise to the level of significance required to fall within the reporting requirement. In considering the issue, the ALJ addressed the statutory basis for the recordkeeping requirement, and specifically rejected OSHA's contention that *all* illnesses be recorded.

5.5.1 Hearing Loss and the Standard Threshold Shift

The BLS guidelines also identify hearing loss as a recordable illness if it is determined to be work-related. One difficulty that has arisen as a result of the 1983 amendments to the OSHA Noise Standard is what degree of change in hearing acuity measured in industrial hearing conservation programs rises to the level of an "illness." Data submitted to the agency in the rulemaking on noise indicated that there are significant problems in the repeatability and precision of hearing tests in the typical industrial situation. The Carter administration, in its last gasp, issued a final rule which would have required the recording of a "Significant Threshold Shift" if it were determined to be permanent on retest.

The rule was stayed and the record reopened, and the present rule adopted in 1983 deleted the requirement. In part, this was due to a change in the definition of STS, now called a "Standard Threshold Shift." The STS was defined by using the smallest change which could be measured reliably by the pure-tone audiometry prescribed by the rule. However, numerous comments in the record, and OSHA's own words in the preamble to the rule, recognized that this measure of hearing loss is insufficient to diagnose occupationally induced hearing loss, and moreover, changes as small as those identified as STS do not rise to the level of a material impairment of health.

OSHA unilaterally changed its policy in 1990, and began to cite employers for failure to record STS absent an affirmative medical determination that the condition was not work-related. This change began its life in a proposed draft compliance instruction that was circulated to area directors, among others. Some area directors began enforcing the interpretation as written while others hesitated. Industry was understandably confused, and in some cases, certain OSHA offices advanced the suggestion of spectacular fines for failure to record barely measurable changes in hearing—in many cases they were neither work-related nor permanent—to coerce companies into recording these cases. The result would have likely been an increase in the reported number of cases of hearing loss on the Form 200 in the face of significant efforts on the part of industry to control the condition through the use of hearing protection. Worse, the increase would have been an artifact of the data collection method. It is hard to see how OSHA can reconcile this action with the explicit statutory duty to "prescribe regulations requiring...accurate records," particularly when its changing interpretations reduce the accuracy of year-to-year comparisons.

OSHA recently issued a letter clarifying its present policy on the recordability of hearing loss pending consideration of the issue in a rulemaking that the Agency expects to initiate this year. OSHA has instructed its inspectors to cite employers for failure to record STS exceeding 25 dB when calculated according to the procedure specified in the current noise standard. As originally drafted, employers would be "encouraged" to record STS between 10 and 25. The inappropriateness of such an approach is obvious. Either the case is recordable or not. If the standards of recordability are to change, it should be through notice and comment rulemaking, according to the terms of the OSH Act. The approach used by OSHA is inappropriate because the changes would result in increased liability on the part of employers for failure to follow the new interpretation. This procedure is contrary to current administrative law governing changes in agency interpretations.

These two examples, the definition of an illness and the recording of STS, illustrate the tendency of OSHA, as well as other agencies, to increase the scope of their authority outside the prescribed method through enforcement and internal policy memoranda. They suggest a material change in agency policy over the last ten years, carried out surreptitiously and, more importantly, without adequate notice and opportunity for comment. This stealth rulemaking is contrary to both OSHA's statute and the Administrative Procedure Act, and undermines the agency's "moral" authority.

5.6 Determination of Work Relatedness

As a general rule, injuries that occur *anywhere* on the employer's premises are considered work-related. Thus, an injury that occurs in a company bathroom or a hallway is an occupational injury. The major exceptions are injuries that occur on company recreational facilities and in company parking lots, which are not recordable unless the employees were engaged in some work-related activity. It is immaterial for recordkeeping purposes whether the employer or employee was at fault for the injury or illness, or whether the injury or illness was preventable.

OSHA argues that the presumption of work-relatedness is necessary when cases occur on the employer's premises to keep the recording criteria simple. Nevertheless, the presumption is rebuttable and the case is not recordable if there is no relationship between the person's presence on the premises and his status as an employee, a point that is frequently overlooked. The basis for OSHA's position is to maintain simplicity in the system. But OSHA's authority is limited to responsibility for *work-related* cases.

Examples used in the BLS guidelines referring to horseplay and employees choking while eating lunch in a company cafeteria are considered recordable by OSHA. But employers must determine whether a case is work-related in other more obscure situations, such as when a condition manifests itself at the job site but is unrelated to the individual's status as an employee.

It is hard to understand OSHA's position that injuries due to non-work related activities should be reported in a system directed toward improving safety in the workplace simply because they occur on the premises. This is inconsistent with the agency's approach that illnesses of equally obvious non-occupational origin are not recordable. OSHA has stated that it plans to consider revising its approach to cases that are not truly work-related as well as eliminating the distinction between illnesses and injuries in the upcoming rulemaking.

5.7 Reporting of Fatality or Multiple Hospitalization Accidents

If a workplace accident causes the death of an employee or the hospitalization of five or more employees, the employer must report the accident orally or in writing within forty-eight hours to the nearest OSHA office. OSHA issued a Notice of Proposed Rulemaking to reduce the permissible reporting period to eight hours or less and to reduce the number of hospitalizations that trigger this requirement in the summer of 1992. Currently, reporting can be accomplished by telephone, telegraph, or facsimile and must include the facts surrounding the accident, the number of fatalities, and the extent of any injuries. OSHA may also require supplemental reports, but more importantly, all catastrophes are investigated by on-site inspections.

It is important to remember that the OSH Act has criminal penalty provisions for willful violations resulting in an employee fatality, and the recordkeeping provisions are supported by a provision involving misdemeanor criminal penalties for knowingly making false statements. Moreover, state and local prosecutors are more actively seeking to apply general criminal codes to situations involving death or serious injury. In light of these provisions, employers should be more circumspect about OSHA inspections, and more cognizant about the potential for both corporate and individual criminal liability. While every OSHA inspection need not be treated as a criminal investigation, certainly fatality and catastrophe investigations should, and OSHA requests for records in these cases should be reviewed by counsel in all cases.

5.7.1 Potential for Criminal Liability

It is also important to highlight the potential for individual criminal liability on the part of supervisors, managers and other staff personnel, and to note that there is often a potential for an ethical conflict between the position of the corporation and that of the individual employee. Attorneys must be wary of this potential, especially in investigations of accidents because of the natural tendency on the part of many individuals to cooperate. Individual Fifth Amendment rights against self-incrimination are often forgotten or ignored. The efforts of certain officials to find and punish "someone" in publicized cases is often counter-productive precisely because it leads to much less cooperation on the part of those closest to the incident. One of the long-standing tenets of accident investigation is to avoid looking only for someone to blame, and to focus on underlying causes over which individuals have some control. Certainly any attorney advising a supervisor in a situation involving severe injuries or fatalities will consider whether his client should seek immunity from criminal prosecution before answering questions. Moreover, in some jurisdictions, any workplace fatality is automatically the subject of a criminal investigation. This approach changes the rules of the game to increase the potential liability of managers and supervisors as well as that of the employers.

5.8 Enforcement of Recordkeeping Requirements

Within recent years, OSHA has initiated aggressive and well-publicized programs of enforcing occupational injury and illness recordkeeping requirements. In the first year of its aggressive recordkeeping enforcement campaign (late 1986 through most of 1987), the agency proposed more substantial fines for recordkeeping violations than it did in the previous six years combined. These efforts have continued through the present time.

OSHA generated headlines by issuing citations and proposing penalties of six figures or more against major corporate employers for recordkeeping violations. Ford Motor Company, Caterpillar Tractor, Yale-New Haven Hospital, Union Carbide, and John Morrell & Co. are among the many firms that faced proposed fines of hundreds of thousands of dollars for recordkeeping problems. Prior to the change in the OSHA penalty structure, the agency assessed proposed penalties of this magnitude through its calculation of the maximum financial penalties under the OSH Act, and applied those penalties to each perceived violation. It remains to be seen whether the agency will calculate the penalties at the maximum permitted now that the ceilings have been raised (that is, $70,000 for "willful" violations). But it can be expected that enforcement efforts will likely continue to be highly visible.

Observers have linked OSHA's recordkeeping enforcement activities to several factors. First, the agency's rule-making and compliance activities came under increased legislative scrutiny throughout the late 1980s. The Democrats' control over both houses of Congress, combined with an increase in the number of workplace fatalities, increased the pressure on OSHA after what was generally perceived as a relaxation of OSHA enforcement during the early years of the Reagan Administration. Legislative consideration of additional worker safety measures—such as the High Risk Occupational Disease Notification and Prevention Act—underscored the concern of many representatives and senators that OSHA was not effectively meeting its statutory goal of enhanced safety and health for all working Americans. In addition, tragic events such as Bhopal, the ARCO refinery fire, the Phillips Petroleum and BASF explosions, and more recent disasters made both employees and the general public aware of the potential dangers that exist in the workplace.

As with previous OSHA policies, the recordkeeping enforcement "offensive" was the target of criticism from both industry and labor groups.

Employers entangled in citations, fines and litigation over recordkeeping practices angrily asserted that emphasis on these "paperwork" obligations does not adequately reflect a firm's substantive safety and health practices. OSHA's method for assessing such violations is considered by industry as regulatory "overkill." Employers believe that illness and injury record-keeping requirements clearly envision the exercise of judgment in classifying a recordable event. Moreover, the courts have repeatedly supported the view that such violations are not serious, holding that they are not directly related to safety and health of employees, where the employer is not impeding the inspection by OSHA. The severity of the case more often turns on the question of employers' bad faith or evidence of numerous prior violations.

5.8.1 Multiple Willful Violations

OSHA's strategy of aggregating multiple willful violations is best illustrated by the proposed penalty assessed against IBP, Inc., a meat-packing firm, in the summer of 1987. The agency cited 1,038 instances in which the company allegedly under-reported or completely failed to report injuries and illnesses at its Dakota City, Nebraska plant over a two-year period. The dollar value of the fine, $2.59 million, was the largest in OSHA's history at that time. The agency's assessment followed extensive and dramatic demands for corrective action by the United Food and Commercial Workers Union.

Former OSHA Administrator John Pendergrass stated that one factor in the agency's decision to seek such a substantial assessment against IBP was the company's alleged alteration of injury and illness logs. According to OSHA, the week before the agency gained access to the company's records, IBP officials directed fifty employees to revise the recordkeeping logs to reflect the actual injuries and illnesses that occurred at the plant. The plant then presented the "corrected" logs to OSHA. However, OSHA had received a copy of the logs as they had actually been maintained by the company. The alleged actions led Pendergrass to declare that IBP's case represented the worst instance of failure to comply with OSHA's recordkeeping requirements.

Another substantial proposed penalty for violations of the recordkeeping regulations occurred in the *General Dynamics* [32] case mentioned above. OSHA alleged 122 willful violations of the recordkeeping regulations and proposed penalties totalling $615,000. The cited violations occurred in 1985 and 1986. Notably, OSHA began its inspection of the company in response to an employee complaint that the injury and illness logs were not available for employees to see and copy, as required by OSHA regulations. The complaint had further alleged that the logs were incomplete. In announcing the proposed penalties, Pendergrass, perhaps stating the obvious in view of the OSHA offensive, noted that "employers must be aware of the importance OSHA places on the accuracy and validity of the injury and illness logs. The

---

[32] 1990 W.L. 122615 (O.S.H.R.C.), 1990 OSHD (CCH) ¶ 29,000.

logs provide vital information for both employers and employees identifying and correcting potential work place hazards."

Chrysler, USX, and Shell Oil are among other major employers cited by OSHA for recordkeeping violations. In each case, the companies denied the agency's allegations and asserted that OSHA's citations and proposed fines were out of proportion to the alleged offenses. While continuing to argue that the disputes related to the interpretation of federal recordkeeping guidelines, most of these companies settled the agency citations at substantially reduced dollar levels.

6.0 THE HAZARD COMMUNICATION STANDARD

In November 1983, the Occupational Safety and Health Administration (OSHA) of the U.S. Department of Labor issued its final "Hazard Communication" Standard. The standard is designed to "reduce the incidence of chemically-related occupational illnesses and injuries among employees in the manufacturing sector." It was developed on the assumption that the wider availability of workplace hazard information required by the standard will allow employers to implement more effective safety measures and provide workers with the information they need to protect themselves.

The Hazard Communication Standard (HCS) establishes uniform hazard communication requirements for manufacturers. Each employee working in a manufacturing facility who is exposed or may potentially be exposed to hazardous chemicals in the workplace must receive information and training which is appropriate for the potential exposures involved. Chemical manufacturers and importers are required to evaluate the hazards of the chemicals which they produce or import, and pass this information to downstream employers through labels on containers and Material Safety Data Sheets (MSDS). Each employer's hazard communication program must provide the necessary hazard chemical information to its employees (through container labels, MSDS, and training) so that they can understand and implement the protective measures developed for their workplaces.

6.1 Exemptions

OSHA's Hazard Communication Standard contains a number of significant exemptions. Certain items are *completely exempt* from the provisions of the OSHA Standard. These include:

(1)   Hazardous waste as defined in the Solid Waste Disposal Act, as amended by the Resource Conservation and Recovery Act, when it is subject to regulations issued under that statute by the Environmental Protection Agency;

(2)   Tobacco or tobacco products;

(3)   Wood or wood products;

(4)   Articles (see discussion below), and

(5)   Foods, drugs or cosmetics intended for personal consumption by employees while in the workplace.

The *labeling requirements* of the OSHA Standard are not applicable to certain substances:

(1)   Pesticides, as defined in the Federal Insecticide, Fungicide and Rodenticide Act, when subject to the labeling requirements of the act and implementing regulations issued by the Environmental Protection Agency;

(2)   Foods, food additives, color additives, drugs and cosmetics (including materials intended for use as ingredients in such products, such as flavors or fragrances), when subject to the labeling requirements of the Food, Drug and Cosmetic Act and the implementing regulations issued by the Food and Drug Administration;

(3)   Distilled spirits, wines or malt beverages intended for non-industrial use, as defined by the Federal Alcohol Administration Act and implementing regulations, when subject to the labeling requirements of that act and the regulations issued by the Bureau of Alcohol, Tobacco and Firearms; and

(4)   Any consumer product as defined in the Consumer Product Safety Act, or hazardous substance as defined in the Federal Hazardous Substances Act, when subject to the labeling requirement of that act and the regulations issued by the Consumer Product Safety Commission.

Other notable exemptions to the HCS have been established. First, the HCS exempts from compliance some hazardous chemicals present in some mixtures.[33] If a mixture has been tested to ascertain its hazards, the test results provide a basis for determining whether the mixture is hazardous and therefore subject to regulation under the HCS. An untested mixture, however, is regulated according to its components. Components that comprise less than one percent of the mixture (0.1% for carcinogens) do not trigger the HCS requirements unless there is clear evidence that such an amount could be released in excess of certain regulatory levels[34] or that such a release would present a health hazard to employees.[35] (See further discussion of mixtures below.)

6.1.1 Articles

Articles are exempt from compliance with the standard. An "article" is defined as:

---

[33]A "mixture" is defined as "any combination of two or more chemicals if the combination is not, in whole or in part, the result of a chemical reaction." 29 C.F.R. § 1910.1200(c) (1990).

[34]OSHA has established permissible exposure limits (PELs) for some hazardous chemicals; the American Conference of Governmental Industrial Hygienists (ACGIH) has established threshold limit values (TLVs) for some hazardous chemicals.

[35]Somewhat incongruously, there is no corresponding rule for "chemicals," as opposed to "mixtures." Thus, a chemical product of a reaction arguably must comply with the HCS for all unreacted hazardous raw materials, even if they comprise a minuscule percentage of the whole.

a manufactured item (i) which is formed to a specific shape or design during manufacture; (ii) which has end use function(s) dependent in whole or in part upon its shape or design during end use; and (iii) which does not release, or otherwise result in exposure to, a hazardous chemical, under normal conditions of use.[36]

The stated purpose of this exemption is to exclude from the hazard communication program items which contain hazardous chemicals in "such a manner that employees won't be exposed to them....Substances inextricably bound in a manufactured item do not present a potential for exposure."[37]

Manufacturers of items which may be considered articles must evaluate their products and the components that are used in their manufacture to determine if any residual amount of a hazardous chemical remains in the article and whether employees of downstream users may be exposed to the chemical. An assessment of the degree of exposure must consider whether the amount released could result in health effects in exposed workers. If so, the effects must be disclosed on the MSDS for the product and the item itself might require a label. OSHA has long used the example of formaldehyde treated fabric as an example of an item which falls outside the exemption for articles.[38]

Whether or not subsection (iii) of the article definition includes a *de minimis* exemption is unclear. Recently, OSHA considered modifying this subsection to read as follows:

> (iii) which under normal conditions of use does not release more than very small quantities, for example, minute or trace amounts, of a hazardous chemical (as determined under paragraph (d) of this section) and does not pose a physical hazard or a health risk to employees.[39]

OSHA stated that the proposed modification "clarifies the definition in accordance with OSHA's enforcement policy to indicate that releases of very small quantities of a hazardous chemical from manufactured items, that do not present a health risk or physical hazard to exposed employees, are not covered by the rule."[40]

Furthermore, in the preamble to a revision of the HCS, OSHA stated:

---

[36] 29 C.F.R. § 1910.1200(c)

[37] OSHA Compliance Instruction (CPL) CPL 2-2.38C, *Inspection Procedures for the Hazard Communication Standard*, 29 C.F.R. §§ 1910.1200, 1915.99, 1917.28, 1918.90, 1926.59, 1928.21, October 1990, page A-2.

[38] This example appeared in the initial version of the OSHA Compliance Instruction, 2-2.38, issued in August 1985. Interestingly, after appearing in the subsequent two issues, the example was dropped in the latest version issued in October 1990, 2-2.38C (the CPL). The import of this change is unclear.

[39] 53 *Fed. Reg.* 29852.

[40] 53 *Fed. Reg.* 29633.

Releases of very small quantities of chemicals are not considered to be covered by the rule. So if a few molecules or a trace amount are released, the item is still an article and therefore exempted.

Similarly, in its manual on inspection procedures of the HCS, OSHA interpreted the article definition as permitting "the release of very small quantities of a hazardous chemical." If the amount released would not produce health effects in exposed employees, the exemption applies. In the compliance instruction, OSHA states that items may "release...very small quantities of a hazardous chemical and still qualify as an article provided that a *physical or health risk* is not posed to employees." Some in OSHA feel that the article exemption is unnecessary and redundant and should be deleted. Many in industry hope that OSHA is moving toward a concept of a "*de minimis* exposure," which implies that exposure assessment is required.

As a practical matter, the definition of the term "very small" is always the determining factor. Each manufacturer must review the scientific evidence to determine at what levels of exposure effects occur. Based on OSHA's interpretation in the recently issued compliance instruction, the definition of very small quantities turns on whether there is a potential for a health or physical risk to exposed employees. If the manufacturer determines that his product is exempt as an article based on the criteria of release of hazardous chemicals, the reasons for the decision should be documented. While there is no requirement that records of such determinations be kept under the standard, the need to prove that the determination was made and the basis for it would suggest that such records be retained. What clearly must be reflected in the manufacturer's written program is a description of the method of determination used.

On the other hand, in *General Carbon Co. v. OSHA*,[41] OSHA argued, and the court agreed, that an electrical brush which released small quantities such that users were exposed to levels of less than 1.6% of the Permissible Exposure Limit of copper dust and less than 6.8% of the PEL of graphite dust was not within the secretary's interpretation of the article definition because of these hazardous chemical releases; thus the brush was not exempt from the HCS requirements. The court found the secretary's interpretation of the HCS reasonable.[42]

6.2 Hazard Determination

Paragraph (d) of the standard,[43] the key to the effectiveness of the HCS, establishes requirements for manufacturers to make a hazard determination for all substances to which employees may be exposed. Paragraph (d)(2) requires manufacturers or employers evaluating chemicals to identify and consider the "available scientific evidence" concerning their hazards. For

---

[41]860 F.2d 479 (D.C. Cir. 1988)

[42]The reasonableness of the Secretary's interpretation was reiterated in *Durez v. OSHA*, 906 F.2d 1 (D.C. Cir. 1990).

[43]29 C.F.R. § 1910.1200.

health hazards, evidence which is statistically significant and which is based on at least one positive study conducted in accordance with established scientific principles is considered sufficient by the agency to establish a hazardous effect if the results of the study meet the definition of "health hazards" in this section.

A "health hazard" is defined by the HCS to mean a chemical for which there is evidence, as defined above, that acute or chronic health effects may occur in exposed employees. The term "health hazard" includes chemicals which are carcinogens, toxic or highly toxic agents, reproductive toxins, irritants, corrosives, sensitizers, hepatotoxins, nephrotoxins, neurotoxins, agents which act on the hematopoietic system, and agents which damage the lungs, skin, eyes, or mucous membranes.

In establishing the definition of health hazard, OSHA identified several sources which presumptively establish that the chemicals listed therein are carcinogenic or otherwise hazardous under the rule. The group of specifically listed substances includes: (1) substances which OSHA regulates; (2) those chemicals identified as carcinogens or potential carcinogens by the International Agency for Research on Cancer or the National Toxicology Program; and, (3) substances on the Threshold Limit Value list of the American Conference of Government Industrial Hygienists (ACGIH).

The results of any studies which are designed and conducted according to established scientific principles, and which report statistically significant conclusions regarding the health effects of a chemical, are a sufficient basis for a hazard determination and must be reported on any material safety data sheet. The chemical manufacturer, importer, or employer may also report the results of other scientifically valid studies which tend to refute the findings of a hazard.

6.2.1 Mixtures and the Threshold Disclosure Concentration

OSHA recognized that most substances to which employees are exposed are not pure chemicals but rather are mixtures. Manufacturers may make the hazard determination of a substance which is a mixture either by testing the mixture as a whole or by assuming that the mixture presents the same health hazards as the individual components which exceed the threshold disclosure concentration (TDC) of the composition. The TDC is set at greater than 0.1% for ingredients meeting the definition of a carcinogen and 1% for all other hazardous ingredients.

Many manufacturers stop at the hazard assessment when they determine that the ingredient is present below the TDC. However, this is not the correct procedure. The standard requires that employers who have "evidence" that a component present below the TDC "could be released in concentrations which would exceed an established OSHA permissible exposure limit [PEL] or and ACGIH Threshold Limit Value [TLV®], or could present a health hazard to employees in those concentrations..." should assume that the mixture has the hazards of the ingredient. Evidence of exposure in the use of a product might include data showing that residual amounts are present at some level combined with calculations that a toxicologically significant amount of the ingredient could be present in a workplace under worst case conditions of use. While exposure calculations are not to be used to determine whether information about ingredients present above the TDC should be included on MSDS and labels, ingredients present below the TDC are not subject to the same evaluation criteria under the standard in the context of making a hazard determination on the mixture as a whole. Thus, it would seem perfectly appropriate to use an exposure-based assessment to determine if the ingredients "present a health hazard to employees in those concentrations...." These provisions are not discussed in the Compliance Instruction issued by OSHA to provide guidance in enforcing the standard, and to some extent manufacturers are required to rely on their own judgement in making the decision on disclosure in these circumstances. The clear thrust of OSHA's oft repeated statements on disclosure is to include any doubtful information.

6.3 The Written Hazard Communication Program

Although OSHA sometimes is very explicit about what is expected, in the HCS, the definition of the written program elements is detailed in very simple language.

> Employers shall develop, implement, and maintain a written hazard communication program for their workplaces which at least describes how the criteria specified in paragraphs (f), (g), and (h) of this section . . . will be met . . . .

However, to meet the standard of describing how these requirements are to be met requires an extensive written program. Simply paraphrasing the language of the standard is not sufficient. OSHA expects to see details, such as responsible managers, descriptions and procedures, written out. In its Compliance Instruction, OSHA has defined what it expects to see in a written Hazard Communication Program (HCP).

In general, the written program should include the following elements where applicable:

(a) Labels and Other Forms of Warning.

   (1) Designation of person(s) responsible for ensuring labeling of in-plant containers.

   (2) Designation of person(s) responsible for ensuring labeling on shipped containers.

   (3) Description of labeling system(s) used.

   (4) Description of written alternatives to labeling of in-plant containers, where applicable.

   (5) Procedures to review and update label information when necessary.

(b) Material Safety Data Sheets.

    (1)   Designation of person(s) responsible for obtaining/maintaining the MSDS.

    (2)   How such sheets are to be maintained (for example, in notebooks in the work area(s), via a computer terminal, in a pick-up truck at the jobsite, via facsimile) and how employees obtain access to them.

    (3)   Procedure to follow when the MSDS is not received at the time of the first shipment.

    (4)   For chemical manufacturers or importers, procedures for updating the MSDS when new and significant health information is found.

(c)   Training[44]

    (1)   Designation of person(s) responsible for conducting training.

    (2)   Format of the program to be used (audiovisuals, classroom instruction, etc.).

    (3)   Elements of the training program—compare to the elements required by the HCS (paragraph (h)).

    (4)   Procedures to train new employees at the time of their initial assignment and to train employees when a new hazard is introduced into the workplace.

    (5)   Procedures to train employees of new hazards they may be exposed to when working on or near another employer's worksite (that is, hazards introduced by other employees).

(d)   Additional Topics To Be Reviewed

    (1)   Does a list of the hazardous chemicals exist and if so, is it compiled for each work area or for the entire worksite and kept in a central location?

    (2)   Are methods the employer will use to inform employees of the hazards of *non-routine* tasks outlined?

    (3)   Are employees informed of the hazards associated with chemicals contained in unlabeled pipes in their work areas?

    (4)   Does the plan include the methods the employer will use at multi-employer worksites to inform other employers of any precautionary measures that need to be taken to protect their employees?

    (5)   For multi-employer workplaces, are the methods the employer will use to inform the other employer(s) of the labeling system used described?

    (6)   Is the written program made available to employees and their designated representatives?

---

[44]Guidelines on training programs prepared by the Office of Training and Education entitled "Voluntary Training Guidelines" (49 *Fed. Reg.* 30290, July 27, 1984) can be used to provide general information on what constitutes a good training program.

The Compliance Safety and Health Officer (CSHO) shall determine whether or not the employer has addressed the issues in sufficient detail to ensure that a comprehensive approach to hazard communication has been developed.

6.4 Material Safety Data Sheets

The Hazard Communication Standard requires chemical manufacturers and importers to develop Material Safety Data Sheets (MSDS) for each hazardous chemical they produce or import, and to provide an MSDS to purchasers of hazardous chemicals in advance of or with their first shipment. Employers using such substances are required to obtain MSDS's from their suppliers for each hazardous chemical used in their workplaces; alternatively, employers may develop their own MSDS's for substances obtained from suppliers. In addition, employers who prepare hazardous chemical mixtures or compounds for use within the plant must develop MSDS's for such substances.

The standard specifies that the following information must be provided, in English, on the MSDS:

(1)   the chemical identity used on the label;

(2)   for single substance—the chemical and common names of the substance;

(3)   for mixtures—the chemical and common names of the mixture and the ingredients which contribute to the hazardous nature of the mixture, and whether the mixture has been tested as a whole to determine its hazards;

(4)   the physical and chemical characteristics of the hazardous chemical;

(5)   the physical hazards of the hazardous chemical, including the potential for fire, explosion and reactivity;

(6)   the health hazards of the hazardous chemical, including signs and symptoms of exposure, and any medical conditions which are generally recognized as being aggravated by exposure to the chemical;

(7)   the primary route(s) of entry;

(8)   the OSHA permissible exposure limit, ACGIH Threshold Limit Value, and any other exposure limit used or recommended;

(9)   whether the hazardous chemical is listed in the National Toxicology Program (NTP) "Annual Report on Carcinogens" latest edition, or has been identified as a potential carcinogen in the International Agency for Research on Cancer (IARC) Monographs, latest edition, or by OSHA;

(10)   any generally applicable precautions for safe handling and use, including appropriate hygienic practices, protective measures

during repair and maintenance of contaminated equipment, and procedures for clean-up of spills and leaks;

(11) any generally applicable control measures such as appropriate engineering controls, work practices, or personal protective equipment;

(12) emergency and first aid procedures;

(13) the date of (i) preparation of the Material Safety Data Sheet or (ii) the latest revision to it; and

(14) the name, address, and telephone number of the chemical manufacturer, importer, employer or other responsible party preparing or distributing the MSDS, who can provide additional information on the hazardous chemical and appropriate emergency procedures, if necessary.

MSDS's may be developed in either of two formats. The first alternative is a single MSDS for each chemical product. The second alternative is to attach the component chemical MSDS received from the company's suppliers to a cover sheet identifying the mixture, listing all hazardous components and referencing the attached MSDS's for further information. Again, the second alternative is acceptable only if the hazards associated with the mixture are not different from those of its components and the preparer of the MSDS is not aware of any additional information which should be included.

The firm which prepares the MSDS must ensure that it accurately reflects the scientific evidence which forms the basis for the hazardous chemical determination. Any significant new information which becomes available to the preparing firm concerning the potential health hazards of the chemical or ways to protect against the hazards must be added to the MSDS within three months of discovering the information. This new information must be provided to distributors and customers with the first shipment after the MSDS is updated, or prior to the time of shipment. As a matter of prudence, the MSDS should be transmitted to distributors with a reminder to distribute them to their downstream customers in accordance with these requirements.

Manufacturers which use hazardous chemicals must maintain copies of the MSDS's, and ensure that they are readily available and accessible to employees and their designated representatives during each work shift.

6.4.1 Which Hazards to Highlight on the MSDS

In its the Compliance Instruction, OSHA states, in pertinent part, as follows:

[T]he selection of hazards to be highlighted on the label will involve some assessment of the weight of the evidence regarding each hazard reported on the data sheet. Assessing the weight of the evidence prior to including a hazard on a label will also necessarily mean consideration of exposures to the chemical that will occur to workers under normal conditions of use, or in foreseeable emergencies.

OSHA further amplifies on this guidance by citing ethanol as an example of a chemical with known carcinogenic effects if ingested, but not if inhaled or absorbed through the skin. Thus, OSHA concludes that while the MSDS for ethanol must disclose its carcinogenic potential, the label need not include a cancer hazard warning where the product's intended use does not involve exposure through ingestion.[45]

6.4.2 Trade Secrets

The OSHA standard defines trade secrets as "any confidential formula, pattern, process, device, information, or compilation of information that is used in an employer's business, and that gives the employer an opportunity to obtain an advantage over competitors who do not know or use it." It provides that a chemical manufacturer, importer or employer may withhold information, such as the specific chemical identity of a hazardous chemical, from a material safety data sheet if: (1) the claim that the information withheld is a trade secret can be supported; (2) the MSDS contains information on the properties and effects of the hazardous chemical; (3) the MSDS indicates that the specific chemical identity is being withheld as a trade secret; and (4) the specific chemical identity is made available to health professionals, employees and designated representatives in accordance with the special provisions of the standard dealing with trade secrets which are outlined below.

Where a treating physician or nurse determines that a medical emergency exists and the specific chemical identity of the hazardous chemical is necessary for emergency or first aid treatment, the information must be released regardless of whether the disclosure is covered by a confidentiality agreement.

In non-emergency, health-related situations, the employer is required to disclose, to a health professional, employee, or designated representative, a specific chemical identity otherwise permitted to be withheld as a trade secret if a request for that information: (1) is in writing; (2) describes in reasonable detail the occupational health need for the information; (3) explains why the disclosure of the specific chemical identity is essential, and why disclosure of alternative information is inadequate; (4) includes a description of the procedures to be used to maintain the confidentiality of the information; and (5) includes a written confidentiality agreement from the health professional, employee or designated representative that the trade secret information will not be used for any purpose other than the health need.

The chemical manufacturer, importer or employer may deny a written request for disclosure of a specific chemical identity. OSHA then has a right

---

[45]OSHA is not always very clear when discussing exposure assessment in making a hazard determination. OSHA staff frequently assert that calculations to determine the *extent* of exposure (versus route or existence of exposure) are not permitted in determining whether a hazard must be disclosed on the MSDS or appear on the label. As noted above, however, not all hazards on the MSDS must appear on the label, and some form of exposure assessment appears to be explicitly required by 29 C.F.R. 1910.1200 (g)(5)(iv).

to review the denial. If OSHA determines that the specific chemical identity requested is *not* a "bona fide" trade secret or is a trade secret but the party requesting the information has a legitimate medical or occupational health need for it, then OSHA may direct disclosure and impose limitations or conditions upon the release of such information so that the health services are provided while the risk to the employer is minimized. Failure to comply with such a directive may result in a citation.

6.5 Warning Labels

Section 1910.1200(f) of the HCS requires that each container of hazardous chemical(s) in the workplace be labeled with the identity of the hazardous chemical(s) and the appropriate hazard warning(s). Chemical manufacturers, importers and distributors are required to ensure that containers of hazardous chemicals leaving their workplace are labeled, tagged or marked with the identity of the substance, appropriate hazard warnings, and the name and address of the manufacturer or other responsible party. The labels may not be in conflict with those used to comply with the Department of Transportation (DOT) regulations under the Hazardous Materials Transportation Act.

Of particular importance is the second requirement that the label provide appropriate hazard warnings. OSHA interprets this language to mean that the hazard warning must identify the specific hazard posed by the chemical, that is, that the warning must include statements of target organ effect when they are known. OSHA does recognize that it may not be necessary to put on the label warnings about every hazard listed on the MSDS.

The standard requires that each of the hazardous chemicals be labeled, tagged or marked with the identity of the substance inside, and that hazard warnings appropriate for employee protection be included on the label. The hazard warning can be any type of message, wording, picture, or symbol, which conveys the hazards of the chemical(s) in the container.

If the substances in the container are regulated by OSHA in a substance-specific health standard, the label must contain the specific language required by that standard. Employees must not remove or deface existing labels on incoming containers of hazardous chemicals unless the container is immediately relabeled with the necessary information. If bulk packages are broken down within the facility, the employer must assure that the individual packages or containers are relabeled. There is a limited exemption from the labeling requirement for portable containers into which hazardous chemicals are transferred from labeled containers if the chemical will be completely used by the person who performs the transfer from a labeled container during the same shift in which the transfer is made.

In-plant labels which refer to updated MSDS's must also be updated accordingly.

6.6 Employee Information and Training

Employers must establish a training and information program for employees exposed to hazardous chemicals in their workplace. The training must be provided at the time of initial assignment, and whenever a new hazard is introduced to the work area. Training also must be provided when new physical or health hazard data on existing chemicals in the work area are developed or discovered.

OSHA expects to see the following subjects covered in an HCS training program:

- Procedures for detecting the presence of hazardous materials, that is monitoring procedures, and/or devices, odors, visibility, etc.
- The physical and health hazards of the chemicals in the work area.
- An explanation of how to determine hazards by reading a label.
- The location of MSDS and the procedure for reviewing them and/or obtaining a copy.
- The method by which MSDS can be obtained for a particular substance, such as the use of a trade name as a key identifier.
- The procedure by which the MSDS and label are updated or the procedure for obtaining updated copies from the chemical manufacturer, importer, or distributor.
- The significance to the employee of each section of information on the MSDS, how to read it, and what it means.
- The fact that information is available on specific hazards of individual chemicals through the MSDS.
- The preventive measures employees can take to protect themselves from chemical exposure.
- The proper use and selection of personal protective equipment.
- Emergency procedures in the event of accidental exposure to hazardous substances, including emergency phone numbers and the location of eye washes and safety showers.
- The emergency measures employees can take to minimize the harm from chemical exposures (for example, eye wash, fresh air, other first aid measures, etc.).

6.5.1 Communication with Contractors

Host employers must take steps to ensure that contractors working in their facilities are advised of the presence of hazardous chemicals to which the contractor employees may be exposed. Likewise, agreements with contractors must require that the contractor advise the host employer of the hazardous chemicals which the contractor will be bringing into the plant. Based on the information provided by the contractor, the host employer must determine whether employees or other contractor's employees may be exposed to the hazardous chemicals, and what additional information concerning the contractor's activities must be communicated to employees and to other contractors. The host employer is responsible for assuring that the contractor has sufficient information to inform the contractor's employees and to protect them from exposure to hazardous chemicals used in the facility or brought into the plant by other contractors. The information provided must include (1) where the MSDS for each chemical presenting an exposure potential for any and all employees may be found; (2) any precautionary measures that need to be taken during normal operating conditions and in foreseeable emergencies; and (3) a description of the labeling system used.

6.6 Coverage of Laboratories[46]

Laboratories are subject to limited coverage under the HCS. Container labels on incoming shipments of hazardous chemicals must not be removed or defaced unless immediately replaced, and MSDS which are received for such substances must be maintained and made available to laboratory personnel. Laboratory personnel must follow good laboratory practices and should label all containers of hazardous chemicals, other than portable containers whose contents will be used immediately, with the identity of their contents.

Laboratory personnel must receive training and instruction concerning the HCS and the hazardous chemicals with which they may have contact and (1) safe methods of handling chemicals in laboratories; (2) physical and health hazards of the chemicals generally; and (3) protective measures which may be relevant to such chemicals, including specialized protective equipment and work practices.

7.0 OSHA REFORM

Comprehensive reform of the Occupational Safety and Health Act of 1970 was actively considered by the 102nd Congress for the first time in its 20 year history. Although none of the changes were passed, the election of Bill Clinton raises expectations that reform bills will receive attention from the 103rd Congress. The following proposed changes will no doubt be included in any new effort:

- increase individual liability of company managers and executives;
- permit OSHA to shut down an operation in the case of an imminent danger without prior judicial review;
- increase criminal penalties by raising the maximum sentence and making the crime a felony instead of a misdemeanor;
- require abatement of serious, willful or repeated violations before adjudication of an employer's challenge of the alleged violation;
- create several new criminal offenses;
- give employees the right to participate in the OSHA enforcement process on substantive issues beyond challenges to the abatement period; and
- give victims of workplace accidents the right to be informed about the progress of an OSHA investigation.

---

[46]Certain laboratories are subject to the Laboratory Standard at 29 C.F.R. § 1910.1450.

8.0 CONCLUSION

The Occupational Safety and Health Act has been in effect for more than twenty years. Numerous lives have been saved and countless others protected from injury and illness by the efforts of government, industry, and labor to improve workplace safety and health practices. While there are many similarities between EPA and OSHA regulatory programs, each agency has a distinct history and mission that results in substantially different approaches. But, the growing inter-relationship of environmental and workplace regulations requires the environmental attorney or regulatory manager to have a general understanding of OSHA's approach.

For a more definitive discussion of this topic, the reader is referred to the OSHA Compliance Handbook *and related books and courses listed at the end of this book.*

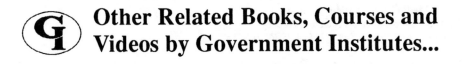# Other Related Books, Courses and Videos by Government Institutes...

BOOKS

For more information on these books and others, please call our Publications Department at (301) 921-2355. Note: prices are subject to change without prior notice.

Federal Environmental Law

Environmental Management Review
Edited by Government Institutes' Staff
Published Quarterly, Code 6000, U.S. $188/year, Outside U.S. $252/year
ISSN: 1041-8182

Environmental Statutes, 1993 Edition
Hardcover, 1,165 Pages, Mar '93, $59 ISBN: 0-86587-352-6

Environmental Regulatory Glossary, 6th Edition
Edited by G. William Frick and Thomas F. P. Sullivan
Hardcover, 544 Pages, May '93, $65 ISBN: 0-86587-353-4

Natural Resources Law Handbook
By Donald C. Baur et al
Softcover, 375 pages, Apr '91, $75 ISBN: 0-86587-243-0

Natural Resources Statutes
Softcover, 600 pages, Apr '91, $49 ISBN: 0-86587-241-4

How the Environmental Legal & Regulatory System Works:
A Business Primer
By Aaron Gershonowitz
Softcover, 128 pages, Mar '91, $24.95 ISBN: 0-86587-244-9

Environmental Management

Environmental, Health & Safety Manager's Handbook, 2nd Edition
Edited by Thomas F.P. Sullivan
Softcover, 242 Pages, Aug '90, $65 ISBN: 0-86587-219-8

Environmental Audits, 6th Edition
By Lawrence Cahill and Raymond Kane
Softcover, 592 Pages, Nov '89, $75 ISBN: 0-86587-776-9

Fundamentals of Environmental Compliance Inspections
By U.S. Environmental Protection Agency
Softcover, 300 Pages, July '89, $69 ISBN: 0-86587-782-3

Multi-Media Investigation Manual
By U.S. Environmental Protection Agency
Softcover, 192 Pages, Sep '92, $69 ISBN: 0-86587-300-3

Environmental Reporting and Recordkeeping Requirements, 2nd Edition
By Theodore W. Firetog et al
Softcover, 288 pages, Mar '92, $69 ISBN: 0-86587-277-5

Environmental Communication and Public Relations Handbook, 2nd Edition
By E. Bruce Harrison et al
Softcover, 194 Pages, Dec '92, $59 ISBN: 0-86587-321-6

The Greening of American Business: Making Bottom-Line Sense of Environmental Responsibility
Edited by Thomas F. P. Sullivan
Softcover, 350 pages, Sep '92, $24.95 ISBN: 0-86587-295-3

Environmental Science

Fundamentals of Environmental Science and Technology
Edited by Porter-C. Knowles
Softcover, 140 pages, Sep '92, $24.95 ISBN: 0-86587-302-X

State Environmental Law

These comprehensive handbooks are written by respected attorneys from each state, with hands-on experience in dealing daily with the maze of state and federal environmental regulations. For more information on available and forthcoming State Environmental Law Handbooks, please call our Publications Department at (301) 921-2355.

RCRA

RCRA Hazardous Wastes Handbook, 9th Edition
By Ridgway M. Hall Jr.
Softcover, 547 Pages, Sep '91, $98 ISBN: 0-86587-270-8

RCRA Inspection Manual, 2nd Edition
By U.S. Environmental Protection Agency
Softcover, 360 Pages, Feb '89, $69 ISBN: 0-86587-762-9

Managing Your Hazardous Waste: A Step-by-Step Guide
By Mary Bauer and Elizabeth Kellar
Softcover, 220 Pages, Jun '92, $65 ISBN: 0-86587-311-9

Treatment Technologies, 2nd Edition
U.S. Environmental Protection Agency
Softcover, 232 Pages, Aug '91, $69 ISBN: 0-86587-263-5

Transportation of Hazardous Materials: A Compliance and Practical Guide for Safe Transportation of Hazardous Materials, 2nd Edition
By William E. Kenworthy
Softcover, 344 Pages, Apr '92, $79 ISBN: 0-86587-286-4

Aboveground Storage Tank Management: A Practical Guide
By Joyce A. Rizzo
Softcover, 220 Pages, Feb '90, $59 ISBN: 0-86587-202-3

Underground Storage Tank Management: A Practical Guide, 4th Edition
By Joyce A. Rizzo
Softcover, 420 Pages, Nov '91, $79 ISBN: 0-86587-271-9

**Used Oil: Disposal Options, Management Practices
and Potential Liability, 3rd Edition**
By John Nolan, Christopher Harris, and Patrick Cavanaugh
Softcover, 321 Pages, Dec. '90, $69 ISBN: 0-86587-234-1

CERCLA/Superfund

Superfund Manual: Legal and Management Strategies, 4th Edition
By Ridgway M. Hall, Jr. et al
Softcover, 442 Pages, Oct. '90, $95 ISBN: 0-86587-229-5

**Emergency Planning and Community Right-to-Know Act Handbook,
4th Edition**
By J. Gordon Arbuckle et al
Softcover, 192 Pages, Jan '92, $67 ISBN: 0-86587-272-4

Pollution Prevention

Facility Pollution Prevention Guide
U.S. Environmental Protection Agency
Softcover, 143 Pages, Oct '92, $34 ISBN: 0-86587-314-3

Case Studies in Waste Minimization
Edited by Government Institutes' Staff
Softcover, 290 Pages, Oct '91, $59 ISBN: 0-86587-267-8

Waste Minimization and Recycling Report
Published monthly, Code 7000, ISSN: 0889-5509 U.S. $198/year; Outside U.S. $252/yr.

Pesticides

Pesticides Inspection Manual
By U.S. Environmental Protection Agency
Softcover, 231 Pages, Sep '89, $69 ISBN: 0-86587-784-X

**Pesticide Poisonings Handbook: Recognition and Management
of Pesticide Poisonings, 4th Edition**
By U.S. Environmental Protection Agency
Softcover, 207 Pages, Sep '89, $49 ISBN: 0-86587-785-8

TSCA

TSCA Handbook, 2nd Edition
By John D. Conner, Jr. et al
Softcover, 490 Pages, Nov '89, $89 ISBN: 0-86587-791-2

Toxicology Handbook
By U.S. Environmental Protection Agency
Softcover, 180 Pages, Sep '86, $55 ISBN: 0-86587-714-6

TSCA Inspection Manual, Part I
By U.S. Environmental Protection Agency
Softcover, 341 Pages, Oct '82, $69 ISBN: 0-86587-541-X

TSCA Inspection Manual, Part II
By U.S. Environmental Protection Agency
Softcover, 216 Pages, Sep '86, $65 ISBN: 0-86587-715-4

Clean Air

Clean Air Handbook
By F. William Brownell and Lee B. Zeugin
Softcover, 336 pages, Mar '91, $79 ISBN: 0-86587-239-2

Control Technologies for Hazardous Air Pollutants
By U.S. Environmental Protection Agency
Softcover, 260 pages, June '92, $69 ISBN: 0-86587-301-1

Building Air Quality
By U.S. Environmental Protection Agency
Softcover, 230 pages, Nov '92, $55 ISBN: 0-86587-312-7

Clean Water

Clean Water Handbook
By J. Gordon Arbuckle et al
Softcover, 446 Pages, June '90, $85 ISBN: 0-86587-210-4

NPDES Permit Handbook, 2nd Edition
By Leonard A. Miller et al
Softcover, 216 Pages, May '92, $74 ISBN: 0-86587-303-8

NPDES Compliance Inspection Manual, 2nd Edition
By U.S. Environmental Protection Agency
Softcover, 234 Pages, Oct '88, $65 ISBN: 0-86587-751-3

Ground Water Handbook, 2nd Edition
By U.S. Environmental Protection Agency
Softcover, 295 Pages, Mar '92, $69 ISBN: 0-86587-279-1

Storm Water: Guidance Manual for the Preparation of NPDES Permit Applications for Storm Water Discharges Associated with Industrial Activity
By U.S. Environmental Protection Agency
Softcover, 180 pages, June '91, $45 ISBN: 0-86587-258-9

Oil Pollution Act of 1990: Special Report
Edited by Government Institutes Staff
Softcover, 210 pages, Mar '91, $79 ISBN: 0-86587-240-6

OSHA

OSHA Compliance Handbook
By W. Scott Railton
Softcover, 448 Pages, May '92, $79 ISBN: 0-86587-290-2

California OSHA Compliance Handbook
By the law firm of Paul, Hastings, Janofsky & Walker
Softcover, 262 pages, Mar '92, $69 ISBN: 0-86587-289-9

Virginia OSHA Compliance Handbook
By the law firm of Mays & Valentine
Softcover, 140 pages, June '92, $72 ISBN: 0-86587-304-6

Health and Safety Audits
By John W. Spencer
Softcover, 336 pages, Apr '92, $65 ISBN: 0-86587-297-X

OSHA Field Operations Manual, 5th Edition
By U.S. Occupational Safety & Health Administration
Softcover, 456 Pages, Nov '92, $69 ISBN: 0-86587-313-5

OSHA Technical Manual, 2nd Edition
By U.S. Occupational Safety & Health Administration
Softcover, 265 Pages, Jun '91, $65 ISBN: 0-86587-255-4

Process Safety Management Standard Inspection Manual
By U.S. Environmental Protection Agency
Softcover, 120 pages, March '93, $49 ISBN: 0-86587-336-4

Hazard Communication Standard Inspection Manual, 3rd Edition
By U.S. Occupational Safety & Health Administration
Softcover, 204 Pages, Jun '91, $59 ISBN: 0-86587-256-2

Environmental References

Directory of Environmental Information Sources, 4th Edition
Edited by Thomas F. P. Sullivan
Softcover, 322 Pages, Nov '92, $74 ISBN: 0-86587-326-7

Book of Lists for Regulated Hazardous Substances, 1993 Edition
Edited by Government Institutes' Staff
Softcover, 345 Pages, Apr '93, $67 ISBN: 0-86587-337-2

Environmental Engineering Dictionary, 2nd Edition
By C.C. Lee, Ph.D.
Hardcover, 630 Pages, Oct '92, $88 ISBN: 0-86587-328-3

Environmental Telephone Directory, 1992-1993 Edition
Edited by Government Institutes' Staff
Softcover, 256 Pages, Nov '91, $59 ISBN: 0-86587-278-3

Real Estate/Environment

Environmental Laws and Real Estate Handbook, 3rd Edition
By Steven A. Tasher et al
Softcover, 290 Pages, Mar '92, $77 ISBN: 0-86587-257-0

Environmental Evaluations for Real Estate Transactions:
A Technical and Business Guide
Edited by Frank D. Goss
Softcover, 250 Pages, Mar '89, $72 ISBN: 0-86587-765-3

Wetlands and Real Estate Development Handbook, 2nd Edition
By Robert E. Steinberg
Softcover, 214 pages, Oct '91, $75 ISBN: 0-86587-269-4

COURSES

For more information on these and other courses, please call our Education Department at (301) 921-2345.

Federal Environmental Law

Environmental Laws and Regulations Compliance Course
Environmental Laws & Regulations Update Course
How Environmental Washington Works Course

Environmental Management

Environmental Audits: Protecting Your Company and Yourself Course
Environmental Management Development Institute
Environmental Management Roundtable
Training Skills for Environmental, Health & Safety Managers Course
Environmental Reporting & Recordkeeping Requirements Course

Environmental Science

Practical Environmental Science: The Science You Need to Know to Comply
with the Law Course

State Environmental Law Compliance Courses

For information on all available state environmental law courses, please call our Education Department at (301) 921-2345.

RCRA

RCRA Regulations Course
Update on RCRA Regulations & Legislation Course
Underground Storage Tanks: Smart Management & Engineering Applications Course
Fundamentals of Aboveground Storage Tanks: Choosing Between Underground
and Aboveground Tanks Course
Industrial Solid Waste Management Regulations Course
How to Manage Your Hazardous Wastes Course

CERCLA/Superfund

CERCLA/Superfund Laws & Regulations Course
EPCRA Laws and Regulations Update Course

Pollution Prevention

Pollution Prevention: National Regulatory Update Course
Pesticides/FIFRA Compliance Course

TSCA

TSCA Compliance Course
Toxicology for Non-Toxicologists Course

Clean Air

Clean Air Operating Permits: The Key to Business Survival Course
The New Air Toxics Program: Compliance Strategies for the '90s Course

Clean Water

Clean Water Act Compliance Course
Storm Water Discharge Regulations Course

OSHA

OSHA Compliance Course
Industrial Hygiene for Non-Industrial Hygienists Course
Health & Safety Auditing: Ensuring Your OSHA Compliance Course

VIDEOS

For more information on these and other videos, please call our Publications Department at (301) 921-2355. Note: prices are subject to change without prior notice.

Our Environment: The Law and You
VHS/23 min./Code 119/1989 $495

Environmental Liability
VHS/18 min./Code 136 $495

Hazwoper Awareness Level Training: Your Role as a First Responder
VHS/15 min./Code 139/1991 $495

Hazwoper Training: Response Levels
VHS/22 min./Code 142/1990 $495

Hazwoper Training: Awareness Level
VHS/20 min./Code 143/1990 $495

Hazardous Waste Manifests
VHS/13 mins./Code 140/1989 $350

Leaking Underground Storage Tanks
VHS/11 min./Code 135 $98

Emergency Planning and Community Right-to-Know Act:
What it Means to You
VHS/15 min./Code 115/1990 $98

Understanding Title III: Emergency Planning & Community Right-to-Know
VHS/15 min./Code 101/1987 $295

Pollution Prevention: Reducing Waste in the Workplace
VHS/24 min./Code 124/1990 $495

Pollution Prevention: The Bottom Line
VHS/24 min./Code 125/1990 $295

Less is More: Pollution Prevention is Good Business
VHS/22 min./Code 109/1989 $98

Beyond Business as Usual: Meeting the Challenge of Hazardous Waste
VHS/28 min./Code 112/ 1989 $98

What Everyone Should Know About Toxicology
VHS/20 min./Code 133/ 1990 $495

Introduction to Water Quality Standards
VHS/15 mins./Code 145 $98

Economic Considerations in Water Quality Standards
VHS/15 mins./Code 146 $98

Groundwater Sampling
VHS/28 min./Code 137/1987 $495

OSHA Legal Liabilities: Thinking it Through:
The Mark of the Professional Supervisor
VHS/22 min./Code 134/1990 $575

Hazard Communication: Employee Introduction
VHS/19 min./Code 117/1985 $495

MSDS: Cornerstone of Chemical Safety
VHS/19 min./Code 116/1986 $495

Essentials of an Environmental Site Assessment
VHS/50 min./Code 114/1989 $198

To receive a free catalog of our books, courses and videos,
please call: (301) 921-2355

or write:
Government Institutes, Inc.
4 Research Place, Suite 200
Rockville, MD 20850